16th
EDITION

Essentials of Marketing

国际市场营销

（第十六版）

A Marketing Strategy Planning Approach

小威廉·D. 佩罗（William D. Perreault Jr.）
[美] 约瑟夫·P. 坎农（Joseph P. Cannon） 著
E. 杰尔姆·麦卡锡（E. Jerome McCarthy）
刘白玉 刘夏青 孙明玉 改编

中国人民大学出版社
·北京·

William D. Perreault Jr., PhD, Joseph P. Cannon, PhD, E. Jerome McCarthy, PhD
Essentials of Marketing: A Marketing Strategy Planning Approach, Sixteenth Edition 9781260405323

北京市版权局著作权合同登记号：01-2019-7291

前　言

《国际市场营销（第十三版）》改编版在 2014 年推出后，深受广大教师和学生的喜爱，全国有 50 多所高校的商务英语专业、市场营销专业、国际商务专业以及 MBA 的学生选用，很多企业也将其作为国际营销人员的培训教材。但是，这几年国际政治、经济、科技、军事、文化都发生了巨大变化，对国际市场环境产生了很大影响，国际市场营销理论与实践也有了新的成果。为了给世界各国教师和学生提供这些最新成果，三位美国著名市场营销教授（北卡罗来纳大学小威廉 · D. 佩罗博士、科罗拉多州立大学约瑟夫 · P. 坎农博士、密歇根州立大学 E. 杰尔姆 · 麦卡锡博士）联合推出了《国际市场营销（第十六版）》，这是目前为止市场营销领域最好的教材，仅从再版十六版就足以证明。为了给广大中国教师和学生提供这些最新成果，刘白玉教授、刘夏青副教授和孙明玉副教授根据中国学生的学习特点及最近 6 年教师和学生的反馈，并征得作者同意，对第十六版教材进行了改编。本教材共分 10 章：第 1 章，营销对消费者、公司及社会的价值；第 2 章，在日新月异的市场环境中评估营销机会；第 3 章，营销战略与市场细分及定位；第 4 章，最终消费者及其购买行为；第 5 章，组织消费者及其购买行为；第 6 章，分销中的顾客服务及物流管理；第 7 章，零售商、批发商及其战略规划；第 8 章，促销与整合营销；第 9 章，定价目标及策略；第 10 章，在以消费者为中心的世界如何进行伦理营销：评估与挑战。需要说明的是，原教材共 19 章，其中还包括产品规划、产品管理及新产品开发等章节，考虑到这部分内容在中国不属于国际营销人员的核心业务，同时考虑到我国高校学时的限制，所以改编时没有列入。但是，这些章节中的一些学生需要掌握的核心理论和成功实践我们都融合到了这 10 章中。

本版教材继续秉承上版教材的五大特点：第一，语言规范、简洁。书的作者都是哲学博士、美国大学教授，同时由于此书针对国际学生，所以所用语言不仅规范，而且简洁易懂。第二，内容全面、具有前沿性。全书共分 10 章，涵盖了国际市场营销的主要领域；同时，作者以营销战略为主线，阐述了营销的实质，属于前沿性的理念。第三，理论与实践有机结合。本书将讲授市场营销、学习市场营销和应用市场营销的知识有机地结合，将理论与实践紧密结合在一起。第四，案例式教学。本书的各个章节都列举了很多成功和失败的营销案例，有助于启发学生思考，学习成功者的经验，汲取失败者的教训。第五，教辅齐全。本书配有 PPT 课件、课后练习答案，便于教师使用。

本教材的设计既可供一个学期 32–36 课时讲授，也可供两个学期 64–72 课时使用。如果讲授一个学期，则只讲每章“学习目标”列出的要点；如果使用两个学期，则可以讲全部内容。教学方法，建议核心内容采用教师讲授法，其他内容采用以问题为导向的小组讨论法。学习方法，建议课前预习提出问题、上课参与解决问题、课后思考再提出问题的“问题学习三步法”。欢迎有志向的教师根据此经典教材录制线上课程，以便让更多学生受益。

本教材既可供商务英语专业、市场营销专业、国际商务专业的学生使用，也可供 MBA 学生使用，亦可作为全校选修课程教材。同时，也欢迎企业管理人员和营销人员使用。

本教材是中外学者第二次合作的结晶，相信会为有志于走向世界的中国精英学生打下英语语言、营销理论与营销实践的坚实基础。

本书配套的教学课件（PPT）以及课后练习题答案，请登录中国人民大学出版社官方网站 http://

www.crup.com.cn，搜索本书后下载使用，或联系 chengzsh@crup.com.cn，wangxw@crup.com.cn，010-62515580，010-62513265 索取。

本书配有相关的网络学习材料。学习中心网址是：http://www.mhhe.com/fourps。

采用本书作教材的教师可向 McGraw-Hill 公司北京代表处联系索取教学课件资料，传真：(010) 62790292，电子邮件：instructorchina@mcgraw-hill.com。

刘白玉　教授

2020 年 2 月 7 日

Authors of Essentials of Marketing, 16/e

William D. Perreault Jr.

William D. Perreault Jr. is Kenan Professor of Business Emeritus at the University of North Carolina. Dr. Perreault is the recipient of the two most prestigious awards in his field: the American Marketing Association Distinguished Educator Award and the Academy of Marketing Science Outstanding Educator Award. He was also selected for the Churchill Award, which honors career impact on marketing research. He was editor of the *Journal of Marketing Research* and has been on the review board of the *Journal of Marketing* and other journals.

The Decision Sciences Institute has recognized Dr. Perreault for innovations in marketing education, and at UNC he has received several awards for teaching excellence. His books include two other widely used texts: *Basic Marketing* and *The Marketing Game!*

Dr. Perreault is a past president of the American Marketing Association Academic Council, served as chair of an advisory committee to the U.S. Census Bureau, and served as a trustee of the Marketing Science Institute. He has also worked as a consultant to organizations that range from GE and IBM to the Federal Trade Commission.

Joseph P. Cannon

Joseph P. Cannon is a Dean's Distinguished Teaching Fellow and professor of marketing at Colorado State University. He has also taught at the University of North Carolina, Emory University, Instituto de Empresa (Madrid, Spain), INSEAD (Fontainebleau, France), and Thammasat University (Bangkok, Thailand). He has received several teaching awards and the N. Preston Davis Award for Instructional Innovation.

Dr. Cannon's research has been published in the *Journal of Marketing, Journal of Marketing Research, Journal of the Academy of Marketing Science, Journal of Operations Management, Journal of Personal Selling and Sales Management, Journal of Public Policy and Marketing, Antitrust Bulletin,* and the *Academy of Management Review,* among others. He is a two-time recipient of the Louis W. and Rhona L. Stern Award for high-impact research on interorganizational issues. He has also written numerous teaching cases. Dr. Cannon has served on the editorial review boards of the *Journal of Marketing, Journal of the Academy of Marketing Science, Journal of Operations Management, Journal of Personal Selling and Sales Management,* and *Journal of Marketing Education*. The *Journal of Marketing* has honored Dr. Cannon with several distinguished reviewer awards. He served as chair of the American Marketing Association's Interorganizational Special Interest Group (IOSIG). Before entering academics, Dr. Cannon worked in sales and marketing for Eastman Kodak Company.

E. Jerome McCarthy

Marketing lost one of its pioneers when E. Jerome "Jerry" McCarthy passed away at his home in East Lansing, Michigan, in 2015.

After earning a PhD at the University of Minnesota, Dr. McCarthy joined the faculty at Notre Dame and became a Fellow in the prestigious Ford Foundation Program at Harvard, an experience that focused on how to make marketing management practice more rigorous and shaped his thoughts on the needs of students and educators. Dr. McCarthy spent most of his career at Michigan State University, gaining a reputation for working with passion and purpose. He received the AMA's Trailblazer Award in 1987 and was voted one of the "top five" leaders in marketing thought by marketing educators.

Dr. McCarthy was well known for his innovative teaching materials and texts, including *Basic Marketing* and *Essentials of Marketing*. These books changed the way marketing was taught by taking a managerial point of view. He also introduced a marketing strategy planning framework, organizing marketing decisions around the Four Ps–Product, Price, Place, and Promotion. As these approaches became the standard in other texts, Dr. McCarthy continued to innovate, including new materials in the digital realm. Today's marketing instructors owe a great debt to this innovative pioneer.

Preface

Essentials of Marketing Is Designed to Satisfy *Your* Needs

This book is about marketing and marketing strategy planning. At its essence, marketing strategy planning is about figuring out how to do a superior job of satisfying customers. We take that point of view seriously and believe in practicing what we preach. So you can trust that this new edition of *Essentials of Marketing*–and all of the other teaching and learning materials that accompany it–will satisfy your needs. We're very excited about this 16th edition of *Essentials of Marketing* and we hope that you will be as well.

In developing this edition, we've made hundreds of big and small additions, changes, and improvements to the text and all the supporting materials that accompany it. We'll highlight some of those changes in this preface, but first we'll provide background on the evolution of *Essentials of Marketing.*

Building on Pioneering Strengths

Basic Marketing (*Essentials of Marketing*'s parent text) pioneered an innovative structure–the "Four Ps" (Product, Price, Promotion, and Place) with a managerial approach–for the introductory marketing course. It quickly became one of the most widely used business textbooks ever published because it organized the best ideas about marketing so that readers could both understand and apply them. The unifying focus of these ideas is: *How does a marketing manager decide which customers to target and what is the best way to meet their needs?*

With each new edition of *Essentials of Marketing,* we update the content based on changes in marketing management and the market environment. This book reflects marketing's best practices and ideas. *Essentials of Marketing* and the supporting materials that accompany it have been more widely used than any other teaching materials for the introductory marketing class. It is gratifying that the Four Ps organizing structure has worked well for millions of students and teachers.

The success of *Essentials of Marketing* is not the result of a single strength–or one long-lasting innovation. Other textbooks have adopted our Four Ps framework, and we have continuously improved the book. The text's Four Ps framework, managerial orientation, and strategy planning focus have proven to be foundation pillars that are remarkably robust for supporting new developments in the field, resulting in innovations in the text and package. Thus, with each new edition of *Essentials of Marketing,* we continue to innovate to better meet the needs of students and faculty. In fact, we have made ongoing changes in how we develop the logic of the Four Ps and the marketing strategy planning process. As always, though, our objective is to provide a flexible, high-quality text and choices from comprehensive and reliable support materials so that instructors and students can accomplish their learning objectives.

What's Different about *Essentials of Marketing?*

The biggest distinguishing factor about *Essentials of Marketing* is our integrative approach to creating a teaching and learning package for the introductory marketing course. This integration makes it easier to learn about marketing, teach marketing, and apply it in the real world. For many students, the introductory marketing course will be the only marketing class they ever take. They need to come away with a strong understanding of the key concepts in marketing and how marketing operates in practice. *Essentials of Marketing:*

1. Examines *what* marketing is and *how* to do it.
2. Integrates special topics such as services, international marketing, big data, social media, ethics, and more across the text–with coverage in almost every chapter.
3. Delivers a supplements package completely developed or closely managed by the authors–so each part connects with the text.

The supplements package is extensive–designed to allow you to *teach marketing your way* (see Exhibit P-1). The integration of these three features delivers a product proven to work for instructors and students. Let us show you what we mean–and why and how instructors and students benefit from the *Essentials of Marketing* teaching and learning package.

What and how marketing? Marketing operates in dynamic markets. Fast-changing global markets, environmental challenges and sustainability, the blurring speed of technological advances–including an explosion in the use of digital tools by consumers and businesses–are just a few of the current trends confronting today's marketing manager. Whereas some marketing texts merely attempt to describe this market environment, *Essentials of Marketing* teaches students *analytical abilities* and *how-to-do-it skills* that prepare them for success.

Exhibit P-1
Essentials of Marketing **Integrates Marketing**

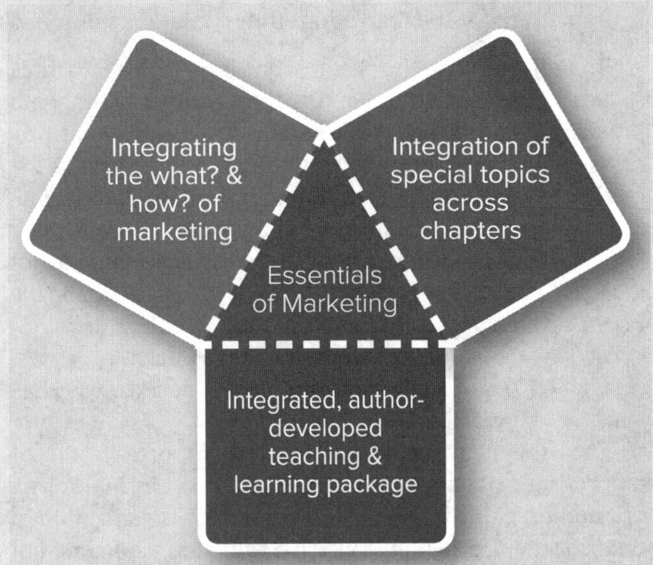

To propel students in this direction, we deliberately include a variety of examples, explanations, frameworks, conceptual organizers, exercises, cases, and how-to-do-it techniques that relate to our overall framework for marketing strategy planning. Taken together, these different learning aids speed the development of "marketing sensibility" and enable students to analyze marketing situations and develop marketing plans in a confident and meaningful way. They are practical and they work. And because they are interesting and understandable, they motivate students to see marketing as the challenging and rewarding area it is. In the end, the *Essentials of Marketing* teaching and learning package prepares students to analyze marketing situations and develop exceptional marketing strategies—not just recite endless sets of lists.

Integration of special topics. In contrast to many other marketing textbooks, we emphasize careful integration of special topics. Some textbooks treat "special" topics—such as marketing relationships, international marketing, services marketing, the Internet, digital lifestyles, nonprofit organizations, marketing ethics, marketing analytics, social issues, and business-to-business marketing—in separate chapters (or parts of chapters). We are convinced that treating such topics separately leads to an unfortunate compartmentalization of ideas. For example, to simply tack on a new chapter covering ethics or marketing analytics completely ignores the reality that these are not isolated topics; rather, they must be considered across the rubric of marketing decisions.

Exhibit P-2 shows the coverage of some key topics across specific chapters.

The teaching and learning materials—designed and developed by the authors—are integrated to work effectively with *Essentials of Marketing.* We don't tack on extras that have been outsourced and therefore don't mix well with our package. Because of this, you have flexible tools for *teaching* and *learning marketing your way.*

Exhibit P-2 Coverage of Special Topics across Chapters*

Special Topic	Chapter									
	1	2	3	4	5	6	7	8	9	10
Marketing relationships	X	X	X	X	X	X	X	X	X	X
International	X	X	X	X	X	X	X	X	X	X
Ethics	X	X	X	X	X	X	X	X	X	X
Services	X	X	X	X	X	X	X	X	X	X
B2B	X	X	X		X	X	X	X	X	X
Marketing analytics	X	X	X	X	X	X	X	X	X	X
Technology, Internet, social media, "Big Data," & digital lifestyle	X	X	X	X	X	X	X	X		X
Environment & sustainability	X	X		X	X	X		X	X	X
Nonprofits	X	X	X		X	X		X	X	X
Quality	X	X	X	X	X	X		X	X	X
Customer value	X	X	X	X	X	X	X	X	X	X
Marketing's link with other functions	X	X	X	X	X	X	X	X	X	X

**X* indicates coverage in the form of a section of the chapter, example, illustration, or discussion.

Marketing can be studied in many ways, and the *Essentials of Marketing* text material is only the central component of our *P*rofessional *L*earning *U*nits *S*ystem (*P.L.U.S.*) for students and for teachers. Instructors and students can select from our units to develop their own personalized teaching and learning systems. Our objective is to offer you a *P.L.U.S.* "menu" so that you can conveniently select units you want—and disregard what you do not want. Many combinations of units are possible depending on course and learning objectives. Later in this preface we highlight each *P.L.U.S.* element (full details can be found in the Instructor's Manual).

Most business students will take only one marketing course in their studies. They deserve the benefits of a highly innovative yet *proven* set of integrated learning materials.

Ten Chapters—with an Emphasis on Marketing Strategy Planning

The emphasis of *Essentials of Marketing* is on marketing strategy planning. Ten chapters introduce the important concepts of marketing and help students see marketing through the eyes of the manager. The organization of the chapters and topics is carefully planned. We took special care in writing so that:

- It is possible to rearrange and use the chapters in many different sequences to fit different needs.
- All topics and chapters fit together into a clear, overall framework for the marketing strategy planning process.

Broadly speaking, the chapters can be grouped into three sections. The first five chapters introduce marketing and provide a broad view of the marketing strategy planning process. Chapters 2–5 each cover different topics, such as the market environment, competition, segmentation, differentiation, and buyer behavior provide information about these topics to improve marketing decisions. The second part of the text (Chapters 6–9) goes into the details of planning the Four Ps, with specific attention to the key strategy decisions in each area. Finally, we conclude with an integrative review (Chapter 10) and a critical assessment of marketing's challenges and opportunities.

The first chapter deals with the important role of marketing—focusing not only on how a marketing orientation guides a business or nonprofit organization in the process of providing superior value to customers, but also on the role of macro-marketing and how a market-directed economy shapes choices and quality of life for consumers.

Chapter 2 introduces students to the importance of evaluating opportunities in the external environments affecting marketing. This chapter also highlights the critical

Exhibit P-3 *Essentials of Marketing* and the Marketing Strategy Planning Process

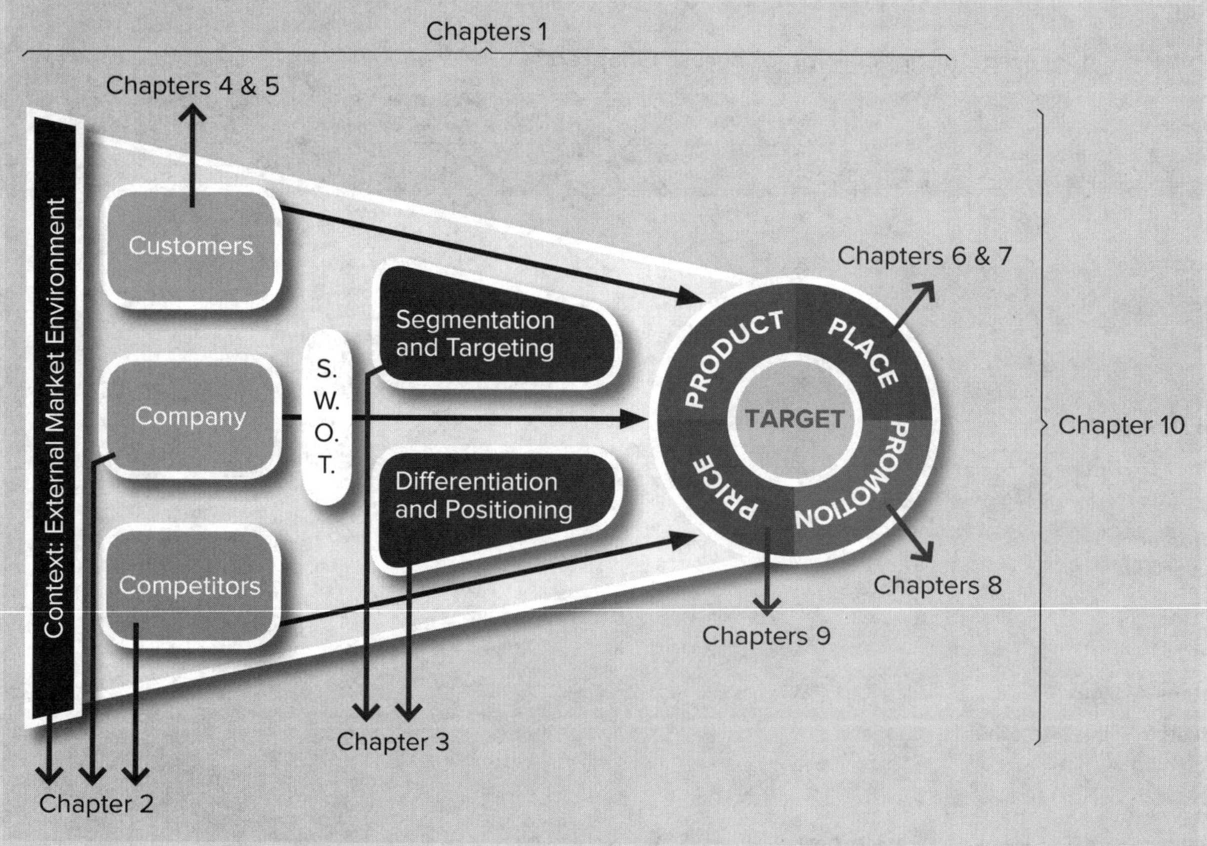

role of screening criteria to narrow down all possible opportunities to those that the firm will pursue. Next Chapter 3 shows how market analysis relates to segmentation and differentiation decisions, as well as the criteria used to narrow down to a specific target market and marketing mix.

It is necessary to understand customers in order to segment markets and satisfy target market needs. So the next two chapters take a closer look at customers. Chapter 4 studies the behavioral aspects of the final consumer market. Chapter 5 looks at how business and organizational customers–such as manufacturers, channel members, and government purchasers–are similar to and different from final consumers.

Chapters 6 and 7 focus on Place. Chapter 6 focuses on the fast-changing arena of logistics and the strides that firms are making in using e-commerce to reduce the costs of storing, transporting, and handling products while improving the distribution service they provide customers. Chapter 7 provides a clear picture of retailers, wholesalers, and their strategy planning, including exchanges taking place via the Internet. This chapter helps students see why the big changes taking place in retailing are reshaping the channel systems for many consumer products.

Chapter 8 deals with Promotion. The chapter builds on the concepts of integrated marketing communications, direct-response promotion, and customer-initiated digital communication, which are introduced in Chapter 8.

Chapter 9 deals with Price. Chapter 9 focuses on pricing objectives and policies, including the use of information technology to implement flexible pricing; pricing in the channel; and the use of discounts, allowances, and other variations from a list price.

The final chapter–Chapter 10–considers how efficient the marketing process is. Here we evaluate the effectiveness of both micro- and macro-marketing–and we consider the competitive, technological, ethical, and social challenges facing marketing managers both now and in the future. Chapter 10 also reinforces the integrative nature of marketing management and reviews the marketing strategy planning process that leads to creative marketing plans.

Most of the 33 short written cases have been updated with new information to make sure they reflect the realities of the current marketplace. The focus of these cases is on problem solving. They encourage students to apply–and really get involved with–the concepts developed in the text. At the end of each chapter, we recommend the cases that best relate to that chapter's content.

I love your book–but there are too many chapters for *my* class. *What can I do?*

We are often asked this question by professors who use the quarter system or prefer to provide students with less breadth of coverage but more depth. Two chapters can easily be dropped from the text without harming understanding of other topics:

- Chapter 6 provides coverage of logistics and customer service. We hear that schools with a required course on supply chain management often find this chapter to be redundant. It can also be dropped if there is less desire for this type of coverage. Dropping it does not have an adverse impact on other Place chapters.
- Chapter 10 provides a critical look at marketing and a review of the marketing strategy planning process. If time is an issue, this can be dropped, though we recommend instructors have a concluding lecture that ties together the course.

What's New in This Edition of *Essentials of Marketing?*

Each revision of *Essentials of Marketing* has a few basic themes–areas we try to emphasize across the book. This edition we focused on (1) marketing analytics, (2) currency, and (3) active learning. There are several big changes to this edition of *Essentials of Marketing* and hundreds of smaller ones. *Essentials of Marketing* is quick to recognize the many dramatic changes in the market environment and marketing strategy; we are also a leader in pedagogical innovations. Here is a quick overview of what we changed for the 16th edition of *Essentials of Marketing.*

Marketing analytics. The last couple of editions of *Essentials of Marketing* have featured growing coverage of big data and marketing analytics. Following marketing practice and feedback from instructors, this edition significantly increases coverage of these topics. Our students–whether marketing majors or in some other area of business–are expected to know what marketing analytics is and how it can be used in marketing strategy planning.

Before revising the text, we had discussions with many different instructors about how to add marketing analytics to the introductory marketing course. While everyone agreed that today's student needs to know more about how businesses use marketing analytics, there was disagreement about how much time and focus it should receive. So our coverage is very flexible–allowing *you* the instructor to decide how much attention marketing analytics will have in your class. Most of our extended treatment of marketing analytics can easily be added or left out–as it involves an in-text boxed element, end-of-chapter and a marketing simulation, Exhibit P-4 shows how each can contribute to the learning objectives you have for your students.

Currency. Every edition of *Essentials of Marketing* focuses on currency. We find that students like to read current examples. And with technology and customer behavior evolving so quickly, a marketing textbook must keep pace. Instructors and students require up-to-date concepts, content, and examples. In this edition:

- We add hundreds of new examples that engage students. Of course, we continue to include the latest earned, owned, and social media examples–but we

Exhibit P-4 You Decide How Much Marketing Analytics to Add to Your Class

I want my students to . . .		Resources in *Essentials of Marketing*
. . . understand the importance of analytics and some key terms.	→	Each chapter features new key terms and/or marketing analytics examples.
. . . understand how marketing managers use analytics.	→	Almost each chapter includes a "Marketing Analytics in Action" activity—a mini-case study of analytics in practice.
. . . calculate some basic marketing analytics.	→	Each chapter includes a Connect homework exercise "Marketing Analytics: Data-to-Knowledge"

also recognize changing consumer behavior, organizational buying behavior, new-product development, the growth and evolution of retail (especially online), advertising, and pricing.

- Current visuals—photos and advertising examples—are particularly important for today's student, so we choose examples that provide a learning experience for the student, not just added color.
- Our *What's Next?* boxes, embedded in each chapter, provide a futuristic perspective on where marketing may be headed.

Active learning exercises. Many instructors count on these to prepare students for class and utilize more active learning activities inside or outside the classroom. We have designed many active learning exercises so students can learn more critical thinking and application of concepts, which helps them understand how marketing really works. This edition of *Essentials of Marketing* features:

- *NEW! Flip Your Marketing Class.* A few years ago, Joe Cannon decided to "flip" his marketing classes. He no longer lectures and now uses about 90 percent of class time on in-class activities. Whether you are ready to completely "flip" your class or are just looking to add more active learning to mix in with your lectures, you will appreciate the materials he has put together. Joe's *Flip Your Marketing Class* e-book can be downloaded from the Instructor's Resource Materials.
- *NEW! In-Class Activities.* As part of the *Flip Your Marketing Class* e-book effort, Joe produced a series of exercises that can be used in class. For each chapter there are two to four In-Class Activities. These exercises can be completed in small groups in class. They reinforce and apply concepts learned from *Essentials of Marketing.* Beyond that, many of the following elements of *Essentials of Marketing* could also be used as in-class activities.
- *NEW! Marketing Analytics in Action*. These in-chapter boxed features place students in the situation facing many managers: analyzing and interpreting marketing analytics. The activities show students how marketing analytics are used—but also ask them questions that force students to use critical thinking skills to make marketing decisions. These exercises work particularly well for in-class discussion.
- *Practice Marketing.* The *Practice Marketing* simulation offers a unique way to learn and apply the Four Ps of marketing. Students take on the role of a marketing manager tasked with creating and launching a new product; they do actual marketing strategy planning around a backpack—analyzing customers, competitors, and company—then deciding on target market, product, place, price, and promotion decisions. After seeing the results of their initial decisions, they can adapt their strategy. The simulation allows students to compete with other students or artificial intelligence characters. Many students have referred to *Practice Marketing* as a virtual internship.
- *What's Next?* Each chapter includes an active learning boxed element. Each *What's Next?* offers an in-depth analysis of some trend or marketing future—and asks students about its implications. These elements have all been updated to make them more forward-looking and active learning focused.
- *Ethical Dilemma.* Many of these critical thinking exercises have been updated from previous editions, with a focus on students making decisions in gray areas, many of which were introduced by the advancing technologies used in marketing.
- *Marketing Analytics*: *Data to Knowledge.* This end-of-chapter exercise—which can be done—shows students how data analysis is used by marketing managers. Using concepts and examples from each chapter, the exercises build higher-order learning skills and demonstrate data-driven marketing decision making. Each practical question walks students through a real-life scenario, shows them how to use a spreadsheet to find answers, and then asks (optional) discussion questions to build critical thinking skills.
- *Cases.* Our short cases continue to provide students with opportunities to explore how real companies conduct the marketing strategy planning process.

Chapter-by-chapter. We updated every chapter's opening case scenario. Although we don't have space to list all our changes, the following are some highlights of the more significant changes we have made to this edition of *Essentials of Marketing:*

Chapter 1. Refreshed with new and updated examples. New key term *marketing metrics. Marketing Analytics in Action* exercise on profits.

Chapter 2. Updates throughout the chapter. Major new elements include (1) *What's Next?* Intelligent agents learn to create and deliver customer value, (2) *Marketing Analytics in Action* on market share, (3) key term *market share,* and (4) extensive coverage of artificial intelligence and intelligent agents as related to marketing.

Chapter 3. Updates throughout this chapter with new examples. Major updates include (1) segmenting draws on Why? What? and Who?; (2) new ethical dilemma; and (3) *Marketing Analytics in Action* on cluster analysis.

Chapter 4. Updates across the chapter and new examples. New content includes (1) websites use artificial intelligence to make recommendations, (2) updates to coverage of ethnic markets, (3) shopping behavior, (4) updates to consumer problem solving, (5) new key term and discussion of *predictive analytics,* and (6) *Marketing Analytics in Action* on analytics and adoption process.

Chapter 5. Updates and refreshed examples. New elements include (1) *What's Next?* Millennials take on organizational buying, and (2) *Marketing Analytics in Action* on supplier scorecards.

Chapter 6. Updated for currency. Major new elements (1) *Marketing Analytics in Action* on trade-offs and customer service level, and (2) *What's Next?* Who's–rather what's–driving that truck?

Chapter 7. We always have a lot of revisions in our coverage of retailing–and this edition is no different. To remain current, every edition requires significant rewriting, especially in our section on retailing and the Internet. We also updated our extended example of the wholesaler Frieda's. Major changes include (1) a new chapter opening case study on Home Depot (very interesting story here), (2) an extended example on Zappos and Foot Locker, (3) department stores update that describes issues around their major decline and closures, (4) major updates to "Retailing and the Internet," (5) the new key term *multichannel shoppers,* (6) information on how technology drives the continued retail evolution, and (7) a new *What's Next?* Psychic retailers?

Chapter 8. This chapter always has a lot of new examples–students notice dated examples and we aim to eliminate them. Changes include (1) adding organizational buying to Exhibit 8-2, (2) examples of encoding-decoding, and (3) updates in budgeting with more attention to the role of analytics.

Chapter 9. Updated for currency as well as major changes that include (1) new key term and coverage of *dynamic pricing,* (2) updated coverage of big data and predictive analytics and how they lead to personalized pricing.

Chapter 10. Modest updates for currency.

Expanded Teaching and Learning Resources for the 16th Edition

The authors of *Essentials of Marketing* and McGraw-Hill Higher Education have put together a variety of resources to supplement your teaching and learning experience. Instructors will find the following resources posted in the Instructor Resources section of the Connect Library for the 16th edition.

- ***NEW! Active Learning Guide and Exercises.*** We hear more and more from instructors seeking to change their marketing course away from being primarily lecture-based to adding more active learning in the classroom. Joe Cannon decided to flip his class and learned a lot in the process. He shares those learnings in an e-book that provides some guidance–see *Flip Your Marketing Class*. The ideas work whether you want to completely flip the class or just add more active learning to your current class sessions. One of the most difficult aspects of making this transition is having high-quality activities for students to work on–activities that reinforce important marketing concepts and critical thinking. We have put together many different resources that can help you make this transition–most with teaching notes.
- ***Connect Interactive Applications***–An online assignment and assessment solution that connects students with the tools and resources they'll need to achieve success.
- ***SmartBook***–Powered by LearnSmart, SmartBook is the adaptive reading experience that helps students learn faster, study more efficiently, and retain more knowledge.
- ***Instructor's Manual and Digital Implementation Guide***–Offers a single resource to make it easier for you to decide which resources to use when covering each chapter in the text.
- ***PowerPoint Presentation Resources:***
  - *Chapter PowerPoint Slides.* For each chapter there is a set of PowerPoint presentations that includes television commercials and short video clip examples, examples of print advertisements that demonstrate important concepts, and questions to use with "clickers" or simply to check if students are getting it. These slides cover all the major topics in the chapter.
  - *Multimedia Lecture Support Guide and Video Guide.* Now integrated into the Instructor's Manual and Digital Implementation Guide, you will find detailed lecture scripts and chapter outlines for the presentation slides to make getting prepared for class fast and easy.
- ***Author Blog***–Connect with the redesigned *Teach the 4 Ps* blog (www.teachthe4ps.com) for links to articles, blog posts, videos, video clips, and commercials–with tips on how to use them with *Essentials of Marketing*. The site is organized by topic–so you can easily find something related to what you are teaching that day–and provides plenty of tips for bringing *active learning* to your classroom.

- ***Practice Marketing Simulation***–An online and fully mobile interactive learning environment that simulates the full marketing mix, as well as market segmentation and targeting. This can be found at www.mhpractice.com and through Connect.
- ***Teaching Videos***–The video package includes 31 full-length videos and video cases that can be shown in class or assigned to students to view outside of class.
- ***Test Bank***–Our test bank includes more than 5,000 objective test questions–every question developed or edited by the authors to ensure it works seamlessly with the text. McGraw-Hill's TestGen program facilitates the creation of tests.

Responsibilities of Leadership

In closing, we return to a point raised at the beginning of this preface. *Essentials of Marketing* has been a leading textbook in marketing since its first edition. We take the responsibilities of that leadership seriously. We know that you want and deserve the very best teaching and learning materials possible. It is our commitment to bring you those materials today with this edition.

We recognize that fulfilling this commitment requires a process of continuous improvement. Because needs change, revisions, updates, and development of new elements must be ongoing. You are an important part of this evolution and of this leadership. We encourage your feedback. The most efficient way to get in touch with us is to send an e-mail message to Joe.Cannon@ColoState.edu. Thoughtful criticisms and suggestions from students and teachers alike have helped make *Essentials of Marketing* what it is today. We hope that you will help us make it what it will be in the future.

William D. Perreault Jr., Joseph P. Cannon, and E. Jerome McCarthy

McGraw Hill Education connect®

McGraw-Hill Connect® is a highly reliable, easy-to-use homework and learning management solution that utilizes learning science and award-winning adaptive tools to improve student results.

- Connect's assignments help students contextualize what they've learned through application, so they can better understand the material and think critically.
- Connect will create a personalized study path customized to individual student needs through SmartBook®.
- SmartBook helps students study more efficiently by delivering an interactive reading experience through adaptive highlighting and review.

Connect's Impact on Retention Rates, Pass Rates, and Average Exam Scores

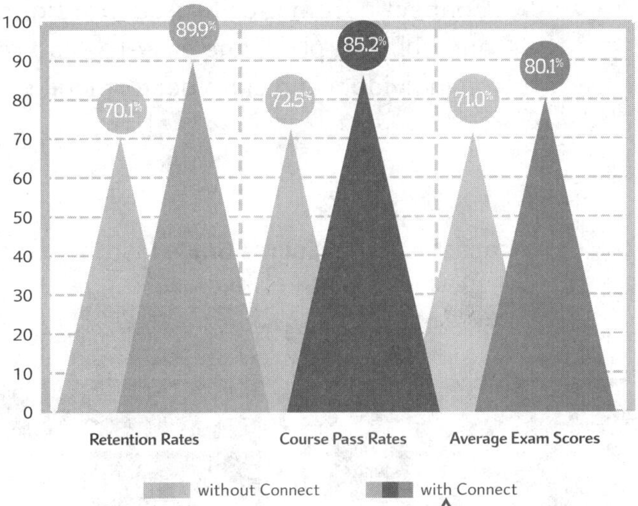

Using **Connect** improves retention rates by **19.8 percentage points,** passing rates by **12.7 percentage points, and** exam scores by **9.1 percentage points.**

Over **7 billion questions** have been answered, making McGraw-Hill Education products more intelligent, reliable, and precise.

73% of instructors who use **Connect** require it; instructor satisfaction **increases** by 28% when **Connect** is required.

Quality Content and Learning Resources

- Connect content is authored by the world's best subject matter experts, and is available to your class through a simple and intuitive interface.
- The Connect eBook makes it easy for students to access their reading material on smartphones and tablets. They can study on the go and don't need internet access to use the eBook as a reference, with full functionality.
- Multimedia content such as videos, simulations, and games drive student engagement and critical thinking skills.

Robust Analytics and Reporting

©Hero Images/Getty Images

- Connect Insight® generates easy-to-read reports on individual students, the class as a whole, and on specific assignments.
- The Connect Insight dashboard delivers data on performance, study behavior, and effort. Instructors can quickly identify students who struggle and focus on material that the class has yet to master.
- Connect automatically grades assignments and quizzes, providing easy-to-read reports on individual and class performance.

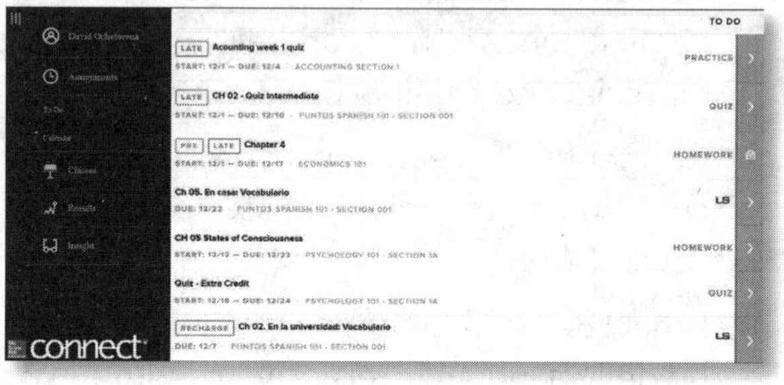

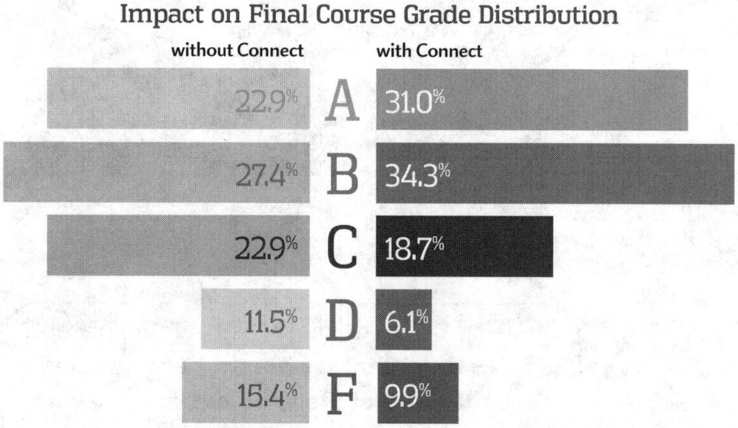

More students earn **As** and **Bs** when they use **Connect**.

Trusted Service and Support

- Connect integrates with your LMS to provide single sign-on and automatic syncing of grades. Integration with Blackboard®, D2L®, and Canvas also provides automatic syncing of the course calendar and assignment-level linking.
- Connect offers comprehensive service, support, and training throughout every phase of your implementation.
- If you're looking for some guidance on how to use Connect, or want to learn tips and tricks from super users, you can find tutorials as you work. Our Digital Faculty Consultants and Student Ambassadors offer insight into how to achieve the results you want with Connect.

www.mheducation.com/connect

Acknowledgments

Essentials of Marketing has been influenced and improved by the input of more people than it is possible to list. We want to express our appreciation to those who have played the most significant roles, especially in this edition.

We are especially grateful to our many students who have critiqued and made comments about materials in *Essentials of Marketing*. Indeed, in many ways, our students have been our best teachers.

Many improvements in recent editions were stimulated by feedback from a number of colleagues around the country. Their feedback took many forms. In particular, we would like to recognize the helpful contributions of:

Cliff Ashmead Abdool, *CUNY College of Staten Island*
Roshan (Bob) Ahuja, *Ramapo College of New Jersey*
Thomas Ainscough, University of South Florida
Ian Alam, Ramapo College of New Jersey
Mary Albrecht, Maryville University
David Andrus, Kansas State University at Manhattan
Chris Anicich, Broome Community College
Maria Aria, Missouri State University
April Atwood, University of Washington
Ainsworth Bailey, University of Toledo
Turina Bakker, University of Wisconsin
Jeff Bauer, University of Cincinnati-Batavia
Leta Beard, Washington University
Amy Beattie, Nichols College of Champlain
Cathleen Behan, Northern VA Community College
Patty Bellamy, Black Hills State University
Suzeanne Benet, Grand Valley State University
Shahid Bhuian, Louisiana Tech University
John S. Bishop Jr., Ohio State University
David Blackmore, University of Pittsburgh
Ross Blankenship, *University of California Berkeley*
Maurice Bode, Delgado Community College
Jonathan Bohlman, Purdue School of Management
William J. Bont, Grand Valley State University
Laurie Brachman, University of Wisconsin
Kit Brenan, Northland Community College
John Brennan, Florida State University
Richard Brien, De Anza College
Elten Briggs, University of Texas-Austin
Denny Bristow, St. Cloud State University
Susan Brudvig, Ball State University
Kendrick W. Brunson, Liberty University
Derrell Bulls, Texas Women's University
Michele Bunn, Collat School of Business, University of Alabama at Birmingham
Helen Burdenski, Notre Dame College of Ohio
Nancy Bush, Wingate University
Carmen Calabrese, University of North Carolina-Pembroke
Catherine Campbell, University of Maryland University College
James Carlson, Manatee Community College
Amy Caponette Pellissippi State Community College
Donald Caudill, *Bluefield State College*
Karen Cayo, Kettering University
Kenny Chan, California State University-Chico
E. Wayne Chandler, Eastern Illinois University
Chen Ho Chao, Baruch College, City University of New York
Valeri Chukhlomin, Empire State College
Margaret Clark, Cincinnati State Technical and Community College
Thomas, Clark University of Houston Downtown
Paris Cleanthous, New York University-Stern School
Thomas Cline, St. Vincent College
Gloria Cockerell, Collin County Community College
Linda Jane Coleman, Salem State College
Brian Connett, California State University-Northridge
Craig Conrad, Western Illinois University
Barbara Conte, Florida Atlantic University
Sherry Cook, Southwest Missouri State
Matt Critcher, University of Arkansas Community College-Batesville
Tammy Crutchfield, Mercer University
Brent Cunningham, Jacksonville State University
Madeline Damkar, Cabrillo Community College/CSUEB
Charles Davies, *Hillsdale College*
J. Charlene Davis, Trinity University
Scott Davis, University of California at Davis
Amy Danley, Wilmington University
Dwane Dean, Manhattan College
Larry Degaris, California State University
Nicholas Didow, University of North Carolina-Chapel Hill
Susan Higgins DeFago, John Carroll University
Oscar W. DeShields Jr., California State University-Northridge
John E. Dillard, University of Houston-Downtown
Les Dlabay, Lake Forest College
Glenna Dod, Wesleyan College
Gary Donnelly, Casper College
Paul Dowling, University of Utah
Laura Downey, Purdue University
Phillip Downs, Florida State University
Michael Drafke, College of DuPage
John Drea, Western Illinois University
Colleen Dunn, Bucks Community College
Sean Dwyer, Louisiana Technical University
Judith Kay Eberhart, *Lindenwood University-Belleville*

Mary Edrington, Drake University
Steven Engel, University of Colorado
Dr. S. Altan Erdem, University of Houston-Clear Lake
Keith Fabes, Berkeley College
Peter Fader, University of Pennsylvania
Ken Fairweather, LeTourneau University
Phyllis Fein, Westchester Community College
Lori S. Feldman, Purdue University
Mark Fenton, University of Wisconsin-Stout
Jodie L. Ferguson, Virginia Commonwealth University
Richard Kent Fields, Carthage College
Lou Firenze, Northwood University
Jon Firooz, Colorado State University
Michael Fitzmorris, Park University
Richard Fogg, Kansas State University
Kim Folkers, Wartburg College
Renee Foster, Delta State University
Frank Franzak, Virginia Commonwealth University
John Gaffney, Hiram College
John Gaskins, *Longwood University*
Carol Gaumer, University of Maryland University College
Karl Giulian, Fairleigh Dickinson University-Madison
Thomas Giese, University of Richmond
J. Lee Goen, Oklahoma Baptist University
Brent G. Goff, University of Houston-Downtown
David Good, Central Missouri State University
Pradeep Gopalakrishna, Pace University
Keith Gosselin, California State University of Northbridge
Rahul Govind, University of Mississippi
Norman Govoni, Babson College
Gary Grandison, Alabama State University
Wade Graves, Grayson County College
Mitch Griffin, Bradley University
Mike Griffith, Cascade College
Alice Griswold, Clarke College
Barbara Gross, California State University-Northridge
Pranjal Gupta, University of Tampa
Susan Gupta, University of Wisconsin at Milwaukee
John Hadjmarcou, University of Texas at El Paso
Khalil Hairston, *Indiana Institute of Technology*
Adam Hall, Western Kentucky University
Bobby Hall, Wayland Baptist University
Joan Hall, Macomb Community College
John Hansen, University of Alabama at Birmingham
David Hansen, Schoolcraft College
Dorothy Harpool, Wichita State University
LeaAnna Harrah, Marion Technical College
James Harvey, George Mason University
John S. Heise, California State University-Northridge
Lewis Hershey, University of North Carolina-Pembroke
James Hess, Ivy Tech Community College
Wolfgang Hinck, Louisiana State University-Shreveport
Pamela Homer, California State University-Long Beach
Ronald Hoverstad, University of the Pacific
John Howard, Tulane University
Doug Hughes, Michigan State University-East Lansing
Deborah Baker Hulse, University of Texas at Tyler
Janet Hunter, Northland Pioneer College
Phil Hupfer, Elmhurst College
Hector Iweka, *Lasell College*
Annette Jajko, Triton College/College of DuPage
Jean Jaymes, West California State University-Bakersfield
Carol Johanek, Washington University
Timothy Johnston, University of Tennessee at Martin
Keith Jones, North Carolina A&T State University
Sungwoo Jung, Saint Louis University
Josette Katz, Atlantic Cape Community College
Fahri Karakaya, University of Massachusetts
Gary Karns, Seattle Pacific University
Pat Karush, Thomas College
Eileen Kearney, Montgomery County Community College
James Kellaris, University of Cincinnati
Robin Kelly, Cuyahoga Community College
Courtney Kernek, Texas A&M University-Commerce
Brian Kinard, PennState University-University Park
Anthony Kim California State Polytechnic University, Pomona
Rob Kleine, Ohio Northern University
Ken Knox, Ohio State University-Athens
Kathleen Krentler, San Diego State University
Claudia Kubowicz-Malhotra, University of North Carolina-Chapel Hill
Dmitri Kuksov, Washington University
Jean Laliberte, Troy State University
Tim Landry, Kutztown University of Pennsylvania
Geoffrey Lantos, Oregon State University
Linda Lamarca, Tarleton State University
Kevin Lambert, Southeast Community College
Richard LaRosa, Indiana University of Pennsylvania
Donald Larson, The Ohio State University
Dana-Nicoleta Lascu, *Richmond University*
Debra Laverie, Texas Tech University
Marilyn Lavin, University of Wisconsin-Whitewater
Freddy Lee, California State University-Los Angeles
Steven V. LeShay, Wilmington University
David Levy, Bellevue University
Dr. Jason Little, Franklin Pierce University
Doug Livermore, Morningside College
Lori Lohman, Augsburg College
Paul James Londrigan, Mott Community College
Guy Lochiatto, California State University
Sylvia Long-Tolbert, University of Toledo
Terry Lowe, Heartland Community College
Harold Lucius, Rowan University
Navneet Luthar, Madison Area Technical College
Richard Lutz, University of Florida
W. J. Mahony, Southern Wesleyan University
Rosalynn Martin, MidSouth Community College
Phyllis Mansfield, Pennsylvania State University-Erie
James McAloon, Fitchburg State University
Lee McCain, *Shaw University*
Christina McCale, Regis University
Michele McCarren, Southern State Community College
Kevin McEvoy, University of Connecticut-Stamford
Rajiv Mehta, New Jersey Institute of Technology
Sanjay Mehta, Sam Houston State University
Matt Meuter, California State University-Chico
Michael Mezja, University of Las Vegas
Margaret Klayton Mi, Mary Washington College
Herbert A. Miller Jr., University of Texas-Austin
Linda Mitchell, Lindon State College
Ted Mitchell, University of Nevada-Reno
Robert Montgomery, University of Evansville

Todd Mooradian, College of William and Mary
Kelvyn A. Moore, Clark Atlanta University
Marlene Morris, Georgetown University
Brenda Moscool, California State University-Bakersfield
Ed Mosher, Laramie Community College
Reza Motameni, California State University-Fresno
Amit Mukherjee, Providence College
Steve Mumsford, *Gwynedd-Mercy College*
Clara Munson, Albertus Magnus
Thomas Myers, University of Richmond
Cynthia Newman, Rider University
Philip S. Nitse, Idaho State University at Pocatello
J. R. Ogden, Kutztown University
David Oh, California State University-Los Angeles
Okey Peter Onyia, Lindenwood University
Sam Okoroafo, University of Toledo
Lisa O'Halloran, Northeast Wisconsin Technical College
Jeannie O'Laughlin, Dakota Wesleyan University
Louis Osuki, Chicago State University
Daniel Padgett, Auburn University
Esther S. Page-Wood, Western Michigan University
Karen Palumbo, University of St. Francis
Terry Paridon, Cameron University
Dr. Amy Patrick, Wilmington University
Terry Paul, Ohio State University
Sheila Petcavage, Cuyahoga Community College
Stephen Peters, Walla Walla Community College
Man Phan, Comsumnes River College
Linda Plank, Ferris State University
Lucille Pointer, University of Houston-Downtown
Brenda Ponsford, Clarion University
Nadia Pomirleanu, *UNLV*
Joel Poor, University of Missouri
Teresa Preston, University of Arkansas at Little Rock
Tracy Proulx, Park University
Brook Quigg, Peirce College
Anthony Racka, Oakland Community College
Kathleen Radionoff, Cardinal Stritch University
Daniel Rajaratnam, Baylor University
Catherine Rich-Duval, Merrimack College
Charles W. Richardson Jr., Clark Atlanta University
Lee Richardson, University of Baltimore
Daniel Ricica, Sinclair Community College
Brent Richard, Ramapo College of New Jersey
Darlene Riedemann, Eastern Illinois University
Sandra Robertson, Thomas Nelson Community College
Kim Rocha, Barton College
Amy Rodie, University of Nebraska-Omaha
Carlos Rodriguez, Governors State University
Robert Roe, University of Wyoming
Ann R. Root, Florida Atlantic University
Mark Rosenbaum, *Northern Illinois University*
Donald Roy, Middle Tennessee State University
Joel Saegert, University of Texas at San Antonio
David Schalow, University of Wisconsin-Stevens Point
Nate Scharff, Grossmont College
Henry Schrader, Ramapo College of New Jersey
C. M. Sashi, Florida Atlantic University
Erika Schlomer-Fischer, California Lutheran University
Lewis Schlossinger, Community College of Aurora
Charles Schwepker, Central Missouri State University
Murphy Sewell, University of Connecticut-Storrs
Kenneth Shamley, Sinclair College
Doris Shaw, Northern Kentucky University
Donald Shifter, Fontbonne College
Jeremy Sierra, New Mexico State University
Lisa Simon, California Polytech-San Luis Obispo
Rob Simon, University of Nebraska
Toye Simmons, University of Houston-Downtown
James Simpson, University of Alabama in Huntsville
Aditya Singh, Pennsylvania State University-McKeesport
Mandeep Singh, *Western Illinois University*
Jill Slomski, Mercyhurst College
Robert Smoot, Lees College
James Smith, University of Houston-Downtown
Don Soucy, University of North Carolina-Pembroke
Roland Sparks, Johnson C. Smith University
Joseph R. Stasio, Merrimack College
Gene Steidinger, Loras College
Jim Stephens, Emporia State University
Tom Stevenson, University of North Carolina
Geoffrey Stewart, University of Louisiana at Lafayette
Karen Stewart, The Richard Stockton College of New Jersey
Stephen Strange, Henderson Community College
Randy Stuart, Kennesaw State University
Rajneesh Suri, Drexel University
John Talbott, Indiana University
Uday Tate, Marshall University
A. J. Taylor, Austin Peay State University
Scott Taylor, McHenry County College
Janice Taylor, Miami University
Kimberly Taylor, *Florida International University*
Steven Taylor, Illinois State University
Jeff Thieme, Syracuse University
Scott Thompson, University of Wisconsin-Oshkosh
Dennis Tootelian, California State University-Sacramento
Gary Tschantz, Walsh University
Fran Ucci, Triton College/College of DuPage
Sue Umashankar, University of Arizona
David Urban, Virginia Commonwealth University
Kristin Uttech, Madison Area Technical College
Laura, Valenti, Nicholls State University
Peter Vantine, Georgia Tech
Steve Vitucci, Tarleton State University
Sharon Wagner, Missouri Western State College
Suzanne Walchli, University of the Pacific
Jane Wayland, Eastern Illinois University
Alan Weber, University of Missouri at Kansas City, Bloch School of Management
Danny "Peter" Weathers, Louisiana State University
Yinghong (Susan) Wei, Oklahoma State University
John Weiss, Colorado State University
M. G. M. Wetzeis, *Universiteit Maastrict, The Netherlands*
Michelle Wicmandy, University of Houston-Downtown
Fred Whitman, Mary Washington College
Judy Wilkinson, Youngstown State University
Phillip Wilson, Midwestern State University
Robert Witherspoon, Triton College
John Withey, Indiana University-South Bend
Brent Wren, Manhattanville College
Doris Wright, Troy University
Jim Wong, Shenandoah University

Joyce H. Wood, N. Virginia Community College
Newell Wright, James Madison University
Joseph Yasaian, McIntosh College
Gary Young, *Worcester State College*

We've always believed that the best way to build consistency and quality into the text and the other P.L.U.S. units is to do as much as possible ourselves. With the growth of multimedia technologies, it's darn hard to be an expert on them all. But we've had spectacular help in that regard.

The lecture-support PowerPoints have been a tremendous effort over many editions. We appreciate the efforts of Luis Torres, Jay Carlson, Mandy Noelle Carlson, David Urban, Milt Pressley, and Lewis Hershey for their creative work on the lecture-support PowerPoint presentation slides. Ellery Miller was a huge help in putting together the YouTube PowerPoints in this edition.

We have had a great team of people work on LearnSmart questions and Connect exercises. I would particularly like to thank Leroy Robinson from University of Houston-Clear Lake for his leadership and work on LearnSmart and Jon Firooz (Colorado State University) who took our Computer-Aided Problems and updated them for use in Connect—they are now titled *Marketing Analytics: Data to Knowledge.*

We consider our "best in the business" video package a true team effort. Although the authors had input, the project has been led in recent years by Nick Childers at Shadows and Light Creative Services. For several editions, Judy Wilkinson has played a big role as producer of the video series for the book. In that capacity, she worked closely with us to come up with ideas, and she provided guidance to the talented group of marketing professors and managers who created or revised videos for this edition.

Of course, like other aspects of *Essentials of Marketing,* the video series has evolved and improved over time, and its current strength is partly due to the insights of Phil Niffenegger, who served as producer for our early video efforts. The video series also continues to benefit from the contributions of colleagues who developed videos in earlier editions. They are:

Gary R. Brockway
James Burley
David Burns
Debra Childers
Martha O. Cooper
Carolyn Costley
Angie Fenton
W. Davis Folsom
Pam Girardo
Brenda Green
Douglas Hausknecht
Jean Jaymes
Linda Mothersbaugh
Michael R. Mullen
Phillip Niffenegger
Scott Johnson
Bart Kittle
Claudia Kubowicz
Gene R. Lazniak
Freddy Lee
Bill Levy
Charles S. Madden
W. Glynn Mangold
Becky Manter
Don McBane
Robert Miller
J. R. Montgomery
Thomas Sherer
Jeanne M. Simmons
Walter Strange
Okey Peter Onyia
Deborah Owens
Thomas G. Ponzurick
George Prough
Peter Rainsford
Jane Reid
Clinton Schertzer
Roger Schoenfeldt
Jeff Tanner
Ron Tatham
Rollie O. Tillman
Carla Vallone
Yinghong (Susan) Wei
Robert Welsh
Holt Wilson
Poh-Lin Yeou

Faculty and students at our current and past academic institutions—Michigan State University, University of North Carolina, Colorado State University, Emory, Notre Dame, University of Georgia, Northwestern University, University of Oregon, University of Minnesota, and Stanford University—have significantly shaped the book. Professor Andrew A. Brogowicz of Western Michigan University contributed many fine ideas to early editions of the text and supplements. Neil Morgan, Charlotte Mason, Rich Gooner, Gary Hunter, John Workman, Nicholas Didow, Barry Bayus, Jon Firooz, Ken Manning, and Ajay Menon have provided a constant flow of helpful suggestions.

We are also grateful to the colleagues with whom we collaborate to produce international adaptations of the text. In particular, Lindsey Meredith, Lynne Ricker, Stan Shapiro, Ken Wong, and Pascale G. Quester have all had a significant impact on *Essentials of Marketing.*

The designers, artists, editors, and production people at McGraw-Hill who worked with us on this edition warrant special recognition. All of them share our commitment to excellence and bring their own individual creativity to the project. First, we should salute Christine Vaughan, who has done a great (and patient) job as content production manager for the project. Without her adaptive problem solving, we could not have succeeded with a (very) rapid-response production schedule—which is exactly what it takes to be certain that teachers and students get the most current information possible.

David Ploskonka worked as product developer on this edition, his insight and project management skills are much appreciated. Our executive brand manager, Meredith Fossel, was new to this edition and brought great enthusiasm, energy, and ideas. We appreciated her valuable perspective on the *Essentials of Marketing* franchise.

The layout and design of the print and online versions of the text included a dedicated team of professionals. Keith McPherson is a long-time creative and valued contributor to *Essentials of Marketing.* He is a great talent and we sincerely appreciate his past efforts that continue to be reflected in the book's design. We sincerely appreciate the talents of Pam Verros who created the interior and Egzon Shaqiri who designed the cover for this edition of *Essentials of Marketing.* We also appreciate Julie De Adder from Photo Affairs, who tracked down photos, ads, and permissions for the images we selected to illustrate important ideas.

We owe an ongoing debt of gratitude to Lin Davis. The book probably wouldn't exist without her—without her help, the book would've been just too overwhelming and we'd have quit! Lin was part of this team for more than 25 years. During that time, she has made contributions in every aspect of the text and package. Kendra Miller was with the team for the 14th and 15th editions of *Essentials of Marketing* and her copyediting and insights were immensely valuable.

This edition of the book brought on two new team members—and they were fantastic additions. Jennifer Collins helped copyedit the manuscript—and brought many ideas and insights to this edition. Shannon LeMay-Finn helped with production, but also brought copyediting, creative ideas, and project management skills to the project. Thank you both!

We are indebted to all the firms that allowed us to reproduce their proprietary materials here. Similarly, we are grateful to associates from our business experiences who have shared their perspectives and feedback and enhanced our sensitivity to the key challenges of marketing management.

Our families have been patient and consistent supporters through all phases in developing *Essentials of Marketing.* The support has been direct and substantive. Pam Perreault and Chris Cannon have provided valuable assistance and more encouragement than you could imagine. Our kids—Suzanne, Will, Kelly, Ally, and Mallory—provide valuable suggestions and ideas as well as encouragement and support while their dads were too often consumed with a never-ending set of deadlines.

Our product must capsulize existing knowledge while bringing new perspectives and organization to enhance it. Our thinking has been shaped by the writings of literally thousands of marketing scholars and practitioners. In some cases, it is impossible to give unique credit for a particular idea or concept because so many people have played important roles in anticipating, suggesting, shaping, and developing it. We gratefully acknowledge these contributors—from the early thought-leaders to contemporary authors and researchers—who have shared their creative ideas. We respect their impact on the development of marketing and more specifically this book.

To all of these persons—and to the many publishers who graciously granted permission to use their materials—we are deeply grateful. Responsibility for any errors or omissions is certainly ours, but the book would not have been possible without the assistance of many others. Our sincere appreciation goes to all who contributed.

William D. Perreault Jr.
Joseph P. Cannon
E. Jerome McCarthy

Brief Contents

Contents

3

CHAPTER THREE

Focusing Marketing Strategy with Segmentation and Positioning 60

4

CHAPTER FOUR

Final Consumers and Their Buying Behavior 86

5

CHAPTER FIVE

Business and Organizational Customers and Their Buying Behavior 114

6

CHAPTER SIX

Distribution Customer Service and Logistics 142

7

8

CHAPTER SEVEN

Retailers, Wholesalers, and Their Strategy Planning 164

CHAPTER EIGHT

Promotion—Introduction to Integrated Marketing Communications 190

CHAPTER NINE

Pricing Objectives and Policies 214

CHAPTER TEN

Ethical Marketing in a Consumer-Oriented World: Appraisal and Challenges 240

Cases

Essentials of Marketing

A Marketing Strategy Planning Approach

1 CHAPTER ONE

Marketing's Value to Consumers, Firms, and Society

When it's time to roll out of bed in the morning, does the Spotify app on your Apple iPhone play your "Waking Up Happy" playlist, or is it your roommate blasting The Chainsmokers? Do you throw on your Nike Flyknit shoes and get in a short run before breakfast? Maybe not this morning. You slept in and now you barely have time to throw on your Levi's jeans, shirt from Zara, and Vans shoes as you race off to class. You do need a quick bite at home before you go. Will it be a Chobani pineapple-flavored Greek yogurt and an Einstein's bagel with Philadelphia Cream Cheese? Or maybe you grab a Chicken Apple Sausage breakfast sandwich at Caribou Coffee in the student union. If you hurry, your roommate can give you a ride to school in her new Ford Fiesta, although you could ride your Big Shot Fixie bike or take the bus that the city bought from Mercedes-Benz. So many choices.

When you think about it, you can't get very far into a day without bumping into marketing—and what the whole marketing system does for you. It affects every aspect of our lives—often in ways we don't even consider.

In other parts of the world, people wake up each day to different kinds of experiences. A family in rural Africa may have little choice about what food they will eat or where their clothing will come from. In some countries, economic decisions are largely made by government officials. But in the world's most developed countries, consumers determine what's on store shelves. If no one buys a particular color, size, or style, then companies stop producing it. So you may have trouble finding a Chicken Apple Sausage sandwich in Hangzhou, China, where the locals are more likely to join the line of people waiting at GanQiShi's for steamed buns.

One brand found around the world is Nike. How has Nike become the choice for so many professional and casual athletes around the world? Is it the more than $1 billion Nike spends each year for endorsements from star athletes like Rory McIlroy and Cristiano Ronaldo? Maybe it's the innovations[1], like Nike's self-lacing sneakers, lightweight Flyknit shoes, and its Nike+ software apps. What part do the 24,000 retailers that carry Nike products play? Do Nike's connections with tens of millions of customers on Twitter, Instagram, and Facebook build customer relationships? And just how much (if at all) do these relationships increase Nike's sales and profits?

Almost 50 years ago, Phil Knight and his college track coach, Bill Bowerman, founded Blue Ribbon Sports (later renamed Nike) to distribute Japanese running shoes. A few years later they were designing, producing, and selling athletic shoes. Today Nike is the 18th most valuable brand in the world, with profits of almost $4 billion on annual sales of more than $32 billion. Part of its success comes from adapting its marketing strategy to changing market conditions—but Nike hasn't always adapted quickly. Back in the early 1980s, Nike was so focused on running shoes that it missed the aerobics shoe craze and fell behind rival Reebok. Nike profits plummeted and only aggressive cost-cutting saved the company.

After Nike signed Michael Jordan to endorse its basketball shoes in 1984, the Air Jordan line took the market by storm. Later, when Nike's advertising agency came up with the "Just Do It!" slogan and an ad campaign that covered television, magazines, and billboards around the world, Nike raced further ahead. "Just Do It" helped carry Nike through the 1990s and its profits soared on rising sales aided by low-cost foreign production.

Then, in the late 1990s, the company came under attack when it was reported that some of its suppliers used child labor. At first Nike denied responsibility, claiming it couldn't control how its suppliers operated. But public protest showed that society expected more from a large, successful corporation, and Nike began to closely monitor its suppliers' labor practices. Since then, Nike's social responsibility efforts have turned around its reputation. For example, Nike recently set an ambitious sustainability goal: from 2015 to 2020 Nike plans to double sales while halving its environmental impact. Already, more than half of its shoes are made (at least in part) with Nike's own manufacturing waste.

These days, Nike targets growth in emerging markets like China. Nike courts Chinese consumers who are crazy about basketball—especially basketball superstar LeBron James—by touting the NBA star in its ads. Nike was one of the first brands to jump onto the Chinese mobile messaging service WeChat—directly connecting with hundreds of millions of Chinese consumers. Nike also targets the fast-growing women's sports apparel market in China. A growing number of Chinese women want to get more fit. So Nike opened stores designed to appeal to Chinese women, featuring softer lighting, boutique-like clothing displays, and in-store fitness classes.

Innovation continues to be an important part of Nike's culture. Some of Nike's recent innovations involve digital tools that create new sources of value for its customers. For example, Nike+ apps that run on iPhone and Android devices are designed for men and women at all fitness levels. The Nike+ Training Club app includes a collection of workouts hosted by athletes like tennis star Serena Williams and Chinese track and field star Su Bingtian who act as virtual trainers. The app also lets users connect with other users who motivate each other to work out. And the apps are free! They help Nike build long-term customer relationships, as well as future sales. Innovations like these need to keep coming if Nike expects to continue to run ahead of a strong field of competitors that includes Adidas, Under Armour, Skechers (now the number two seller of athletic footwear in the United States), and Chinese upstart Li Ning.

LEARNING OBJECTIVES

In this chapter, you'll learn what marketing is all about and why it's important to you as a consumer. We'll also explore why it is so crucial to the success of individual firms and nonprofit organizations and the impact that it has on the quality of life in different societies.

When you finish this chapter, you should be able to

1. know what marketing is and why you should learn about it.
2. understand the difference between marketing and macro-marketing.
3. know the marketing functions and why marketing specialists—including intermediaries and collaborators—develop to perform them.
4. understand what a market-driven economy is and how it adjusts the macro-marketing system.
5. know what the marketing concept is—and how it should guide a firm or nonprofit organization.
6. understand what customer value is and why it is important to customer satisfaction.
7. know how social responsibility and marketing ethics relate to the marketing concept.
8. understand the important new terms (shown in boldface).

Marketing—What's It All About?

Marketing is more than selling or advertising

Many people think that marketing means "selling" or "advertising." It's true that these are parts of marketing. But *marketing is much more than selling and advertising.*

How did all those bicycles get here?

To illustrate some of the other important things that are included in marketing, think about all the bicycles being pedaled with varying degrees of energy by bike riders around the world. Most of us don't make our own bicycles. Instead, they are made by firms such as Trek, Specialized, Mongoose, and Electra.

Most bikes do the same thing—get the rider from one place to another. But a bike rider can choose from a wide assortment of models. They are designed in different sizes and with or without gears. Off-road bikes have large knobby tires. Kids and older people may want more wheels—to make balancing easier. Some bikes need baskets or even trailers for cargo. You can buy a basic bike for less than $100. Or you can spend more than $5,000 for a custom frame.

This variety of styles and features complicates the production and sale of bicycles. The following list shows some of the things a manager should do before and after deciding to produce and sell a bike.

1. Analyze the needs of people who might buy a bike and decide if they want more or different models.
2. Determine how many of these people will want to buy bicycles, where in the world they live, and when they will want to buy.
3. Identify competing companies that also produce bikes, what kind they sell, and at what prices.
4. Predict the designs of bikes–frame and handlebar styles, derailleurs, types of wheels, brakes, and other accessories–different customers will want, and decide which of these people the firm will try to satisfy.
5. Determine whether to sell bikes directly to consumers or through retailers–and if retailers, which ones should be used.
6. Decide how to tell potential customers about the firm's bikes.
7. Estimate the prices potential customers are willing to pay for their bikes and if the firm can make a profit selling at those prices.
8. Figure out how to provide customer service if a customer has a problem after buying a bike.

The above activities are not part of **production**–actually *making* goods or *performing* services. Rather, they are part of a larger process–called *marketing*–that provides needed direction for production and helps make sure that the right goods and services are produced and find their way to consumers.

For now, it's enough to see that marketing plays an essential role in providing consumers with need-satisfying goods and services and, more generally, in creating customer satisfaction. Simply put, **customer satisfaction** is the extent to which a firm fulfills a customer's needs, desires, and expectations.

Marketing Is Important to You

Marketing is important to every consumer

Marketing affects almost every aspect of your daily life. The choices you have among the goods and services you buy, the stores where you shop, and the radio and TV programs you tune in to are all possible because of marketing. In the process of providing all these choices, marketing drives organizations to focus on what it takes to satisfy you, the customer. Most of the things you want or need are available conveniently *when* and *where* you want or need them.

Some courses are interesting when you take them but not directly relevant to your life once they're over. That's not so with marketing–you'll be a consumer dealing with marketing for the rest of your life regardless of what career you pursue. Moreover, as a consumer, you pay for the cost of marketing activities. In advanced economies, marketing costs about 50 cents of every consumer dollar. For some goods and services, the percentage is much higher. It makes sense to be an educated consumer and to understand what you get and don't get from all that spending.

Marketing will be important to your job

Another reason for studying marketing is that it offers many exciting and rewarding career opportunities. Throughout this book, you will find information about opportunities in different areas of marketing.

If you're aiming for a nonmarketing job, knowing about marketing will help you do your job better. Throughout the book, we'll discuss ways that marketing interacts with other parts of the company–including finance, accounting, human resources, computer information systems, research and development, and more. Further, marketing is important to the success of every organization.

Beyond that, the same basic principles used to sell soap or breakfast cereal are used to "sell" ideas, politicians, health care services, environmental sustainability, museums, and even colleges. No matter what job you end up in, you are very likely to have to understand others' needs, and perhaps persuade people to behave differently or change their minds about something. Doctors and nurses often need to persuade patients to take their medicine and change their eating habits. Managers have to understand people that work with them and convince them to change behaviors to increase their job performance. Marketing principles will help you achieve those goals and maybe help you get your next job.

Use a marketing approach to get your next job

You will probably be seeking a job sometime soon, offering your services–as an accountant, a salesperson, a computer programmer, a financial analyst, or perhaps a store manager. Or maybe you will be looking for an opportunity with more responsibility or higher pay where you currently work. You will have more success getting what you want when you take a marketing approach and try to figure out how to best satisfy the needs, interests, and desires of a current or prospective employer the same way a business looks at its customers. Much of what you learn about how businesses market their products and services to customers can be applied in the job market. Even your job résumé is part of a marketing campaign to sell yourself to an employer.

Marketing affects innovation and standard of living

An even more basic reason for studying marketing is that marketing plays a big part in economic growth and development. One key reason is that marketing encourages research and **innovation**–the development and spread of new ideas, goods, and services. As firms offer new and better ways of satisfying consumer needs, customers have more choices among products, which fosters competition for consumers' money. This competition drives down prices. Moreover, when firms develop products that really satisfy customers, fuller employment and higher incomes can result. The combination of these forces means that marketing has a big impact on consumers' standard of living–and it is important to the future of all nations.

How Should We Define Marketing?

There are micro and macro views of marketing

In our bicycle example, we saw that a producer of bicycles has to perform many customer-related activities besides just making bikes. The same is true for an insurance company or an art museum. This supports the idea of marketing as a set of activities done by an individual organization to satisfy its customers.

On the other hand, people can't survive on bicycles and art museums alone! In advanced economies, it takes goods and services from thousands of organizations to satisfy the many needs of society. Further, a society needs some sort of marketing system to organize the efforts of all the producers, wholesalers, and retailers required to satisfy the varied needs of all its citizens. So marketing is also an important social process.

We can view marketing in two ways: *from a micro view as a set of activities performed by organizations* and also *from a macro view as a social process.* Yet, in everyday use when people talk about marketing, they have the micro view in mind. So that is the way we will define marketing here. However, the broader macro view that looks at the whole production-distribution system is also important, so later we will provide a separate definition and discussion of macro-marketing.

Marketing defined

Marketing is the performance of activities that seek to accomplish an organization's objectives by anticipating customer or client needs and directing a flow of need-satisfying goods and services from producer to customer or client. Let's look at this definition.

Applies to profit and nonprofit organizations

Marketing applies to both profit and nonprofit organizations. Profit is the objective for most business firms. But other types of organizations may seek more members or acceptance of an idea. Customers or clients may be individual consumers, business firms, nonprofit organizations, government agencies, or even foreign nations. Although most customers and clients pay for the goods and services they receive, others may receive them free of charge or at a reduced cost through private or government support.

Marketing aims to identify customer needs and meet those needs so well that the product sells itself. Help Remedies found many customers looking for simple solutions to minor health problems.
Source: Help Remedies Inc.

More than just persuading customers

Marketing isn't just selling and advertising. Unfortunately, some executives still think of it that way. They feel that the job of marketing is to "get rid of" whatever the company happens to produce. In fact, the aim of marketing is to identify customers' needs and meet those needs so well that the product almost "sells itself."

Begins with customer needs

Marketing should begin with potential customer needs–not with the production process. Marketing should try to anticipate needs. And then marketing, rather than production, should determine what goods and services are to be developed–including decisions about product features; design and packaging; prices or fees; transporting and storing policies; advertising and sales tactics; and, after the sale, installation, customer service, warranty[2], and perhaps even disposal and recycling policies.

Does not do it alone

This does not mean that marketing should try to take over production, accounting, and financial activities. Rather, it means that marketing–by interpreting customers' needs–should provide direction for these activities and try to coordinate them.

Marketing involves exchanges

The idea that marketing involves a flow of need-satisfying offerings from a producer to a customer implies that there is an exchange of the need-satisfying offering for something else, such as the customer's money. Marketing focuses on facilitating exchanges. In fact, *marketing doesn't occur unless two or more parties are willing to exchange something for something else.* For example, in a **pure subsistence**[3] **economy**–where each family unit produces everything it consumes–there is no need to exchange goods and services and no marketing is involved. (Although each producer-consumer unit is totally self-sufficient in such a situation, the standard of living is typically relatively low.)

Builds a relationship with the customer

Keep in mind that a marketing exchange is usually part of an ongoing relationship, not just a single transaction. Rather, the goal is continuing sales and an ongoing *relationship* with the customer. In the future, when the customer has the same need again–or some other need that the firm can meet–other sales will follow. A consumer does not visit her local Shell station once, but perhaps every week or two–as long as Shell's gas, coffee, or service satisfies her, she is likely to keep going to the same gas station. This *flow* of need-satisfying goods and services builds a long-lasting relationship that benefits both the firm and the customer.

The focus of this text—management-oriented micro-marketing

Because you are probably preparing for a career in management, the main focus of this text will be on managerial marketing, or the micro view of marketing. We will see marketing through the eyes of the marketing manager.

The marketing ideas we will be discussing throughout this text apply to a wide variety of situations. They are important for new ventures started by one person as well as big corporations, in domestic and international markets, and regardless of whether the focus is on marketing physical goods, services, or an idea or cause. They are equally critical whether the relevant customers or clients are individual consumers, businesses, or some other type of organization.

One of the challenges for many of today's consumer products companies involves addressing the needs of a growing market in developing countries. Makers of many health and beauty products, for example, have found a potential market with the rural poor. For an example of how effective micro-marketing can be used to appeal to this growing market, read *What's Next?* Marketing to developing countries' rural poor.

Although marketing within individual firms (micro-marketing) is the primary focus of the text, marketing managers must remember that their organizations are just small parts of a larger macro-marketing system. Therefore, next we will briefly look at the macro view of marketing. Then we will develop the managerial view more fully in later chapters.

Macro-Marketing

Macro-marketing is a social process that directs an economy's flow of goods and services from producers to consumers in a way that effectively matches supply and demand and accomplishes the objectives of society.

Emphasis is on whole system

With macro-marketing we are still concerned with the flow of need-satisfying goods and services from producer to consumer. However, the emphasis with macro-marketing is not on the activities of individual organizations. Instead, the emphasis is on *how the whole marketing system works.* This includes looking at how marketing affects society and vice versa.

Every society needs a macro-marketing system to help match supply and demand. Different producers in a society have different objectives, resources, and skills. Likewise, not all consumers share the same needs, preferences, and wealth.

An effective macro-marketing system delivers the goods and services that consumers want and need. It gets products to them at the right time, in the right place, and at a price they're willing to pay. It keeps consumers satisfied after the sale and brings them back to purchase again when they are ready. That's not an easy job—especially if you think about the variety of goods and services a highly developed economy can produce and the many kinds of goods and services consumers want.

Separation between producers and consumers

Effective marketing in an advanced economy is difficult because producers and consumers are often separated in several ways. As Exhibit 1-1 shows, exchange between producers and consumers is hampered by *spatial separation; separation in time; separation of information; separation in values;* and *separation of ownership.* You may love your cell phone, but you probably don't know when or where it was produced or how it got to you. The people in the factory that produced it don't know about you or how you live. The producer knows it wants to make that phone at a low cost and isn't sure what features and benefits you are seeking.

In addition, most firms specialize in producing and selling large amounts of a narrow assortment of goods and services. This allows them to take advantage of mass production with its **economies of scale**—which means that as a company produces larger numbers of a particular product, the cost of each unit of the product goes down. Yet most

What's Next? Marketing to developing countries' rural poor

In recent decades India has experienced rapid economic growth. Many of its citizens have more income and enjoy a higher quality of life. That helps explain why Unilever's Indian subsidiary, Hindustan Unilever Limited (HUL), has worked hard to build a 40 percent share of the Indian market with its product lines that include soaps, toothpaste, and packaged foods.

Previously, HUL focused on India's cities. Yet, almost three-fourths of India's one *billion* plus people still live in rural areas. About a third of these rural villagers still lack access to electricity—and less than half have basic sanitation. Many of them have an income of less than $2 a day. Conventional wisdom suggests that these poor rural villagers have too little money to be an attractive market. And it's expensive to distribute products to far-flung villages.

But now that is changing. HUL's marketing managers decided that Indian villagers represent an opportunity for growth—and that villagers might benefit if they could purchase the soaps, toothpaste, and packaged food products that HUL is successfully selling in urban areas of India.

HUL tailored a new marketing strategy to this target market. Many products are repackaged in "sachets"—small bags that contain a one- or two-day supply. HUL prices the small sachets so that villagers can afford them—and that in turn gives customers a chance to try quality products that were previously priced out of their reach.

HUL created its "Shakti Ammas" (women entrepreneurs) program to communicate the benefits of its products and distribute them in remote rural areas. The program sets up rural women as home-based distributors and sales agents. These women stock HUL products at their homes and go door-to-door to sell them. They also organize meetings in local schools and at village fairs to educate fellow villagers on health and hygiene issues.

This program continues to evolve[4]. To provide wider distribution, male entrepreneurs (Shaktimaan) were recruited and given bicycles. The bikes allow each Shaktimaan to cover five or six nearby villages—far more than the Shakti Amma previously covered on foot. A partnership with a leading Indian telecom provider gives Shakti entrepreneurs an additional product to sell while on their rounds.

Today, more than than 70,000 Shakti Ammas and 48,000 Shaktimaans operate in 162,000 villages, and reach over four million rural households across India. The Indian success spurred Unilever to adapt the model to developing countries around the globe. The Shakti have a new source of income and are learning about business—while they bring the health benefits of improved hygiene to rural villages. And, of course, HUL hopes to clean up with a new source of growth.

Based on Unilever's success, many of its competitors are following suit. This may reflect the immediate future of marketing to the rural poor.

How do we see parts of the definition of marketing represented in this case study? What customer needs does the Shakti Ammas program address? How does it build a relationship between HUL and the customer?

consumers want to buy only a small quantity; they also want a wide assortment of different goods and services. Apple makes millions of iPhones in a few factories in China, but most customers want to buy just one. And most smartphone buyers like to go to a store with several different phones from different companies. These "discrepancies of quantity" and "discrepancies of assortment" further complicate exchange between producers and consumers (Exhibit 1-1). That is, each producer specializes in producing and selling large amounts of a narrow assortment of goods and services, but each consumer wants only small quantities of a wide assortment of goods and services.

The purpose of a macro-marketing system is to overcome these separations and discrepancies. The "universal functions of marketing" help do this.

Marketing functions help narrow the gap

The **universal functions of marketing** are buying, selling, transporting, storing, standardization[5] and grading, financing, risk taking, and market information. They must be performed in all macro-marketing systems. *How* these functions are performed—and *by whom*—may differ among nations and economic systems. But they are needed in any macro-marketing system. Let's take a closer look at them now.

Any kind of exchange usually involves buying and selling. The **buying function** means looking for and evaluating goods and services. The **selling function** involves promoting the product. It includes the use of personal selling, advertising, customer service, and other direct and mass selling methods to tell customers about the product. This is probably the most visible function of marketing.

The **transporting function** means the movement of goods from one place to another. The **storing function** involves holding goods until customers need them.

Standardization and grading involve sorting products according to size and quality. This makes buying and selling easier because it reduces the need for inspection and sampling. **Financing** provides the necessary cash and credit to produce, transport, store, promote, sell, and buy products. **Risk taking** involves bearing the uncertainties that are part of the marketing process. A firm can never be sure that customers will want to buy its products. Products can also be damaged, stolen, or outdated. The **market information function** involves the collection, analysis, and distribution of all the information needed to plan, carry out, and control marketing activities, whether in the firm's own neighborhood or in a market overseas. Together these universal functions of marketing address the discrepancies and separations in Exhibit 1-1.

Producers, consumers, and marketing specialists perform functions

Producers and consumers sometimes handle some of the marketing functions themselves. However, exchanges are often easier or less expensive when a marketing specialist performs some of the marketing functions. For example, both producers and consumers may benefit when an **intermediary**[6]—someone who specializes in trade rather than production—plays a role in the exchange process. Imagine what it would be like to shop at many different factories and farms for the wide variety of

Exhibit 1-1 Marketing Facilitates Production and Consumption

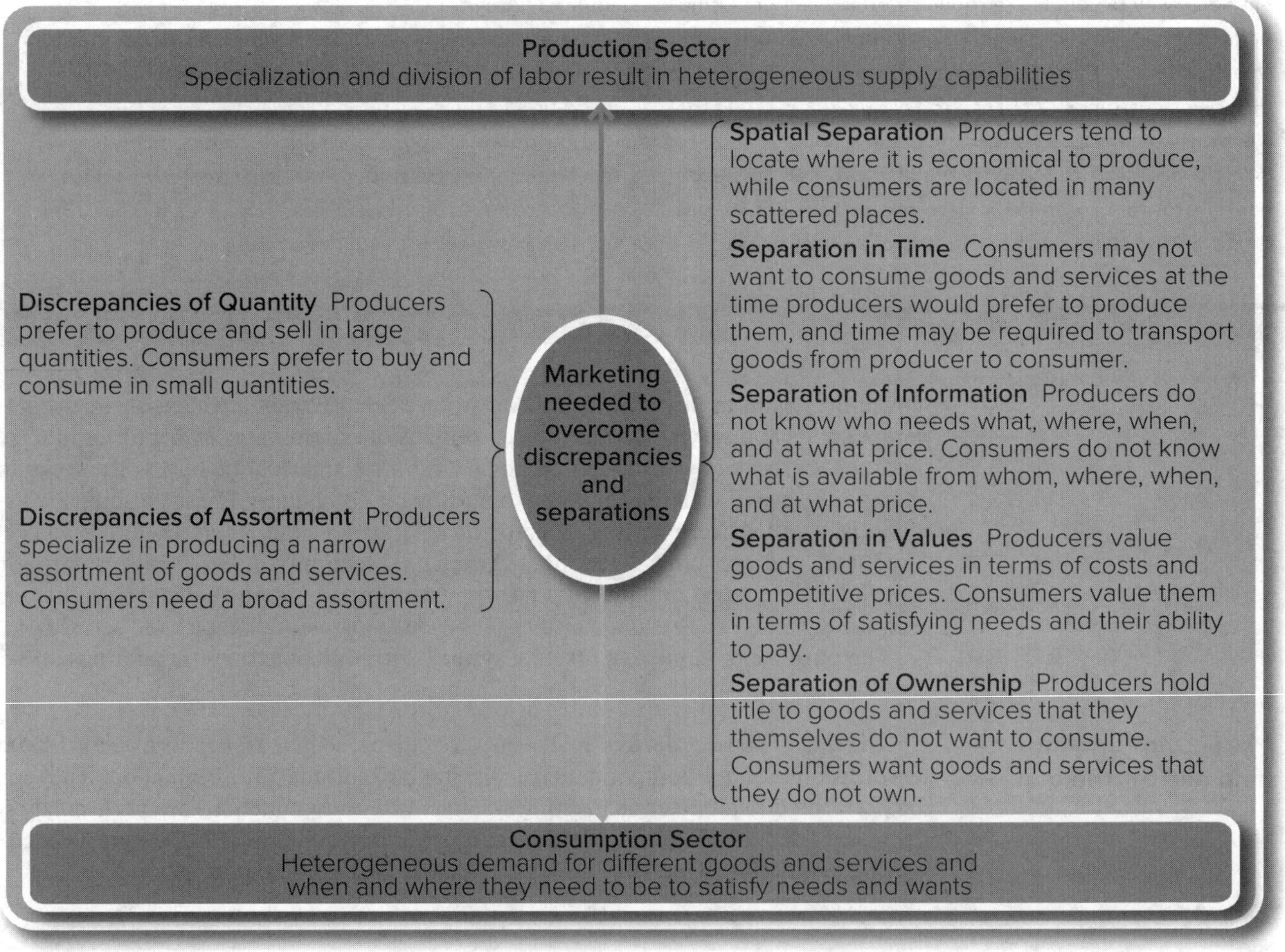

Intermediaries and collaborators develop and offer specialized services that facilitate exchange between producers and consumers. Companies that produce building supplies work with an intermediary such as Home Depot to better serve the electricians, plumbers, and carpenters that buy and use its products. EMMA helps organizations create, send, and track e-mail campaigns and online surveys. EMMA is a collaborator; it facilitates its clients selling and marketing information functions.
(left): Source: Homer TLC, Inc.; (right): Used with permission of myemma.com

brands of packaged foods that you like rather than at a well-stocked local grocery store. Although wholesalers and retailers must charge for services they provide, this charge is usually offset by the savings of time, effort, and expense that would be involved without them. So these intermediaries can help make the whole macro-marketing system more efficient and effective.

A wide variety of other marketing specialists may also help smooth exchanges among producers, consumers, or intermediaries. These specialists are **collaborators**—firms that facilitate or provide one or more of the marketing functions other than buying. These collaborators include advertising agencies, marketing research firms, independent product-testing laboratories, Internet service providers, public warehouses, transporting firms, communications companies, and financial institutions (including banks).

New specialists develop to fill market needs

New types of marketing specialists develop or evolve when there are opportunities to make exchanges between producers and consumers more efficient or effective. The growth of the Internet provided one such opportunity and resulted in the rapid growth of e-commerce. **E-commerce** refers to exchanges between individuals or organizations—and activities that facilitate these exchanges—based on applications of information technology. Internet-based intermediaries—such as Amazon.com and eBay.com—help cut the costs of many marketing functions. Other marketing specialists have popped up online: Search engines such as Google facilitate information search, PayPal reduces consumer risks associated with paying for goods purchased online, and chat-based customer service firms help any company provide 24/7 customer support. Collectively, developments in e-commerce have significantly increased the efficiency and effectiveness of our macro-marketing system. At the same time, many individual firms take advantage of these innovations to improve profitability and customer satisfaction.

Through innovation, specialization[7], or economies of scale, marketing intermediaries and collaborators are often able to perform the marketing functions better–and at a lower cost–than producers or consumers can. This allows producers and consumers to spend more time on production, consumption[8], or other activities–including leisure.

Functions can be shifted and shared

From a macro-marketing viewpoint, all of the marketing functions must be performed by someone–an individual producer or consumer, an intermediary, a marketing collaborator, or, in some cases, even a nation's government. No function can be completely eliminated. However, from a micro viewpoint, not every firm must perform all of the functions. Rather, responsibility for performing the marketing functions can be shifted and shared in a variety of ways. Further, not all goods and services require all the functions at every level of their production.

Regardless of who performs the marketing functions, in general they must be performed effectively and efficiently or the performance of the whole macro-marketing system will suffer. With many different possible ways for marketing functions to be performed in a macro-marketing system, how can a society hope to arrive at a combination that best serves the needs of its citizens? To answer this question, we can look at the role of marketing in different types of economic systems.

The Role of Marketing in Economic Systems

All societies must provide for the needs of their members. Therefore, every society needs some sort of **economic system**–the way an economy organizes to use scarce resources to produce goods and services and distribute them for consumption by various people and groups in the society.

How an economic system operates depends on a society's objectives and the nature of its political institutions. But regardless of what form these take, all economic systems must develop some method–along with appropriate economic institutions–to decide what and how much is to be produced and distributed by whom, when, to whom, and why.

Government officials may make the decisions

In a **command economy**, government officials decide what and how much is to be produced and distributed by whom, when, to whom, and why. These decisions are usually part of an overall government plan, so command economies are also called "planned" economies. It sounds good for a government to have a plan, but as a practical matter, attempts by a government to dictate an economic plan often don't work out as intended.

Producers in a command economy generally have little choice about what goods and services to produce. Their main task is to meet the production quotas assigned in the plan. Prices are also set by government planners and tend to be very rigid–not changing according to supply and demand. Although consumers usually have some freedom of choice–it's impossible to control every single detail–the assortment of goods and services may be limited.

Government planning in a command economy may work fairly well as long as an economy is very simple, with little variety in goods and services. However, modern first- and second-world economies are more complex, and government planning tends to break down. Although countries such as North Korea, Cuba, and Iran rely largely on command-oriented economic systems, there is a trend toward market-directed economic systems. They have proven more effective in meeting consumer needs.

Artists and craftworkers in developing economies do not often have a large local market for their products. Ten Thousand Villages operates retail stores and an e-commerce website that help artisans reach more customers and promote economic development in their communities.
Source: Ten Thousand Villages

A market-directed economy adjusts itself

In a **market-directed economy**, the individual decisions of the many producers and consumers make the macro-level decisions for the whole economy. In a pure market-directed economy, consumers make a society's production decisions when they make their choices in the marketplace. They decide what is to be produced and by whom—through their dollar "votes."

Price is a measure of value

Prices in the marketplace are a rough measure of how society values particular goods and services. If consumers are willing to pay the market prices, then apparently they feel they are getting at least their money's worth. Similarly, the cost of labor and materials is a rough measure of the value of the resources used in the production of goods and services to meet these needs. New consumer needs that can be served profitably—not just the needs of the majority—will probably be met by some profit-minded businesses.

Greatest freedom of choice

Consumers in a market-directed economy enjoy great freedom of choice. They are not forced to buy any goods or services, except those that must be provided for the good of society—things such as national defense, police and fire protection, roads, public schools, and public-health services. These are provided by the community—and citizens' taxes pay for them.

Similarly, producers are free to do whatever they wish—provided that they stay within the rules of the game set by government *and* receive enough dollar "votes" from consumers. If they do their job well, they earn a profit and stay in business. But profit, survival, and growth are not guaranteed.

The role of government

The American economy and most other Western economies are mainly market-directed—but not completely. Society assigns supervision of the system to the government. For example, besides setting and enforcing the "rules of the game," government agencies control interest rates and the supply of money. They also set import and export rules that affect international competition, regulate radio and TV broadcasting, sometimes control wages and prices, and so on. Government also tries to be sure that property is protected, contracts are enforced, individuals are not exploited, no group unfairly monopolizes[9] markets, and producers deliver the kinds and quality of goods and services they claim to be offering.

Public interest groups and consumers spread the word

In many Western economies, public interest groups and consumers provide an additional check on a market-directed economy. For example, the Center for Science in the Public Interest (CSPI) is a consumer watchdog group that pressures food companies to make healthier products.

Consumers can also report their satisfaction or dissatisfaction with companies by posting reviews on websites. Some customers make sure their dissatisfaction is heard. When musician Dave Carroll's guitar was damaged by United Airlines–and baggage handlers and the airline refused to compensate him–Carroll's band made a YouTube video. The funny video, "United Breaks Guitars," went viral, millions saw it, and lo and behold, United offered Carroll a new guitar. Prospective customers often search the web to learn about companies before buying. They can easily find positive and negative information on the Internet, giving firms an extra incentive[10] to play by the socially accepted rules of the game.

Macro-marketing systems adjust over time

So far, we have described how a market-directed macro-marketing system adjusts to become more effective and efficient by responding to customer needs (see Exhibit 1-2).

Marketing's Role Has Changed a Lot over the Years

It's clear that marketing decisions are very important to a firm's success. But marketing hasn't always been so complicated. In fact, understanding how marketing thinking has evolved makes the modern view clearer. So we will discuss five stages in marketing evolution: (1) the simple trade era, (2) the production era, (3) the sales era, (4) the marketing department era, and (5) the marketing company era. We'll talk about these eras as

Exhibit 1-2 Model of a Market-Directed Macro-Marketing System

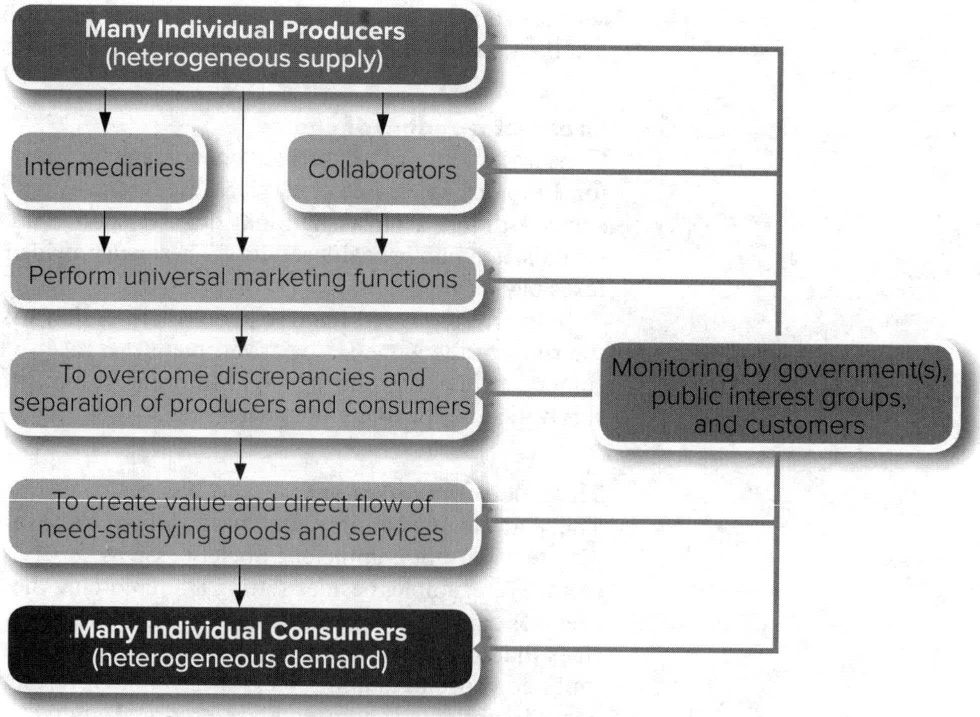

if they applied generally to all firms—but keep in mind that *some managers still have not made it to the final stages.* They are stuck in the past with old ways of thinking.

Simple trade era to production era

When societies first moved toward some specialization of production and away from a subsistence economy where each family raised and consumed everything it produced, traders played an important role. Early "producers for the market" made products that were needed by themselves and their neighbors. As bartering became more difficult, societies moved into the **simple trade era**—a time when families traded or sold their "surplus[11]" output to local distributors. These specialists resold the goods to other consumers or other distributors. This was the early role of marketing—and it is still the focus of marketing in many of the less-developed areas of the world. In fact, even in the United States, the United Kingdom, and other more advanced economies, marketing didn't change much until the Industrial Revolution brought larger factories more than 150 years ago.

From the production to the sales era

From the Industrial Revolution until the 1920s, many companies were in the production era—some still are today. The **production era** is a time when a company focuses on production of a few specific products—perhaps because few of these products are available in the market. "If we can make it, it will sell" is management thinking characteristic of the production era. Because of product shortages, many nations—including some of the postcommunist republics of eastern Europe—continue to operate with production era approaches.

By about 1930, most companies in the industrialized Western nations had more production capability than ever before. Now the problem wasn't just to produce—but to beat the competition and win customers. This led many firms to enter the sales era. The **sales era** is a time when a company emphasizes selling because of increased competition.

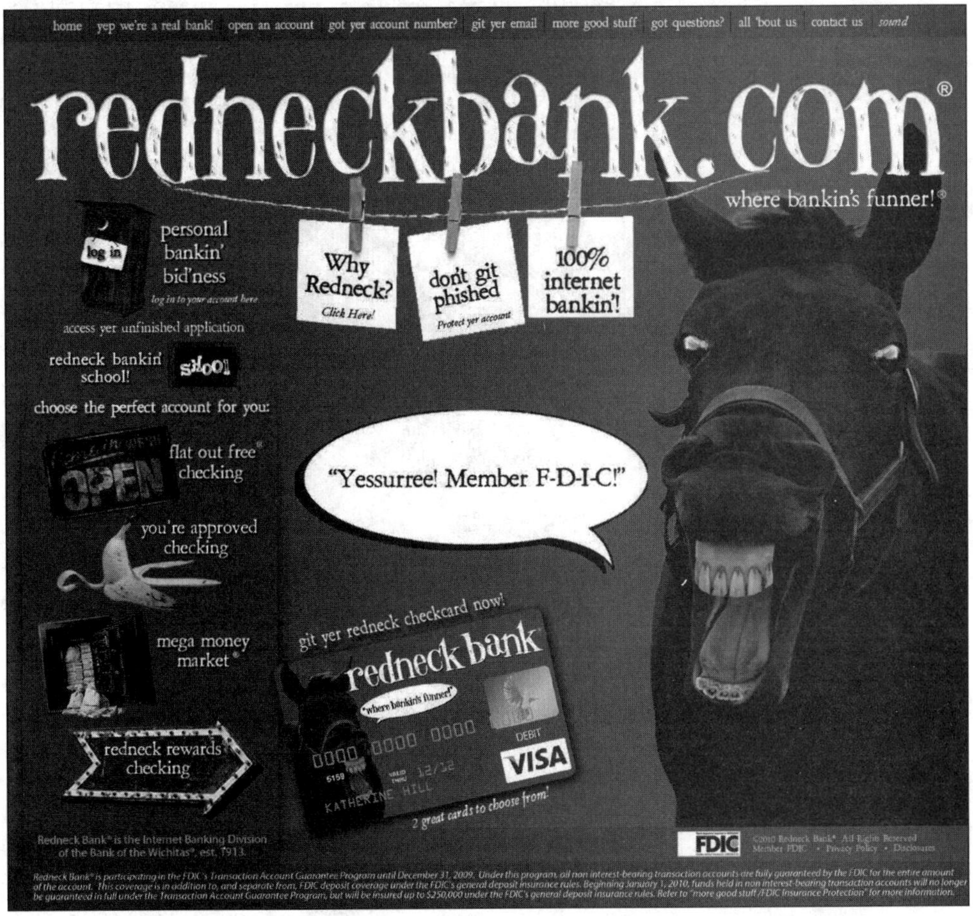

In the past, many banks created products but left it to the marketing department to sell them. In today's more competitive environment, banks conduct research to discover customer needs, then develop products that meet their users' needs. This leads to more satisfied customers. When Bank of the Wichitas added an online branch, it decided to use an untraditional approach and called it Redneck Bank. Redneck Bank offers customers "flat out free checking" and convenience served with a healthy dollop of humor. The approach has been successful and the small bank from Oklahoma quickly added customers from all over the United States.
Source: Bank of the Wichitas®

To the marketing department era

For most firms in advanced economies, the sales era continued until at least 1950. By then, sales were growing rapidly in most areas of the economy. The problem was deciding where to put the company's effort. Someone was needed to tie together the efforts of research, purchasing, production, shipping, and sales. As this situation became more common, the sales era was replaced by the marketing department era. The **marketing department era** is a time when all marketing activities are brought under the control of one department to improve short-run policy planning and to try to integrate the firm's activities.

To the marketing company era

Since 1960, most firms have developed at least some managers with a marketing management outlook. Many of these firms have even graduated from the marketing department era into the marketing company era. The **marketing company era** is a time when, in addition to short-run marketing planning, marketing people develop long-range plans–sometimes five or more years ahead–and the whole-company effort is guided by the marketing concept.

What Does the Marketing Concept Mean?

The **marketing concept** means that an organization aims *all* of its efforts at satisfying its *customers*–at a *profit.* The marketing concept is a simple but very important idea.

The marketing concept is not a new idea–it's been around for a long time. But some managers show little interest in customers' needs. These managers still have a **production orientation**[12]–making whatever products are easy to produce and *then* trying to sell them. They think of customers existing to buy the firm's output rather than of firms existing to serve customers and–more broadly–the needs of society.

Well-managed firms have replaced this production orientation with a marketing orientation. A **marketing orientation** means trying to carry out the marketing concept. Instead of just trying to get customers to buy what the firm has produced, a marketing-oriented firm tries to offer customers what they need.

Three basic ideas are included in the definition of the marketing concept: (1) customer satisfaction, (2) a total company effort, and (3) profit–not just sales–as an objective. See Exhibit 1-3. These ideas warrant further discussion.

Exhibit 1-3
Organizations with a Marketing Orientation Carry Out the Marketing Concept

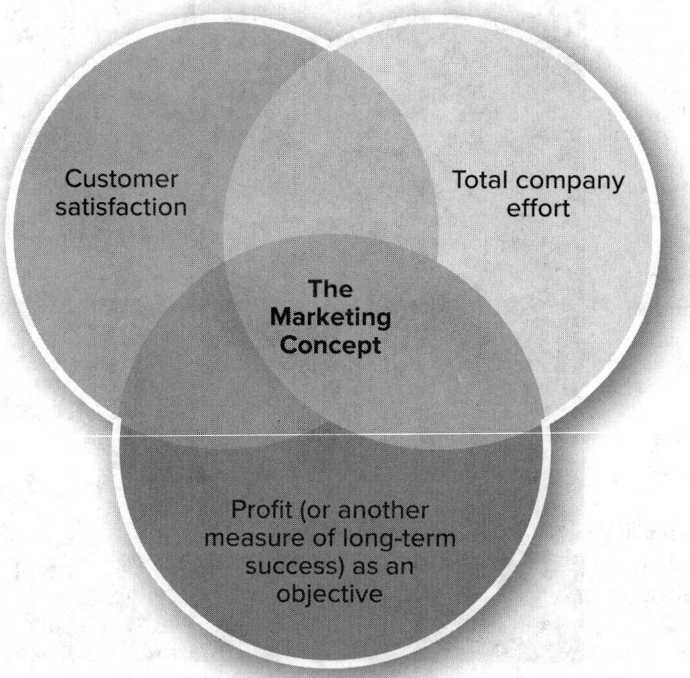

Customer satisfaction guides the whole system

"Give the customers what they need" seems so obvious that it may be hard for you to see why the marketing concept requires special attention. However, people don't always do the logical thing—especially when it means changing what they've done in the past. When customers have choices, they choose companies that best meet their needs, desires, and expectations. They purchase again from these companies and they tell their friends about the great experience. This all starts with customer satisfaction.

The whole company works together to satisfy customers

Ideally, all managers should work together as a team. Every department may directly or indirectly impact customer satisfaction. But some managers tend to build "fences" around their own departments. There may be meetings to try to get them to work together—but they come and go from the meetings worried only about protecting their own turf.

We use the term *production orientation* as a shorthand way to refer to this kind of narrow thinking—and lack of a central focus—in a business firm. But keep in mind that this problem may be seen in sales-oriented sales representatives, advertising-oriented agency people, finance-oriented finance people, directors of nonprofit organizations, and so on. It is not a criticism of people who manage production. They aren't necessarily any more guilty of narrow thinking than anyone else.

The fences come down in an organization that has accepted the marketing concept. There may still be departments because specialization often makes sense. But the total system's effort is guided by satisfying customers' needs and wants—instead of what each department would like to do. The marketing concept provides a guiding focus that *all* departments adopt. It must be a philosophy of the whole organization, not just an idea that applies to the marketing department.

Profit, revenues, and costs are examples of **marketing metrics** which refer to numeric data that allow marketing managers to evaluate performance, often against a set target or goal. At a basic level, marketing managers use these metrics to calculate how well a strategy performs. For example, consider a student who wants to sell T-shirts on campus to support a student organization. The student could estimate profits in advance and then evaluate the profits later. The *Marketing Analytics in Action: Revenue, Cost, and Profit* exercise describes this in more detail.

Survival and success require a profit

Firms must satisfy customers. But keep in mind that it may cost more to satisfy some needs than any customers are willing to pay. Or it may be much more costly to try to

Marketing Analytics in Action: Revenue, Cost, and Profit

Marketing managers pay close attention to profit—that also means monitoring revenues and costs. And while marketing managers want to know a company's overall profits, they are also likely to examine revenues, costs, and profits for individual products, perhaps in different geographic markets. This suggests some simple metrics that can be calculated with the following formulas:

- Revenue = Price × Quantity sold
- Profit = Revenue − Cost

To better understand how a marketing manager might use these numbers, let's look at a simple example. Julie Tyler is a college student in charge of fundraising for a student organization. Last year the group successfully sold T-shirts to raise money and awareness for the group. They made 250 T-shirts for $12 each and sold them at a price of $20 per T-shirt. This year Julie wants to buy a higher-quality shirt that will cost $15, and she believes she can sell them for $30. However, at the higher price she expects to sell only 200 shirts.

1. *Calculate the profits the group earned last year.*
2. *Calculate the profits Julie would earn this year using these prices and assuming her sales projections are accurate.*
3. *What else could Julie do to increase profits?*

attract new customers than it is to build a strong relationship with—and encourage repeat purchases from—existing customers. So profit—the difference between a firm's revenue and its total costs—is the bottom-line measure of the firm's success and ability to survive. It is the balancing point that helps the firm determine what needs it will try to satisfy with its total (sometimes costly!) effort.

Some organizations have other measures of long-term success. Most nonprofit organizations need revenues to exceed costs to survive long term—but they may have other goals valued by employees and supporters. For example, a food bank may measure success by the number of meals it serves to the homeless. Many for-profit organizations consider more than profit; for example, many are concerned with the environment or their community.

Many organizations go beyond profit

Some organizations explicitly consider a **triple bottom line**—which measures an organization's economic, social, and environmental outcomes—as a measure of long-term success. Profit is the economic outcome. Social refers to how the company's business activities affect its employees and other people in the communities where it operates. The third bottom line takes into account environmental responsibility, usually seeking to at least not harm the natural environment. Together, these are sometimes referred to as measures of people, planet, and profit.

Consider Namaste Solar, which actively seeks economic profits while also measuring the impact on its local community and the planet. For example, the company gives 20 percent of its after-tax earnings to support projects such as a community bicycle-recycling program or the local children's museum. Namaste Solar's core products help the planet, but it also offers grants of up to $30,000 to help schools and nonprofits install their own solar systems. The company also self-monitors and reduces its waste. It recycles or reuses 90 percent of its office supplies and employs a zero waste company kitchen. Many of Namaste Solar's customers and employees value its triple bottom line orientation.

Adoption of the marketing concept is not universal

The marketing concept may seem obvious, but it is easy to maintain a production-oriented way of thinking. Producers of industrial commodities such as steel, coal, and chemicals have tended to remain production-oriented in part because buyers see little difference among competitors. Some industries with limited competition, including electric utilities and cable television providers, have also been slow to adopt the marketing concept. When an industry gets competitive, consumers have choices and flock to those that deliver customer satisfaction. This provides an incentive for more firms to practice the marketing concept.

Take a look at Exhibit 1-4. It shows some differences in outlook between adopters of the marketing concept and typical production-oriented managers. As the exhibit suggests, the marketing concept forces the company to think through what it is doing—and why.

The Marketing Concept and Customer Value

Take the customer's point of view

A manager who adopts the marketing concept sees customer satisfaction as the path to profits. To better understand what it takes to satisfy a customer, it is useful to take the customer's point of view.

A customer may look at a market offering from two perspectives. One deals with the potential benefits of that offering; the other concerns what the customer has to give up to get those benefits. Consider a student who has just finished an exam and is thinking about getting an iced coffee from Starbucks. Our coffee lover might see this as a great-tasting treat, a quick pick-me-up, a quiet place to relax and meet friends, or as a way to get to know an attractive classmate. Clearly, different needs are associated with these different benefits. The cost of getting these benefits would include the price of the coffee

Exhibit 1-4 Some Differences in Outlook between Adopters of the Marketing Concept and Typical Production-Oriented Managers

Topic	Marketing Orientation	Production Orientation
Attitudes toward customers	Customer needs determine company plans	They should be glad we exist, trying to cut costs and bringing out better products
Product offering	Company makes what it can sell	Company sells what it can make
Role of marketing research	To determine customer needs and how well company is satisfying them	To determine customer reaction, if used at all
Interest in innovation	Focus is on locating new opportunities	Focus is on technology and cost cutting
Customer service	Satisfy customers after the sale and they'll come back again	An activity required to reduce consumer complaints
Focus of advertising	Need-satisfying benefits of goods and services	Product features and how products are made
Relationship with customer	Customer satisfaction before and after sale leads to a profitable long-run relationship	Relationship ends when a sale is made
Costs	Eliminate costs that do not give value to customer	Keep costs as low as possible

and any tip to the server, but there might be other nonmonetary costs. For example, how difficult it is to find parking is a convenience cost. Slow service could be an aggravation.

Customer value reflects benefits and costs

As this example suggests, both benefits and costs can take many different forms. They also may vary depending on the situation. However, it is the *customer's view* of the various benefits and costs that is important. We want to repeat this important distinction: it is the *customer's view* of costs and benefits that is important. A company may want to offer a more fun atmosphere at its coffee shop—but whether it succeeds depends on the customer's perception.

This leads us to the concept of **customer value**—the difference between the benefits a customer sees from a market offering and the costs of obtaining those benefits. Exhibit 1-5 shows the wide range of different types of benefits; for example *functional benefits* could save a customer time or effort, *emotional benefits* might deliver fun and

Exhibit 1-5 Customer Value Equals Benefits Minus Costs

Customer Value = Benefits − Costs

Examples of different types of benefits

Functional
- Save time
- Simplify
- Provide information
- Reduce cost

Emotional
- Provide fun/entertainment
- Lower anxiety
- Offer superior design/aesthetics
- Provide rewards in some form

Life changing
- Give hope
- Offer motivation
- Provide sense of affiliation/belonging

Examples of different types of costs

Monetary
- Money
- Interest rate
- Fees

Inconvenience
- Time delay to receive the benefit
- Effort required to receive benefit

entertainment or design and aesthetics, and *life changing benefits* could increase motivation or feelings of belonging.

Exhibit 1-5 also recognizes costs. Some people think that higher customer value comes from a low price. But that may not be the case at all. A good or service that doesn't meet a customer's needs results in low customer value, even if the price is very low. A high price may be more than acceptable when it obtains the desired benefits. Think again about our Starbucks example. You can get a cup of coffee for a much lower price, but Starbucks offers more than just a cup of coffee.

Our definition of customer value might help you start thinking about how Starbucks could offer more customer value. Starbucks probably needs to start by providing a great tasting cup of coffee—but what else can increase customer value? Although Starbucks could easily increase value by lowering prices, it prefers to seek out ways to increase benefits. Do some Starbucks customers experience benefits when a drive-through window saves them time in the morning? Does the Starbucks app, with the option of preordering your coffee and skipping the line, save a customer time and reduce effort? Does the Starbucks Rewards program, which leads to free cups of coffee, deliver benefits? Any of these potential value-enhancing activities depends on Starbucks' customers' interpretation of their value.

Customers may not think about it very much

It is useful for a manager to evaluate ways to improve the benefits, or reduce the costs, of what the firm offers customers. However, this doesn't mean that customers stop and compute some sort of customer value score before making each purchase. If they did, there wouldn't be much time in life for anything else. So a manager's objective and thorough analysis may not accurately reflect the customer's impressions. Yet it remains the customer's view that matters—even when the customer has not thought about it.

Where does competition fit?

You can't afford to ignore competition. Consumers usually have choices about how they will meet their needs. If a firm hopes to win and keep customers over the long haul, that firm must offer a level of customer value greater than that offered by competitors. Consumers have choices—and they tend to choose options that deliver the most value.

Companies recognize that an offering with high value can change if the competition offers something better. Competition drives innovation and continuous improvements in most markets. When Uber entered the "taxi" market with a more convenient way to hail a ride, many taxi companies developed their own apps and improved service. After Tesla introduced its $50,000 Model S60 electric car with a range of 208 miles per charge, General Motors (GM) upped its game to bring out the $30,000 Chevrolet Bolt with a 238-mile range. Of course, there are other benefits to car ownership, and Tesla hopes its newest model delivers what some customers see as a better value than the Bolt.

Build relationships with customer value

Firms that embrace the marketing concept seek ways to build a profitable long-term relationship with each customer. Even the most innovative firm faces competition sooner or later. Trying to get new customers by taking them away from a competitor is usually more costly than retaining current customers by really satisfying their needs. Satisfied customers buy again and again whereas dissatisfied customers often tell others not to buy. With a long-term relationship, the customer's buying job is easier, and it also increases the selling firm's profits.

Building relationships with customers requires that everyone in a firm work together to provide customer value before *and after* each purchase. If there is a problem with a customer's bill, the accounting people can't just leave it to the salesperson to straighten it out or, even worse, act like it's "the customer's problem." These hassles[13] raise customers' costs of doing business. The long-term relationship with the customer—and the lifetime value of the customer's future purchases—is threatened unless everyone works together to make things right for the customer. Similarly, the firm's advertising might encourage a customer to buy once, but if the firm doesn't deliver on the benefits promised in its ads, the customer is likely to go elsewhere the next time the need arises. In other words, anytime the customer value is reduced—because the benefits to the customer decrease or the costs increase—the relationship is weakened.

Exhibit 1-6 summarizes these ideas. In a firm that has adopted the marketing concept, everyone focuses on customer satisfaction. They look for ways to offer superior customer value. That helps attract customers in the first place—and keeps them satisfied after they buy. So when they are ready to make repeat purchases, the firm is able to keep them as customers. Sales may increase further because satisfied customers are likely to buy other products offered by the firm. In this way, the firm builds profitable relationships with its customers. In other words, when a firm adopts the marketing concept, it wins and so do its customers.

The Marketing Concept Applies in Nonprofit Organizations

Newcomers to marketing thinking

The marketing concept is as important for nonprofit organizations as it is for business firms. In fact, marketing applies to all sorts of public and private nonprofit organizations—ranging from government agencies, health care organizations, educational institutions, and religious groups to charities, political parties, and fine arts organizations.

Support may not come from satisfied "customers"

As with any business firm, a nonprofit organization needs resources and support to survive and achieve its objectives. Yet support often does not come directly from those who receive the benefits the organization produces. For example, the World Wildlife Fund protects animals. If supporters of the World Wildlife Fund are not satisfied with its efforts—if they don't think the benefits are worth what it costs to provide them—they will put their time and money elsewhere.

Just as most firms face competition for customers, most nonprofits face competition for the resources and support they need. The Air Force faces a big problem if it can't attract new recruits. A shelter for homeless individuals may fail if supporters decide to focus on some other cause, such as AIDS education.

Exhibit 1-6 Satisfying Customers with Superior Customer Value to Build Profitable Relationships

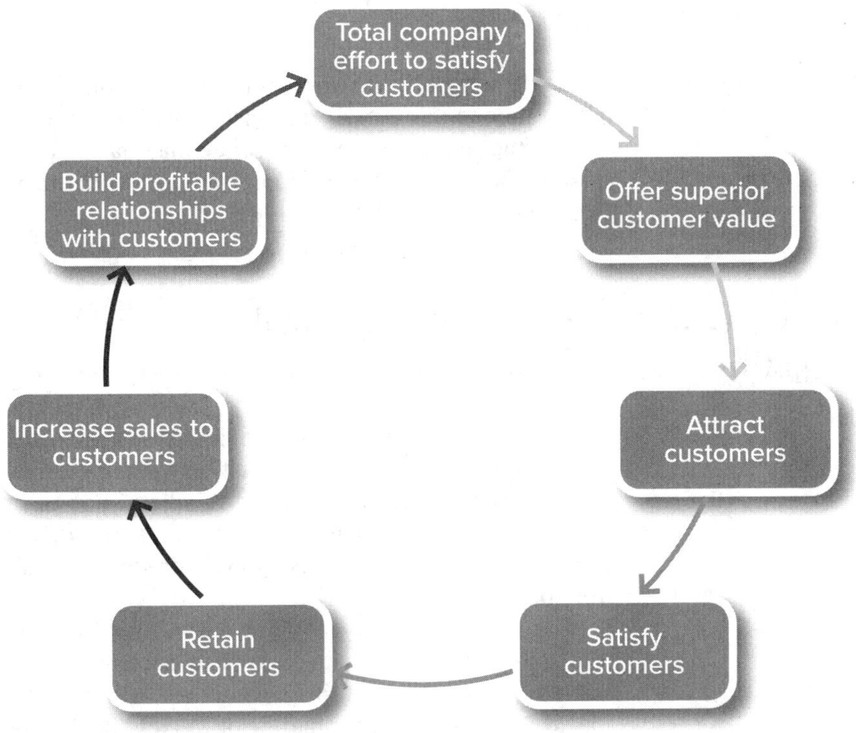

While nonprofits are newcomers to marketing, some are finding creative approaches to raise money. The United Nations' World Food Programme (WFP) aims to fight hunger. WFP used marketing to reduce the number of hungry children. It developed a smartphone app that allows people to "share their meals" with hungry children. Each time they "tap" the gold medallion, they donate $0.50, which feeds one child for a day. The app has led to sharing of more than 10 million meals, with many more each day.
Source: World Food Program; (smartphone frame): ©Oleg GawriloFF/Shutterstock RF

What is the "bottom line"?

As with a business, a nonprofit must take in as much money as it spends or it won't survive. However, a nonprofit organization does not measure "profit" in the same way as a firm. And its key measures of long-term success are also different. The YMCA, colleges, symphony orchestras, and the United Way, for example, all seek to achieve different objectives and need different measures of success. When everyone in an organization agrees to *some* measure(s) of long-run success, it helps the organization focus its efforts.

May not be organized for marketing

Some nonprofits face other challenges in organizing to adopt the marketing concept. Often no one has overall responsibility for marketing activities. Even when some leaders do the marketing thinking, they may have trouble getting unpaid volunteers with many different interests to all agree with the marketing strategy. Volunteers tend to do what they feel like doing!

The Marketing Concept, Social Responsibility, and Marketing Ethics

Society's needs must be considered

The marketing concept is so logical that it's hard to find fault with it. Yet when a firm focuses its efforts on satisfying some consumers–to achieve its objectives–there may be negative effects on society. For example, producers and consumers making free choices can cause conflicts and difficulties. This is called the **micro-macro dilemma**[14]. What is "good" for some firms and consumers may not be good for society as a whole.

For instance, many people in New York City buy bottled water because they like the convenience of easy-to-carry disposable bottles with spill-proof caps. On the other hand, the city already provides citizens with good tasting, safe tap water at a fraction of the cost. Is this just a matter of free choice by consumers? It's certainly a popular choice! Yet, critics point out that it is an inefficient use of resources to waste oil making and transporting millions of plastic bottles that end up in landfills where they leach chemicals into the soil. That kind of thinking, about the good of society as a whole, explains why New York City has run ads that encourage consumers to "get your fill" of free city water. What do you think? Should future generations pay the environmental price for today's consumer conveniences?

Source: New York City Department of Health/ DCF Advertising

Questions like these are not easy to answer. The basic reason is that many different people may have a stake in the outcomes—and social consequences—of the choices made by individual managers *and* consumers in a market-directed system. This means that marketing managers should be concerned with **social responsibility**—a firm's obligation to improve its positive effects on society and reduce its negative effects. As you read this book and learn more about marketing, you will also learn more about social responsibility in marketing—and why it must be taken seriously. You'll also see that being socially responsible sometimes requires difficult trade-offs.

Social responsibility can be difficult to assess when the effects on society are mixed. Take hydraulic fracturing (fracking), a process that sends pressurized liquid deep into the ground to remove oil and natural gas. Some argue that fracking helps America become more energy independent, produces cleaner fuel compared to alternatives, and lowers gas prices, thus stimulating the economy. On the other hand, the chemicals and procedures used in fracking may harm the environment and cause earthquakes. The government and many oil and gas producers are working to minimize the negative effects, but as you can imagine there are no easy answers for these conflicts.

The issue of social responsibility in marketing also raises other important questions—for which there are no easy answers.

Should all consumer needs be satisfied?

Some consumers want products that may not be safe or good for them in the long run. Some critics argue that businesses should not offer high-heeled shoes, alcoholic beverages, marijuana, gambling, or sugar-coated cereals because they aren't "good" for some consumers in the long run. Similarly, bicycles and roller blades are among the most dangerous products identified by the Consumer Product Safety Commission. Who should decide if these products will be offered to consumers?

Think about sugary soft drinks—consumers love them, but they add to a growing global obesity problem. Most consumers know the drinks are not good for them, and that they need to cut back, but some have trouble with this. New York City passed a law (later overturned in court) prohibiting the sale of sweetened drinks of more than 16 ounces. France passed a soda tax. Coca-Cola has, on its own, limited advertising to children, increased promotion of diet drinks, and promoted physical activity programs. Should governments or consumers make decisions about what products are offered to consumers?

Do all marketers act responsibly?

Not all marketers act in a socially responsible manner. Sometimes firms or individuals advance their own short-term interests at the expense of customers. For example, during the housing boom in the mid-2000s, some mortgage[15] brokers took advantage of trusting customers and sold them mortgages they could not afford while earning large commissions for themselves. As a result, many homebuyers were unable to pay for their homes, and this contributed to a global economic recession. When products are complicated, consumers may be vulnerable to unscrupulous[16] sellers. In these circumstances we can debate whether it is better to "let the buyer beware" or enact stricter government regulation.

What if it cuts into profits?

There are times when being socially responsible can increase not only a firm's profits, but also its costs. Even though some consumers will pay premium prices to buy "fair trade" coffee, napkins made from recycled paper, hybrid[17] cars that pollute less, or products made in overseas factories that pay a "fair wage," these items may cost more to produce. At the same time, other consumers attach little or no value to these social measures and refuse to pay a higher price for such products. Consequently, many firms selling to this second group are reluctant to be more socially responsible.

When a society feels that the social benefits are important, it may add regulations to create a level playing field for all firms and to assure that these benefits are provided. For example, there are laws that protect rivers from water pollution and that restrict the use of child labor. Still, it is difficult for governments to impose regulations that govern all circumstances where such trade-offs occur. So is the marketing concept really desirable?

Socially conscious marketing managers are trying to answer these questions. Their definition of customer satisfaction includes long-range effects—as well as immediate customer satisfaction. They try to balance consumer, company, and social interests.

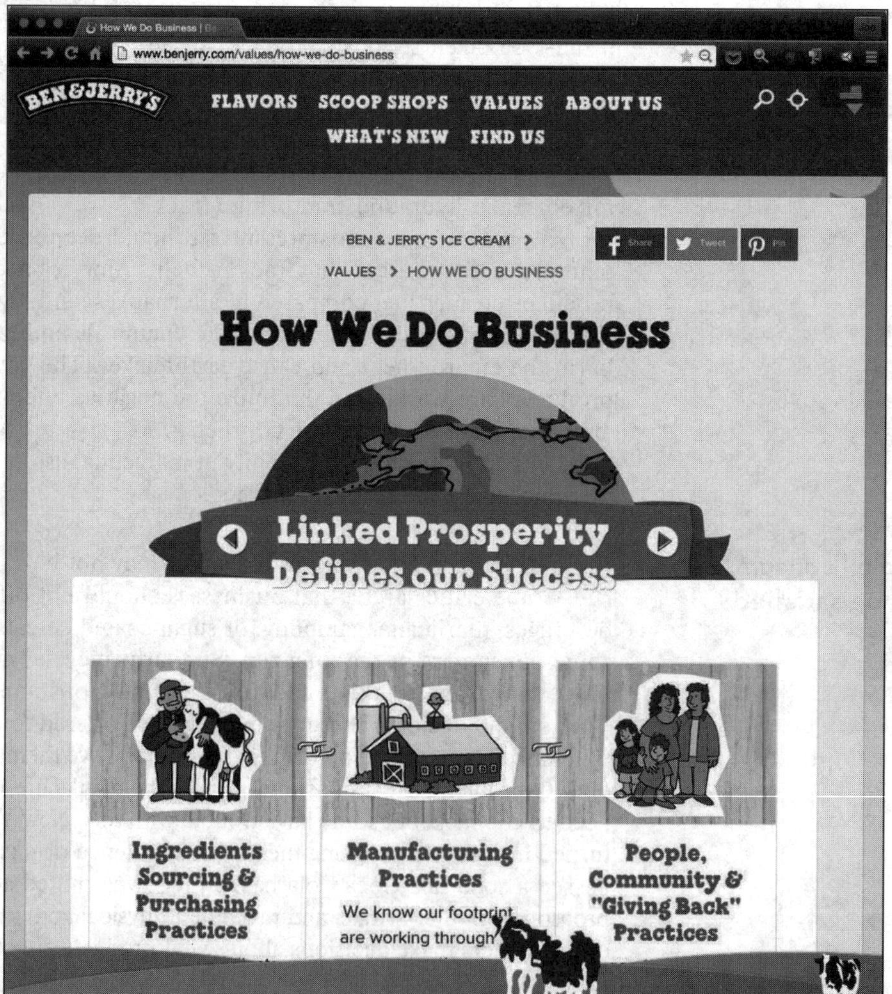

Ben & Jerry's runs its business with a very clear set of values. These values guide the ice cream maker's employees, including its marketing managers' ethics—the moral standards that guide marketing decisions and actions.

Source: Ben & Jerry's United States, Inc.

The marketing concept guides marketing ethics

A manager cannot be truly consumer-oriented and at the same time intentionally unethical. However, at times, problems and criticism may arise because a manager did not fully consider the ethical implications of a decision. In either case, there is no excuse for sloppiness[18] when it comes to **marketing ethics**—the moral standards that guide marketing decisions and actions. Each individual develops moral standards based on his or her own values. That helps explain why opinions about what is right or wrong often vary from one person to another, from one society to another, and among different groups within a society. It is sometimes difficult to say whose opinions are "correct." Even so, such opinions may have a very real influence on whether an individual's (or a firm's) marketing decisions and actions are accepted or rejected. So marketing ethics are not only a philosophical issue; they are also a pragmatic concern.

Problems may arise when one or a few individual managers don't share the same marketing ethics as others in the organization. A small number of people—or even one person operating alone—can damage a firm's reputation and even survival. Consider the scandal faced by Volkswagen when it came to light that the company found a way to "cheat" on emissions tests. When the company could not find a way to meet emissions reduction targets in its diesel vehicles, a few supervisors approved development of software designed to "cheat" emission testing systems. For years, about 11 million Volkswagen cars spewed as much as 40 times the allowable amount of pollutants. After this was discovered, Volkswagen paid out more than $23 billion in fines and fixes.

To be certain that standards for marketing ethics are as clear as possible, many organizations have developed their own written codes of ethics. These codes usually state—at least at a general level—the ethical standards that everyone in the firm should follow in dealing with customers and other people. Many professional societies also have such codes. For example, the American Marketing Association's code of ethics—see Exhibit 1-7—sets specific ethical standards for many aspects of marketing.

Exhibit 1-7 Summary of American Marketing Association Statement of Ethics

Preamble

The American Marketing Association commits itself to promoting the highest standard of professional ethical norms and values for its members (practitioners, academics, and students). Norms are established standards of conduct that are expected and maintained by society and/or professional organizations. Values represent the collective conception of what communities find desirable, important, and morally proper. Values also serve as the criteria for evaluating our own personal actions and the actions of others. As marketers, we recognize that we not only serve our organizations but also act as stewards of society in creating, facilitating, and executing the transactions that are part of the greater economy. In this role, marketers are expected to embrace the highest professional ethical norms and the ethical values implied by our responsibility toward multiple stakeholders (e.g., customers, employees, investors, peers, channel members, regulators, and the host community).

Ethical Norms

As Marketers, we must:

- Do no harm.
- Foster trust in the marketing system.
- Embrace ethical values.

Ethical Values

- Honesty—to be forthright in dealings with customers and stakeholders.
- Responsibility—to accept the consequences of our marketing decisions and strategies.
- Fairness—to balance justly the needs of the buyer with the interests of the seller.
- Respect—to acknowledge the basic human dignity of all stakeholders.
- Transparency—to create a spirit of openness in marketing operations.
- Citizenship—to fulfill the economic, legal, philanthropic, and societal responsibilities that serve stakeholders.

Ethical Dilemma

What would you do? A customer purchases a Canon digital camera that comes with a 90-day manufacturer's warranty on parts and labor. The salesperson suggests that the customer consider the store's three-year extended service to cover any problems with the camera. The customer replies, "I'm getting a Canon because it's a reputable brand—and at $98 the service agreement is one-third the cost of the camera." Four months later, the customer returns to the store and complains that the camera no longer takes pictures and that "the store needs to make it right."

If you were the store manager, what would you say? Would your response be any different if you knew that the customer was going to post his complaint on a consumer website?

Throughout the text, we will be discussing the types of ethical issues individual marketing managers face. But we won't be moralizing and trying to tell you how you should think on any given issue. Rather, by the end of the course we hope that *you* will have some firm personal opinions about what is and is not ethical in micro-marketing activities.

Fortunately, the prevailing practice of most businesspeople is to be fair and honest. However, not all criticisms of marketing focus on ethical issues.

Marketing has its critics

We must admit that marketing—as it exists in the United States and other developed societies—has many critics. Marketing activity is especially open to criticism because it is the part of business most visible to the public.

A number of typical complaints about marketing are summarized in Exhibit 1-8. Think about these criticisms and whether you agree with them or not. What complaints do you have that are not covered by one of the categories in Exhibit 1-8?

Such complaints should not be taken lightly. They show that many people are unhappy with some parts of the marketing system. Certainly, the strong public support for consumer protection laws proves that not all consumers feel they are being treated like royalty.

As you consider the various criticisms of marketing, keep in mind that not all of them deal with the marketing practices of specific firms. Some of the complaints about marketing really focus on the basic idea of a market-directed macro-marketing system—and these criticisms often occur because people don't understand what marketing is or how it works. As you go through this book, we'll discuss some of these criticisms. Then in our final chapter, we will return to a more complete appraisal of marketing in our consumer-oriented society.

Exhibit 1-8 Sample Criticisms of Marketing

- Advertising is everywhere, and it's often annoying, misleading, or wasteful.
- The quality of products is poor and often they are not even safe.
- There are too many unnecessary products.
- Retailers add too much to the cost of distribution and just raise prices without providing anything in return.
- Marketing serves the rich and exploits the poor.
- Marketers overpromise service, and when a consumer has a problem, nobody cares.
- Marketing creates interest in products that pollute the environment.
- Private information about consumers is collected and used to sell them things they don't need.
- Marketing makes people too materialistic and motivates them toward "things" instead of social needs.
- Easy consumer credit makes people buy things they don't need and can't afford.

CONCLUSION

The basic purpose of this chapter is to introduce you to marketing and highlight its value for consumers, firms, and society. This chapter sets the stage for that by introducing basic principles that guide marketing thinking.

You've learned about two views of marketing, both of which are important. One takes a micro view and focuses on marketing activities by an individual business (or other type of organization). This is what most people (including most business managers) have in mind when they talk about marketing. But it's important to understand that marketing also plays a more macro role. Macro-marketing is concerned with the way the whole marketing system works in a society or economy. It operates to make exchanges and relationships between producers and their customers more effective.

We discussed the functions of marketing and who performs them. This includes not only producers and their customers but also marketing specialists who serve as intermediaries between producers and consumers and other specialists (such as product-testing labs and advertising agencies) who are collaborators and facilitate marketing functions.

We explained how a market-directed economy works, through the macro-marketing system, to provide consumers with choices. We introduced macro-marketing in this chapter, and we'll consider macro-marketing issues throughout the text. But the major focus of this book is on marketing by individual organizations. Someone in an organization must plan and manage its activities to make certain that customer needs are satisfied.

That's why understanding the marketing concept is another objective. The marketing concept is the basic philosophy that provides direction to a marketing-oriented firm. It stresses that the company's efforts should focus on satisfying some target customers—at a profit. Production-oriented firms tend to forget this. The various departments within a production-oriented firm let their natural conflicts of interest get in the way of customer satisfaction.

We also introduced the customer value concept. It is marketing's responsibility to make certain that what the firm offers customers really provides them with value that is greater than they can obtain somewhere else. In today's competitive markets, a firm must offer superior customer value if it wants to attract customers, satisfy them, and build beneficial long-term relationships with them.

A final objective was for you to see how social responsibility and marketing ethics relate to the marketing concept. The chapter ends by considering criticisms of marketing—both of the way individual firms work and of the whole macro system. When you have finished reading this book, you will be better able to evaluate these criticisms.

By learning more about marketing-oriented decision making, you will be able to make more efficient and socially responsible decisions. This will help improve the performance of individual firms and organizations (your employers). Eventually it will help our macro-marketing system work better.

JOYFUL MOMENT

What Is Marketing?

You see a gorgeous girl at a party. You go up to her and say, "I am very rich. Marry me!" That's Direct Marketing.

You're at a party with a bunch of friends and see a gorgeous girl. One of your friends goes up to her and pointing at you says, "He's very rich. Marry him." That's Advertising.

You see a gorgeous girl at a party. You go up to her and get her telephone number. The next day you call and say, "Hi, I'm very rich. Marry me." That's Telemarketing.

You're at a party and see a gorgeous girl. You get up and straighten your tie; you walk up to her and pour her a drink. You open the door for her, pick up her bag after she drops it, offer her a ride, and then say, "By the way, I'm very rich. Will you marry me?" That's Public Relations.

You're at a party and see a gorgeous girl. She walks up to you and says, "You are very rich...?" That's Brand Recognition.

You see a gorgeous girl at a party. You go up to her and say, "I'm rich. Marry me." She gives you a nice hard slap on your face. That's Customer Feedback.

WORDS AND EXPRESSIONS

1. **innovation**: *n.* the act of starting something for the first time; introducing something new 创新；革新
   —Large numbers of machine tools have been rushed out since the implementation of technological innovation.
   自从实行技术革新以来，大批机床迅速地生产出来。
2. **warranty**: *n.* a written assurance that some product or service will be provided or will meet certain specifications 保修单，担保
   —This warranty is good for one year after the date of the purchase of the product.
   本保证书自购置此产品之日起有效期为一年。
3. **subsistence**: *n.* the condition of just having enough money or food to stay alive 维持生活；生存，生计
   —Many Namibians are subsistence farmers who live in the

arid borderlands.
许多纳米比亚人都是自给自足的农民，他们居住在干旱的边境地区。

4. **evolve**: *vi.* to undergo development or evolution 发展，进化
—Popular music evolved from folk songs.
流行音乐由民歌演变而来。

5. **standardization**: *n.* the condition in which a standard has been successfully established 标准化
—On one hand, standardization reduces flexibility and the freedom of choice.
标准化一方面会降低灵活性和选择的自由度。

6. **intermediary**: *n.* a person or organization that tries to help two other people or groups to agree with each other 中间人
—Jackson acted as an intermediary between the two parties.
杰克逊充当了双方的中间人。

7. **specialization**: *n.* the act of specializing; making something suitable for a special purpose 专业化，专门化
—It will continue on this path driven by globalization and specialization.
它将继续行进在由全球化和专业化驱动的道路上。

8. **consumption**: *n.* (economics) the utilization of economic goods to satisfy needs or in manufacturing 消费
— They were prepared to put people out of work and reduce consumption by strangling the whole economy.
他们准备让人们失业、降低消费，由此来遏制整个经济。

9. **monopolize**: *v.* to have and control fully and exclusively 垄断
— They are controlling so much cocoa that they are virtually monopolizing the market.
控制着那么多可可粉，他们实际上是在垄断市场。

10. **incentive**: *n.* something that encourages sb. to do 激励，奖励
—A little bonus will give the employees an incentive to work harder.
一点奖金可以刺激雇员更加努力地工作。

11. **surplus**: *n.* a quantity much larger than is needed 剩余，盈余
—Norway's budget surplus has fallen from 5.9% in 1986 to an expected 0.1% this year.
挪威的预算盈余已从 1986 年的 5.9% 下降到今年预计的 0.1%。

12. **orientation**: *n.* the type of activity or subject that a person or organization seems most interested in and gives most attention to 目标，方向，目的
— The company needs to develop a stronger orientation towards marketing its products.
公司需要针对其产品的营销定立一个更为明确的目标。

13. **hassle**: *n.* a situation that is difficult and involves problems, effort, or arguments with people 困难的事情；麻烦的事情；争论
—Weddings are so much hassle that you need a good break afterwards.
婚礼真是件折腾人的事，办完后得好好休息才行。

14. **dilemma**: *n.* state of uncertainty or perplexity especially as requiring a choice between equally unfavorable options 困境；进退两难
—He was faced with the dilemma of whether or not to return to his country.
他面临着是否回国的艰难选择。

15. **mortgage**: *n.* a conditional conveyance of property as security for the repayment of a loan 抵押
— The bank refused to accept any mortgage on land.
银行拒绝接受任何土地抵押。

16. **unscrupulous**: *adj.* behaving in an unfair or dishonest way 不讲道德的
— These kids are being exploited by very unscrupulous people.
这些孩子正被极不道德的人利用。

17. **hybrid**: *n.* a hybrid or a hybrid car is a car that can be powered by either petrol or electricity 混合动力汽车
—Hybrids, unlike pure electric cars, never need to be plugged in.
混合动力汽车，不像纯电动汽车，从不需要接电源。

18. **sloppiness**: *n.* carelessness 马虎
—This time the cause is not the recklessness of their lending, but the sloppiness with which they are dealing with the resulting defaults.
这一次的起因并不是他们不计后果地放贷，而是马虎地处理那些无法结算还清的欠款。

EXERCISES

1. **Multiple choices**

(1) According to the text, marketing means ____.
A. making a good product that sells itself　　B. much more than selling and advertising
C. selling and advertising　　D. producing goods and/or services

(2) Customer satisfaction is the extent to which a firm fulfills a consumer's ____.
A. needs　　B. desires
C. expectations　　D. all of the above

(3) Marketing is NOT needed in a ____ economy.
A. consumer-oriented　　B. command
C. pure subsistence　　D. market-directed

(4) Which of the following statements by a U.S. president best reflects a MICRO view of marketing? ____

A. "A tax cut will give consumers more spending money."
B. "With interest rates low, many young people can now afford to buy a new home."
C. "My administration will spend 75 percent more on purchases related to domestic security during the next year."
D. "Tourism firms should advertise more to attract more international visitors."

(5) ___ should be at the center of a company's marketing strategy.

A. Customers　B. Profits　C. Products　D. Employees

2. Terms translation

(1) marketing　(2) financing　(3) customer satisfaction　(4) command economy
(5) social responsibility　(6) intermediary　(7) collaborator　(8) sales era
(9) marketing ethics　(10) economics of scale

3. True or false

(1) If a firm produces the right goods or services, marketing has little role to play in creating customer satisfaction. ______
(2) The micro view of marketing sees it as the performance of activities that seek to accomplish an organization's objectives by anticipating customer or client needs and directing a flow of need-satisfying goods and services from producer to customer or client. ______
(3) Marketing does not occur unless there are two or more parties who want to exchange something for something else. ______
(4) In addition to delighting customers, companies today should also harness technology, think globally and be ethnically and socially responsible. ______
(5) During the "production era" a company focuses on production—because few products are available in the market. ______
(6) A marketing-oriented firm would try to produce what customers want, while a production-oriented firm would try to get customers to buy what the firm has produced. ______
(7) Setting a low price for a firm's offering is a sure way of creating high customer value. ______
(8) To develop lasting relationship with customers, marketing-oriented firms need to focus on customer satisfaction both before and after each sale. ______
(9) The marketing concept cannot be applied to nonprofit organization because they are not profit-oriented. ______
(10) Each individual develops moral standards based on his or her values, so it is sometimes difficult to say whose opinions are correct. ______

4. Fill in the blanks

(1) __________ means that as a company produces more of a product the total cost of each unit produced goes down.
(2) __________ refers to exchanges between individuals and organizations—and the activities that facilitate those exchanges—based on applications of information technology.
(3) __________ is the difference that a customer sees between the benefits of a firm's offering and the costs of obtaining those benefits.
(4) The primary purpose of the transporting and storing functions of marketing is to overcome __________ .
(5) __________ involve(s) sorting products according to size and quality.
(6) Firms that specialize in providing marketing functions other than buying and selling are known as __________ .
(7) An economic system in which government officials determine production levels is known as __________ .
(8) During the __________ era, concern about increased competition lead firms to focus on selling to attract customers.
(9) Accepting the "marketing concept" means that a firm should have a __________ orientation.
(10) The term "__________" means that what is "good" for some producers and consumers may not be good for society as a whole.

5. Answer the following questions

(1) Define the functions of marketing in your own words.
(2) Define the marketing concept in your own words.
(3) Distinguish between the micro and macro views of marketing. Then explain how they are interrelated, if they are.
(4) Distinguish between production orientation and marketing orientation.
(5) Give an example of a recent purchase you made where the purchase wasn't just a single transaction but rather part of an ongoing relationship with the seller. Discuss what the seller has done (or could do better) to strengthen the relationship and increase the odds of your being a loyal customer in the future.

SUGGESTED CASES

1. McDonald's "Seniors" Restaurant
2. Nature's Own Foods, Inc.
16. Hanratty Company

MARKETING ANALYTICS: DATA TO KNOWLEDGE

connect

CHAPTER 1: REVENUE, COST, AND PROFIT RELATIONSHIPS

This problem introduces you to the Marketing Analytics exercises, which are available in Connect (may require a separate purchase) for this text—and gets you started with the use of spreadsheet analysis for marketing decision making. Connect creates a spreadsheet to help you focus on the use of marketing analytics and not spreadsheet creation. In this case the problem is relatively simple. In fact, you could work it without the software. But by starting with a simple problem, you will learn how to use the program more quickly and see how it will help you with more complicated problems.

Sue Cline, the business manager at Magna University Student Bookstore, is developing plans for the next academic year. The bookstore is one of the university's nonprofit activities, but any "surplus" (profit) it earns is used to support the student activities center.

Two popular products at the bookstore are the student academic calendar and notebooks with the school name. Sue thinks that she can sell calendars to 90 percent of Magna's 3,000 students, so she has had 2,700 printed. The total cost, including artwork and printing, is $11,500. Last year the calendar sold for $5.00, but she is considering changing the price this year.

Sue thinks that the bookstore will be able to sell 6,000 notebooks if they are priced right. But she knows that many students will buy similar notebooks (without the school name) from stores in town if the bookstore price is too high.

Sue has entered the information about selling price, quantity, and costs for calendars and notebooks in the spreadsheet program so that it is easy to evaluate the effect of different decisions. The spreadsheet is also set up to calculate revenue and profit, based on:

Revenue = (Selling price) × (Quantity sold)

Profit = (Revenue) − (Total cost)

See Connect for the spreadsheet and questions needed to analyze this scenario.

CHAPTER TWO

Evaluating Opportunities in the Changing Market Environment

Back in 1995, when Amazon.com first went online, its founder Jeff Bezos saw a breakthrough opportunity in changing the retail shopping experience. Amazon's strategy took advantage of trends Bezos observed, especially a growing number of consumers shopping on the Internet. Laws back then didn't require the collection of sales tax on online sales, which offset charges for shipping and handling. Early investors were patient as Amazon lost $3 billion from 1995 to 2003. They shared Bezos' belief that if Amazon consistently delivered value and satisfaction, customers would come back, buy more, and tell their friends. Bezos' and his investors' predictions were on target.

Amazon wasn't just "lucky" to be in the right place and time. Bezos pushes his firm to be innovative in every aspect of the customer experience. He urges employees to keep the company's mission statement in mind: "We strive to offer our customers the lowest possible prices, the best available selection, and the utmost convenience." With this focus, Amazon pioneered community features such as customer reviews and customer questions and answers, which help customers discover new products and make more informed decisions. Amazon Marketplace gives many sellers the opportunity to compete directly with Amazon. Amazon also expanded into new product markets, over time adding electronics, home and garden, health and beauty aids, industrial tools, clothing and shoes, cloud computing services, and more.

Amazon quickly pursued global growth, initially launching new sites in both the United Kingdom and Germany. Like the United States, these markets offered a large number of customers with access to the Internet and high incomes. Amazon is now in 14 countries, including Australia, Canada, France, India, and China. Although most of these efforts have gone well, Amazon has struggled to gain a foothold in the important and fast-growing Chinese market. While many Chinese have access to the Internet and a growing income, Amazon's share of China's e-commerce sales is estimated at only about 2 percent. By comparison, Amazon's market share of U.S. e-commerce sales is 43 percent and growing. Amazon believes that in order to turn things around in China, it needs to better customize[1] its marketing strategy to the local culture.

Amazon's a leader in using customer data and artificial intelligence to deliver personalized shopping experiences to every customer. For example, Amazon knows how its customers behave on the site—what pages they visit, what they buy and don't buy, and whether they read reviews or shop around before purchasing. These insights, combined with knowledge gained from observing hundreds of millions of other customers, help Amazon anticipate its customers' wants and needs. Computer programs then deliver personalized advertising and product recommendations to Amazon customers.

Amazon continually strives to make shopping convenient. For a $99 annual fee, all Amazon Prime customers receive free two-day shipping on select products and free access to select videos, music, and more. Amazon is also setting up warehouses near major metro areas and is testing different delivery approaches. For example, local inventory enables Amazon's Prime Now program, which offers customers one-hour delivery in some markets and same-day delivery in others. Amazon hopes to someday use drone aircraft to deliver small packages in 30 minutes or less. Right now, local regulations—rather than technology limitations—are holding up this plan.

Striving for "utmost convenience," Amazon realized it needed to build physical stores, too. Amazon hopes to leverage[2] two of its greatest resources—its technological expertise[3] and financial resources—and find ways to improve the in-store shopping experience. In its hometown of Seattle, Amazon is testing a new grocery store concept called Amazon Go. This store lets customers walk in, grab what they want, and walk out—without having to swipe[4] a card or stand in a checkout line. These customers are not getting everything for free—after all, Amazon is in business to make a profit. Artificial intelligence and sensors placed throughout the store track items customers place in their physical baskets, and the Amazon Go app places those same items in their virtual shopping carts. When finished shopping, a customer simply walks out and everything is charged to his or her Amazon account. Is this what's next for retail?

Another innovation, Amazon Echo, was created to make life (and shopping) better for Amazon customers. Echo is a nine-inch-tall smart speaker. When a customer calls out "Alexa," Echo wakes up and connects to a personal digital assistant. From there, a user can ask Alexa to play music, deliver news and sports scores, play rock, paper, scissors, report the weather—and of course place an order on Amazon. It's so easy a six-year-old can do it—and one did. When a little girl from Dallas, Texas, asked Alexa to "send me a KidKraft Sparkle Mansion dollhouse and some sugar cookies," they arrived at her home two days later. After the surprise delivery, Mom and Dad activated parental controls to add another step to the ordering process.

Amazon's diverse product line means it needs to monitor a wide range of strong competitors. Amazon engages in price wars with Walmart over books, toys, and DVDs; fights Netflix and Hulu in video downloads; and battles Apple and Spotify in online music. Amazon has never been afraid to tackle markets with strong competitors. To the contrary, it seeks large and growing markets where it can leverage its competitive strengths—company size, technology skills, efficient operations, and creative personnel. To grow in these competitive and fast-changing market environments, Amazon must continue to anticipate market trends and adjust its marketing strategies.

LEARNING OBJECTIVES

The Amazon case shows that a marketing manager must understand customer needs and choose marketing strategy variables within the framework of a changing market environment. Opportunities need to fit with a firm's objectives and resources, and managers should screen for opportunities where there is a chance for competitive advantage and, if possible, favorable trends in the external environment.

When you finish this chapter, you should be able to

1 know the variables that shape the environment of marketing strategy planning.

2 understand why company objectives are important in guiding marketing strategy planning.

3 see how the resources of a firm affect the search for opportunities.

4 know how to conduct a competitor analysis and how different types of competition affect strategy planning.

5 understand how the economic and technological environments can affect strategy planning.

6 know how elements of the political and legal environment affect marketing strategy planning.

7 understand the cultural and social environment and how demographic[5] trends affect strategy planning.

8 understand how to screen and evaluate marketing strategy opportunities.

9 understand the important new terms (shown in boldface).

The Market Environment

The marketing strategy planning process (see Exhibit 2-1) requires narrowing down to the best opportunities and developing a strategy that gives the firm a competitive advantage and provides target customers with superior customer value. This narrowing-down process should consider the important elements of the market environment and how they are shifting.

A large number of forces shapes the market environment. The direct market environment includes customers, the company, and competitors. The external market environment is broader and includes four major areas:

1. Economic environment
2. Technological environment
3. Political and legal environment
4. Cultural and social environment

Exhibit 2-1 Overview of Marketing Strategy Planning Process

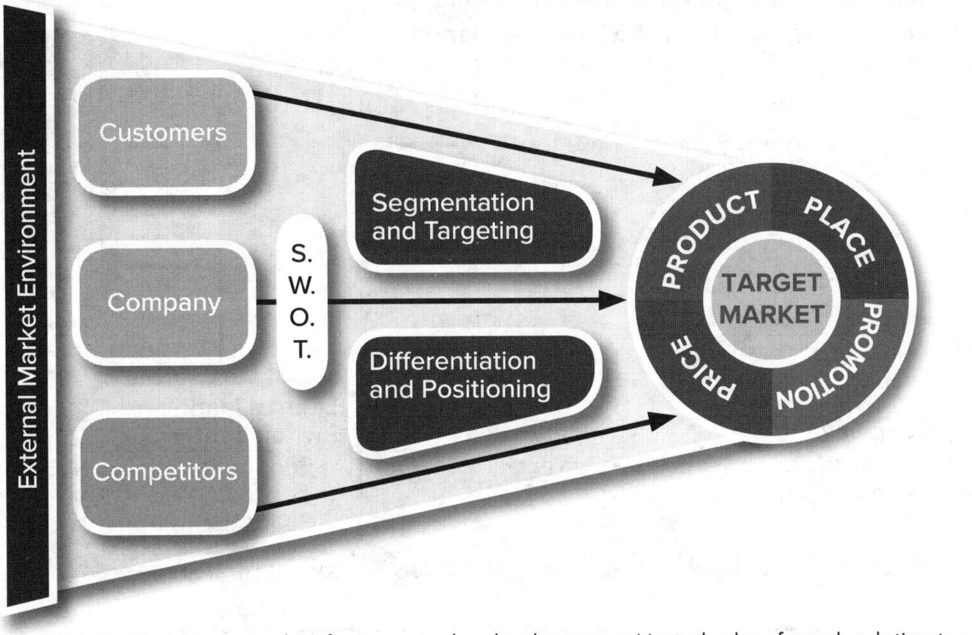

Note: Marketing manager narrows down from screening broad market opportunities to develop a focused marketing strategy. S.W.O.T. denotes Strengths, Weaknesses, Opportunities, and Threats.

In this chapter we'll look at the key market environment variables shown in Exhibit 2-2 in more detail. We'll see how they shape opportunities–limiting some possibilities but making others more attractive. Managers can't alter the variables of the market environment. That's why it's useful to think of them as uncontrollable variables. On the other hand, a manager should analyze the environment when making decisions that can be controlled. For example, a manager can select a strategy that leads the firm into a market where competition is not yet strong or where trends in the external market are likely to support market growth.

Objectives Should Set Firm's Course

A company must decide where it's going, or it may fall into the trap expressed so well by the quotation: "Having lost sight of our objective, we redoubled our efforts." Company objectives should shape the direction and operation of the whole business.

It is difficult to set objectives that really guide the present and future development of a company. The marketing manager should be heard when the company is setting objectives. But setting whole-company objectives–within resource limits–is ultimately the responsibility of top management. Top management must look at the whole business, relate its present objectives and resources to the external environment, and then decide what the firm wants to accomplish in the future.

A mission statement helps set the course

Each firm needs to develop its own objectives based on its own situation. This is important, but top executives often don't state their objectives clearly. If objectives aren't clear from the start, different managers may hold unspoken and conflicting objectives.

Many firms try to avoid this problem by developing a **mission statement**, which sets out the organization's basic purpose for being. A good mission statement focuses on a few key goals rather than embracing everything. It should guide managers in determining which opportunities to pursue.

The mission statement for the American Red Cross provides this direction: "The American Red Cross prevents and alleviates human suffering in the face of emergencies by mobilizing the power of volunteers and the generosity of donors." This tells a Red Cross employee she should not pursue a grant that supports children's literacy–even if

Exhibit 2-2 Marketing Strategy Planning, Competitors, Company, and External Market Environment

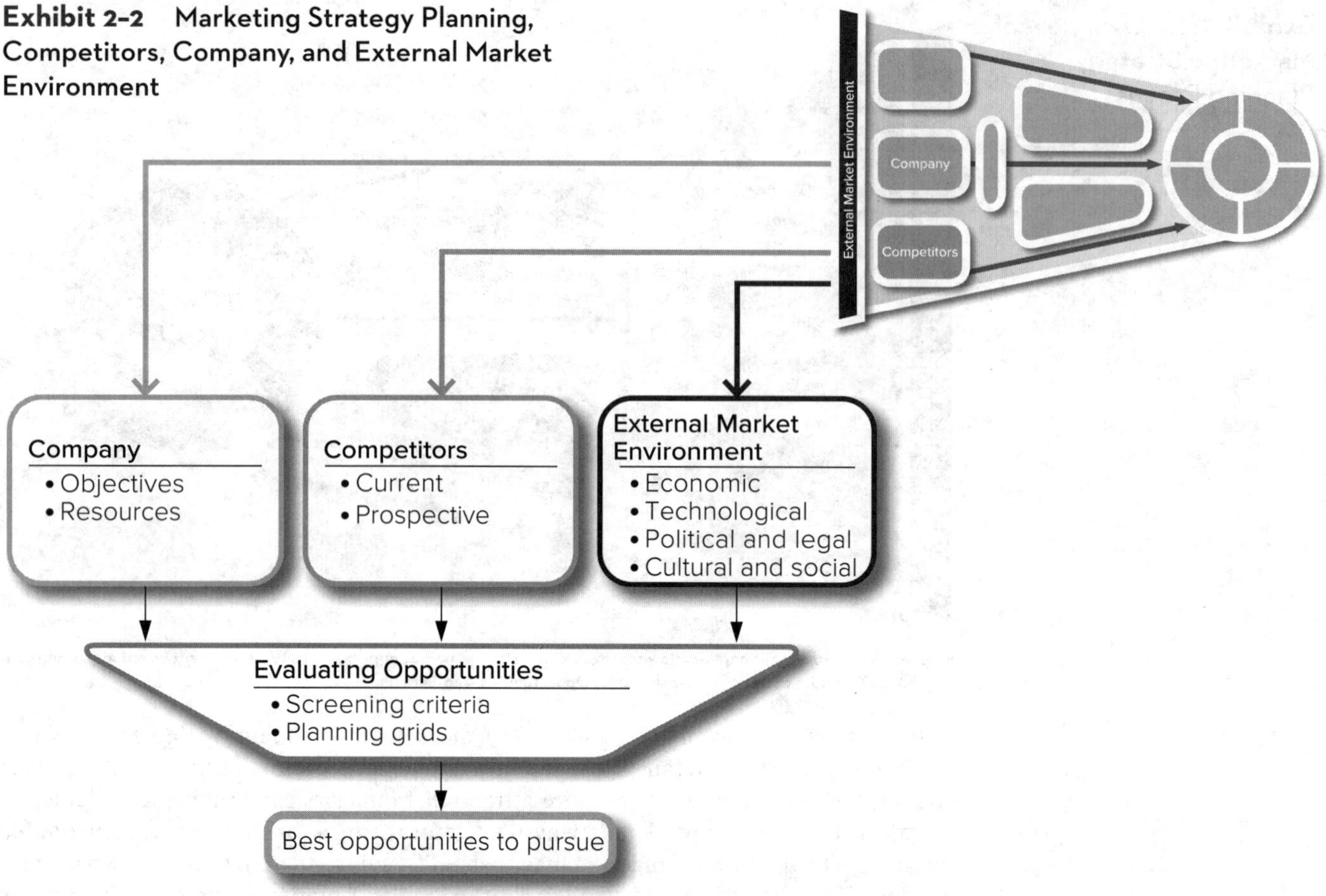

it's a good cause. On the other hand, the opportunity to develop a smartphone app that accepts donations for aid to Nepal following an earthquake fits right in this charity's mission. A mission statement may need to be revised as new market needs arise or as the market environment changes. This would be a fundamental change and not one that is made casually.

The whole firm must work toward the same objectives

A mission statement is important, but it is not a substitute for more specific objectives that provide guidance in screening possible opportunities. For example, top management might set objectives such as "earn 25 percent annual return on investment" and "introduce at least three innovative and successful products in the next two years."

Of course, when there are a number of specific objectives stated by top management, it is critical that they be compatible. For example, the objective of introducing new products is reasonable. However, if the costs of developing and introducing the new products cannot be recouped[6] within one year, the return on investment objective is impossible.

Company objectives should lead to marketing objectives

To avoid such problems, the marketing manager should at least be involved in setting company objectives. Company objectives guide managers as they search for and evaluate opportunities–and later plan marketing strategies. Particular *marketing* objectives should be set within the framework of larger company objectives. As shown in Exhibit 2-3, firms need a hierarchy[7] of objectives–moving from company objectives to marketing department objectives. For each marketing strategy, firms also need objectives for each of the Four Ps–as well as more detailed objectives. For example, in the Promotion area, we need objectives for personal selling, mass selling, *and* sales promotion.

Exhibit 2-3 A Hierarchy of Objectives

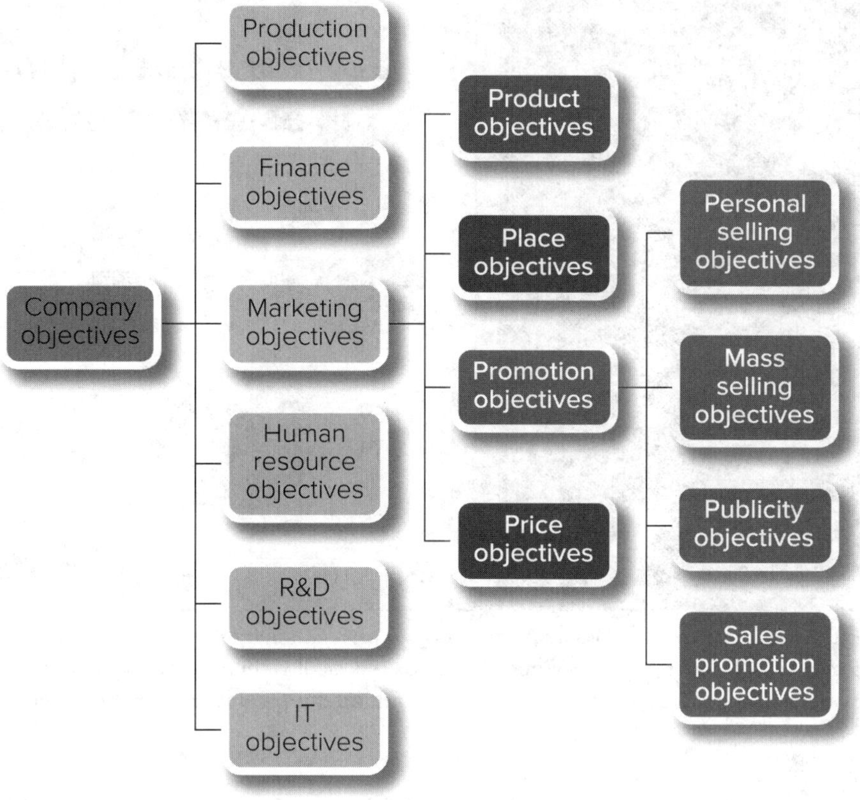

Insurance company USAA provides an example. One of USAA's top objectives is to deliver high levels of customer satisfaction. Because customer service is a key driver of satisfaction, it is critical to have highly qualified and well-trained customer service representatives (CSRs) responding to customers' questions or problems. This leads to human resource objectives that guide the hiring and training of CSRs. Similarly, it's imperative[8] for USAA's information technology group to develop software that increases the effectiveness of CSRs in their dealings with customers. So new software was designed to allow CSRs to view the same online screens as customers see on their PCs at home. With these capabilities, CSRs can solve customer problems more efficiently. USAA expects these efforts to deliver even higher levels of customer satisfaction and customer retention[9] in the competitive insurance market.

Both company objectives and marketing objectives should be realistic and achievable. Overly ambitious objectives are useless if the firm lacks the resources to achieve them.

Company Resources May Limit Search for Opportunities

Every firm has some resources—hopefully some unique ones—that set it apart. Breakthrough opportunities—or at least some competitive advantage—come from making use of these strengths while avoiding direct competition with firms having similar strengths.

To find its strengths or recognize weaknesses, a firm must evaluate its functional areas (production, research and engineering, marketing, general management, and finance) as well as its present products and markets. The knowledge of people at the firm can also be a unique resource. By analyzing successes or failures in relation to the firm's resources, management can discover why the firm was successful—or why it failed—in the past. Let's take a closer look at three specific types of resources that guide marketing strategy planning—financial, production, and marketing.

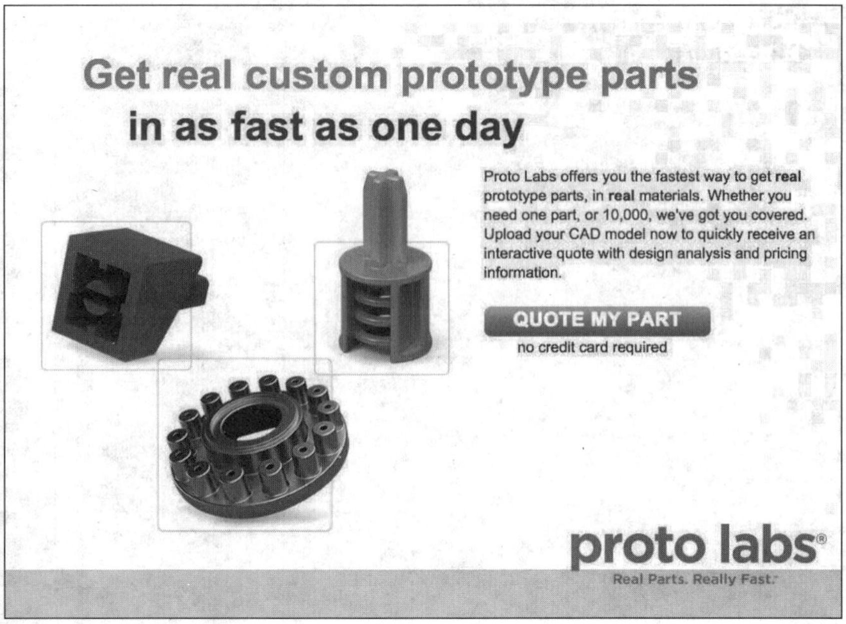

The opportunities a firm decides to pursue may depend on its resources and capabilities. For example, General Mills was already producing a key ingredient for its new Chocolate Chex Mix, so it went ahead and launched Chex Mix Turtle. When 3-D printing technology became increasingly practical, Proto Labs added this production capability and faster services for its customers.
(left): Source: General Mills, Inc.; (right): Used with permission of Proto Labs, Inc.

Financial resources determine opportunities

Some opportunities require large amounts of capital just to get started. Money may be required for R&D, production facilities, marketing research, or advertising before a firm makes its first sale. And even a really good opportunity may not be profitable for years—so cash flow matters, too. If financial resources are limited, a firm may have to develop lower-cost and potentially riskier marketing plans. So lack of financial strength is often a barrier to entry into an otherwise attractive market.

What and how many can be produced? At what cost?

Production resources also affect opportunities. In many businesses, the cost of producing and selling each unit decreases as the quantity increases. This can place smaller firms at a production cost disadvantage when seeking to win business from larger competitors. On the other hand, new—or smaller—firms sometimes have the advantage of flexibility. They are not handicapped with large, special-purpose facilities that are obsolete or poorly located.

Many firms increase flexibility by not having any "in-house" manufacturing for their brands. Hanes is a good example. At one point, Hanes had U.S. factories for its underwear and T-shirts. But the factories were sold when most textile-related manufacturing moved to other countries with lower labor costs. Top managers for the brand said that they didn't have a competitive advantage in manufacturing anyway. Now, as Hanes' needs change, it has the flexibility to work with whatever suppliers around the world are best able to meet its specifications.

Marketing strategies often build on existing marketing resources

Marketing resources can create opportunities for a firm. In the product area, for example, a familiar brand can be a big strength. Starbucks is famous for its coffee beverages. When Starbucks introduced its coffee ice cream, many people quickly tried it because they knew what Starbucks flavor meant.

Good relations with wholesalers and retailers can also be an important marketing resource—especially when introducing new products. Marketing managers at Clorox relied on this when they introduced the Green Works line of household cleaners. After years of working with the company on well-established products such as Clorox Bleach, retailers trusted Clorox to create an effective marketing strategy for Green Works. This trust opened doors that would've been closed to a new company. Other firms have a strong sales force or expertise in advertising, which should be recognized when developing a marketing strategy.

Firms can and often do develop new resources and capabilities when entering new markets. The lack of such resources should not rule out an opportunity, but an organization should recognize the costs required to develop the new capabilities.

Analyzing Competitors and the Competitive Environment

Avoid head-on competition

The **competitive environment** affects the number and types of competitors the marketing manager faces and how they may behave. Although marketing managers usually can't control these factors, they can choose strategies that avoid head-on competition. And where competition is inevitable, they can plan for it.

Kinds of competitive situations

Economists describe four basic kinds of market (competitive) situations: monopoly[10], oligopoly[11], pure competition, and monopolistic[12] competition. Understanding the differences among these market situations is helpful in analyzing the competitive environment, and our discussion assumes some familiarity with these concepts.

Competitor-free environments are rare

Monopoly situations occur when one firm completely controls a broad product-market. These are relatively rare in market-directed economies. When monopolies are necessary, monopolists often face a great deal of government regulation. For example, in many parts of the world prices set by utility companies (electricity and water) must be approved by a government agency. Monopolists can be tempted to ignore customer needs, but a customer orientation can fend off increased government regulation and help the firm if competitors later enter the market.

Pure competition and oligopoly when there is little or no differentiation

Many product-markets head toward *pure competition*—or *oligopoly*—over the long run. In these situations, competitors offer very similar marketing mixes, and customers see the alternatives as close substitutes. In other words, competitors have failed to differentiate their offerings. In this situation, managers usually compete on low prices, and profit margins[13] shrink. In oligopoly there are a few large firms competing, whereas in pure competition there are often many firms.

Avoiding these competitive situations is sensible and fits with our emphasis on finding a competitive advantage. Marketing managers can't just adopt the same "good" marketing strategy being used by other firms. That leads to head-on competition and a downward spiral in prices and profits. So target marketers try to offer a marketing mix better suited to target customers' needs than competitors' offerings.

Monopolistic competition is typical and a challenge

In *monopolistic competition,* different firms offer marketing mixes that at least some customers see as different. Each competitor tries to get control (a monopoly) in its "own" target market. But competition still exists because some customers see the various alternatives as substitutes. Most marketing managers in developed economies face monopolistic competition.

In monopolistic competition, marketing managers sometimes try to differentiate very similar products by relying on other elements of the marketing mix. For example, many consumers believe that most brands of gasoline are similar. This makes it difficult for a Texaco station to attract customers by claiming it offers better gasoline. So a Texaco station might compete on other parts of its offering, perhaps by serving Seattle's Best Coffee, giving discounted car washes, or maintaining longer hours of operation. Yet such approaches may not work for long if they are easily copied by competitors. So marketing managers should actively seek **sustainable competitive advantage**, a marketing mix that customers see as better than a competitor's mix and cannot be quickly or easily copied.

Analyze competitors to find competitive advantage

The best way for a marketing manager to avoid head-on competition is to find new or better ways to satisfy customers' needs and provide value. The search for a breakthrough opportunity—or some sort of competitive advantage—requires an understanding not only of customers but also of competitors. That's why marketing managers turn to **competitor analysis**—an organized approach for evaluating the strengths and weaknesses of current or potential competitors' marketing strategies.

The basic approach to competitor analysis is simple. You compare the strengths and weaknesses of your current (or planned) target market and marketing mix with what competitors are currently doing or are likely to do in response to your strategy.

The initial step in competitor analysis is to identify potential competitors. It's useful to start broadly and from the viewpoint of target customers. Companies may offer quite different products to meet the same needs, but they are competitors if customers see them as offering close substitutes. For example, disposable diapers, cloth diapers, and diaper rental services all compete in the same broad market concerned with baby care. Identifying a broad set of potential competitors helps marketing managers understand the different ways customers are currently meeting needs and sometimes points to new opportunities. Even parents who usually prefer the economy of cloth diapers may be interested in the convenience of disposables when they travel.

Keep a closer eye on competitive rivals

Marketing managers usually narrow the focus of their analysis to the set of **competitive rivals**[14] that are their closest competitors. Rivals offering similar products are usually easy to identify. However, with a really new and different product concept, the closest competitor may be a firm that is currently serving similar needs with a different type of product. Although such firms may not appear to be close competitors, they are likely to fight back—perhaps with a directly competitive product—if another firm starts to take away customers.

Marketing managers will often assess their progress against competitive rivals by monitoring market share. **Market share** is the portion of total sales in a product category accounted for by a particular brand. So the market share of the Apple iPhone in the United States is the portion of iPhones sold in the United States in a given period of time as compared to all smartphones sold in the United States in the same time period. It is usually expressed as a percentage. Market share may be based on units or dollars sold. Marketing managers often track market share over time to monitor how well a product is doing in a particular market. The *Marketing Analytics in Action: Market Share* activity next provides an example of this.

Marketing Analytics in Action: Market Share

Marketing managers often keep a close eye on market share, comparing how market share changes over time and typically sorting out market share in different geographic locations. Consider the data below, which show the Apple iPhone's market share in four countries from September to November in 2015 and 2016.

	iPhone Market Share		
Country	**November 2015**	**November 2016**	**Market Share Change**
United States	37.1%	43.5%	+6.4%
Great Britain	39.8	48.3	+9.1
Germany	23.8	20.6	−3.2
China	25.3	19.9	−5.4

During this period, we can see that the iPhone was doing much better—as measured by market share and market share change—in some countries (the United States and Great Britain) as compared to others (Germany and China).

1. *What insights would this provide for a marketing manager for the iPhone with responsibility for global sales?*
2. *What other analysis could be done to help develop a marketing strategy for the iPhone in each of these countries?*

Actively seek information about competitors

A marketing manager should actively seek information about current and potential competitors. Although most firms try to keep the specifics of their plans secret, much public information may be available. Sources of competitor information include trade publications, sales reps, suppliers, and other industry experts. In business markets, customers may be quick to explain what competing suppliers are offering.

Ethical issues may arise

The search for information about competitors can raise ethical issues. For example, people who change jobs and move to competing firms may have a great deal of information, but is it ethical for them to use it? Similarly, some firms have been criticized for going too far—like waiting at a landfill for competitors' trash to find copies of confidential company reports or "hacking" a competitor's computer network.

Beyond the moral issues, spying on competitors to obtain trade secrets is illegal. Damage awards can be huge. In one example, the courts ordered competing firms to pay Procter & Gamble about $125 million in damages for stealing secrets about its Duncan Hines soft cookies.

Ethical Dilemma

What would you do? You are a salesperson for a company that manufactures industrial lighting used in factories. During a recent sales call, an engineer at your customer firm comments about a new energy-saving light bulb that his company is testing for a competing supplier. Your company was not aware of the competitor's new product—which you think may make one of your product lines obsolete.

Should you pass this competitive intelligence to your sales manager? Should you question the engineer or others at the customer firm to learn more? If you gather more information, should you share that with your company?

The Economic Environment

The **economic environment** refers to macro-economic factors, including national income, economic growth, and inflation[15], that affect patterns of consumer and business spending. The rise and fall of the economy in general, within certain industries, or in specific parts of the world can have a big impact on what customers buy.

Economic conditions change rapidly

The economic environment can, and does, change quite rapidly. The effects can be far-reaching and require changes in marketing strategy.

Even a well-planned marketing strategy may fail if a country or region goes through a rapid business decline. You can see how quickly this can occur by considering what happened in the U.S. housing market just a few years ago. Earlier in the decade the economy was growing, household incomes were increasing, and interest rates were low. As a result, the housing market was hot. Manufacturers of building materials, home-builders, real estate firms, and mortgage companies all enjoyed strong profits as they scrambled[16] to keep up with demand. By 2008 the economy was in a recession and the housing market abruptly collapsed. Firms that had done so well a year earlier were suffering huge losses—and many went bankrupt. Worse, millions of people lost their homes when they could not afford rising payments for variable-rate mortgages.

Interest rates and inflation affect buying

Changes in the economy are often accompanied by changes in the interest rate—the charge for borrowing money. Interest rates directly affect the total price borrowers must pay for products. So the interest rate affects when, and if, they will buy. This is an especially important factor in some business markets. But it also affects consumer purchases of homes, cars, and other items usually bought on credit.

Consider the situation of a homebuyer borrowing $150,000 on a 30-year mortgage at 4 percent interest. Monthly payments would be $716 (not including taxes). If the interest rate on that same 30-year loan was 7 percent, monthly payments would be $998–almost $300 more per month. You can see how high interest rates can cause many consumers to not buy a home, buy a smaller home, or buy the home but not new furniture or landscaping.

Interest rates usually increase during periods of inflation, and inflation is a fact of life in many economies. Inflation refers to the general increase in prices in an economy. In some Latin American countries, inflation has exceeded 400 percent a year in recent years. In contrast, recent U.S. levels–3 to 20 percent–seem low. Inflation must be considered in strategy planning. When consumers anticipate fast-rising prices, they behave differently, usually spending money as soon as they get it. When price increases outpace income gains, consumers have no choice but to buy less. When businesses' costs are rising rapidly a marketing manager may have to increase prices. For example, airlines and freight carriers can raise prices sharply in response to spiraling fuel costs.

Marketing managers must watch the economic environment carefully. In contrast to the cultural and social environment, economic conditions can move rapidly and require immediate strategy changes.

The Technological Environment

Technology affects opportunities

Technology is the application of science to convert an economy's resources to output. Technology affects marketing in two basic ways: it creates opportunities for new products and it drives the development of new processes (ways of doing things). Throughout this book we offer many examples, so let's start by showing how anticipating technologies helps firms spot threats and opportunities.

Anticipate technologies and plan for the future

Although most technological developments don't come out of nowhere, it is not always clear how a technology just over the horizon might change a business. For example, producers of cameras and GPS might not have seen how quickly smartphones would cut into their business. Marketing managers should monitor technologies that might impact their industry–and engage in contingency planning for potential opportunities and threats.

Consider the pending impact of driverless cars. Many expect that by the late 2020s, most of us will be transported in robot-driven cars. Automakers need to prepare new vehicles with this technology. Robots are expected to be much better drivers than we humans, so auto insurance companies need to prepare for lower premiums. Beyond that, did you know that in the United States, auto accidents account for 2 million emergency room visits each year? Driverless cars may reduce hospital demand for emergency services. Also, the nation's older adults might be able to live on their own longer if they can get around without having to drive, slowing demand for nursing homes while increasing the need for in-home health care. Bars and restaurants may see more business–and sell more alcohol–when patrons don't need to worry about driving home under the influence. Marketing managers who anticipate the impact of new technology can plan and adapt marketing strategies for the future.

Artificial intelligence changes marketing processes

Many of the fastest-growing new technologies use **artificial intelligence (AI)**, which refers to having machines operate like humans with respect to learning and decision making. Artificial intelligence is implemented by an **intelligent agent**, a device that observes an environment and acts to achieve a goal. Many companies today utilize AI to deliver better service to customers; for example, AI is behind the driverless car we just discussed. The car operates as an intelligent agent that makes decisions about when to stop, accelerate, brake, and turn. Over time it can learn if a

What's Next? Intelligent agents learn to create and deliver customer value

Faster computer processing and more data allow intelligent agents—powered by artificial intelligence—to deliver more value to customers. To some degree, intelligent agents are not new. For example, a basic home thermostat is an intelligent agent. Since 1927, thermostats have been able to sense a room's temperature and turn on or turn off the heating and air conditioning to maintain a constant temperature. These days, the thermostat is smarter and delivers more value. The Nest Thermostat automatically learns a customer's schedule and preferences—its sensors observe when you go to sleep (to dial the temperature down), when you wake up (to warm up the house or specific rooms just before you wake up) and when you go to work (again, to dial the temperature down). Customers save money by not using heat or air conditioning when they don't need it.

Let's look at a few more examples of how intelligent agents deliver customer value.

Facebook has become so ubiquitous that many users have hundreds or thousands of "friends." Yet most users really want to see just a small subset of those friends. Facebook's intelligent agent learns whose posts you are most interested in and places those at the top of your newsfeed. Facebook's image-recognition software learns your friends and suggests names for tagging your photos. By making the program more relevant, Facebook enhances the value of the program and encourages users to visit more often.

Intelligent agents also help shoppers monitor prices—so they know when something is a good deal. For example, car shopping site iSeeCars analyzes comparable car sales across the web to suggest a fair "market price" for a particular used car. iSeeCars sorts your search for a used Ford Escape so the "best deals" (priced most below the "market price") sort to the top of the list. When customers search for flights from Atlanta to Dallas, online travel agent Kayak uses current pricing and demand information to predict whether and when the ticket price might rise or drop.

All of these examples are here now, so *What's Next?* Soon intelligent agents will deliver value by taking on marketing activities—perhaps doing a better job at a lower cost than humans. For example, intelligent agents will answer every customer service phone call on the first ring—computers can handle unlimited customers at the same time. The agents will be smart enough to answer most questions in any language. Other intelligent agents will operate like salespeople. Someday soon, a customer might simply tell her smartphone, "I need red sneakers." The phone will respond with follow-up questions to better narrow down her needs: "What will you use them for?" "How important is comfort?" "What athletic shoes have you liked in the past?" The intelligent agent will "remember" the customer wears a size 8, is price sensitive, and loves free shipping and easy returns. The agent will then search online for coupons and compare retailer offers before presenting the customer with the best "red sneaker" options given her wants and needs. She can reply "buy these" and the agent will place the order.

The use of artificial intelligence and intelligent agents in marketing is just beginning. As intelligent agents learn more about customers, their recommendations and advice will improve. Buyers will save time and money when intelligent agents offer personalized recommendations and wise buying advice.

customer prefers a slower "driver" or taking the scenic route. The Amazon Echo includes an intelligent agent that learns where a customer lives, so it chooses the right city when it is asked about "today's weather" or "local news." In the *What's Next?* Intelligent agents learn to create and deliver customer value box we take a closer look at AI and intelligent agents.

Technology changes marketing processes

Technology changes how customers and marketers do things. Facebook was founded in 2004 and by 2017 had over 2 billion users. Now many organizations have Facebook pages or run highly targeted ads on the social network—fans of the Pittsburgh Steelers usually say that right on their Facebook page, identifying them as

Researchers at Coca-Cola developed a new technology for the plastic bottles used for many of its products. PlantBottle packaging looks and functions just like traditional PET plastic bottles—and it is recyclable. But because these bottles are partially made from plant material, they have a much smaller carbon footprint, making them better for the environment. Coke works with Ford, Heinz, Nike, and Procter & Gamble (not Pepsi) to accelerate future development of plant-based plastics.
Source: The Coca-Cola Company

a target for ads for gear with their favorite football team's logo. The Internet has changed the nature of retailing as many consumers shop from their keyboard—or tablet device—and have purchases delivered to their homes. Hotels and airlines change prices depending on supply and demand on specific dates. Throughout this textbook you will read about how marketing is changing because of new applications of technology.

Technology comes with challenges

Although technological change opens up many new opportunities, it also poses challenges for marketers. For some marketing managers new technology is scary, so they avoid what they do not understand. For others it is easy to fall in love with the latest thing—whether from the firm's R&D lab or a consultant selling social media tools—and blindly add it to the firm's marketing strategy. Both approaches can lead to a production-oriented way of thinking. That makes it more important than ever for a marketing orientation to guide the process. Finding the best applications of technology still require that marketing managers begin with customer needs.

Technology can pose ethical dilemmas

Breakthrough products can raise questions—do the benefits outweigh the costs? For example, whereas some genetically modified foods increase crop yields and provide greater nutrition, critics wonder about human safety. Aseptic drink boxes are convenient but difficult to recycle.

New technologies give marketers new ways to track consumers and perhaps deliver a more tailored experience—but does that invade consumers' privacy? Website visitors may not be aware that small computer files (called cookies) are often placed on their computers. Cookies allow the company to track what the customer does on the web. This information can give a web surfer a better online experience, perhaps serving up useful information, advertising, and discounts. On the other hand, users are often tracked without their knowledge and may prefer to retain their privacy. Marketing managers should keep these debates in mind as they evaluate new technologies.

The Political Environment

The attitudes and reactions of people, social critics, and governments all affect the political environment. Consumers in the same country usually share a common political environment, but the political environment can also affect opportunities at a local or international level.

Nationalism can be limiting in international markets

Strong sentiments of **nationalism**—an emphasis on a country's interests before everything else—affect how macro-marketing systems work. They can affect how marketing managers work as well. Nationalistic feelings can reduce sales—or even block all marketing activity—in some international markets.

The "Buy American" policy in many government contracts and business purchases reflects this same attitude in the United States. There is broad consumer support for protecting U.S. producers—and jobs—from foreign competition. Automaker Chrysler drew on this sentiment in its "Imported from Detroit" campaign, which included Detroit rap music artist Eminem and a two-minute Super Bowl commercial "Halftime in America" featuring Clint Eastwood. Both promoted Chrysler's ties to Detroit, Michigan, Chrysler's American home.

Trade agreements lower costs of trade

Important dimensions of the political environment are likely to be similar among nations that have banded together to have common regional economic boundaries. **Free trade** refers to agreements between countries to not restrict imports and exports. Some countries have restrictions that raise the costs of importing, but free trade agreements drop those barriers. Since its inception in 1994, the North American Free Trade Agreement (NAFTA) has reshaped the rules of trade among the United States, Canada, and Mexico. Similar agreements exist among countries within Asia and Europe. Trade deals can change with new government policies and may significantly change a firm's costs in different markets.

Adero wants marketers to keep in mind that a website that targets prospects from all over the world won't be successful in turning them into customers if it ignores nationalism and cultural differences.
Source: Adero, Inc.

The unification of European markets

Twenty years ago, each country in Europe had its own unique trade rules and regulations. These differences made it difficult and expensive to move products from one country to another. Now, the almost 30 countries of the European Union (EU) are reducing conflicting laws, taxes, and other obstacles to trade within Europe. This, in turn, is reducing costs and prices, and it is creating new jobs. Many of the member countries use the same currency (the euro), simplifying inter-European commerce and trade yet more.

Although Europe is becoming a large unified[17] market, marketers may still encounter differences among European countries. What happened to Lands' End, the Wisconsin-based Internet and mail-order retailer, illustrates the issues. To better reach European consumers, Lands' End set up shop in England and Germany. As in the United States, its promotion and website touted[18] the unconditional lifetime guarantee that is a key part of its strategy. However, German consumer protection rules prohibited promotion of the guarantee; the Germans argued that the promotion was a misleading gimmick (on the logic that the cost of the guarantee was "hidden" in higher prices that consumers would pay). German officials wanted this ban to apply even if the German consumer purchased the product from a Lands' End website in England. Local rules like this could erode some of the benefits that should come from more European unification.

The Legal Environment

Changes in the political environment often lead to changes in the legal environment and in the way existing laws are enforced. To illustrate the effects of the legal environment, we will discuss how it has evolved in the United States. However, laws often vary from one country to another.

Trying to encourage competition

American economic and legislative thinking is based on the idea that competition among many small firms helps the economy. Therefore, attempts by businesses to limit competition are considered contrary to the public interest.

Starting in 1890, Congress passed a series of antimonopoly laws. Exhibit 2-4 shows the names and dates of these laws. Although the specific focus of each law is different, in general they are all intended to encourage competition.

Antimonopoly law and marketing mix planning

In later chapters, we will specifically apply antimonopoly law to the Four Ps. For now you should know what kind of proof the government must have to get a conviction under each of the major laws. You should also know which of the Four Ps are most affected by each law. Exhibit 2-4 provides such a summary—with a phrase following each law to show what the government must prove to get a conviction.

Prosecution is serious—you can go to jail

Businesses and *individual managers* are subject to both criminal and civil laws. Penalties for breaking civil laws are limited to blocking or forcing certain actions—along with fines. Where criminal law applies, jail sentences can be imposed. For example, several managers at Beech-Nut Nutrition Company were fined $100,000 each and sent to jail. In spite of ads claiming that Beech-Nut's apple juice was 100 percent natural, they tried to bolster profits by secretly using low-cost artificial ingredients.

Consumer protection laws are not new

Although antimonopoly laws focus on protecting competition, the wording of the laws in Exhibit 2-4 has, over time, moved toward protecting consumers. Some consumer protections are also built into the English and U.S. common law systems. A seller has to tell the truth (if asked a direct question), meet contracts, and stand behind the firm's product (to some reasonable extent). Beyond this, it is expected that vigorous competition in the marketplace will protect consumers—*so long as they are careful.*

Exhibit 2-4 Focus (Mostly Prohibitions) of Federal Antimonopoly Laws on the Four Ps

Law	Product	Place	Promotion	Price
Sherman Act (1890) Monopoly or conspiracy in restraint of trade	Monopoly or conspiracy to control a product	Monopoly or conspiracy to control distribution channels		Monopoly or conspiracy to fix or control prices
Clayton Act (1914) Substantially lessens competition	Forcing sale of some products with others—tying contracts	Exclusive dealing contracts (limiting buyers' sources of supply)		Price discrimination by manufacturers
Federal Trade Commission Act (1914) Unfair methods of competition		Unfair policies	Deceptive ads or selling practices	Deceptive pricing
Robinson-Patman Act (1936) Tends to injure competition			Prohibits "fake" advertising allowances or discrimination in help offered	Prohibits price discrimination on goods of "like grade and quality" without cost justification, and limits quantity discounts
Wheeler-Lea Amendment (1938) Unfair or deceptive practices	Deceptive packaging or branding		Deceptive ads or selling claims	Deceptive pricing
Antimerger Act (1950) Lessens competition	Buying competitors	Buying producers or distributors		
Magnuson-Moss Act (1975) Unreasonable practices	Product warranties			

Yet focusing only on competition didn't protect consumers very well in some areas. So the government found it necessary to pass other laws. For example, various laws regulate packaging and labels, telemarketing, credit practices, and environmental claims. Usually, however, the laws focus on specific types of products.

Foods and drugs are controlled

Consumer protection laws in the United States go back to 1906 when Congress passed the Pure Food and Drug Act. Unsanitary meatpacking practices in the Chicago stockyards stirred consumer support for this act. Before the law, it was assumed that common law and the old warning "let the buyer beware" would take care of consumers.

Later acts corrected some loopholes in the law. The law now bans the shipment of unsanitary and poisonous products and requires extensive testing of drugs. The Food and Drug Administration (FDA) attempts to control manufacturers of these products. It can seize products that violate its rules–including regulations on branding and labeling.

Product safety is controlled

The Consumer Product Safety Act (of 1972), another important consumer protection law, set up the Consumer Product Safety Commission. This group has broad power to set safety standards and can impose penalties for failure to meet these standards. There is some question as to how much safety consumers really want–the commission found the bicycle the most hazardous product under its control!

But given that the commission has the power to *force* a product off the market–or require expensive recalls to correct problems–it is obvious that safety must be considered in product design. And safety must be treated seriously by marketing managers. There is no more tragic example of this than the recalls of Firestone tires used as original equipment on Ford's Explorer SUV. Hundreds of consumers were killed or seriously injured in accidents.

State and local laws vary

Besides federal legislation[19]—which affects interstate commerce—marketers must be aware of state and local laws. There are state and city laws regulating minimum prices and the setting of prices, regulations for starting up a business (licenses, examinations, and even tax payments), and in some communities, regulations prohibiting certain activities—such as telephone selling or selling on Sundays or during evenings.

When electric carmaker Tesla Motors tried to bypass auto dealers and sell its vehicles directly to consumers, many states enacted laws prohibiting direct sales. And Airbnb, a service that allows people to temporarily rent rooms in their apartments and homes, was found to violate housing regulations in New York City. This tapestry of state and local laws may lead firms to specifically adapt marketing strategies to local requirements.

The Cultural and Social Environment

The **cultural and social environment** affects how and why people live and behave as they do—which affects customer buying behavior and eventually the economic, political, and legal environments. Many variables make up the cultural and social environment. Some examples are the languages people speak; the type of education they have; their religious beliefs; what type of food they eat; the style of clothing and housing they have; and how they view work, marriage, and family. Because the cultural and social environment has such broad effects, most people don't stop to think about it—how it may be changing or how it may differ for other people.

Social cultural trends today

Some social cultural trends reflect broad changing attitudes. For example, many consumers are becoming more careful about the food they eat; organic foods have become more popular. You would think that might work well for Whole Foods Market, which has been selling organic groceries for more than 30 years. Unfortunately, as consumer demand grew, so did the interest of other retailers. Now Kroger sells its Simple Truth line of natural and organic foods—and Walmart stores carry some Wild Oats items. Although that expansion might harm Whole Foods' bottom line, it helps organic farmers who are having trouble keeping up with demand.

Where people are around the world

Other social cultural changes relate to demographic trends. We examine evolving trends related to population, age, income, literacy, and technology adoption across the globe and within the United States. This type of demographic data is also important to marketing strategy planning.

Exhibit 2-5 summarizes data for a number of representative countries from different regions around the world. Even with a population of more than 316 million, the United States makes up only 4.9 percent of the world's over 7 billion people. Marketing managers in any country may seek growth opportunities in other countries.

Although the size of a market is important, the population trend also matters. The world's population is growing fast, but that population growth varies dramatically from country to country. For example, between 2013 and 2025, the population is projected to grow 35 percent or more in Ethiopia and Nigeria and about 25 percent in Egypt, Singapore, and Bangladesh. During this same period, growth will be about 9 percent in the United States and 3 percent in China, whereas the population is predicted to decline in Japan, Russia, Germany, and Finland. These trends have many marketing managers paying increased attention to fast-growing developing countries in Africa and Southeast Asia.

A shift from rural to urban areas

Just 50 years ago, about two-thirds of the world's population lived in rural areas. Today about half live in urban areas, as more people move to cities for better job opportunities. The extent of urbanization varies widely across countries. While about 82 percent of U.S. residents live in urban areas, more than 90 percent do in Japan, Singapore, Israel, and Argentina (Exhibit 2-5). By contrast, in Ethiopia and Kenya, 26 percent or

Exhibit 2-5 Demographic Dimensions and Characteristics for Selected Countries

Country	2013 Population (000s)	2025 Projected Population (000s)*	2013–2025 Projected Population Change (%)	Population Density per Square Km	Percent of Population in Urban Areas	GNI per Capita (U.S. $)	GDP (billions of $U.S.)	Estimated Literacy % of Population (age 15+)	Mobile Phones/100 Inhabitants, 2015	% Mobile Phone/100 Growth, 2010–2015	% Population Using Internet, 2015	% Internet User Growth, 2010–2015
Algeria	39,210	45,841	17	17	71	4,870	167	80	113	28	38	206
Argentina	41,450	47,165	14	16	92	12,460	583	98	144	2	69	54
Australia	23,130	25,054	8	3	89	60,070	1,339	99	133	32	85	11
Bangladesh	156,600	197,674	26	1,237	34	1,190	195	61	83	85	14	289
Brazil	200,400	218,259	9	25	86	9,850	1,775	93	127	25	59	45
Canada	35,160	37,559	7	4	82	47,540	1,551	99	82	8	88	10
China	1,357,000	1,394,639	3	146	56	7,930	11,008	96	93	47	50	47
Egypt	82,060	103,742	26	92	43	3,340	331	76	111	23	36	66
Ethiopia	94,100	131,261	39	99	19	590	62	49	43	443	12	1,447
Finland	5,439	5,251	–4	18	84	46,550	232	99	135	–13	93	7
France	6,031	68,860	4	122	80	40,540	2,419	99	103	12	85	10
Germany	80,620	79,226	–2	234	75	45,940	3,363	99	117	10	88	7
Haiti	10,320	11,252	9	389	59	810	9	61	70	73	12	46
India	1,252,000	1,396,046	12	441	33	1,600	2,095	72	79	26	26	247
Iran	77,450	90,481	17	49	73	n/a	n/a	87	93	29	44	177
Israel	8,059	8,984	12	387	92	35,770	299	97	133	9	79	17
Italy	59,830	62,591	5	206	69	32,810	1,821	99	151	–2	66	22
Japan	127,300	123,386	–3	348	93	38,840	4,383	99	125	29	93	19
Kenya	4,350	53,196	20	81	26	1,340	63	78	81	32	46	226
Libya	6,202	7,375	19	4	79	n/a	n/a	91	157	-13	19	36
Mexico	122,300	134,829	9	65	79	9,710	1,144	95	85	10	57	85
Nigeria	173,600	234,363	35	200	48	2,820	481	90	82	50	47	98
Norway	5,084	5,682	11	14	80	93,740	387	100	114	–1	97	4
Pakistan	182,100	228,385	20	245	39	1,440	271	56	67	17	18	125
Romania	19,960	20,872	5	86	55	9,500	178	99	107	–4	56	40
Russia	143,500	128,180	–11	9	74	11,450	1,331	100	160	–3	73	71
Saudi Arabia	28,830	31,877	11	15	83	23,550	646	95	177	–7	70	70
Singapore	5,399	6,733	25	7,807	100	52,090	293	97	146	1	82	16
Spain	46,650	51,415	10	93	80	28,530	1,199	98	108	–3	79	20
Turkey	74,930	90,498	21	102	73	9,950	718	96	96	12	54	35
United Kingdom	64,100	67,244	5	269	83	43,390	2,858	99	126	2	92	8
United States	316,100	346,407	9	35	82	55,980	18,037	99	118	29	75	4
Vietnam	89,710	102,459	14	296	34	1,990	194	95	131	4	53	72

Note: Data from 2013. Internet users are individuals who have used the Internet (from any location) in the last 12 months. Internet can be used via a computer, mobile phone, personal digital assistant, games machine, digital TV, etc.

Sources: Data for projected population are from U.S. Census Bureau International Data Base. Urbanization data and literacy data are from the CIA *World Factbook* and World Bank. All other data are from the World Bank.

less of the population lives in urban areas. The concentration of people in major cities often simplifies Place and Promotion decisions.

There's no market when there's no income

Profitable markets require income as well as people. The amount of money people can spend affects the products they are likely to buy. When considering international markets, income is often one of the most important demographic dimensions. There are a variety of different measures of national income. One widely used measure is **gross domestic product (GDP)**—the total market value of all goods and services provided in a country's economy in a year by both residents and nonresidents of that country. **Gross national income (GNI)** is a measure that is similar to GDP, but GNI does not include income earned by foreigners who own resources in that nation. By contrast, GDP does include foreign income.

When you compare countries with different patterns of international investment, the income measure you use can make a difference. For example, Ford has a factory in Thailand. The GDP measure for Thailand would include the profits from that factory because they were earned in that country. However, Ford is not a Thai firm, and most of its profit will ultimately flow out of Thailand. The Thai GNI would not include those profits. You should see that using GDP income measures can give the impression that people in less-developed countries have more income than they really do. In addition, in a country with a large population, the income of the whole nation must be spread over more people. So *GNI per capita* (per person) is a useful figure because it gives some idea of the income level of people in the country.

Exhibit 2-5 gives an estimate of GNI per capita and GDP for each country listed. You can see that the larger and more developed industrial nations—including the United States, China, Japan, and Germany—account for the biggest share of the world's GDP. In these countries, except for China, the GNI per capita is also quite high. This explains why so much trade takes place among these countries—and why many firms see them as the more important markets. In general, markets like these offer the best potential for products that are targeted at consumers with higher income levels. The GNI per capita in the United States is $55,980.

Many managers, however, see great potential—and less competition—where GNI per capita is low. For example, Coca-Cola has made a push in Africa, where it hopes to establish a relationship with consumers now and turn that brand loyalty into profitable growth as consumer incomes rise.

Reading, writing, and marketing problems

The ability of a country's people to read and write has a direct influence on the development of its economy—and on marketing strategy planning. The degree of literacy affects the way information is delivered, which in marketing means promotion. The United Nations estimated that 16 percent of adults (aged 15 or older) in the world cannot read and write. About two-thirds of them are women. But that is changing; among youth aged 15 to 24 only 9 percent cannot read and write. You may be surprised by the low literacy rates for some of the countries in Exhibit 2-5. Illiteracy creates challenges for product labels, instructions, and print advertising.

Technology adoption races across continents

Cell phone and Internet usage have increased rapidly around the world. These technologies may have their greatest impact in developing countries where, for example, they've completely skipped the adoption of landline phones and instead moved directly to a reliance on mobile phones.

Let's look at this phenomenon more closely. With the introduction of cell phones to the developing world came an ability to instantly communicate supply and demand to buyers and sellers. This has dramatically increased efficiency in some markets. For example, after fishermen in India began using cell phones, they called ashore to find out which ports had the most demand for their catch. This helped match supply and demand, lowering waste and stabilizing prices.

Adoption of these technologies varies across the globe (see Exhibit 2-5). Take cell phones, for example. In many countries, people have separate phones for work and personal use, so the number of cell phones actually exceeds the population. While penetration is lower in many of the poorest nations, those countries are experiencing very fast adoption rates. In Ethiopia, for instance, the 2015 ownership rate of 43 phones per 100 people represents a more than 443 percent increase from just five years earlier. Similar differences can be observed in Internet access. Marketing managers need to recognize how target markets utilize this technology to determine its role in marketing strategy. For example, setting up a website in another language may be more useful in some countries than others.

Population trends in the U.S. consumer market

While the U.S. population is not growing as quickly as in some other countries, current population and population growth vary a lot in different regions of the country. The greatest growth is in the west and southeastern United States. These different rates of growth are important to marketers. Sudden growth in one area may create a demand for new shopping centers and furniture stores—whereas retailers in declining areas face tougher competition for a smaller number of customers.

Boomers drive the graying of America

Another important dimension of U.S. society is its age distribution. In 1980, the median age of the U.S. population was 30—but by 2010 the median age rose to 37. The median age is growing because the percentage of the population in older age groups has increased. Exhibit 2-6 shows population trends by age groups. The graphic shows the number of people in the United States at various age groups in 2005, 2015, and 2025.

In Exhibit 2-6, these changes can be seen most dramatically when looking at the population of those older than age 60. The three age bands (60-69, 70-79, and 80+) each show a large increase by 2025. This will significantly increase the number of

Exhibit 2-6 Population Distribution by Age Group in 2005, 2015, and 2025

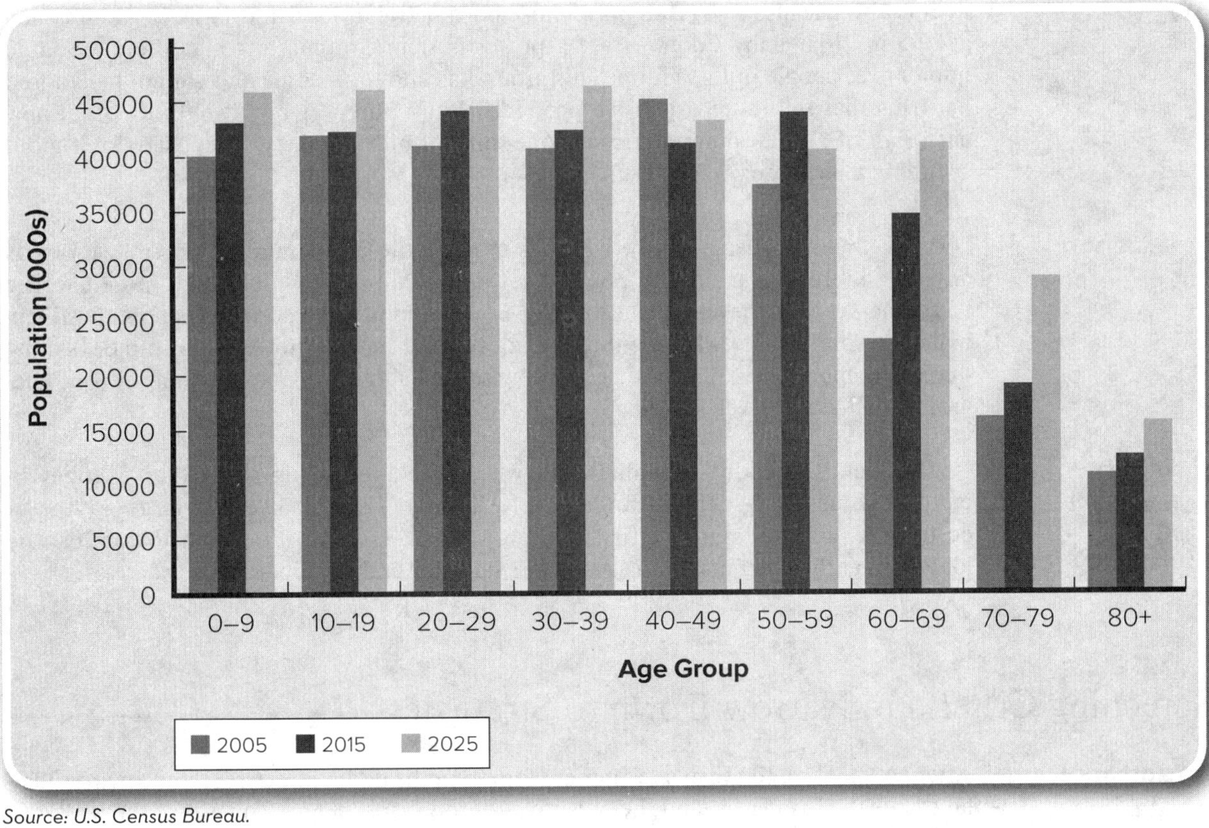

Source: U.S. Census Bureau.

Sales of minivans declined when new Gen X parents thought they were "uncool." Toyota responded with an online campaign featuring a couple rapping about life in the suburbs and driving their kids in their "Swagger Wagon." The campaign generated millions of online views and sales of Toyota's Sienna minivan jumped. Watch the videos at https://youtu.be/pUG3Z8Hxa5I.
Source: Toyota Motor Corporation

senior citizens (people older than 65). This increase is partly due to better health care and Americans living longer lives.

It is also because **Baby Boomers**, those born between 1946 and 1964, began to reach age 65 in 2011. Baby Boomers are a powerful demographic force, as there are large numbers of people in this group. This group has a lot of income and cannot be ignored by firms that sell more expensive products. Baby Boomers buy two-thirds of all new cars, half of all new computers, and one-third of movie tickets. They also don't mind spending a bit more on their pets.

Don't generalize too much about generations

Marketing managers must be cautious in using these generational generalizations as anything more than a starting point. They should ultimately focus on a more specific target market when developing a strategy. For example, whereas about half of all Millennials are comfortable with technology, more than half do not feel the same. If most marketing managers follow the "general wisdom" about Millennials, there will be subgroups that are not well-served.

Social and cultural changes come slowly

The trends and demographic data we've been reviewing show that changes in cultural values and social attitudes evolve slowly. They also reflect large groups of customers–not necessarily a firm's target market. Opportunities and threats can be identified early when marketing managers monitor and anticipate these changes.

Using Screening Criteria to Narrow Down to Strategies

Developing and applying screening criteria

After you analyze the firm's resources (for strengths and weaknesses), the environmental trends the firm faces, and the objectives of top management, you merge them all into a set of product-market screening criteria. These criteria should include both quantitative and qualitative components. The quantitative components summarize the firm's objectives: sales, profit, and return on investment (ROI) targets. The qualitative components summarize what kinds of businesses the firm wants to be in, what businesses it wants to exclude, what weaknesses it should avoid, and what resources (strengths) and trends it should build on.

Developing screening criteria is difficult but worth the effort. They summarize in one place what the firm wants to accomplish. When a manager can explain the specific criteria that are relevant to selecting (or screening out) an opportunity, others can understand the manager's logic. Thus, marketing decisions are not just made or accepted based on intuition[20] and gut feel. The criteria should be realistic—that is, they should be achievable. Opportunities that pass the screen should be viable strategies that the firm can implement with the resources it has.

Sustainability matters

Sometimes screening criteria can help bring focus to opportunities that fit well with trends in the external market environment. For example, General Electric (GE) operates many types of businesses, from jet aircraft engines and water treatment facilities to medical imaging and lightbulbs. Top management at GE believes that the really crucial needs of society relate to protecting the environment. It believes that efforts in this arena are so critical that they should be supported across all dimensions of the external environment. Thus, it wants all GE managers to look for opportunities that fit what GE calls "ecomagination"—applying GE's creativity to solve problems related to ecology. GE is not alone in this kind of thinking. Many organizations now screen opportunities on **sustainability**—the idea that it's important to meet present needs without compromising the ability of future generations to meet their own needs. In many lines of business, that is a tall order. At GE that means lightbulbs that use less energy, medical images with no toxic waste, jets that burn less fuel, and new ways to turn seawater into drinking water.

Whole plans should be evaluated

You need to forecast the probable results of implementing a marketing strategy to apply the quantitative part of the screening criteria because only implemented plans generate sales, profits, and return on investment. For a rough screening, you need to estimate only the likely results of implementing each opportunity over a logical planning period. If a product's life is likely to be three years, for example, a good strategy may not produce profitable results for 6 to 12 months. But evaluated over the projected three-year life, the product may look like a winner. When evaluating the potential of possible opportunities (product-market strategies), it is important to evaluate similar things—that is, whole plans over longer time periods.

Planning Grids[21] Help Evaluate a Portfolio of Opportunities

When a firm has many scenarios to evaluate, comparisons are best made with graphical approaches—such as the nine-box strategic planning grid developed by General Electric (GE) and used by many other companies. Such grids can help evaluate a firm's whole portfolio of strategic plans or businesses.

General Electric looks for green positions

GE's strategic planning grid—see Exhibit 2-7—forces company managers to make three-part judgments (high, medium, and low) about the business strengths and industry attractiveness of all proposed or existing product-market plans. As you can see from Exhibit 2-7, this approach helps a manager organize information about the company's marketing environments (discussed earlier in this chapter) along with information about its strategy and translate it into relevant screening criteria.

Exhibit 2-7 General Electric's Strategic Planning Grid

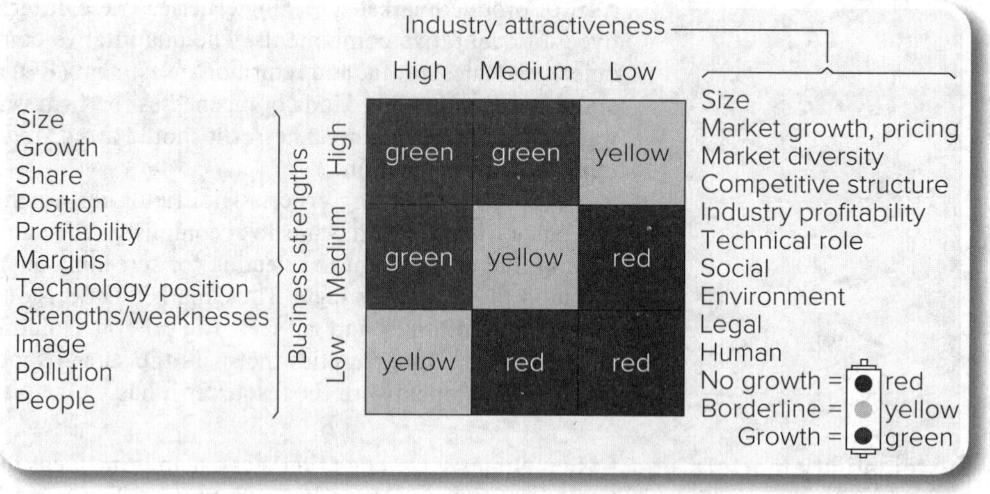

The industry attractiveness dimension helps managers answer the question: Does this product-market plan look like a good idea? To answer that question, managers have to judge such factors (screening criteria) as the size of the market and its growth rate, the nature of competition, the plan's potential environmental or social impact, and how laws might affect it. Note that an opportunity may be attractive for *some* companies—but not well suited to the strengths (and weaknesses) of a particular firm. That is why the GE grid also considers the business strengths dimension.

The business strengths dimension focuses on the ability of the company to pursue a product-market plan effectively. To make judgments along this dimension, a manager evaluates whether the firm has people with the right talents and skills to implement the plan, whether the plan is consistent with the firm's image and profit objectives, and whether the firm could establish a profitable market share given its technical capability, costs, and size. Here again, these factors suggest screening criteria specific to this firm and market situation.

GE feels opportunities that fall into the green boxes in the upper left-hand corner of the grid are its best growth opportunities. Managers give these opportunities high marks on both industry attractiveness and business strengths. The red boxes in the lower right-hand corner of the grid, on the other hand, suggest a no-growth policy. Existing red businesses may continue to generate earnings, but they no longer deserve much investment. Yellow businesses are borderline cases—they can go either way. GE may continue to support an existing yellow business but will probably reject a proposal for a new one. It simply wouldn't look good enough on the relevant screening criteria.

GE's "stoplight" evaluation method is a subjective, multiple-factor approach. It avoids the traps and possible errors of trying to use oversimplified, single-number criteria—such as ROI or market share. Instead, top managers review detailed written summaries of many different screening criteria that help them make summary judgments. This approach helps everyone understand why the company supports some new opportunities and not others.

General Electric considers factors that reflect its objectives. Another firm might modify the evaluation to emphasize other screening criteria—depending on its objectives and the type of product-market plans it is considering.

Evaluating Opportunities in International Markets

Evaluate the risks

The approaches we've discussed so far apply to international markets just as they do to domestic ones. But in international markets it is often harder to fully understand the market environment variables. This may make it more difficult to see the risks involved in particular opportunities. Some countries are politically unstable; their governments and constitutions come and go. An investment safe under one government might become a takeover target under another.

To reduce the risk of missing some basic variable that may help screen out a risky opportunity, marketing managers sometimes need a detailed analysis of the market environment they are considering entering. Such an analysis can reveal facts about an unfamiliar market that a manager in a distant country might otherwise overlook. Further, a local citizen who knows the market environment may be able to identify an "obvious" problem ignored even in a careful analysis. Thus, it is very useful for the analysis to include inputs from locals—perhaps cooperative distributors.

Risks vary with environmental sensitivity

The farther you go from familiar territory, the greater the risk of making big mistakes. But not all products, or marketing mixes, involve the same risk. Think of the risks as running along a "continuum of environmental sensitivity." See Exhibit 2-8.

Some products are relatively insensitive to the economic and cultural environment into which they're placed. These products may be accepted as is—or they may require just a little adaptation to make them suitable for local use. Most industrial products are near the insensitive end of this continuum.

At the other end of the continuum, we find highly sensitive products that may be difficult or impossible to adapt to all international situations. Consumer products closely linked to other social or cultural variables are at this end. For example, some cultures view dieting as unhealthy; that explains why products such as Diet Pepsi, although popular in the United States, have sometimes done poorly in other countries. Many American quick-serve restaurants succeed in international markets only after adapting their menus to foreign tastes. McDonald's in India sells the Maharaja Mac, which is made from lamb or chicken, and in Japan it sells the Ebi Filet-O, which is a kind of shrimp burger.

This continuum helps explain why many of the early successes in international marketing were basic commodities such as gasoline, soap, transportation vehicles, mining equipment, and agricultural machinery. It also helps explain why some consumer products firms have been successful with basically the same promotion and products in different parts of the globe.

Yet some managers don't understand the reason for these successes. They think they can develop a global marketing mix for just about *any* product. They fail to see that firms producing and/or selling products near the sensitive end of the continuum should carefully analyze how their products will be seen and used in new environments—and plan their strategies accordingly.

What if risks are still hard to judge?

If the risks of an international opportunity are hard to judge, it may be wise to look first for opportunities that involve exporting. This gives managers a chance to build experience, know-how, and confidence over time. Then the firm will be in a better position to judge the prospects and risks of taking further steps.

Exhibit 2-8 Continuum of Environmental Sensitivity

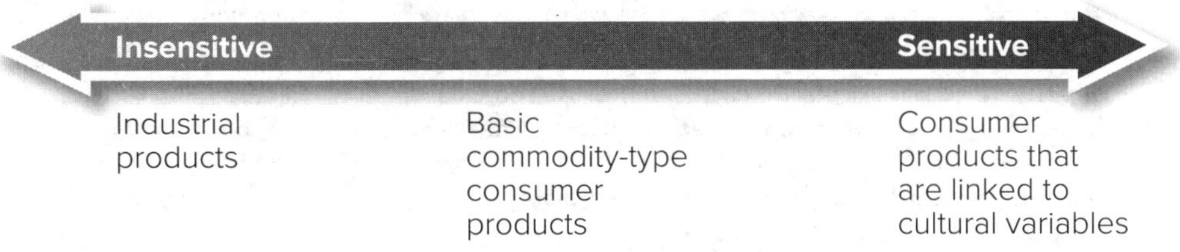

CONCLUSION

Businesses need innovative strategy planning to survive in our increasingly competitive markets. In this chapter, we discussed the variables that shape the broad environment of marketing strategy planning and how they may affect opportunities. First we looked at how the firm's own resources and objectives may help guide or limit the search for opportunities. Then we went on to look at the need to understand competition and how to do a competitive analysis. Next we shifted our focus to the external market environments. They are important because changes in these environments present new opportunities, as well as problems, that a marketing manager must deal with in marketing strategy planning.

The economic environment—including chances of recession or inflation—also affects the choice of strategies. And the marketer must try to anticipate, understand, and deal with these changes—as well as changes in the technology underlying the economic environment. We saw how emerging technology around artificial intelligence might impact how marketing managers deliver value in the future.

The marketing manager must also be aware of legal restrictions and be sensitive to changing political climates. The acceptance of consumerism has already forced many changes.

The cultural and social environment affects how people behave and what marketing strategies will be successful.

Demographic data, including trends in population, income, and technology usage, provide an indicator of social trends. So we looked at these more closely.

Developing good marketing strategies within all these environments isn't easy. You can see that marketing planning is a challenging job that requires integration of information from many disciplines.

Eventually, managers need procedures for screening and evaluating opportunities. We explained an approach for developing qualitative and quantitative screening criteria—from an analysis of the strengths and weaknesses of the company's resources, the environmental trends it faces, and top management's objectives. We also discussed ways for evaluating and managing quite different opportunities—using the GE strategic planning grid.

Now we can go on in the rest of the book to discuss how to turn opportunities into profitable marketing plans and programs.

JOYFUL MOMENT

"When the CEO dropped a brownie on his calculator, he was accused of fudging the numbers."

WORDS AND EXPRESSIONS

1. **customize**: *vt.* to make or change something. to suit the needs of the owner 定做，按客户具体要求制造
   —You can, of course, customize the page as you like.
   当然，您可以根据自己的喜好来定制页面。
2. **leverage**: *vt.* to use something that you already have in order to achieve something new or better 借助已有的…实现新（或更好）的目标
   —We can gain a market advantage by leveraging our network of partners.
   我们可以借助合伙人网络获得市场优势。
3. **expertise**: *n.* special skill or knowledge that is acquired by training, study, or practice 专门知识；专门技术；专家的意见
   —Not only do they have a strong voice with decision makers, many of them also have essential technical expertise.
   他们不仅对决策者有很强的影响力，他们中许多人也有必要的技术专长。
4. **swipe**: *v./n.* to pass a plastic card, such as a credit card, through a special machine that is able to read the information that is stored on it 刷（卡）
   —Swipe your card through the phone, then dial.
   在电话机上刷卡，然后拨号。
5. **demographic**: *adj./n.* relating to demography (= the study of populations and the different groups that make them up) 人口的；人口统计的；人口学的
   —There have been monumental social and demographic changes in the country.
   该国的社会和人口状况已经发生了巨大的变化。
6. **recoup**: *vt.* to get back money that you have spent or lost 补偿；弥补；收回（成本）
   —It takes a while to recoup the initial costs of starting up a business.
   要收回开创新公司投入的先期成本需要一段时间。
7. **hierarchy**: *n.* a system in which people or things are arranged according to their importance 等级制度
   —He rose quickly through the political hierarchy to become party leader.
   他的政治地位迅速上升，成了党的领导人。
8. **imperative**: *adj.* extremely important or urgent 极重要的；紧急的；迫切的
   —The president said it was imperative that the release of all hostages be secured.
   总统说当前要务是确保所有人质都获释。

9. **retention**: *n.* the act of keeping in your possession 保留；记忆力，保持力
—The company needs to improve its training and retention of staff.
公司需要改进对员工的培训和留用工作。

10. **monopoly**: *n.* (an organization or group that has) complete control of something, especially an area of business, so that others have no share 垄断（机构）；专卖；独占
—The government is determined to protect its tobacco monopoly.
政府下决心保护其烟草专卖权。

11. **oligopoly**: *n.* a situation in which a small number of organizations or companies has control of an area of business, so that others have no share 寡头垄断
—This big business establishment resists innovations because they might undermine their oligopoly, margins or special privileges.
大企业抵制创新，这是因为创新可能有损它们的垄断、利润或特权。

12. **monopolistic**: *adj.* having or trying to have complete control of something, especially an area of business, so that others have no share 垄断的
—Excess capacity is a characteristic of natural monopoly or monopolistic competition.
过剩产能是自然垄断或垄断竞争的一个特点。

13. **profit margin**: the ratio gross profits divided by net sales 利润率
—The firm had shaved profit margins.
公司调低了利润率。

14. **rival**: *n.* a person, business, or organization who you are competing or fighting against in the same area or for the same things 对手
—Aggressive pricing in one market may elicit a competitive response from a rival in another market.
在一个市场上的攻击性定价可能会招致对手在另一个市场上的反击。

15. **inflation**: *n.* a general increase in the prices of goods and services in a country 通货膨胀
—Inflation erodes the value of our money.
通货膨胀使我们的货币贬值了。

16. **scramble**: *v./n.* to bring into random order; an unceremonious and disorganized struggle 攀登，扰乱；混乱
—Tourists were scrambling over the rocks looking for the perfect camera angle.
旅行者们爬上岩石，寻找最完美的拍摄角度。

17. **unify**: *v.* to bring separate parts of something together so that they are one 使成一体；统一
—His strong voice on the issue has helped unify the cabinet.
他在该问题上的坚定立场有助于统一议会的意见。

18. **tout**: *vt.* to advertise, talk about, or praise something or someone repeatedly, especially as a way of encouraging people to like, accept, or buy something（尤指为了提高销售额、知名度或推动发展）给…做广告，宣传，赞扬，吹捧
—A local car dealership was touting its services on the radio.
一家地方汽车特许经销商正在当地电台作宣传。

19. **legislation**: *n.* a law or set of laws suggested by a government and made official by a parliament 法律；立法
—The government has promised to introduce legislation to limit fuel emissions from cars.
政府许诺将通过立法来限制汽车尾气排放。

20. **intuition**: *n.* unexplained feelings that something is true even when you have no evidence or proof of it 直觉
—Her intuition was telling her that something was wrong.
她的直觉在告诉她事情有些不对头。

21. **grid**: *n.* a pattern or structure made from horizontal and vertical lines crossing each other to form squares 网格，方格
—GE's Strategic Business-Planning Grid: it is an analytical tool for classifying a firm's businesses by profit potential.
通用电气公司法采用“多因素投资组合矩阵”对企业的战略业务单位加以分类和评价。

EXERCISES

1. **Multiple choices**

(1) The direct market environment includes ____, the company, and competitors.
A. country　B. cost　C. customer　D. culture

(2) The external market environment includes economic environment, ____, political and legal environment, cultural and social environment.
A. natural environment　B. technological environment
C. demographic environment　D. domestic environment

(3) GDP does include foreign income, but ____ does not include income earned by foreigners who own resources in that nation.
A. GDP　B. FDA　C. NAFTA　D. GNI

(4) For each marketing strategy, the Four Ps objectives are Product objectives, Place objectives, ____ objectives, and Price objectives.
A. Personal　B. Promotion　C. Publicity　D. Production

(5) The economic environment refers to ____ factors, including national income, economic growth, and inflation.
A. macro-economic　B. micro-economic　C. direct market　D. segmented market

2. **Terms translation**

(1) mission statement　(2) competitive environment
(3) sustainable competitive advantage　(4) competitor analysis

(5) economic environment
(6) cultural and social environment
(7) gross national income (GNI)
(8) intelligent agent
(9) nationalism
(10) sustainability

3. **True or false**

(1) Firms need a hierarchy of objectives, such as company objectives and marketing department objectives. ______
(2) A good mission statement focuses on a few key goals rather than embracing everything. ______
(3) A mission statement is important, and it is a substitute for more specific objectives that provide guidance in screening possible opportunities. ______
(4) In pure competition there are a few large firms competing, whereas in oligopoly there are often many firms. ______
(5) Technology is the application of science to convert an economy's resources to output. ______
(6) Some countries have restrictions that raise the costs of importing, and free trade agreements raise those barriers. ______
(7) Gross domestic product (GDP)—the total market value of all goods and services provided in a country's economy in a year by both residents and nonresidents of that country. ______
(8) Baby Boomers are a powerful demographic force, and this group has a lot of income and cannot be ignored by firms that sell more expensive products. ______
(9) The farther you go from familiar territory, the smaller the risk of making big mistakes. ______
(10) If the risks of an international opportunity are hard to judge, it may be wise to look first for opportunities that involve exporting. ______

4. **Fill in the blanks**

(1) Developing a ________ sets out the organization's basic purpose for being.
(2) Four basic kinds of market (competitive) situations are ________, oligopoly, pure competition, and monopolistic competition.
(3) Technology affects marketing in two basic ways: it creates ________ for new products and it drives the development of new processes.
(4) ________ refers to having machines operate like humans with respect to learning and decision making.
(5) Artificial intelligence is implemented by an ________, a device that observes an environment and acts to achieve a goal.
(6) ________ refers to an emphasis on a country's interests before everything else.
(7) ________ refers to agreements between countries to not restrict imports and exports.
(8) American economic and legislative thinking is based on the idea that ________ among many small firms helps the economy.
(9) ROI is an abbreviation of ________.
(10) ________ refers to the idea that it's important to meet present needs without compromising the ability of future generations to meet their own needs.

5. **Answer the following questions**

(1) Who will be responsible for setting whole-company objectives and what are their responsibilities?
(2) If company objectives aren't clear from the start, different managers may hold unspoken and conflicting objectives. How do many firms try to avoid this problem?
(3) To find its strengths or recognize weaknesses, what must a firm evaluate?
(4) What does sustainable competitive advantage refer to? What should marketing managers do to find some competitive advantage?
(5) Do the benefits of new technologies outweigh their costs? What is your opinion about this?

SUGGESTED CASES

2. **Nature's Own Foods, Inc.**
6. **Dynamic Steel**
22. **Bright Light Innovations: The Starlight Stove**
29. **Kennedy & Gaffney (K&G)**

CHAPTER 2: COMPETITOR ANALYSIS

Mediquip, Inc. produces medical equipment and uses its own sales force to sell the equipment to hospitals. Recently, several hospitals have asked Mediquip to develop a laser-beam "scalpel" for eye surgery. Mediquip has the needed resources, and 200 hospitals will probably buy the equipment. But Mediquip managers have heard that Laser Technologies—another quality producer—is thinking of competing for the same business. Mediquip has other good opportunities it could pursue—so it wants to see if it would have a competitive advantage over Laser Tech.

Mediquip and Laser Tech are similar in most ways, but there are a few important differences. Laser Technologies already produces key parts that are needed for the new laser product—so its production costs would be lower. It would cost Mediquip more to design the product—and getting parts from outside suppliers would result in higher production costs.

On the other hand, Mediquip has marketing strengths. It already has a good reputation with hospitals—and its sales force calls on only hospitals. Mediquip thinks that each of its current sales reps could spend some time selling the new product and that it could adjust sales territories so only four more sales reps would be needed for good coverage in the market. In contrast, Laser Tech's sales reps call on only industrial customers, so it would have to add 14 reps to cover the hospitals.

Hospitals have budget pressures—so the supplier with the lowest price is likely to get a larger share of the business. But Mediquip knows that both suppliers' prices will be set high enough to cover the added costs of designing, producing, and selling the new product—and leave something for profit.

Mediquip gathers information about its own likely costs and can estimate Laser Tech's costs from industry studies and Laser Tech's annual report. Mediquip has set up a spreadsheet to evaluate the proposed new product.

See Connect for the spreadsheet and questions needed to analyze this scenario.

CHAPTER THREE

Focusing Marketing Strategy with Segmentation and Positioning

In the early 1930s in Billund, Denmark, carpenter Ole Kirk Christiansen started a company that built wooden toys. He named his company LEGO, combining the first two letters from each word in the Danish phrase *leg godt*, which means "play well." Christiansen believed in quality—"only the best is good enough"—a value that stays with LEGO to this day.

During the 1950s, LEGO articulated its plastic bricks as part of a "system of play," based on learning through imagination, creativity, and problem solving. By 1958 LEGO had refined the design of the classic LEGO brick; those 1958 bricks still click and lock with any of the billions of bricks LEGO has made since. Buoyed by the tail end of the baby boom generation, LEGO grew rapidly in the 1960s and 1970s. That growth slowed during the 1980s when the "construction toy market" lost favor to electronic toys and software.

LEGO reacted by broadening its market. In the 1990s, LEGO opened three LEGOLAND theme parks, developed video games and electronic toys, produced books and TV shows, and licensed watches and clothing. Although the new product lines increased sales, costs rose even more quickly. In 2004, LEGO lost more than $300 million. LEGO needed a strategy to turn things around—and fast!

To address the immediate financial weakness, LEGO sold off LEGOLAND theme parks, outsourced production, and consolidated its product lines. In assessing its strengths, LEGO recognized (1) its brand name was widely trusted; and (2) its enduring system of play, building with bricks, provided a platform for innovation. To focus its new strategy, LEGO redefined its market around the iconic brick with a vision to equip children for the future through creative, playful learning. LEGO thought it could profitably grow in the "active play market."

LEGO next sought to get to know its customers better. So the company set loose teams of researchers who embedded with families to understand how seven- to nine-year-old boys in Germany and the United States lived and played. One finding showed LEGO that it had taken the wrong lessons from the growth of video games. LEGO assumed kids wanted immediate gratification in play, so it dumbed down many of its toys. But the new research found that kids wanted opportunities to demonstrate mastery—evidenced by the scoring, ranking, and sharing common in many computer games. LEGO also discovered that while kids lived very scheduled lives, they appreciated time to themselves.

Guided by these insights, LEGO introduced new kits. For example, it introduced LEGO City's fire station and police station kits and *Star Wars* movie-themed kits targeting the previously studied seven- to nine-year-old boys segment. Some of these kids (and their parents) were looking for products to bridge the physical and digital worlds, so LEGO introduced Boost. LEGO Boost kits include simple motors and sensors and introduce kids to basic computer coding through a smartphone or tablet app. With the Boost kit, kids can make Vernie—a robot with a bowtie and moving eyebrows—Frankie the Cat, or three other models. At $160, the Boost kit is not cheap. But LEGO knows the kit delivers what many parents want from their kids' toys. LEGO's research found German and American parents (much more than Japanese parents, for example) seek out toys that combine play *and* learning. For older boys seeking more of a challenge, LEGO Mindstorms provide advanced robotics construction kits.

The *Star Wars* kits and LEGO Mindstorm robots struck a chord with another market segment—adults. Thanks to the Internet, the dispersed adult fans of LEGO (they call themselves by the acronym AFOLs) found they weren't alone. At first, LEGO didn't design a marketing mix for the AFOL segment. That changed when it discovered that some AFOLs spent thousands of dollars a year on LEGO. When LEGO introduced the 3,104-piece, $299 Imperial Star Destroyer kit, it flew off store shelves. LEGO Architecture, which lets users build replicas of famous buildings such as the Eiffel Tower and Sydney Opera House, also appeals to adults. AFOLs account for 5 to 10 percent of all LEGO sales and influence even more.

Over the years, LEGO has made several failed attempts to crack the "girls active play market." LEGO research showed that after age 5, most girls lose interest in LEGO products. LEGO knew a big opportunity awaited if it could figure out this market. Its researchers spent time observing girls at play; their findings drove decisions for the LEGO Friends line. Research showed that whereas boys like to complete a kit before they start playing make-believe, girls prefer to play and pretend as they build. So the Friends kits come with bagged parts, allowing the girls to start storytelling and rearranging sooner. Girls also had opinions about the LEGO figurines (LEGO calls them "mini-figs"). Whereas boys play with the mini-figs in the third person, girls project themselves onto each figure; further, girls found the traditional stubby mini-fig ugly, so Friends mini-figs look more like real people. The main mini-fig characters in LEGO Friends come with names and backstories described in accompanying books. LEGO Friends work across cultures—showing strong sales in the United States, Germany, and the fast-growing Chinese market. Thanks to Friends, sales to girls went from 9 percent to 27 percent of LEGO's total sales.

In 2014, LEGO entered a new product-market when it released its first feature-length movie. *The LEGO Movie* and a sequel *The LEGO Batman Movie* were hits—on screen and off with accompanying kits. Success across product markets helped LEGO earn annual profits of more than $1 billion on sales of more than $4 billion. By "playing well" with boys, girls, and adults, LEGO constructed the most valuable company in the toy business.

LEARNING OBJECTIVES

As the LEGO case illustrates, a manager who develops an understanding of the needs and characteristics of specific groups of target customers within the broader market may see new, breakthrough opportunities. But it's not always obvious how to identify the real needs of a target market—or the marketing mix that those customers will see as different from, and better than, what is available from a competitor. This chapter covers concepts and approaches that will help you succeed in the search for those opportunities.

When you finish this chapter, you should be able to

1 be familiar with the Four Ps in a marketing mix.

2 define and describe generic markets and product-markets.

3 know what market segmentation is and how to segment product-markets into submarkets.

4 know three approaches to market-oriented strategy planning.

5 know dimensions that may be useful for segmenting markets.

6 recognize how some computer-aided methods are used in segmenting.

7 know what positioning is and why it is useful.

8 understand the important new terms (shown in boldface).

Search for Opportunities Can Begin by Understanding Markets

At first, let's focus on marketing strategy planning which means finding attractive opportunities and developing profitable marketing strategies. But what is a "marketing strategy"? We have used these words rather casually so far. Now let's see what they really mean.

A **marketing strategy** specifies a target market and a related marketing mix. It is a big picture of what a firm will do in some market. Two interrelated parts are needed:

1. A **target market**—a fairly homogeneous (similar) group of customers to whom a company wishes to appeal.
2. A **marketing mix**—the controllable variables the company puts together to satisfy this target group.

The "Four Ps" make up a marketing mix

It is useful to reduce all the variables in the marketing mix to four basic ones:

Product—is the good or service for the target's needs.

Place–is concerned with all the decisions involved in getting the right product to the target market's Place.

Promotion–is concerned with telling the target market or others in the channel of distribution about the right product.

Price–must make it right.

And a **marketing plan** is a written statement of a marketing strategy and the time-related details for carrying out the strategy.

In this chapter, we discuss concepts that can guide the selection of specific target customers. See Exhibit 3-1 for an overview.

Because this chapter is about bringing focus to the search for market opportunities, a good place to start is by discussing what we really mean when we use the term *market.*

What is a company's market?

Identifying a company's market is an important but sticky issue. In general, a **market** is a group of potential customers with similar needs who are willing to exchange something of value with sellers offering various goods or services–that is, ways of satisfying those needs. However, within a general market, marketing-oriented managers develop marketing mixes for *specific* target markets. Getting the firm to focus on specific target markets is vital.

Don't just focus on the product

Some production-oriented managers don't understand this narrowing-down process. They get into trouble because they ignore the tough part of defining markets. To make the narrowing-down process easier, they just describe their markets in terms of *products* they sell. For example, producers and retailers of greeting cards might define their market as the "greeting card" market. But this production-oriented approach ignores customers–and customers make a market! This leads to missed opportunities.

Hallmark isn't missing these opportunities. Instead, Hallmark aims at the "personal expression" market. The Hallmark.com online store, its Gold Crown stores, and other dealers offer all kinds of products that allow people to express their feelings by capturing and saving memories. As opportunities related to these needs change, Hallmark changes, too. For example, at a Hallmark store you can find both cards and picture frames. Hallmark also sells photo albums that allow customers to attach voice recordings to each picture. At Hallmark.com, subscribers find tips about what to write in a

Exhibit 3-1 Focusing Marketing Strategy with Segmentation and Positioning

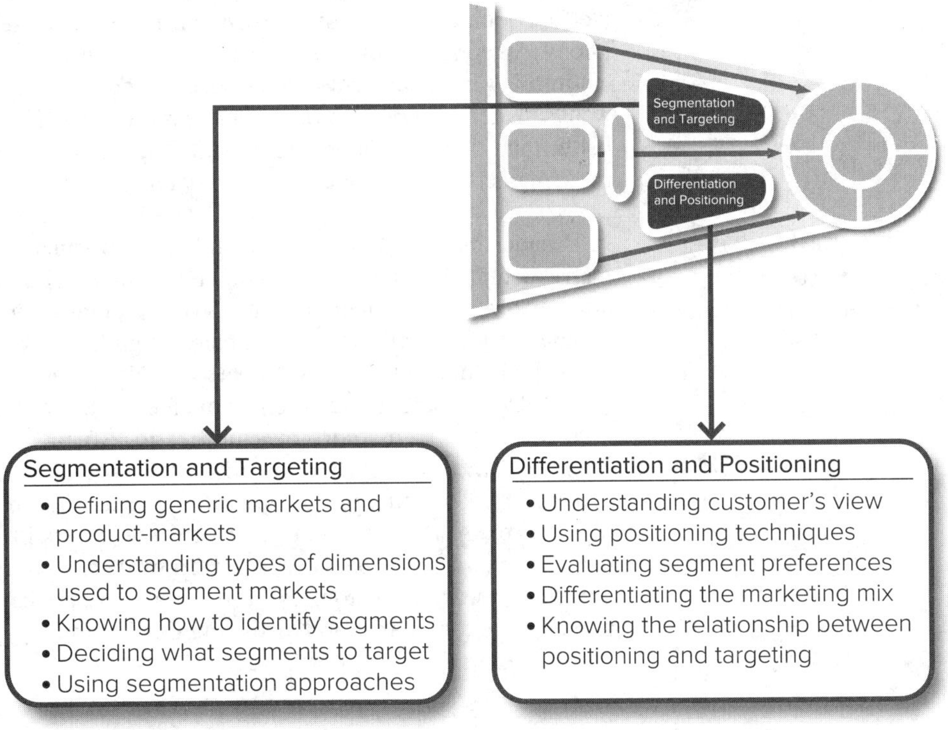

Nestlé targets customers in many different geographic markets around the world, but often the product-markets in one country are different than in another. For example, Nestlé created banana-flavored milk ice on a stick to fit the local tastes and preferences of Chinese consumers. The same product would probably not have a following in other places.
Source: Société des Produits Nestlé S.A.,Vevey, Switzerland

graduation or birthday card, the etiquette to follow in writing a birth announcement, and a blog post on how to "Banish boredom with a Summer Fun List." A smartphone app lets users customize Hallmark eCards—they can even include video greetings from their favorite characters in *Modern Family* or *Star Wars*. They can send the card by e-mail or post the wishes on Facebook.

From generic markets to product-markets

To understand the narrowing-down process, it's useful to think of two basic types of markets. A **generic**[1] **market** is a market with *broadly* similar needs and sellers offering various, *often diverse,* ways of satisfying those needs. In contrast, a **product-market** is a market with *very* similar needs and sellers offering various *close substitute* ways of satisfying those needs.

A generic market description looks at markets broadly and from a customer's viewpoint. Entertainment-seekers, for example, have many very different ways to satisfy their needs. An entertainment-seeker might buy a high-definition TV (HDTV) and subscribe to Netflix, book a vacation on Carnival Cruise Line, or reserve season tickets for the symphony. Any one of these *very different* products may satisfy this entertainment need. Sellers in this generic entertainment-seeker market have to focus on the need(s) customers want satisfied—not on how one seller's product (HDTV system, vacation, or live music) is better than that of another producer. It is sometimes hard to understand and define generic markets because *product types that are quite different may compete with one another.*

Broaden market definitions to find opportunities

Broader market definitions—including both generic market definitions and product-market definitions—can help firms find opportunities. But deciding *how* broad to go isn't easy. Too narrow a definition limits a firm's opportunities—but too broad a definition makes the company's efforts and resources seem insignificant. Consider, for example, the mighty Coca-Cola Company. It has great success and a huge market share in the U.S. soft drink market. On the other hand, its share of all beverage drinking worldwide is very small.

Here we try to match opportunities to a firm's resources and objectives. So the *relevant market for finding opportunities* should be bigger than the firm's present product-market—but not so big that the firm couldn't expand and be an important competitor. A small manufacturer of screwdrivers in Mexico, for example, shouldn't define its market as broadly as "the worldwide tool-users market" or as narrowly as "our present screwdriver customers." But it may have the capabilities to consider "the repairperson hand-tool market in North America." Carefully naming your product-market can help you see possible opportunities.

Naming Product-Markets and Generic Markets

Some managers think about markets only in terms of the product they already produce and sell. But this approach can lead to missed opportunities. For example, marketing managers at Eastman Kodak paid too much attention to competition in the photographic film market and failed to see how quickly digital imaging was replacing it. The music industry, long defined by sales of physical records, cassettes, or CDs, failed to anticipate how digital downloads would change how consumers buy music.

As this suggests, when evaluating opportunities, product-related terms do not—by themselves—adequately describe a market. A complete product-market definition includes a four-part description:

What:	**1. Product type (type of good and type of service)**
To meet what:	**2. Customer (user) needs**
For whom:	**3. Customer types**
Where:	**4. Geographic area**

We refer to these four-part descriptions as product-market "names" because most managers label their markets when they think, write, or talk about them. Such a four-part definition can be clumsy, however, so we often use a nickname. And the nickname should refer to people—not products—because, as we emphasize, people make markets! For example, LEGO's "active play market" describes kids who enjoy toys that foster creative, playful learning.

Product market definition

Product type describes the goods and/or services that customers want. Sometimes the product type is strictly a physical good or strictly a service. But marketing managers who ignore the possibility that *both* are important can miss opportunities.

Customer (user) needs refer to the needs the product type satisfies for the customer. At a very basic level, product types usually provide functional benefits such as nourishing, protecting, warming, cooling, transporting, cleaning, holding, and saving time. Although we need to identify such "basic" needs first, in advanced economies, we usually go on to emotional needs—such as needs for fun, excitement, pleasing appearance, or status. Correctly defining the need(s) relevant to a market is crucial and requires a good understanding of customers.

Customer type refers to the final consumer or user of a product type. Here we want to choose a name that describes all present (possible) types of customers. To define customer type, marketers should identify the final consumer or user of the product type, rather than the buyer—if they are different. For instance, producers should avoid treating intermediaries as a customer type—unless intermediaries actually use the product in their own business.

The *geographic area* is where a firm competes, or plans to compete, for customers. Naming the geographic area may seem trivial, but understanding the geographic boundaries of a market can suggest new opportunities. A firm aiming only at the domestic market, for example, may want to expand to other countries.

Product-market boundaries provide focus

This idea of making a decision about the boundaries of a market applies not just to geographic areas served but also to decisions about customer needs and product and customer types. Thus, naming the market is not simply an exercise in assigning labels. Rather, the manager's market definition sets the limits of the market(s) in which the firm will compete. For example, Canon targets a wide range of photographic needs and might approach a product-market named the "digital photographers market," defined as digital cameras (product type) that are easy to use and take high-quality digital photographs (customer needs) for amateur photographers (customer types) in developing countries (geographic area). Canon's product line should appeal to this broad product-market. On the other hand, camera maker GoPro focuses on a more specific set of customer needs and has tighter boundaries on its market definition. GoPro might define the "adventure video market" as digital video cameras (product type) that are rugged, waterproof, and don't need to be operated by hand (customer needs) for adventure sports enthusiasts (customer types) who live anywhere in the world (geographic area). GoPro's video cameras attach to surfboards, handlebars, or helmets so that adventure sport enthusiasts can capture all the action. These product-market definitions give each company a focus that sharpens marketing strategy.

No product type in generic market names

A generic market description *doesn't include any product-type terms.* It consists of only three parts of the product-market definition. This emphasizes that any product type that satisfies the customer's needs can compete in a generic market. Exhibit 3-2 shows the relationship between generic market and product-market definitions.

Later we'll study the many possible dimensions for segmenting markets. But for now you should see that defining markets only in terms of current products is not the best way to find new opportunities. Instead, the most effective way to find opportunities is to use market segmentation.

Market Segmentation Defines Possible Target Markets

Market segmentation is a two-step process

Market segmentation is a two-step process of (1) *naming* broad product-markets and (2) *segmenting* these broad product-markets in order to select target markets and develop suitable marketing mixes.

For example, although it might be easy to call Millennials "digital extroverts spreading trends and experiences," a recent study found only 42 percent fit that stereotype. Other Millennials use technology differently and have different attitudes about social media.

Naming broad product-markets is disaggregating

The first step in effective market segmentation involves naming a broad product-market of interest to the firm. Marketers must break apart—disaggregate—all possible needs into some generic markets and broad product-markets in which the firm may be able to operate profitably (see Exhibit 3-3). No one firm can satisfy everyone's needs. So the naming–disaggregating–step involves brainstorming about very different solutions to various generic needs and selecting some broad areas—broad product-markets—where the firm has some resources and experience. This means that a car manufacturer would probably ignore all the possible opportunities in food and clothing markets and focus on the generic market, "transporting people in the world," and probably on the broad product-market, "cars, trucks, and utility vehicles for transporting people in the world."

Market grid is a visual aid to market segmentation

Assuming that any broad product-market (or generic market) may consist of submarkets, picture a market as a rectangle with boxes that represent the smaller, more homogeneous product-markets.

Exhibit 3-4, for example, represents the broad product-market of bicycle riders. The

Exhibit 3-2
Relationship between Generic and Product-Market Definitions

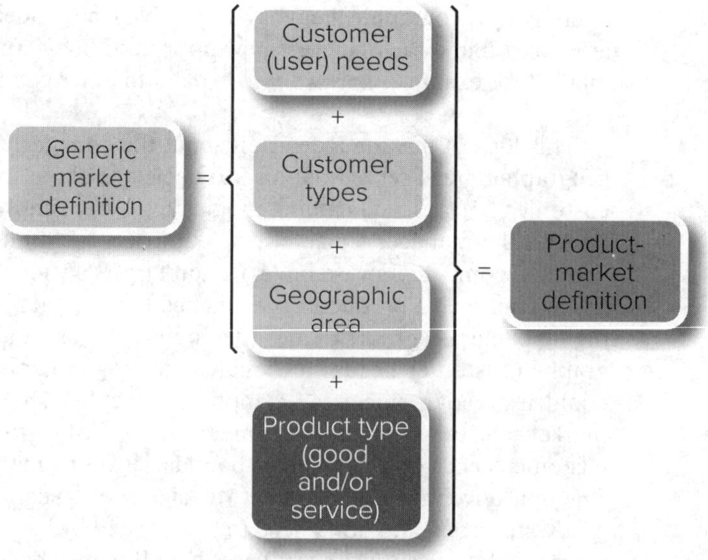

Exhibit 3-3 Narrowing Down to Target Markets

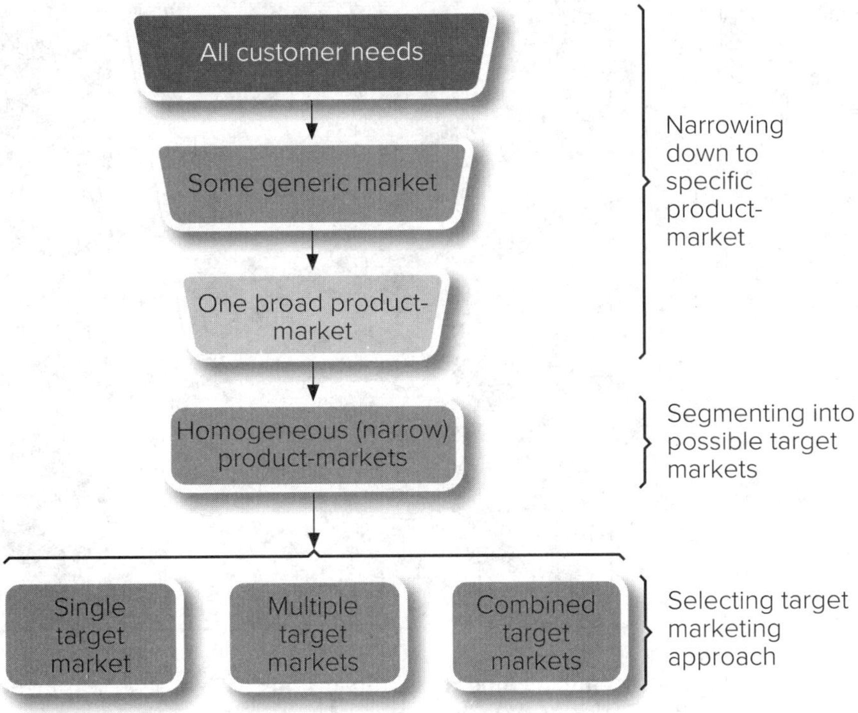

boxes show different submarkets. One submarket might focus on people who want to commute to work or school, another on people who want exercise, and so on. Alternatively, in the generic "transporting market" discussed earlier, we might see different product-markets of customers for bicycles, motorcycles, cars, airplanes, ships, buses, and "others."

Segmenting is an aggregating process

Marketing-oriented managers think of **segmenting** as an aggregating process—clustering people with similar needs into a "market segment." A **market segment** is a (relatively) homogeneous group of customers who will respond to a marketing mix in a similar way.

The number of segments that should be formed depends more on judgment than on some scientific rule. But the following guidelines can help.

Criteria for segmenting a broad product-market

Ideally, "good" market segments meet the following criteria:

1. *Homogeneous*[2] *(similar) within*—the customers in a market segment should be as similar as possible with respect to their likely responses to marketing mix variables *and* their segmenting dimensions.
2. *Heterogeneous*[3] *(different) between*—the customers in different segments should be as different as possible with respect to their likely responses to marketing mix variables *and* their segmenting dimensions.
3. *Substantial*[4]—the segment should be big enough to be profitable.
4. *Operational*—the segmenting dimensions should be useful for identifying customers and deciding on marketing mix variables.

It is especially important that segments be *operational*. This leads marketers to in-

Exhibit 3-4 A Market Grid Diagram with Submarkets

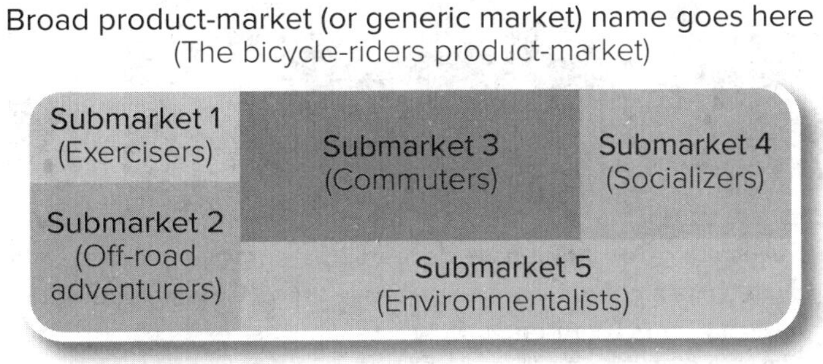

Consumers associate the Clorox brand with strong cleaning power and bleach. Clorox uses the Green Works brand to target customers who want natural cleaning products that don't have harsh chemical fumes or residue.
Source: The Clorox Company

clude demographic dimensions such as age, sex, income, location, and family size. In fact, it is difficult to make some Place and Promotion decisions without such information. For example, magazines, websites, and television shows have data on the demographic characteristics of their readers, visitors, and viewers. This makes it easier for a marketing manager to match these qualities with its target market.

Avoid segmenting dimensions that have no practical operational use. For instance, you may find a personality trait such as moodiness among the traits of heavy buyers of a product, but how could you use this fact? Salespeople can't give a personality test to each buyer. Similarly, advertising couldn't make much use of this information. So although moodiness might be related in some way to previous purchases, it would not be a useful dimension for segmenting.

Target marketers aim at specific targets

Once you accept the idea that broad product-markets may have submarkets, you can see that target marketers usually have a choice among many possible target markets.

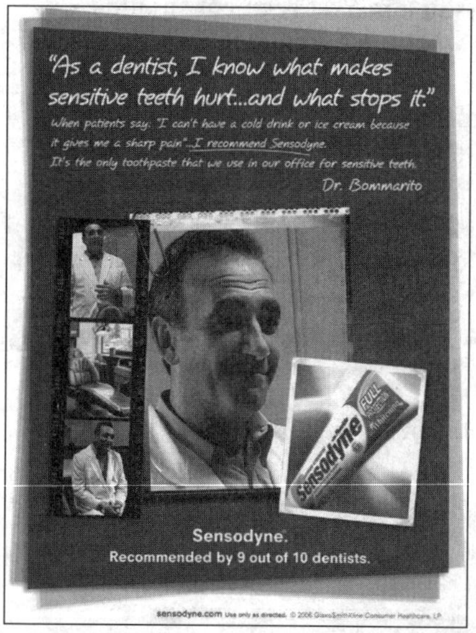

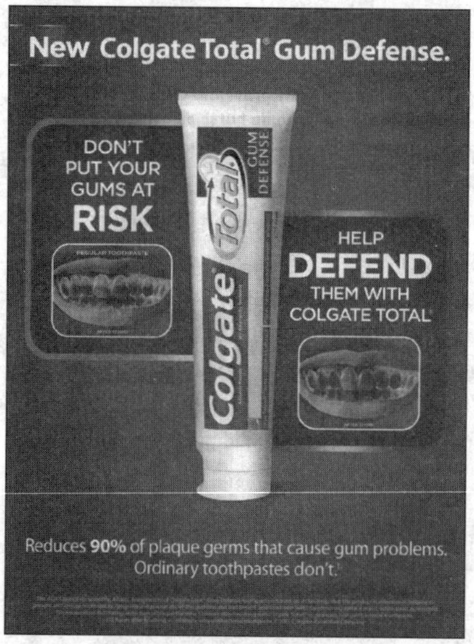

Firms that compete in the oral health care market have developed a variety of products that appeal to the needs of different customer segments. Sensodyne targets consumers with sensitive teeth, Colgate Total Gum Defense aims at those concerned about the health of their gums, and Tom's Children's toothpaste emphasizes its use of natural ingredients.
(left) Source: GlaxoSmithKline group of companies; (middle) Source: Colgate-Palmolive Company; (right) Source: Tom's of Maine

There are three basic ways to develop market-oriented strategies in a broad product-market.

1. The **single target market approach**—segmenting the market and picking one of the homogeneous segments as the firm's target market.
2. The **multiple target market approach**—segmenting the market and choosing two or more segments, and then treating each as a separate target market needing a different marketing mix.
3. The **combined target market approach**—combining two or more submarkets into one larger target market as a basis for one strategy.

Note that all three approaches involve target marketing. They all aim at specific, clearly defined target markets (see Exhibit 3-5). For convenience, we call people who follow the first two approaches the "segmenters" and people who use the third approach the "combiners."

Combiners try to satisfy "pretty well"

Combiners try to increase the size of their target markets by combining two or more segments. Combiners look at various submarkets for similarities rather than differences. Then they try to extend or modify their basic offering to appeal to these "combined" customers with just one marketing mix. For example, a combiner who faces the broad bicycle-riders product-market shown in Exhibit 3-4 might try to develop a marketing mix that would do a pretty good job of appealing to both the *Exercisers* and the *Off-road adventurers.* The combined market would be bigger than either segment by itself. And although both submarkets might like fatter tires and multiple speeds, the *Off-road adventurer* prefers a wider range of gears, a suspension system to handle bumps, and a more durable frame than the *Exerciser* might want or need. On the other hand, comfort is more important to the *Exerciser* who favors a more upright seating position. A single model of bicycle designed for both segments might not be the *best bike* for either segment.

Thus, a combiner makes compromises in developing the marketing mix. The combiner doesn't try to fine-tune each element of the marketing mix to appeal to each of the smaller submarkets. Rather, the marketing mix is selected to work fairly well with each segment.

A combined target market approach may help achieve some economies of scale. It may also require less investment than developing different marketing mixes for different segments—making it especially attractive for firms with limited resources.

Exhibit 3-5
Segmenters and Combiners Aim at Specific Target Markets

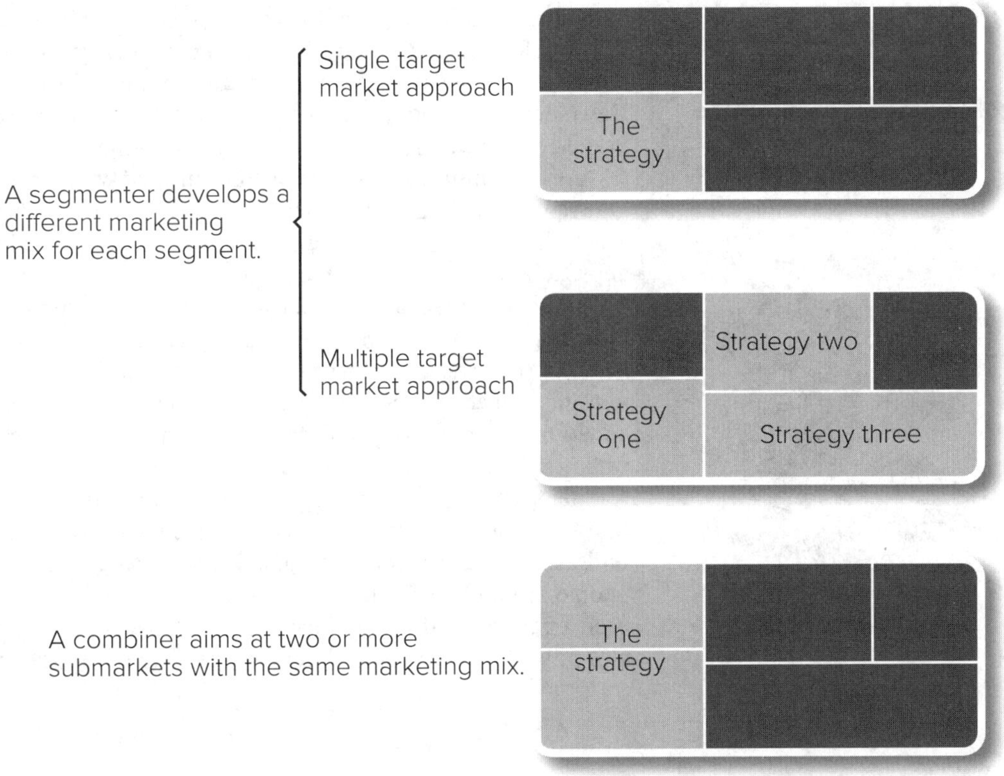

Segmenters try to satisfy "very well"

Segmenters aim at one or more homogeneous segments and try to develop a different marketing mix for each segment. Segmenters usually fine-tune their marketing mixes for each target market—perhaps making basic changes in the product itself—because they want to satisfy each segment very well.

Instead of assuming that the whole market consists of a fairly similar set of customers (like the mass marketer does) or merging various submarkets together (like the combiner), segmenters believe that aiming at one, or some, of these smaller markets makes it possible to provide superior value and satisfy them better. This then provides greater profit potential for the firm.

Segmenting may produce bigger sales

Note that segmenters are not settling for a smaller sales potential or lower profits. Instead, they hope to increase sales by getting a much larger share of the business in the market(s) they target. A segmenter who really satisfies the target market can often build such a close relationship with customers that he or she faces no real competition. A segmenter who offers a marketing mix precisely matched to the needs of the target market can often charge a higher price, thus producing higher profits. Customers are willing to pay a higher price because the whole marketing mix provides better customer value.

Consider the success of the Aeron desk chair developed by Herman Miller (HM), an 80-year-old company that makes office furniture. Most firms that sell office furniture offered similar lines of executive desk chairs that were padded for comfort and conveyed the look of success. Marketing managers at HM realized that some customers felt that these traditional chairs were boring. Further, in an e-commerce world, even top executives sit at computers and want a chair that provides both good support and good looks. So to satisfy this upscale segment, HM designed a new type of chair from scratch. There's no fabric or padding, but everything about it adjusts to your body. It's so comfortable that HM positions it as "the chair you can wear." With a price tag of $750 or more, the Aeron chair became a status symbol for high-tech managers and has been as profitable as it is popular.

Should you segment or combine?

Which approach should a firm use? This depends on the firm's resources, the nature of competition, and—most important—the similarity of customer needs, attitudes, and buying behavior.

It's usually safer to be a segmenter—that is, to try to satisfy some customers *very* well instead of many just *fairly* well. That's why many firms use the single or multiple target market approach instead of the combined target market approach. For example, Procter & Gamble (P&G) uses the multiple target market approach with its dishwashing liquids. P&G targets those wanting to cut through grease on pots, pans, and dishes with its Dawn detergent; those seeking long-lasting suds might prefer Joy. Even within the Dawn brands, different formulas serve customer segments with different needs. Dawn Escapes features different scents, Dawn Platinum provides extra grease-cleaning power, and Dawn Free & Gentle removes dyes and strong perfumes. Product, Promotion, and Place differ across these Dawn dishwashing soaps. Though extremely effective, this approach may not be possible for a smaller firm with more limited resources.

A smaller firm may have to use the single target market approach, focusing all its efforts at a smaller segment where it sees the best opportunity. For example, sneaker maker Kaepa's all-purpose sneaker sales plummeted as Nike and Reebok stole customers with a multiple target market approach. Nike and Reebok developed innovative products and aimed their promotion at specific needs, such as jogging, aerobics[5], cross-training, and walking. Kaepa turned things around by catering to the needs of cheerleaders. Cheerleading squads can order Kaepa shoes with custom team logos and colors. The soles of the shoes feature finger grooves that make it easier for cheerleaders to build human pyramids. Kaepa also carefully targets its marketing research and promotion. Kaepa salespeople attend cheerleading camps each summer that draw 40,000 enthusiasts. Kaepa even arranges for the cheering teams it sponsors to do demos at retail stores. This generates publicity and pulls in buyers, so retailers put more emphasis on the Kaepa line.

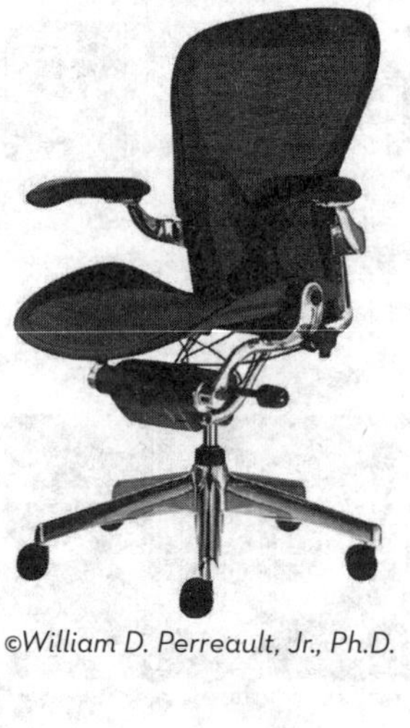

©William D. Perreault, Jr., Ph.D.

Profit is the balancing point

In practice, cost considerations often encourage more aggregating and favor combining submarkets as costs often drop due to economies of scale. On the other hand, many customers prefer to have their needs satisfied more exactly—and will be more satisfied by a segmenter that develops a marketing mix that more closely matches their needs. When the rest of the marketing mix better matches their needs, customers are often willing to pay a higher price. Profit is the balancing point. It determines how unique a marketing mix the firm can afford to offer to a particular market segment.

What Dimensions Are Used to Segment Markets?

Segmenting dimensions guide marketing mix planning

Market segmentation forces a marketing manager to decide which product-market dimensions might be useful for planning marketing strategies. Ideally, we want to describe any potential product-market in terms of all three types of customer-related dimensions—plus a product-type description—because these dimensions help us develop better marketing mixes.

Segmenting draws on why, what, and who

As a marketing manager narrows down to particular segmenting dimensions, some basic questions can help guide the process. First, a marketing manager should understand *why* customers are making a purchase decision. This might take into account customers' needs, preferences, and consumer decision process. Second, a manager wants to know *what* customers have done before making a decision. For example, are customers buying this product for the first time or are they repeat customers? How frequently do they make this purchase? Finally, *who* are the customers? Where do they live and shop, what is their age or gender, and so on? Answering these why, what, and who questions allows a marketing manager to better identify the dimensions on which customers are similar and different.

Many segmenting dimensions may be considered

Customers can be described by many specific dimensions. Exhibit 3-7 shows some dimensions useful for segmenting consumer markets. A few are behavioral dimensions; others are geographic and demographic. We discuss these final consumer segmenting dimensions in Chapters 2 and 4. Exhibit 3-8 shows some additional dimensions for

Exhibit 3-6 Relation of Potential Target Market Dimensions to Marketing Strategy Decision Areas

Potential Target Market Dimensions	Effects on Strategy Decision Areas
1. Behavioral needs, attitudes, and how present and potential goods and services fit into customers' consumption patterns.	Affect *Product* (features, packaging, product line assortment, branding) and *Promotion* (what potential customers need and want to know about the firm's offering, and what appeals should be used).
2. Urgency to get need satisfied and desire and willingness to seek information, compare, and shop.	Affect *Place* (how directly products are distributed from producer to customer, how extensively they are made available, and the level of service needed) and *Price* (how much potential customers are willing to pay).
3. Geographic location and other demographic characteristics of potential customers.	Affect size of *target markets* (economic potential), *Place* (where products should be made available), and *Promotion* (where and to whom to target with advertising, publicity, sales promotion, and personal selling).

Exhibit 3-7 Possible Segmenting Dimensions and Typical Breakdowns for Consumer Markets

Behavioral	Needs, benefits sought, thoughts (attitudes), rate of use, purchase relationship, brand familiarity, kind of shopping, type of problem solving, information required, purchase situation, psychographics or lifestyle (see Chapter 4)
Geographic	Country, region, city, size of city, urban/rural (see Chapter 2)
Demographic	Income, gender, age, marital status, family size, family life cycle (see Chapter 4), occupation, education, ethnicity, social class (see Chapter 2)

Exhibit 3-8 Possible Segmenting Dimensions for Business/Organizational Markets

Kind of relationship	Weak/strong loyalty to vendor, single source/multiple vendors, "arm's length"/close partnership
Type of customer	Manufacturer, service producer, government agency, military, nonprofit, wholesaler or retailer
Geographic	Region of world, country, region within country, urban/rural
Demographic	Size (number of employees or sales volume), primary business or industry (NAICS), number of facilities
How product will be used	Installations, components, accessories, raw materials, supplies, professional services
Type of buying situation	Decentralized/centralized, buyer/multiple buying influence, straight rebuy/modified rebuy/new-task buying
Purchasing methods	Vendor analysis, purchasing specifications, Internet bids, negotiated contracts

segmenting markets when the customers are businesses, government agencies, or other types of organizations. These dimensions for segmenting organizational customers are covered in Chapter 5. Regardless of whether customers are final consumers or organizations, segmenting a broad product-market *usually* requires using several different dimensions at the same time.

What are the qualifying and determining dimensions?

To select the important segmenting dimensions, think about two different types of dimensions. **Qualifying dimensions** are those relevant to including a customer type in a product-market. **Determining dimensions** are those that actually affect the customer's purchase of a *specific* product or brand in a product-market.

A prospective car buyer, for example, has to have enough money—or credit—to buy a car and insure it. Our buyer also needs a driver's license. This still doesn't guarantee a purchase. He or she must have a real need—such as a job that requires "wheels" or kids who have to be carpooled. This need may motivate the purchase of *some* car. But these qualifying dimensions don't determine what specific brand or model car the person might buy. That depends on more specific interests—such as the kind of safety, performance, or appearance the customer wants. Determining dimensions related to these needs affect the specific car the customer purchases. If safety is a determining dimension for a customer, a Volvo wagon that offers side impact protection, air bags, and all-wheel drive might be the customer's first choice.

Consider Ford's efforts to sell cars in Vietnam. When Ford arrived in the country a few years ago, many consumers didn't even know how to drive a car—an important *qualifying* dimension when you are selling cars. To increase the size of its market, Ford created a free driving school for Vietnamese wanting to learn how to drive. Ford hoped that training drivers using Ford cars would build brand preference that would become a *determining* dimension for future Vietnamese drivers.

Determining dimensions may be very specific

How specific the determining dimensions are depends on whether you are concerned with a general product type or a specific brand (see Exhibit 3-9). The more

Exhibit 3-9 Finding the Relevant Segmenting Dimensions

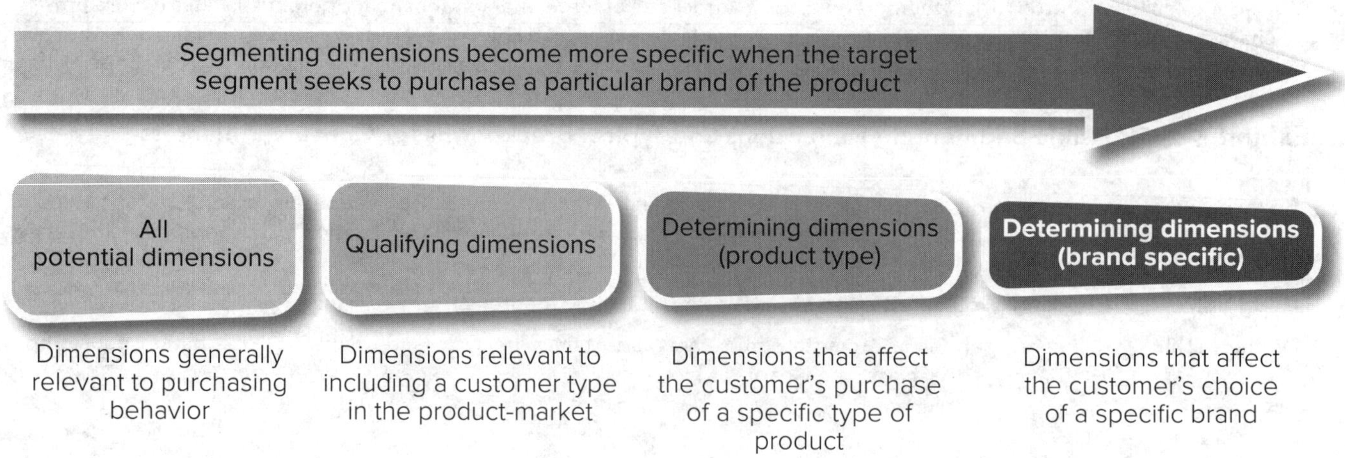

specific you want to be, the more particular the determining dimensions may be. In a particular case, the determining dimensions may seem minor. But they are important because they *are* the determining dimensions.

For example, marketing managers at Chicago South Loop Hotel know that some customers drive to into downtown Chicago and worry about the cost of parking. For these customers, manner of arrival might be a determining dimension in choosing a particular hotel for their next trip to the Windy City. So Chicago South Loop Hotel offers free parking to encourage this segment to choose its hotel.

Qualifying dimensions are important too

The qualifying dimensions help identify the "core benefits" that must be offered to everyone in a product-market. For example, people won't choose to stay at the Chicago South Loop Hotel unless they have plans to travel to the city of Chicago. Qualifying and determining dimensions work together in marketing strategy planning.

Different dimensions needed for different submarkets

Note that each different submarket within a broad product-market may be motivated by a different set of dimensions. In the snack food market, for example, health food enthusiasts are interested in nutrition, dieters worry about calories, and economical shoppers with lots of kids may want volume to "fill them up."

Sometimes a marketing manager must decide whether a firm should serve customers it really doesn't want to serve. For example, banks sometimes offer marketing mixes that are attractive to wealthy customers but drive off low-income consumers.

Personas give segments life

After creating segments, some firms create *buyer personas*–fictional depictions of customers illustrative of each target segment. These depictions often turn into elaborate background "stories" that describe a typical segment member's demographic characteristics and behavior patterns–related (and unrelated) to buying, motivations, and goals. A buyer persona emerges from customer research, usually personal interviews with several members of the target market segment.

For example, a bicycle maker might develop buyer personas for different target segments. If it targets commuters, the following might reflect the beginnings of a buyer persona:

> Sam is a single 29-year-old male who lives in Seattle, Washington. He rides 10 miles each way to his job where he earns $85,000 a year as a computer programmer. On weekends he likes to hang with his girlfriend and race mountain bikes. Sam is price sensitive with his commuter bike (he spends more lavishly on his mountain bikes). The commuter bike must be safe and reliable; it should have fenders and a chain guard to deal with the regular rains in Seattle.

People who are out in the sun should protect their skin. This safety need is a qualifying dimension of consumers in the market for sunscreen products. However, parents may especially seek Banana Boat Baby and Kids Sunblock Lotion and Baby Sprays because they are easy on kids' eyes and don't cause tearing. For these parents this is a determining need. There are a variety of ways that Coffee-Mate is different from cream, but this ad focuses on the idea that it does not need to be refrigerated. For some consumers, that determines what they will buy.
(left) Source: Edgewell; (right) Source: Creative Director/Copywriter: Emily Smeraldo; Art Director: Wayne Kan & Jonathan Lee; School: School of Visual Arts, New York; Instructors: Richard Pels & Paul Jarvi

This description of Sam might continue with details on Sam's favorite websites, social media behavior, reading selections, long- and short-term goals, and his history of riding. Personas often include a photo. Because people relate best to people (rather than abstract "segments"), personas help everyone across the organization (research and development, customer service, advertising, website development, and more) to better empathize with target customers and develop a marketing orientation.

International marketing requires even more segmenting

Success in international marketing requires even more attention to segmenting. There are more than 192 nations with their own unique cultures! And they differ greatly in language, customs (including business ethics), beliefs, religions, race, and income distribution patterns. (We discuss some of these differences in Chapters 2, 4, and 5.) These additional differences can complicate the segmenting process. Even worse, critical data are often less available—and less dependable—as firms move into international markets. This is one reason why some firms insist that local operations and decisions be handled by natives. They, at least, have a feel for their markets.

Segmenting international markets may require more dimensions. But one practical method adds just one step to the approach discussed earlier. First, marketers segment by country or region—looking at demographic, cultural, and other characteristics, including stage of economic development. This may help them find regional or national submarkets that are fairly similar. Then—depending on whether the firm is aiming at final consumers or business markets—they apply the same basic approaches presented before.

Smart segmenters win in international markets

Many firms make only modest changes to marketing mixes when they enter developing countries. So sellers can really stand out when they show a respect for and focus on local customers. A few years ago Korea's LG Electronics started tailoring products to the Indian market. As one example, LG's Charcoal Lighting Heater Microwave includes an autocook menu with settings for more than 130 Indian dishes. The move paid off when LG was chosen as the most trusted consumer durable brand in India.

Ethical issues in selecting segmenting dimensions

Marketing managers sometimes face ethical decisions when selecting segmenting dimensions. Problems may arise if a firm targets customers who are somehow at a disadvantage in dealing with the firm or who are unlikely to see the negative effects of their own choices. For example, some people criticize athletic shoe companies for targeting poor, inner-city kids who see expensive athletic shoes as an important status symbol. Many firms, including producers of infant formula, have been criticized for targeting consumers in less-developed nations. Some nutritionists criticize firms that market soft drinks, candy, and snack foods to children.

Ethical Dilemma

What would you do? You have just started working as assistant brand manager for Silky Smooth skin cream, and you are responsible for one southeast Asian country. Silky Smooth is a skin moisturizer that also lightens skin tone. To this point, the lightening feature has not been noted on Silky Smooth product packaging or in advertising. In this country there is discrimination against people with darker skin tones, so many consumers actively seek to lighten their skin. Two major skin cream competitors promote "skin lightening" by showing ads featuring an unhappy woman who starts using the product and becomes very happy and more successful with her lighter skin. Activists have protested against skin-lightening products because they reinforce a negative stereotype. Silky Smooth's consumer research predicts that promoting skin lightening benefits to customers with darker skin tones would increase Silky Smooth sales by 20 percent in less than a year. You are wondering whether to target the market segment of women seeking lighter skin with advertising and packaging that emphasizes these benefits. Your boss says it is your call, while also reminding you of the bonus you receive for growing sales by 10 percent or more.

Do you have any concerns about this issue? Would you target this darker-skinned segment of the population? Why or why not?

More Sophisticated Techniques May Help in Segmenting and Targeting

Marketing researchers and managers often turn to computer-aided methods for help with the segmenting job.

Clustering usually requires a computer

Clustering techniques try to find similar patterns within sets of data. Clustering groups customers who are similar on their segmenting dimensions into homogeneous segments. Clustering approaches use computers to do what previously was done mainly with intuition and judgment.

The data to be clustered might include such dimensions as demographic characteristics, the importance of different needs, attitudes toward the product, and past buying behavior. The computer searches all the data for homogeneous groups of people. When it finds them, marketers study the dimensions of the people in the groups to see why the computer clustered them together. The results sometimes suggest new, or at least better, marketing strategies. Check out *Marketing Analytics in Action: Cluster Analysis* to see the results of a cluster analysis and segmentation of holiday gift shoppers.

A customer database can focus the effort

A variation of the clustering approach relies on **customer relationship management (CRM)**, where the seller fine-tunes the marketing effort with information from a detailed customer database. The database stores information that is useful for segmentation. Analytic software aids in identifying customer segments, so that each can be delivered to a different marketing mix.

Safeway gathers customer data from its shoppers' use of customer loyalty cards. These data are used to tailor marketing mixes to each customer. So a customer who has purchased Kellogg's Corn Flakes may get a different coupon than someone who regularly purchases Quaker Oatmeal. These offers can be seen on the customer's smartphone and the Safeway Just for U™ app.
Source: Safeway.com

Marketing Analytics in Action: Cluster Analysis

A few years ago, Forbes Consulting Group surveyed 612 Americans aged 18 to 64 who are personally responsible for holiday shopping. The survey was conducted in mid-November, just before typical holiday shopping begins. The research used cluster analysis to identify three groups of shoppers:

- "Giving Is Love": These people give gifts as a way of expressing love and affection and want to be admired for picking great gifts. Eighty-three percent pride themselves on giving unique gifts, and 52 percent splurge on luxury items.
- "Obligated Posers": These people mostly just want to avoid being scorned by peers. They are most likely to view shopping as an obligation (53 percent) and don't want to spend a lot of money, but they want to look like they did.
- "Utilitarian Grinches": These people feel a great deal of anxiety about gift-giving, prefer to give practical gifts that someone "really needs," and prefer to buy online.

1. *Name a retail store where each segment might be more likely to shop.*
2. *Give an example of a product that might be bought by each shopper type.*
3. *Describe a buyer persona (covered earlier in the chapter) for each of these groups.*

What's Next? Target reads its customers' minds

A few years ago, a man walked into a Target store outside Minneapolis demanding to see a manager. The man was upset that Target was sending his teenage daughter coupons for baby clothes and cribs. "Are you trying to encourage her to get pregnant?" he asked the manager. The store manager promised to look into it, but a few days later the father called back and sheepishly admitted that there was more going on in his house than he knew about. His daughter was due in August. How did Target know? Why would Target care?

Consumers' shopping habits are hard to break. Once customers start shopping at a particular store for groceries, personal care products, or greeting cards, they get into a routine and don't even consider shopping at other stores. It turns out that a few major life events—new job, new home, marriage, and yes, new baby—significantly weaken those habits, at least for a short time. At those vulnerable moments, a competing store has an opportunity to steal a customer away— perhaps encouraging a switch with some well-timed promotions—and maybe help the customer develop a new shopping habit.

So how does a retail store such as Target segment its market and target pregnant shoppers? Target's marketing managers wondered if their customer relationship management (CRM) database might hold an answer. The database includes information on the shopping behavior of customers who sign up for the store's loyalty card or use a credit card. Along with additional data Target purchases from third parties, the database offers a detailed profile of millions of Target customers.

A small number of these customers told Target they were pregnant by signing up for the store's baby registry, where they also recorded the date the baby was due to be born. Target's statisticians used data from the customers they knew were pregnant and "mined" their CRM data to try to determine how their shopping behavior changed during pregnancy.

The statisticians discovered 25 products that were purchased more frequently during pregnancy. For example, although many people buy lotions, about six months before their due date purchases of unscented lotions bump up. Around that same time pregnant women stock up on supplements such as calcium, magnesium, and zinc. A few months later there is an uptick in purchases of scent-free soap, extra-large bags of cotton balls, hand sanitizers, and washcloths.

The statisticians use this information to develop a prediction score for each customer in Target's CRM database—predicting whether each is pregnant and when she will deliver. Customers with high scores receive customized direct mailings with coupons for a new crib or disposable diapers. Target wants these customers to start buying groceries and other products at Target, too. So it makes sure the mailings also include other products these customers haven't yet bought at Target. Many of these customers soon have a new habit and make Target their primary shopping location. So the next time you open a promotion for something you are thinking about buying, the store may be reading your mind—via its CRM database.

When this story became public, some customers questioned whether Target had crossed an ethical line. They found Target's behavior creepy. *What do you think? Are Target's practices ethical? Should a retailer use data to predict customer behavior? Why or why not?*

Netflix's CRM database includes the specific shows and movies each customer has actually streamed to his or her TV, computer, or mobile device. Netflix has found that these behavioral data predict future viewing behavior much better than demographic information such as age, gender, or geographic location. So Netflix uses analytics software and artificial intelligence to decide what TV shows and movies appear as suggestions on each customer's Netflix home page. Target's CRM combines previous purchases with demographic data to predict customers' future needs. Read more in *What's Next?* Target reads its customers' minds.

Targeting a segment of one

The ultimate in personalization occurs when firms consider each customer as its own segment. Business-to-business markets, with very large customers, have typically treated customer firms individually as "segments of one." Many CRM systems use artificial intelligence to do the same for large numbers of consumers. For example, Macy's mines customer data to adapt marketing communications to *individual* customers. Macy's CRM database includes a great deal of insight about each customer: previous purchases, responses to e-mails, online shopping behavior, and other information collected over time. Macy's uses these data to customize promotions in e-mails and direct mail. For example, Macy's sent out 30,000 different versions of a catalog mailing; the pieces varied from 32 to 76 pages long and featured merchandise designed to appeal to each customer. As a result, a footwear fanatic saw more shoes and moms saw more kids' clothes.

Smartphones help target customers by current location

Many marketing managers would like to know when target customers are near their stores. With that information, they might be able to make those customers an offer to get them to visit the store and make a purchase. That kind of information is becoming a reality.

Today more than two-thirds of Americans and Europeans have smartphones. These phones send out signals, so an advertiser knows where the phone (and presumably its owner) is at any given moment. This helps retailers send messages to potential customers when they get within set distances of their stores. For example, customers who download the Macy's app to their phones are reminded of products they "liked" in the app when they enter a Macy's store. Audi's mobile ads direct customers to their nearest Audi dealer. Marketing managers and advertising agencies are just figuring out how to use location data—but we can expect this to grow, allowing marketers to more easily identify and reach customers.

Differentiation and Positioning Take the Customer Point of View

Differentiate the marketing mix—to serve customers better

As we've emphasized throughout, the reason for focusing on a specific target market—by using marketing segmentation approaches or tools such as cluster analysis or CRM—is so that you can fine-tune the whole marketing mix to provide some group of potential customers with superior value. By *differentiating* the marketing mix to do a better job meeting customers' needs, the firm builds competitive advantage. When this happens, target customers view the firm's marketing mix as uniquely suited to their preferences and needs.

Although the marketing manager may want customers to see the firm's offering as unique, that is not always possible. Me-too imitators may come along and copy the firm's strategy. Further, even if a firm's marketing mix is different, consumers may not know or care. They're busy and, simply put, the firm's product may not be that important in their lives. This is where another important concept, *positioning,* comes in.

Positioning is based on customers' views

Positioning refers to how customers think about proposed or present brands in a market. Without a realistic view of how customers think about offerings in the market, it's hard for the marketing manager to differentiate. At the same time, the manager should know how he or she *wants* target customers to think about the firm's marketing mix. Positioning issues are especially important when competitors in a market appear to be very similar. For example, many people think that there isn't much difference between one provider of home owner's insurance and another. But State Farm Insurance uses advertising to emphasize the value of the service and personal attention from its agents, who live right in the customer's neighborhood. Low-price insurers who sell from websites or toll-free numbers can't make that claim.

Figuring out what customers really think about competing products isn't easy, but there are approaches that help. Most of them require some formal marketing research. The results are usually plotted on graphs to help show how consumers view the competing products. Usually, the products' positions are related to two or three product features that are important to the target customers.

Sanuk wants customers to think about its shoes as "fun." The brand takes its name from the Thai word for fun, its products are known for a funky sense of style, and its promotion is creative and humorous. These contribute to the brand's positioning and Sanuk's target customers perceive the brand as fun and irreverent.
Source: Deckers Brands

Managers make the graphs for positioning decisions by asking consumers to make judgments about different brands–including their "ideal" brand–and then use computer programs to summarize the ratings and plot the results. The details of positioning techniques–sometimes called *perceptual*[6] *mapping*–are beyond the scope of this text. But Exhibit 3-10 shows the possibilities.

Exhibit 3-10 **"Product Space" Representing Consumers' Perceptions for Different Brands of Bar Soap**

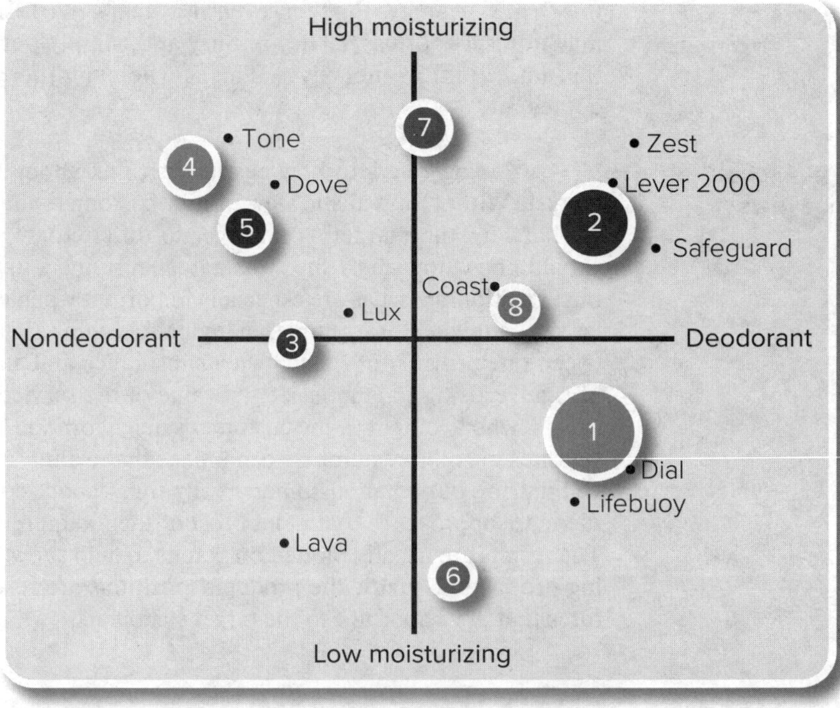

Exhibit 3-10 shows the "product space" for different brands of bar soap using two dimensions–the extent to which consumers think the soaps moisturize and deodorize their skin. For example, consumers see Dove as quite high on moisturizing but low on deodorizing. Dove and Tone are close together–implying that consumers think of them as similar on these characteristics. Dial is viewed as different from Dove and Tone and at a distance from them on the graph. Remember that positioning maps are based on *customers' perceptions*–the actual characteristics of the products (as determined by a chemical test) might be different!

Each segment may have its own preferences

The circles in Exhibit 3-10 show different sets (submarkets) of consumers clustered near their ideal soap preferences. Groups of respondents with a similar ideal product are circled to show apparent customer concentrations. In this graph, the size of the circles suggests the size of the segments for the different ideals.

Ideal clusters 1 and 2 are the largest and are close to two popular brands–Dial and Lever 2000. It appears that customers in cluster 2 want more moisturizing than they see in Dial. However, exactly what this brand should do about this isn't clear. Perhaps Dial should leave its physical product alone–but emphasize moisturizing more in its promotion to make a stronger appeal to those who want moisturizers. A marketing manager talking about this approach might simply refer to it as "positioning the brand as a good moisturizer." Of course, whether the effort is successful depends on whether the whole marketing mix delivers on the promise of the positioning communication.

Note that ideal cluster 7 is not near any of the present brands. This may suggest an opportunity for introducing a new product–a strong moisturizer with some deodorizers. A firm that chooses to follow this approach would be making a segmenting effort.

Combining versus segmenting

Positioning analysis may lead a firm to combining–rather than segmenting–if managers think they can make several general appeals to different parts of a "combined" market. For example, by varying its promotion, Coast might try to appeal to segments 8, 1, and 2 with one product. These segments are all quite similar (close together) in what they want in an ideal brand. On the other hand, there may be clearly defined submarkets–and some parts of the market may be "owned" by one product or brand. In this case, segmenting efforts may be practical–moving the firm's own product into another segment of the general market area where competition is weaker.

Positioning as part of broader analysis

A positioning analysis helps managers understand how customers see their market. It is a visual aid to understanding a product-market. The first time such an analysis is done, managers may be shocked to see how much customers' perceptions of a market differ from their own. For this reason alone, positioning analysis may be crucial. But a positioning analysis usually focuses on specific product features and brands that are close competitors in the product-market. Thus, it is a product-oriented approach. Important *customer*-related dimensions–including needs and attitudes–may be overlooked.

Premature[7] emphasis on product features is dangerous in other ways as well. As our bar soap example shows, starting with a product-oriented definition of a market and how bar soaps compete against other bar soaps can make a firm miss more basic shifts in markets. For example, bars have lost popularity to liquid soaps. Other products, such as bath oils or body washes for use in the shower, are now part of the relevant competition also. Managers wouldn't see these shifts if they looked only at alternative bar soap brands–the focus is just too narrow.

It's also important to realize that the way consumers look at a product isn't just a matter of chance. Let's return to our bar soap example. Although many consumers do think about soap in terms of moisturizing and deodorizing, other needs shouldn't be overlooked. For example, some consumers are especially concerned about wiping out germs. Marketers for Dial soap recognized this need and developed ads that positioned Dial as "the choice" for these target customers. This helped Dial win new customers, including those who switched from Lifebuoy–which was otherwise similar to Dial (see Exhibit 3-10). In fact, what happened to Lifebuoy highlights what happens if managers don't update their marketing strategy as customer needs and competition change. Lifebuoy was the first deodorant soap on the market; it was a leading brand for more than 100 years. But it gradually lost sales to competitors with stronger marketing mixes (clearer differentiation, better positioning, and superior customer value) until sales declined and Lever stopped selling it.

Sometimes repositioning is needed

Sometimes research shows the marketing manager that target customers are not viewing the brand in the desired way—it needs to be *repositioned*[8]. Changing customers' perceptions of a brand is not easy—and requires changes to the marketing mix. In the mid-2000s Korean carmaker Hyundai found that its positioning was not helping it sell more vehicles. It conducted research that showed pictures of the Hyundai Veracruz, with the Hyundai name hidden, to a group of potential car buyers—71 percent said they would buy one. Another group of buyers was shown the same pictures *with* the Hyundai name—only 52 percent were interested this time. Hyundai learned that it had a reputation as a "cheap low quality" car, even though data showed its vehicles among the best made in the world. To reposition the brand, Hyundai gave buyers a 10-year, 100,000-mile warranty on every car and ran ads that emphasized its high safety and quality ratings. Soon Hyundai wasn't seen as cheap; instead, it was "more value for your money." With the new positioning, Hyundai's market share jumped 70 percent in three years.

Positioning statement provides direction for marketing strategy

Sometimes marketing managers use a positioning statement to provide focus for a marketing mix. A **positioning statement** concisely identifies the firm's desired target market, product type, primary benefit or point of differentiation, and the main reasons a buyer should believe the firm's claims. The one or two benefits highlighted in the statement should be those most important to the target market—and unique to the brand. It's important that everyone involved in planning the marketing strategy agree with the positioning statement because it helps narrow options and guide the selection of a marketing mix.

Some firms use a template like the following to aid in preparation of a positioning statement:

> For (*our target market*), (*our brand*) of all (*product type*) delivers (*key benefit or point of differentiation*) because (*our brand*) is (*reasons to believe*).

A few years ago, marketing managers for Mountain Dew used this template to develop the following positioning statement:

> For 16- to 24-year-old males, who embrace excitement, adventure, and fun, Mountain Dew of all carbonated soft drinks, delivers great taste that exhilarates like no other because Mountain Dew is energizing, thirst-quenching, and has a one-of-a-kind citrus flavor.

The positioning statement provided Mountain Dew's advertising agency with a direction to follow that led to a series of television and print advertisements that reinforced this positioning. The statement guided decisions about packaging, point-of-purchase promotion, sponsorships, the look and feel of a website, and choices for new flavors. The marketing strategy based on this positioning helped Mountain Dew gain market share with this target market.

As we emphasize throughout the text, you must understand potential needs and attitudes when planning marketing strategies. If customers treat different products as substitutes, then a firm has to position itself against those products too. Customers won't always be conscious of all of the detailed ways that a firm's marketing mix might be different, but careful positioning can help highlight a unifying theme or benefits that relate to the determining dimensions of the target market. Thus, it's useful to think of positioning as part of the broader strategy planning process—because the purpose is to ensure that the whole marketing mix is positioned for competitive advantage.

Source: Pepsico Inc.

CONCLUSION

The basic purpose of this chapter is to show how marketing managers use market segmentation and positioning to guide that narrowing-down process.

Now that you've read this chapter you should understand how to carefully define generic markets and product-markets and how that can help in identifying and evaluating opportunities. We stressed the shortcomings of a too-narrow, product-oriented view of markets and explained why it's better to take a broader view that also includes consideration of customer needs, the product type, the customer type, and the geographic area.

We also discussed approaches for market segmentation—the process of naming and then segmenting broad product-markets to find potentially attractive target markets. Some people try to segment markets by starting with the mass market and then dividing it into smaller submarkets based on a few demographic characteristics. But this can lead to poor results. Instead, market segmentation should first focus on a broad product-market and then group similar customers into homogeneous submarkets. The more similar the potential customers are, the larger the submarkets can be. Four criteria for evaluating possible product-market segments were presented.

Once a broad product-market is segmented, marketing managers can use one of three approaches to market-oriented strategy planning: (1) the single target market approach, (2) the multiple target market approach, or (3) the combined target market approach. In general, we encourage marketers to be segmenters rather than combiners.

We also cover computer-aided approaches such as clustering techniques, CRM, and positioning. We emphasize the role of positioning in providing a focus or theme to the various elements of a differentiated marketing mix that fits the preferences of target customers.

In summary, good marketers should be experts on markets and the dimensions that segment them. By thoughtfully segmenting markets, they may spot opportunities—even breakthrough opportunities—and help their firms succeed against aggressive competitors offering similar products.

In Chapters 4 and 5 you'll learn more about the buying behavior of final consumers and organizational customers. As you enrich your understanding of customers and how they behave, you will develop command of a broader set of dimensions that are important for segmentation and positioning.

JOYFUL MOMENT

The Best Salesman in the World

Harry saw an ad in a window. It said: "Wanted. The Best Salesman in the World. Top Pay."

"I'm a great salesman." Harry told himself. "I can sell anything. I'll go in and ask for that job." He went into the building and spoke to the manager. "I'm the best salesman in the world," he said. "Give me the job."

"You must prove you're the best," the manager said.

"I'll pass every test you give me." Harry told him.

"Good."

The manager took a box of candy out of his desk. "Last week, I bought a thousand boxes of this candy. If you can sell them all before the end of the week, you can have the job."

"That's easy," Harry said. He took the box of candy and left the office. Every day and all day, he went from shop to shop, trying to sell boxes of the candy. He couldn't sell one. The candy was so bad he couldn't even give it away. At the end of the week he went back to the manager.

"I'm sorry, sir," he said, "I was wrong about myself. I'm not the best salesman in the world, but I know who is."

"Oh", said the manager, "Who?"

"The person who sold you a thousand boxes of this candy." Harry said.

WORDS AND EXPRESSIONS

1. **generic**: *adj.* to describe something that refers or relates to a whole class of similar things 通用的
   —Parmesan is a generic term used to describe a family of hard Italian cheeses.
   巴尔马干酪是一个用来描述一类坚硬的意大利奶酪的通用名称。
2. **homogeneous**: *adj.* consisting of things or people that are all the same or all of the same type 由相同（或同类型）事物（或人）组成的；同种类的
   —Not only is America's market the largest, but that market is homogeneous: a firm that works in one state can probably work in any other.
   美国市场不仅全球最大，而且市场同质性最高：在美国其中一州经营成功的企业，几乎可以转战任何其他州。
3. **heterogeneous**: *adj.* consisting of elements that are not of the same kind or nature 异质的
   —In the real world of human action, virtually all historical events are unique and heterogeneous, though often similar, to all other historical events.
   在人行动的真实世界里，尽管历史事件常常很相似，但其实每一个事件都独一无二，它们是异质的。
4. **substantial**: *adj.* fairly large, having substance or capable of

being treated as fact; not imaginary 大量的；实质的
—This sounds promising, but as far as we know, substantial investigation of the applicable rules has yet to be done.
这听起来十分有前途，但是据我所知，人们对可应用的规则已经进行了大量的研究。

5. **aerobics**: *n.* exercise that increases the need for oxygen 有氧运动
—I'd like to join an aerobics class to improve my fitness.
我想进一个有氧运动班来增强我的体质。

6. **perceptual**: *adj.* relating to the way people interpret and understand what they see or notice 感知的，理解的
—Some children have more finely trained perceptual skills than others.
一些孩子比其他孩子具备更为训练有素的感知技能。

7. **premature**: adj. too soon or too hasty 过早的
—We think this kind of variability must have something to do with premature aging.
我们认为，这种发病年龄的差异一定与过早老化有关。

8. **reposition**: *v.* to reposition something such as a product or service means to try to interest more or different people in it, for example by changing certain things about it or the way it is marketed 重新定位（如产品或服务）
—Mazda needs to reposition itself to boost its sales and reputation.
要想提升销量和名声，马自达公司需要对自己重新定位。

EXERCISES

1. Multiple choices

(1) The main difference between a generic market and a product-market is that ___.
A. a generic market involves a less similar set of needs than does a product-market
B. a product-market is usually larger than a generic market
C. product-markets usually don't involve competition, but generic markets do
D. sellers in a generic market are more concerned with prices than sellers in a product-market

(2) A "product-market" is a market in which ___.
A. all sellers offer exactly the same product
B. one firm has achieved a competitive advantage
C. all sellers offer products that are unique and innovative
D. sellers offer very close substitute ways of satisfying potential customer's needs

(3) Market segmentation ___.
A. means the same thing as marketing strategy planning
B. assumes that most submarkets can be satisfied by the same marketing mix
C. is the same thing as positioning
D. tries to identify homogeneous submarkets within a product-market

(4) Saying that a "good" product-market segment should be substantial means ___.
A. that the company does not have to worry about substantial competition for a long time
B. that people should have substantially different reactions to marketing mix variables
C. it should be large enough to be profitable
D. that people in different market segments should be as different as possible

(5) Segmenting and combining are two alternate approaches to developing market-oriented strategies. Which of the following statements concerning these approaches is true?
A. Combiners treat each submarket as a separate target market.
B. Segmenters try to develop a marketing mix that will have general appeal to several market segments.
C. A combiner looks at various submarkets for similarities rather than differences.
D. A segmenter assumes that the whole market consists of a fairly homogeneous group of customers.

2. Terms translation

(1) market segmentation	(2) submarket	(3) positioning	(4) CRM
(5) product market	(6) differentiation	(7) positioning statement	(8) generic market
(9) combiner	(10) brand familiarity		

3. True or false

(1) The main difference between a "product-market" and a "generic market" is whether customer needs are similar or different. ______

(2) Marketing segmentation says that target marketers would develop one good marketing mix aimed at a fairly large market. ______

(3) The correct number of submarkets in a broad product-market is usually obvious, so the likelihood of managerial error is small. ______

(4) Market segmentation applies only to consumer goods and services; it cannot be applied to business products. ______

(5) The first step in segmenting international markets is to group countries that are close to each other into "common markets." ______

(6) Marketing-oriented managers see segmenting as a process of aggregating people with similar needs into a group. ______

(7) A firm's relevant market for finding opportunities should be bigger than the present product market but not so large that it could not expand and still be an important competitor. ______

(8) Ideally, segmenters should start with the idea that each person is "one of a kind" and can be described by a special set of dimensions that may be used to aggregate customers together. ______

(9) With the "multiple target market approach" the marketer combines two or more homogeneous submarkets into one larger market as a basis for one strategy. ______

(10) Firms that operate on the Internet are at a disadvantage when it comes to using approaches like CRM. ______

4. Fill in the blanks

(1) Effective market segmentation is a two-step process that starts with naming broad product-market and then goes on to segmenting these broad product-market into more homogeneous __________.

(2) "Good" market segments should be homogeneous (similar) within, __________ (different) between, substantial, and operational.

(3) __________ technique can be used in segmenting to help find similar patterns within sets of data—to identify homogeneous groups of people.

(4) __________ aim at one or more homogeneous segments and try to develop a different marketing mix for each segment.

(5) A __________ market is a market with broadly similar needs and sellers offering various—and often diverse—ways of satisfying those needs.

(6) __________ is the process of naming broad product-markets and then segmenting these broad product-market in order to select target markets and develop suitable marketing mixes.

(7) Market segmentation is a two-step process of (a)__________ broad product-markets and (b)__________ these broad product-markets in order to select target markets and develop suitable marketing mixes.

(8) __________ segmenting dimensions help decide whether a person might be a potential customer—but not which specific products or brands that person might buy.

(9) __________ segmenting dimension are those which actually affect a person's purchase of a specific product type or brand in a product-market.

(10) __________ is a marketing management aid which refers to how customers think about proposed and/or present brands in a market.

5. Answer the following questions

(1) Distinguish between a generic market and a product-market.

(2) Explain what market segmentation is.

(3) How to develop market-oriented strategies in a product market?

(4) Illustrate at least five dimensions used to segment market.

(5) Explain how positioning analysis can help a marketing manager identify target market opportunities.

SUGGESTED CASES

2. Nature's Own Foods, Inc.
3. NOCO United Soccer Academy
7. Lake Pukati Lodge
10. Cousin's Ice Center
14. Schrock & Oh Design
27. Canadian Mills, Ltd.

CHAPTER 3: SEGMENTING CUSTOMERS

The marketing manager for Audiotronics Software Company is seeking new market opportunities. He is focusing on the voice recognition market and has narrowed down to three segments: the Fearful Typists, the Power Users, and the Professional Specialists. The Fearful Typists don't know much about computers—they just want a fast way to create e-mail messages, letters, and simple reports without errors. They don't need a lot of special features. They want simple instructions and a program that's easy to learn. The Power Users know a lot about computers, use them often, and want a voice recognition program with many special features. All computer programs seem easy to them—so they aren't worried about learning to use the various features. The Professional Specialists have jobs that require a lot of writing. They don't know much about computers but are willing to learn. They want special features needed for their work—but only if they aren't too hard to learn and use.

The marketing manager prepared a table summarizing the importance of each of three key needs in the three segments (see table that follows).

	Importance of Need (1 = not important; 10 = very important)		
Market Segment	Features	Easy to Use	Easy to Learn
Fearful Typists	3	8	9
Power Users	9	2	2
Professional Specialists	7	5	6

Audiotronics' sales staff conducted interviews with seven potential customers who were asked to rate how important each of these three needs were in their work. The manager prepared a spreadsheet to help him cluster (aggregate) each person into one of the segments—along with other similar people. Each person's ratings are entered in the spreadsheet, and the clustering procedure computes a similarity score that indicates how similar (a low score) or dissimilar (a high score) the person is to the typical person in each of the segments. The manager can then "aggregate" potential customers into the segment that is most similar (that is, the one with the *lowest* similarity score).

	Importance of Need (1 = not important; 10 = very important)			
Potential Customer	Features	Easy to Use	Easy to Learn	Type of Computer
A.	8	1	2	Dell laptop
B.	6	6	5	HP desktop
C.	4	9	8	Apple
D.	2	6	7	Apple
E.	5	6	5	HP desktop
F.	8	3	1	Dell laptop
G.	4	6	8	Apple

See Connect for the spreadsheet and questions needed to analyze this scenario.

4 CHAPTER FOUR

Final Consumers and Their Buying Behavior

When Sony introduced its Walkman in the late 1970s, it quickly became a popular way for music lovers to play cassette tapes with their favorite songs—anywhere they went. Competing players quickly emerged, but Sony kept its lead by improving its Walkman and then offering models for CDs when that medium came on the market.

In the late 1990s, the new MP3 format offered quality music from a digital file that played on a computer or portable player. Diamond Multimedia's Rio was the first MP3 player. The Rio was innovative, but users had to download music from virus-ridden websites such as Napster—or use special software to "rip" CDs to MP3 format. Many music buffs liked the idea of having songs at their fingertips, but getting the digital files was just too complicated. Further, music companies filed lawsuits charging some with illegally downloading MP3 music files. All of this slowed the initial adoption of MP3 players.

Attitudes quickly changed when Apple offered an innovative marketing mix that addressed these customer needs. The online iTunes store offered legal downloads of songs at a reasonable price without the risk of viruses. Apple's free iTunes software made it easy to organize digital music on a computer and transfer it to Apple's iPod. The iPod was stylish and easy to use. Apple's ads generated awareness and interest of the new concept among customers with the promise of "a thousand songs in your pocket." Even skeptics who ignored the ads couldn't help but notice the distinctive white iPod cords dangling from the ears of a friend who was "in" on this cool new product. That prompted a lot of product conversations and on-the-spot iPod demos. Testimonials on blogs, online consumer reviews, and posts on social media also helped spread the word.

Apple also reinvented the cell phone market when it introduced the iPhone. More than just a cell phone that also played music, the iPhone's colorful touchscreen display, web browsing, and music player wowed consumers. Soon iPhone owners customized their phones with software applications ("apps") from the iTunes store that let them play games such as *Angry Birds* and *Minecraft: Pocket Edition*, watch YouTube videos, or check Facebook or Snapchat on their iPhones.

These days most American consumers already own a smartphone, and growth has slowed. So Apple looks to international markets for new growth opportunities. Here it finds consumers with different needs. For example, in India, where consumers have less disposable income, Apple lowers prices and provides interest-free loans. Chinese consumers are influenced a great deal by what their friends buy. So Apple's strategy focuses on getting opinion leaders and celebrities to use the iPhone.

The iPhone's success created opportunities for other Apple products. Once someone owns an iPhone, he or she pays more attention to Apple—lingering at a store display, watching an Apple ad, or asking friends about their iPad. A positive iPhone experience raises a customer's expectations and trust in the entire Apple product line; many iPhone buyers went on to buy a Macbook, iPad, or Apple Watch, and maybe subscribed to Apple TV and Apple Music.

Apple's iPod and iTunes were innovative, but over time consumer attitudes on how to buy and listen to music changed. Many were happy just to "rent" music rather than buy and "own" a digital file. Streaming music services from Pandora and Spotify offered customers subscriptions to large music catalogs. Soon there were similar services from Google, Amazon, and Apple.

By the time Apple Music launched, consumers had more choice among streaming services. Customers with economic concerns often chose the free advertising-supported option from Spotify. Others wanted more information before deciding. While researching, they might have found that Spotify didn't carry Taylor Swift's music catalog, and that Tidal had exclusive access to some music from Kanye and Beyoncé. Decisions, decisions. More chose Spotify, which had a head start, but Apple Music made up ground to emerge as the number two player in the United States.

Looking ahead, the iPhone may be key to a big opportunity for Apple: delivering targeted advertising to customers' iPhones. In the "online ad delivery" market, Apple competes with Google, Facebook, and Amazon—each of which collects and analyzes data that predict customers' needs and interests to deliver advertising they might care about. Accurate predictions allow marketing managers to direct the right promotional messages to customers at the appropriate stage in the consumer decision process.

Making predictions requires customer data, and the iPhone knows a lot about its owner, including which apps are used and what they are used for, online searches, and the questions customers ask Siri, the iPhone's intelligent assistant. The iPhone also tracks a customer's location. All of these data can help Apple deliver targeted, timely promotion for brands. Let's look at an example.

Say Peet's Coffee & Tea wants to target loyal Starbucks customers like Mallory Moog. It wants to encourage Mallory to try Peet's in hopes that she changes her coffee habits. Apple knows Mallory uses the Starbucks app three to four mornings a week to buy a Caffé Mocha. When Mallory gets within a block of a Peet's Coffee & Tea store—and only if it's morning—Peet's sends Mallory's iPhone a text message with a coupon for 50 percent off a Peet's Caffé Mocha. The text conveniently includes a link with Apple Map directions to the nearby store.

Apple faces strong, fast-moving competition—all seeking a piece of Apple's pie. To stay ahead, it must continue to innovate in music, wearable technology, computers, phones, and advertising delivery. Success will continue to be based on its ability to anticipate customer needs and exceed customer expectations.

LEARNING OBJECTIVES

Many variables influence consumer buying behavior. As the Apple case highlights, successful marketing strategy planning requires a clear understanding of how target consumers buy—and what factors affect their decisions. The learning objectives for this chapter will help you develop that understanding.

When you finish this chapter, you should be able to

1 describe how economic needs influence the buyer decision process.

2 understand how psychological variables affect an individual's buying behavior.

3 understand how social influences affect an individual's buying behavior.

4 describe how culture and ethnicity influence consumer buying behavior.

5 explain how characteristics of the purchase situation influence consumer behavior.

6 explain the process by which consumers make buying decisions.

7 understand important new terms (shown in boldface).

Consumer Behavior: Why Do They Buy What They Buy?

The Apple case shows the in-depth customer knowledge needed for effective marketing strategy planning. Without that understanding, it would be difficult to zero in on the right target market, or to develop and adapt a marketing mix that will be the best value for customers.

Understanding consumer behavior can be a challenge. Specific behaviors vary a great deal for different people, products, and purchase situations. In today's global markets the variations are countless. That makes it impractical to catalog all the possibilities. But there are general behavioral principles—frameworks—that marketing managers can apply to better understand their specific target markets. In this chapter our approach focuses on developing your skill in working with these frameworks by exploring thinking from economics, psychology, sociology, and other behavioral disciplines. We'll take a look at the topics overviewed in Exhibit 4-1, which includes a simplified model of consumer behavior.

We will begin with a discussion of influences on the consumer decision process: economic needs, psychological variables, social influences, culture/ethnicity, and the purchase situation. Exhibit 4-2 provides an expanded look at these influences. Following our discussion of these different categories of influences, we will look more closely at the consumer decision process.

Exhibit 4-1 Consumer Behavior for Marketing Strategy Planning

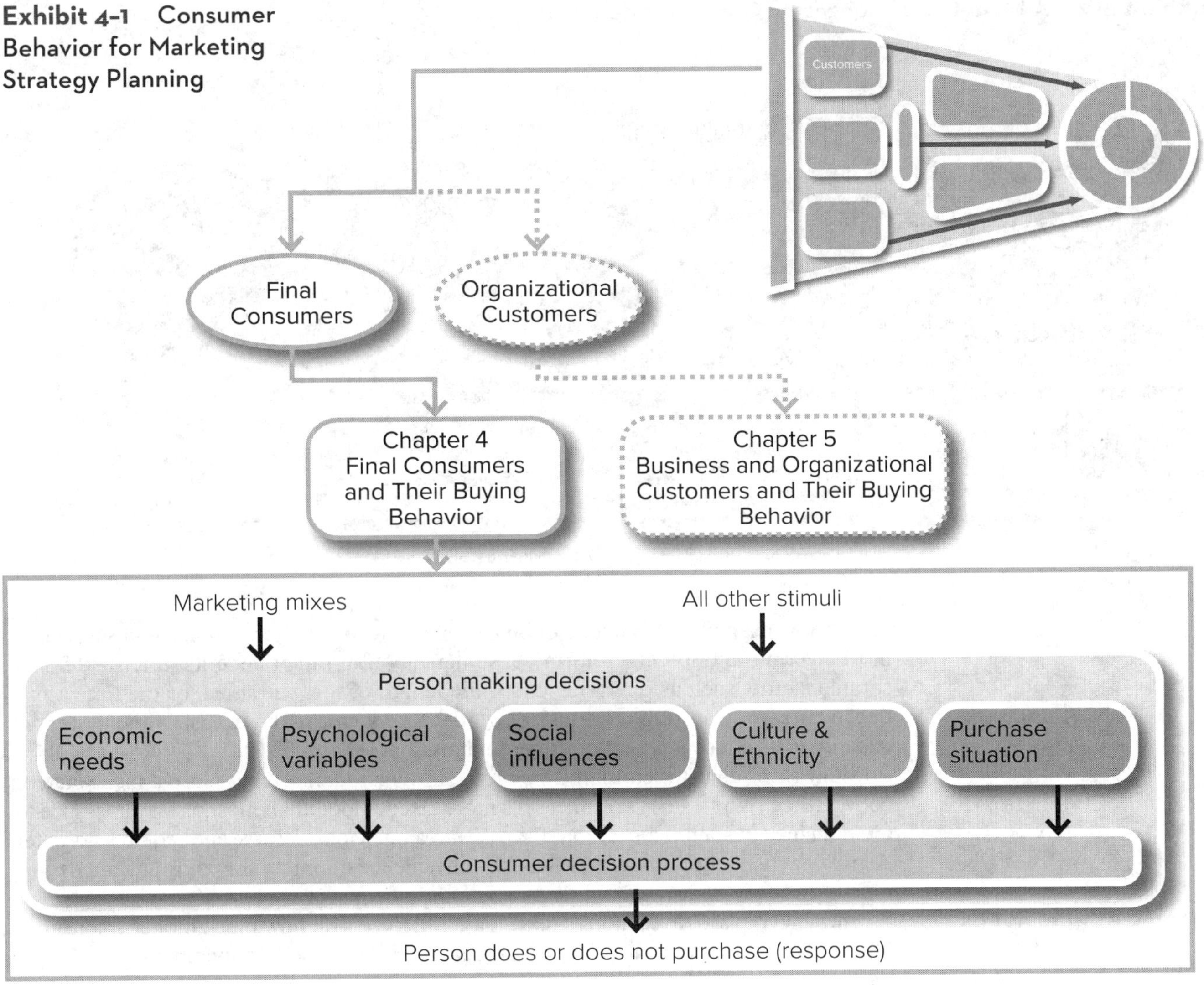

Economic Needs Affect Most Buying Decisions

Economic buyers seek the best uses of time and money

Most economists assume that consumers are **economic buyers**—people who know all the facts and logically compare choices to get the greatest satisfaction from spending their time and money. The economic-buyer theory says that consumers decide what to buy based on **economic needs**, which are concerned with making the best use of a consumer's time and money—as the consumer judges it. Some consumers look for the lowest price. Others will pay extra for convenience. And others may weigh price and quality for the best value. Some economic needs include:

1. Economy of purchase or use (buying a less expensive store brand of frozen pizza)
2. Efficiency in operation or use (a Miele vacuum cleaner's power makes for faster cleanup)
3. Dependability in use (Toyotas have lower repair costs over the years)
4. Improvement of earnings (Ally Bank offers a better interest rate)
5. Convenience (a drive-through lane at a Starbucks makes it convenient to pick up coffee on the way to work in the morning)

Clearly, marketing managers must be alert to new ways to appeal to economic needs. Most consumers appreciate firms that offer them improved economic value for the money they spend. But improved value does not just mean offering lower and lower

Exhibit 4-2 A Model of Influences on Consumer Behavior

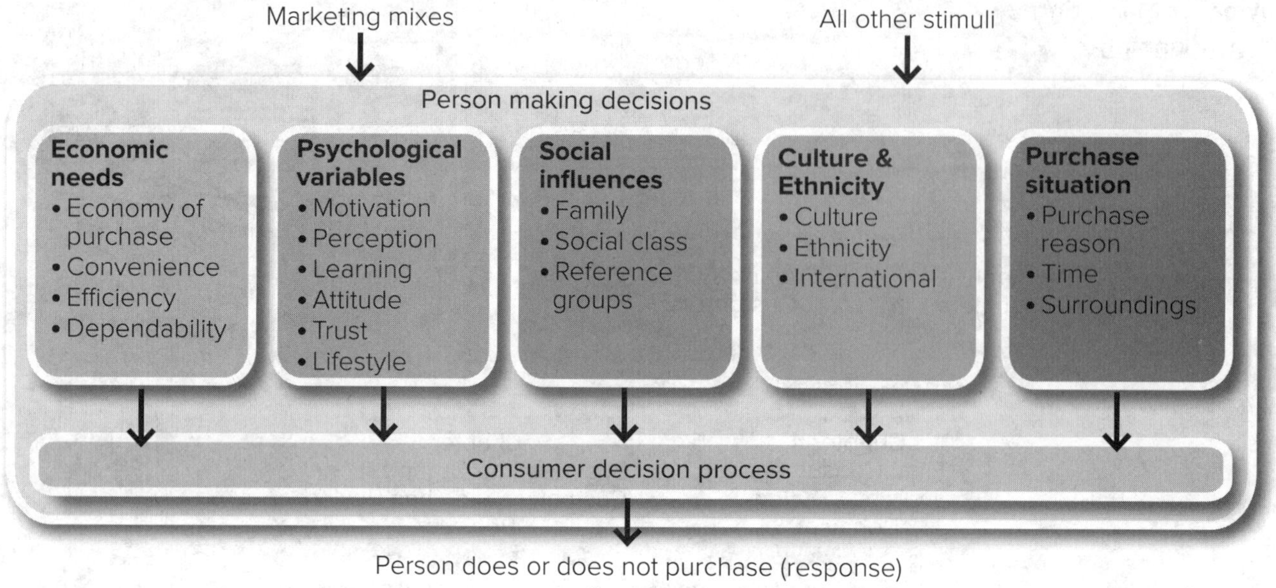

prices. For example, products can be designed to work better, require less service, or last longer. Promotion can inform consumers about product benefits in terms of measurable factors such as operating costs, the length of the guarantee, or the time a product will save. Carefully planned Place decisions can make it easier and faster for customers who face a poverty of time to make a purchase.

Many firms adjust their marketing mixes for target markets that place a high value on convenience. Whole Foods Market sells more takeout food than most restaurants. Tide-to-Go is an instant stain remover that fits easily in a purse or briefcase and requires no water. A growing number of consumers like the convenience of online shopping at Zappos.

Income affects needs

The ability to satisfy economic needs largely depends on how much money a consumer has available–which in turn depends a great deal on household income. In the United

Economic needs affect many buying decisions. GEICO knows that some customers are looking for low rates when shopping for car insurance. Dependability is another economic need that car shoppers seek out. Chevrolet wants its target market to know that its Malibu won awards for initial quality and long-term dependability.
Left: All text and images are copywritten with permission from GEICO. Right: Source: General Motors Company, Chevrolet

States, income distribution varies widely. In 2015, 22 percent of households reported an income of less than $25,000, and the median income—where half the households earned more and half earned less—was $56,516. After taking account of inflation, the median income has been flat over the last decade and is about 2.5 percent less than its peak in 1999. During this same period, America's middle-income consumers have been hit hard by the rising costs of necessities.

In most households, people don't have enough income to buy everything they want. For many products, these people can't be customers even if they want to be. For example, most families spend a good portion of their income on such necessities as food, rent or house payments, home furnishings, transportation, and insurance. A family's purchase of "luxuries" comes from **discretionary[1] income**—what is left of income after paying taxes and paying for necessities.

Discretionary income is an elusive[2] concept because the definition of necessities varies from family to family and over time. It depends on what they think is necessary for their lifestyle. High-speed Internet service purchased out of discretionary income by a lower-income family may be considered a necessity by a higher-income family.

Consumer confidence affects spending

Economic conditions affect consumer confidence and spending. In a strong economy, consumers feel confident and secure in their jobs, so they are more likely to borrow money to buy a larger house, a new car, or vacation in an exotic locale. On the other hand, when consumers worry about job prospects or their retirement savings decline, they are more cautious spenders.

Economic value and income are important factors in many purchase decisions. But most marketing managers think that buyer behavior is not as simple as the economic-buyer model suggests. Consumer confidence shows how economic factors are related to psychological influences. So let's look more closely at the psychological variables that influence buying behavior (see Exhibit 4-2).

Psychological Influences within an Individual

Needs motivate consumers

Everybody is motivated by needs and wants. **Needs** are the basic forces that motivate a person to do something. Some needs involve a person's physical well-being; others the individual's self-view and relationship with others. Needs are more basic than wants. **Wants** are "needs" that are learned during a person's life. For example, everyone needs water or some kind of liquid, but some people also have learned to want Clearly Canadian's raspberry-flavored sparkling water.

Whether a product is a want or a need depends on what a consumer has learned during his or her life.
Source: Nissan Motor Company

When a need is not satisfied, it may lead to a drive. The need for liquid, for example, leads to a thirst drive. A **drive** is a strong stimulus[3] that encourages action to reduce a need. Drives are internal—they are the reasons behind certain behavior patterns. In marketing, a product purchase results from a drive to satisfy some need.

Some critics imply that marketers can somehow manipulate[4] consumers to buy products against their will. But trying to get consumers to act against their will is a waste of time. Instead, a good marketing manager studies what consumer drives, needs, and wants already exist and how they can be satisfied better.

Consumers seek benefits to meet needs

We're all a bundle of needs and wants. Exhibit 4-3 lists some important needs that might motivate a person to some action. This list, of course, is not complete. But thinking about such needs can help you see what *benefits* consumers might seek from a marketing mix.

When a marketing manager defines a product-market, the needs may be quite specific. For example, the food need might be as specific as wanting a Domino's thick-crust pepperoni pizza—delivered to your door hot and ready to eat.

Marketing managers appeal to customer needs

Consumer psychologists often argue that a person may have several reasons for buying—sometimes at the same time. Maslow is well known for his five-level hierarchy of needs. We will discuss a similar four-level hierarchy that is easier to apply to consumer behavior. Exhibit 4-4 illustrates the four levels along with an example showing how a company has tried to appeal to each need. Generally, lower-level needs must be addressed before consumers seek to satisfy the higher-level needs. The lowest-level needs are physiological, then come safety, social, and personal needs (PSSP).

Physiological needs are concerned with biological needs—food, liquid, rest, and sex. Marketers that offer *solutions* to consumer problems build brand loyalty. Charmin addressed such a need for holiday shoppers in New York City. Because it can be difficult to find a public restroom—and coffee shops don't like it when noncustomers use their facilities—Charmin's "holiday gift to the City" was luxury public restrooms located in Times Square. Many users will remember Charmin's gift the next time they buy toilet tissue.

Safety needs are concerned with protection and physical well-being (perhaps involving health, financial security, medicine, and exercise). Under Armour's wide range of fitness products promote health and exercise. Northwestern Mutual Life offers life insurance and financial planning for those seeking financial security.

Social needs are concerned with love, friendship, status, and esteem—things that involve a person's interaction with others. Marketers that help people *connect* with others inspire positive feelings about their own brands. Coca-Cola addressed this need with a series of viral videos around the theme of delivering happiness. One featured a bright red Coca-Cola truck that stopped on streets in Brazil. A sign on the back of the truck told consumers to "Push" a large button. When they did, the truck dispensed happiness in the form of Cokes and fun items such as T-shirts, soccer balls, and even a surfboard. The truck created on-the-street social connections. The fun video created more social connection when viewers forwarded a link to friends and family.

Personal needs, on the other hand, are concerned with an individual's need for personal satisfaction—unrelated to what others think or do. Examples include accomplishment,

Exhibit 4-3 Possible Needs Motivating a Person to Some Action

Types of Needs	Specific Examples			
Physiological needs	Food Sex	Rest Liquid	Activity Self-preservation	Sleep Warmth/coolness
Psychological needs	Nurturing Playing/relaxing Self-identification	Curiosity Order Power	Independence Personal fulfillment Pride	Love Playing/competition Self-expression
Desire for . . .	A better world Acceptance Affiliation[5] Esteem Knowledge	Respect Status Achievement Appreciation Sympathy	Beauty Happiness Self-satisfaction Variety Affection	Companionship Distinctiveness Recognition Sociability Fun
Freedom from . . .	Fear Pain	Depression Stress	Loss Sadness	Anxiety Illness

Exhibit 4-4 The PSSP Hierarchy of Needs

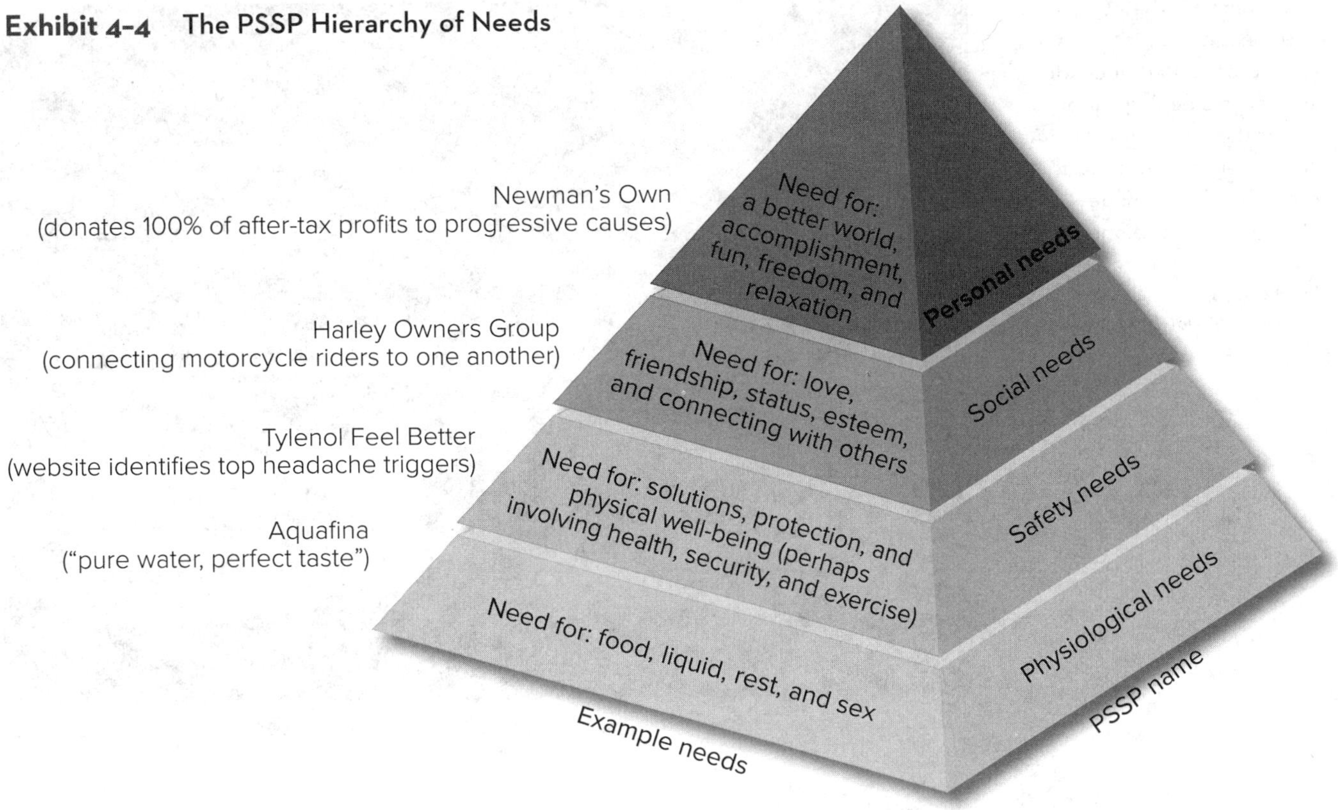

fun, freedom, and relaxation—as well as a desire to make the world a better place. Many people want to make food choices that enable them to achieve a healthier balance in their lives. So ConAgra Foods (maker of healthy foods such as SmartPop! Popcorn and Egg Beaters) developed an online tool to help. Members complete a survey at "Start Making Choices" and then receive feedback and advice on nutrition, activity, and well-being based on a calculated "Balanced Life Index." Weekly contact between the company and its customers keeps the relationship alive.

Often marketing managers try to address multiple needs. Consider the California Milk Processing Board (creators of the infamous "Got Milk?" campaign) and its online game *Get the Glass*. The game appealed to kids—the group that needs milk the most. Besides being fun (personal needs), it educated players on why milk is important (safety needs). It could be played with family—or forwarded to friends (social needs). Of course drinking milk addresses thirst (physiological needs) and promotes strong bones (safety needs). In the online game's first two months, more than 6 million people visited the site, with 650,000 reaching the Glass at Fort Fridge. The game was credited with helping boost sales of milk by more than 10 million gallons compared to the same period a year earlier.

Perception determines what consumers see and feel

Consumers select varying ways to meet their needs sometimes because of differences in **perception**—how we gather and interpret information from the world around us.

We are constantly bombarded by marketing stimuli—ads, products, signs, stores—yet we notice only a small number of these. This is because we apply the following selective processes:

1. **Selective exposure**—our eyes and minds seek out and notice only information that interests us. This often relates to current needs. So when we are hungry, we notice signs for restaurants; when we are looking for a new sports car, we notice ads for sports cars.
2. **Selective perception**—we screen out or modify ideas, messages, and information that conflict with previously learned attitudes and beliefs. So if we believe that Apple products are cool, we ignore ads by Samsung that suggest Apple is uncool.
3. **Selective retention**—we remember only what we want to remember. Even when we notice stimuli in the market, we may not place it in memory if we don't believe it or

The Consumer Safety Institute in the Netherlands wants to remind parents that children see those cleaning supplies under the sink differently. As consumers approached this outdoor ad, the image changed from the one on the left to the one on the right (and back).
Source: eiligheidNL; Agency: Lemz/ Netherlands

The ad shows two different images when viewed from different angles (lenticular effect).

don't feel that information will be useful to us. If we read an article about Panera Bread (restaurant) removing artificial ingredients from its food, but we don't eat at Panera, then we won't commit this new information to memory.

Recognizing that consumers use these selective processes, marketing managers try to engage with customers when they are likely to be open to their messages. So Mazda advertises its sports car on websites such as Edmunds.com where consumers research cars. A marketing manager for Dreyer's brand ice cream sends a $1.00 off coupon[6] to a customer's smartphone just as they walk into their local grocery store.

Learning determines what response is likely

Learning is a change in a person's thought processes caused by prior experience. Learning is often based on direct experience: A little girl tastes her first cone of Ben & Jerry's Cherry Garcia flavor ice cream, and learning occurs! Learning may also be based on indirect experience or associations. If you watch an ad that shows other people enjoying Ben & Jerry's Chocolate Fudge Brownie low-fat frozen yogurt, you might conclude that you'd like it too.

Consumer learning may result from things that marketers do, or it may result from stimuli that have nothing to do with marketing. Either way, almost all consumer behavior is learned.

Exhibit 4-5 The Learning Process

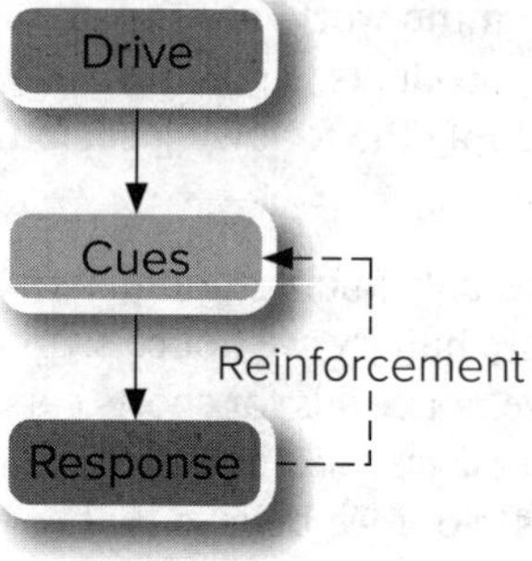

Experts describe a number of steps in the learning process. We've already discussed the idea of a drive as a strong stimulus that encourages action. Depending on the **cues**[7]—products, signs, ads, and other stimuli in the environment—an individual chooses some specific response. A **response** is an effort to satisfy a drive. The specific response chosen depends on the cues and the person's past experience.

Reinforcement of the learning process occurs when the response is followed by satisfaction—that is, reduction in the drive. Reinforcement strengthens the relationship between the cue and the response. And it may lead to a similar response the next time the drive occurs. Repeated reinforcement leads to development of a habit—making the individual's decision process routine. Exhibit 4-5 shows the relationships of the important variables in the learning process.

Sales take off after Febreze learns a lesson

Marketing managers for Febreze used the learning process to develop a best-selling product, but first they had to get the drive, cue, response, and reinforcement just right. Febreze contains a chemical very effective at eliminating odors–spray it on clothing, furniture, or carpet and smells magically disappear. Febreze's marketing managers figured that most consumers desired a home free of offensive odors (drive), so the first television ads for Febreze focused on smells around the house. For example, one showed a dog on a couch and a woman saying, "Sophie will always smell like Sophie, but now my couch doesn't have to" (cue). In the ad, the woman sprays Febreze on the couch (response) and the dog smell disappears (reinforcement).

In spite of an aggressive advertising campaign, Febreze sold poorly when it was initially launched. To learn why, marketing researchers interviewed customers in their homes. They discovered two problems. First, many people living in the smelliest homes simply didn't realize their homes smelled at all. They had become desensitized to the smells of their pets, cigarette smoke, or other odors, so for them, the desired cue didn't exist. Second, what Febreze provided–lack of a smell–didn't provide positive reinforcement for the customer.

So Febreze's marketing managers went back to the drawing board. They interviewed more customers and reviewed video tape of people cleaning their homes. They identified another market, people who wanted a clean house (drive). When they saw a messy home (cue), they cleaned the house (response) and finished by rewarding themselves with something relaxing or happy–maybe just a smile (reinforcement). Here marketing managers realized that a scented version of Febreze might provide positive reinforcement–something that could signal the cleaning job was done. So Febreze added scents and new advertising that showed homemakers spraying a room with Febreze after cleaning (reinforcement). Sales took off; now Febreze sells more than $1 billion a year. And Febreze's marketing managers learned a valuable lesson.

Many needs are culturally learned

Many needs are culturally (or socially) learned. The need for food, for instance, may lead to many specific food wants. Many Japanese enjoy sushi (raw fish), and their children learn to like it. Fewer Americans, however, have learned to enjoy it.

Ethics question: do consumers learn needs from marketing?

Some critics argue that marketing efforts encourage people to spend money on learned wants totally unrelated to any basic need. Consumer needs are internal, but advertising can make consumers aware of their needs–and suggest a way to satisfy these needs. For example, a customer may have thirst as a basic need; advertising helps him become aware of Simply Lemonade brand as a tasty way to satisfy his need. The next time he is thirsty, he may want Simply Lemonade. So advertising does not create needs–but it can make consumers more aware of an existing need and create a want for a specific product.

Attitudes relate to buying

An **attitude** is a person's point of view toward something. The "something" may be a product, an advertisement, a salesperson, a firm, or an idea. Attitudes are an important topic because they affect the selective processes, learning, and the buying decisions.

Because attitudes are usually thought of as involving liking or disliking, they have some action implications. Beliefs are not so action-oriented. A **belief** is a person's opinion about something. Beliefs may help shape a consumer's attitudes but don't necessarily involve any liking or disliking. It is possible to have a belief–say, that Listerine PocketPak strips have a medicinal taste–without really caring what they taste like. On the other hand, beliefs about a product may have a positive or negative effect in shaping consumers' attitudes. For example, promotion for Splenda, a no-calorie sweetener in a yellow packet, informs consumers that it's "made from sugar so it tastes like sugar." A dieter who believes that Splenda will taste better because it is made from sugar might try it instead of just routinely rebuying another brand, like Equal. On the other hand, a person with diabetes might believe that he should avoid Splenda–like he avoids other products made from sugar–even though Splenda is actually suitable for people with diabetes.

Consumer attitudes can affect their purchasing (and donating) behavior. The World Wildlife Fund knows consumers have more favorable attitudes toward panda bears as compared to bluefin tuna—but both species are endangered and need support.
Source: World Wildlife Fund

In an attempt to relate attitude more closely to purchase behavior, some marketers stretch the attitude concept to include consumer "preferences" or "intention to buy." Managers who must forecast how much of their brand customers will buy are particularly interested in the intention to buy. Forecasts would be easier if attitudes were good predictors of intentions to buy. Unfortunately, the relationships usually are not that simple. A person may have a positive attitude toward hot tubs, but have no intention to buy one.

"Green" attitudes and beliefs change marketing mixes

A growing number of consumers believe that making "greener" purchases has a positive effect on the environment. Marketing managers have responded by developing marketing mixes to address these ecological interests. Subway sandwich shops have added recycling bins. GM and Nissan introduced all-electric cars. Malt-O-Meal breakfast cereals, a low-cost brand that has always been packaged in bags, touted the environmental benefits of this packaging. Its "Bag the Box" campaign garnered publicity on a small budget. Many consumers have positive attitudes toward brands that try to make a difference in this area.

Follow changing attitudes

Customers are beginning to change attitudes about ownership. Whether driven by environmental concerns or economic factors, many consumers are *sharing* instead of *owning*. Read more about how that is changing the automobile market in *What's Next?* Will sharing replace owning?

It is not easy to change existing consumer attitudes

As those offering new services, like car sharing, have discovered, it's not easy to change customer attitudes. That challenge does not keep some companies from trying. Many American consumers have negative attitudes toward frozen (as compared to fresh) vegetables. B&G Foods bought the Green Giant brand of frozen vegetables with hopes of changing those attitudes. B&G plans a significant advertising campaign to support the brand and turn around a decade-long decline in sales.

Ethical issues may arise

Part of the marketing job is to inform and persuade consumers about a firm's offering. An ethical issue sometimes arises, however, if consumers have *inaccurate* beliefs. For example, promotion of a "children's cold formula" may play off parents' fears that adult medicines are too strong—even though the basic ingredients in the children's formula are the same and only the dosage is different.

What's Next? Will sharing replace owning?

In much of the United States and Europe customers have long viewed car *ownership* as a necessity. That is starting to change with evolving needs, attitudes, and lifestyles. Whether seeking a simpler life, a desire to save the planet, or just plain economics, many consumers are becoming more comfortable with car *sharing*.

There is an economic case for turning in the keys. Monthly payments, insurance, parking, gas, depreciation, and maintenance add up to an average of $8,000 per year for car owners. Let's look at a few new ways customers are getting around in cars without owning one.

Car-sharing services like Zipcar are growing fast. Signing up for Zipcar is simple: Customers hop online, fill out an application, and pay a $25 one-time application fee. Applicants with a good driving record receive a Zipcard in the mail a few days later. Renting a car is even easier. A member (called a Zipster) logs on to Zipcar's website, searches for cars in his or her area, and makes a reservation. Cars are typically parked on a street, gas station, or parking lot, making them easy to locate. At the reserved time, a Zipster unlocks the car with a wave of a smartphone (equipped of course with the Zipcar app) and drives off, returning the car to the same general area when done.

Another approach lets individual car owners share their vehicles (and earn a few bucks) through a *peer-to-peer* network. Car (or truck) owners can list a vehicle at Turo.com by posting photos and a brief description. They also set daily and weekly rental rates. Prescreened renters search the site, click on a car, and wait to hear if it's available from the owner. Turo takes a cut and provides insurance coverage. The company facilitates hundreds of thousands of transactions a year. Car owners can earn $4,000 or more a year.

Some non-car owners are *ridesharing*. Although carpooling has been around a long time, ridesharing uses the Internet to connect riders with drivers going on the same route at the same time. Frédéric Mazzella, founder of BlaBlaCar (more on the name in a moment), came up with the idea on a holiday trip to see his family. Mazzella noticed that most of the cars on the road contained only the driver. He thought there had to be a way to fill some of those empty seats.

BlaBlaCar members create a brief profile with a photo and an indication of how much they like to talk—a single "Bla" means not very chatty, "BlaBla" people are talkative, and "BlaBlaBlas" can't shut up. Drivers post where they are going, when, and how much a customer needs to "chip in" on expenses (usually a fraction of the cost of a corresponding rail or bus ticket). Passengers search for rides, and drivers have a choice about whom they carry. After the ride, drivers and passengers rate each other to help future riders make better choices.

Consumers' attitudes on sharing have been changing. Recorded music has largely moved from owning physical goods—records, tapes, and CDs—to renting music from streaming services like Spotify and Apple Music. Others share a bedroom or their entire home on services such as Airbnb and VRBO.

Identify other product-markets where consumers are sharing, borrowing, or renting instead of owning. What product-markets do you think might see a shift from ownership to sharing? Why?

Marketers must also be careful about promotion that might encourage false beliefs, even if the advertising is not explicitly misleading. For example, ads for Ultra Slim-Fast low-fat beverage don't claim that anyone who buys the product will lose weight and look like the slim models who appear in the ads—but some critics argue that the advertising gives that impression.

Meeting expectations is important

Attitudes and beliefs sometimes combine to form an **expectation**—an outcome or event that a person anticipates or looks forward to. Consumer expectations often focus on the benefits or value that the consumer expects from a firm's marketing mix. This is an important issue for marketers because a consumer is likely to be dissatisfied if his or her expectations are not met. Promotion that overpromises can create this problem. Finding the right balance, however, can be difficult. A few years ago Van Heusen came up with a new way to treat its wash-and-wear shirts so that they look better when they come out of the wash. Van Heusen promoted these shirts as "wrinkle-free." The new shirt was an improvement, but consumers who expect it to look as if it had been ironed were disappointed.

Ethical Dilemma

What would you do? You are a marketing assistant for Auntie Em's Cookie Company, which makes and distributes packaged cookies through grocery stores. Your company recently ran a test market for a new brand of low-fat cookies called Tastee DeeLites. The new brand meets government standards to be labeled and advertised as "low fat," so the ads and package used in the test market highlighted that benefit. Test-market sales were very promising. However, now a consumer activist group has created a website (www.TasteeDeeLIES.com) that claims Tastee DeeLites package and ads are misleading because the product's high calories make it even more fattening than most other cookies. Your boss has asked you to recommend how Auntie Em's should handle this situation.

Drawing on what you've learned about consumer behavior, do you think consumers are being misled? Does your company have any responsibility to respond to these charges? Should changes be made to the product, package, or promotion?

Building trust builds sales

Trust is the confidence a person has in the promises or actions of another person, brand, or company. Trust drives expectations because when people trust, they *expect* the other party to fulfill promises or perform capably.

Customers may come to trust through experience with a company or person. For example, if your dog always happily chows down Purina dog food—and remains healthy and active—you might come to trust the Purina brand. A customer might trust a travel agent who previously planned enjoyable vacations for her family. Trust can also relate to recommenders—for example, many consumers trust *Consumer Reports* magazine and put a lot of stock in its product reviews and ratings.

Morton knows that consumers have positive attitudes toward trusted brands. Because the Morton brand is trusted, customers are more likely to try its new Safe-T-Plus and other products to melt icy sidewalks and driveways. This ad is directed at retailers, encouraging them to order the new product.
Source: Morton Salt, Inc.

Highly trusted people, brands, and companies have many advantages in the marketplace. Consumers prefer to buy from and are more loyal to brands they trust. Trusted brands are less susceptible to price-based competition. For example, few people would switch from a trusted hair stylist just to save a few dollars.

Trust takes time to build, but it can be destroyed quickly. Consider what happened to Samsung when some of its Galaxy Note 7 smartphones started catching on fire. Customers were justifiably worried. While Samsung quickly recalled the bad phones, many consumers lost faith in a brand they previously trusted. Trust can be fragile and companies must work to maintain customer trust that has been built—sometimes over many decades.

Psychographics focus on activities, interests, and opinions

Psychographics or **lifestyle analysis** is the analysis of a person's day-to-day pattern of living as expressed in that person's *A*ctivities, *I*nterests, and *O*pinions—sometimes referred to as *AIOs.* Exhibit 4-6 shows a number of variables for each of the AIO dimensions—along with some demographics used to add detail to the lifestyle profile of a target market.

Understanding the lifestyle of target customers has been especially helpful in providing ideas for advertising themes. Let's see how it adds to a typical demographic

Exhibit 4-6 Lifestyle Dimensions (and Some Related Demographic Dimensions)

Dimension	Examples		
Activities	Work Hobbies Social events	Vacation Entertainment Club membership	Surfing web Shopping Sports
Interests	Family Home Job	Community Recreation Fashion	Food Media Achievements
Opinions	Themselves Social issues Politics	Business Economics Education	Products Future Culture
Demographics	Income Age Family life cycle	Geographic area Ethnicity Dwelling	Occupation Family size Education

description. It may not help Dodge marketing managers much to know that an average member of the target market for a Dodge Dart is 34.8 years old, married, lives in a three-bedroom home, and has 2.3 children. Lifestyles help marketers paint a more human portrait of the target market. For example, lifestyle analysis might show that the 34.8-year-old is also a community-oriented consumer with traditional values who especially enjoys spectator sports and spends a lot of time in other family activities. An ad might show the Veracruz being used by a happy family at a ball game so the target market could really identify with the ad. And the ad might be placed on an ESPN show whose viewers match the target lifestyle profile.

Social Influences Affect Consumer Behavior

We've been discussing some of the ways needs, attitudes, and other psychological variables influence the buying process. Now we'll look at how a consumer's family, social class, and reference groups influence the consumer decision process.

Family life cycle influences needs

Relationships with other family members influence many aspects of consumer behavior. Family members may share many attitudes and values, consider one another's opinions, and divide various buying tasks. Marital status, age, and the age of any children in the family have an especially important effect on how people spend their income. Put together, these dimensions tell us about the life-cycle stage of a family. Exhibit 4-7 shows a summary of stages in the family life cycle. Let's take a closer look at how a few of these stages influence buying behavior.

Schwan's home delivery of food products and complete meals appeals to dual-career families and professionals who place a high value on their time.
Source: Schwan's Home Service, Inc.

Exhibit 4-7 Stages in Modern Family Life Cycles

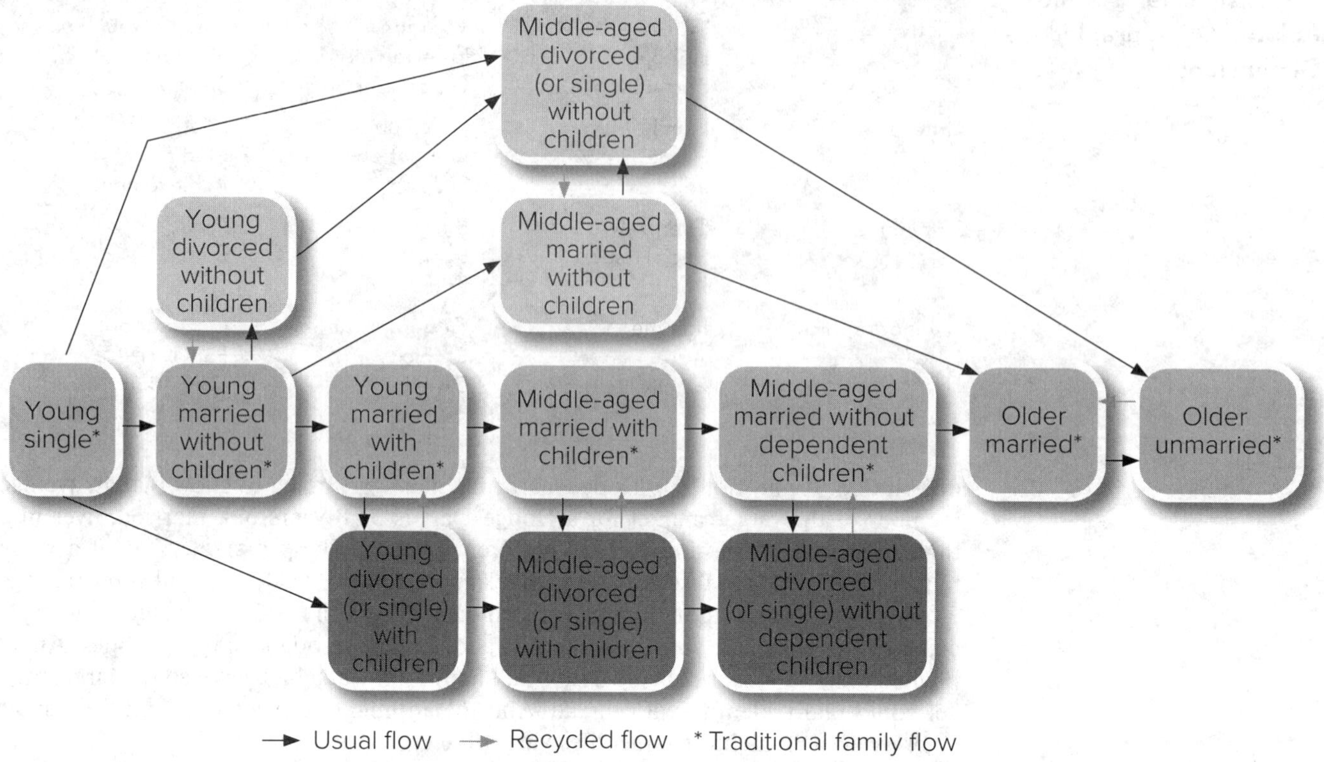

Young people and families accept new ideas

Singles and young couples seem to be more willing to try new products and brands—and they are careful, price-conscious shoppers. Although many young people are waiting longer to marry, most tie the knot eventually. These younger families—especially those with no children—are still accumulating durable goods, such as automobiles and home furnishings. Only as children arrive and grow does family spending shift to soft goods and services, such as education, medical, and personal care. To meet expenses, people in this age group often make more purchases on credit, and they save less of their income.

Divorce—increasingly a fact of American life—disrupts the traditional family life-cycle pattern. The mother usually has custody of the children, and the father may pay child support. The mother and children typically have much less income than two-parent families. Such families spend a larger portion of their income on housing, child care, and other necessities, leaving little for discretionary purchases. If a single parent remarries, the family life cycle may start over again.

Reallocation for teenagers

Once children become teenagers, further shifts in spending occur. Teenagers eat more, want to wear expensive clothes, like music, and develop recreation and education needs that are hard on the family budget. American teens currently spend almost $200 billion a year. They are a target for many firms; Bausch & Lomb's contact-lens sales hit record levels when the firm refocused its marketing efforts on teens.

Selling to the empty nesters

Another important category is the **empty nesters**—people whose children are grown and who are now able to spend their money in other ways. This tends to be a high-income period, especially for white-collar workers. Empty nesters are an attractive market for many items. Often they spend more on travel and other things they couldn't afford earlier in life. Much depends on their income, of course.

Who is the real decision maker in family purchases?

In years past, most marketers in the United States targeted the wife as the family purchasing agent. Now, with sex-role stereotypes changed and with night and weekend shopping more popular, men and older children take more responsibility for shopping and decision making. Family roles vary from one culture to another.

Buying responsibility and influence vary greatly depending on the product and the family. Although often only one family member goes to the store for a specific purchase, other family members may influence the decision or really decide what to buy. Still others may use the product.

It is estimated that teenagers make or directly influence more than $200 billion in spending in the United States. Tyson recognizes this fact and appeals to parents who have heard their teens cry, "I'm still hungry."
Source: Tyson Foods, Inc.

Social class affects attitudes, values, and buying

Up to now, we've been concerned with individuals and their family relationships. Now let's consider how society looks at an individual and perhaps the family—in terms of social class. A **social class** is a group of people who have approximately equal social position as viewed by others in the society.

Almost every society has some social class structure. In most countries, social class is closely related to a person's occupation, but it may also be influenced by education, community participation, where a person lives, income, possessions, social skills, and other factors—including what family a person is born into.

In most countries—including the United States—there is *some* general relationship between income level and social class. But people with the same income level may be in different social classes. So income by itself is usually not a good measure of social class. And people in different social classes may spend, save, and borrow money in very different ways.

The U.S. class system is far less rigid than those in most countries. Children start out in the same social class as their parents—but they can move to a different social class depending on their education and job. By contrast, India's social structure is much more rigid, and individuals can't easily move up in the class system.

Marketers want to know what buyers in various social classes are like. In the United States, simple approaches for measuring social class groupings are based on a person's *occupation, education,* and *type and location of housing.* By using marketing research surveys or available census data, marketers can get a feel for the social class of a target market.

What do these classes mean?

Although many people think of America as a middle-class society, studies suggest that in many marketing situations distinctive social class groups do exist. Various classes shop at different stores. They prefer different treatment from salespeople. They buy different brands of products—even though prices are about the same. And they have different attitudes toward spending and saving—even when they have the same income level.

Reference groups help people form attitudes

A **reference group** refers to the people to whom an individual looks when forming attitudes about a particular topic. People normally have several reference groups for different topics. Some they meet face-to-face; others they just wish to imitate—for example, performers or athletes. In either case, they may take values from these reference groups and make buying decisions based on what the group might accept.

Reference influence is stronger for products that others "see" and which relate to status in the group. For example, whereas one group might view owning a fur coat as a sign of "having arrived," a group of animal lovers may see the same purchase as bad judgment.

Opinion leaders influence buyers

An **opinion leader** is a person who influences others. Opinion leaders aren't necessarily wealthier or better educated. And opinion leaders on one subject aren't necessarily opinion leaders on another. For example, you may have a friend who is ahead of the curve in knowing about videogames, but you might not want that friend's opinion about new clothing styles and cosmetics. Opinion leaders can influence both what product categories a consumer considers and what brands he or she purchases.

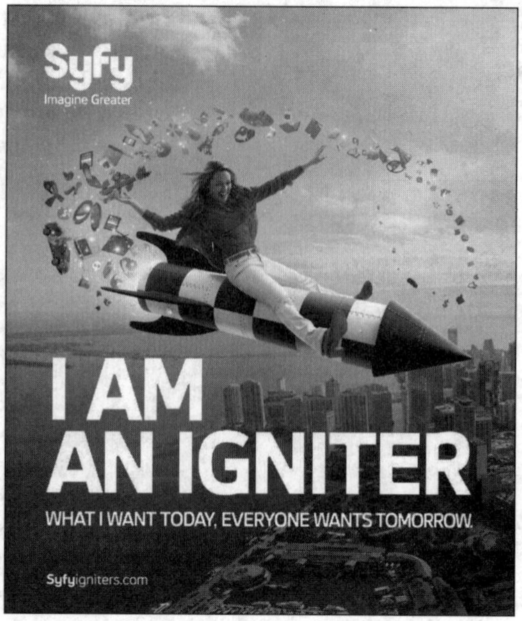

Marketing managers often target opinion leaders because they influence others. The Syfy television network wants advertisers to know that many of its viewers are opinion leaders.
Source A Division of NBCUniversal

Social media boosts social influence

Social media such as Facebook, Twitter, Instagram, and Snapchat make it easier for consumers to influence one another. On social media it is easy to follow people from various reference groups whether that means Justin Bieber's Twitter feed or an old high school friend's Facebook posts. These give consumers access to new reference groups that may influence their buying decision process.

Social media can also amplify the voices of opinion leaders. A traveler can have a lot of influence by posting a long, detailed review of a sight that "can't be missed" in Thailand. A friend can rave (or rage) about the new *Star Wars* movie–and influence who goes (and who stays home). Marketing managers are trying to figure out how to manage this type of influence.

Facebook advertising tries to leverage social influence. Let's say that John Doe has liked Home Depot on Facebook. Home Depot can use this endorsement[8] by paying for Facebook ads that appear in John Doe's friends' Facebook newsfeeds and report "John Doe likes Home Depot." This ad is more powerful when a friend appears to endorse Home Depot.

Websites use artificial intelligence to make recommendations

Some websites use artificial intelligence that analyzes a customer's own online search and shopping behavior as well as what other customers do to make more targeted product recommendations. For example, news websites like CNN.com show "ads" at the end of an article with a headline, "If you liked this, you might also like..." followed by links to articles from other sites. Amazon.com combines a user's own behavior with that of other shoppers to make recommendations. When a customer is considering a particular purchase, the page shows "Customers Who Bought This Item Also Bought..." followed by suggested additional purchases. It is estimated that about a third of Amazon's sales follow from such recommendations.

Culture, Ethnicity, and Consumer Behavior

Cultural variation across ethnic groups or countries can result in differences in how consumers make purchase choices. These differences create opportunities for resourceful firms. In this section we discuss how culture, ethnicity, and international boundaries influence consumer behavior.

Culture surrounds the other influences

Culture is the whole set of beliefs, attitudes, and ways of doing things of a reasonably homogeneous set of people.

We can think of the American culture, the French culture, or the Chinese culture. People within these cultural groupings tend to be more similar in outlook and behavior. But often it is useful to think of subcultures within such groupings. For example, within the American culture, there are various religious, ethnic, and regional subcultures.

Failure to consider cultural differences, even subtle ones, can result in problems.

Do ethnic groups buy differently?

America may be called the melting pot, but ethnic groups deserve special attention when analyzing markets. One basic reason is that people from different ethnic groups may be influenced by very different cultural variables. They may have quite varied needs and their own ways of thinking. Moreover, many Americans value diversity and the United States is becoming a multicultural market. As a result, rather than disappearing in a melting pot, some important cultural and ethnic dimensions are being preserved and highlighted. This creates both opportunities and challenges for marketers.

Ethnic markets are increasingly important

Marketers are paying more attention to ethnic groups because the number of ethnic consumers is growing at a much faster rate than the rest of the United States. Although some of this growth results from immigration, a much larger share follows from higher birthrates among ethnic minorities. Asian Americans, African Americans, and Hispanics are also seeing their wealth grow. Together these trends point to growing buying power for these ethnic groups. Ethnic and cultural groups often cluster in certain areas and share buying patterns that can be important to some businesses. Let's take a closer look at the three largest ethnic groups in the United States.

Hispanic market is large and growing

In 2015, 56.6 million Hispanics (18 percent of the U.S. population) represented the largest ethnic group in the United States. In 2015, the median household income of Hispanics grew to $45,148. By 2019, Hispanic buying power in the United States will total $1.7 trillion. More than half of all Hispanics in the United States live in three states–California, Texas, and Florida. That concentration makes promotion easier. Hispanics are known for embracing technology, and they often buy brands and products reflecting their family values. Data show that Hispanics are disproportionately likely to buy vegetables and dried grains, hot sauce, and women's fragrances. About 51 percent of Hispanics speak Spanish more than English.

Many companies are responding to this trend. For example, Wells Fargo branches in the Southwest have added Latin-style decor, bicultural tellers, and Spanish-language promotion. Efforts such as these have significantly increased Wells Fargo's business. P&G found Hispanic consumers like using fragrances in their homes and developed Febreze Destinations Collections, a line of air fresheners targeting this market.

African Americans appreciate cultural traditions

Forty-four million African Americans comprise almost 14 percent of the U.S. population–but in some southern states that percentage is about 30 percent. African Americans have a median household income of $36,898; by 2019 they are expected to have $1.4 trillion in buying power. African American consumers often buy products tied to cultural traditions and family gatherings. African Americans are more likely to buy unprepared meat and juice drinks, among other products.

P&G launched a campaign specifically targeting African American women. "My Black Is Beautiful" includes a cable TV show, website, and a Facebook page with more than 2 million members. These efforts have helped P&G brands reach out to African Americans.

Asian Americans are smaller in number, higher in income

There are about 19 million Asian Americans in the United States, and about a third of those live in California. Although just 6 percent of the population, this groups boasts the highest average household income at $77,166, which projects to $1 trillion in buying power by 2018. Asian Americans disproportionately purchase more fresh produce, organic foods, and electronic goods, and are also more likely to shop online as compared to other groups. Many Asian Americans are first or second generation in the United States, and three-quarters speak a language other than English at home.

Online news and entertainment site BuzzFeed has targeted the fast-growing Asian American segment with content appealing to this group. BuzzFeed, known for its listicles (articles composed of lists), has recently published "22 Signs You Grew Up with Immigrant Chinese Parents," "21 Annoying Comments Filipinos Are Tired of Hearing," and more to get Asian Americans to click through.

Stereotypes are common and misleading

A marketer needs to carefully study ethnic dimensions, because they can be subtle and fast-changing. For example, second-generation immigrants—those born in the United States—often differ significantly from their parents who immigrated to the country. And marketing managers must be careful not to stereotype ethnic consumers. Hispanics include people with roots in the Caribbean Islands and Mexico as well as Central and South America. The "black market" is not a single group; marketing managers should use other segmenting dimensions to more accurately reflect the great variability in African American households. The 19 million Asian Americans include people with Chinese, Filipino, Indian, and other backgrounds—yet no single group makes up more than 20 percent of this total. Marketing managers might start with these general categories, but other segmenting variables should be used to better understand and target customers.

Customer behavior differs across international markets

Planning strategies that consider cultural and behavior differences across international markets can be a challenge. Marketing managers need to understand the differences. Each foreign market may need to be treated as a separate target market with its own submarkets. Ignoring cultural differences—or assuming that they are not important—almost guarantees failure in international markets.

Consider the situation faced by marketers as they introduced Swiffer, the fast-selling wet mop, in Italy. Research showed that Italian women wash their floors four times more often than Americans. Based on that, you might predict a big success for Swiffer in Italy. Yet many new cleaning products flop[9] there. Fortunately, the research suggested a reason. Many Italians have negative attitudes about ad claims that a product makes cleaning *easier*. Although this benefit has wide appeal in the United States, many Italian women doubt that something that works easily will meet their standards for cleanliness. So for the Italian market, Swiffer was modified and beeswax was added to polish floors after they have been mopped. Now Swiffer is a top seller in Italy.

Sometimes an understanding of local culture points out new ways to blend the Four Ps. For example, Nestlé knew that free samples would kickstart the adoption process of its new line of food flavorings in Brazil. In the United States, it's common to distribute free samples at stores, but that would seem strange to Brazilians. Local Nestlé managers in Brazil posed a more culturally acceptable approach to distribute the samples. In Brazil, people cook on gas stoves and deliverymen regularly bring canisters[10] of gas to their homes. So Nestlé paid these local gas deliverypeople to offer their customers sam-

Many firms are developing strategies to appeal to the fast-growing Hispanic market. Goya wants to let grocers know that demand for coconut milk spikes during the holidays because it is a vital part of many Hispanic celebrations. Nestlé's Coffee-Mate brand is bringing flavors popular in Mexico and South America to the United States.
(left) Source: Goya Foods, Inc; (right) Source: Nestlé S.A

ples of the flavorings and explain how to use them. Consumers showed more interest in the samples when the conversation took place with someone they trusted right by the stove where the flavorings would be used.

Individuals Are Affected by the Purchase Situation

The **purchase situation** takes into account the purpose, time available, and location where a purchase is made.

Consumers consider the purpose for the purchase

Consumers can buy the same type of product, yet they have completely different *purposes* for the purchase. This influences buying behavior. For example, how a consumer buys a bunch of flowers depends on whether they are for a mother who lives far away, the host of a dinner party, or a girlfriend following a little disagreement. The reason for the purchase influences how the buyer evaluates options and, ultimately, the choice made.

Time affects what happens

Time influences a purchase situation. When consumers make a purchase—and the time they have available for shopping—will influence their behavior. Socializing with friends at a Starbucks induces different behavior than grabbing a quick cup of 7-Eleven coffee on the way to work. The urgency of the need is another time-related factor. Shopping for tires is much more urgent when one has a flat as compared to when one notices that the tread is just starting to wear thin. When the need is urgent, customers will be less inclined to evaluate a range of options—and place more emphasis on speed and convenience.

Some retail stores have discovered that customers spend more when they shop slower. Origins stores found that customers who sat spent 40 percent more than those who did not, and the beauty care retailer took notice. Its stores were redesigned to slow down the shopping experience—adding a wall specially lit for selfies, a large sink to facilitate sampling soaps, and plenty of seating.

Consumer behavior varies with situational factors. Consumers shop differently when buying gifts—and BoConcept tries to make gift-buying easier by presenting a range of ideas. The time a consumer has available to shop also affects his or her behavior. Woot uses this to its advantage. The online retailer offers one deeply discounted product each day—customers must buy that day or forget about it.
(left) Source: BoConcept; (right) Source: Woot Inc.

Surroundings affect buying too

Where a purchase is made and the surrounding location can affect buying behavior. The excitement at an on-site auction may stimulate impulse buying. Checking out an auction online might lead to a different response. Consider how the warehouse-like setting in a Sam's Club store signals low-cost operations and price reductions.

Needs, benefits sought, attitudes, motivation, and even how a consumer selects certain products all vary depending on the purchase situation. So different purchase situations may require different marketing mixes—even when the same target market is involved.

The Consumer Decision Process

The model in Exhibit 4-2 organizes the many different influences on consumer behavior. It helps explain *why* consumers make the decisions they make. Now, we'll expand that model with a closer look at the steps in the consumer decision process and a focus on *how* consumers make decisions. See Exhibit 4-8.

Recognizing a need creates a problem for the consumer

The consumer decision process begins when a consumer becomes aware of an unmet need. The consumer's problem-solving process then focuses on how best to meet that need. Problem recognition often happens quickly. A student on the way to class, for example, may realize that she's thirsty and wants something to drink. Or problem recognition may take shape over time. For example, a recent grad with a new apartment might want a comfortable place to sit while watching TV in the evening. These situations present problems that may be solved with a purchase. But what purchase would it be?

Steps in consumer problem solving

How a consumer solves the problem depends on the situation. Exhibit 4-9 highlights the four basic problem solving steps a consumer may go through to satisfy a need. As the exhibit indicates, consumers do not always move forward in this process—sometimes they will postpone a decision or start over later. Marketing managers want their

Exhibit 4-8 An Expanded Model of Consumer Behavior

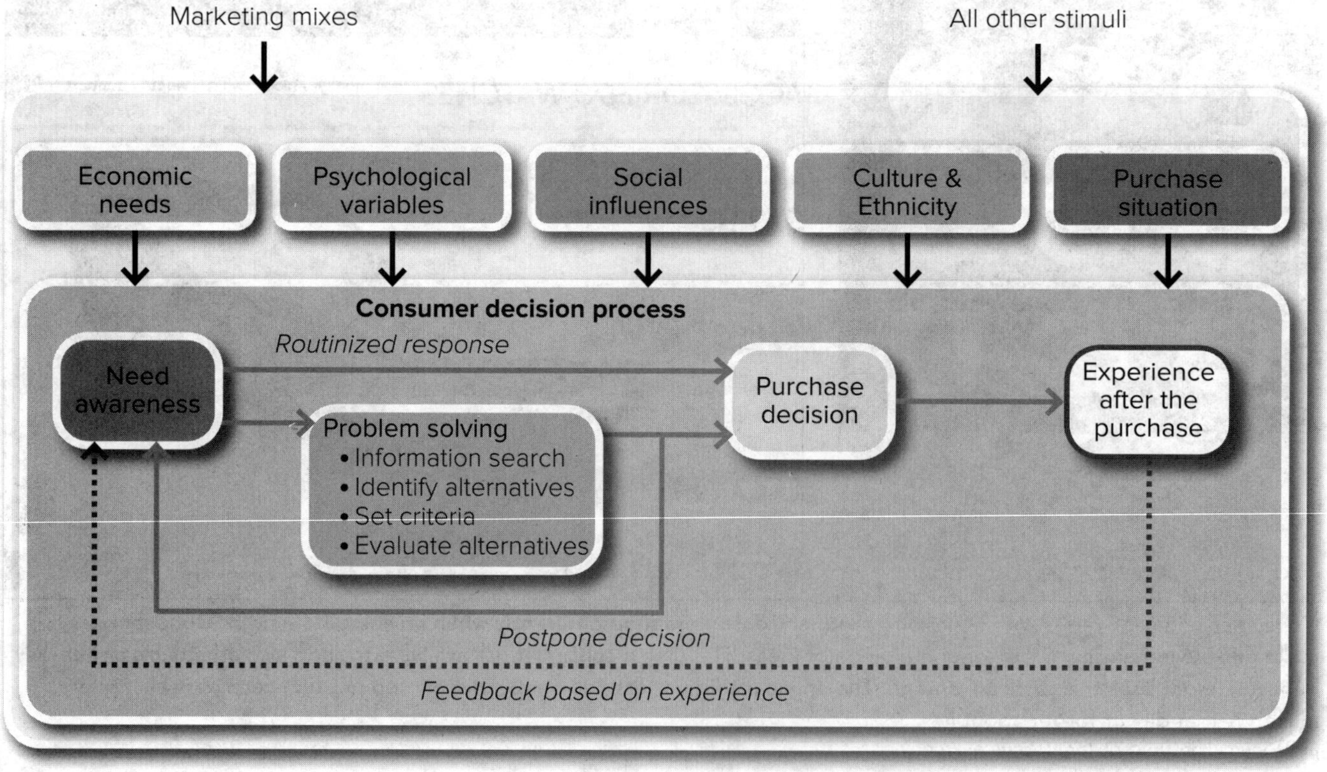

product to be in consumers' minds when they engage in these steps:

1. *Information search:* During this step, customers seek information about a solution for their problem or about specific brands. Customers may find information from other customers, experts, or a company's promotion (advertising, salespeople, or website, for example).
2. *Identify alternatives:* During this step, customers recognize available options for meeting a need.
3. *Set criteria:* During this step, customers identify criteria and the relative importance of each in preparation for the final step.
4. *Evaluate alternatives:* During this step, customers consider the costs and benefits of various alternatives.

Exhibit 4-9 Consumer Problem Solving

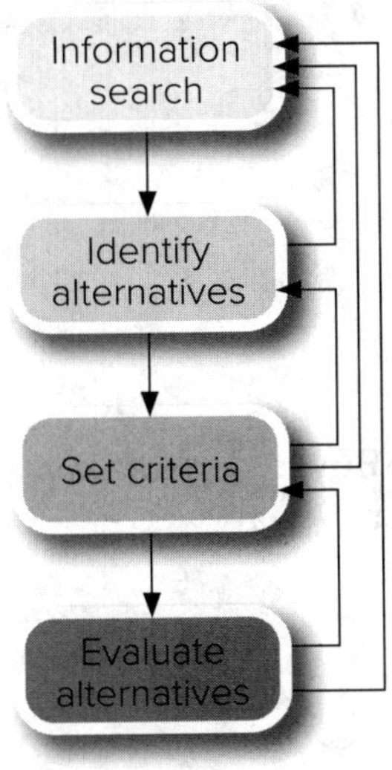

Three levels of problem solving are useful

These activities may require a lot of time and effort on the part of a consumer, very little time, or they may be skipped altogether. How much effort is put into a buying decision depends in part on the economic needs, psychological variables, social influences, and purchase situation factors discussed earlier in this chapter. It's also tied to the amount of risk a buyer sees in making a wrong choice. For instance, when a buyer has little involvement in the purchase or the expense is small, a poor buying decision will result in little financial or social risk. Under these circumstances the buyer usually puts little effort into the buying decision. On the other hand, when a buyer is highly involved and cares deeply about the choice, or when the price is high, there may be more risk in making a bad decision. So the buyer often extends more effort in order to be more confident. Exhibit 4-10 suggests three levels of problem solving that relate to the amount of effort the buyer puts into the decision.

Consumers use **extensive problem solving** when they put much effort into deciding how to satisfy a need—as is likely for a completely new purchase or to satisfy an important need. At this level of problem solving, consumers conduct more information search, identify more alternatives, have more criteria for evaluation, and spend more time evaluating options (see Exhibit 4-9). For example, an avid computer "gamer" may put a great deal of effort into buying a new gaming computer. Our gamer might solicit[11] friends' opinions about the graphics speed and audio quality for different models before going online to compare options and prices and read technical reviews. Then, the gamer might visit a local store for a hands-on demo of a favorite game on a few computers. To narrow down to a final choice, the gamer could evaluate customer service support and warranties. This is certainly not an impulse purchase! The decision to buy—and what to buy—comes only after an extensive effort.

Limited problem solving is used by consumers when *some* effort is required in deciding the best way to satisfy a need. This is typical when the consumer has some previous experience with a product but isn't quite sure which choice to make at the moment. A seasoned computer gamer, for instance, may already know that he likes sports games and what store has the newest releases. At the store he might get the salesperson's advice and check out the video quality on a few games before deciding which to buy. This

Exhibit 4-10 Problem-Solving Continuum

is a deliberate purchase, but only a limited amount of effort is expended before making the decision.

A consumer uses **routinized response behavior** when he or she regularly selects a particular way of satisfying a need when it occurs. Routinized response is typical when a consumer has considerable experience in how to meet a specific need and requires no new information. For example, our gamer might automatically buy the latest version of *Madden NFL* as soon as EA Sports makes it available. Routinized response also may occur when a buyer trusts a company, brand, or a friend's recommendation. Because trust lowers the risk of making the wrong choice, less effort is required from the buyer.

Routinized response behavior is also typical for **low-involvement purchases**—purchases that have little importance or relevance for the customer. Let's face it, for most of us, buying a box of salt is probably not one of the burning issues in our life.

Buying isn't always rational

The idea of a decision process does *not* imply that consumers always apply *rational* processes in their buying decisions. To the contrary, consumers don't always seek accurate information or make smart choices that provide the best economic value. This is often because of the influences on consumer behavior that we discussed earlier in the chapter. For example, most sport-utility vehicles never leave the paved road, but buyers like the image of driving an SUV and *knowing* they can get off the paved road if they want to. When a tourist spends 1,000 euros on a Loewe leather purse, it may simply be that she loves the style, can afford it, and "has to have it." Needs are operating in such a purchase, but they are higher-level needs and not some sort of functional "requirement."

To buy or not to buy

A customer who is ready to buy may have to decide which brand to purchase and where to make the purchase (that is, which store or location). There may be related decisions about colors, features, or other options as well. Buying can be complicated—and sometimes the complexity of all the choices causes customers to delay the purchase.

When a consumer decides to delay a purchase, oftentimes the sale is lost. He or she may never return. For that reason, some marketers make it easy for customers to come back later and purchase. For example, Walmart recently instituted a Christmas layaway program. When using layaway, a customer makes incremental payments on a purchase—and does not take it home until it is paid in full. Similarly, online retailers often allow customers to place items on a "Wish List" or "Save to Favorites" so they are easy to find when they return to the site.

When a customer gets close to making a purchase, marketing managers want to help "tip the scales." At this point, offers of special financing or free delivery might be helpful in overcoming a delayed purchase.

Consumers can have second thoughts after a purchase

After making a purchase, buyers often have second thoughts and wonder if they made the right choice. The resulting tension is called **dissonance**[12]—a feeling of uncertainty about whether the correct decision was made. (In layman's terms, this is known as "buyer's remorse.") This may lead a customer to seek additional information to confirm the wisdom of the purchase.

Post-purchase regret is a bigger problem

Sometimes uncertainty isn't the issue. Rather the consumer is certain about being unhappy with a purchase. When a post-purchase experience fails to live up to expectations, a customer will be disappointed. For example, going out for an expensive dinner—and then getting slow service and cold food—results in considerable dissatisfaction and regret over the choice. The diner is much less likely to visit that restaurant again. A consumer may regret making a purchase for a variety of reasons that the consumer didn't anticipate when making the purchase. But, whatever the reason, regret is not likely to lead to the same decision in the future.

Some consumers spread the word after they buy

Many consumers talk about their purchases and share opinions about their good and bad experiences. Recommendations from friends can have a big influence on whether we try a new restaurant, buy a hybrid car, or choose a veterinarian. Consumers are even more likely to share stories about being dissatisfied than satisfied. This is important for a marketer to remember. At times, his or her career might call for countering negative publicity—damage control—to save a product's image.

Predictive analytics and the consumer decision process

Some firms already utilize marketing analytics and intelligent agents during different stages of the consumer decision making process. Many firms compile data useful for **predictive analytics**—a process to analyze data to make predictions about unknown future events. For a marketing manager, unknown future events include customers' future needs, the information useful to problem solving, and whether a customer is considering a switch to a competitor. Let's look at a few examples of how such predictive analytics could operate in consumer decision making:

- *Needs awareness.* A sporting goods store might gather mileage data from a customer's fitness app to predict when the customer will be ready for a replacement set of running shoes. Under Armour and Nike have already invested in fitness tracking apps.
- *Information search.* Based on a customer's past car shopping behavior, a website for an automaker could present features the customer is most concerned with. For example, a customer whose previous behavior indicated a concern for gas mileage and rear seat legroom might have this information presented first.
- *Alternatives identification.* A customer's Netflix home page offers viewing recommendations based on their past viewing behavior.
- *Post-purchase.* Marketing managers often try to predict if customers will stop using a product. For example, if a cell phone provider knows a customer is considering a switch to a rival network, it could make the customer an offer to keep its service.

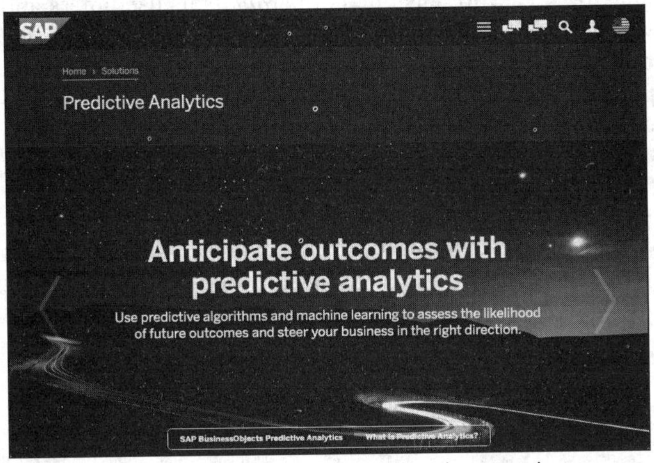

SAP is one of many software companies that use data to make predictions about future events—including consumers' purchasing plans.
Source: SAP SE

New concepts require an adoption process

When consumers face a really new concept, their previous experience may not be relevant. These situations involve the **adoption process**—the steps individuals go through on the way to accepting or rejecting a new idea. Although the adoption process is similar to the decision-making process, learning plays a clearer role, and promotion's contribution to a marketing mix is more visible.

In the adoption process, an individual moves through some fairly definite steps:

1. *Awareness*—the potential customer comes to know about the product but lacks details. The consumer may not even know how it works or what it will do.
2. *Interest*—if the consumer becomes interested, he or she will gather general information and facts about the product.
3. *Evaluation*—a consumer begins to give the product a mental trial, applying it to his or her personal situation.
4. *Trial*—the consumer may buy the product to experiment with it in use. A product that is either too expensive to try or isn't available for trial may never be adopted.
5. *Decision*—the consumer decides on either adoption or rejection. A satisfactory evaluation and trial may lead to adoption of the product and regular use. According to psychological learning theory, reinforcement leads to adoption.
6. *Confirmation*—the adopter continues to rethink the decision and searches for support for the decision—that is, further reinforcement.

Dropbox had to work with the adoption process when it introduced cloud (online) data storage—an idea that was not familiar to many computer users. Dropbox lets users create a file folder on their devices—say their laptop, tablet, or smartphone—and share it with the others. For example, if a consumer places a photo, song, or document in the Dropbox folder on their laptop, it would automatically be replicated on his or her phone and tablet computer. The file is also backed up on the Internet. Furthermore, folders can also be shared with friends or work colleagues.

Dropbox first targeted techies, people who are comfortable with technology. The techies quickly downloaded Dropbox because it filled a need—these users tend to have many digital devices. Dropbox came with 2 GB of free online storage. To encourage early customers to spread *awareness* and generate *interest* in Dropbox, they were given additional storage space for each person they referred to Dropbox. Many techies found good value in Dropbox and were happy to spread the word. A video on its website demonstrated how Dropbox works, making it easy for customers to *evaluate* its usefulness and show how easy (low cost) it was to install. This and the free 2 GB of storage made *trial* easy, too. As others used Dropbox, many began to share files with friends, family, and coworkers. Some found Dropbox so useful they made the *decision* to buy more storage space on a subscription basis (paying each year). As others adopted Dropbox it became easier to share large files, which provided users with *confirmation* of Dropbox's value, leading them to renew their subscription.

Marketing analytics can monitor adoption

Marketing managers may use analytics to monitor how a new idea is being adopted by the market. Marketing metrics at each step can be used to evaluate this progress. *Marketing Analytics in Action: Adoption Process* examines how this might be useful in the case of Dropbox.

Marketing Analytics in Action: Adoption Process

The adoption process might be modeled using marketing analytics. Let's see how this might work in the previous example for Dropbox, which might use this information to forecast sales or to fine-tune a marketing mix. Let's examine possible metrics in four steps along the adoption process. (Note that to simplify, we have left off the confirmation and renewal steps.)

- *Awareness:* An advertising campaign might initially be used to make customers aware. Assume an advertising campaign makes 1,000,000 people in the target market ("techies") aware of Dropbox.
- *Interest and evaluation:* In this case, interest and evaluation could be inferred from the number of customers who visit the website and view the video describing the product. Assume 10 percent of the 1,000,000 (in step 1) who were made aware from the advertising subsequently visit the website and watch the video.
- *Trial:* In this case, trial could be measured as the percentage of people who watch the video and subsequently download and install the Dropbox free trial. Assume 10 percent of people who watch the video go on to install the free software.

Using the numbers above, Dropbox could estimate the number of users and the number of initial sales it would make. The equation using the assumptions in steps 1–4 is as follows:

Number of customers buying Dropbox = 1,000,000 × 10% (who watch the video) × 10% (who download the software) × 5% (who purchase the software)

Use this equation and the insights just discussed to answer the following questions:

1. *Using the numbers presented above, how many of the initial 1,000,000 aware customers eventually make a purchase?*
2. *Assume Dropbox makes a new video that customers find more compelling. This increases the 10% in step 3 to 15%. What is the number of buying customers with this new assumption?*
3. *Besides a more compelling video, identify two other changes a marketing manager might make to change the percentages shown in steps 2 to 4. Describe how your proposed change will affect the percentage.*

CONCLUSION

In this chapter, we analyzed the individual consumer as a problem solver who is influenced by economic needs, psychological variables, social influences, cultural factors, and the purchase situation. We showed how these variables influence the consumer decision process, what the steps in that process are, and why it is important to consider these steps when planning a marketing strategy. For example, we discussed three levels of problem solving that you can use to evaluate how consumers approach different types of purchase decisions—from the simple, routinized response behavior to the complex, extensive problem-solving behavior. We also discussed how the consumer's experience after the purchase impacts what that consumer will do in the future.

From a broader perspective, this chapter makes it clear that each consumer and purchase decision is somewhat unique. It isn't possible to catalog all of the individual possibilities. Rather, the overall focus of this chapter is to provide general frameworks you can use to analyze consumers regardless of the particular product or decision. This also helps you identify the dimensions of consumer behavior most important for segmenting the market and developing a targeted marketing mix.

By now it should be clear that expensive marketing errors can be made when you assume that other consumers will behave in the same manner as you or your family and friends. That's why we rely on the social and behavioral sciences for insight about consumer behavior and why marketing research is so important to marketing managers when they are developing a marketing strategy for a particular target market. When managers understand how and why consumers behave the way they do, they are better able to develop effective marketing mixes that really meet the needs of their target market.

JOYFUL MOMENT

Repeat Tactic

In a sales company, the boss said to one of his employees, "The main thing to remember is repetition, repetition, repetition! That's the key! If you have a product to sell, keep harping on it in every way possible. Repeat it; cram it down people's throats. Even make yourself sickening and repulsive if you have to, but don't ever forget to repeat, repeat, repeat. It's the only way to get results and sell our products!" So, the employee said, "Yes, sir!" Then the boss said, "Now, what was it you came to see me about?" And the employee replied, "Well, sir, it's about a raise, a raise, a raise!"

WORDS AND EXPRESSIONS

1. **discretionary**: *adj.* having or using the ability to act or decide according to your own discretion or judgment 任意的；自由决定的
   —An essential characteristic is the possession of a reasonable amount of discretionary income.
   其中的一个重要特征是拥有一份合理的可自由支配收入。
2. **elusive**: *adj.* be difficult to detect or grasp by the mind; difficult to describe 难以捉摸的；不易记住的
   —Try to catch the elusive charm of the original in translation.
   翻译时设法把握住原文中难以捉摸的风韵。
3. **stimulus**: *n.* any stimulating information or event; acts to arouse action 刺激物；刺激因素
   —Interest rates could fall soon and be a stimulus to the U.S. economy.
   利率可能很快就会下调，从而刺激美国经济。
4. **manipulate**: *v.* influence or control shrewdly or deviously 巧妙地控制；操纵
   —The technology uses a pen to manipulate a computer.
   这项技术使用一支笔来操作电脑。
5. **affiliation**: *n.* a close or official connection with 加入；联系或关系；接纳
   —There is no affiliation between our organization and theirs, even though our names are similar.
   尽管两个组织的名称相似，但我们之间并没有关系。
6. **coupon**: *n.* a piece of printed paper which allows you to pay less money than usual for a product, or to get it free 赠券，优惠券
   —Bring the coupon below to any Tecno store and pay just £10.99.
   持下面的优惠券到任意一家 Tecno 专卖店，只需付 10.99 英镑。
7. **cue**: *n.* a stimulus that provides information about what to do 暗示，提示；线索
   —When she coughs, it's my cue to come onto the stage.
   她一咳嗽，就是给我暗号出场。
8. **endorsement**: *n.* the act of endorsing, formal and explicit approval 代言；认可，支持；背书
   —His commercial endorsements for everything from running shoes to breakfast cereals will take his earnings to more than ten million dollars a year.
   他的商业代言从跑鞋到早餐麦片一应俱全，令其年收入达到一千多万美元。
9. **flop**: *n.* a complete failure 彻底失败；惨败
   —It is the public who decide whether a film is a hit or a flop.
   决定一部电影会走红还是惨败的是大众。

10. canister: *n.* a strong metal container used to hold gases or chemical substances（储存气体或化学品的）金属罐，金属桶
—The canister is filled with activated charcoal.
回收罐中充满了活性炭。

11. solicit: *v.* ask for money, help, support, or an opinion from someone 恳求；征求
—They were planning to solicit funds from a number of organizations.
他们正计划向一些机构募集资金。

12. dissonance: *n.* a lack of agreement or harmony between things 不和谐音，不一致
—Dissonance among the three partners doomed the project.
三个股东间的不调和注定了计划的失败。

EXERCISES

1. Multiple choices

(1) Which of the following is not consumers' economic need? ___
A. economy of purchase or use B. esteem
C. dependability in use D. convenience

(2) Psychological variables in making consumer decisions include the following except ___.
A. motivation B. perception C. social class D. lifestyle

(3) A ___ is strong stimulus that encourages action to reduce a need.
A. need B. want C. desire D. drive

(4) ___ needs are concerned with biological needs—food, liquid, rest, and etc.
A. Physiological B. Social C. Personal D. Safety

(5) ___ are people whose children are grown and are now able to spend their money in other ways.
A. Full nesters B. Empty nesters C. DINK D. Traditional family

2. Terms translation

(1) consumer buying behavior (2) economic needs
(3) hierarchy of needs (4) empty nesters
(5) reference group (6) safety needs
(7) selective retention (8) physiological needs
(9) discretionary income (10) reinforcement

3. True or false

(1) Research allows marketers to determine relatively easily "what people buy," while determining "why people buy" is more difficult. ______
(2) Marketers want and need to understand how the various marketing and environmental stimuli are changed into responses. ______
(3) Consumer purchases are more influenced by economic factors than cultural, social, personal and psychological factors. ______
(4) Growing up in a society, a child learns basic values, perceptions, wants and behaviors from the family and other important institutions. ______
(5) It is considered unethical for a marketer to enlist the aid of opinion leaders to spread the word about their brands. ______
(6) Marketers study consumer behavior in an effort to determine new products that might be wanted. ______
(7) Most responsible marketers avoid segmenting a market on such variables as nationality, religion or race to avoid the possibility of discrimination. ______
(8) Marketers would prefer to target younger buyers as opposed to mature buyers because the younger consumers control over 50 percent of discretionary income. ______
(9) Social classes in the United States are not fixed and rigid; people can easily move to a higher social class or drop to a lower one. ______
(10) A customer is an individual who has both the ability to buy (income, savings, and borrowing power) and the willingness to spend. ______

4. Fill in the blanks

(1) __________ is a change in behavior based on experience.
(2) A (n) __________ leader is a person who influences others.
(3) All marketing and environmental __________ impact a buyer and are transformed into a set of observable responses.

(4) __________ buyer behavior refers to the buying behavior of final consumers, individuals, and households who buy products and services for personal consumption.

(5) __________ needs are concerned with love, friendship, status, and esteem.

(6) Social __________ are society's relatively permanent and ordered divisions whose members share similar values, interests and behaviors.

(7) The __________ is the most important consumer buying organization in society.

(8) A(n) __________ is a person's point of view toward something.

(9) According to Maslow, __________ needs are the primary level of human needs.

(10) __________ is the process by which people select, organize and interpret information to form a meaningful picture of the world.

5. **Answer the following questions**

(1) How to distinguish want, need and drive?

(2) What is Maslow's hierarchy of needs?

(3) What is the learning process?

(4) What are the traditional stages in modern family cycles?

(5) Explain the three levels of problem solving that relate to the amount of effort the buyer puts into the decision.

SUGGESTED CASES

1. McDonald's "Seniors" Restaurant
3. NOCO United Soccer Academy
8. Carmine's Italian Restaurant
9. Quiet Night Motel
10. Cousin's Ice Center
11. Running On
12. DrV.com—Custom Vitamins
27. Canadian Mills, Ltd.

MARKETING ANALYTICS: DATA TO KNOWLEDGE

Mc Graw Hill Education connect®

CHAPTER 4: SELECTIVE PROCESSES

Submag, Inc. uses direct-mail promotion to sell magazine subscriptions. Magazine publishers pay Submag $3.12 for each new subscription. Submag's costs include the expenses of printing, addressing, and mailing each direct-mail advertisement plus the cost of using a mailing list. There are many suppliers of mailing lists, and the cost and quality of different lists vary.

Submag's marketing manager, Shandra Debose, is trying to choose between two possible mailing lists. One list has been generated from phone directories. It is less expensive than the other list, but the supplier acknowledges that about 10 percent of the names are out-of-date (addresses where people have moved away). A competing supplier offers a list of active members of professional associations. This list costs 4 cents per name more than the phone list, but only 8 percent of the addresses are out-of-date.

In addition to concerns about out-of-date names, not every consumer who receives a mailing buys a subscription. For example, *selective exposure* is a problem. Some target customers never see the offer—they just toss out junk mail without even opening the envelope. Industry studies show that this wastes about 10 percent of each mailing—although the precise percentage varies from one mailing list to another.

Selective perception influences some consumers who do open the mailing. Some are simply not interested. Others don't want to deal with a subscription service. Although the price is good, these consumers worry that they'll never get the magazines. Submag's previous experience is that selective perception causes more than half of those who read the offer to reject it.

Of those who perceive the message as intended, many are interested. But *selective retention* can be a problem. Some people set aside the information and then forget to send in the subscription order.

Submag can mail about 25,000 pieces per week. Shandra Debose has set up a spreadsheet to help her study effects of the various relationships discussed earlier and to choose between the two mailing lists.

See Connect for the spreadsheet and questions needed to analyze this scenario.

5 CHAPTER FIVE

Business and Organizational Customers and Their Buying Behavior

MetoKote Corporation specializes in protective coating applications, such as powder-coat and liquid paint, that other manufacturers need for the parts and equipment they make. For example, when you see John Deere agricultural, construction, or lawn-care equipment, many of the components have likely been coated (painted) in a MetoKote facility. In fact, Deere and MetoKote have a close buyer-seller relationship. Although Deere uses a variety of methods to identify suppliers and get competitive bids for many items it needs, it's different with MetoKote. Deere isn't going to switch to some other supplier just because other options provide cheaper coatings. MetoKote not only provides protective coatings for many Deere products, it also has built facilities right next to some Deere plants. When it's time for a component to be coated, a conveyer belt moves the part out of the Deere plant and into the MetoKote facility. A short time later it's back—and it's green or yellow.

Many people were involved in the decision to purchase coating services in this way. The responsibility for choosing a painting vendor didn't rest only with Deere's purchasing department but involved input from people in finance, quality control, and production. They worked together—often with MetoKote personnel—to figure out exactly what was needed to provide the high-quality protective finish Deere's customers expect on each piece of Deere equipment. A decision like this was not easy, so before selecting MetoKote, Deere's buying team gathered information and reviewed different suppliers.

Once the team decided to work with MetoKote, it was a long-term decision. Deere trusts that MetoKote will consistently offer quality paint jobs, but also appreciates that the supplier's experts keep up with all of the environmental regulations and new technologies for coatings.

Deere does all this because it knows how demanding the customers in its agricultural, commercial, and construction equipment markets can be. Deere's organizational customers differ from the consumers that buy its riding lawnmowers. There are fewer business customers, but many of them spend more than $100,000 a year on Deere equipment. And they often conduct an economic analysis to ensure those investments pay off in the long run. Like Deere, they want good value—and Deere is known for delivering that. These business buyers are experts, too, highly trained in what they buy.

How do John Deere products create value for modern farmers? Competition in agriculture has put pressure on farmers to produce more with less. Data and analytics are keys to more efficient and effective farm operations. John Deere is at the forefront of this trend, offering technology and data analytic tools to today's farmers. For example, with John Deere Field Connect technology, farmers can precisely monitor soil moisture, rainfall, and wind in particular sites within their fields. Data from Field Connect is wirelessly shared with the farmer through a mobile app or via the web. John Deere software combines these data with weather forecasts to provide exact recommendations for irrigating and fertilizing fields.

Data from different pieces of John Deere equipment flow seamlessly into the farmer's MyJohnDeere.com site, creating an "operations center" for the farm. A farm's JDLink (another John Deere tool) manages all of a farmer's equipment (even non-Deere equipment). For example, JDLink tracks usage and tells a farmer when a piece of equipment needs maintenance. Optimizing equipment reduces downtime and lowers service costs—delivering tangible economic value to farmers. A farmer can also share this information with another team member or the local John Deere dealer.

John Deere's dealer network is also critical to its success. Although some customers buy directly from John Deere, most purchase from one of the 2,000-plus John Deere dealers located in more than 100 countries. These dealers buy and stock what their customers want. And the dealers know that John Deere's reputation for quality service is just as important as the company's reputation for quality products. So Deere has streamlined distribution with the goal of giving customers and dealers better service. It's dropping dealers who don't measure up to its goals for customer satisfaction—and encouraging the dealers that remain to consolidate. Consolidation gives dealers greater economies of scale in purchasing, allows them to add specialists in important areas like e-commerce, and facilitates sharing inventory among multiple locations. Dealers appreciate that Deere set up the website www.machinefinder.com and Facebook page, which help customers find used Deere equipment sold by its dealers. Deere even finances used purchases through John Deere Credit.

Deere designs marketing strategies that solve particular customer problems. For example, golf course managers buy Deere equipment to maintain their fairways, greens, and sand traps because they value the reliability and durability of the brand's products. However, they also need a variety of operating supplies—ranging from grass seed and irrigation equipment to ball washers and chemicals. Golf course managers have many responsibilities besides purchasing, so Deere introduced its One Source service, which provides golf course managers with a "one-stop shop" for the things they need—all backed by the trusted Deere name. One Source saves time and strengthens Deere's relationships with both its dealers and their golf course customers. Of course, it creates new challenges for Deere's purchasing department. It must identify, evaluate, monitor, and recommend the suppliers for the products that golf courses need. Deere's dealers and golf course customers rely on Deere's purchasing specialists to make the right decisions, but that's part of the value that Deere provides.

Innovative approaches to delivering customer value make Deere the supplier of choice for all kinds of business customers.

LEARNING OBJECTIVES

As the John Deere case illustrates, the buying behavior of organizational customers can be very different from the buying behavior of final consumers. Marketing strategy planning requires a solid understanding of who these organizational customers are and how they buy.

When you finish this chapter, you should be able to

1 name and give examples of the different types of business and organizational buyers.

2 describe how organizational and business markets differ from consumer markets.

3 describe each step in the model of organizational/business buying.

4 explain the different types of buying processes.

5 understand the different types of buyer-seller relationships and their benefits and limitations.

6 know about the number and distribution of manufacturers and why they are an important customer group.

7 know how buying by service firms, retailers, wholesalers, and governments is similar to—and different from—buying by manufacturers.

8 understand important new terms (shown in boldface).

Business and Organizational Customers—A Big Opportunity

Most people think about an individual final consumer when they hear the term *customer.* But many marketing managers aim at customers who are not final consumers. In fact, the dollar value of purchases made by businesses and other organizations in the United States is more than double that made by final consumers.

Business and organizational customers are any buyers who buy for resale or to produce other goods and services. There are many different types of organizational customers, including the following:

- *Producers of goods and services*—including manufacturers, farmers, real estate developers, hotels, banks, and even doctors and lawyers
- *Intermediaries*—wholesalers and retailers
- *Government units*—federal agencies in the United States and other countries as well as state and local governments
- *Nonprofit organizations*—national organizations such as the American Red Cross and Girl Scouts as well as local organizations such as museums and churches

As this suggests, not all organizational customers are business firms. Even so, they are sometimes loosely referred to as *business buyers, intermediate buyers,* or *industrial buyers*—and marketing managers often refer to organizational customers collectively as the "business-to-business" market, or simply, the *B2B market.*

In this chapter, we'll focus on organizational customers and their buying behavior (see Exhibit 5-1). In Chapter 4 we focused on buying by final consumers, so here we'll start by covering important ways that organizational buying differs from buying by final consumers. Next, we will look at a model of business and organizational buying. Finally, we'll focus on some key differences among the specific types of organizational customers.

So keep in mind that, for many firms, marketing strategy planning is about meeting the needs of organizational customers, not final consumers. A firm can target both final consumers and organizations, but different marketing mixes may be needed. As you learn about the buying behavior of organizations, think about how a firm's marketing mix may need to be different and how it may be adjusted.

Organizational Customers Are Different

In some ways, organizational buying is similar to the model of consumer behavior introduced in Chapter 4. Businesses and organizations make purchases to solve problems, they seek information, and the decision-making process varies depending on the nature of the purchase. Yet organizational customers and their buying behaviors differ from final consumers and their buying behaviors. These differences have important implications for the marketing strategy planning process (see Exhibit 5-2).

Exhibit 5-1 Understanding Business and Organizational Customers for Marketing Strategy Planning

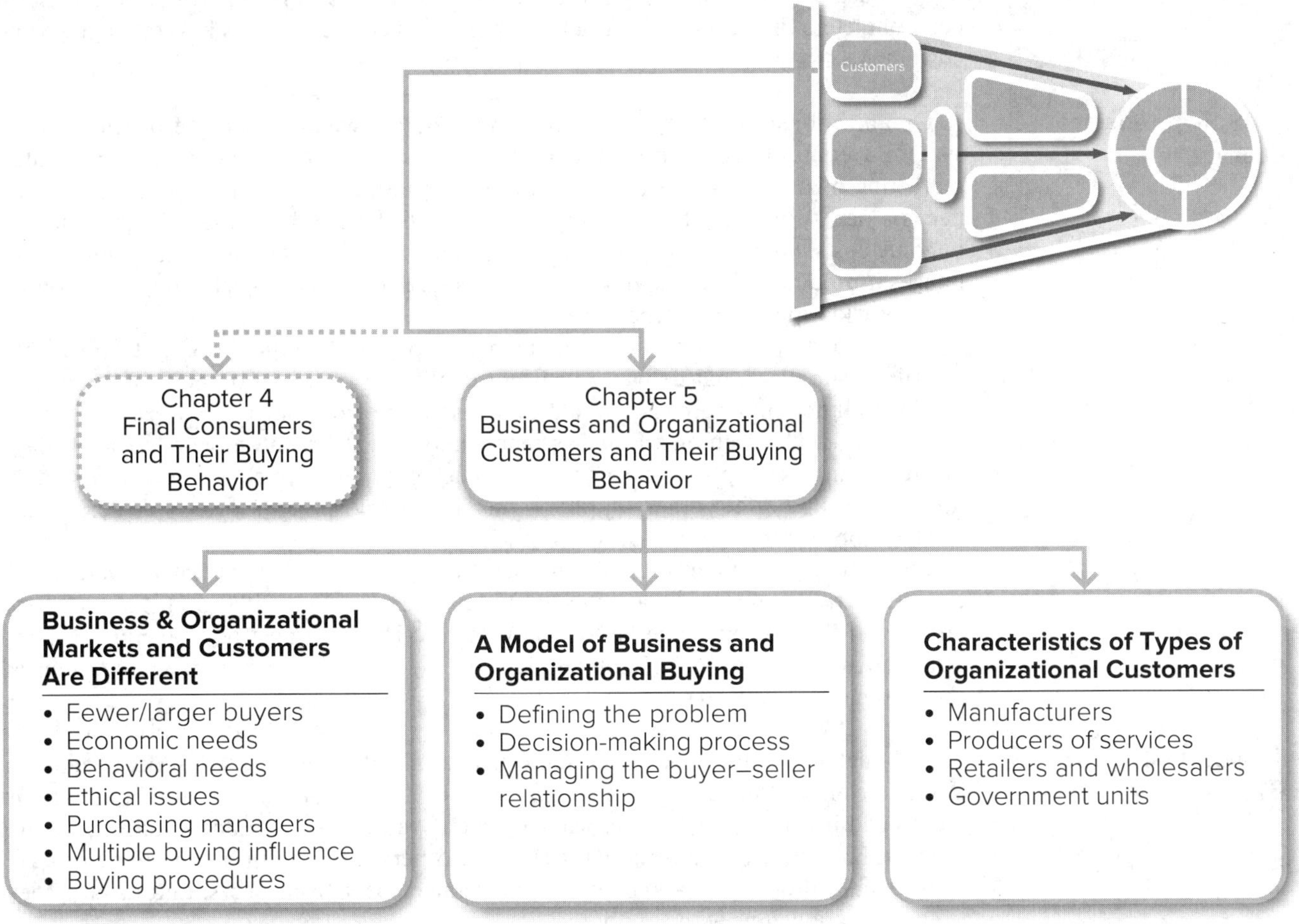

Exhibit 5-2 Differences between Organizational Customers and Final Consumers

Customers are fewer in number but each spends more dollars

As compared to the consumer market, the organizational market includes far fewer buyers–yet the dollars spent by each are, on average, much greater. Consider that Procter & Gamble sales to Walmart are more than $11 billion. Although that case reflects an extreme, most B2B sellers have many customers that provide each of them with thousands–if not hundreds of thousands–of dollars in revenue. This allows business marketers the opportunity to invest more marketing resources into satisfying each customer.

Economic needs are primary

Organizations intently focus on economic factors when they make purchase decisions. Buyers try to account for the total cost of selecting a supplier and its particular marketing mix, not just the initial price of the product. For example, a hospital that needs a new type of digital X-ray equipment might look at both the original cost and ongoing costs, how it would affect doctor productivity, and, of course, the quality of the images it produces. The hospital might also consider the seller's reliability and its ability to provide speedy maintenance and repair.

The matter of reliability deserves further emphasis. Companies count on reliable suppliers–suppliers that deliver consistent quality on time. An organization may not be able to function if purchases don't arrive when they're expected. For example, imagine what would happen on a Buick assembly line if Nexteer Automotive was a few days late delivering its adaptive steering wheels. Buick might have to shut down the assembly line. This would affect other suppliers–raising their costs–and Buick's dealers might not be happy if they lost car sales.

The cost of poor quality can also be significant. Airbags made by Takata were found to be defective[1]–but that was after 30 million cars (in the United States alone) were already on the road with the faulty safety device. The total cost of replacing all those airbags was more than half a billion dollars, not counting the harm to the reputations of the automakers involved.

Behavioral needs still matter

Although economic needs are usually primary, B2B sellers know that organizational buyers are also influenced by noneconomic factors. Some of the behavioral dimensions mentioned in Chapter 4, such as security, status, and a sense of accomplishment, are relevant here, too. Purchasing managers and others involved in buying decisions are also human–they worry about their jobs, want respect from peers, and usually seek friendly relationships with suppliers.

A seller's marketing mix may need to consider both the needs of the company and the individual. Buyers want to avoid taking risks that reflect badly on their decisions. Honda reminds customers that its reputation for reliability is something they can count on—that lowers the risk a buyer might feel buying an unknown brand. A.O. Smith knows that organizational buyers want to save their company money, but they also want to feel good about their choices.
(left) Source: American Honda Motor Co., Inc.; (right) Source: A.O. Smith

For example, some purchasing people want to be seen—inside and outside their company—as more forward thinking. These buyers are often eager to imitate progressive competitors or even to be the first to try new products. Such innovators deserve special attention when new products are being introduced. Organizational buyers want to do their jobs well, and good suppliers try to help them accomplish that. Along those lines, a recent survey found that buyers are more motivated to receive and open e-mails from marketers who offer fresh insight and ideas.

For many purchases, organizational buyers know that choosing a supplier that provides inconsistent quality or late deliveries can be very costly—but it also means the buyer may be blamed. Buyers want to avoid this risk—and a marketer who develops a marketing mix that lowers the buyer's personal risk puts himself or herself in a stronger position.

A seller's marketing mix should satisfy *both* the needs of the customer company and the needs of individuals who influence the purchase. Therefore, sellers need to find an overlapping[2] area where both can be satisfied. See Exhibit 5-3 for a summary of this idea.

Exhibit 5-3
Overlapping Needs of Individual Influencers and the Customer Organization

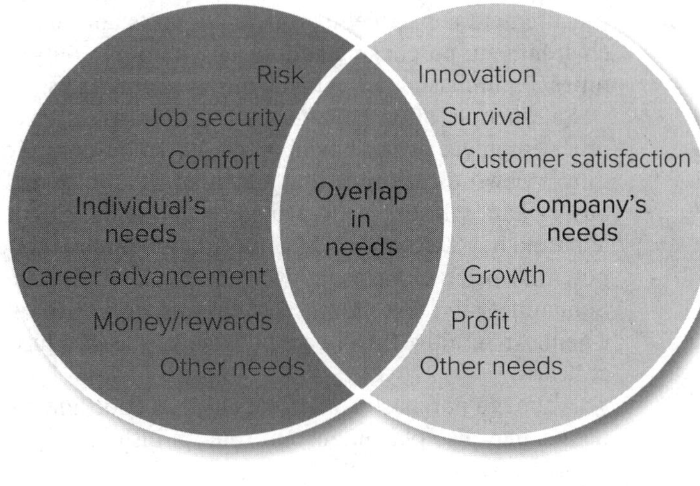

Ethical conflicts may arise

While consumers have ethical issues to consider when making purchases, organizational buyers must be careful to avoid a conflict between their own self-interest and company outcomes. This can be difficult; sometimes the ethical line can be blurry. Consequently, some firms set strict ethical guidelines. Marketers must be careful here. A salesperson offering a company pen to a prospect may view the giveaway as part of the promotion effort—but the customer firm may have a policy against employees accepting any gift from a supplier.

Although most organizational buyers act in an ethical manner, there have been highly publicized abuses. For example, Omnicare Inc., which provides pharmaceutical drugs to customers that include nursing homes, was charged with soliciting and receiving kickback payments from its nursing home customers and drug maker suppliers, including Johnson & Johnson (J&J). J&J and Omnicare apparently sold the drug Risperdal to nursing homes as a treatment for dementia and anxiety, conditions for which it was not approved. The two companies also agreed to downplay risks of diabetes and weight gain when talking to patients and doctors. The case may cost the two firms more than $1 billion in fines and other charges—plus untold damage to their reputations.

Marketers need to take concerns about conflict of interest very seriously. Part of the promotion job is to persuade different individuals who may influence an organization's purchase. Yet the whole marketing effort may be tainted if it even *appears* that a marketer has encouraged a person who influences a decision to put personal gain ahead of company interest. The pressure marketing managers feel to make sales goals must be tempered by ethical choices.

Ethical Dilemma

What would you do? Assume that you are a salesperson in a small company. For months you've been trying to get a big order from a large firm. A purchasing manager at the firm casually mentions that she is trying to help two friends find tickets for a big hockey game. Your boss has season tickets for entertaining customers, but you know that the purchasing manager's company strictly prohibits any gift to employees. When you ask your boss what to do, the reply is, "Well, the tickets would be used by the friends and not the customer firm's employee, so you can offer them if you think you should."

What should you do? What are the pros and cons of your decision?

Purchasing managers are specialists

Many organizations rely on specialists to ensure that purchases are handled sensibly. These specialists have different titles in different firms (such as procurement officer, supply manager, purchasing agent, or buyer), but basically they are all **purchasing managers**—buying specialists for their employers. In large organizations, they usually specialize by product area and are real experts.

Some people think purchasing is handled by clerks who sit in cubicles[3] and do the paperwork to place orders. That view is out of date. Today, most firms look to their procurement departments to help cut costs and provide competitive advantage. In this environment, purchasing people have a lot of clout[4]. And there are good job opportunities in purchasing for capable business graduates.

Salespeople often have to see a purchasing manager first—before they contact any other employee at the buying firm. These buyers hold important positions and take a dim[5] view of sales reps that try to go around them. Rather than being "sold," these buyers want salespeople to provide accurate information that will help them solve problems and buy wisely. They like information on new goods and services, as well as tips on potential price changes, supply shortages, and other changes in market conditions. Sometimes all it takes for a sales rep to keep a buyer up to date is to send an occasional e-mail. An intuitive buyer can tell when a sales rep has the customer firm's best interests at heart.

Although purchasing managers usually coordinate relationships with suppliers, other people may also play important roles in influencing the purchase decision.

Multiple buying influence in a buying center

Multiple buying influence means that several people—perhaps even top management—play a part in making a purchase decision. Possible buying influences include the following:

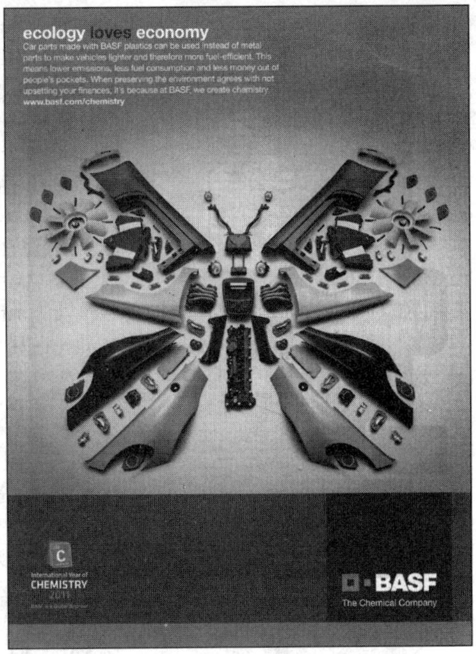

BASF plastics can be used in automobile parts—replacing heavier metal parts. The lower weight can increase fuel efficiency. BASF personnel work with purchasing managers and engineers at automakers to determine where plastic parts offer the greatest benefit to the end user (car buyer).
Source: BASF Corporation 2015

1. *Users*—perhaps production line workers or their supervisors.
2. *Influencers*—perhaps engineering or R&D people who help write specifications or supply information for evaluating alternatives.
3. *Buyers*—the purchasing managers who have the responsibility for working with suppliers and arranging the terms of the sale.
4. *Deciders*—the people in the organization who have the power to select or approve the supplier—often a purchasing manager but perhaps top management for larger purchases.
5. *Gatekeepers*—people who control the flow of information within the organization. Gatekeepers might include purchasing managers, receptionists, secretaries, research assistants, bookkeepers, and many more.

The following example portrays how different buying influences work in the purchase of a corporate jet. A company that already owns a corporate jet may decide it is time to lease a new one. The current lease is expiring and a newer jet would have better fuel efficiency and be more reliable. Middle and upper management (users) would be likely to provide comments on features they would like to see in the new model. Thus, they play the roles of influencers. The expert knowledge of the chief pilot and the airplane mechanic would make them significant influencers on the purchase. The chief pilot might also serve as gatekeeper by deciding which information and how much of his expertise he shares with others. A finance executive would also be likely to weigh in (another influencer) with thoughts on costs and financing the purchase. An assistant to the purchasing manager (gatekeeper) does online searches for information and decides what information to put into a report. After recommendations have been made, a large multimillion-dollar purchase like a corporate jet might go before the board of directors (deciders) for final approval. After all these buying influences are considered and a particular jet is selected, one of the

A company's purchase of a corporate jet is likely to involve multiple buying influence—meaning several people from the buying firm will play a part in making a purchase decision.
Source: Cessna Aircraft Company

purchasing agents for the firm (the buyer) works with the chosen supplier to arrange the terms of the sale, including delivery dates, payment, installation, and after-sale service.

It is helpful to think of a **buying center** as all the people who participate in (or influence) a purchase. Because different people may make up a buying center from one decision to the next, the salesperson must study each case carefully. Just learning whom to talk with may be hard, but thinking about the various roles in the buying center can help.

The salesperson may have to talk to every member of the buying center—stressing different topics for each. This not only complicates the promotion job but also lengthens it. Approval of a routine order may take anywhere from a day to several months. On very important purchases—a new building, major equipment, or a new information system—the selling period may take a year or more.

Buying procedures are standardized

Buying organizations often establish formal procedures governing how purchases are made. For example, if a contract exists with an office supply vendor, everyone in the organization may be required to make their purchases through a special website. A person who needs to purchase something may have to complete a **requisition**[6]—a request to buy something. For larger purchases, there may be rules requiring that multiple suppliers are contacted so that prices can be compared.

If a large organization has facilities at dispersed locations, much of the purchasing work may be done at a central location. With centralized buying, a sales rep may be able to sell to facilities all over a country—or even across several countries—without leaving the base city. Walmart handles many of the purchase decisions for stores in its retail chain from its headquarters in Arkansas. Many purchasing decisions for agencies of the U.S. government are handled in Washington, DC.

The general procedures for organizational buying are outlined in the next section.

A Model of Business and Organizational Buying

Business and organizational buying generally follows the three-step approach shown in Exhibit 5-4. Depending on the nature of the purchase, how each step plays out can vary—and the third step is not always routinely reviewed. The next few sections of this chapter will examine more closely these three steps. Let's begin by looking at how organizations define the problem by narrowing down from problem recognition to specifying a particular solution.

Exhibit 5-4 A Model of Organizational Buying

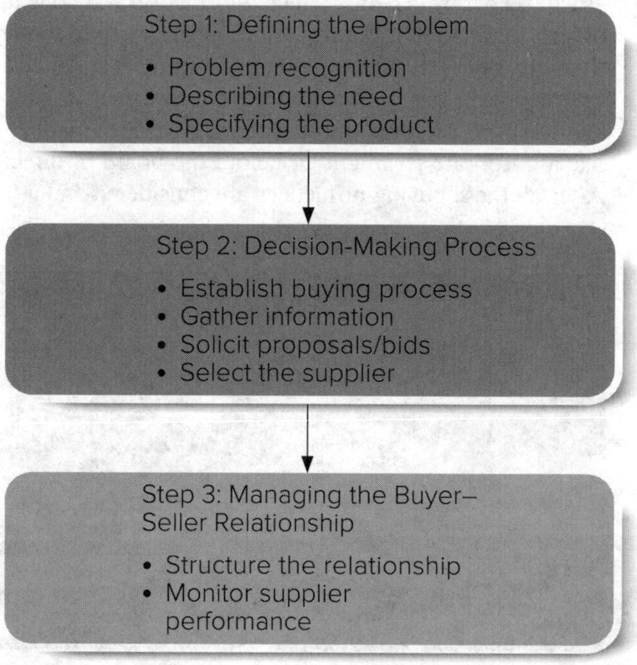

Step 1: Defining the Problem

Organizations make purchases to satisfy needs. Generally speaking, most organizations make purchases for the same basic reason: They buy goods and services that will help them meet the demand for the goods and services that they in turn supply to their markets. In other words, their basic need is to satisfy their own customers and clients. A producer buys because it wants to earn a profit by making and selling goods or services. A wholesaler or retailer buys products it can profitably resell to its customers. A town government wants to meet legal and social obligations to its citizens.

From recognizing problems to describing needs

At their earliest stages, problems may not be well understood. A manufacturer might be seeking a way to speed up production. A dentist might wonder if there is a better way to bill her customers. A clothing retailer may be looking for spring fashions to appeal to its target market. A school district may be seeking a way to provide more students with access to computers. Each of these realizations can trigger the organization to seek more details about the problem at hand.

Ultimately, the problem should be narrowed down to a more specific need. What product or service can solve the client's problem? Selling organizations often try to get in at this stage. Some sellers even help the buyer realize they have a problem—for example, a seller of medical office management software might send direct mail to dentists describing the benefits other dental offices have received after using its software.

Specifications describe the product

In other situations, an organization may simply decide what it wants and move quickly through this stage. Often larger organizations, with formal procedures, spend more time detailing the purchase requirements. In this case, organizational buyers may buy on the basis of a set of **purchasing specifications**—a written description of what the firm wants to buy. When quality is highly standardized, as is often the case with manufactured items, the specification may simply consist of a brand name or part number.

Often, however, when the purchase requirements are more complicated, the specifications may set out detailed information about the performance standards the product must meet. Purchase specifications for services tend to be detailed because services are less standardized and usually are not performed until after they're purchased.

Eastman Chemical Co. developed Eastman Tritan, an innovative copolyester (plasticlike) material. Tritan is durable, heat resistant, and offers design flexibility and ease of processing. It is ideal for the molded parts needed by kitchen appliance manufacturers. Promotion from Eastman Chemical, possibly through ads like this one or a salesperson calling on a buyer, will help the buying firm recognize a need and see that Tritan is the solution.
Source: Eastman Chemical Company

Step 2: The Decision-Making Process

After the buying organization recognizes the problem, describes the need, and specifies the product, the next step involves the decision-making process—how a firm decides whether to buy, what to buy, and what criteria to consider when evaluating suppliers. Buyers then gather information, solicit proposals from suppliers, and finally choose a supplier. The decision-making process can vary depending on the nature of the purchase—so we start by looking at different buying processes (see Exhibit 5-5).

Three kinds of buying processes are useful

New-task buying occurs when a customer organization has a new need and wants a great deal of information. The company may have never purchased this type of product before. For example, an automaker that was just starting an electric car project may be purchasing large batteries for the first time. New-task buying involves setting product specifications, evaluating sources of supply, and establishing an order routine that can be followed in the future if results are satisfactory. Multiple buying influence is most often found in new-task buying.

A **straight rebuy** is a routine repurchase that may have been made many times before. Buyers probably don't bother looking for new information or new sources of supply. Most of a company's small or recurring purchases are of this type—but they take only a small part of an organized buyer's time. Think of a grocery store placing an order to refill 21-ounce boxes of Cheerios because supply is low. Important purchases may be made this way too—but only after the firm has decided what procedure will be "routine."

The **modified rebuy** is the in-between process where some review of the buying situation is done—though not as much as in new-task buying. This might be a buying decision that has not been done before, or the criteria used to make a purchase decision may have changed. For example, the firm may have new objectives around sustainability that were not part of previous buying decisions.

Straight rebuys often use e-commerce order systems

E-commerce computer systems *automatically* handle a large portion of straight rebuys. Buyers program decision rules that tell the computer how to order and leave the details of following through to the computer. For example, when a machine tool maker receives an order that requires certain materials or parts, the computer information system automatically orders them from the appropriate suppliers, sets the delivery date, and schedules production.

If conditions change, buyers modify the computer instructions. When nothing unusual happens, however, the computer system continues to routinely rebuy as needs develop—electronically sending purchase orders to the regular supplier.

New-task buying requires the most information

Whereas buyers want to stay current on all facets of purchasing, new-task buying situations motivate them to seek specific information. Often a new-task buy starts with a *user* who becomes aware of a need and begins researching solutions. Even though a

Exhibit 5-5
Organizational Buying Processes

Characteristics	Type of Process		
	New-Task Buying	Modified Rebuy	Straight Rebuy
Time Required	Much	Medium	Little
Multiple Influence	Much	Some	Little
Review of Suppliers	Much	Some	None
Information Needed	Much	Some	Little

wide variety of information sources are available (see Exhibit 5-6), business buyers will use the sources they trust. To build trust, a marketer must make sure its information is reliable and useful to the buyer. Sellers should present information objectively; if it appears too self-serving and biased toward the suppliers' offering, it may not be trusted or used by the buyer.

How much information a customer collects depends on the importance of the purchase and the level of uncertainty about what choice might be best. The time and expense of searching for information may not be justified for a minor purchase. But a major purchase often involves real detective work by the buyer.

New-task buying situations provide a good opportunity for a new supplier to make inroads with a customer. With a buyer actively searching for information, the seller's promotion has a much greater chance of being noticed and having an impact. Advertising, trade show exhibits, e-mails, and salespeople can all help build the buyer's attention, but an informative website may be essential for getting attention in the first place.

Search engines—a first step to gathering information

Most purchasing managers start with an Internet search when they need to identify new suppliers, better ways to meet needs, or information to improve decisions. Buyers often rely on highly specialized search engines–like one that finds all types of steel that meet certain technical specifications and then compares prices. But buyers also use general-purpose search engines such as Google. A search across the whole web can often locate off-the-shelf products that eliminate the need to buy expensive, custom-made items. For example, a firm in Saudi Arabia ordered $1,000 worth of tiny rubber grommets[7] from Allstates Rubber & Tool, a small firm in the suburbs of Chicago. If the buyer's search hadn't located Allstates' website, the only alternative would have been to pay much more for custom-made grommets–and Allstates wouldn't have picked up a new customer.

Marketing managers know that it is critical to have a website that buyers can find. That's why suppliers often pay for a sponsored link (an ad) that appears when certain keywords are included in a search. A supplier might also change its website so that it is more likely to appear high on a list of searches.

Buyers want sites with useful content

Having useful content on a website not only moves it higher on the buyer's search results, but also gives buyers a reason to fully explore the seller's website. Instead of trying to sell the customer, a supplier needs to educate buyers about their needs and present the advantages and disadvantages of the seller's products. Buyers like to read targeted **white papers** (an authoritative report or guide that addresses important issues in an industry and offers solutions). White papers may advocate a seller's solution, but if they appear objective, they can help establish a firm as a thought leader in a particular area. Buyers also like to read case studies to learn about how other companies have addressed similar needs. Video content and blogs can also make a seller's website more useful.

Exhibit 5-6 Major Sources of Information Used by Organizational Buyers

	Marketing sources	Nonmarketing sources
Personal sources	• Salespeople • Others from supplier firms • Trade shows	• Buying center members • Outside business associates • Consultants and outside experts
Impersonal sources	• Online events and virtual trade shows • Sales literature and catalogs • E-mails and newsletters • Website content including blogs, video, case studies, and white papers • Social media (a company LinkedIn page)	• Online searches • Rating services • Trade associations • News publications • Product directories • Online communities • Social media (comments on LinkedIn)

Buyers share experiences in online communities

Buyers especially value recommendations from others who have already dealt with a similar need. Sometimes they turn to their LinkedIn network (an online social media site for business people) to solicit advice from colleagues. Others turn to online communities. For example, at Spiceworks Community (www.spiceworks.com), IT professionals ask and answer technical questions, research best practices, and learn what others think about a product or service they are considering. Buyers trust this source of information, and similar online communities have developed around other industries. As buyers rely more on social networks, communications from marketers may have less influence on buyers' attitudes and choices.

Solicit proposals from suppliers

When buyers in B2B markets identify potential suppliers, they contact one or more suppliers for proposals. A supplier may simply send a brochure or product catalog, or it may have a salesperson contact the buyer over the phone. In more complex buying situations, there may be formal presentations from different suppliers that also submit detailed proposals.

To learn more about how the next generation of B2B buyers gathers information, researches, and buys, check out *What's Next?* Millennials take on organizational buying.

Buyers ask for competitive bids to compare offerings

Sometimes buyers will ask suppliers to submit a **competitive bid**—the terms of sale offered by the supplier in response to the purchase specifications posted by a buyer. If different suppliers' quality, dependability, and delivery schedules all meet the specs, the buyer will select the low-price bid. But a creative marketer needs to look carefully at the buyer's specs—and the need—to see if changing other elements of the marketing mix could provide a competitive advantage.

Source: State of California

Rather than search for suppliers, buyers sometimes post their requirements and invite qualified suppliers to submit a bid. Some firms set up or participate in a procurement website that directs suppliers to companies (or divisions of a company) that need to make purchases. These sites make it easy for suppliers to find out about the purchase needs of the organizations that sponsor the sites. This helps increase the number of suppliers competing for the business and that can drive down prices or provide more beneficial terms of sale. For example, when the California Department of Transportation was planning $4 billion in new construction projects, it established a procurement site so that potential suppliers knew each project's requirements for submitting a competitive bid.

Evaluating and selecting suppliers

Considering all of the factors relevant to a purchase decision can be very complex. A supplier or product that is best in one way may not be best in others. To try to deal with these situations, many firms use **vendor analysis**—a formal rating of suppliers on all relevant areas of performance. The purpose isn't just to get a low price from the supplier on a given part or service. Rather, the goal is to lower the *total costs* associated with purchases. Analysis might show that the best vendor is the one that helps the customer reduce costs of excess inventory[8], retooling of equipment, or defective parts.

Sustainability matters, too

Many buying firms find that adding sustainability to a vendor analysis is more than just the "right thing to do." Attention to sustainability often identifies unexpected savings. For example, when Falconbridge Limited's aluminum smelter changed to more efficient (but more expensive) lightbulbs, it saved almost $100,000 per year in energy bills. When the Fairmont Hotel in Vancouver searched for alternative swimming pool chemicals, an environmentally friendly option proved healthier for guests and cut costs.

Some progressive firms don't need to see financial benefits; they simply make sustainability an essential buying criterion. New Belgium Brewing Company put sustainable values in its mission statement; that means its purchasing people select more

What's Next? Millennials take on organizational buying

In Chapter 2 we described how the large number of Millennials—Americans born between 1978 and 1994—and their particular worldview affects *consumer* buying behavior. These days, Millennials are increasingly responsible for *organizational* buying—and they bring new attitudes and approaches. Three surveys of more than 5,000 organizational buyers sheds some light on how the rise of Millennials may affect *What's Next?* in organizational buying and, consequently, B2B marketing strategy planning. Let's look more closely at a few Millennial practices and how some suppliers are responding.

It's no surprise that Millennials are more likely to jump online when researching a potential supplier. This group is comfortable with the Internet and Google. One study found that search engines or a vendor's website were the single most important information source for almost half of Millennial respondents. In fact, buyers report conducting an average of 12 online searches *before* even clicking on a supplier's website. Connecting with vendor salespeople occurs even further along in many organizational buying situations.

It might be a surprise that "social media" was named most important by 11 percent of Millennial buyers. The social media channel used most often was Facebook (40 percent), followed by YouTube (16 percent) and Google+ (13 percent), with LinkedIn lagging behind (7 percent). Millennial buyers visit a supplier's Facebook page to read customer comments and company replies.

Millennials have pretty clear preferences about how they like their information presented—video please! When asked their first choice for content delivery, 29 percent chose video, well ahead of "text" case studies (19 percent), white papers (16 percent), and brochures (15 percent). Research also showed that videos do more than create awareness; 70 percent of organizational buyers watch videos throughout the buying process, with almost half watching more than 30 minutes of total video content while researching a purchase.

Some B2B suppliers already see *What's Next?* Take General Electric (GE), a $125 billion company that builds aircraft engines, medical imaging equipment, locomotives, and a whole lot more. GE's Facebook page is inviting: "We love science, technology, innovation, and hearing from you! So, say hello." The GE Facebook page (just one of its many social media channels) posts questions, pictures, and videos. Some campaigns build GE's brand. For example, the video *What If Millie Dresselhaus, Female Scientist, Was Treated Like a Celebrity* has almost a million views and promotes women in science. Videos also promote specific products; the GE Digital YouTube channel features *GE Digital's APM Enables Intelligent Asset Strategies*. Although this video has less than 5,000 views, those viewers are often researchers and decision makers influencing multimillion-dollar software purchases.

Big budgets and highly produced videos are not required to connect with customers. Jeanine Blackwell's small business helps companies create online training programs. She regularly records two- to three-minute videos with her phone in places like her car or office. She posts them on her Facebook page and website where customers appreciate her inspiration and tips.

The bottom line: Marketing managers who adapt marketing strategies to better fit the needs of the new Millennial buyers will see long-term benefits.

What could a company that sells automobile parts to auto manufacturers do to better appeal to Millennial organizational buyers? What about a computer maker that buys hard drives?

energy-efficient (but higher-priced) brew kettles, buy wind-powered electricity, and build facilities that are more costly but use the latest green ideas.

Buying procedures can vary

From our earlier discussion, you can see that buyers make important decisions about how to deal with one or more suppliers. At one extreme, a buying firm might want to rely on competition among all available vendors to get the best price on every order it places. The buyer cares little about which supplier fills the order; only the price and delivery time matter, and maybe a different vendor is chosen to fill each order. On the other hand, there are situations where it makes sense to routinely buy everything from a single vendor with which a buyer already has a good relationship. In practice, there are many important and common variations between these extremes. To better understand the variations, let's take a closer look at the benefits and limitations of different types of buyer–seller relationships.

Step 3: Managing Buyer–Seller Relationships in Business Markets

After selecting a supplier, the buyer and seller must figure out how to structure and manage the relationship. Many organizational purchases are ongoing–a buyer will make regular purchases. Other purchases, might involve a single transaction–buying a replacement part for example. Buyers and suppliers should work together to figure out the best way to structure the relationship. In this section we look at the many different considerations for managing buyer-seller relationships.

Close relationships may produce mutual benefits

There are often significant benefits of a close working relationship between a supplier and a customer firm. And such relationships are becoming common. Many firms are reducing the number of suppliers with whom they work–expecting more in return from the suppliers that remain. The best relationships involve real partnerships where there's mutual trust and a long-term outlook. Closely tied firms often share tasks at lower total cost than would be possible working at arm's length.

The partnership between AlliedSignal and Betz Laboratories, for example, shows the benefits of a good relationship. Awhile back, Betz was just one of several suppliers that sold Allied chemicals to keep the water in its plants from gunking up pipes and rusting machinery. But Betz didn't stop at selling commodity powders. Teams of Betz experts and Allied engineers studied each plant to find places where water was being wasted. In less than a year, a team in one plant found $2.5 million in potential cost savings. For example, by adding a few valves to recycle the water in a cooling tower, Betz was able to save 300 gallons of water a minute, resulting in savings of more than $100,000 a year and reduced environmental impact. Because of ideas like this, Allied's overall use of water treatment chemicals decreased. However, Betz sales to Allied doubled because it became Allied's only supplier of water chemicals.

Relationships can involve many from both sides

As the Allied-Betz Laboratories collaboration shows, some buyer-seller relationships can involve multiple buying influence–more than just a purchasing agent and a salesperson. To develop effective solutions, those closest to the problems should be directly involved. This may mean bringing people together from accounting, finance, production, information systems, and/or other functional areas of both the buyer and seller firms.

Relationships may not make sense

Although close relationships can produce benefits, they are not always best. For buyers, long-term commitments can also reduce flexibility. When competition drives down prices and spurs innovation, customers may be better off letting suppliers compete for their business. It may not be worth the customer's investment to build a relationship for purchases that are not particularly important or made that frequently. Besides that, close relationships take time and attention to build and manage.

In today's business markets, many suppliers of goods and services seek to build long-term relationships that provide value for their customers. Kaleidoscope provides services to help its customers with brand strategy and design. In this ad, Kaleidescope says "'Bite-sized' relationships are a dime a dozen. But there is nothing sweeter than working with people you like who deliver consistent results year after year... ."
Courtesy of Kaleidoscope

Sellers don't usually want closer relationships with all of their customers either. Some customers may place orders that are too small or require so much special attention that the relationship would never be profitable for the seller. Also, in situations where a customer doesn't want a relationship, trying to build one may cost more than it's worth. Buyers and sellers should choose closer relationships where the benefits outweigh the costs.

Relationships have many dimensions

Relationships are not "all or nothing" arrangements. Many firms may have a close relationship in some ways and not in others. Thus, it's useful to think about five key dimensions that help characterize most buyer–seller relationships: cooperation, information sharing, operational linkages, legal bonds, and relationship-specific adaptations. Purchasing managers for the buying firm and salespeople for the supplier usually coordinate the different dimensions of a relationship. However, as shown in Exhibit 5–7, close relationships often involve direct contacts between a number of people from other areas in both firms.

Cooperation treats problems as joint responsibilities

In cooperative relationships, the buyer and seller work together to achieve both mutual and individual objectives. The two firms treat problems that arise as a joint responsibility. National Semiconductor (NS) and Siltec, a supplier of silicon wafers, found clever ways to cooperate and cut costs. Workers at the NS plant used to throw away the expensive plastic cassettes that Siltec uses to ship the silicon wafers. Now Siltec and NS cooperate to recycle the cassettes. This helps the environment and also saves more than $300,000 a year. Siltec passes along most of that to NS as lower prices.

Shared information is useful but may be risky

Some relationships involve open sharing of information. This might include the exchange of proprietary[9] cost data or demand forecasts or working jointly on new product designs. Information might be shared in discussions between personnel, or through information systems connected via the Internet, a key facet of B2B e-commerce. The electronic approach has a big advantage in that it is fast and easy to update the information. It also saves time. A customer can check detailed product specs or the status of a job on the production line without having to wait for someone to respond.

Information sharing can lead to better decisions and better planning. However, firms don't want to share information if there's a risk that a partner might misuse it. For example, one of General Motors' suppliers shared some of its planned technology to the automaker. It later found out that General Motors' purchasing chief showed blueprints of that secret technology to competing suppliers. Violations of trust in a relationship are an ethical matter and should be taken seriously.

Suppliers can be wary of sharing bad news with an important customer. For example, a supplier may wait to tell a customer of financial problems—and that can cause trouble. When Edscha, a German supplier of sunroofs to BMW, unexpectedly filed for insolvency[10], BMW had a crisis in the making. BMW was about to launch its new Z4 convertible—and

Exhibit 5–7 Key Dimensions of Relationships in Business Markets

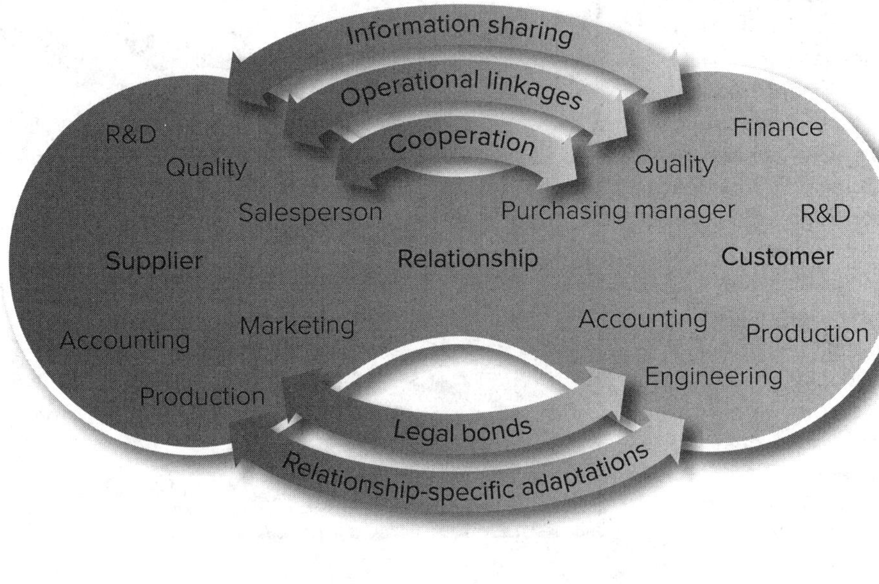

Edscha supplied all the tops. Getting a new supplier up-to-speed would have taken six months, so BMW scrambled to support Edscha and launch the Z4 on schedule. A more trusting and open relationship might have provided more lead time to work out problems.

Operational linkages share functions between firms

Operational linkages are direct ties between the internal operations of the buyer and seller firms. These linkages usually involve ongoing coordination of activities between the firms. Shared activities are especially important when neither firm, working on its own, can perform a function as well as the two firms can working together.

Business customers often require operational linkages to reduce total inventory costs, maintain adequate inventory levels, and keep production lines moving. On the other hand, keeping too much inventory is expensive. Providing a customer with inventory when it's needed may require that a supplier be able to provide **just-in-time delivery**—reliably getting products there *just* before the customer needs them. For now, it's enough to know that closer relationships between buyers and sellers involve operational linkages that lower costs and increase efficiency.

Contracts spell out obligations

Many purchases in business markets are simple transactions. The seller's responsibility is to transfer title to goods or perform services, and the buyer's responsibility is to pay the agreed price. However, more complex relationships may be spelled out in detailed legal contracts. An agreement may apply only for a short period, but long-term contracts are also common.

For example, a customer might ask a supplier to guarantee a 6 percent price reduction for a particular part for each of the next three years and pledge to virtually eliminate defects. In return, the customer might offer to double its orders and help the supplier boost productivity.

Sometimes the buyer and seller know roughly what is needed but can't fix all the details in advance. For example, specifications or total requirements may change over time. Then the relationship may involve **negotiated contract buying**, which means agreeing to contracts that allow for changes in the purchase arrangements. In such cases, the general project and basic price are described but with provision for changes and price adjustments up or down.

Some managers figure that even a detailed contract isn't a good substitute for regular good-faith reviews to make sure that neither party gets hurt by changing business conditions. Harley-Davidson used this approach when it moved toward closer relationships with a smaller number of suppliers. Purchasing executives tossed out detailed contracts and replaced them with a short statement of principles to guide relationships between Harley and its suppliers.

Spain's EmpordAigua offers consulting services to help firms manage water quality and usage. EmpordAigua believes that no two drops of water are alike—nor are any two customers' water needs. So EmpordAigua develops close buyer-seller relationships based on cooperation, information sharing, and relationship-specific adaptations to develop custom water solutions for each of its client's needs.
Source: EmpordAigUA® Water Design & Technology

Specific adaptations invest in the relationship

Relationship-specific adaptations involve changes in a firm's product or procedures that are unique to the needs or capabilities of a relationship partner. Industrial suppliers often custom design a new product for just one customer; this may require investments in R&D or new manufacturing technologies. MetoKote, in its relationship with John Deere in the case at the beginning of this chapter, made a specific adaptation by building its coating plant right next door to Deere's factory.

Buying firms may also adapt to a particular supplier. When Apple designed MacBook computers with an Intel computer chip, it made it difficult later to change to a different chipmaker. However, buyers are often hesitant to make big investments that increase dependence on a specific supplier. Typically, they do it only when there isn't a good alternative—perhaps because only one or a few suppliers are available to meet a need—or if the benefits of the investment are clear before it's made.

Specific adaptations are usually made when the buying organization chooses to **outsource**[11] contract with an outside firm to produce goods or services rather than to produce them internally. Many firms have turned to outsourcing to cut costs—and that's why much outsourcing is handled by suppliers in countries where labor costs are lower. For example, many American companies are outsourcing production to firms in China and customer service to India.

A powerful customer may control the relationship

Although a marketing manager may want to work in a cooperative partnership, that may be impossible with large customers who have the power to dictate how the relationship will work. Often a powerful customer negotiates lower prices from suppliers. For example, when Hewlett-Packard started selling personal computers through Walmart stores, it knew a rock-bottom price would be required. So it used its large sales volume to demand lower prices from its suppliers and the contract manufacturers that assembled the PCs. This helped H-P offer lower-priced computers while maintaining higher profit margins than its competition.

Buyers usually use several sources to spread their risk

Even if a marketing manager develops the best marketing mix possible and cultivates a close relationship with the customer, the customer may not give *all* of its business to one supplier. Buyers often look for several dependable sources of supply to protect themselves from unpredictable events such as strikes, fires, or floods in one of their suppliers' plants. For example, Western Digital, the world's largest provider of hard-disk drives, produces most of its drives in Thailand. When flooding in Thailand closed down many of Western Digital's manufacturing plants, it significantly tightened the world's supply of personal computers.

Even when buyers don't want a single source of supply, a good marketing mix is still likely to win a larger share of the total business—which can prove to be very important. From a buyer's point of view, it may not seem like a big deal to give a particular supplier a 40 percent share of the orders rather than a 20 percent share. But for the seller that doubles their sales with that one customer—a 100 percent increase.

Buyers monitor supplier performance

Organizations routinely monitor supplier performance. Suppliers that fail to meet a buyer's performance expectations may be dropped. The process can be good for both buyer and supplier. Suppliers that perform well may find their share of a buyer's purchases go up. Suppliers that listen to feedback from customers can learn how to improve and increase the value of the relationship. Good buying organizations provide regular feedback to their suppliers without being asked—and smart suppliers listen closely and respond to them. Honda, for example, provides a monthly *scorecard* that details the supplier's performance in five areas: quality, delivery, quantity delivered, performance history, and any special incidents. The report fosters an ongoing dialogue between Honda suppliers about ways that both Honda and the supplier can work together to improve supplier performance.

Let's take a closer look at how a supplier scorecard works in practice in the *Marketing Analytics in Action: Supplier Scorecards* activity.

Marketing Analytics in Action: Supplier Scorecards

HighFly Drones is a manufacturer of drone aircraft for the hobbyist market. A particular printed circuit board (part number PX5534) is used in three of HighFly's most popular drone models. Because this product is so important, HighFly regularly purchases it from two different suppliers: Ace Electronics and Charter Components. The price for each PX5534 is $9.62, and each supplier is paid that same price.

Last year, each supplier received half of HighFly's orders. For the coming year, HighFly wants to work more closely with one PX5334 supplier, giving it 75 percent of the orders, while the other supplier would receive 25 percent. To help decide which supplier will get the greater part of the orders, the purchasing manager reviews the scorecards shown below for the two suppliers over the last three months. The suppliers are rated on three performance dimensions using a 0 to 100 scale, with 100 being the highest level of performance.

	Ace Electronics			Charter Components		
	Sept.	**Oct.**	**Nov.**	**Sept.**	**Oct.**	**Nov.**
Quality	85	88	92	98	86	78
Communication	81	72	84	92	94	92
Delivery	71	94	82	92	96	94
Average	**79**	**78**	**86**	**97**	**92**	**88**

Review the performance of Ace Electronics and Charter Components over the last three months, then answer the following questions:

1. *What kind of feedback do you think is warranted for Ace Electronics? What concerns do you have with its performance?*
2. *What kind of feedback do you think is warranted for Charter Components? What concerns do you have with its performance?*
3. *Which supplier should receive the larger share of HighFly's business, and why? Under what circumstances would you be inclined to choose the other supplier to receive the larger share?*

Variations in buying by customer type

We've been discussing aspects of relationships and buying approaches that generally apply with different types of customer organizations–in both the United States and internationally. However, it's also useful to have more detail about specific types of customers. Knowing the size, number, geographic location, and buying procedures of manufacturers, service firms, retailers, wholesalers, and governments helps marketing managers segment markets, identify targets, and create more effective marketing mixes.

Manufacturers Are Important Customers

There are not many big ones

One of the most striking facts about manufacturers is how few there are compared to final consumers. This is true in every country. In the United States, for example, there are about 250,000 factories. The majority of these are quite small–less than 2 percent have more than 500 employees and about three-quarters have fewer than 20 employees. Smaller manufacturing firms have a much less formal buying process than large firms.

Customers cluster in geographic areas

In addition to concentration by company size, industrial markets are concentrated in certain geographic areas. Internationally, industrial customers are concentrated in countries that are at the more advanced stages of economic development. From all the talk in the news about the United States shifting from an industrial economy to a service and information economy, you might conclude that the United States is an exception–that the industrial market in this country is shrinking. It is true that the number of people employed in manufacturing has been shrinking, but U.S. manufacturing output is higher than at any other time in the nation's history. The rate of growth, however, is fastest in countries where labor is cheapest.

Within a country, there is often further concentration of manufacturing in specific areas. In the United States, many factories are concentrated in big metropolitan areas—especially in New York, Pennsylvania, Ohio, Illinois, Texas, and California. There is also concentration by industry. In Germany, for example, the steel industry is concentrated in the Ruhr Valley. Most automobile manufacturing occurs in Michigan, Indiana, and Ohio.

Business data often classify industries

The products an industrial customer needs to buy depend on the business it is in. Because of this, sales of a product are often concentrated among customers in similar businesses. For example, apparel manufacturers are the main customers for zippers. Marketing managers must focus their marketing mixes on prospective customers who exhibit characteristics similar to their current customers.

Detailed information is often available to help a marketing manager learn more about customers in different lines of business. The U.S. government collects and publishes data by the **North American Industry Classification System (NAICS) codes**—groups of firms in similar lines of business. (NAICS is pronounced like "nakes.") The number of establishments, sales volumes, and number of employees—broken down by geographic areas—are given for each NAICS code. A number of other countries collect similar data, and some of them try to coordinate their efforts with an international variation of the NAICS system. However, in many countries data on business customers are incomplete or inaccurate.

So let's take a closer look at how the NAICS codes work. The NAICS code breakdowns start with broad industry categories such as construction (23), manufacturing (31), retail trade (44), and so on (see Exhibit 5-8). Within each two-digit industry breakdown, much more detailed data may be available for three-digit industries (that is, subindustries of the two-digit industries). For example, within the two-digit manufacturing industry (code 31) there are manufacturers of food (311), leather (316), and others, including apparel manufacturers (315). Then each three-digit group of firms is further subdivided into more detailed four-, five-, and six-digit classifications. For instance, within the three-digit (315) apparel manufacturers there are four-digit subgroups for knitting mills (3151), cut and sew apparel (3152), and producers of apparel accessories (3159). Exhibit 5-8 illustrates that breakdowns become more detailed as you move to codes with more digits. However, detailed data (say, broken down at the four-digit level) aren't available for all industries in every geographic area. The government does not provide detail when only one or two plants are located in an area.

Many firms find their *current* customers' NAICS codes and then look at NAICS-coded lists for similar companies that may need the same goods and services. Other companies look at which NAICS categories are growing or declining to discover new opportunities.

Producers of Services—Smaller and More Spread Out

The service side of the U.S. economy is large and has been growing fast. Service operations are also growing in some other countries. There are many good opportunities to provide these service companies with the products they need to support their operations. But there are also challenges.

The United States has almost 6 million service firms—more than 17 times as many as it has manufacturers. Some of these are big companies with international operations. Examples include AT&T, Hilton Hotels, Prudential Insurance, PricewaterhouseCoopers, Wells Fargo, and Accenture. These firms have purchasing departments that are like those in large manufacturing organizations. But as you might guess given the large number of service firms, most of them are small—Evans Dental Group, North Coast Maid Service, and Affordable Computer Repair. They're also more spread out around the country than manufacturing concerns. Factories often locate where transportation facilities are good, raw materials are available, and it is less costly to produce goods in quantity. Service operations, in contrast, often have to be close to their customers.

Exhibit 5-8 Illustrative NAICS Code Breakdown for Apparel Manufacturers

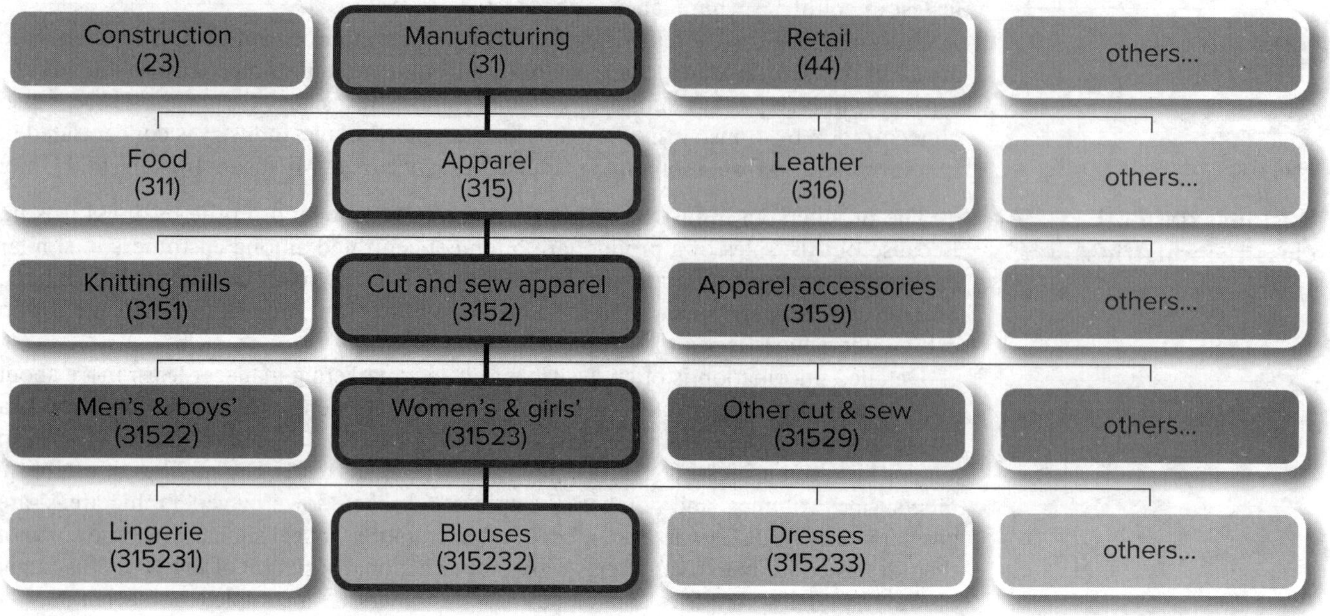

Buying may not be as formal

Purchases by small service firms are often handled by whoever is in charge or their administrative assistant. This may be a doctor, lawyer, owner of a local insurance agency, hotel manager, or office manager. Suppliers who usually deal with purchasing specialists in large organizations may have trouble adjusting to this market. Personal selling is still an important part of promotion, but reaching these customers in the first place often requires more advertising. And small service firms may need much more help in buying than a large corporation.

Small service customers like Internet buying

Small service companies that don't attract much personal attention from salespeople often rely on e-commerce for many of their purchases. Purchases by small customers can add up—so for many suppliers these customers are an important target market. Increasingly suppliers cater to the needs of these customers with specially designed websites. A well-designed website can be efficient for both customers and suppliers. Customers can get information, place orders, or follow up with a call or e-mail for personal attention from a salesperson or customer service rep when it's needed.

In a smaller service organization, purchases may be made by the person who is in charge rather than a person with full-time responsibility for purchasing. This ad recognizes this reality and tries to make renting from Hertz for this target market easy.
Source: The Hertz Corporation

Retailers and Wholesalers Buy for Their Customers

Most retail and wholesale buyers see themselves as purchasing agents for their target customers—remembering the old saying that "Goods well bought are half sold." For example, the buying specialist at Walgreens drug stores who handles products targeted at ethnic consumers is a real expert. He knows what ethnic customers want and won't be persuaded by a sales rep for a manufacturer who can't provide it. He might also work closely with Televisa, a manufacturer of hair care and skin care products, to produce a line of products targeting the growing Hispanic market.

Committee buying is impersonal

Space in retail stores is limited, and buyers for retail chains simply are not interested in carrying every product that some salesperson wants them to sell. In an average week, 150 to 250 new items are offered to the buying offices of a large chain such as Safeway. If the chain accepted all of them, it would add 10,000 new items during a single year! Obviously, these firms need a way to deal with this overload. Most retailers carefully evaluate products. A product has to prove itself before gaining widespread adoption.

Decisions to add or drop lines or change buying policies may be handled by a *buying committee.* The seller still calls on and gives a pitch to a buyer—but the buyer does not have final responsibility. Instead, the buyer prepares forms summarizing proposals for new products and passes them on to the committee for evaluation. The seller may not get to present her story to the buying committee in person. This rational, almost cold-blooded, approach certainly reduces the impact of a persuasive salesperson. On the other hand, it may favor a firm that has hard data on how its whole marketing mix will help the retailer attract and keep customers.

The entrepreneurs who started PenAgain (a uniquely shaped writing tool), for example, had to have more than a distinct product to get shelf space at Walmart. Their presentation to Walmart had to include hard data showing their marketing mix already worked well in other retail stores and evidence of their ability to supply the large quantities a retailer the size of Walmart would need. After that, Walmart might sell PenAgain in a limited number of stores, seeking evidence the product met sales targets, before selling it in all its stores.

Buyers watch computer output closely

Most larger firms use sophisticated computerized inventory replenishment[12] systems. Scanners at retail checkout counters keep track of what goes out the door—and computers use these data to update the records. Even small retailers and wholesalers use automated control systems that create daily reports showing sales of every product. Buyers with this kind of information know, in detail, the profitability of the different competing products. If a product isn't moving, the retailer isn't likely to be impressed by a salesperson's request for more in-store attention or added shelf space.

Reorders are straight rebuys

Retailers and wholesalers usually carry a large number of products. A drug wholesaler, for example, may carry up to 125,000 products. Because they deal with so many products, most intermediaries buy their products on a routine, automatic reorder basis—straight rebuys—once they make the initial decision to stock specific items. Au-

Retailers see themselves as buying agents for their target customers—but they also have to determine what they can profitably sell. Retailers are attracted to well-known brands such as Dove because they know their consumers are more likely to buy brands they know. Chiquita wants to remind convenience stores that selling bananas can bring profits.
(left) Source: Mars, Incorporated; (right) Source: Chiquita Brands L.L.C.

tomatic computer ordering is a natural outgrowth of computerized checkout systems. Sellers to these markets must understand the size of the buyer's job and have something useful to say and do when they call.

The Government Market

Size and diversity

Some marketers ignore the government market because they think that government red tape[13] is more trouble than it's worth. They probably don't realize how big the government market really is. Government is the largest customer group in many countries–including the United States. About 30 percent of the U.S. gross domestic product is spent by various government units. Different government units buy almost every kind of product. They run not only schools, police departments, and military organizations, but also supermarkets, public utilities, research laboratories, offices, hospitals, and even liquor stores. These huge government expenditures cannot be ignored by an aggressive marketing manager.

The City of San Jose worked with a number of suppliers when it built the Lake Cunningham Regional Skate Park. Among the city's vendors for this project:

1. California Skateparks of Upland, California, used 800 cubic yards of a special spray concrete mixture to create the park's bowls, halfpipes, and walls.
2. Robert A. Bothman, Inc., from San Jose, California, created planters that were filled with wildflowers, native grasses, and palms to give the park more color and shade.
3. Musco Lighting from Oskaloosa, Iowa, lit the park with 50-foot poles, each bearing three 1,500-watt fixtures.

Courtesy of Dan Sparagna

Competitive bids may be required

Government buyers in the United States are expected to spend money wisely–in the public interest–so their purchases are usually subject to much public review. To avoid charges of favoritism, most government customers buy by specification using a competitive bidding procedure. Often the government buyer must accept the lowest bid that meets the specifications. You can see how important it is for the buyer to write precise and complete specifications. Otherwise, sellers may submit a bid that fits the specs but doesn't really match what is needed. By law, a government unit might have to accept the lowest bid–even for an unwanted product.

The approved supplier list

Specification and bidding difficulties aren't problems in all government orders. Items that are bought frequently–or for which there are widely accepted standards–are purchased routinely. The government unit simply places an order at a previously approved price. To share in this business, a supplier must be on the list of approved suppliers and agree on a price that will stay the same for a specific period–perhaps a year.

Learning what government wants

In the United States, there are about 90,000 local government units (school districts, cities, counties, and states) as well as many federal agencies that make purchases. Some firms sell directly to government agencies; others work with prime contractors that resell to the government. Both are good opportunities for many businesses. Often small and medium-size businesses find it easier to sell to prime contractors rather than win a contract with a large government agency. Potential suppliers should focus on the government units or prime contractors they want to cater to and learn the bidding methods of those units. Then, they should monitor websites where government contracts are advertised. Target marketing can make a big contribution here—making sure the marketing mixes are well matched with the different bid procedures.

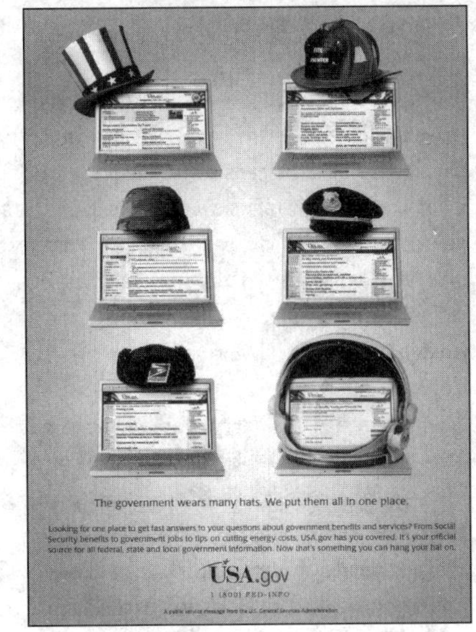

Source: USA.gov

Because government agencies want to promote competition for their business, marketers are provided with a lot of information—in print form and online. The U.S. government has a central source and USA.gov is a great place to start. There are also resources at FedBizOpps.gov (www.fbo.gov), including videos, publications, and a search tool to find opportunities to fit a firm's strategy. The General Services Administration handles vendor contracts for off-the-shelf goods and services; information for vendors is available at www.gsa.gov. Every federal government agency has a separate office devoted to small businesses with direct links to prime contractors. Various state and local governments also offer guidance, as do government units in other countries.

Dealing with foreign governments

Foreign governments offer a good opportunity for some organizations. But sellers should recognize that selling to government units in foreign countries can be a real challenge, one that should be approached with caution. In many cases, a firm must get permission from the government in its own country to sell to a foreign government. Moreover, most government contracts favor domestic suppliers if they are available. Even if such favoritism is not explicit, public sentiment may make it very difficult for a foreign competitor to get a contract. Or the government bureaucracy may simply bury a foreign supplier in so much red tape that there's no way to win.

Is it unethical to "buy help"?

In some countries, government officials expect small payments (grease money) just to speed up processing of routine paperwork, inspections, or decisions from the local bureaucracy. Outright influence peddling—where government officials or their friends request bribe money to sway a purchase decision—is common in some markets. In the past, marketers from some countries have looked at such bribes as a cost of doing business. However, the **Foreign Corrupt Practices Act**, passed by the U.S. Congress in 1977, prohibits U.S. firms from paying bribes to foreign officials. A person who pays bribes, or authorizes an agent to pay them, can face stiff penalties. However, the law was amended in 1988 to allow small grease money payments if they are customary in a local culture. Since 1998, the law applies to foreign firms or foreign individuals who accept payments while in the United States. In recent years, prosecutions under this statute have increased thanks to more rigorous enforcement and greater cooperation with foreign governments. For example, in 2012 more than 80 firms were under investigation for violating the Foreign Corrupt Practices Act. This included Wal-Mart Stores, Inc., which was alleged to have bribed officials in Mexico to quickly obtain permits to open stores. The Sarbanes-Oxley Act of 2002 makes individual executives responsible for their company's financial disclosures; and a bribe mischaracterized as a legitimate expense may violate the law. Managers need to be careful and up-front about such payments.

CONCLUSION

In this chapter, we examined organizational buying and how it differs from final consumer buying. We saw that organizational buyers rely heavily on economic factors and cost-benefit analysis to make purchase decisions. Organizational buyers generally prefer to avoid risk. This chapter showed how multiple influences are important in buying decisions—and how marketing managers must recognize and attend to the needs of all members of the buying center.

The chapter introduced a three-step model of business and organizational buying. The first step—defining the problem—described how buyers recognize problems and then find solutions by determining buying needs. The second step—the decision-making process—examined three organizational buying processes: new-task buying, modified rebuy, and the straight rebuy. Each process involves different levels of information gathering, and this section reviewed how buyers gather information for buying. The third step—managing the buyer-seller relationship—looked at different aspects of these relationships in practice. Buying behavior and marketing opportunities may change when there's a close relationship between a supplier and a customer. There are different ways that a supplier can build close relationships with its customers. We identified key dimensions of relationships and their benefits and limitations.

We saw that organizational buyers buy for resale or to produce other goods and services—this group includes manufacturers, farmers, distributors, retailers, government agencies, and nonprofit organizations. The chapter concluded by providing insights about buying practices particular to manufacturers, service firms, intermediaries, and governments.

Understanding how organizations buy can help marketing managers identify logical dimensions for segmenting markets and developing marketing mixes. The unique nature of each product will likely require further adjustments in the mix. Variations by product may provide additional segmenting dimensions to help a marketing manager fine-tune a marketing strategy.

JOYFUL MOMENT

Bad Business

A salesman was chatting with the owner of a motel.

"Business is terrible," said the motel owner, "Really bad."

"But every time I drive by here you have the 'no vacancy' sign on." said the salesman.

"That's true," replied the motel owner. "But I used to turn away 30 to 35 people a night. Now, I only turn away ten to 15."

WORDS AND EXPRESSIONS

1. **defective**: *adj./n.* having a fault or flaw 有缺陷的；不完美的
—Retailers can return defective merchandise.
零售商可以退回有瑕疵的商品。
2. **overlap**: *v.* to coincide partially or wholly 重叠；与…部分相同
—His duties and mine overlap.
他的任务和我的任务有重叠。
3. **cubicle**: *n.* a very small enclosed area 小卧室，斗室
—She studies in a cubicle in the school library.
她在学校图书馆的小自习室里学习。
4. **clout**: *n.* special advantage or influence 影响力；权势
—The queen may have privilege but she has no real political clout.
女王有特权，但无真正的政治影响力。
5. **dim**: *adj.* lacking clarity or distinctness 暗淡的，不光明的；看不清的
—The light is too dim for me to read easily.
光线太暗，我很难阅读。
6. **requisition**: *n.* an official form on which a request is made 申请书；征用令
—The army made a requisition on the villagers for provisions.
军方向村民下了征购粮食的命令。
7. **grommet**: *n.* fastener consisting of a metal ring for lining a small hole to permit the attachment of cords or lines 金属扣眼，索环；垫环
—Complete the holes install the grommets as per manufacturers' instructions.
按制造商的指示完成安装扣眼孔。
8. **inventory**: *n.* a detailed list of all the items in stock 存货；详细目录
—This concept appears in manufacturing where they count both scrap and inventory.
此概念会出现在制造业，在其中会计算废料和存货。
9. **proprietary**: *adj.* protected by trademark or patent or copyright 专有的，专利的
—We had to take action to protect the proprietary technology.
我们必须采取措施保护专利技术。
10. **insolvency**: *n.* the state of not having enough money to pay your debts 破产；倒闭；无偿债能力
—The company is on the verge of insolvency.
该公司快要破产了。
11. **outsource**: *v.* to obtain goods or services from an outside supplier; to contract work out 外购；外包（工程）
—We outsource all our computing work.

我们把全部计算机技术工作包给外边去做。

12. **replenishment**: *n.* the process by which something is made full or complete again 补给，补充
—The company developed forecasts and replenishment strategy with supplier and buyers.
公司和供应商及采购商制定销售预测和补货策略。

13. **red tape**: *n.* needlessly time-consuming procedure 繁文缛节；官僚作风
—Because of all red tape at immigration I missed my connecting flight.
由于移民局方面令人讨厌的繁琐公事程序，我误了联程航班。

EXERCISES

1. **Multiple choices**

(1) All of the following statements about organizational buyers are true except ____.
A. business and organizational clients are "customers"
B. not all organizational customers are business firms
C. organizational buyers rarely focus on economic factors
D. organizational buyers make purchases primarily to satisfy their own customers and clients

(2) Procurement officer, supply manager, purchasing agent, and buyer are titles for an organization's ____.
A. marketing managers B. purchasing managers
C. executive officers D. warehouse managers

(3) Close buyer-seller relationships have many advantages for a firm, but one key disadvantage is ____.
A. buyer-seller relationships foster mutual trust and a long-term outlook
B. long-term commitments to another organization reduce flexibility for a firm
C. closely-tied firms often share tasks at lower total cost
D. information sharing can lead to efficient decisions and better planning

(4) Large wholesale and retail buyers typically ____.
A. use new-task buying for most product purchases
B. don't trust automatic inventory control methods
C. see themselves as selling agents for manufacturers
D. buy most of their products as straight rebuys

(5) When selling to ____, marketers must expect to use advertising, rely heavily on e-commerce for purchases and customer service, and make pitches to whomever is in charge (or their administrative assistant).
A. small service firms B. big box retailers
C. large manufacturers D. governments

2. **Terms translation**

(1) business customers (2) organizational buyers (3) buying center (4) new-task buying
(5) purchasing manager (6) vendor analysis (7) straight rebuy (8) outsource
(9) requisition (10) competitive bid

3. **True or false**

(1) Suppliers do not play roles in the purchase decision process for business buying. ______
(2) A gatekeeper in a buying center is one who controls the flow of money to others in the decision-making process. ______
(3) Interpersonal factors and group dynamics do not enter into or affect the outcome of the buying procedure. ______
(4) A performance review may lead a buyer to continue, modify, or drop the buying arrangement. ______
(5) Business Buying Behavior refers to the buying behavior of organizations that buy goods and services for use in the production of other goods and services that are sold. ______
(6) Compared with consumer purchases, a business purchase usually involves more decision participants and a more professional purchasing effort. ______
(7) Within a Buying Center, the Gatekeeper helps define specifications and evaluates alternative proposals. ______
(8) When suppliers' offers are very similar, buyers may allow personal factors to influence their buying decision. ______
(9) When purchasing capital equipment, most buyers prefer a blanket contract rather than periodic purchase orders, to simplify the purchasing process. ______
(10) Vendor analysis is a formal rating of suppliers on all relevant areas of performance. ______

4. **Fill in the blanks**
   (1) Business demand ultimately comes from the demand for consumer goods. This is known as __________ demand.
   (2) Margo Lane, purchasing agent for Locker Industries, found that her firm's supply of company letterhead paper was low. She reordered 10,000 sheets from her usual supplier. Lane was engaged in __________ rebuy.
   (3) As compared with consumer purchases, an organizational purchase involves __________ buyers and more __________ purchasing.
   (4) __________ buying occurs when a customer organization has a new need and wants a great deal of information.
   (5) Government buying organizations are found at the state or __________ level.
   (6) __________ contract buying means agreeing to contracts that allow for changes in the purchase arrangements.
   (7) The decision-making unit of a buying organization is called its __________.
   (8) The business marketer normally deals with fewer but more geographically __________ buyers than the consumer marketer does.
   (9) In large organizations, __________ managers usually specialize by product area and are real experts.
   (10) Within the buying center, the __________ have the power to select or approve final suppliers.

5. **Answer the following questions**
   (1) What are the major types of organizational customers?
   (2) Who play a part in making a business purchase decision?
   (3) Explain the differences between a straight rebuy and a modified rebuy.
   (4) What is NAICS code?
   (5) What are the major personal sources of information used by organizational buyers?

SUGGESTED CASES

5. Resin Dynamics
6. Dynamic Steel
14. Schrock & Oh Design
21. GeoTron International

MARKETING ANALYTICS: DATA TO KNOWLEDGE

CHAPTER 5: VENDOR ANALYSIS

CompuTech Inc. makes circuit boards for personal computers. It is evaluating two possible suppliers of electronic memory chips.

The chips do the same job. Although manufacturing quality has been improving, some chips are always defective. Both suppliers will replace defective chips. But the only practical way to test for a defective chip is to assemble a circuit board and "burn it in"—run it and see if it works. When one chip on a board is defective at that point, it costs $2 for the extra labor time to replace it. Supplier 1 guarantees a chip failure rate of not more than 1 per 100 (that is, a defect rate of 1 percent). The second supplier's 2 percent defective rate is higher, but its price is lower.

Supplier 1 has been able to improve its quality because it uses a heavier plastic case to hold the chip. The only disadvantage of the heavier case is that it requires CompuTech to use a connector that is somewhat more expensive.

Transportation costs are added to the price quoted by either supplier, but Supplier 2 is farther away so transportation costs are higher. And because of the distance, delays in supplies reaching CompuTech are sometimes a problem. To ensure that a sufficient supply is on hand to keep production going, CompuTech must maintain a backup inventory—and this increases inventory costs. CompuTech figures inventory costs—the expenses of finance and storage—as a percentage of the total order cost.

To make its vendor analysis easier, CompuTech's purchasing agent has entered data about the two suppliers on a spreadsheet. He based his estimates on the quantity he thinks he will need over a full year.

See Connect for the spreadsheet and questions needed to analyze this scenario.

6

CHAPTER SIX

Distribution Customer Service and Logistics[1]

If you want a Coca-Cola, there's usually one close by—no matter where you might be in the world. And that's no accident. An executive for the best-known brand name in the world stated the goal simply: "Make Coca-Cola available within an arm's reach of desire." To achieve that level of customer service, Coke works with many different channels of distribution. But that's just the start. Think about what it takes for a bottle, can, or cup of Coke to be there whenever you're thirsty. In warehouses and distribution centers, on trucks, in restaurants and sports arenas, and in thousands of other retail outlets, Coke handles, stores, and transports more than 600 billion soft drink servings per year. Getting all of its product to consumers is a huge undertaking, but Coke does it effectively and at a low cost.

Readily accessible information about what the market needs helps keep Coke's distribution on target. Coke uses an Internet-based data system that links about 1 million retailers and other sellers to Coke and its bottlers. The system lets Coke bottlers and retailers exchange orders, invoices, and pricing information online. Coke sells more than 500 brands and 3,500 products in 206 countries, making for what could be a logistical nightmare. But Coke's marketing and logistics managers coordinate with its computer information systems group to integrate this system worldwide.

It works. Computer systems show Coke managers exactly what's selling in each market, and sophisticated software programs accurately predict future sales. Analytics help factor in the effects of seasonal changes, weather forecasts, and planned promotions to fine-tune and plan inventories and deliveries. Orders are processed instantly, so sales to consumers at the end of the channel aren't lost because of stock-outs. Coke moves products efficiently through the channel. In Cincinnati, for example, Coke built the beverage industry's first fully automated distribution center. And when Coke's truck drivers get to a retail store, they knowingly stock the shelves with the correct mix of products.

Coke's strategies in international markets have similar objectives. But because cultural differences and the stage of market development vary across countries, Coke's emphasis varies as well. To increase sales in France, for example, Coke installed thousands of soft drink coolers in French supermarkets. In Great Britain, Coke emphasizes multipacks because it wants to have more inventory at the point of consumption—in consumers' homes. In Japan, by contrast, Coke relies heavily on an army of truck drivers to constantly restock 1 million Coke vending machines, more per capita than anywhere else in the world. Japanese customers can even use their cell phones to buy a Coke from one of these vending machines. In Thailand, Coke's bottlers are buying more trucks and increasing the frequency of delivery to keep up with fast growth.

In less-developed areas, the focus may be on different challenges—especially if the limitations of the Place system can make Coke products hard to find or costly. In Africa, where per capita consumption of Coke products is one-tenth of that in the United States, Coca-Cola wants its products to be cold and available everywhere—even in the lowest-income areas. For example, in Kabira, a Kenyan slum, a local distributor uses three shipping containers as a portable warehouse. Dirt and gravel roads make it easier to deliver by hand, so delivery personnel stack a couple dozen crates onto two-wheeled carts and fan out to 345 small shops delivering Coke, Fanta, and Stoney Ginger Beer. Deliveries might occur once or twice a day because the small shops hold so little inventory. Coke provides shops with plenty of "red"—Coke signage, tablecloths, and refrigerated coolers. Returnable glass bottles help keep down costs and at prices of less than 25 cents (U.S.), Coke becomes a treat on hot days.

While technology facilitates Coke's complex distribution system, retailers and wholesalers in developing countries don't always have scanner checkout systems and electronic data interchange. So Coke utilizes a technology readily accessible to most channel partners: cell phones. For example, in Vietnam, Coke uses an app to help retailers and wholesalers manage inventory and ordering and speed up order fulfillment. When a retailer uses the app to order a case of Coke, the message immediately goes to multiple wholesalers. The wholesaler that can fill the order most quickly responds; deliveries—often by motorcycle—now happen in hours instead of days. This means local retailers don't run out and more consumers have a Coke within that "arm's reach of desire."

Fortune magazine recently put the spotlight on Coca-Cola's commitment to sustainability. Its decisions in the logistics area have had big environmental effects. For example, Coca-Cola helped develop vending machines that are HFC-free and 40 to 50 percent more energy efficient than conventional beverage equipment. Similarly, in the United States and Canada, Coca-Cola's gas-electric hybrid delivery trucks cut emissions[2] and fuel consumption by a third.

In spite of positive steps like these, Coca-Cola still faces some challenges concerning sustainability and logistics. Critics argue that in a society where there is already a safe supply of tap water, it doesn't make sense to bottle water (Coke's brand is Dasani), transport it in trucks that consume fuel and contribute to pollution, and then add worry about how best to dispose of the empty bottles and bottle tops.

Coca-Cola's worldwide distribution network delivers a sustainable competitive advantage. Of course, Pepsi, Dr Pepper, and Hansen's Natural Sodas are competing for distributors' attention and retail shelf space. Coke is pushing new products as well. The battle to quench customers' thirsts depends on each brand's marketing programs—but clearly Place has an important role to play.

LEARNING OBJECTIVES

Choosing the right distribution channels is crucial in getting products to the target market's Place. But, as the Coca-Cola case shows, that alone doesn't ensure that products are placed "within an arm's reach of desire"—when, where, in the quantities that customers want them, and at a price they're willing to pay. In this chapter, we discuss how marketing managers ensure that they also have physical distribution systems that meet their customers' needs—at both an acceptable service level and an affordable cost.

When you finish this chapter, you should be able to

1. understand why logistics (physical distribution) is such an important part of Place and marketing strategy planning.
2. understand why the physical distribution customer service level is a key marketing strategy variable.
3. understand the physical distribution concept and why the coordination of storing, transporting, and related activities is so important.
4. see how firms can cooperate and share logistics activities that will provide added value to their customers.
5. know about the advantages and disadvantages of various transportation methods.
6. know how inventory and storage decisions affect marketing strategy.
7. understand the distribution center concept.
8. understand important new terms (shown in boldface).

Physical Distribution Gets It to Customers

Whenever Product includes a physical good, Place requires logistics decisions. **Logistics** is the transporting, storing, and handling of goods in ways that match target customers' needs with a firm's marketing mix—both within individual firms and along a channel of distribution. **Physical distribution (PD)** is another common name for logistics.

There are many different combinations of logistics decisions. Each combination can result in a different level of distribution service and different costs. So companies must determine the best way to provide the level of distribution service that customers want and are willing to pay for. We start this chapter by considering these critical logistics decisions (see Exhibit 6-1). Next, we describe the choice among different modes of transportation. Each has its own costs and benefits. We conclude with decisions about inventory and the use of distribution centers.

Exhibit 6-1 The Role of Logistics and Physical Distribution Customer Service in Marketing Strategy

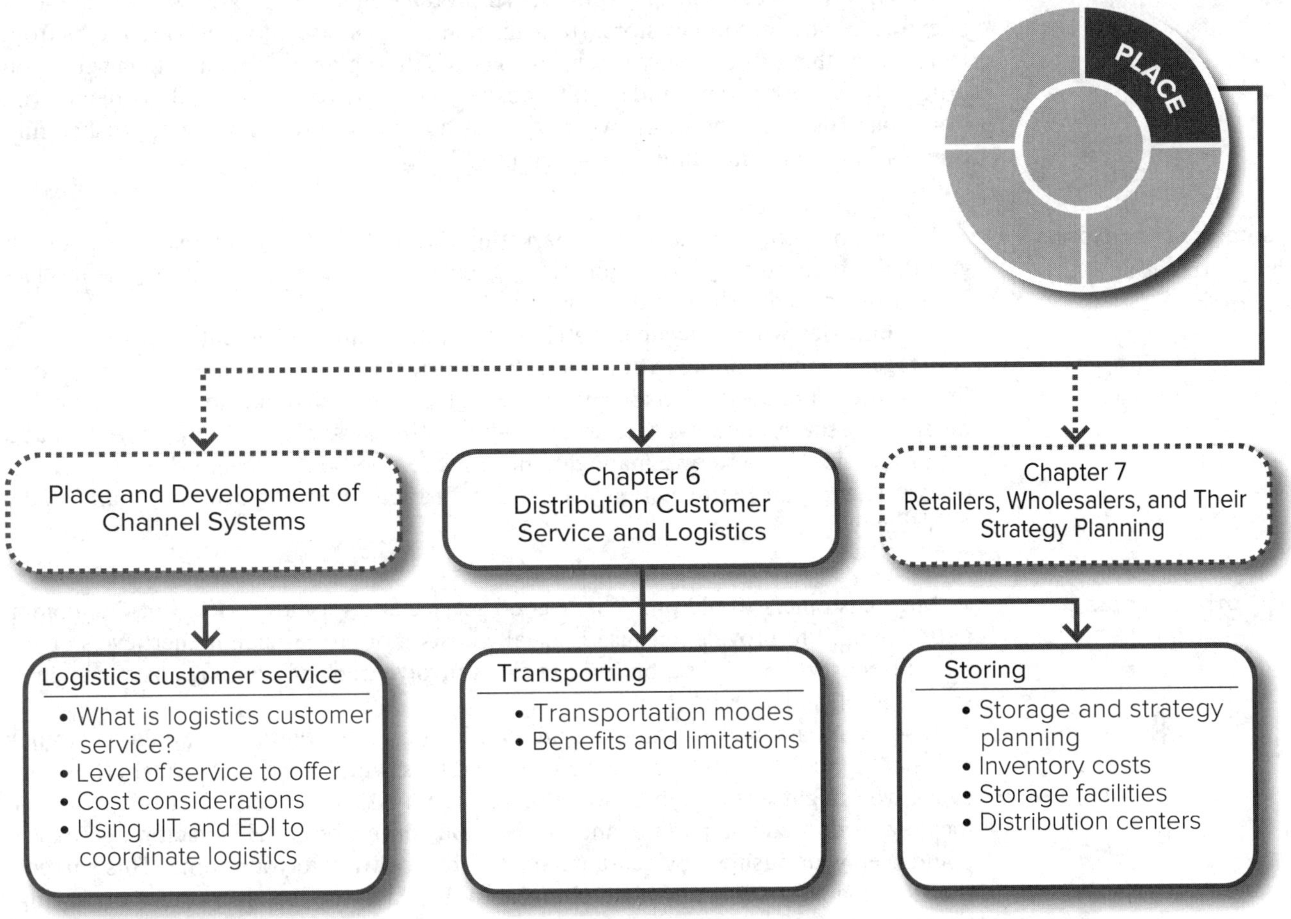

Logistics costs are very important to both companies and consumers. These costs vary from firm to firm and, from a macro-marketing perspective, from country to country. For some products, a company may spend half or more of its total marketing dollars on physical distribution activities. As lawmakers debate the high cost of health care, logistics costs represent more than one-third the expense attached to hospital supplies. Although this is down from about 50 percent a few decades ago, there's still room for improvement.

Differences in logistics costs around the world can be substantial. Developed economies in the United States and Europe spend about 9 to 15 percent of GDP on logistics-related costs—whereas in the developing economies of Latin America and Africa, costs are 30 percent or more. Marketing managers must carefully consider these costs when entering new markets.

Physical Distribution Customer Service

From the beginning, we've emphasized that marketing strategy planning is based on meeting customers' needs. Planning for logistics and Place is no exception. So let's start by looking at logistics through a customer's eyes.

Customers want products, not excuses

Customers don't care how a product was moved or stored or what some channel member had to do to provide it. Rather, customers think in terms of the physical distribution **customer service level**—how rapidly and dependably a firm can deliver what they, the customers, want.

What does this really mean? It means that Toyota wants to have enough windshields delivered to make cars *that* day—not late so production stops *or* early so there are a lot of extras to move around or store. It means that business executives who rent cars from Hertz want them to be ready when they get off their planes. It means that when you order a blue shirt at the Lands' End website you receive blue, not pink. It means you want your Tostitos to be whole when you buy a bag at the snack bar—not crushed into crumbs from rough handling in a warehouse.

Physical distribution is invisible to most consumers

PD is, and should be, a part of marketing that is "invisible" to most consumers. It gets their attention only when something goes wrong. At that point, it may be too late to do anything that will keep them happy.

In countries where physical distribution systems are inefficient, consumers face shortages of the products they need. By contrast, most consumers in the United States and Canada don't think much about physical distribution. This probably means that these market-directed macro-marketing systems work pretty well—that a lot of individual marketing managers have made good decisions in this area. But it doesn't mean that the decisions are always clear-cut or simple. In fact, many trade-offs[3] may be required.

Trade-offs of costs, service, and sales

Most customers would prefer very good service at a very low price. But that combination is hard to provide because it usually costs more to provide higher levels of service. So most physical distribution decisions involve trade-offs among costs, customer service level, and sales.

If you want a new HP computer and the Best Buy store where you would like to buy it doesn't have it on hand, you're likely to buy it elsewhere; or if that model HP is hard to get, you might just switch to some other brand. Assuming your Best Buy store can locate your desired computer at another Best Buy or in stock at HP's factory, perhaps it could keep your business by guaranteeing two-day delivery to your home. This will cost the store manager some airfreight charges. In this case, the manager trades the savings of storing inventory for the extra cost of speedy delivery. Missing one sale may not seem that important, but it all adds up; consider, a few years ago a computer company lost more than $500 million in sales because its computers weren't available when and where customers were ready to buy them.

Exhibit 6-2 illustrates trade-off relationships like the one highlighted in the HP example just mentioned. The exhibit shows costs on the vertical axis and customer service

Exhibit 6-2 Trade-Offs among Physical Distribution Costs, Customer Service Level, and Sales

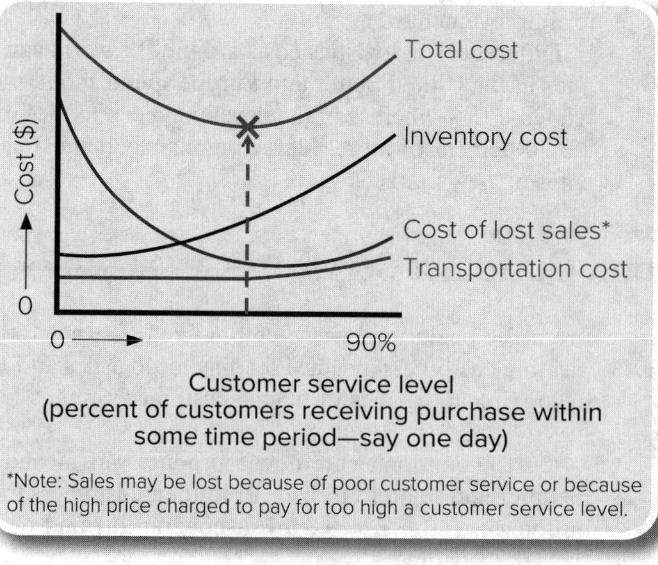

*Note: Sales may be lost because of poor customer service or because of the high price charged to pay for too high a customer service level.

Marketing Analytics in Action: Trade-Offs and Customer Service Levels

Customer service levels are a major challenge for stores that sell shoes. Consider that for each style, the store may stock different colors and many sizes. In this case, we define customer service level as the percentage of customers who find the shoe style, color, and size they wish to purchase in stock on the day they shop. All the possible combinations can make 100 percent customer service costly. How might a store selling shoes decide on the best level of customer service?

Ronnie Chin is a marketing manager for Wanderlust Outdoor, a small chain of outdoor shops. She manages the availability of outdoor shoes and boots for all stores. Ronnie generated the following table from internal data. The left side of the table shows the current costs for transportation, inventory, and lost sales, as well as the total cost.

Ronnie is considering adding in-store kiosks that would make ordering out-of-stock shoes easier and faster—plus Wanderlust would include free two-day shipping to a customer's home on all kiosk orders. This would change the customer service cost structure. The right side of table lists costs at different customer service levels using the kiosks. Note the following:

- With kiosks, transportation costs are higher at lower levels of customer service. Because Wanderlust pays for the two-day shipping to a customer's home, this raises its transportation costs. This happens more often at low customer service levels.
- The kiosks would not change inventory cost.
- With kiosks, costs for lost sales would fall, especially at lower levels of customer service. Because more customers make a kiosk purchase instead of leaving the store emptyhanded, fewer sales are lost at lower levels of customer service.

Customer Service Level	Current Costs* at Different Customer Service Levels				Costs at Different Customer Service Levels with Kiosks			
	Transport	Inventory	Lost Sales	Total Cost	Transport	Inventory	Lost Sales	Total Cost
50%	$12	$22	$60	**$ 94**	$14	$22	$38	**$ 74**
60%	$12	$24	$50	**$ 86**	$14	$24	$30	**$ 68**
70%	$12	$27	$43	**$ 82**	$14	$27	$30	**$ 71**
80%	$13	$31	$37	**$ 81**	$14	$31	$31	**$ 76**
90%	$14	$37	$44	**$ 95**	$14	$37	$42	**$ 93**
100%	$15	$45	$50	**$110**	$15	$45	$50	**$110**

1. *What customer service level do you recommend? Why?*
2. *What other factors might Ronnie want to consider before making her decision regarding desired customer service level?*
3. *Do you recommend buying the kiosks? Why or why not?*

level (measured as the percentage of customers receiving delivery within one day) on the horizontal axis. Note the following:

- As service level increases (moving left to right), transportation cost is flat for a bit before increasing as shipments become more frequent to ensure there are no stockouts.
- Inventory cost rises as the retailer carries more computers to meet any level of demand.
- Cost of lost sales initially falls because customers are not likely to buy a different product when the model they want is in stock. However, as customer service climbs to higher levels (mostly a result of rising inventory carrying costs), the seller must raise prices to cover the higher service levels. This leads to some customers choosing alternatives–and raises the cost of lost sales.

- When all of these costs are added together, the total cost falls as service level increases—but then rises. The optimum level of customer service (based on cost) occurs where the total cost is minimized (X on the graph).

Exhibit 6-2 provides a starting point to discuss the trade-offs marketing managers must make. Often transportation and inventory carrying costs can be reliably determined, but the cost of lost sales is an estimate. Marketing managers should work closely with distribution managers to discuss and monitor the trade-offs. To better understand how this analysis occurs in practice, complete the *Marketing Analytics in Action: Trade-Offs and Customer Service Levels* activity.

Trade-offs more complicated with more products

Trade-offs that must be made in physical distribution can be even more complicated. The approach demonstrated in Exhibit 6-2 focuses on the sale of a single item. But a customer dissatisfied by not finding the item she wanted may soon shop elsewhere—reducing the lifetime customer value. For example, a few years ago cost-cutting efforts at Walmart resulted in reduced inventory—and some empty shelves. Some of those disappointed Walmart customers decided to shop elsewhere, and losses were far greater than the failure to sell particular items on a particular day or two. Similar problems occurred when Target entered Canada a few years ago. Target could not deliver quickly enough and empty shelves made a bad first impression. Target never recovered and closed all 133 stores it operated there.

Information technology, data, and analytics can improve service levels and cut costs at the same time. Better information flows make it easier to coordinate activities, improve efficiency, and add value for the customer.

Physical Distribution Concept Focuses on the Whole Distribution System

The physical distribution concept

The **physical distribution (PD) concept** says that all transporting, storing, and product-handling activities of a business and a whole channel system should be coordinated as one system that seeks to minimize the cost of distribution for a given customer service level. Both lower costs and better service help increase customer value. This seems like common sense, but until recently most companies treated physical distribution functions as separate and unrelated activities.

Traditionally, responsibility for different logistics activities was spread among various departments in a firm—production, shipping, sales, warehousing, purchasing, and others. No one person was responsible for coordinating storing and shipping decisions or customer service levels. It was even rarer for different firms in the channel to collaborate. Each just did its own thing. Unfortunately, in too many firms these old-fashioned ways persist—with a focus on individual functional activities rather than the whole physical distribution system.

Decide what service level to offer

With broader adoption of the physical distribution concept, this is changing. Firms work together to decide what aspects of service are most important to customers at the end of the channel. Then they focus on finding the least expensive way to achieve the target level of service.

Exhibit 6-3 shows a variety of factors that may influence the customer service level (at each level in the channel). The most important aspects of customer service depend on target market needs. Xerox might focus on how long it takes to deliver copy machine repair parts once it receives an order. When a copier breaks down, customers want the repair "yesterday." The service level might be stated as "we will deliver 90 percent of all emergency repair parts within 24 hours." This might require that commonly needed parts be available on the service truck, that order processing be very fast, and that parts not available locally be sent by air-

Exhibit 6-3 Examples of Factors That Affect PD Service Levels

- Advance information on product availability
- Time to enter and process orders
- Backorder procedures
- Where inventory is stored
- Accuracy in filling orders
- Damage in shipping, storing, and handling
- Online status information
- Advance information on delays
- Time needed to deliver an order
- Reliability in meeting delivery date
- Compliance with customer's instructions
- Defect-free deliveries
- How needed adjustments are handled
- Procedures for handling returns

Sauder tries to help customer firms do a better job of tracking the status of orders and making certain that products are where they are needed at the right time.
Source: Sauder Woodworking Company

freight. Obviously, supplying this service level will affect the total cost of the PD system. But it may also beat competitors.

Fast PD service can be critical for retailers that appeal to consumers who are eager to get a new product that is in hot demand—the latest movie release, bestselling book, or popular toy or video game.

Customers increasingly expect more convenience and speed as part of their PD service—and at a low cost. After examining their own strengths and weaknesses, as well as the needs of their target customers, two of the largest retailers in the United States have taken divergent strategic paths. As an almost completely online player, Amazon continues to focus on offering its customers faster delivery. Amazon Prime customers (numbering in the tens of millions) already get free two-day delivery with a low-cost option to upgrade to next-day delivery. Now with investments in warehouses around the country, Amazon offers same-day delivery to many customers. Amazon's Prime Pantry program allows customers to pay a $5.99 flat fee to receive low-priced grocery, household, and pet care items.

In contrast, Walmart has chosen to more tightly integrate its stores and online offerings; instead of faster home delivery it uses the web to make for a faster in-store experience. Walmart's site to store program allows customers to shop online and get free shipping to a Walmart store or select FedEx Office locations, where customers pick up their order. The store is also testing Walmart To-Go, where customers order groceries (and other merchandise) online and pick them up at a local store (for free) or have them delivered for $5 to $7.

Find the lowest total cost for the right service level

In selecting a PD system, the **total cost approach** involves evaluating each possible PD system and identifying *all* of the costs of each alternative. This approach uses the tools of cost accounting and economics. Costs that otherwise might be ignored—like inventory carrying costs—are considered. The possible costs of lost sales due to a lower customer service level may also be considered.

For example, Vegpro Kenya compared different PD systems for shipping ready-to-eat fresh produce from fields in Kenya to grocery stores in major European cities. The analysis showed that the costs of airfreight transportation were significantly higher than using trucks and ships. But the firm also found that costs of spoilage and inventory could be much lower when airfreight is used. The faster airfreight-based PD system brought customers fresher produce at about the same total cost. So Vegpro cleans, chops, and packages vegetables in its 27,000 square-foot air-conditioned facility at the Nairobi airport—using low-cost African labor. And the next day, fresh beans, baby carrots, and other vegetables are on store shelves in Madrid, London, and Paris.

Coordinating Logistics Activities among Firms

Functions can be shifted and shared in the channel

As a marketing manager develops the Place part of a strategy, it is important to decide how physical distribution functions can and should be divided within the channel. Who will store, handle, and transport the goods–and who will pay for these services? Who will coordinate all of the PD activities?

There is no right sharing arrangement. Physical distribution can be varied endlessly in a marketing mix and in a channel system. And competitors may share these functions in different ways–with different costs and results.

How PD is shared affects the rest of a strategy

How the PD functions are shared affects the other three Ps–especially Price. The sharing arrangement can also make (or break) a strategy. Consider Channel Master, a firm that wanted to take advantage of the growing market for the dishes used to receive TV signals from satellites. The product looked like it could be a big success, but the small company didn't have the money to invest in a large inventory. So Channel Master decided to work only with wholesalers who were willing to buy (and pay for) several units–to be used for demonstration and to ensure that buyers got immediate delivery.

In the first few months Channel Master earned $2 million in revenues–just by providing inventory for the channel. And the wholesalers paid the interest cost of carrying inventory–more than $300,000 the first year. Here the wholesalers helped share the risk of the new venture, but it was a good decision for them, too. They won many sales from a competing channel whose customers had to wait several months for delivery. And by getting off to a strong start, Channel Master became a market leader.

JIT requires a coordinated effort

If firms in the channel do not plan and coordinate how they will share PD activities, PD is likely to be a source of conflict rather than a basis for competitive advantage. Let's consider this point by taking a closer look at *just-in-time (JIT) delivery* systems.

A key advantage of JIT for business customers is that it reduces their PD costs–especially storing and handling costs. However, if the customer doesn't have any backup inventory, there's no security blanket if a supplier's delivery truck gets stuck in traffic, there's an error in what's shipped, or there are any quality problems. Thus, a JIT system requires that a supplier have extremely high quality control in every PD activity.

A JIT system usually requires that a supplier respond to very short order lead times and the customer's production schedule. Thus, e-commerce order systems and information sharing over computer networks are often required. JIT suppliers often locate their facilities close to important customers. Trucks may make smaller and more frequent deliveries–perhaps even several times a day.

A JIT system shifts greater responsibility for PD activities backward in (up) the channel. If the supplier can be more efficient than the customer could be in controlling PD costs–and still provide the customer with the service level required–this approach can work well for everyone in the channel. However, JIT is not always the best approach. It may be better for a supplier to produce and ship in larger, more economical quantities–if the savings offset the distribution system's total inventory and handling costs.

Supply chain may involve even more firms

In our discussion, we have taken the point of view of a marketing manager. This focuses on how logistics should be coordinated to meet the needs of customers at the end of the channel of distribution. Now, however, we should broaden the picture somewhat because the relationships within the distribution channel are sometimes part of a broader network of relationships in the **supply chain**–the complete set of firms and facilities and logistics activities that are involved in procuring materials, transforming them into intermediate or finished products, and distributing them to customers.

For example, Manitowoc is one of the world's largest manufacturers of cranes. Its huge mobile cranes are used at construction sites all around the world. Robert Ward, who is in charge of purchasing for Manitowoc, must ensure an unbroken flow of parts and materials so that Manitowoc can keep its promises to customers regarding crane delivery dates. This

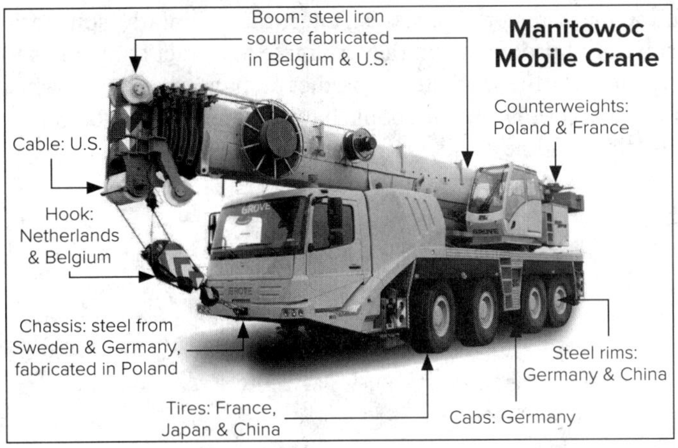

Source: Manitowoc Company, Inc.

is difficult because each crane has component parts from many suppliers around the globe. Further, any supplier may be held up by problems with its own suppliers. In one case, Manitowoc's German factory was having trouble getting key chassis parts from two suppliers in Poland. Ward traced the problem back to a Scandinavian steel mill that was behind on shipments to the Polish firms. Manitowoc buys a lot of steel and has a lot of leverage with steel distributors, so Ward scoured Europe for distributors who had extra inventory of steel plate. The steel he found was more expensive than buying the steel directly from the mill, but the mill couldn't keep supplies flowing and the distributors could. By helping coordinate the whole supply chain, Manitowoc was able to keep its promises and deliver cranes to its customers on schedule.

Work to meet the needs of the customer at the end of the supply chain

Ideally, all of the firms in the supply chain should work together to meet the needs of the customer at the very end of the chain. That way, at each link along the chain, the shifting and sharing of logistics functions and costs are handled to result in the most value for the final customer. This makes a supply chain more efficient and effective–giving it a competitive advantage against other supply chains competing to serve the same target market.

Better information helps coordinate PD

Coordinating all of the elements of PD has always been a challenge–even in a single firm. Trying to coordinate orders, inventory, and transportation throughout the whole supply chain is even tougher. But information shared over the Internet and at websites has been important in finding solutions to these challenges. Physical distribution decisions will continue to improve as more firms are able to have their computers "talk" to each other directly and as websites help managers get access to up-to-date information whenever they need it.

Electronic data interchange sets a standard

Until recently, differences in computer systems from one firm to another hampered the flow of information. Many firms attacked this problem by adopting **electronic data interchange (EDI)**–an approach that puts information in a standardized format easily shared between different computer systems. In many firms, purchase orders, shipping reports, and other paper documents were replaced with computerized EDI. With EDI, a customer transmits his or her order information directly to the supplier's computer. The supplier's computer immediately processes the order and schedules production, order assembly, and transportation. Inventory information is automatically updated, and status reports are available instantly. The supplier might then use EDI to send the updated information to the transportation provider's computer. In fact, most international transportation firms rely on EDI links with their customers.

Improved information flow and better coordination of PD activities is a key reason for the success of Pepperidge Farm's line of premium cookies. Most of the company's delivery truck drivers use handheld computers to record the inventory at each stop along their routes. They use a wireless Internet connection to instantly transmit the information into a computer at the bakeries, and cookies in short supply are produced. The right assortment[4] of fresh cookies is quickly shipped to local markets, and delivery trucks are loaded with what retailers need that day. Pepperidge Farm moves cookies from its bakeries to store shelves in about three days; most cookie producers take about 10 days. That means fresher cookies for consumers and helps support Pepperidge Farm's high-quality positioning and premium price.

Ethical issues may arise

Some ethical issues that arise in the PD area concern communications about product availability. For example, some critics say that Internet sellers too often take orders for products that are not available or which they cannot deliver as quickly as customers expect. Yet a marketing manager can't always know precisely how long it will take before a product will be available. It doesn't make sense for the marketer to lose a customer if it appears that he or she can satisfy the customer's needs. But the customer may be inconvenienced or face added cost if the marketer's best guess isn't accurate. Similarly, some critics say that stores too often run out of products that they promote to attract consumers to the store. Yet it may not be possible for the marketer to predict demand or to know when placing an ad that deliveries won't arrive. Different people have different views about how a firm should handle such situations. Some retailers just offer rain checks.

Ethical Dilemma

What would you do? Many major firms, ranging from Nike and Starbucks to Walmart and IKEA, have been criticized for selling products from overseas suppliers whose workers toil in bad conditions for long hours and at low pay. Defenders of the companies point out that overseas sourcing provides jobs that are better than what workers would have without it. Critics think that companies that sell products in wealthy countries have a social responsibility to see that suppliers in less-developed nations pay a fair wage and provide healthy working conditions.

What do you think? Should U.S. firms be required to monitor the employment practices of suppliers in their supply chains? Should all suppliers be held to Western legal or moral standards? What solutions or compromises might be offered?

The Transporting Function Adds Value to a Marketing Strategy

Transporting aids economic development and exchange

Transporting is the marketing function of moving goods. Transportation makes products available when and where they need to be–at a cost. But the cost is less than the value added to products by moving them, or there is little reason to ship in the first place.

Transporting can help achieve economies of scale in production. If production costs can be reduced by producing larger quantities in one location, these savings may more than offset the added cost of transporting the finished products to customers. Without low-cost transportation, both within countries and internationally, there would be no mass distribution as we know it today.

Transporting can be costly

Transporting costs limit the target markets a marketing manager can serve. Shipping costs increase delivered cost–and that's what really interests customers. Transport costs add little to the cost of products that are already valuable relative to their size and weight. A case of medicine, for example, might be shipped to a drugstore at low cost. But transporting costs can be a large part of the total cost for heavy products of low value–such as many minerals and raw materials. You can imagine that shipping a massive roll of aluminum to a producer of soft drink cans is an expensive proposition. Exhibit 6-4 shows transporting costs as a percentage of total sales dollars for several products.

Exhibit 6-4
Transporting Costs as a Percentage of Selling Price for Different Products

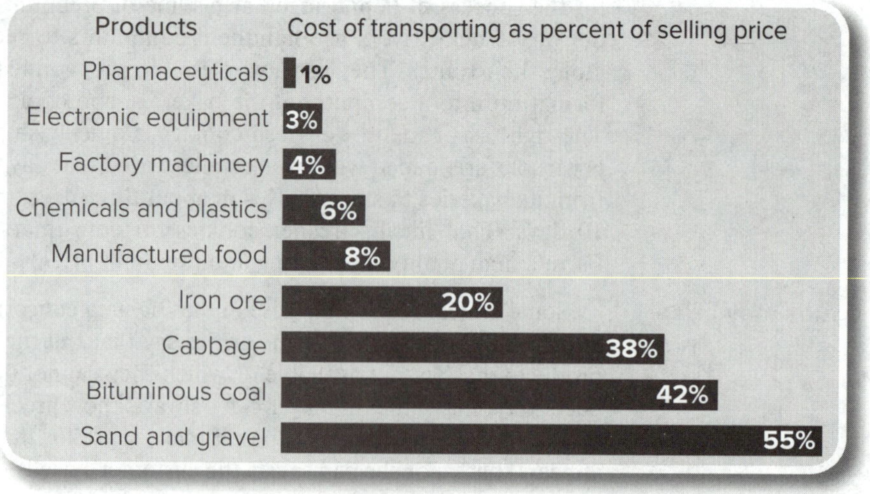

Governments may influence transportation

Government often plays an important role in the development of a country's transportation system, including its roads, harbors, railroads, and airports. And different countries regulate transportation differently, although regulation has in general been decreasing.

As regulations decreased in the United States, competition in the transportation industry increased. As a result, a marketing manager generally has many carriers in one or more modes competing for the firm's transporting business. Or a firm can do its own transporting. So knowing about the different modes is important.

Which Transporting Alternative Is Best?

Transporting function must fit the whole strategy

The transporting function should fit into the whole marketing strategy. But picking the best transporting alternative depends on the product, other physical distribution decisions, and what service level the company wants to offer. The best alternative should provide the level of service (for example, speed and dependability) required at as low a cost as possible. Exhibit 6-5 shows that different modes of transportation have different strengths and weaknesses. Low transporting cost is *not* the only criterion for selecting the best mode.

Railroads—large loads moved at low cost

Railroads are still the workhorse of the U.S. transportation system. They carry more freight over more miles than any other mode. However, they account for less than 10 percent of transport revenues. They carry heavy and bulky goods–such as coal, steel, and chemicals–over long distances at relatively low cost. Because railroad freight usually moves more slowly than truck shipments, it is not as well suited for perishable[5] items or those in urgent demand. Railroads are most efficient at handling full carloads of goods. Less-than-carload (LCL) shipments take a lot of handling, which means they usually move more slowly and at a higher price per pound than carload shipments.

Trucks are more expensive, but flexible and essential

The flexibility and speed of trucks make them better at moving small quantities of goods for shorter distances. They can travel on almost any road. They go where the rails can't. They are also reliable in meeting delivery schedules, which is an essential requirement for logistics systems that provide rapid replenishment of inventory after a sale. In combination these factors explain why at least 75 percent of U.S. consumer products travel at least part of the way from producer to consumer by truck. And in countries with good highway systems, trucks can give extremely fast service. Trucks compete for high-value items. Trucks are essential for firms that deliver to people's homes–the so-called last mile for e-commerce. They will become even more critical as online sales and same-day delivery become important parts of some retailers' marketing strategies.

Exhibit 6-5 Benefits and Limitations of Different Transport Modes

	Transporting Features					
Mode	Cost	Delivery Speed	Number of Locations Served	Ability to Handle a Variety of Goods	Frequency of Scheduled Shipments	Dependability in Meeting Schedules
Rail	Medium	Average	Extensive	High	Low	Medium
Truck	High	Fast	Very extensive	High	High	High
Water	Very low	Very slow	Limited	Very high	Very low	Medium
Pipeline	Low	Slow	Very limited	Very limited	Medium	High
Air	Very high	Very fast	Extensive	Limited	High	High

Ship it overseas, but slowly

Water transportation is the slowest shipping mode, but it is usually the lowest-cost way of shipping heavy freight. Water transportation is very important for international shipments and often the only practical approach. This explains why port cities such as Boston, New York City, Rotterdam, Osaka, and Singapore are important centers for international trade.

Inland waterways are important too

Inland waterways (such as the Mississippi River and Great Lakes in the United States and the Rhine and Danube in Europe) are also important, especially for bulky, nonperishable products such as iron ore, grain, and gravel. However, when winter ice closes freshwater harbors, alternate transportation must be used.

Pipelines move oil and gas

Pipelines are used primarily to move oil and natural gas. So pipelines are important both in the oil-producing and oil-consuming countries. Only a few major cities in the United States, Canada, Mexico, and Latin America are more than 200 miles from a major pipeline system. However, the majority of the pipelines in the United States are located in the Southwest, connecting oil fields and refineries.

Airfreight is expensive, but fast and growing

The most expensive cargo transporting mode is airplane—but it is fast! Airfreight rates are on average three times higher than trucking rates—but the greater speed may offset the added cost.

High-value, low-weight goods—such as high-fashion clothing and parts for the electronics industry—are often shipped by air. Perishable products that previously could not be shipped are now being flown across continents and oceans. Flowers and bulbs from Holland, for example, now are jet-flown to points all over the world. And airfreight has become very important for small emergency deliveries, like repair parts.

But airplanes may cut the total cost of distribution

Using planes may reduce the cost of packing, unpacking, and preparing goods for sale and may help a firm reduce inventory costs by eliminating outlying warehouses. Valuable benefits of airfreight's speed are less spoilage, theft, and damage. Although the *transporting* cost of air shipments may be higher, the *total* cost of distribution may be lower. As more firms realize this, airfreight firms—such as DHL Worldwide Express, FedEx, and Emery Air Freight—have enjoyed rapid growth.

Will drones deliver soon?

Small unmanned aircraft, called drones, have been used in the military and by hobbyists. They are now being used for delivery services. In Germany, DHL uses drones to deliver medicine to a small island off the German coast. Swiss Post has been testing drone delivery of mail. And Amazon is testing drones for delivery in Canada (the Federal Aviation Administration in the United States has slowed testing here).

Put it in a container—and move between modes easily

Products often move by several different modes and carriers during their journey. This is especially common for international shipments. Japanese firms, like Sony, ship stereos to the United States, Canada, and Europe by boat. When they arrive at the dock, they are loaded on trains and sent across the country. Then the units are delivered to a wholesaler by truck or rail.

To better coordinate the flow of products between modes, transportation companies like CSX offer customers a complete choice of different transportation modes. Then CSX, not the customer, figures out the best and lowest-cost way to shift and share transporting functions among the modes.

Loading and unloading goods several times used to be a real problem. Parts of a shipment would become separated, damaged, or even stolen. It would take a week and many hours of high-priced labor to unload a cargo ship. All this handling of the goods, perhaps many times, raised costs and slowed delivery. Many of these problems are reduced with **containerization**[6]—grouping individual items into an economical shipping quantity and sealing them in protective containers for transit to the final destination. This protects the products and simplifies handling during shipping. Shipping containers also facilitate intermodal transport. Some containers are as large as truck bodies.

Transportation costs higher in developing countries

Transportation choices are usually not so good in developing countries. Roads are often poor, rail systems may be limited, and ports may be undeveloped. Local firms that specialize in logistics services may not exist at all. Even so, firms that are willing to invest the effort can reap benefits and help their customers overcome the effects of these problems.

Metro AG, a firm based in Germany that has opened wholesale facilities in Bangalore and several other major cities in India, illustrates this point. Metro focuses on selling food products and other supplies to the thousands of restaurants, hotels, and other small businesses in the markets it serves. When Metro started in India, 40 percent of the fruits and vegetables it purchased from farmers were spoiled, damaged, or lost by the time they got to Metro. These problems piled up because the produce traveled from the fields over rough roads and was handled by as many as seven intermediaries along the way. To overcome these problems, Metro gave farmers crates to protect freshly picked crops from damage and to keep them away from dirt and bacteria that would shorten their shelf life. Further, crates were loaded and unloaded only once because Metro bought its own refrigerated trucks to pick up produce and bring it directly to its outlets. Metro used the same ideas to speed fresh seafood from fishermen's boats. Many of Metro's restaurant customers previously bought what they needed from a variety of small suppliers, many of whom would run out of stock. Now the restaurant owners save time and money with one-stop shopping at Metro. Metro is growing fast in India because it has quality products that are in stock when they're needed, and it's bringing down food costs for its customers.

Transportation choices have environmental costs too

Marketing managers should be sensitive to the environmental effects of transportation decisions. Trucks, trains, airplanes, and ships contribute to air pollution and global warming; estimates suggest that on average more than half of most firms' total carbon emissions come from transportation. Other environmental issues may spring from transportation as well. For example, a damaged pipeline or oil tanker can spew thousands of gallons of oil before it can be repaired.

Many firms are taking steps to reduce such problems. FedEx and UPS are revamping their fleets to use more electric and alternative-fuel vehicles. Whereas rail is usually the cleanest way to move land freight a long distance, General Electric's recently introduced Evolution locomotives have 5 percent better fuel economy and 40 percent

When Metro set up its cash-and-carry wholesale operations in India, it could not rely on the same logistics systems it used in Germany. Rather, Metro had to create its own fleet of refrigerated trucks to pick up produce directly from farmers. However, this reduced stock-outs and helped Metro offer customers better-quality produce at lower prices.
Source: METRO Cash & Carry India Pvt. Ltd.

What's Next? Who's—or rather what's—driving that truck?

Someday not too far in the future, you are going to be driving down the highway in your car. You'll look to your right as you pass a truck. But there will be nobody sitting in the driver's seat. Who will be driving this truck? As it turns out, what's driving that truck will be a better question because artificial intelligence may be doing the driving—and it will be safer than most truck drivers. That might sound a bit far-fetched, but tests are already under way. Experts in the field have little doubt that driverless trucks are *What's next?* in transportation. So let's take a closer look at what is happening with this technology.

There are many benefits to removing drivers from [illegible] is economic. About 75 percent of the cost of shipping a truckload of goods across the United States goes to paying the driver. Most truck drivers have a built-in incentive to drive faster because they are paid by the mile; but by driving slower, driverless trucks can optimize fuel economy. Federal regulations also limit human truckers to 11 hours of driving a day before a required 8-hour break. A driverless truck can operate practically 24/7, making much better utilization of an expensive capital asset. Another benefit is safety. Each year about 350,000 accidents and 4,000 fatalities on U.S. roads are attributed to large trucks. About 90 percent of those are caused by human error and AI will drive much more safely.

The move to driverless trucks is under way. In fact, mining companies Rio Tinto and BHP Billiton already use autonomous vehicles on their private land. Controlled road tests have been conducted on highways in Europe and the United States. Right now, truck producer Freightliner's demonstrations include a "highway pilot" or driver on board—though drivers will disappear as the artificial intelligence learns from early experience and gets smarter.

Big truck makers like Daimler and Volvo, together with tech startups, are helping to quickly make this a reality. For example, Otto, a firm founded by former Google executives, developed a $30,000 retrofit kit that adds driverless functionality to any truck built since 2013. That beats buying a new truck for $200,000. Another startup, Peloton Technology, produces software that helps self-driving vehicles facilitate multiple self-driving trucks driving closely behind one another in a convoy, allowing multiple trucks to drive as a "platoon." Sensors and direct vehicle-to-vehicle communications allow trucks to drive closer together, operating as a single unit. The "drafting" effects of planned "tailgating" lowers wind resistance and saves 10 to 15 percent on fuel.

Experts estimate that by 2025, autonomous trucks will be widespread and you won't even look twice when passing one on that cross-country drive. *What's next* after that? Safer roads, cleaner air, and cheaper deliveries if this AI technology delivers on its promises.

lower emissions compared to previous models. Truck manufacturers are also working to improve fuel efficiency and environmental impact. Peterbilt and International are among firms working to build diesel-hybrid 18-wheelers. The U.S. government supports these initiatives[7] with the Environmental Protection Agency's SmartWay program (www.epa.gov/smartway/learn-about-smartway). It helps freight carriers, shippers, and logistics companies improve fuel efficiency and reduce environmental impact. Today the public *expects* companies to manufacture, transport, sell, and dispose of products in an environmentally sound manner.

Transportation analytics aid the environment and lower costs

Transportation is also made more efficient with analytics. Transportation companies routinely place sensors on trucks and train cars to monitor their movement. These sensors generate a lot of data. Managers use this to identify opportunities to more effectively manage the economic and environmental costs of transportation.

For example, UPS uses global positioning data to learn and recommend routes for its drivers—routes that maximize service and minimize fuel consumption. The system even adapts on the fly to changes in traffic or if a customer asks for a delivery before noon. Soon this type of analysis may not be relayed to a *human* driver. To learn more, see *What's Next?* Who's—or rather what's—driving that truck?

The Storing Function and Marketing Strategy

Store it and smooth out sales and increase profits and consumer satisfaction

Storing is the marketing function of holding goods so they're available when they're needed. **Inventory** is the amount of goods being stored.

Storing is necessary when production of goods doesn't match consumption. This is common with mass production. Nippon Steel, for example, might produce thousands of steel bars of one size before changing the machines to produce another size. It's often cheaper to produce large quantities of one size, and store the unsold quantity, than to have shorter production runs. Thus, storing goods allows the producer to achieve economies of scale in production.

Menasha, a supplier of innovative packaging, wants its client firms to realize that its package designs can help reduce both logistics costs and environmental impacts.
Source: Menasha Corporation

Storing varies in the channel system

Storing allows producers and intermediaries to keep stocks at convenient locations, ready to meet customers' needs. In fact, storing is one of the major activities of some intermediaries.

Most channel members provide the storing function for some length of time. Even final consumers store some things for their future needs. Which channel members store the product, and for how long, affects the behavior of all channel members. For example, the producer of Snapper lawn mowers[8] tries to get wholesalers to inventory a wide selection of its machines. That way, retailers can carry smaller inventories because they can be sure of dependable local supplies from wholesalers. And the retailers might decide to sell Snapper—rather than Toro or some other brand that they would have to store at their own expense.

If consumers "store" the product, more of it may be used or consumed. That's why Breyer's likes customers to buy its half-gallon packages. The "inventory" is right there in the freezer—and ready to be eaten—whenever the impulse hits.

Goods are stored at a cost

Storing can increase the value of goods, but *storing always involves costs* too. Different kinds of cost are involved (see Exhibit 6-6). Car dealers, for example, must store

Exhibit 6-6 Many Expenses Contribute to Total Inventory Cost

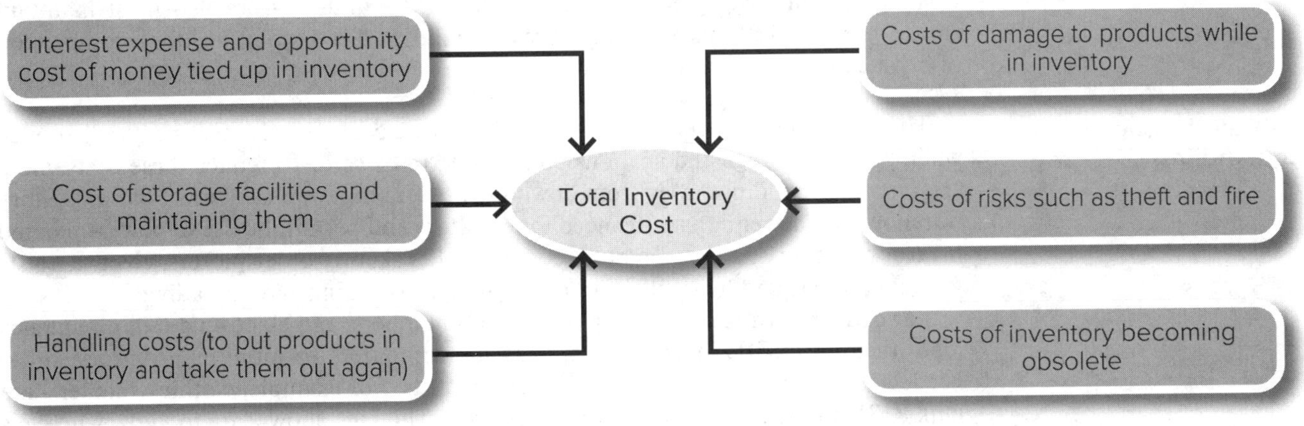

cars on their lots—waiting for the right customer. The interest expense of money tied up in the inventory is a major cost. In addition, if a new car on the lot is dented or scratched, there is a repair cost. If a car isn't sold before the new models come out, its value drops. There is also a risk of fire or theft—so the retailer must carry insurance. And, of course, dealers incur the cost of leasing or owning the display lot where they store the cars.

In today's competitive markets, most firms watch their inventories closely. They try to cut unnecessary inventory because it can make the difference between a profitable strategy and a loser. On the other hand, a marketing manager must be very careful in making the distinction between unnecessary inventory and inventory needed to provide the distribution service level customers expect. Shipments of Boeing's 787 Dreamliner aircraft were significantly delayed by a shortage of bolts that hold the jet airplanes together. The lack of availability of this relatively small part cost Boeing millions of dollars.

Rapid response cuts inventory costs

Many firms are finding that they can cut inventory costs and still provide the desired customer service level—if they can reduce the time it takes to replace items that are sold. This is one important reason that JIT [illegible]. The firms involved use EDI, the Internet, and similar computerized approaches to share information and speed up the order cycle and delivery process.

Specialized Storing Facilities May Be Required

New cars can be stored outside on the dealer's lot. Fuel oil can be stored in a specially designed tank. Coal and other raw materials can be stored in open pits. But most products must be stored inside protective buildings. Often, firms can choose among different types of specialized storing facilities. The right choice may reduce costs and serve customers better.

Private warehouses are common

Private warehouses are storing facilities owned or leased by companies for their own use. Most manufacturers, wholesalers, and retailers have some storing facilities either in their main buildings or in a separate location. A sales manager often is responsible for managing a manufacturer's finished-goods warehouse, especially if regional sales branches aren't near the factory.

Firms use private warehouses when a large volume of goods must be stored regularly. Yet private warehouses can be expensive. If the need changes, the extra space may be hard, or impossible, to rent to others.

Public warehouses fill special needs

Public warehouses are independent storing facilities. They can provide all the services that a company's own warehouse can provide. A company might choose a public warehouse if it doesn't have a regular need for space. For example, Tonka Toys uses public warehouses because its business is seasonal. Tonka pays for the space only when it is used. Public warehouses are also useful for manufacturers that must maintain stocks in many locations, including foreign countries. See Exhibit 6-7 for a comparison of private and public warehouses.

Warehousing facilities cut handling costs too

The cost of physical handling is a major storing cost. Goods must be handled once when put into storage and again when removed to be sold. To reduce these costs, modern one-story buildings away from downtown traffic have replaced most old multistory warehouses. They eliminate the need for elevators and permit the use of power-operated lift trucks, battery-operated motor scooters, roller-skating order pickers, electric hoists for heavy items, and hydraulic[9] ramps[10] to speed loading and unloading.

Bar codes, Universal Product Code (UPC) numbers, and electronic radio frequency identification (RFID) tags make it easy for computers to monitor inventory, order needed stock, and track storing and shipping costs. For example, clothing retailer Zara puts RFID tags on every piece of merchandise. The tags allow Zara to know where ev-

Exhibit 6-7
A Comparison of Private Warehouses and Public Warehouses

Characteristics	Type of Warehouse: Private	Type of Warehouse: Public
Fixed investment	Very high	No fixed investment
Unit cost	High if volume is low; very low if volume is very high	Low: charges are made only for space needed
Control	High	Low managerial control
Adequacy for product line	Highly adequate	May lack convenience
Flexibility	Low: fixed costs have already been committed	High: easy to end arrangement

ery piece of merchandise is at any given time—greatly simplifying the process of taking inventory. Each time Zara sells a garment, the tag immediately notifies the stockroom to bring up another from the stockroom. Chips in the tags make it easier to find similar garments—in the store or at a nearby store.

The Distribution Center—A Different Kind of Warehouse

Is storing really needed?

Discrepancies of assortment or quantity between one channel level and another are often adjusted at the place where goods are stored. It reduces handling costs to regroup and store at the same place—*if both functions are required.* But sometimes regrouping is required when storing isn't.

Don't store it; distribute it

A **distribution center** is a special kind of warehouse designed to speed the flow of goods and avoid unnecessary storing costs. Today, the distribution center concept is widely used by firms at all channel levels. Many products buzz through a distribution center without ever tarrying on a shelf; workers and equipment immediately sort the products as they come in and then move them to an outgoing loading dock and the vehicle that will take them to their next stop. Technology is key to making distribution centers efficient.

Consider how food distributor Sysco addresses the challenge of shipping more than 21.5 million tons of fruit, vegetables, meats, and other food-related products each year. Sysco's customers include one in every three restaurants, school cafeterias, and other food service outlets in the United States and Canada. Because Sysco delivers so many products in so many different forms—from boxes of frozen French fries, crates of Granny Smith apples, and 80-pound tubs of flour to pots, pans, and utensils—its handling needs vary widely.

To move all these goods efficiently and quickly, Sysco relies on technology. It uses supply chain management software and an EDI system to automatically direct supplies from vendors such as Kraft and Kellogg to one of two Sysco "redistribution centers." There, orders are quickly consolidated[11] and moved to one of Sysco's 177 distribution centers. The 400,000+ square-foot distribution centers are organized by weight and temperature; heavier items—such as cans weighing 40 to 50 pounds—are housed on one side, and lighter items—such as boxes of potato chips—on the other. To fill orders, custom software supplies fork-lift drivers with printouts telling them which items to pick first and how to stack them on a pallet[12] based on the weight of the items, their location in the distribution center, and their ultimate destination. After calculating delivery routes that optimize time and fuel use, the software also provides instructions for loading the trucks.

Sysco delivers more than food to its customers. On the "Customer Solutions" section of Sysco's website, restaurateurs are connected with business resources (such as payroll and marketing tools) and managers of school lunch programs or nursing home meals can learn about Sysco's profitability consultation, menu analysis, and safety training. Together Sysco's combination of efficient operations, service and support, and quality products provide excellent value for its target market.

Direct store delivery skips the distribution center

Some firms prefer to skip the distribution center altogether and ship products directly from where they are manufactured to retail stores. This may move products more quickly, but usually at a higher cost. Frito-Lay uses this approach. It handles more than 10,000 direct delivery routes to more than 200,000 small-store customers. The route drivers build close relationships with the many small retailers. That helps Frito-Lay better understand end consumers and adapt product mixes to particular stores. These extra services result in more shelf space and higher prices at the small stores.

Managers must be innovative to provide customers with superior value

More competitive markets, improved technology, coordination among firms, and efficient new distribution centers are bringing big improvements to the PD area. Yet the biggest challenges may be more basic. As we've emphasized here, physical distribution activities [illegible] So taking advantage of ways to improve often requires cooperation all along the channel system. Too often, such cooperation doesn't exist–and changing ingrained[13] ways of doing things is hard. But marketing managers who push for innovations in these areas are likely to win customers away from firms and whole channel systems that are stuck doing things the old way.

CONCLUSION

This chapter explained the major logistics activities and how they contribute to the value of products by getting them to the place that customers want or need them. If the distribution customer service level meets their needs and can be provided at a reasonable cost, customers may not even think about the logistics activities that occur behind the scenes. But if products are not available when and where they need to be, a strategy will fail. So decisions in these areas are an important part of Place and marketing strategy planning.

We emphasized the relation between customer service level, transporting, and storing. The physical distribution concept focuses on coordinating all the storing, transporting, and product-handling activities into a smoothly working system—to deliver the desired service level and customer value at the lowest total cost.

Marketing managers often want to improve service and may select a higher-cost alternative to improve their marketing mix. The total cost approach might reveal that it is possible both to reduce costs and to improve customer service—perhaps by working closely with other members of the supply chain.

We discussed various modes of transporting and their advantages and disadvantages. We also discussed ways to reduce inventory costs. For example, distribution centers are an important way to cut storing and handling costs, and computerized information links—within firms and among firms in the channel—are increasingly important in blending all of the logistics activities into a smooth-running system.

Effective marketing managers make important strategy decisions about physical distribution. Creative strategy decisions may result in lower PD costs while maintaining or improving the customer service level. And production-oriented competitors may not even understand what is happening.

JOYFUL MOMENT

Keep Your Head!

A young man was working in the production section of a grocery store when a customer asked him for half a head of cabbage.

"Sir, we don't sell half heads of anything."

"Well, I insist; I only want half a head."

"I'll ask the manager."

The young man walked to the manager's office and, not realizing that the customer had followed him, said to the manager, "Sir, some asshole wants to buy just half a head of cabbage."

Turning and noticing the customer, he quickly added, "And this gentleman wants the other half."

WORDS AND EXPRESSIONS

1. **logistics**: *n.* handling an operation that involves providing labor and materials as needed 物流；后勤
—Logistics is the entity flow process of the commodity from provide place to the accepted place.
物流是指物品从供应地向接受地的实体流动过程。
2. **emission**: *n.* the release of something such as gas orradiation 排放，散发物
—Sulfur emissions from steel mills become acid rain.
炼钢厂排放出的硫形成了酸雨。
3. **trade-off**: *n.* an exchange that occurs as a compromise 交易；权衡
—The newspaper's headline indicates that there was a trade-off at the summit.
报纸的大字标题表明峰会上大家作出了妥协。
4. **assortment**: *n.* a collection containing a variety of sorts of things 分类；搭配；花色品种
—This shop has a good assortment of goods to choose from.
该店各色货物俱全，任君选择。
5. **perishable**: *adj.* liable to perish; subject to destruction or death or decay 易腐坏的；易毁灭的
—Unlike perishable agricultural products, oil can be stored in the ground.
不同于易腐烂的农产品，石油可以长期埋在地下。
6. **containerization**: *n.* transportation by containers 货柜运输
—I think containerization is one of the best loading methods at present.
我认为集装箱运输是目前最佳运输方法之一。
7. **initiative**: *n.* the first of a series of actions 主动性；首创；主动权
—We have the initiative and we intend to keep it.
我们拥有主动权并且我们不打算放弃它。
8. **mower**: *n.* a lawn mower or machine that has sharp blades for cutting something such as corn or wheat 割草机；收割机
—We need a lawn mower to cut the grass.
我们需要一台草坪修剪机来割草。
9. **hydraulic**: *adj.* involving or operated by a fluid that is under pressure 水压的，液压的
—The boat has no fewer than five hydraulic pumps.
这艘船配备至少 5 个液压泵。
10. **ramp**: *n.* an inclined surface or roadway that moves traffic from one level to another 斜道;（装车或上下飞机的）活动梯或活动坡道
—That driver drove the car up the ramp.
那司机将车开上了斜坡。
11. **consolidate**: *v.* to bring together into a single whole or system 合并；巩固，统一；合计金额
—The two banks will consolidate in July next year.
这两家银行明年 7 月将合并。
12. **pallet**: *n.* a portable platform for storing or moving goods that are stacked on it 托盘；平台；运货板
—The warehouse will hold more than 90,000 pallets storing 30 million Easter eggs.
那间仓库将用 9 万多个货盘装 3000 万只复活节彩蛋。
13. **ingrained**: *adj.* deeply rooted; firmly fixed or held 根深蒂固的；难以根除的
—The belief that one should work hard is ingrained in our culture.
人人都应该努力工作这个信念在我们的文化中根深蒂固。

EXERCISES

1. **Multiple choices**

(1) About ___ of the cost of health care supplies in the U.S. is a result of logistics.

A. 5%　　B. 15%　　C. 35%　　D. 60%

(2) When planning physical distribution, the marketing manager should ___.

A. meet the delivery needs of every customer

B. minimize the cost of distribution for a given customer service level

C. minimize the cost of transportation

D. maximize the speed of delivery

(3) The "total cost approach" to physical distribution management ____.
A. seeks to eliminate the storing function
B. seeks to minimize the cost of transportation
C. might suggest a high-cost transporting mode if storing costs could be reduced enough to lower total distribution costs
D. ignores inventory carrying costs

(4) Within the United States, the largest amount of goods is transported by which of the following methods?
A. Truck. B. Rail. C. Water. D. Air.

(5) Compared to shipping by truck, the high cost of shipping by air freight may be offset by which of the following?
A. Reduced storage capacity on newer planes.
B. Job growth involved with staffing outlying warehouses.
C. Greater speed of delivering goods.
D. Greater ability to handle different types of goods.

2. Terms translation

(1) logistics system (2) physical distribution (3) customer service level (4) supply chain
(5) EDI (6) containerization (7) public warehouses (8) private warehouses
(9) inventory (10) transportation mode

3. True or false

(1) Logistics costs vary from firm to firm and from country to country. ______
(2) Customers care much about how a product was moved or stored. ______
(3) Most customers would prefer very good delivery service at a low price, but it is hard to provide. ______
(4) There are trade-off relationships among physical distribution costs, customer service level and sales. ______
(5) The total cost approach ignores inventory carrying costs. ______
(6) Marketing managers should decide how physical distribution functions can be divided within the channel. ______
(7) Transportation makes products available when and where they need to be. ______
(8) The transportation cost is usually more than the value added to products by moving them. ______
(9) Railroads carry large loads at low cost. ______
(10) Airplane is most suitable for carrying low-value, and low weight goods. ______

4. Fill in the blanks

(1) Physical distribution is another name for __________.
(2) Most physical distribution decisions involve __________ between costs, the customer service and sales.
(3) Supply __________ is the complete set of firms and facilities and logistics activities that are involved in procuring materials, transforming them into intermediate or finished products, and distributing them to customers.
(4) Transporting can help achieve __________ of scale in production.
(5) Transport costs add little to the cost of products that are already __________ relative to their size and weight.
(6) Railroads are most efficient at handling full __________ of goods.
(7) The flexibility and speed of trucks make them better at moving small quantities pf goods for shorter __________.
(8) Water transportation is the __________ shipping mode, but is usually the lowest-cost way of shipping heavy freight.
(9) Inland waterways are important for carrying bulky, __________ products such as iron ore, grain, and gravel.
(10) __________ are used primarily to move oil and natural gas.

5. Answer the following questions

(1) Discuss the types of trade-offs involved in physical distribution costs, service levels, and sales.
(2) What is a just-in-time delivery system?
(3) What are the factors that affect PD service levels?
(4) Explain the total cost approach and why it may cause conflicts in some firms.
(5) Discuss the relative advantages and disadvantages of railroads, trucks, and airlines as transporting methods.

SUGGESTED CASES

16. Hanratty Company

24. Fresh Harvest

MARKETING ANALYTICS: DATA TO KNOWLEDGE

McGraw Hill Education connect

CHAPTER 6: TOTAL DISTRIBUTION COST

Proto Company has been producing various items made of plastic. It recently added a line of plain plastic cards that other firms (such as banks and retail stores) will imprint to produce credit cards. Proto offers its customers the plastic cards in different colors, but they all sell for $40 per box of 1,000. Tom Phillips, Proto's product manager for this line, is considering two possible physical distribution systems. He estimates that if Proto uses airfreight, transportation costs will be $7.50 a box, and its cost of carrying inventory will be 5 percent of total annual sales dollars. Alternatively, Proto could ship by rail for $2 a box. But rail transport will require renting space at four regional warehouses—at $26,000 a year each. Inventory carrying cost with this system will be 10 percent of total annual sales dollars. Phillips prepared a spreadsheet to compare the cost of the two alternative physical distribution systems.

See Connect for the spreadsheet and questions needed to analyze this scenario.

7

CHAPTER SEVEN

Retailers, Wholesalers, and Their Strategy Planning

Back in the late 1970s, Bernie Marcus and Arthur Blank ran a chain of Southern California home improvement centers called Handy Dan. While running some pricing experiments, they found that lower prices raised sales revenue and lowered costs as a percentage of sales. They thought the lower prices could increase Handy Dan's profits compared to the "buy low and sell high" pricing commonly practiced in their industry. However, before they could expand the experiment to more stores, new ownership at Handy Dan came in and swept out most of top management—including Marcus and Blank.

From a Los Angeles coffee shop, the two drafted a business plan for a new kind of home improvement center. A New York City investment firm funded the idea, and the first two Home Depot stores opened outside of Atlanta, Georgia. Marcus and Blank helped usher in a new "mass-merchandising" approach to retail, demonstrating that low prices could generate high sales volume and profitability.

Even in the company's early days, Home Depot's 100,000-square-foot warehouse stores featured a wide variety of merchandise—from paint to plumbing to electrical and lumber. Experienced contractors and serious do-it-yourselfers loved the wide selection and low prices. To appeal to a less experienced and less confident target market, Home Depot hired and trained a knowledgeable staff who could teach customers how to lay a tile floor, handle a power tool, or build a fence. As this target market gained confidence, they tackled more household jobs—after going to Home Depot, of course. Sales grew quickly. By the late 1990s, Home Depot generated sales of over $38 billion from more than 900 stores.

After Marcus and Blank retired in the early 2000s, Home Depot sought to grow profits by opening stores in international markets like China and cutting costs at home. These strategies were not successful. After six years of disappointing sales in China, Home Depot pulled out, citing cultural differences. The company found that Chinese consumers were not ready for the warehouse store, preferring to shop at smaller, specialty shops. Back in the United States, cost control efforts included cutting the number and training of its sales associates. Although this increased profits in the short term, it alienated employees. And when customers couldn't find knowledgeable help at their local Home Depot, many headed to rival Lowe's, which offered better service. Sales lagged and then dropped when the economic recession and housing crash came in 2008.

At this point, Home Depot returned to a familiar marketing strategy: low prices and high customer service. More sales associates and spruced-up stores created a better shopping experience. Store managers' incentives emphasized customer satisfaction. Soon employee morale improved; customers noticed the changes and returned to Home Depot.

Home Depot faces a wide range of competitors. Fellow home improvement center Lowe's goes after a similar target market. Other competitors seek a slice of Home Depot's business. For example, Sherwin-Williams Paint Stores offer a limited product line of paint, stain, painting supplies, and wallpaper. Many formerly independent hardware stores joined the Ace Hardware cooperative, where pooling purchases and marketing expenses lowers costs. When seeking just a few items for a small project, many customers like the convenient easy-in, easy-out of Ace's smaller stores. Other customers pick up those supplies at their local Walmart or Target supercenter.

For many retailers, the most feared competitor is Amazon. The store's name has even become a verb; for example, department stores like Macy's have been "Amazoned"—losing significant market share to the online retail giant. Supermarkets appear to be the next type of store in Amazon's sights. Home Depot's marketing strategy tries to avoid direct competition with Amazon. This strategy starts with those knowledgeable folks in the orange aprons. It also seeks to build brand preference for exclusive store brands like Ryobi power tools, Hampton Bay fans, and Behr paints.

Home Depot also understands the advantages and disadvantages of online shopping. It recognizes online shopping can offer customers access to a rich variety of information, customer reviews, and 24/7 shopping. On the other hand, some products need to be seen and touched before making a purchase, and others don't ship well via UPS. In addition, some customers like to talk to a knowledgeable salesperson before buying. Most importantly for Home Depot, many customers want the best of both worlds. These multichannel shoppers shift back and forth between a cell phone, computer, and local store before making a purchase.

Home Depot appeals to multichannel shoppers with "interconnected retail," which combines the best of online and in-store shopping for a better shopping experience. For example, a recent redesign of Home Depot's website improves search capabilities, facilitates comparison shopping, and speeds up online checkout. A new feature offers customers fast, accurate delivery dates and times, and Home Depot's 2,000+ stores have become "distribution centers." A customer can go online and search for a refrigerator, compare models and prices, and then go to a store to open those French doors and see how the freezer drawers actually work. They can then purchase from their smartphone and arrange a two-hour window for delivery the next day. For other purchases, customers buy online and pick up their order at their local store, where they often make additional purchases. Home Depot management is finding that improving customers' online experience offers a better return on investment than opening new stores. In fact, most of the company's growth now comes from online shopping, which accounts for more than 6 percent of its sales.

Professional contractors remain an important growth opportunity for Home Depot. Although only 3 percent of Home Depot's customers, these B2B buyers account for 40 percent of Home Depot sales. Over the years, Home Depot has used different strategies for this target market. For example, a separate wholesale channel (HD Supply) targeted the housing supply market. Eventually, it sold off HD Supply, which now targets different customers than Home Depot and sells maintenance, repair, and operations supplies. Today, Home Depot sells to its contractor target market through its retail stores with a different marketing mix. For example, its Pro Xtra Loyalty Program offers contractors volume pricing discounts and free direct-to-job delivery services.

Home Depot credits its success to an almost "paranoid" focus on target customers and eliminating friction in the shopping process. Measures of retail success suggest the company's tactics are working. Recently, comparable store sales—which measure sales growth at stores open a year or more—were an impressive 4.5 percent, double that of Lowe's. And in 2016, Home Depot revenues topped $94 billion with profits of almost $8 billion.

LEARNING OBJECTIVES

Retail and wholesale organizations exist as members of marketing channel systems. But they also do their own strategy planning as they compete for target customers. As the Home Depot case shows, these firms make decisions about Product, Place, Promotion, and Price. This chapter overviews the strategy planning decisions of different types of retailers and wholesalers. The chapter shows how retailing and wholesaling are evolving—to give you a sense of how things may change in the future.

When you finish this chapter, you should be able to

1 understand the nature and basic structure of retailing.

2 understand how retailers plan their marketing strategies.

3 know about the many kinds of retailers that work with producers and wholesalers as members of channel systems.

4 understand what is different about retailing on the Internet.

5 understand how and why retailers evolve, including the roles of technology, scrambled merchandising, and the "wheel of retailing."

6 understand some of the differences in retailing in different nations.

7 know what progressive wholesalers are doing to modernize their operations and marketing strategies.

8 know the various kinds of merchant and agent wholesalers and the strategies they use.

9 understand important new terms (shown in boldface).

Retailers and Wholesalers Plan Their Own Strategies

As we saw in previous chapters, retailers and wholesalers perform a vital role in channel systems. Now we'll look at the decisions that retailers and wholesalers make in developing their own strategies. But first, study Exhibit 7-1 for a visual of how everything fits together.

Exhibit 7-1 Marketing Strategy Planning for Retailers and Wholesalers

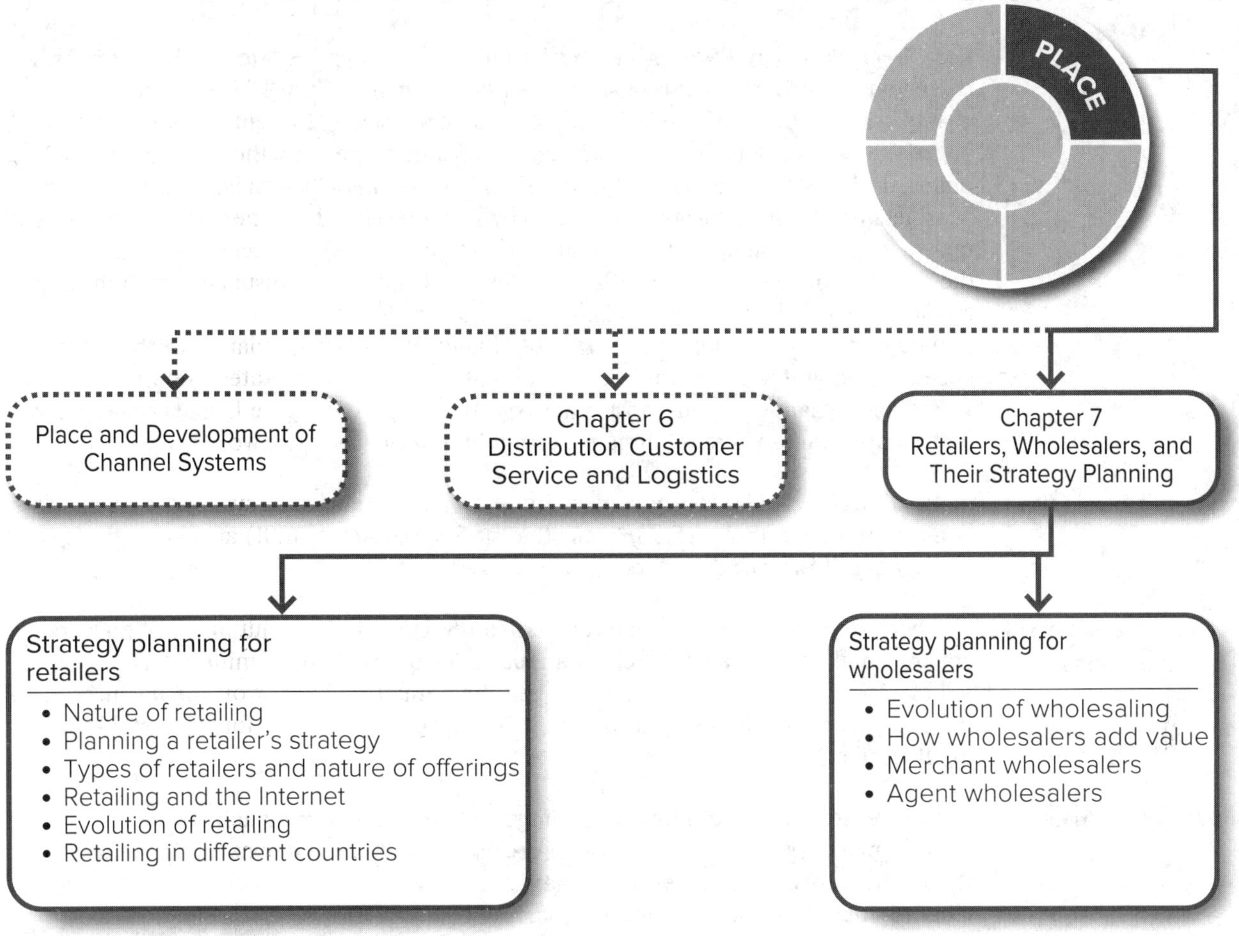

Producers can choose a variety of different paths to make goods and services available to customers when, where, and in the right quantities (see Exhibit 7-2). In Chapter 6 we discussed how some producers deliver goods or services directly to customers. We also saw how in some industries, retailers and/or wholesalers add value so it makes sense to use indirect channels. And of course, many producers use more than one of these paths to get products to customers.

When marketing managers decide to use intermediaries in their marketing strategy, they can choose among many different types of retailers and wholesalers. Retailers and wholesalers have different target markets and different marketing mixes, and a producer should select intermediaries that best facilitate its strategy.

To better understand these options, it helps to understand strategy planning for retailers (see Exhibit 7-1). Retailers create a marketing mix that provides value for a target market. We also discuss how retailing has evolved and where it is heading, including some important international differences.

Exhibit 7-2 Wholesalers and Retailers in a Typical Channel of Distribution

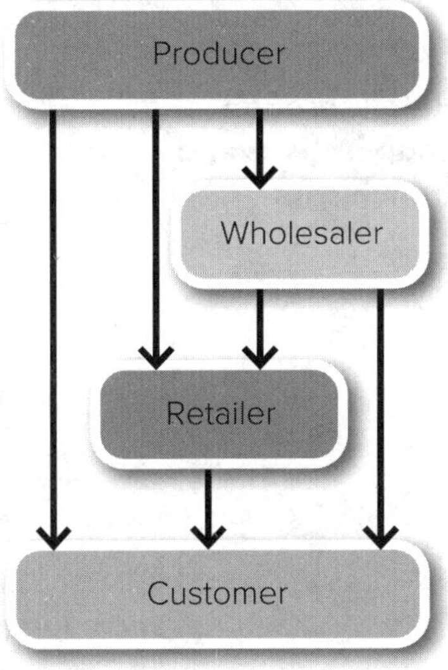

The Nature of Retailing

Retailing covers all of the activities involved in the sale of products to final consumers. Retailers range from large chains of specialized stores, such as Toys "R" Us, to individual merchants like the woman who sells baskets from an open stall in the central market in Ibadan, Nigeria. Some retailers operate from stores and others operate without a store–by selling online, on TV, with a printed catalog, from vending machines, or even in consumers' homes. Most retailers sell physical goods produced by someone else. But in the case of service retailing–such as dry cleaning, fast food, tourist attractions, online bank accounts, or hair salons–the retailer is often the producer. Because they serve individual consumers, even the largest retailers face the challenge of handling many small transactions.

The nature of retailing and its rate of change are generally related to the stage and speed of a country's economic development. In the United States, retailing is more varied and dynamic than in most other countries. By studying the U.S. system, you will better understand where retailing is headed in other parts of the world.

Retailing is big business

Retailing is crucial to consumers in every macro-marketing system. For example, consumers spend about $5.5 *trillion* (that's $5,500,000,000,000!) a year buying goods and services from U.S. retailers.

A few big retailers do most of the business

There are more than a million retailers in the United States, but most of these retailers are small; more than half report annual sales of less than $1 million. The larger retail stores–those selling more than $5 million annually–do most of the business. Less than 15 percent of the retail stores are this big, yet they account for almost 75 percent of all retail sales.

Big chains have market clout

One reason for the dominance of large retailers is that many achieve economies of scale from a corporate chain. A **corporate chain** is a firm that owns and manages more than one store–and often it's many. Chains–including Nordstrom, Walmart, Kroger, 7-Eleven, and Chipotle–have grown rapidly and now account for about half of all retail sales. Chains can buy in larger quantities and earn lower prices, they get operational efficiencies from running many stores, and they can apply advertising and other promotion costs over many stores. You can expect chains to continue to grow and take business from independent stores.

Some businesspeople like to open retail franchises with brand names consumers already know–brands with track records of success, like Dunkin' Donuts and Baskin Robbins.
Source: DD IP Holder LLC AND BR IP Holder LLC

Retail through cooperatives and franchisors

Because size offers such an advantage, many retailers not connected to a chain join cooperatives or franchises[1]. Retailers' cooperatives pool purchasing and marketing expenses to increase efficiency and effectiveness. Piggly Wiggly grocery, Ace Hardware, NAPA Auto Parts stores, and Carpet One are examples of cooperatives.

In a **franchise operation**, the franchisor develops a good marketing strategy, and the retail franchise holders carry out the strategy in their own units. Each franchise holder benefits from its relationship with the larger company and its experience, buying power, promotion, and image. In return, the franchise holder signs a contract, agreeing to pay fees and commissions and strictly follow franchise rules designed to continue the successful strategy. Franchise holders' sales account for about a third of all retail sales. Hampton Hotels, Anytime Fitness, Subway, and Supercuts are examples of franchises.

Small retailers specialize

While big chains and franchises dominate the sales volume, 85 percent of all retailers are small. But it is not easy for small retailers; the failure rate of small retailers is high. A recent study found less than half were operating four years after starting in business. Without the same economies of scale, small retailers that survive usually develop a specialty and become highly knowledgeable about a market niche. For example, online retailer Wicker Central specializes in outdoor wicker furniture. With four toy stores in Charleston, South Carolina, Wonder Works survives because it offers visitors a unique experience on each visit. These stores compete with larger competitors based on intimate knowledge of their markets and high levels of customer service.

Planning a Retailer's Strategy

Retailers interact directly with final consumers, so strategy planning is critical to their survival. If a retailer loses a customer to a competitor, the retailer is the one that suffers. Producers and wholesalers still make *their* sale regardless of which retailer sells their product. Let's take a closer look at strategy planning for retailers.

Consumers have reasons for buying from particular retailers

Different consumers favor different kinds of retailers. But many retailers either don't know or don't care why. Successful retailers identify possible target markets and try to understand why these people buy where they do. They also understand their own company's strengths and weaknesses as well as those of its competitors. These insights guide the retailer's efforts to fine-tune its marketing mix to the needs of specific target markets.

Marketing mix decisions for retailers

In developing a strategy, a retailer should identify its target market and consciously make decisions on each of the Four Ps; Exhibit 7-3 outlines some of the options available. The chosen combination determines how target customers perceive the retailer's

Exhibit 7-3 Examples of Marketing Strategy Decisions for Retailers

Product
- Product selection (width and depth of assortment, brands, quality)
- After-sale service
- Special services (special orders, entertainment, gift wrap)

Place
- Physical stores and/or sales over the Internet
- Number and location of stores
- Shopping atmosphere (comfort, safety)
- Store size, layout, and design
- Store hours

Price
- Credit cards—whether to offer a store card
- Discount policies
- Frequency and level of sales prices
- Charge (or not) for delivery or other services

Promotion
- Advertising
- Publicity (Facebook, Twitter, Pinterest)
- Salespeople (number and training)
- Helpful information (demonstrations, displays, online videos, online reviews)

offering (its positioning) and how it is differentiated from other retailers. The marketing mix must provide superior value to some target market, or the retailer will fail.

Strategy planning for two successful shoe retailers

Consider the marketing strategies for two very different, yet successful, shoe retailers. Usually located in malls, Foot Locker is a specialty shop that sells athletic footwear and some athletic apparel. Its primary target market is young males aged 12 to 20, though it also sells to other active individuals. Other segments are targeted more directly through its Lady Foot Locker and Kids Foot Locker stores. Although its shoes can be ordered online, most sales occur in one of the 3,400+ stores located around the world. Each store typically carries less than 300 styles of athletic shoes with a focus on those designed for running, basketball, and casual wear. Whereas Foot Locker carries several brands, about three-quarters of its sales are of Nike shoes. Its promotion includes a sales staff at each store and advertising featuring famous athletes like basketball player Russell Westbrook and football player Tom Brady. Foot Locker's biggest fans—almost 6 million of them—follow the store on Facebook. Foot Locker's prices are competitive, and regular sales offer larger discounts. The formula seems to work; Foot Locker's same store sales have grown every quarter for more than six years.

Zappos.com offers a different marketing mix to a different target market. Zappos operates several online storefronts in addition to its core website—including Zappos Couture, selling high-fashion shoes, and Zappos Running, selling athletic footwear. Although Zappos recently added clothing, handbags, housewares, and beauty supplies to its product assortment, its core product line remains shoes. Zappos' wide product line includes more than 150,000 styles and 1,400 brands—including well-known brands such as Nike, Timberland, and Bandolino. Because many shoppers are reluctant to buy shoes without first trying them on, Zappos devotes a whole page to each shoe it sells. Each page features eight or more photos from different angles, a video, customer reviews, detailed descriptions, and suggestions for other shoes "You may also like." Zappos also offers free shipping and free returns—for up to 365 days after purchase! The retailer wins praise for its customer service, which is available 24/7 on the phone or the web. That service helps build positive word-of-mouth for Zappos, and more than 75 percent of its customers are repeat buyers. It has a relatively small budget for its advertising, seen on television, print, online, and even on the bottom of the plastic bins in airport security lines. Zappos and Foot Locker developed very different marketing mixes, but each keeps target customers coming back.

Zappos creatively utilizes its small advertising budget—in this case, placing ads at the bottom of airport security bins. Foot Locker advertises on television using well-known athletes like New England Patriots quarterback Tom Brady.
Top: Source: Zappos.com; Bottom: Source: Foot Locker Retail, Inc.

Different types of retailers emphasize different strategies

Retailers have an almost unlimited number of ways to alter their offerings—their marketing mixes—to appeal to a target market. Because of all the variations, it's oversimplified to classify retailers and their strategies based on a single characteristic—such as merchandise, services, sales volume, or even whether they operate in cyberspace. But a good place to start is by considering basic types of retailers and some differences in their strategies.

Conventional Retailers—Try to Avoid Price Competition

Single-line, limited-line retailers specialize by product

About 150 years ago, **general stores**—which carried anything they could sell in reasonable volume—were the main retailers in the United States. But with the growing number of consumer products after the Civil War, general stores couldn't offer enough variety in all their traditional lines. So some stores began specializing in dry goods, apparel, furniture, or groceries.

Now most *conventional* retailers are **single-line** or **limited-line stores**—stores that specialize in certain lines of related products rather than a wide assortment. Many specialize not only in a single line, such as clothing, but also in a *limited line* within the broader line. Within the clothing line, a retailer might carry *only* shoes, formal wear, or even neckties but offer depth in that limited line.

Single-line, limited-line stores are being squeezed

The main advantage of limited-line retailers is that they can satisfy some target markets better. Perhaps some are just more conveniently located, but most adjust to suit specific customers. They build a relationship with their customers and earn a position as *the* place to shop for a certain type of product. But these retailers face the costly problem of having to stock some slow-moving items in order to satisfy their target markets. Many of these stores are small—with high expenses relative to sales. So they try to keep their prices up by avoiding competition on identical[2] products.

Conventional retailers like this have been around for a long time and are still found in every community. They are a durable lot and clearly satisfy some people's needs. In fact, in most countries conventional retailers still handle the vast majority of all retailing sales. However, this situation is changing fast. Nowhere is the change clearer than in the United States. Conventional retailers are being squeezed by retailers who modify their mixes in the various ways suggested in Exhibit 7-4. Let's look closer at some of these other types of retailers.

Exhibit 7-4 Types of Retailers and the Nature of Their Offerings (*with examples*)

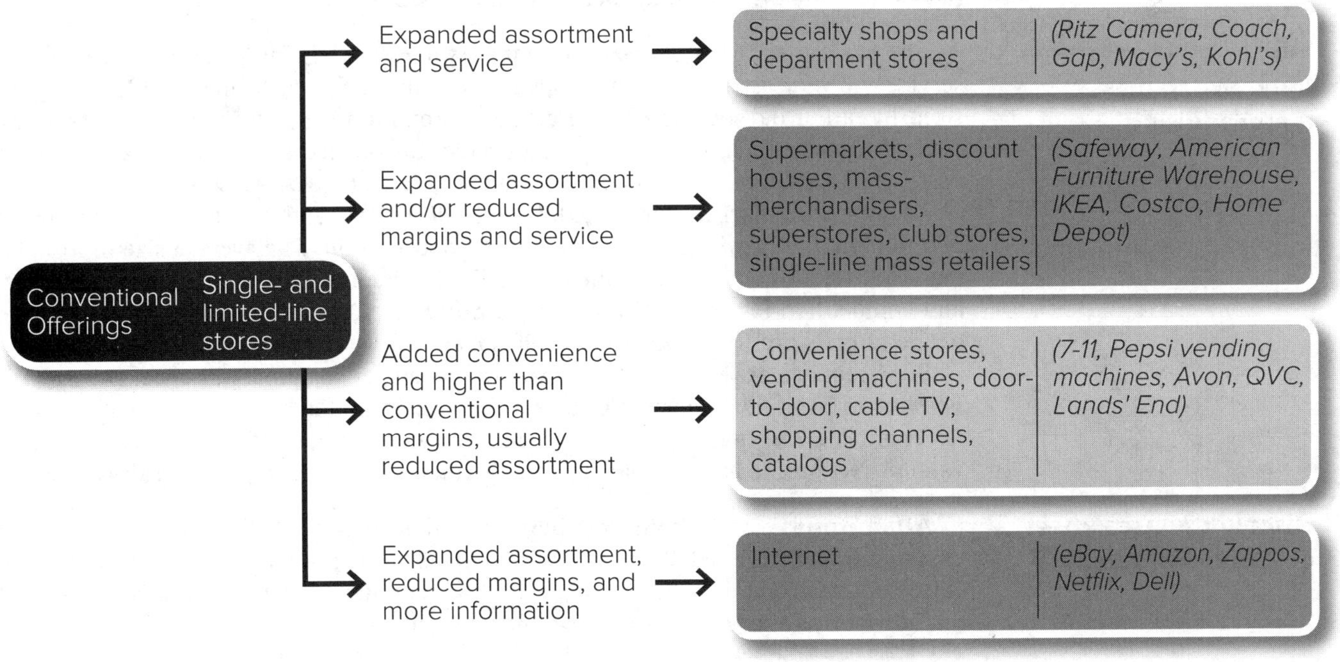

Expand Assortment and Service–To Compete at a High Price

Specialty shops usually sell shopping products

A **specialty shop**–a type of conventional limited-line store–is usually small and has a distinct "personality." Specialty shops sell special types of shopping products, such as high-quality sporting goods, exclusive clothing, baked goods, or even antiques. They aim at a carefully defined target market by offering a unique product assortment, knowledgeable salesclerks, and better service.

Catering to certain types of customers whom the management and salespeople know well simplifies buying, speeds turnover, and cuts costs due to obsolescence[3] and style changes. Specialty shops probably will continue to be part of the retailing scene as long as customers have varied tastes and the money to satisfy them.

Department stores combine many limited-line stores and specialty shops

Department stores are larger stores that are organized into many separate departments and offer many product lines. Each department is like a separate limited-line store and handles a wide variety of shopping products, such as men's wear or housewares. They are usually strong in customer services, including credit, merchandise return, delivery, and sales help. Leading department store chains include Macy's, Dillard's, and Nordstrom.

Department stores are still a major force in big cities. However, in the United States, the number of department stores as well as the average sales per store and their share of retail business have declined significantly since the 1970s. Well-run limited-line stores compete with good service and often carry the same brands. In the United States and many other countries, mass-merchandising and online retailers have posed an even bigger threat.

Evolution of Mass-Merchandising Retailers

Mass-merchandising is different from conventional retailing

The conventional retailers just discussed think that demand in their area is fixed–and they have a "buy low and sell high" philosophy. Many modern retailers reject these ideas. Instead, they accept the **mass-merchandising concept**–which says that retailers should offer low prices to get faster turnover and greater sales volumes–by appealing to larger markets. The mass-merchandising concept applies to many types of retailers, including both those that operate stores and those that sell online. But to understand mass-merchandising better, let's look at its evolution from the development of supermarkets and discounters to modern mass-merchandisers such as Walmart in the United States, Tesco in the UK, and Amazon.com on the Internet.

Supermarkets started the move to mass-merchandising

The basic idea for **supermarkets**, large stores specializing in groceries with self-service and wide assortments, developed in the United States during the 1930s Depression. In earlier days, customers entered a store and a clerk, from behind a counter, fetched requested items. Then some innovators introduced self-service as a way to cut costs while also providing a broad assortment in large bare-bones stores.

Today's supermarkets carry 20,000 to 40,000 items and per-store sales are about $20 million a year, with about 75 percent of that in food. The average size of a supermarket is 40,000 square feet. In the United States, there are about 35,000 supermarkets, and competition in most areas is intense. More recently, supermarket operators have opened superstores of 50,000 to 100,000 square feet with extensive selection.

Supermarkets are planned for maximum efficiency. Scanners at checkout make it possible to carefully analyze the sales of each item and allocate more shelf space to faster-moving and higher-profit items. Survival depends on efficiency and high sales volume. Net profits in supermarkets usually run a thin 1 to 2 percent of sales or less!

Discount houses upset conventional retailers

After World War II, some retailers started to focus on discount prices. These **discount houses** offered "hard goods" (cameras, TVs, and appliances) at substantial price cuts to customers who would go to the discounter's low-rent store, pay cash, and take care of any service or repair problems themselves. These retailers sold at 20 to

30 percent off the list price being charged by conventional retailers. From these origins evolved today's mass-merchandisers.

Mass-merchandisers are more than discounters

Mass-merchandisers are large self-service stores with many departments that emphasize "soft goods" (housewares, clothing, and fabrics) and staples (like health and beauty aids) but still follow the discount house's emphasis on lower margins to get faster turnover. Mass-merchandisers, such as Walmart and Target, have checkout counters in the front of the store and little sales help on the floor. Today, the average mass-merchandiser has nearly 60,000 square feet of floor space, but many new stores are 100,000 square feet or more. Mass-merchandisers grew rapidly—and they've become the primary place to shop for many frequently purchased consumer products. To move into new markets—big cities or small towns—some of these retailers are opening stores with smaller footprints.

Supercenters meet all routine needs

Some supermarkets and mass-merchandisers have moved toward becoming **supercenters (hypermarkets)**—very large stores that try to carry not only food and drug items but all goods and services that the consumer purchases *routinely.* These superstores look a lot like a combination of the supermarkets, drugstores, and mass-merchandisers from which they have evolved, but the concept is different. A supercenter is trying to meet *all* the customer's routine needs at a low price. Supercenter operators include Meijer, Fred Meyer, Target, and Walmart. In fact, Walmart's supercenters have turned it into the largest food retailer in the United States.

Supercenters average more than 150,000 square feet and carry about 50,000 items. Their assortment in one place is convenient, but many time-pressured consumers think that the crowds, lines, and "wandering around" time in the store are not. Some supercenters have responded by reducing product line depth. For example, Walmart recently decided that it didn't need to carry 24 tape measures and now carries just four.

New mass-merchandising formats keep coming

The warehouse club is another retailing format that quickly gained popularity. Sam's Club and Costco are two of the largest. Consumers usually pay an annual membership fee to shop in these large, no-frills facilities. Among the 3,500 items per store, they carry food, appliances, yard tools, tires, and other items that many consumers see as homogeneous shopping items and want at the lowest possible price. The growth of these clubs has also been fueled by sales to small-business customers. That's why some people refer to these outlets as wholesale clubs. However, when half or more of a firm's sales are to final consumers, it is classified as a retailer, not a wholesaler.

Single-line mass-merchandisers rise and fall

Since 1980, many retailers focusing on single product lines have adopted the mass-merchandisers' approach with great success. Toys "R" Us pioneered this trend. Similarly, IKEA (furniture), Lowe's (home improvements), Best Buy (electronics), and Staples (office supplies) attract large numbers of customers with their large assortment and low prices in specific product categories. These stores are called *category killers* because it's so hard for less specialized retailers to compete. Now online retailers offering greater assortment and even lower prices threaten the category killers.

Analytics for mass-merchandising

We have seen the growth and evolution of mass-merchandising, with its focus on low prices and fast turnover. To monitor that turnover, retailing managers utilize a measure of **stockturn rate** (also called inventory turnover)—the number of times the average inventory is sold in a year. For now, it helps to understand that stockturn rate is one indication of the health of a retailer as it measures how quickly its inventory sells. Rising inventory (and a lower stockturn rate) means that product is not selling quickly enough. Retailing managers often monitor stockturn rate from month to month or in comparison to similar retailers.

Some Retailers Focus on Added Convenience

Convenience (food) stores must have the right assortment

Convenience (food) stores are a convenience-oriented variation of the conventional limited-line food stores. Instead of expanding their assortment, however, convenience stores limit their stock to pickup or fill-in items such as bread, milk, beer, and eat-on-the-go snacks. Many also sell gas. Stores such as 7-Eleven and Stop-N-Go aim to fill consumers' needs between trips to a supermarket, and many of them are competing with fast-food outlets. They offer convenience, not assortment, and often charge prices 10 to 20 percent higher than nearby supermarkets. However, as many other retailers have expanded their hours, intense competition is driving down convenience store prices and profits.

Vending machines are convenient

Automatic vending is selling and delivering products through vending machines. Vending machine sales account for only about 1.5 percent of total U.S. retail sales. Yet for some target markets this retailing method can't be ignored.

Although vending machines can be costly to operate, consumers like their convenience. Many vending machines are becoming more convenient by accepting credit cards and mobile payment. Traditionally, soft drinks, candy bars, and snack foods have been sold by vending machines. Now some higher-margin products are beginning to use this channel. For example, Standard Hotels uses poolside vending machines to sell bathing suits.

Stores come to the home—in person, on television, and in catalogs

In-home shopping in the United States started in the pioneer days with **door-to-door selling**—a salesperson going directly to the consumer's home. Variations on this approach are still important for firms such as Amway Global and Mary Kay. It meets some consumers' need for convenient personal attention. Although gaining popularity in some international markets such as China and parts of Africa, it now accounts for less than 1 percent of retail sales in the United States.

Customers can also shop at home by watching cable television channels dedicated[4] to shopping and then calling in their orders by phone. QVC and Home Shopping Network operate in the United States, Japan, and some European countries. Similarly, catalogs allow customers to page through merchandise and place orders on the phone or online. Deliveries will usually occur a few days later. These home shopping methods often use a multichannel approach by adding a website.

Internet retailing has quickly become the most popular way to shop at home (and sometimes at work). Let's take a closer look at online retailing.

Retailing and the Internet

Internet retailing is growing fast, but varies by category

Internet retailing is growing fast; online sales are growing about 15 percent per year whereas total retail sales are growing around 4 percent. In 2016, online sales in the United States topped $350 billion. Although that sounds like a lot—and it is—online sales still make up only about 9 percent of all retail sales.

Online shopping is not very common for many of the most frequent purchases people make—groceries and health and beauty, for example. The share of online sales is much greater in some categories; more than half of all computer hardware and software and more than a third of books, movies, and music are sold online. Over time, people are getting more used to online shopping; currently about half of all American consumers buy online at least a few times per month. The impact of the Internet on retail sales is even greater; many shoppers gather information on the Internet—often at online retailers—before purchasing in a physical store.

Online retailers versus "brick-and-mortar" stores

These days there are online retailers, physical stores (sometimes called brick-and-mortar retailers), and many stores that use both approaches. **Online retailers** are stores that sell exclusively or almost exclusively online. These stores do not have a physical store that consumers can visit.

Consumers see advantages and disadvantages to shopping online as compared to shopping in a physical store. Exhibit 7-5 offers a comparison of these two shopping methods. These days many innovative online retailers are finding ways to offset many of the advantages of physical stores—at the same time physical stores are utilizing the Internet to add value to their offerings. This battle for consumer dollars is fueling a period of innovation and evolution unlike anything retailing has ever seen. Let's take a closer look at how online and brick-and-mortar retailers use the Internet to improve customers' shopping experiences.

Online retail offers low prices and wide assortment

With no storefront and limited sales help, online retailers often have lower operating costs than brick-and-mortar stores. These cost advantages lead many online stores to use low prices to attract customers. But because the Internet makes it easy to compare products and prices from different online sellers, price-sensitive shoppers often choose the store with the lowest price. That puts constant price pressure on Internet sellers to figure out how to differentiate their offerings.

Online stores can also offer a very wide assortment of products—often from different sellers. It is easy to click from site to site or simply conduct a search for a specific brand/model and find multiple sites offering the same thing. Amazon and eBay bring different sellers together to offer customers more choices on a single retail platform. To counter that online advantage, many brick-and-mortar stores are adding in-store computer terminals (kiosks) that connect to the Internet so customers can access a store's website and buy what they might not find in the store.

Lowering the risk of shopping online

Some customers still see risk in online shopping. They worry about unexpected shipping costs, whether their purchase will look the same when it arrives as it did online, how easy it will be to return, or whether an online retailer will mishandle personal information such as credit card numbers.

Successful online retailers are overcoming these customer concerns. Most sell well-known brands and provide free shipping. Some now include bar-coded return labels with the original shipment to simplify returns—which may be even more convenient than returning them to a local store. Many online stores provide excellent customer service and build a good reputation—because word-of-mouth matters online. And as customers do more online shopping, they gain confidence. Together these are eliminating the worries and hassles of online shopping.

Obtaining purchase information

For many purchases, consumers seek information to help them make a purchase decision. This is especially important when a customer is buying in a product category for the first time. It also matters more with clothing or fashion items, where fit matters. Physical stores offer the advantage of being able to touch, feel, and perhaps try some-

Exhibit 7-5 Comparing the Advantages of Shopping Online with Shopping at a Physical Store

Advantages of Shopping Online	Advantages of Shopping at a Physical Store
• Rich variety of product information from many sources	• Ability to hold, try on, or test products before purchase
• Reviews and tips from customers who've already used the product	• Personal help and interaction
• Wide assortment	• Edited assortment—easier to decide
• Fast and convenient purchase/checkout	• Convenient product returns
• Simplified price and product feature comparison	• Help with setup and ongoing service needs
• Anytime and anywhere access	• Instant access to products and instant gratification
	• Shopping with friends or family as a social activity

thing on before purchasing. And physical stores have a salesperson there to answer customer questions. Online retailers are addressing many of these customers concerns as well. Online reviews, virtual salesclerks, and "fit guides" provide information to make buying easier. Many sites post photos and video demonstrations to give customers more information. At online eyeglass retailer EyeBuyDirect.com, customers can upload a photo of themselves and then see what they look like when they virtually "try on" different frames. Another eyeglass retailer, Warby Parker, encourages customers to choose five frames and try them on at home before placing an order.

What is convenience?

Traditional thinking about retail stores considered shopping convenience from the perspective of product assortment, store location, and store hours. By contrast, when shopping online, a customer can access a wide assortment on a single retailer's site or by clicking from one website to another. In addition, online stores are always open—and a customer does not even need to leave home to shop.

However, the Internet makes shopping inconvenient in other ways. You have to plan ahead. When you buy something, you've actually just ordered it and you have to wait for delivery. Online retailers are trying to overcome these disadvantages with faster shipping. It started with low-cost two-day shipping; then one-day shipping became more reasonable. Now some online retailers offer same-day delivery in a few large cities.

Big data and analytics personalize shopping

Online retailers have lots of information on their customers' shopping behavior. For example, online retailers can track (and retain) data showing how a customer moves through their website, which product pages a customer views, whether she reads the reviews or watches a video, what competitive products she considers, and what (if anything) she ultimately purchases. Cookies (small data files placed on a customer's computer) can even tell a retailer what a shopper does at a competitor's website, pull information from a customer's Facebook page, and even track his movements around town via his cell phone. All these data potentially offer a retailer a great deal of information on each customer.

The ability to collect and analyze big data in real time (before that next "click") gives online retailers the opportunity to deliver a personalized shopping experience. Using predictive analytics, retailers anticipate their customers' needs. For example, a customer known to have shopped at a competitor's site might be seen as a "price-oriented shopper" and could receive a targeted (only for that customer) discount. Knowing that a customer previously purchased a sweater from the store, an online retailer might show more sweaters of a similar style on the front page of its site when the customer returns. When a customer shops for a movie at Amazon, the site makes recommendations for other videos based on that customer's previous purchases and past purchases of movie buyers with similar interests. This stored customer knowledge makes recommendations more on-target and relevant—and more likely to encourage more purchases. All of these activities deliver customers a shopping experience tailored to their needs and interests.

Multichannel shoppers shop across channels . . .

With so many online and physical store options, some customers become **multichannel shoppers** who use different channels as they move through a purchase process. The consumer decision process can occur over time as a consumer recognizes a need and researches a purchase. For example, a multichannel shopper seeking a new tennis racquet might read customer reviews of the Wilson Blade tennis racquet at Amazon.com, go to a pro shop at a local tennis club to hit some balls with the Blade, and then purchase the tennis racquet at a steep discount from TennisExpress.com.

. . . but only buy at one

Multichannel shopping causes problems for retailers. When consumers go to a brick-and-mortar store to inspect a product and then purchase from an online retailer with a lower price, this practice is called *showrooming.* One retailer acts as a showroom (providing a customer with a real product to view) for another (lower-priced) competitor. Smartphone apps make the practice easy; with Amazon's app, customers scan product bar codes in a retail store and see the Amazon price. With one click they can make the purchase online.

The practice also works in reverse. *Webrooming* occurs when a customer gathers information at an online store (perhaps by reading reviews) and then purchases at a brick-and-mortar store. Of course, the only retailer making money on this shopping trip is the one the customer buys from, not the others from whom the customer gleaned information along the purchase journey.

Physical retailers add online feature

With the rise in multichannel shopping, many physical retailers are adding online features to offset the advantages of online stores. These days most brick-and-mortar retailers have an online presence. The website may simply provide product information or it may be a full-blown e-commerce website. Earlier in this chapter, we described how Foot Locker and Home Depot use their online stores to carry a wider product assortment than can be carried in a single store. Target, Walmart, Macy's, and Best Buy all do substantial sales volume through their online stores. An important marketing strategy planning decision for a retailer with physical stores involves deciding what online capabilities (if any) to build.

Smartphones are a new channel

Consumers—especially Millennials—are increasingly comfortable shopping on their smartphones. The behavior may be as simple as texting a photo of a pair of shoes to a friend for feedback or researching prices across stores. Some brick-and-mortar retailers see an opportunity to leverage this trend with websites and apps that deliver extra services to customers in physical stores. For example, Sam's Club's Scan & Go app lets customers skip the checkout line. They scan products as they shop and click a button to pay directly from the app. Shopping on mobile devices is a new consumer behavior, and leading retailers are watching closely for opportunities to develop services that enhance target customers' shopping experience.

Omnichannel: the seamless multichannel shopping experience

Many brick-and-mortar retailers view these trends—shopping online, on mobile devices, and webrooming—as an opportunity. These retailers connect their physical store with online channels to create a competitive advantage. **Omnichannel** is a multichannel selling approach in which a retailer provides a seamless customer shopping experience from computer, mobile device, or brick-and-mortar store. Omnichannel is an example of multichannel distribution designed to appeal to a single consumer who prefers to shop across channels.

For example, when a customer shops on Crate & Barrel's website from her laptop and later uses the store's mobile app, anything the customer already placed in her virtual shopping cart carries over to the app; it also remembers what other products she viewed on her laptop. Other retailers allow customers to use their site to check what is in stock at their local store. Home Depot and Best Buy do this and allow customers to buy online and pick up in the store. Omnichannel strategies are winning over multichannel shoppers.

Online retailers open physical stores

Online retailers are fighting back, too. A few formerly online-only retailers are investing in brick-and-mortar stores to deliver a better shopping experience to their customers. For example, after struggling to build its grocery business through its online channel, Amazon decided that having physical stores might be helpful and it purchased Whole Foods Market. Amazon has also opened physical bookstores in malls and on some college campuses. Online glasses retailer Warby Parker has opened 25 stores, too. The future may lead to more retailers that try to combine the best in online and physical stores to better serve customers.

Why Retailers Evolve and Change

The Internet and online shopping and the competitive threat it poses to traditional retailing has been a big motivator of evolution and change in retailing. In this section, we discuss some broader retailing trends and consider how in-store technology influences shopping.

The wheel of retailing keeps rolling

The **wheel of retailing theory** says that new types of retailers enter the market as low-status, low-margin, low-price operators and then, if successful, evolve into more conventional retailers offering more services with higher operating costs and higher prices. Then they're threatened by new low-status, low-margin, low-price retailers—and the wheel turns again. Department stores, supermarkets, and mass-merchandisers went through this cycle. Some Internet sellers are on this path.

The wheel of retailing theory doesn't explain all major retailing developments. Vending machines enter as high-cost, high-margin operations. Convenience food stores are high-priced. Suburban shopping centers don't emphasize low price.

Scrambled merchandising—mixing product lines for higher profits

Conventional retailers tend to specialize by product line. But many modern retailers are moving toward **scrambled merchandising**—carrying any product lines they think they can sell profitably. Supermarkets and drugstores sell anything they can move in volume—panty hose, phone cards, one-hour photo processing, motor oil, potted plants, and computer software. Mass-merchandisers don't just sell everyday items but also cell phones, computer printers, and jewelry.

Product life-cycle concept applies to retailer types too

A retailer with a new idea may have big profits—for a while. But if it's a really good idea, the retailer can count on speedy imitation and a squeeze on profits. Other retailers will copy the new format or scramble their product mix to sell products that offer them higher margins or faster turnover. That puts pressure on the original firm to change or lose its market.

Some conventional retailers are in decline as these life and death cycles continue. Recent innovators, like the Internet merchants, are still in the market growth stage (see Exhibit 7-6). Some retailing formats that are mature in the United States are only now beginning to grow in other countries.

Technology drives continued retail evolution

Beyond the Internet, retailers are turning to other types of technology to find a competitive advantage. For example, Kroger is a forerunner in the use of technology to enhance customers' in-store shopping experience. A few years ago, the average wait in a checkout line at its supermarkets was four minutes. Then Kroger installed special infrared cameras at each store entrance and above cash registers. A computer algorithm interprets the camera data and software automatically signals a manager when more than two customers are waiting in line. The store manager can then open additional checkout lanes—and the home office monitors service levels at every Kroger store. Average wait time fell to less than 30 seconds.

Brick-and-mortar retailers saw the advantage online retailers gained by analyzing data showing how customers shopped. Now in-store tracking provides information that guides store layout, merchandising, and sales promotion. Some stores utilize video cameras; others use sensors or track cell phones to monitor customer movement around stores. Jeweler Alex & Ani learned where customers lingered longer and which items were picked up most often—leading to changes in product placement. Retailers are only

Exhibit 7-6 Retailer Life Cycles—Timing and Years to Market Maturity

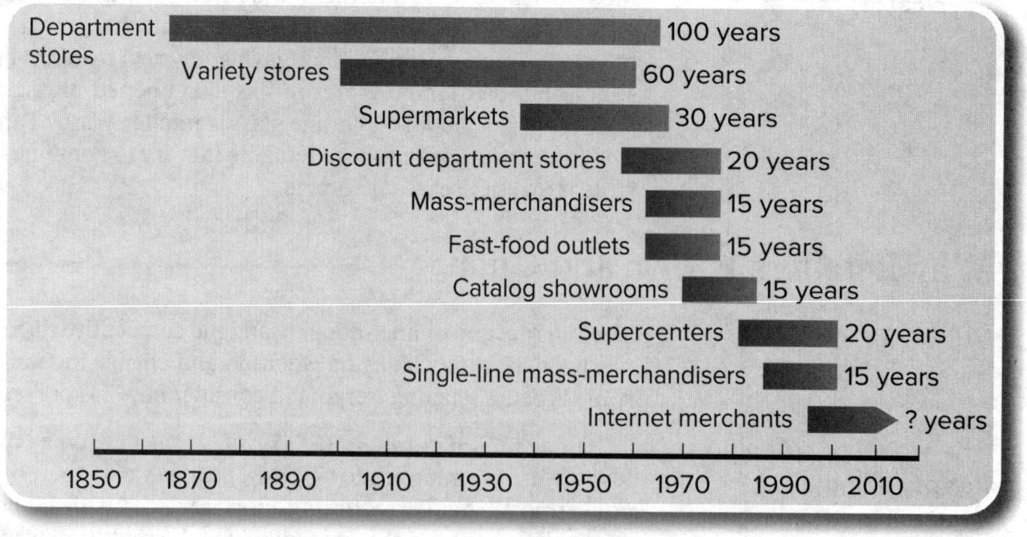

What's Next? Psychic retailers

Brick-and-mortar retailers are afraid of online retailers. Online retailers can track and monitor customers' movement and behavior across the web and integrate that data with social media and other purchase information. As online retailers figure out how to apply predictive analytics to these data, it could put brick-and-mortar retailers at a significant disadvantage. Online competition is inspiring some brick-and-mortar retailers to collect data of their own. And this might be *What's Next?* in retailing—a future where brick-and-mortar retailers use customers' smartphones, apps, and in-store technology to deliver customized marketing mixes for each customer.

The first step for brick-and-mortar retailers is to collect data to learn more about customer needs and shopping behaviors. This data collection begins with loyalty cards. Many retailers give customers who use loyalty cards discounts—enticing customers to sign up. Add to that a retailer's shopping app, which is used to track customer movement through the store. The app knows which aisles a customer visits and where they linger. Some retailers are experimenting with video data that will let them know what products customers pick up, how long they look at them—even whether they are smiling or frowning. Someday soon, you may find yourself stopping at the lawn mower display in Home Depot, smiling as you look at an electric mower. You don't buy, but the next day Home Depot's app sends you a message suggesting it's time to buy a new electric Greenworks lawn mower. If that doesn't work, a week later you'll be offered a 10 percent discount.

To learn even more about consumers, retailers can add data from other sources to create a "big data" file. They can purchase credit card data to add in a customer's purchase history from any store. A mapping app shares how many times a customer has visited the store's main competitor. And mining a customer's social media gives additional insights. When all those data are run through predictive analytics, retailers can decide what products to show each customer and what discounts will encourage a customer to buy.

For example, the store downloads the purchase history from your credit card company and information from social media. These are combined with in-store tracking and loyalty card data, creating a "big data" salad. From these data, a retailer might know you "Liked" an Instagram photo of a friend's new shirt. Previous history suggests your favorite colors are red and blue—and that 15 percent discounts are usually enough to motivate you to buy. The next time you visit the mall, a clothing store there could send you a text message with a photo of a blue and red sweater stating "15% off today only."

That is not all. Someday retailers may know what you want—before you even want it. Amazon has a patent for "anticipatory shipping" where it ships customers' orders *before* they click "buy." Perhaps someday soon, as you walk into your favorite Nordstrom store, a clerk will call you by name and bring you to a changing room where you'll find three outfits in your size and style. You love them and purchase them on the spot! Psychic retailing. Maybe that's *What's Next?*

Technologies that save customers money or time or create a more pleasant in-store shopping experience are changing the future of shopping. *Consider a McDonald's restaurant and a college bookstore—how could some of these ideas discussed be used to improve customer experiences at each of these locales? What other technologies could they employ?*

scratching the surface of possibilities with technologies like these; to get a peek into the future, check out *What's Next?* Psychic retailers.

Ethical issues for retailers

Let's look more closely at the ethical challenges that emerge from these new technologies and other retail practices. As you read in our discussion of online retailing and in the *What's Next?* box, retailers are gathering and using information to offer customers more personalized shopping experiences. This appears to be consistent with the marketing concept. But is it ethical to monitor customers' shopping behavior without their knowledge? Do retailers need customers' permission? Does it depend on how this information is used? And is it fair to offer discounts to some customers but not others? The marketing concept should guide firms away from unethical treatment of customers. However, a retailer on the edge of going out of business may lose perspective on the need to satisfy customers in both the short and the long term.

Ethical Dilemma

What would you do? Farmers in poor countries get very little money for crops—such as coffee, cocoa, and bananas—that they grow for export. Some consumers in prosperous nations are willing to pay retailers higher prices for "fair trade" goods so that the farmers receive greater compensation. But critics question whether fair trade works as it should. For example, Sainsbury's is a popular British food retailer. It was charging $2.74 per pound for "fair trade" bananas versus only $0.69 per pound for regular bananas. Farmers, however, got only $0.16 extra from that $2.05 price premium. Critics charge that Sainsbury's makes more from the "fair trade" promotion than the farmers it is supposed to help. Many retailers have similar programs.

Do you think that Sainsbury's is acting ethically? What do you think Sainsbury's and other similar retailers should do? Why?

Differences in Retailing in Different Nations

New ideas spread across countries

New retailing approaches that succeed in one part of the world are often quickly adapted to other countries. Self-service approaches that started with supermarkets in the United States are now found in retail operations worldwide. The supercenter concept, on the other hand, initially developed in Europe.

Mass-merchandising requires mass markets

The low prices, selections, and efficient operations offered by mass-merchandisers might be attractive to consumers everywhere, but consumers in less-developed nations often don't have the income to support mass distribution. The small shops that survive in these economies sell in very small quantities, often to a small number of consumers.

Retailers moving to international markets must adapt marketing strategies

Slow growth at home has prompted some large retail chains to move into international markets. They think that the competitive advantages that worked well in one market can provide a similar advantage in another country. But legal and cultural differences in international markets can make success difficult. Despite success in Latin America and Canada, Walmart has struggled in Germany and Japan. Similarly, French mass-merchandiser Carrefour expanded in Europe and South America, but its U.S. stores failed and it experienced legal problems in Indonesia.

Other retailers, such as California-based My Dollarstore, have successfully adapted for quick international growth. My Dollarstore franchises the "dollar store" concept worldwide and adapts its marketing strategy to local markets. In India, the price of each product is 99 rupees or about two dollars. Dollar stores in the United States target lower-income consumers, but in India the "Made in America" label attracts many higher-income consumers. Initially the merchandise in the Indian stores was the same as in U.S. stores. However, My Dollarstore quickly discovered what sold (Hershey's syrup is a hit) and what didn't (papaya and carrot juice). It also offered money-back guarantees, an unusual practice in India. Adaptations like these helped entice[5] consumers into My Dollarstore's Indian franchises.

Online retailing varies across nations

Online shopping behavior, and therefore online retailing, varies considerably across countries. For example, in the United Kingdom about half of all consumers regularly purchase online, whereas in emerging markets online sales are almost nonexistent. The most obvious prerequisite for online retailing is access to the Internet—in particular, broadband (fast) connections. Chapter 2 discussed technology and the uneven adoption of the Internet and mobile phones across the globe. A reliable national postal system (lacking in many countries) is also needed for delivering online purchases.

Even when infrastructure is in place, cultural factors influence preferences for online shopping. For example, a European study of 20,000 clothing shoppers identified seven segments based on their shopping needs. One segment, nicknamed "time-pressed optimizers," was particularly interested in online shopping. With very busy lives, this group had less time for in-store shopping so they sought the best possible product by doing research online. Yet only 3 percent of Italian shoppers and 6 percent of French shoppers fell into this segment—as compared to 16 percent of Brits and 18 percent of Germans. Another segment, "price-oriented bargain hunters," enjoyed going to many stores and rummaging to find bargain merchandise. This group was most common in Italy (31 percent of shoppers), and helps explain why only about 10 percent of Italians regularly purchased online.

What Is a Wholesaler?

It's hard to define what a wholesaler is because there are so many different wholesalers doing different jobs. Some of their activities may even seem like manufacturing. As a result, some wholesalers describe themselves as "manufacturer and dealer." Some like to identify themselves with such general terms as *merchant, agent, dealer,* or *distributor.* And others just take the name commonly used in their trade—without really thinking about what it means.

To avoid a long technical discussion on the nature of wholesaling, we'll use the U.S. Census Bureau definition: **Wholesaling** is concerned with the *activities* of those persons or establishments that sell to retailers and other merchants, or to industrial, institutional, and commercial users, but that do not sell in large amounts to final consumers. So **wholesalers** are firms whose main function is providing wholesaling activities. Wholesalers sell to all of the different types of organizational customers described in Chapter 5.

Wholesaling activities are just variations of the basic marketing functions—gathering and providing information, buying and selling, grading, storing, transporting, financing, and risk taking—we discussed in Chapter 1. You can understand wholesalers' strategies better if you look at them as members of channels. They add value by doing jobs for their customers and for their suppliers.

Wholesaling Is Changing with the Times

A hundred years ago wholesalers dominated distribution channels in the United States and most other countries. The many small producers and small retailers needed their services. This situation still exists in less-developed economies.

Wholesaling is in decline

However, in developed nations, as producers became larger many bypassed[6] the wholesalers. Cost-conscious buyers at some large retail chains, including Walmart and Lowe's, even refuse to deal with some wholesalers who represent small producers. Efficient delivery services from UPS and FedEx make it easier for many producers to ship directly to their customers, even those in foreign markets. The Internet also puts pressure on wholesalers whose primary role is providing information to bring buyers and sellers together. These factors have combined to decrease the number of wholesalers in the United States; there are about 400,000 wholesalers today—following a steady decline over the last 20 years.

Opportunities remain for progressive wholesalers

Those that have survived are adapting their marketing strategies and finding new ways to add value in the channel. Progressive wholesalers are becoming more concerned with their customers and with channel systems. Many of the same strategies used by retailers are also being utilized by wholesalers; for example, some wholesalers are using omnichannel because their customers are multichannel shoppers. Some of the biggest B2B e-commerce sites are wholesaler operations, and many wholesalers are enjoying significant growth. Others develop voluntary chains that bind them more closely to their customers.

Frieda's innovates in wholesale produce

Frieda's Inc. is a good example; it is a wholesaler that supplies supermarkets and food service distributors with $30 million worth of exotic fruits and vegetables every year. It was started by Frieda Caplan in 1962; today her daughters Karen and Jackie run the company. It is a sign of the marketing savvy[7] of these women that artichokes, Chinese donut peaches, alfalfa sprouts, and spaghetti squash no longer seem very exotic. All of these crops were once viewed as unusual. Few farmers grew them, supermarkets didn't handle them, and consumers didn't know about them. Caplan helped change all of that. She realized that some supermarkets wanted to attract less price-sensitive consumers who preferred more interesting choices in the produce department. So she looked for products that would help her retailer-customers meet this need. For example, the funny-looking kiwi fruit with its fuzzy brown skin was popular in New Zealand but virtually unknown to U.S. consumers. Caplan worked with small farmer-producers to ensure that she could provide her retailer-customers with a steady supply. She packaged kiwi with interesting recipes and promoted it to consumers. Because of her efforts, demand has grown, and most supermarkets now carry kiwi. That has attracted competition from larger wholesalers. But that doesn't bother the Caplans. When one of their specialty items becomes a commodity with low profit margins, another novel item replaces it. In a typical year, Frieda's introduces about 40 new products–some of the latest include Kiwano Melons and Stokes Purple Sweet Potatoes.

Frieda's also has an advantage because of the special services it provides. It was the first wholesaler to routinely use airfreight for orders and send produce managers a weekly "hot sheet" about its best sellers. Today the Caplans use online videos and a blog to let customers know what's new. Frieda's website attracts final consumers with helpful tips and recipes. And now that more consumers are eating out, Frieda's has established a separate division to serve the special needs of food service distributors.

Wholesalers need to add value

Progressive wholesalers need to be efficient, but that doesn't mean they all have low costs. Some wholesalers' higher operating expenses result from the strategies they select, including the special services they offer to some customers. Let's look more closely at different types of wholesalers and the different ways they add value to channels of distribution.

Wholesalers Add Value in Different Ways

Exhibit 7-7 compares the number, sales volume, and costs of some major types of wholesalers. The differences in operating costs suggest that each of these types performs, or does not perform, certain wholesaling functions. But which ones and why? And why do manufacturers use merchant wholesalers–costing 13.1 percent of sales–when agent wholesalers cost only 3.7 percent?

Exhibit 7-7 U.S. Wholesale Trade by Type of Wholesale Operation

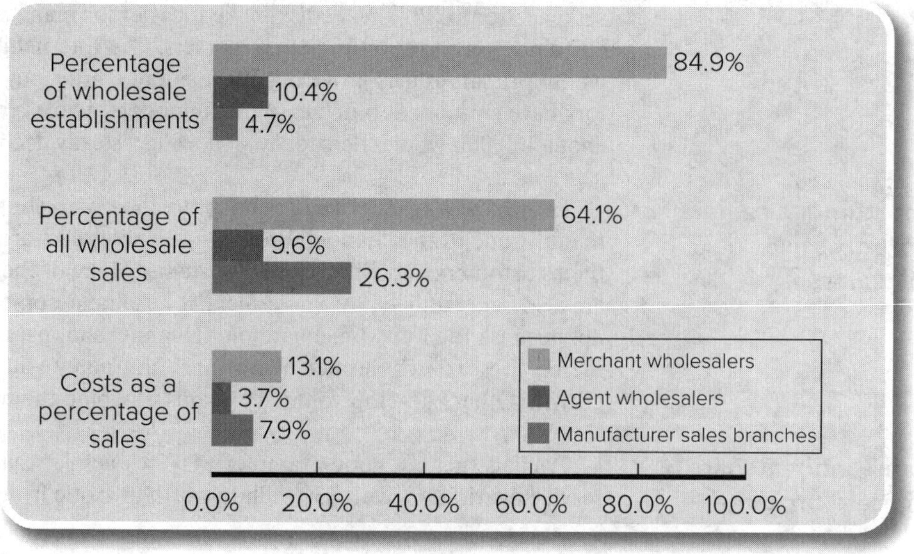

To answer these questions, we must understand what these wholesalers do and don't do. Exhibit 7–8 gives a big-picture view of the major types of wholesalers we'll be discussing. There are lots more specialized types, but our discussion will give you a sense of the diversity. Note that a major difference between merchant and agent wholesalers is whether they *own* the products they sell. Before discussing these wholesalers, we'll briefly consider producers who handle their own wholesaling activities.

Manufacturers' sales branches are considered wholesalers

Manufacturers who just take over some wholesaling activities are not considered wholesalers. However, when they have **manufacturers' sales branches**—warehouses that producers set up at separate locations away from their factories—they're classified as wholesalers by the U.S. Census Bureau and by government agencies in many other countries.

In the United States, these manufacturer-owned branch operations account for about 4.7 percent of wholesale facilities—but they handle 26.3 percent of total wholesale sales. One reason sales per branch are so high is that the branches are usually placed in the best market areas. This also helps explain why their operating costs, as a percentage of sales, are often lower. It's also easier for a manufacturer to coordinate information and logistics functions with its own branch operations than with independent wholesalers.

Merchant Wholesalers Are the Most Numerous

Merchant wholesalers own (take title to) the products they sell. They often specialize by certain types of products or customers. For example, Fastenal is a wholesaler that specializes in distributing threaded fasteners used by a variety of manufacturers. It owns (takes title to) the fasteners for some period before selling to its customers. If you think all merchant wholesalers are fading away, Fastenal is proof that they can serve a needed role. In the last decade Fastenal's profits have grown at about the same pace as Microsoft's.

Exhibit 7–7 shows that almost 85 percent of the wholesaling establishments in the United States are merchant wholesalers—and they handle more than 64 percent of wholesale sales. Merchant wholesalers are even more common in other countries. Japan is an extreme example. Products are often bought and sold by a series of merchant wholesalers on their way to the business user or retailer.

Exhibit 7–8 Types of Wholesalers

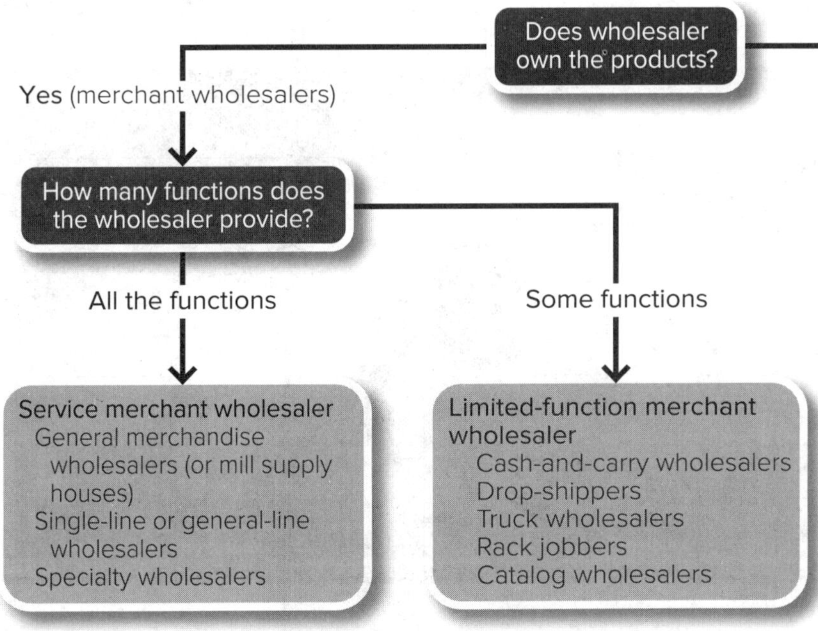

Service wholesalers provide all the functions

Service wholesalers are merchant wholesalers that provide all the wholesaling functions. Within this basic group are three types: (1) general merchandise, (2) single-line, and (3) specialty.

General merchandise wholesalers are service wholesalers that carry a wide variety of nonperishable items such as hardware, electrical supplies, furniture, drugs, cosmetics, and automobile equipment. With their broad line of convenience and shopping products, they serve hardware stores, drugstores, and small department stores. *Mill supply houses* operate in a similar way, but they carry a broad variety of accessories and supplies to serve the needs of manufacturers.

Single-line (or general-line) wholesalers are service wholesalers that carry a narrower line of merchandise than general merchandise wholesalers. For example, they might carry only food, apparel, or certain types of industrial tools or supplies. In consumer products, they serve the single- and limited-line stores. In business products, they cover a wider geographic area and offer more specialized service.

Specialty wholesalers are service wholesalers that carry a very narrow range of products and offer more information and service than other service wholesalers. For example, a firm that produces specialized lights for vehicles might rely on specialty wholesalers to help reach automakers in different countries. A consumer products specialty wholesaler might carry only health foods instead of a full line of groceries. Some limited-line and specialty wholesalers are growing by helping independent retailer-customers compete with mass-merchandisers. But in general, many consumer-products wholesalers have been hit hard by the growth of retail chains that set up their own distribution centers and deal directly with producers.

A specialty wholesaler of business products might limit itself to fields requiring special technical knowledge or service. Richardson Electronics is an interesting example. One of its specialties is in distributing replacement parts, such as electron tubes, for old equipment that many manufacturers still use on the factory floor. Richardson describes itself as "on the trailing edge of technology," but many of its customers operate in countries where new technologies are not yet common. Richardson gives them easy access to information from its website (www.rell.com) and makes its products available quickly by stocking them in locations around the world.

Henry Schein is the largest distributor of health care products and services to office-based practitioners in North America. It also serves many international countries. It operates as a full-service wholesaler for medical, dental, and veterinary professionals.
Source: Henry Schein, Inc.

Limited-function wholesalers provide some functions

Limited-function wholesalers provide only *some* wholesaling functions. In the following paragraphs, we briefly discuss the main features of these wholesalers. Although less numerous in some countries, these wholesalers are very important for some products.

Cash-and-carry wholesalers want cash

Cash-and-carry wholesalers operate like service wholesalers—except that the customer must pay cash. In the United States, big warehouse clubs have taken much of this business. But cash-and-carry operators are common in less-developed nations where very small retailers handle the bulk of retail transactions. Full-service wholesalers often refuse to grant credit to small businesses that may have trouble paying their bills.

Drop-shippers do not handle the products

Drop-shippers own (take title to) the products they sell—but they do *not* actually handle, stock, or deliver them. These wholesalers are mainly involved in selling. They get orders and pass them on to producers. Then the producer ships the order directly to the customer. Drop-shippers commonly sell bulky products (like lumber) for which additional handling would be expensive and possibly damaging. Drop-shippers in the United States are already feeling the squeeze from buyers and sellers connecting directly via the Internet. But the progressive ones are fighting back by setting up their own websites and getting fees for referrals.

Truck wholesalers deliver—at a cost

Truck wholesalers specialize in delivering products that they stock in their own trucks. Their big advantage is that they promptly deliver perishable products that regular wholesalers prefer not to carry. A 7-Eleven store that runs out of potato chips on a busy Friday night doesn't want to be out of stock all weekend! They help retailers keep a tight rein on inventory, and they seem to meet a need.

Rack jobbers sell hard-to-handle assortments

Rack jobbers specialize in hard-to-handle assortments of products that a retailer doesn't want to manage—and rack jobbers usually display the products on their own wire racks. For example, a grocery store or mass-merchandiser might rely on a rack jobber to decide which paperback books or magazines it sells. The wholesaler knows which titles sell in the local area and applies that knowledge in many stores.

Catalog wholesalers reach outlying areas

Catalog wholesalers sell through catalogs that may be distributed widely to smaller industrial customers or to retailers that might not be called on by other wholesalers. Customers place orders at a website or by mail, e-mail, fax, or telephone. These wholesalers sell lines such as hardware, jewelry, sporting goods, and computers. For example, Inmac uses a catalog that is printed in six languages and a website (www.inmac.com) to sell a complete line of computer accessories. Many of its customers don't have a local wholesaler, but they can place orders from anywhere in the world. Most catalog wholesalers quickly adapted to the Internet. It fits what they were already doing and makes it easier. But they're facing more competition too; the Internet allows customers to compare prices from more sources of supply.

Agents Are Strong on Selling

They don't own the products

Agent wholesalers are wholesalers that do *not* own the products they sell. Their main purpose is to help in buying and selling. Agent wholesalers normally specialize by customer type and by product or product line. But they usually provide even fewer functions than the limited-function wholesalers. They operate at relatively low cost—sometimes 2 to 6 percent of their selling price—or less in the case of website-based agents who simply bring together buyers and sellers.

They are important in international trade

Agents are common in international trade. Many markets have only a few well-financed merchant wholesalers. The best many producers can do is get local representation through agents and then arrange financing through banks that specialize in international trade.

Agent wholesalers are usually experts on local business customs and regulations in their own countries. Sometimes a marketing manager can't work through a foreign government's red tape without the help of a local agent.

Manufacturers' agents provide selling expertise

A **manufacturers' agent** sells similar products for several noncompeting producers—for a commission on what is actually sold. Such agents work almost as members of each company's sales force, but they're really independent wholesalers. More than half of all agent wholesalers are manufacturers' agents. Their big plus is that they already call on some customers and can add another product line at relatively low cost—and at no cost to the producer until something sells! If an area's sales potential is low, a company may use a manufacturers' agent because the agent can do the job at low cost. Small producers often use agents everywhere because their sales volume is too small to justify their own sales force.

Agents can be especially useful for introducing new products. For this service, they may earn 10 to 15 percent commission. (In contrast, their commission on large-volume established products may be quite low—perhaps only 2 percent.) A 10 to 15 percent commission rate may seem small for a new product with low sales. Once a product sells well, however, a producer may think the rate is high and begin using its own sales reps.

Export and import agents are experts in international trade

Export agents and **import agents** are basically manufacturers' agents who specialize in international trade. These agent wholesalers operate in every country and help international firms adjust to unfamiliar market conditions in foreign countries.

Manufacturers' agents will continue to play an important role in businesses that need an agent to perform order-getting tasks. But manufacturers' agents everywhere are feeling pressure when it comes to routine business contacts. More producers are turning to telephone selling, websites, e-mail, teleconferencing, and faxes to contact customers directly.

Brokers offer market information and knowledge

Brokers bring buyers and sellers together. Brokers usually have a *temporary* relationship with the buyer and seller while a particular deal is negotiated. They are especially useful when buyers and sellers don't come into the market very often. The broker's product is information about what buyers need and what supplies are available. If the transaction is completed, they earn a commission from whichever party hired them. **Export brokers** and **import brokers** operate like other brokers, but they specialize in bringing together buyers and sellers from different countries. Smart brokers quickly saw new opportunities to expand their reach by using the Internet. As the Internet causes consolidation, it will also provide more value. A smaller number of cyberbrokers will cut costs and dominate the business with larger databases of buyers and sellers.

Selling agents—almost marketing managers

Selling agents take over the whole marketing job of producers—not just the selling function. A selling agent may handle the entire output of one or more producers, even competing producers, with almost complete control of pricing, selling, and advertising. In effect, the agent becomes each producer's marketing manager.

Financial trouble is one of the main reasons a producer calls in a selling agent. The selling agent may provide working capital and may also take over the affairs of the business. But selling agents also work internationally. A **combination export manager** is a blend of manufacturers' agent and selling agent—handling the entire export function for several producers of similar but noncompeting lines.

Auction companies speed up the sale

Auction companies provide a place where buyers and sellers can come together and bid to complete a transaction. Traditionally they were important in certain lines—such as livestock, fur, tobacco, and used cars—where demand and supply conditions change rapidly.

CONCLUSION

In this chapter, we explored evolving approaches to retailing and wholesaling. We also examined how marketers are finding an efficient and effective balance of technology and the personal touch that works for their target markets.

There are many different types of retailers, each offering different marketing mixes to appeal to different target customers. Lower margins and faster turnover are the modern philosophy for mass-merchandisers, but this is no guarantee of success as retailers' life cycles mature. Online retailing is growing quickly, and many brick-and-mortar retailers are taking advantage of the Internet to create more appealing marketing mixes.

Retailing tends to evolve in predictable patterns—and we discussed the wheel of retailing theory to help understand this. But the growth of chains and scrambled merchandising continues as retailing evolves to meet changing consumer demands.

Wholesalers can provide functions for those both above and below them in a channel of distribution. These services are closely related to the basic marketing functions. There are many types of wholesalers. Some provide all the wholesaling functions—whereas others specialize in only a few. Eliminating wholesalers does not eliminate the need for the functions they now provide, but technology is helping firms to perform these functions in more efficient ways.

One thing is certain, the evolving Internet and yet-to-emerge technologies won't allow marketers to rest on their laurels. Successes will be short-lived as retail and wholesale competitors keep looking for new ways to satisfy customer needs. The most agile retailers and wholesalers are the most likely to survive.

JOYFUL MOMENT

Early Big Shopping

An offender was brought to trial before a judge. The judge asked him, "What is the crime you have committed?"

The offender said, "I went shopping too early during the New Year."

The judge said, "This is not a crime! Is there a mistake, perhaps? So how early did you go shopping?"

He answered, "The shop was not yet open for business, and I was already inside."

WORDS AND EXPRESSIONS

1. **franchise**: *n./v.* (to give) an authorization to sell a company's goods or services in a particular place 特权，经销权；给…以特许（或特权）
   —She has recently franchised her business.
   她最近已出售了其公司的特许经营权。
2. **identical**: *adj.* exactly alike; incapable of being perceived as different 同一的；完全相同的
   —He is identical in character with his wife.
   他的品性和他的夫人相同。
3. **obsolescence**: *n.* the process of becoming obsolete; falling into disuse or becoming out of date [生物] 退化，荒废
   —The aircraft was nearing obsolescence by early 1942.
   这种飞机在 1942 年年初就濒临淘汰了。
4. **dedicate**: *vt.* to give entirely to a specific person, activity, or cause 致力，献身
   —She vowed to herself that she would dedicate her life to scientific studies.
   她默默地发誓要献身于科学研究。
5. **entice**: *vt.* to provoke someone to do something through (often false or exaggerated) promises or persuasion 诱使；怂恿
   —On the one hand, low rates entice investors out of cash and into riskier assets.
   一方面，低利率引诱投资者拿出现金投资风险较大的资产。
6. **bypass**: *vt.* to avoid something unpleasant or laborious 绕开；忽视
   —A growing number of employers are trying to bypass the unions altogether.
   越来越多的雇主试图完全置工会于不顾。
7. **savvy**: *n.* the cognitive condition of someone who understands 悟性；理解能力
   —He is known for his political savvy and strong management skills.
   他以其政治洞察力和高超的管理手段著称。

EXERCISES

1. **Multiple choices**

   (1) ____ decisions include choices about what products to carry, how much assortment to offer, and which services to support.
   A. Place　　B. Promotion　　C. Product　　D. Price

(2) ___ are larger stores that are organized into many separate departments and offer many product lines.

A. Department stores B. Specialty shops C. Mass-merchandisers D. Limited-line stores

(3) These ___ offered "hard goods" (cameras, TVs, and appliances) at substantial price cuts to customers.

A. mass-merchandisers B. discount houses C. supercenters D. retailers

(4) The ___ theory says that new types of retailers enter the market as low-status, low-margin, low-price operators and then, if successful, evolve into more conventional retailers offering more services with higher operating costs and higher prices.

A. wheel of retailing B. marketing mix C. market failure D. segmented market

(5) ___ wholesalers operate like service wholesalers—except that the customer must pay cash.

A. Service B. Limited-function C. Cash-and-carry D. Single-line

2. Terms translation

(1) single-line store (2) mass-merchandising concept (3) discount house (4) mass-merchandiser

(5) wheel of retailing theory (6) franchise operation (7) specialty wholesaler (8) drop-shipper

(9) manufacturers' agent (10) brokers

3. True or false

(1) Retailing is crucial to consumers in every macromarketing system. ______

(2) Product decisions include where stores will be located—online and/or brick-and-mortar. ______

(3) Now most conventional retailers are single-line or limited-line stores. ______

(4) The large number of retailers might suggest that retailing is a field of small businesses. ______

(5) Voluntary chains are retailer-sponsored groups that work with "independent" retailers. ______

(6) New retailing approaches that succeed in one part of the world cannot be adapted to other countries. ______

(7) Progressive wholesalers need to be efficient, so that means that they all have low costs. ______

(8) Manufacturers who just take over some wholesaling activities are not considered wholesalers. ______

(9) Merchant wholesalers don't own the products they sell. ______

(10) Limited-function wholesalers provide only some wholesaling functions. ______

4. Fill in the blanks

(1) __________ are the stores that specialize in certain lines of related products rather than a wide assortment.

(2) A __________ is a type of conventional limited-line store, and is usually small and has a distinct "personality."

(3) __________ is selling and delivering products through vending machines.

(4) In-home shopping in the United States started in the pioneer days with __________ selling—a salesperson going directly to the consumer's home.

(5) In a __________, the franchisor develops a good marketing strategy, and the retail franchise holders carry out the strategy in their own units.

(6) __________ is concerned with the activities of those persons or establishments that sell to retailers and other merchants, or to industrial, institutional, and commercial users, but that do not sell in large amounts to final consumers.

(7) __________ are merchant wholesalers that provide all the wholesaling functions.

(8) __________ own (take title to) the products they sell—but they do not actually handle, stock, or deliver them.

(9) __________ bring buyers and sellers together. They usually have a temporary relationship with the buyer and seller while a particular deal is negotiated.

(10) A combination export manager is a blend of manufacturers' agent and __________—handling the entire export function for several producers of similar but noncompeting lines.

5. Answer the following questions

(1) What sort of a "product" are specialty shops offering?

What are the prospects for organizing a chain of specialty shops?

(2) According to your own experience, what are some advantages and disadvantages to using the Internet for shopping?

(3) What advantages does a retail chain have over a retailer who operates with a single store?

(4) Explain "The manufacturers' agents are the free-wheeling sales reps."

(5) Why would a manufacturer set up its own sales branches if established wholesalers were already available?

SUGGESTED CASES

11. Running On
12. DrV.com—Custom Vitamins
14. Schrock and Oh Design
15. The Scioto Group
16. Hanratty Company

MARKETING ANALYTICS: DATA TO KNOWLEDGE

connect

CHAPTER 7: SELECTING CHANNEL INTERMEDIARIES

Art Glass Productions, a producer of decorative glass gift items, wants to expand into a new territory. Managers at Art Glass know that unit sales in the new territory will be affected by consumer response to the products. But sales will also be affected by which combination of wholesalers and retailers Art Glass selects. There is a choice between two wholesalers. One wholesaler, Giftware Distributing, is a merchant wholesaler that specializes in gift items; it sells to gift shops, department stores, and some mass-merchandisers. The other wholesaler, Margaret Degan & Associates, is a manufacturers' agent who calls on many of the gift shops in the territory.

Art Glass makes a variety of glass items, but the cost of making an item is usually about the same—$5.20 a unit. The items would sell to Giftware Distributing at $12.00 each—and in turn the merchant wholesaler's price to retailers would be $14.00—leaving Giftware with a $2.00 markup to cover costs and profit. Giftware Distributing is the only reputable merchant wholesaler in the territory, and it has agreed to carry the line only if Art Glass is willing to advertise in a trade magazine aimed at retail buyers for gift items. These ads will cost $8,000 a year.

As a manufacturers' agent, Margaret Degan would cover all of her own expenses and would earn 8 percent of the $14.00 price per unit charged the gift shops. Individual orders would be shipped directly to the retail gift shops by Art Glass, using United Parcel Service (UPS). Art Glass would pay the UPS charges at an average cost of $2.00 per item. In contrast, Giftware Distributing would anticipate demand and place larger orders in advance. This would reduce the shipping costs, which Art Glass would pay, to about $0.60 a unit.

Art Glass' marketing manager thinks that Degan would be able to sell only about 75 percent as many items as Giftware Distributing—because she doesn't have time to call on all of the smaller shops and doesn't call on any department stores. On the other hand, the merchant wholesaler's demand for $8,000 worth of supporting advertising requires a significant outlay.

The marketing manager at Art Glass decided to use a spreadsheet to determine how large sales would have to be to make it more profitable to work with Giftware and to see how the different channel arrangements would contribute to profits at different sales levels.

See Connect for the spreadsheet and questions needed to analyze this scenario.

CHAPTER EIGHT

Promotion—Introduction to Integrated Marketing Communications

Back in the 1930s, during the depths of the Great Depression, Leo and Lillian Goodwin started the Government Employees Insurance Company—GEICO. GEICO kept operating costs low by selling auto insurance only to two low-risk target markets: federal employees and military personnel. GEICO passed on the savings in the form of lower premiums—and sales steadily grew for decades.

After becoming a wholly owned subsidiary[1] of Berkshire Hathaway in 1996, GEICO's management sought to accelerate earnings growth by targeting new markets. However, getting growth in the mature auto insurance market meant that GEICO would need to take customers away from better-known competitors such as Allstate and State Farm. As if that wasn't difficult enough, many prospects didn't even know about GEICO. Ted Ward, GEICO's vice president of marketing, discussed this situation with the firm's ad agency, the Martin Agency of Richmond, Virginia. Together they decided that an aggressive advertising campaign could achieve the objectives of increasing awareness of GEICO and bringing in new customers.

The GEICO campaign that emerged used an animated[2], talking lizard to help get attention and communicate the firm's message. In the first commercial, the charming reptile[3] with the British accent stated, "I am a gecko, not to be confused with GEICO, which could save you hundreds on car insurance. So stop calling me!" The humorous ads quickly achieved GEICO's objectives: generating awareness and interest among target customers. The original plan was for the Gecko campaign to run for a short time, but research showed that customers loved the Gecko, and the company saw a bump in its sales. The Gecko continues to be an important part of GEICO's image and promotions.

GEICO wants customers to know it offers good value—great car insurance at low prices. But to prove this, customers must reach out for a price quote. It's quick and easy to get a quote at GEICO's website, so to spur the target audience to action, GEICO ads remind them that "15 minutes could save you 15 percent or more on car insurance." GEICO likes to have a variety of ads—and has had all kinds of animals and inanimate objects talking in its ads; pigs, camels, bumper stickers, and dinner plates star in its humorous television spots. GEICO also posts many of its ads on YouTube—where ads play immediately before videos. Because YouTube lets customers skip the ads after watching for five seconds, GEICO makes sure its ads get the point across before customers skip over them. All that advertising works. GEICO was recently ranked number one in the United States in advertising awareness across all brands.

Although GEICO aims to reach its target market with advertising, it knows that many customers interested in insurance start the information gathering process on their own. GEICO knows when people type "auto insurance" into Google, they are probably looking to buy car insurance. GEICO uses various techniques to make sure GEICO.com appears near the top of the organic search results. Just in case customers don't see that, it also pays for a sponsored link (advertisement) ensuring that GEICO will join other ads at the top of the search results. GEICO pays around $30 each time a customer clicks on one of these ads, so keeping customers interested is important; the page customers land on after clicking one of these ads asks for their ZIP code, the first step toward getting a price quote from GEICO. Interested customers can also visit GEICO's website to learn more about the company and its portfolio of insurance products.

All this promotion helped make GEICO a familiar name, but many insurance buyers still want to talk to a real person before deciding what to do. These customers can visit with a GEICO salesperson at one of its local offices or at an event. They might prefer to call GEICO's national call center and talk with an inside sales rep. GEICO selects capable salespeople who are licensed insurance agents, and then trains them to develop an understanding of each customer's needs and concerns so that the agents can then explain GEICO's benefits to the customer in a persuasive way.

Of course, GEICO seeks to build an ongoing relationship with customers after they sign up for a policy. Regular contacts and updates are handled with promotional e-mails. Customers can call a GEICO salesperson to learn more about other GEICO products, such as less familiar umbrella insurance policies. Later, if a customer who purchases a policy has a problem, GEICO's highly rated customer service team quickly works to resolve it. Customers can also turn to their GEICO Mobile App for roadside assistance or to talk to its artificial intelligence-powered virtual assistant "Kate." Kate answers questions about policy coverage, billing information, and more.

GEICO's website also fosters that relationship with current customers. The website is a type of "owned media"—GEICO owns and manages it—unlike television and radio *advertising* that GEICO pays to access. Many current customers use GEICO.com to manage and update their policy or make an insurance claim. They can also learn more about GEICO's other insurance products, various discounts, local gas prices, and more. The site also links to GEICO's social media pages.

GEICO's social media, including a blog, Facebook pages, a YouTube channel (www.youtube.com/GEICO), and a Twitter feed, also build relationships with its current customers and connect with potential new customers. Its most popular social media tool is its Facebook page, which more than 400,000 people have "Liked"—though some customers (more than 250,000 of them) prefer the Gecko's personal Facebook page. The Facebook pages let customers see the latest television ads and photos of the Gecko. Customers can also "Like" or "share" an ad or other post with their own Facebook friends. Potential customers are more likely to consider GEICO when they have seen a friend "Like" the brand.

GEICO's promotion brings together advertising, personal selling, and online media; in combination, they help GEICO acquire and retain customers. That recipe—along with a great product—has moved GEICO from less than a 3 percent share of the auto insurance market in 1996 to more almost 12 percent share and the industry's number two position today.

LEARNING OBJECTIVES

As the GEICO example shows, there are many decisions that a marketing manager must make concerning Promotion, and it is an important part of marketing strategy planning. Marketing managers usually blend a variety of different promotion methods to achieve promotion objectives because each method has its own strengths and limitations. In this chapter we introduce the major promotion options and how to integrate them into an effective whole.

When you finish this chapter, you should be able to

1. know the advantages and disadvantages of the promotion methods a marketing manager can use in strategy planning.
2. understand the integrated marketing communications concept and why firms use a blend of different promotion methods.
3. understand the importance of promotion objectives.
4. know how the traditional communication process affects promotion planning.
5. understand how customer-initiated interactive communication affects promotion planning.
6. know how typical promotion plans are blended to get an extra push from wholesalers and retailers, as well as help from customers in pulling products through the channel.
7. understand how promotion blends typically vary over the adoption curve and product life cycle.
8. understand how to determine how much to spend on promotion efforts.
9. understand important new terms (shown in boldface).

Promotion Communicates to Target Markets

Promotion is communicating information between the seller and potential buyer or others in the channel to influence attitudes and behavior. The promotion part of the marketing mix involves telling target customers that the right Product is available at the right Place at the right Price. Just as Promotion must be fine-tuned for a specific target market, it must fit with the other variables of the marketing mix and reinforce the strategy's differentiation and positioning.

This is the first of four chapters that discuss issues pertinent to Promotion. We begin with an overview of the major promotion methods. Marketing managers can choose from several basic types of promotion: personal selling, mass selling, sales promotion, and publicity (see Exhibit 8-1). Because these methods have different strengths and limitations, a marketing

Exhibit 8-1 Promotion and Marketing Strategy Planning

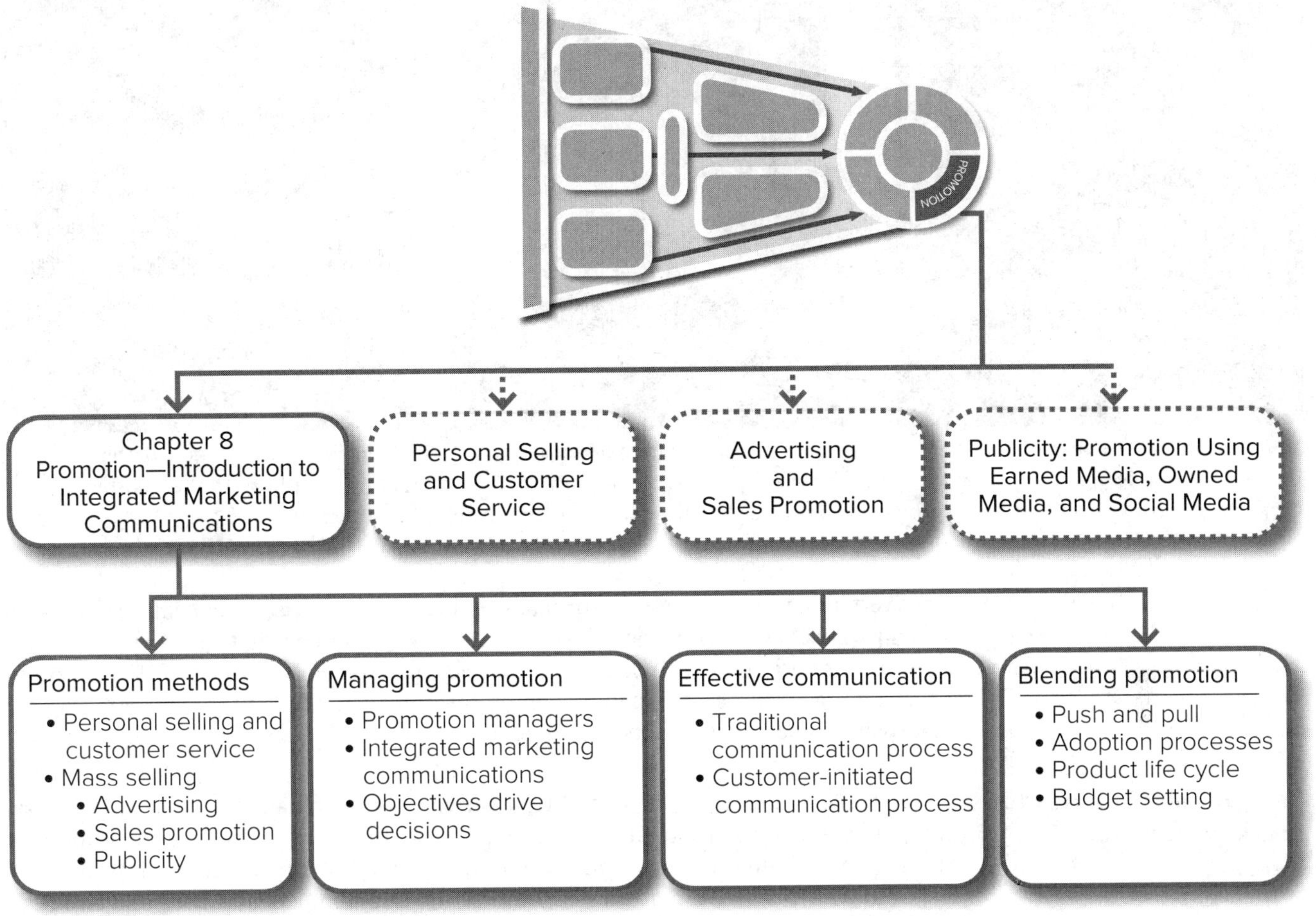

manager typically uses them in combination to achieve specific objectives. We also discuss the specialists who are involved in managing different types of promotion and why it is important for them to work together as a team. This chapter also provides models that will help you understand how communication works–including when companies broadcast information to target markets and when target customers seek information on their own. Finally, we look at some concepts that help marketing managers develop the best promotion blend.

In this chapter we'll go into some detail about the different promotion methods–a key challenge for marketing managers is how best to blend them. So it's helpful to begin with a brief overview of the promotion methods available.

Several Promotion Methods Are Available

Personal selling—flexibility is its strength

Personal selling involves direct spoken communication between sellers and potential customers. Customer service is a form of personal communication between a customer and seller to resolve a problem with a purchase. Salespeople get immediate feedback, which helps them adapt. Although some personal selling is included in most marketing mixes, it can be very expensive. So it's often desirable to combine personal selling with advertising, sales promotion, and/or publicity.

Mass selling involves advertising and publicity

Mass selling is communicating with large numbers of potential customers at the same time. It's less flexible than personal selling, but when the target market is large and scattered, mass selling can be less expensive.

Everyone loves free snacks, so it's not surprising that many customers engaged with McDonald's outdoor ad. Customers use their cell phone to snap a picture of a particular snack (on this day a sundae), then they bring the photo to the nearby McDonald's for their reward. Sales promotion activities like this stimulate consumer interest and trial.
Source: McDonald's

Advertising is a primary form of mass selling. **Advertising** is any *paid* form of nonpersonal presentation of ideas, goods, or services by an identified sponsor. It includes the use of traditional media such as magazines, newspapers, radio and TV, signs, and direct mail as well as new media such as the Internet. Marketing managers pay for advertising to be placed on specific media.

Sales promotion tries to spark immediate interest

Sales promotion refers to promotion activities—other than advertising, publicity, and personal selling—that stimulate interest, trial, or purchase by final customers or others in the channel. Sales promotion may be aimed at consumers, at intermediaries, or at a firm's own employees. Examples include contests and coupons aimed at consumers, trade shows or calendars for wholesalers or retailers, or sales contests and meetings aimed at a company's own sales force. Relative to other promotion methods, sales promotion can usually be implemented quickly and get results sooner. In fact, most sales promotion efforts are designed to produce immediate results.

Publicity avoids media costs

Publicity is any *unpaid* form of nonpersonal presentation of ideas, goods, or services. Of course, publicity people are paid. But they try to attract attention to the firm and its offerings *without having to pay media costs.* Publicity includes a wide range of different types of media: a company's website and the material it posts on the website, viral videos, word-of-mouth communication, a company's Facebook page, and its "tweets" on Twitter. It can also include coverage it receives in the press—for example, when a movie is reviewed in the newspaper.

Less is spent on advertising than personal selling or sales promotion

Many people incorrectly believe that promotion money gets spent primarily on advertising—because advertising is all around them. But all the special sales promotions—coupons, sweepstakes, trade shows, and the like—add up to even more money. Similarly, much personal selling goes on in the channels and in other business markets. In total, firms spend less money on advertising than on personal selling or sales promotion.

Someone Must Plan, Integrate, and Manage the Promotion Blend

Each promotion method has its own strengths and weaknesses. In combination, they complement one another. Each method also involves its own distinct activities and requires different types of expertise. As a result, it's usually the responsibility of specialists—such as sales managers, advertising managers, sales promotion managers, public relations managers, and social media managers—to develop and implement the detailed plans for the various parts of the overall promotion blend.

Sales managers manage salespeople

Sales managers are concerned with managing personal selling. Often the sales manager is responsible for building good distribution channels and implementing Place policies. In smaller companies, the sales manager may also act as the marketing manager and be responsible for advertising and sales promotion.

Advertising managers work with ads and agencies

Advertising managers manage their company's mass-selling effort—in television, newspapers, magazines, and other media. Their job is choosing the right media and developing the ads. Advertising may be handled in-house, by departments existing within the firms, or it may be contracted to outside advertising agencies.

Sales promotion managers need many talents

Sales promotion managers manage their company's sales promotion effort. In some companies, a sales promotion manager has independent status and reports directly to the marketing manager. If a firm's sales promotion spending is substantial, it probably *should* have a specific sales promotion manager. Sometimes, however, the sales or advertising departments handle sales promotion efforts—or sales promotion is left as a responsibility of individual brand managers. Regardless of who the manager is, sales promotion activities vary so much that many firms use both inside and outside specialists.

Publicity may be managed by many

An advertising manager may handle publicity, but in larger firms there may be someone who manages **public relations**—communication with noncustomers, including the press, labor, public interest groups, stockholders, and the government. A *social media manager* may be in charge of a company's social media (Facebook page, Twitter feed, LinkedIn page, etc.) and possibly its website. Any of these jobs may be outsourced—though a firm that manages public relations probably differs from one that manages social media or a firm's website.

Marketing manager talks to all, blends all

Although many specialists may be involved in planning for and implementing specific promotion methods, determining the blend of promotion methods is a strategy decision—and it is the responsibility of the *marketing manager.* With all of the promotion options, determining the best blend is a challenging responsibility.

The marketing manager must weigh the pros and cons of the various promotion methods and then devise an effective promotion blend—fitting in the various departments and personalities and coordinating their efforts. Then the advertising, sales, and sales promotion managers should develop the details consistent with what the marketing manager wants to accomplish.

Send a consistent and complete message with integrated marketing communications

Effective blending of all of the firm's promotion efforts should produce **integrated marketing communications**—the intentional coordination of every communication from a firm to a target customer to convey a consistent and complete message.

The GEICO case at the start of this chapter is a good example of integrated marketing communications. Different promotion methods handle different parts of the job. Yet the methods are coordinated so that the sum is greater than the parts. The separate messages are complementary, but also consistent.

It seems obvious that a firm's different communications to a target market should be consistent. However, when a number of different people are working on different promotion elements, they are likely to see the same big picture only if a marketing manager ensures that it happens. Getting consistency is harder when different firms handle different aspects of the promotion effort. For example, different firms in the channel may have conflicting objectives.

To get effective coordination, everyone involved with the promotion effort must clearly understand the plan for the overall marketing strategy. They all need to understand how each promotion method will contribute to achieve specific promotion objectives.

Which Methods to Use Depends on Promotion Objectives

Overall objective is to affect behavior

A marketing manager usually has to set priorities for the promotion objectives. The ultimate objective is to encourage customers to choose a *specific* product. However, which promotion objectives are of highest priority will depend on the market situation and target market. For example, as we saw in Chapters 4 and 5, customers often move along a step-by-step buying path—and the path may differ for different types of purchases. Sometimes customers are familiar with the product and sometimes it is completely new to them. Sometimes customers are buying a product for the very first time and sometimes they have bought it many times before. Objectives should be guided by what we know about target customers. In this section, we discuss different types of promotion objectives and tie them to frameworks describing the purchase process.

Informing, persuading, and reminding are basic promotion objectives

Promotion objectives must be clearly defined—because the right promotion blend depends on what the firm wants to accomplish. It's helpful to think of three basic promotion objectives: *informing, persuading,* and *reminding* target customers about the company and its marketing mix. All try to affect buyer behavior by providing customers with information.

It's also useful to set more specific promotion objectives that state *exactly whom* you want to inform, persuade, or remind, and *why.* This is unique to each company's strategy—and specific objectives vary by promotion method. Here we'll focus on the three basic promotion objectives and then link them to the adoption process and a new model.

Informing is educating

Potential customers must know something about a product if they are to buy it. A firm with a really new product may not have to do anything but inform consumers of the product's features and benefits. An *informing* objective can show that it meets consumer needs better than other products can. Imagine a customer moving to a new town with an interest in joining a health club where he can work out. A health club might place brochures in local apartment complexes or run ads in the newspaper to let target customers know about the features at its facility. A small business might want to have a service regularly clean its offices. The owner might begin by searching on the Internet. There she might find a local cleaning company's website with information about various services.

Persuading usually becomes necessary

When competitors offer similar products, the firm must not only inform customers that its product is available but also persuade them to buy it. A *persuading* objective means the firm will try to develop a favorable set of attitudes so customers will buy, and keep buying, its product. A persuading objective often tries to demonstrate how one brand is better than others. To convince consumers to buy Brawny paper towels, ads show Brawny as the towel that's best for tough cleanup jobs. A salesperson for Andersen Windows tries to convince homebuilders about the quality and affordability of

The Boston Celtics Instagram page *reminds* fans of their favorite team.
Source: NBA Media Ventures, LLC

Andersen Windows as compared to those of a competitor, so the builder chooses Andersen for future housing projects.

Reminding may be enough

If target customers already have positive attitudes about a firm's marketing mix—or a good relationship with a firm—a *reminding* objective might be suitable. Customers who have been attracted and sold once are still targets for competitors' appeals. Reminding them of their past satisfaction may keep them from shifting to a competitor. An accountant working for a small local firm might phone her customers once every few months to "check in" and see if they have any questions. This serves as a reminder that the accountant is there and available.

Promotion objectives relate to adoption processes

In Chapter 4, we looked at consumer buying as a step-by-step problem-solving process through which buyers go on the way to adopting (or rejecting) an idea or product. The three basic promotion objectives relate to these steps. See the first two columns in Exhibit 8-2. *Informing* and *persuading* may be needed to affect the potential customer's knowledge and attitudes about a product and then bring about its adoption. Later, promotion can simply *remind* the customer about that favorable experience and confirm the adoption decision.

The AIDA model is a practical approach

The basic promotion objectives and adoption process fit very neatly with another action-oriented model—called AIDA—that we will use in this chapter to guide some of our discussion. The **AIDA model** consists of four promotion jobs: (1) to get *Attention,* (2) to hold *Interest,* (3) to arouse *Desire,* and (4) to obtain *Action.*

The first and third columns in Exhibit 8-2 show the relationship of the promotion objectives and adoption process to the AIDA jobs. Getting attention is necessary to make consumers aware of the company's offering. Holding interest gives the communication a chance to build the consumer's interest in the product. Arousing desire affects

Exhibit 8-2 Relation of Promotion Objectives, Adoption Process, AIDA Model, and Organizational Buying Model

Promotion Objectives	Adoption Process	AIDA Model	Organizational Buying Model
Informing	Awareness Interest	Attention Interest	Defining the problem
Persuading	Evaluation Trial	Desire	Making the decision
Reminding	Decision Confirmation	Action	Managing the buyer-seller relationship

What's Next? Once upon a time . . .

Does telling a story get customers' attention and interest? Research finds that people remember stories more than statistics. Another study discovered that the most popular Super Bowl ads follow a classic story pattern: exposition, rising action, climax, falling action, dénouement (resolution). Budweiser's "Lost Dog" Super Bowl ad follows this arc. The ad begins on a ranch, showing the connection between a puppy and one of the Budweiser Clydesdale horses (exposition). When the puppy gets lost in the city, the rancher posts "lost dog" posters (rising action). The puppy journeys toward home but with the ranch in the distance, we see a wolf stalking the pup (more rising action). Back at the ranch, the Clydesdales hear the pup, so they escape the barn, coming to the puppy's rescue (climax). The Clydesdales and puppy run home together (falling action) and the muddy puppy gets a bath (dénouement). That one-minute story won the *USA Today Super Bowl Admeter*—a survey of viewers—and generated lots of attention for Budweiser.

Lifebuoy soap used story to focus people on an important problem. Each year diarrhea and pneumonia claim the lives of two million children before they reach age five. Research shows that regular handwashing with soap significantly cuts the risk of diarrhea and infection. Lifebuoy soap wanted to get this message to people in third-world countries, so it created its "Help a Child Reach 5" campaign. As a demonstration, Lifebuoy adopted Thesgora, a village in rural India, and showed how handwashing lowered diarrhea incidence from 36 percent to 5 percent. Lifebuoy created a three-minute video story (see https://youtu.be/UF7oU_YSbBQ) showing a father walking on his hands through town to a religious shrine to offer thanks. We then see that this is his son's fifth birthday—a milestone his previous children never reached. This is also the Lifebuoy story—the essence of the brand—that handwashing can save lives.

Other stories get customers' interest because they explain how a company solves problems. This approach is behind many B2B firms' use of case studies that describe how they solved a specific customer's problems. Networking hardware giant Cisco Systems' "Never Better" campaign creates digital stories that combine video, photography, and text to tell powerful stories that provide emotional resonance. The documentary style demonstrates how Cisco's technology helps save rhinos (https://goo.gl/cDGNIz), make cities smarter (https://goo.gl/Vadxsp), and more.

What's Next? A full-length movie feature? No, wait, LEGO has already done that—twice! Maybe we can expect a mystery novel from construction machinery company Caterpillar. Probably not soon—but you should see its Jenga ad (Google it). Stories that resonate with target markets grab attention and interest; many are passed on to friends and family. But it isn't easy coming up with a good story. Do you remember the 2013 flop *Movie 43*? Almost no one does. And marketing stories that fail to resonate will not help a brand either.

Describe a story your college or university could tell that might resonate with prospective students. How could that story be turned into a short television ad or YouTube video?

the evaluation process, perhaps building preference. And obtaining action includes gaining trial, which may lead to a purchase decision. Continuing promotion is needed to confirm the decision and encourage an ongoing relationship and additional purchases.

British marketers for Pampers disposable diapers generated attention and interest with TV ads that showed the world from a baby's perspective. To encourage desire and action, they used creative in-store and point-of-purchase advertising. For example, on the doors of restrooms with baby-changing facilities, fake door knobs were placed unreachably high, with the message: "Babies have to stretch for things. That's why they like the extra stretchiness of Pampers Active fit." And on store shelves, in a play on babies' disobedient[4] nature, pull-out Pampers information cards were marked "Do Not Pull."

Promotion objectives and B2B

In Chapter 5 we showed how organizational buyers go through a similar step-by-step process on the way to purchase. The three steps in our organizational buying model also correspond to the three basic promotion objectives; see Exhibit 8-2.

These two images were part of an advertisement in the social media app Snapchat. They demonstrate elements of the AIDA model. The image on the left showed a camel chewing his cud. It was funny and grabbed attention. When the viewer clicked "READ" at the bottom of this screen, the image on the right appeared. The headline, photo, and details below hold interest and arouse desire for a trip to Dubai—hopefully on an Emirates flight.
Source: Emirates; smartphone frame: ©Oleg GawriloFF/ Shutterstock RF

Stories grab attention and hold interest

While there is growing interest in data and analytics among marketing managers, they have not forgotten the power of a good story in getting customers' attention, holding their interest, and arousing desire. Many managers believe that *What's Next?* is actually a return to good storytelling—see *What's Next?* Once upon a time...

Promotion Requires Effective Communication

Communication starts with a trusted source and a receiver

Promotion is wasted when it doesn't communicate effectively. There are many reasons why a promotion message can be misunderstood or not heard at all. To understand this, it's useful to think about a whole **communication process**—which means a source trying to reach a receiver with a message. Exhibit 8-3 shows the elements of the communica-

Exhibit 8-3 The Traditional Communication Process

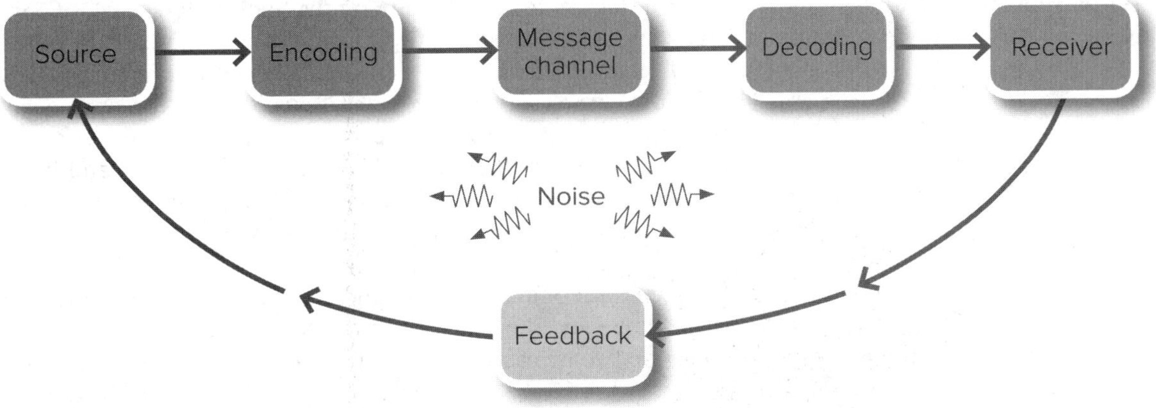

tion process. Here we see that a **source**—the sender of a message—is trying to deliver a message to a **receiver**—a potential customer.

Customers evaluate the source of the message in terms of trustworthiness and credibility. For example, American Dental Association (ADA) studies show that Listerine mouthwash helps reduce plaque buildup on teeth. Listerine mentions the ADA endorsement in its promotion to help make the promotion message credible. If a salesperson (source) is not trusted, then the message being delivered will not be used by the receiver.

A major advantage of personal selling is that the source—the seller—can get immediate feedback from the receiver. It's easier to judge how the message is being received and to change it if necessary. Mass sellers usually must depend on marketing research or total sales figures for feedback—and that can take too long. Many marketers include toll-free telephone numbers and website addresses as ways of building direct-response feedback from consumers into their mass-selling efforts.

Noise distracts the message

The **noise**—shown in Exhibit 8-3—is any distraction that reduces the effectiveness of the communication process. Conversations and snack-getting during TV ads are noise. An industrial buyer reading a text message during a salesperson's presentation is noise. Advertisers who plan messages must recognize that many possible distractions—noise—can interfere with communications.

Encoding[5] and decoding[6] depend on a common frame of reference

The basic difficulty in the communication process occurs during encoding and decoding. **Encoding** is the source deciding what it wants to say and translating it into words or symbols that will have the same meaning to the receiver. **Decoding** is the receiver translating the message. This process can be very tricky. The meanings of various words and symbols may differ depending on the attitudes and experiences of the two groups. People need a common frame of reference to communicate effectively (see Exhibit 8-4).

Exhibit 8-4 This Same Message May Be Interpreted Differently

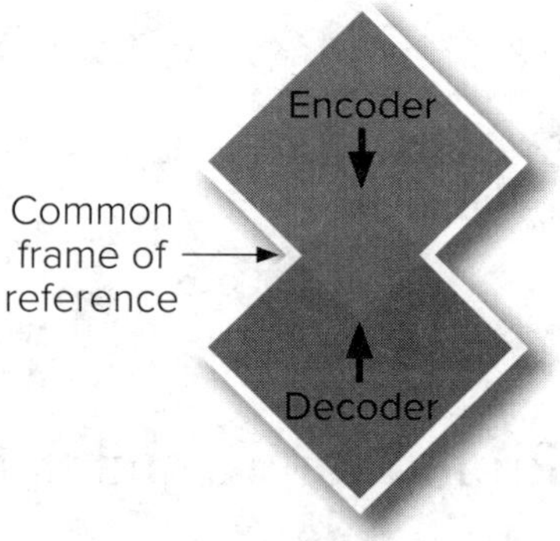

Pepsi encountered this problem with a recent advertisement featuring fashion model Kendall Jenner. In the ad, Jenner is involved in a photo shoot but becomes distracted by a passing group of protesters. She joins the protest and later brings a smile to the face of a stoic police officer by giving him a can of Pepsi. While Pepsi was "trying to project a global message of unity, peace, and understanding," it ended up missing the mark in the eyes of many viewers—and was roundly criticized in the media. Many thought that it downplayed and commercialized protests on important social issues. The message Pepsi encoded was not the one decoded by many in its target market.

The same message may be interpreted differently

Different audiences can interpret a message differently. Such differences are common in international marketing where cultural differences and translation are problems. KFC's "finger-lickin' good" chicken turned into "eat your fingers off" when first translated to Chinese. The Swedish brand Samarin thought it would avoid these problems with ads showing three simple drawings—and no words. The first picture shows a man holding his stomach in obvious pain, in the second he is drinking Samarin, and in the last he is smiling and happy. Worked great—except in the Middle East where people read from right to left. Uh oh! Many firms run into problems like this.

Message channel is important too

The communication process is complicated even more because the message is coming from a source through some **message channel**—the carrier of the message. A source can use many message channels to deliver a message. The salesperson does it in person with voice and action. Advertising must do it with media such as magazines, TV, e-mail, or Internet websites. A particular message channel may enhance or detract from a message. A TV ad, for example, can *show* that Dawn dishwashing detergent "takes the grease away"; the same claim might not be convincing if it arrived in a consumer's e-mail.

Feedback takes many forms

The last element in the traditional communication process is *feedback*—communication from the receiver back to the source. Feedback may take many different forms: a customer may simply have a different attitude, seek more information, visit a store, or purchase the product. For this reason, objectives should state the desired feedback and marketing managers should measure whether the communication is having the anticipated response.

Integrated direct response seeks immediate feedback

Sometimes marketing managers want to get immediate feedback from *specific* customers. This prompts firms to turn to direct marketing—direct communication between a seller and an individual customer using a promotion method other than face-to-face personal selling. Most direct marketing communications are designed to prompt immediate feedback—a direct response—by customers. That's why this type of communication is often called *direct-response promotion.*

Direct mail and e-mail are two tools commonly used for direct-response promotion. A carefully selected mailing list—perhaps from the firm's customer relationship management (CRM) database—allows advertisers to reach customers with specific interests. For the best response, marketing managers carefully segment their customers and use mail or e-mail to deliver targeted messages.

E-mail can be low cost and targeted

Most customers use e-mail these days, and communicating via e-mail offers benefits to buyers and sellers. Sellers like the relatively low cost compared to direct mail. E-mails give customers a chance to click through to photos and videos. Media tools such as these help them decide whether to make a donation or place an order.

Of course getting to the message in the e-mail necessitates a customer opening the e-mail. Personalized and creative messages can get customers' attention in a crowded e-mail inbox. To get opened, an e-mail subject line should grab target customers' attention. For example, when a customer buys eyeglasses at Warby Parker, the retailer asks when the prescription expires. Two weeks before it expires, you get an e-mail with the subject line: "Uh-oh your prescription is expiring." This catches the reader's attention—the subject line is true—and increases the odds of the e-mail being opened.

When Customers Initiate the Communication Process

The traditional process in Exhibit 8-3 assumes that it's the seller ("source") who initiates communication. Let's look closer at another communication model, shown in Exhibit 8-5, where a customer ("receiver") initiates the communication process. For example, a consumer enters "pizza delivery" into Google or asks a retail salesperson for help, and organizational buyers phone salespeople to ask questions or request bids. The growth of the Internet makes it more common for buyers to start the information gathering process. Although this "customer-initiated" process has many of the same components as the traditional process we considered earlier, the differences and implications for Promotion are significant.

Customer initiates communication with a search process

In the process in Exhibit 8-5, a customer (*receiver*) initiates communication with a decision to *search* for information in a particular message channel. The most common and far-reaching *message channel* used for information searching is the Internet—usually queried through a search engine such as Google or Bing and accessed by a personal computer, tablet, or cell phone. Sometimes a buyer immediately links to a particular seller's web page to

Exhibit 8-5 A Model of Customer-Initiated Interactive Communication

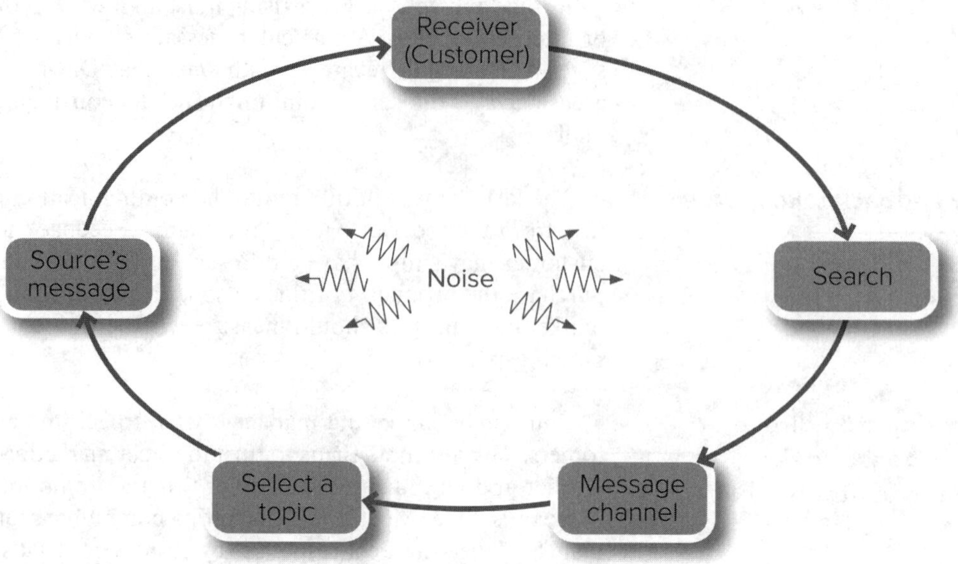

seek out information. The message channel is still the carrier of the message, as was the case before, but searchable message channels usually feature an archive[7] of existing messages on a number of topics. There may be many available topics—even millions.

Customer decides how much information to get

The receiver then reviews and screens the various options and decides which messages to pursue. A search engine returns a list of results that includes paid advertisements and free listings. A search can also occur at the website of a producer, retailer, or wholesaler. For example, a business customer may visit a distributor of janitorial supplies and search for industrial cleaning solutions—and then click on pricing information or perhaps the safety of the ingredients. Similarly, a consumer might visit Netflix and search for horror movies and then look for the director, actors, or the comments of people who have already seen the movie. The customer chooses the information of interest to her—not the marketing manager.

Marketers must grab attention to be selected

Because a customer now has so many options, it's important for a marketer to be among the first to grab that customer's attention. That means that an online retailer that sells golf gear wants to be near the top of the search results when someone searches for "Big Bertha golf," Callaway's popular line of golf clubs. In this case, the retailer can pay a search engine company to put a sponsored (advertising) link near the top of the list or make changes to its website so it appears near the top of search results.

When the receiver looks more closely at the information on screen, he decides whether to stay or leave the site. Usually more information is just a click away—and that click can be to dig deeper into the marketer's site or to click away to another website. Marketing managers need to make sure that the page holds the receiver's interest or begins to arouse desire. Noise can still be a problem as well—and lead the searcher in a different direction. For example, a confusing website may make it difficult to figure out a retailer's return policy and discourage a customer from buying.

As this short scenario depicts, consumers can collect information from a wide range of sources before making purchase decisions. Although many of those are outside the control of a marketing manager, that doesn't mean those sources should be ignored. Marketing managers can still make sure that they have plenty of product pictures—and that they are easy to post on Pinterest and Instagram. They can also monitor what is being said about the brand online. Whereas online compliments let the firm know what it is doing well, complaints can highlight unmet customer needs—and give managers a chance to turn things around.

Promotion timing and relevance have an impact

Communication that customers receive during the customer-initiated communication process is usually timely—it often occurs when a customer is actively gathering purchase information. Consequently, customers more readily pay attention and are more likely to be interested in promotional information.

When customers surf the Internet, they often signal they are ready to make a purchase. For example, reading articles about different kinds of bicycles, visiting a couple of websites, and "Liking" the local bike shop on Facebook might all be indications of an impending bicycle purchase. There are companies that monitor and track consumers as they surf the web. Customers often leave telltale signs that they might be interested in buying certain products. Marketing managers can identify target customers interested in buying their products and deliver timely and relevant online (and offline) advertising to these customers.

Prepare for customers who initiate communication

When customers have the power to decide where to click next, marketing managers need to create a different kind of promotion. The first challenge is for marketing managers to figure out how to appear high on target customers' searches. Second, the marketing managers must have truly useful information—or customers will quickly click to something that will help them make a better purchase decision. And finally, promotion needs to keep them there to learn more about the seller's offering.

An example will demonstrate what we mean by capturing and retaining the inbound customer. The travel agency Discover Africa creates content that attracts customers to its website and keeps them coming back. Discover Africa started by identifying nine different target markets that it thought it could serve (for example, "Mr. Business," "The Campers," and "The Student/Backpacker"). Then Discover Africa created articles, blog posts, videos, and travel guides for its website—each designed to appeal to one or more target groups. With a little outbound promotion of the discoverafrica.com website and its content, others started noticing and linking to the site. This helped Discover Africa appear near the top of online searches related to travel in Africa. Discover Africa was soon viewed as an authority on African travel, and sales began to climb.

Ethical issues in marketing communications

Promotion is one of the most frequently criticized areas of marketing. Many criticisms focus on whether communications are honest and fair. Marketers must sometimes make ethical judgments in considering these charges and in planning their promotion.

For example, we often look to the source of a communication to decide whether we believe it is credible. When a TV news program broadcasts a video publicity release, consumers don't know it was prepared to achieve marketing objectives. They think the news staff is the source. That may make the message more credible, but is it fair? Many say yes—as long as the publicity information is truthful. Similar concerns are raised about the use of celebrities in advertisements. A person who plays the role of an honest and trustworthy person on a popular TV series may be a credible message source in an ad, but is using such a person misleading to consumers? Some critics believe it is. Others argue that consumers recognize advertising when they see it and know celebrities are paid for their endorsements.

The most common criticisms of promotion relate to exaggerated claims. If an advertisement or a salesperson claims that a product is the "best available," is that just a personal opinion or should every statement be backed up by proof? What type of proof should be required? Some promotions do misrepresent the benefits of a product. Customers look to online reviews for objective opinions. What about posting fake favorable reviews for your company or its products—or negative reviews about a competitor? Real reviews offer a way for consumers to see beyond potential exaggerated claims. But if consumers feel that at least some reviews are phony, they may distrust all reviews. Some people believe that the Internet will eventually expose dishonest players in the market. This question is not always easy to answer; see the following Ethical Dilemma.

Ethical Dilemma

What would you do? A friend of your family owns an upscale Italian restaurant called Giupetto's. Because you are a student of marketing, he asks for your help. Business has suddenly fallen off, except for the "regulars"—they don't see as many new customers as before. His cook has heard that the owner of a competing restaurant has been pressuring his employees to post negative reviews of Giupetto's food, service, and prices. When you check the website, there are a number of unfavorable, anonymous reviews. You also notice that there are about 30 very upbeat reviews of the competing restaurant. Your friend wants you to help give the competitor "what he deserves" and write some negative reviews about that restaurant.

Would you do what he asks? Why or why not? What else could you do?

There are also issues related to consumer privacy. Most consumers are unaware that their web-surfing habits are being tracked. Many websites place "cookies" (electronic files) on a customer's computer so that when the customer revisits their site, the system "remembers" the customer. Although this sort of tracking offers them the potential benefit of more personalized communications, some consumers might want to remain anonymous.

Most marketing managers realize that the ultimate proof comes when the customer makes the purchase. Customers won't spread positive word-of-mouth or come back if the marketing mix doesn't deliver what the promotion promises. As a result, most marketing managers work to make promotion claims specific and believable.

How Typical Promotion Plans Are Blended and Integrated

There is no one right blend

There is no one *right* promotion blend for all situations. Each one must be developed as part of a marketing mix and should be designed to achieve the firm's promotion objectives in each marketing strategy. So let's take a closer look at typical promotion blends in different situations.

Get a push in the channel with promotion to intermediaries

When a channel of distribution involves intermediaries, their cooperation can be crucial to the success of the overall marketing strategy. **Pushing** (a product through a channel) means using normal promotion effort—personal selling, advertising, and sales promotion—to help sell the whole marketing mix to possible channel members. This approach emphasizes the importance of securing the wholehearted cooperation of channel members to promote the product in the channel and to the final user.

Producers usually take on much of the responsibility for the pushing effort in the channel. However, wholesalers often handle at least some of the promotion to retailers. Similarly, retailers often handle promotion in their local markets. The overall effort is most likely to be effective when all of the individual messages are carefully integrated.

Promotion to intermediaries emphasizes personal selling and sales promotion

Salespeople handle most of the important communication with wholesalers and retailers. These clients don't want empty promises. They want to know what they can expect in return for their cooperation and help. A salesperson can answer questions about what promotion will be directed toward the final consumer, each channel member's part in marketing the product, and important details on pricing, markups, promotion assistance, and allowances. A salesperson can also help the firm determine when it should adjust its marketing mix from one intermediary to another.

When suppliers offer similar products and compete for attention and shelf space, intermediaries usually pay attention to the one with the best profit potential. So sales promotions targeted at intermediaries usually focus on short-term arrangements that will improve the intermediary's profits. For example, a soft drink bottler might offer a convenience store a free case of drinks with every two cases it buys. The free case improves the store's profit margin on the whole purchase.

Green Mountain Coffee uses both push and pull to support its coffees. Green Mountain's website and membership program promote a "Deal of the Week" directly to consumers. The ad on the right targets purchasing agents at grocery stores, letting them know that Green Mountain's family of brands will bring volume and profits to their stores.
Source: Keurig Green Mountain, Inc.

Firms run ads in trade magazines to recruit new intermediaries or to inform channel members about a new offering. Trade ads usually encourage intermediaries to contact the supplier for more information, and then a salesperson takes over.

Push within a firm—with promotion to employees

Some firms emphasize promotion to their own employees—especially salespeople or others in contact with customers. This type of *internal marketing* effort is basically a variation on the pushing approach. One objective of an annual sales meeting is to inform reps about important elements of the marketing strategy—so they'll work together as a team to implement it. Some firms use promotion to motivate employees to provide better customer service or achieve higher sales. This is typical in services where the quality of the employees' efforts is a big part of the product. For example, at one time, advertising for McDonald's used the theme "We love to see you smile." The ads communicate to customers but also remind employees that the service they provide is crucial to customer satisfaction.

Pulling policy—customer demand pulls the product through the channel

Most producers focus a significant amount of promotion on customers at the end of the channel. This helps stimulate demand and pull the product through the channel of distribution. **Pulling** means getting customers to ask intermediaries for the product.

Pulling and pushing are usually used in combination (see Exhibit 8-6). However, if intermediaries won't work with a producer—perhaps because they're already carrying a competing brand—a producer may try to use a pulling approach by itself. This involves highly aggressive promotion to final consumers or users—perhaps using coupons or samples—temporarily bypassing intermediaries. If the promotion works, the intermediaries are forced to carry the product to satisfy customer requests. However, this approach is risky. Customers may lose interest before reluctant intermediaries make the product available. At a minimum, intermediaries should be told about the planned pulling effort—so they can be ready if the promotion succeeds.

Who handles promotion to final customers at the end of the channel varies in different channel systems, depending on the mix of pushing and pulling. Further, the promo-

Exhibit 8-6 Promotion May Encourage Pushing in the Channel, Pulling by Customers, or Both

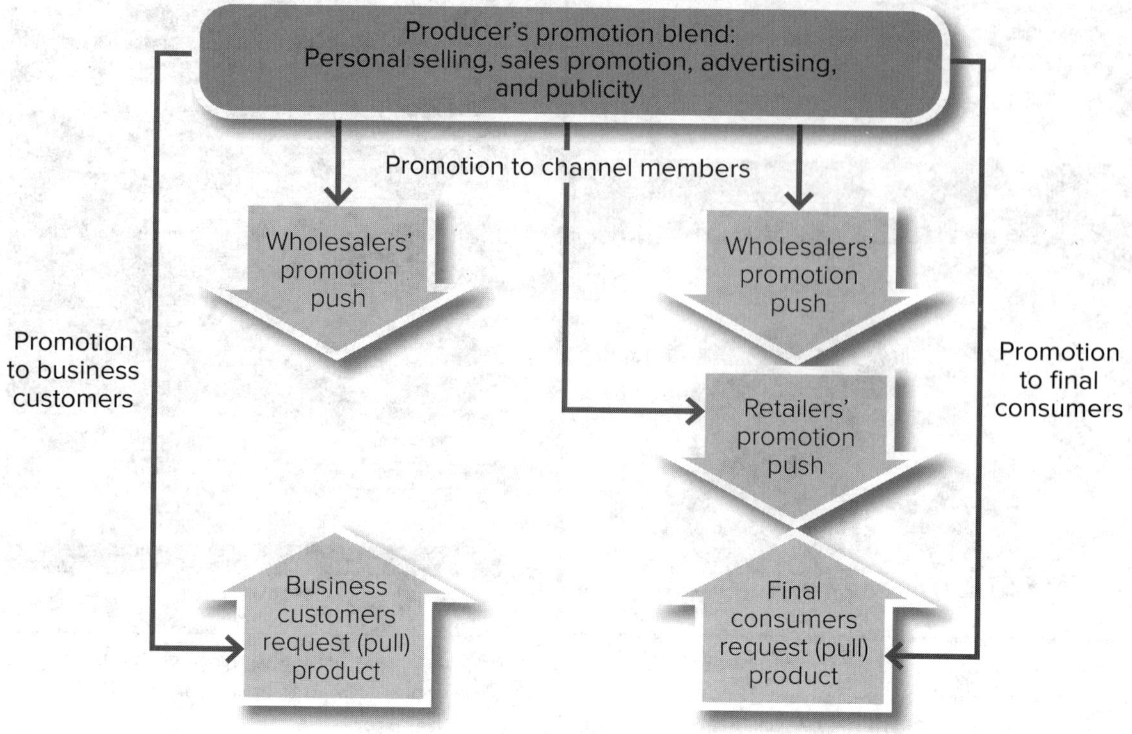

tion blend typically varies depending on whether customers are final consumers or business users.

Promotion to final consumers

The large number of consumers almost forces producers of consumer products and retailers to emphasize advertising, publicity, and sales promotion. Sales promotion—such as coupons, contests, or free samples—builds consumer interest and short-term sales of a product. An informative website that includes customer reviews and video demonstrations helps customers build favorable impressions of a company and its products. Effective mass selling may build enough brand familiarity so that little personal selling is needed, as in self-service and discount operations.

Personal selling can be effective too. Aggressive personal selling to final consumers usually is found in channel systems for expensive products, such as those for financial services, furniture, fine jewelry, consumer electronics, designer clothing, and automobiles.

Promotion to business customers

Producers and wholesalers that target business customers often emphasize personal selling. This is practical because there are fewer of these customers and their purchases are typically larger. Sales reps can be more flexible in adjusting their companies' appeals to suit each customer—and personal contact is usually required to close a sale. A salesperson is also able to call back later to follow up, resolve any problems, and nurture the relationship with the customer.

Although personal selling dominates in business markets, mass selling is necessary too. A typical sales call on a business customer costs about $500. That's because salespeople spend less than half their time actually selling. The rest is consumed by such tasks as traveling, paperwork, sales meetings, and strictly service calls. So it's seldom practical for salespeople to carry the whole promotion load.

Business buyers often engage in Internet search to identify solutions for current needs. So it's important for a seller's website to appear near the top of the search results. Otherwise, it has no opportunity to draw buyers' attention and build interest for the firm's products. Ads in trade magazines or at a B2B e-commerce website, for instance, can inform potential customers that a product is available. Most trade ads give a toll-free telephone number and an e-mail or website address to stimulate direct inquiries. Domestic and international trade shows also help identify prospects.

Combine promotion methods to move B2B buyers through the purchase process

Although mass selling does not consume a large portion of the promotion budget, if used effectively, it can make personal selling more effective. Mass selling can be a first step in an integrated marketing communications program; a website, advertisement, or e-mail targets potential customers. Those customers who express interest in the mass selling become "leads" that a salesperson tries to convert to customers.

Each market segment may need a unique blend

Knowing what type of promotion is typically emphasized with different targets is useful in planning the promotion blend. But each unique market segment may need a separate marketing mix and a different promotion blend. You should be careful not to slip into a shotgun approach (using a single promotion across market segments) when what you really need is a rifle approach (a specific mix for a particular target market). This can result from too much combining.

Marketing managers blend push and pull activities because of the specific needs of those target markets. Another way to segment a market depends on where customers are in the adoption process, and we discuss these needs next.

Adoption Processes Can Guide Promotion Planning

The AIDA and adoption processes (for review, see Exhibit 8-2) look at individuals. This emphasis on individuals helps us understand how promotion affects the way that people behave. But it's also useful to look at markets as a whole. Different segments of customers within a market may behave differently—with some taking the lead in trying new products and, in turn, influencing others.

Promotion must vary for different adopter groups

Research on how markets accept new ideas has led to the adoption curve model. The **adoption curve** shows when different groups accept ideas. It emphasizes the relations among groups and shows that individuals in some groups act as leaders in accepting a new idea. Promotion efforts usually need to change over time to adjust to differences among the adopter groups.

Exhibit 8-7 shows the adoption curve for a typical successful product. Some of the important characteristics of each of these customer groups are discussed next. Which one are you? Does your group change for different products?

Exhibit 8-7 The Adoption Curve

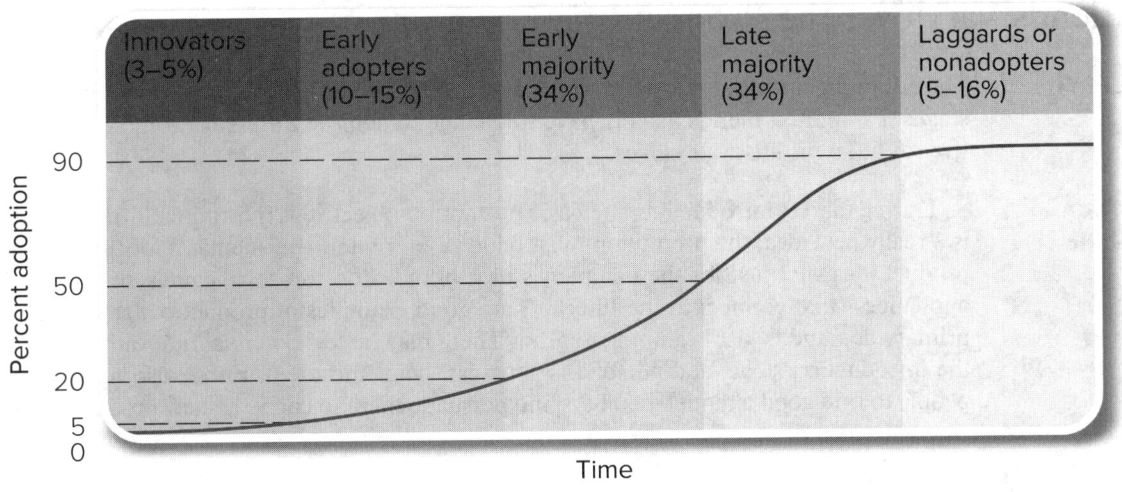

Innovators don't mind taking some risks

The **innovators** are the first to adopt. They are eager to try a new idea and willing to take risks. Innovators tend to be young and well educated. They are likely to be mobile and have many contacts outside their local social group and community. Business firms in the innovator group are often specialized and willing to take the risk of doing something new.

Innovators tend to rely on impersonal and scientific information sources, or other innovators, rather than salespeople. They often search for information on the Internet, read articles in technical publications, or look for informative ads in special-interest magazines.

Early adopters are often opinion leaders

Early adopters are well respected by their peers and often are opinion leaders. They tend to be younger, more mobile, and more creative than later adopters. But unlike innovators, they have fewer contacts outside their own sociai group or community. Business firms in this category also tend to be specialized.

Of all the groups, this one tends to have the greatest contact with salespeople. Mass media are important information sources too. Marketers should be very concerned with attracting and selling to the early adopter group. Their acceptance is crucial. The next group, the early majority, look to the early adopters for guidance. The early adopters can help the promotion effort by spreading *word-of-mouth* information and advice among other consumers.

Early majority group is deliberate

The **early majority** avoids risk and waits to consider a new idea after many early adopters have tried it—and liked it. Average-sized business firms that are less specialized often fit in this category. If successful companies in their industry adopt the new idea, they will too.

The early majority have a great deal of contact with mass media, salespeople, and early adopter opinion leaders. Members usually aren't opinion leaders themselves.

Late majority is cautious

The **late majority** is cautious about new ideas. Often they are older and more set in their ways, so they are less likely to follow early adopters. In fact, strong social pressure from their own peer group may be needed before they adopt a new product. Business firms in this group tend to be conservative, smaller-sized firms with little specialization.

The late majority makes little use of marketing sources of information—mass media and salespeople. They tend to be oriented more toward other late adopters rather than outside sources they don't trust.

Laggards or nonadopters hang on to tradition

Laggards or **nonadopters** prefer to do things the way they've been done in the past and are very suspicious of new ideas. They tend to be older and less well educated. The smallest businesses with the least specialization often fit this category. They cling to the status quo and think it's the safe way.

The main source of information for laggards is other laggards. This certainly is bad news for marketers. In fact, it may not pay to bother with this group.

Promotion Blends Vary over the Product Life Cycle

Stage of product in its life cycle

The adoption curve helps explain why a new product goes through the product life-cycle stages. Promotion blends usually have to change to achieve different promotion objectives at different life-cycle stages.

Market introduction stage—"this new idea is good"

During market introduction, the basic promotion objective is informing. If the product is a really new idea, the promotion must build **primary demand**—demand for the general product idea—not just for the company's own brand. Rooftop solar panels and "smart" appliances (that connect to the Internet) are good examples of product concepts where primary demand is just beginning to grow. There may be few potential innovators during the introduction stage, and personal selling can help find them. Firms also need salespeople to find good channel members and persuade them to carry the new product. Sales promotion may be targeted at salespeople or channel members to get them interested in selling the new product. And sales promotion may also encourage customers to try it.

Market growth stage—"our brand is best"

In the market growth stage, more competitors enter the market, and promotion emphasis shifts from building primary demand to stimulating **selective demand**—demand for a company's own brand. The main job is to persuade customers to buy, and keep buying, the company's product.

Now that there are more potential customers, mass selling becomes more economical. But salespeople and personal selling must still work in the channels, expanding the number of outlets and cementing relationships with channel members.

The evolution of promotion for Banquet Homestyle Bakes illustrates these first two stages. When ConAgra Foods introduced Homestyle Bakes, it was the first shelf-stable meal kit with the meat already in the package. ConAgra, also the producer of Armour processed meats, had the expertise to create a tasty product that a consumer could prepare in a few minutes and then just stick in the oven. When Homestyle Bakes came out, there was no direct competition. The sales force used marketing research data to convince retailers to give the product shelf space, and ads used humor to highlight that the package was unusually heavy because it already included meat. However, over time new competition entered the market with similar offerings. So promotion shifted to emphasize why Homestyle Bakes was better, with a variety of new flavors and 10 percent more meat. Similarly, to keep customers interested in the Homestyle brand, the sales force shifted its efforts to get retailers to participate in Homestyle Bakes' "Super Meals/Super Moms" contests, which offered harried moms prizes such as a visit to a spa.

Market maturity stage—"our brand is better, really"

In the market maturity stage, mass selling and sales promotion may dominate the promotion blends of consumer products firms. Business products may require more aggressive personal selling—perhaps supplemented by more advertising. The total dollars allocated to promotion may rise as competition increases.

If a firm already has high sales—relative to competitors—it may have a real advantage in promotion at this stage. For example, sales of Tylenol tablets are about four times the sales of Motrin competing tablets. If both Tylenol and Motrin spend the same percentage of sales (say 35 percent) on promotion, Tylenol will spend four times as much as its smaller competitor and will probably communicate to more people.

Firms that have differentiated their marketing mixes may favor mass selling because they have something to talk about. For instance, a firm with a strong brand may use reminder-type advertising or target frequent-buyer promotions at current customers to strengthen the relationship and keep customers loyal. This may be more effective than costly efforts to win customers away from competitors.

However, as a market drifts toward pure competition, some companies resort to price-cutting. This may temporarily increase the number of units sold, but it is also likely to reduce total revenue and the money available for promotion. The temporary sales gains disappear and prices are dragged down even lower when competitors retaliate with their own short-term sales promotions, like price-off coupons. As cash flowing into the business declines, spending may have to be cut back.

Sales decline stage—"let's tell those who still want our product"

During the sales decline stage, the total amount spent on promotion usually decreases as firms try to cut costs to remain profitable. Because some people may still want the product, firms need more targeted promotion to reach these customers.

On the other hand, some firms may increase promotion to try to slow the cycle, at least temporarily. Crayola had almost all of the market for children's crayons, but sales were slowly declining as new kinds of markers came along. Crayola increased ad spending to urge parents to buy their kids a "fresh box."

Setting the Promotion Budget

Size of budget affects promotion efficiency and blend

There are some economies of scale in promotion. An ad on national TV might cost less *per person* reached than an ad on local TV. Similarly, citywide radio, TV, and newspapers may be cheaper than neighborhood newspapers or direct personal contact. But the *total cost* for some mass media may force small firms, or those with small promotion budgets, to use promotion alternatives that are more expensive per contact. For example, a small retailer might want to use local television but finds that there is only enough money for a web page, a neon sign, and an occasional newspaper ad.

Find the task, budget for it

The most common method of budgeting for promotion expenditures is to compute a percentage of either past sales or sales expected in the future. The virtue of this method is its simplicity. However, just because this mechanical approach is common doesn't mean that it's smart. It leads to expanding marketing expenditures when business is good and cutting back when business is poor. When business is poor, this approach may just make the problem worse—if weak promotion is the reason for declining sales.

In light of our continuing focus on planning marketing strategies to reach objectives, the most sensible approach to budgeting promotion expenditures is the **task method**—basing the budget on the job to be done. It helps a marketing manager to set priorities so that the money spent on promotion produces specific and desired results. In fact, this approach makes sense for *any* marketing expenditure, but here we'll focus on promotion.

A practical approach is to determine which promotion methods are most economical and effective for the tasks that need to be completed to achieve communication objectives. The costs of these tasks are then totaled to determine how much should be budgeted for promotion (just as money is allocated for other marketing activities required by the strategy). In other words, the firm can assemble its total promotion budget directly from detailed plans rather than by simply relying on historical patterns or ratios.

Marketing research clarifies budgeting estimates

Some promotion activities and objectives can be readily measured. Often a firm has measured the results and return on investment from previous promotion efforts. These can provide a good estimate of the cost to achieve a similar objective. For example, if Taco Bell sets a target of adding 10,000 new "Likes" to its Facebook page and has used coupons to grow it in the past, it has some previous results to compare new campaigns to. Or perhaps a firm's advertising agency has experience that can provide better estimates. Taco Bell can measure the cost of the promotion (coupons plus any advertising) and the number of new "Likes" on the Facebook page. Figuring out the value of a "Like" might be more difficult.

Other objectives can be more challenging to predict and measure. What if the objective is to raise the level of brand familiarity of Bonobos pants for fashion-conscious men by running ads in select men's magazines? And Bonobos has never run magazine ads. Although not impossible, predicting the results of the advertising for the first time can be a challenge. Even when evaluation is difficult, marketing managers should still try to evaluate costs and returns to develop a realistic budget.

CONCLUSION

Promotion is an important part of any marketing mix. Most consumers and intermediate customers can choose from among many products. To be successful, a producer must not only offer a good product at a reasonable price but also inform potential customers about the product and where they can buy it. Further, producers must tell wholesalers and retailers in the channel about their product and marketing mix. These intermediaries, in turn, must use promotion to reach their customers. And the promotion blend must fit with the rest of the marketing mix and the target market.

In this chapter, we introduced different promotion methods and we discussed the advantages and disadvantages of each method. We also discussed the integrated marketing communications concept and explained why most firms use a blend of different promotion methods. Although the overall promotion objective is to affect buying behavior, the basic promotion objectives are informing, persuading, and reminding. These objectives help guide the marketing manager's decisions about the promotion blend.

Models from the behavioral sciences help us understand the communication process and how it can break down. These models recognize different ways to communicate. We discussed direct-response promotion for developing more targeted promotion blends. And we described an approach where customers initiate and interact with the marketer's communications. It provides new and different challenges for marketing managers.

This chapter also recognized other factors that influence decisions about promotion blends. Marketing managers must make decisions about how to split promotion that is directed at final consumers or business customers—and at channel members. Promotion blends are also influenced by the adoption curve and the product life-cycle stages. Finally, we described how promotion budgets are set and influence promotion decisions.

In this chapter, we considered some basic concepts that apply to all areas of promotion.

JOYFUL MOMENT

Letter of Recommendation

When Peters learned that he was being fired, he went to see the head of human resources. "Since I've been with the firm for so long," he said, "I think I deserve at least a letter of recommendation."

The human resources director agreed and said he'd have the letter the next day.

The following morning, Peters found a letter on his desk. It read, "Jonathan Peters worked for our company for 11 years. When he left us, we were very satisfied."

WORDS AND EXPRESSIONS

1. **subsidiary**: *adj./n.* of or relating to or being a subsidy; a company that is completely controlled by another company 附属的，辅助的；子公司
   —The marketing department has always played a subsidiary role to the sales department.
   营销部一直都扮演着销售部的辅助角色。
2. **animate**: *vt./adj.* to make lively; belonging to the class of nouns that denote living beings 使有生气；鼓舞；有生命的
   —There was precious little about the cricket to animate the crowd.
   这场板球比赛极少有让观众兴奋的地方。
3. **reptile**: *n.* any cold-blooded vertebrate of the class Reptilia including tortoises, turtles, snakes, lizards, alligators, crocodiles and extinct forms 爬虫类
   —Mammals arose from a fairly primitive reptile in the Mesozoic era.
   哺乳类起源于中生代宛若原始的爬虫类。
4. **disobedient**: *adj.* not obeying or complying with commands of those in authority 不服从的；违背的；不孝的
   —Her tone was that of a parent to a disobedient child.
   她的声音听上去好像家长在教训不听话的小孩。
5. **encode**: *vt.* to convert ordinary language into code [计] 编码，译码
   —The two parties encode confidential data in a form that is not directly readable by the other party.
   双方把机密数据写成一种不能被对方直接读懂的密码。
6. **decode**: *v.* to convert code into ordinary language [计][通信] 译码，解码
   —All he had to do was decode it and pass it over.
   他所要做的就是解译它，然后把它发过去。
7. **archive**: *n./vt.* a depository containing historical records and documents 档案馆；档案文件；把…存档
   —The system will archive the information so agencies can review it in detail.
   该系统会将该信息存档，以便各代理机构能对其详细审阅。

EXERCISES

1. Multiple choices

(1) ___ involves direct spoken communication between sellers and potential customers.
A. Personal selling B. Mass selling C. Advertising D. Marketing

(2) ___ manage their company's mass-selling effort—in television, newspapers, magazines and other media.
A. Sales managers B. Advertising managers
C. Sales promotion managers D. Marketing managers

(3) A(n) ___ objective can show that it meets consumer needs better than other products.
A. persuading B. reminding C. supporting D. informing

(4) We see that a source—the sender of a message—is trying to deliver a message to a ___—the potential customer.
A. receiver B. sender C. promoter D. seller

(5) ___ means using normal promotion effort—personal selling, advertising, and sales promotion—to help sell the whole marketing mix to possible channel members.
A. Pulling B. Selling C. Planning D. Pushing

2. Terms translation

(1) promotion (2) publicity (3) sales promotion (4) public relations
(5) integrated marketing communications (6) AIDA model (7) encoding
(8) message channel (9) adoption curve (10) primary demand

3. True or false

(1) It's not desirable to combine personal selling with mass selling and sales promotion. ______
(2) Mass selling is more flexible than personal selling, but when the target market is large and scattered, mass selling can be less expensive. ______
(3) Publicity is any paid form of nonpersonal presentation of ideas, goods, or services. ______
(4) Most sales promotion efforts are designed to produce immediate results. ______
(5) The sales promotion managers are concerned with managing personal selling. ______
(6) It seems obvious that a firm's different communications to a target market should be consistent. ______
(7) A persuading objective means the firm will try to develop a favorable set of attitudes so customers will buy and keep buying its products. ______
(8) If target customers already have positive attitudes about a firm's marketing mix—or a good relationship with a firm—an informing objective might be suitable. ______
(9) Encoding is the source deciding what it wants to say and translating it into words or symbols that will have the same meaning to the receiver. ______
(10) The most common criticisms of promotion relate to exaggerated claims. ______

4. Fill in the blanks

(1) Traditional thinking about promotion—and for that matter about the communication process—has usually been based on the idea that it's the __________ who initiates communication.
(2) __________ means getting customers to ask intermediaries for the product.
(3) Research on how markets accept new ideas has led to the __________ model.
(4) The __________ are the first to adopt. They are eager to try a new idea and willing to take risks.
(5) The __________ avoids risk and waits to consider a new idea after many early adopters have tried it and liked it.
(6) In the market growth stage, more competitors enter the market, and promotion emphasis shifts from building primary demand to stimulating __________—demand for a company's own brand.
(7) In the light of our continuing focus on planning marketing strategies to reach objectives, the most sensible approach to budgeting promotion expenditures is the __________—basing the budget on the job to be done.
(8) __________ is communicating information between the seller and potential buyers or others in the channel to influence attitudes and behavior.
(9) __________ is communicating with large numbers of potential customers at the same time.
(10) If target customers already have positive attitudes about a firm's marketing mix—or a good relationship with a firm—a __________ objective might be suitable.

5. **Answer the following questions**
   (1) Who will be responsible for planning, integrating, and managing the promotion blend and what are their responsibilities?
   (2) What methods does a marketing manager usually use to promote depending on promotion objectives?
   (3) What is the AIDA model? How does it work?
   (4) The promotion blends vary over the life cycle. How to adopt different promotion blends?
   (5) How is the promotion budget set and how does it influence the promotion decisions?

SUGGESTED CASES

14. Schrock & Oh Design
18. West Tarrytown Volunteer Fire Department (WTVFD)
19. MyOwnWedding.com

MARKETING ANALYTICS: DATA TO KNOWLEDGE

McGraw Hill Education connect

CHAPTER 8: SELECTING A COMMUNICATIONS CHANNEL

Helen Troy, owner of three Sound Haus stereo equipment stores, is deciding what message channel (advertising medium) to use to promote her newest store. Her current promotion blend includes direct-mail ads that are effective for reaching her current customers. She also has knowledgeable salespeople who work well with consumers once they're in the store. However, a key objective in opening a new store is to attract new customers. Her best prospects are professionals in the 25–44 age range with incomes over $38,000 a year. But only some of the people in this group are audiophiles who want the top-of-the-line brands she carries. Troy has decided to use local advertising to reach new customers.

Troy narrowed her choice to two advertising media: Pandora, a music streaming service that offers localized advertising services, and a biweekly magazine that focuses on entertainment in her city. Many of the magazine's readers are out-of-town visitors interested in concerts, plays, and restaurants. They usually buy stereo equipment at home. But the magazine's audience research shows that many local professionals do subscribe to the magazine. Troy doesn't think that the objective can be achieved with a single ad. However, she believes that ads in six issues will generate good local awareness with her target market. In addition, the magazine's color format will let her present the prestige image she wants to convey in an ad. She thinks that will help convert aware prospects to buyers. Specialists at a local advertising agency will prepare a high-impact ad for $2,000, and then Troy will pay for the magazine space.

Pandora can target an audience similar to Troy's own target market. She knows repeated ads will be needed to be sure that most of her target audience is exposed to her ads. Troy thinks it will take daily ads for several months to create adequate awareness among her target market. Pandora will provide an announcer and prepare a recording of Troy's ad for a one-time fee of $200. All she has to do is tell them what the message content for the ad should say.

Both Pandora and the magazine gave Troy reports summarizing recent audience research. She decides that comparing the two media in a spreadsheet will help her make a better decision.

See Connect for the spreadsheet and questions needed to analyze this scenario.

9 CHAPTER NINE

Pricing Objectives and Policies

Twenty-somethings Adam Lowry and Eric Ryan shared a San Francisco apartment and an interest in starting a business. Back in 2000, after studying chemistry, Lowry was a climate scientist with a passion for sustainability. Ryan had studied marketing and worked in the advertising business; his interest was design. While hanging out drinking beer and on road trips to the mountains, the two talked about products they thought were cool and uncool—and what markets might be ripe for disruption.

They spotted opportunity in the $17 billion household cleaning product-market. They saw a mature market with little differentiation among brands. Dealer brands were viewed as lower quality at lower prices. National brands gave retailers price deals and advertising allowances in exchange for shelf space. Competitive advertising debated minor differences in cleaning efficacy, with coupons and sale prices used to woo shoppers whose brand loyalty was more habit than commitment.

The external market environment suggested a path building on the entrepreneurs' strengths. Scientific studies showed that many household cleaning chemicals had unhealthy side effects associated with long-term use. The green movement was picking up momentum. Mass-merchandiser Target was successfully selling everyday items with a designer flair. Lowry and Ryan thought a line of stylish, sustainable products made with safe ingredients that "cleaned like heck and smelled like heaven" could find a niche in this market.

Soon Method Products was born. Lowry and Ryan tested batches of cleaning products they mixed in their bathtub and stored in beer pitchers labeled "Do Not Drink." They filled clear spray bottles with samples of their first four products—cleaners for the kitchen, shower, bath, and glass. Then they ambushed independent grocery store managers in early morning hours and pitched their products. That's how their first customer, the owner of Mollie Stone's Market, discovered Method.

As sales began to take off later that summer, Ryan revisited packaging design. Without money to advertise, he thought something unique would garner attention and interest at the point-of-purchase. Method approached well-known industrial designer Karim Rashid with a pitch to "reinvent soap." Intrigued, Rashid came on board. Rashid's designs got Method noticed. A lot of Method customers discover the brand in a store—they love the cool package and figure at least the soap looks good sitting on the counter. Then customers find they like how well the cleaners work and keep buying.

Method's green promise also resonates with customers. Method's People against Dirty campaign tells the brand's story: most cleaners leave behind toxic chemical residues, leaving homes "dirty" after being cleaned. And when these chemicals go down the drain, they contaminate the natural environment. People against Dirty got the message across to Method's target market. Design and green proved to be powerful differentiators and allowed Method to charge a premium[1] price about 20 percent higher than leading brands.

Their first big sale was to Target. Method's stylish packaging was a perfect fit with Target's target market. Following successful test markets in San Francisco and Chicago, Target took Method nationwide. But Method doesn't appeal to every retailer. For example, Walmart customers thought Method was too expensive, and the line was dropped.

Despite high prices and impressive retail contracts, Method struggled to be profitable. By 2006, the brand held only 0.5 percent in market share and less than $100 million in sales. The problem: Method's production and operating costs were higher than giant, mega-brand competitors such as Procter & Gamble; brands like Dawn's retail prices were less than Method's production cost. Suppliers didn't give Method the same quantity discounts and it didn't have similar manufacturing economies of scale.

Growth had other costs. For example, retailers and wholesalers expected up-front cash payments or a few free cases of product before taking a chance on Method. New products are risky; retailers don't know how much they'll sell.

Fortunately for Method, its financial backers were initially concerned with market share and sales volume rather than profitability. They continued to invest in building support for the brand and developing innovative new products.

Method's innovations in the laundry category show how a little company can influence a big—make that huge—market. When Method introduced a laundry soap three times as concentrated as market leader Tide, most consumers thought Method was much more expensive than the larger bottles on the shelf. Method had to teach customers that it took less Method to get the same clean. After learning how to properly "dose" Method, customers appreciated the smaller bottles' convenience. Retailers immediately recognized the value of lower handling costs and a smaller shelf footprint (so they could stock more products) and pressured Method's competitors to offer similar concentrates.

A few years later, Method launched an improved laundry detergent. Its "smartclean technology" was eight times the concentration of regular detergent. Moms could hold a 20-ounce bottle (50 loads) in one hand and their baby in the other.

For price-sensitive shoppers, Method's $15.49 list price ($12.99 at Target) might not look like a great deal next to Target's own Up & Up brand for $8.38 (75 loads of laundry) or Tide's 100-ounce, 64-load jug at $11.99. Even after a coupon, a package bundled with fabric softener, or a refill with the Method pouch, customers pay more per load of laundry for Method. So how is Method growing? Method's whole marketing mix offers superior value to its narrow target market. Customers might try Method because of its stylish packaging and green roots, or its clever advertising, sales promotion, and publicity efforts attracted their attention. They keep buying because the products clean well and protect the environment, and they can find the brand where they shop. With Method's focus, that little corner of the market where they're cleaning up continues to grow.

LEARNING OBJECTIVES

The Method case demonstrates the importance of Price and how it interacts with the other marketing mix variables to create value and influence customer behavior. This chapter will help you better understand pricing objectives and policies that influence how firms make pricing decisions.

When you finish this chapter, you should be able to

1. explain the dimensions of price and value.
2. understand how pricing objectives should guide strategy planning for pricing decisions.
3. understand choices marketing managers must make about price flexibility.
4. know what a marketing manager should consider when setting the price level for a product in the early stages of the product life cycle.
5. understand the many possible variations of a price structure, including discounts, allowances, and who pays transportation costs.
6. understand the value pricing concept and its role in obtaining a competitive advantage by offering target customers superior value.
7. understand the legality of price-level and price-flexibility policies.
8. understand important new terms (shown in boldface).

Price Has Many Strategy Dimensions

Price is one of the four major strategy decision variables that a marketing manager controls. Pricing decisions affect both the number of sales a firm makes and how much money it earns. Price is what a customer must give up to get the benefits offered by the rest of a firm's marketing mix, so it plays a direct role in shaping customer value.

Guided by the company's objectives, marketing managers develop specific pricing objectives (see Exhibit 9-1). These objectives drive decisions about key pricing policies: (1) how flexible prices will be, (2) the level of prices over the product life cycle, (3) to whom and when discounts and allowances will be given, and (4) how transportation costs will be handled. After we've looked at these specific areas, we will discuss how they combine to impact customer value as well as laws that are relevant.

It's not easy to define price in real-life situations because price reflects many dimensions. People who don't realize this can make big mistakes.

Exhibit 9-1 Strategy Planning and Pricing Objectives and Policies

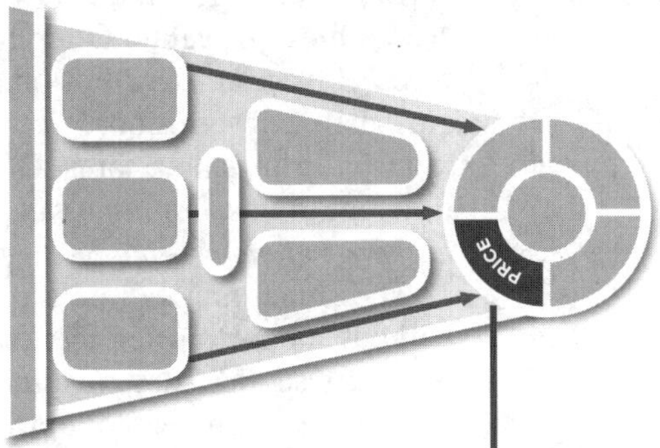

Chapter 9 Pricing Objectives and Policies

Price Setting in the Business World

Pricing objectives
- Profit-oriented
- Sales-oriented
- Status quo -oriented

Pricing policies
- Price flexibility
- Prices over the product life cycle
- Discounts and allowances
- Transportation costs

Pricing and customer value
- Value pricing
- Meeting competition

Legal issues and pricing policies
- Minimum prices
- List prices
- Price fixing
- Price discrimination

Suppose you've been saving to buy a new car and you see in an ad that, after a $1,000 rebate[2], the base price for the new-year model is $16,494–5 percent lower than the previous year. At first this might seem like a real bargain. However, your view of this deal might change if you found out you also had to pay a $400 transportation charge and an extra $480 for an extended service warranty. The price might look even less attractive if you discovered that the navigation system, side air bags, and moonroof that were standard the previous year are now options that cost $1,900. The cost of the higher interest rate on the car loan and the sales tax on all of this might come as an unpleasant surprise too. Further, how would you feel if you bought the car anyway and then learned that a friend who just bought the exact same model got a much lower price from the dealer by using a broker he found on the Internet?

IKEA's clever—and carefully located—promotional signs remind customers that its price is a good value compared to what they pay for other everyday goods and services.
Source: Inter IKEA Systems

The price equation: Price equals something of value

This example emphasizes that when a seller quotes a price, it is related to *some* assortment of goods and services. So **Price** is the amount of money that is charged for "something" of value. Of course, price may be called different things in different settings. Colleges charge tuition. Landlords collect rent. Motels post a room rate. Magazines have subscriptions. Country clubs get dues. Banks ask for interest when they loan money. Airlines have fares. Doctors set fees. Employees want a wage. People may call it different things, but *almost every business transaction in our modern economy involves an exchange of money—the Price—for something.*

The something can be a physical product in various stages of completion, with or without supporting services, with or without quality guarantees, and so on. Or it could be a pure service—dry cleaning, a lawyer's advice, or insurance on your car.

The nature and extent of this something determine the amount of money exchanged. Some customers pay list price. Others obtain large discounts or allowances because something is *not* provided. Exhibit 9-2 summarizes some possible variations for consumers or users, and Exhibit 9-3 does the same for channel members. These variations are discussed more fully below, and then we'll consider the customer value concept more fully—in terms of competitive advantage. But here it should be clear that Price has many dimensions. How each of these dimensions is handled affects customer value. If

Exhibit 9-2 Price Exchanged for Something of Value (as seen by consumers or users)

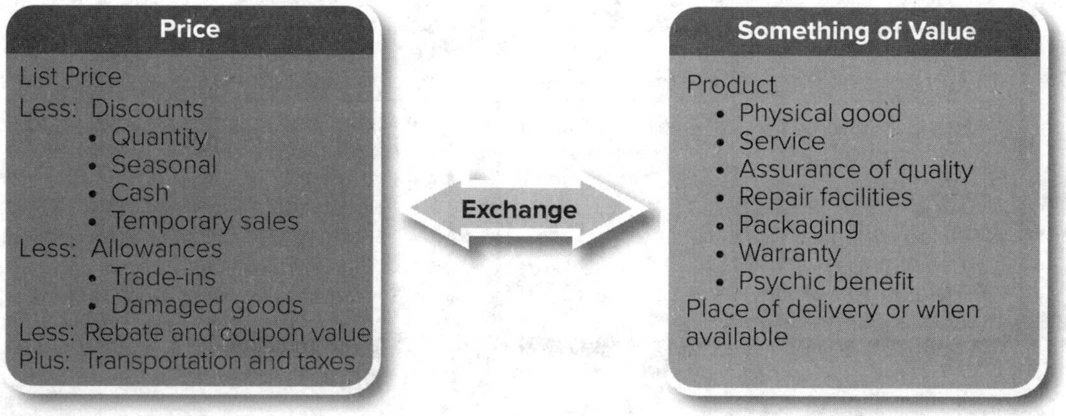

Exhibit 9-3 Price Exchanged for Something of Value (as seen by channel members)

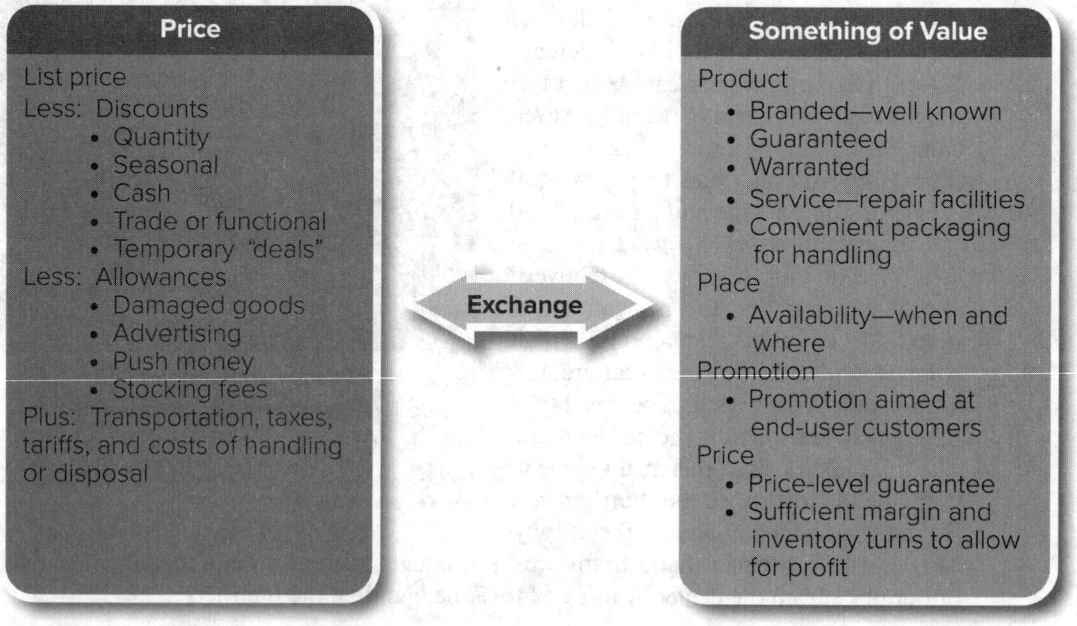

a customer sees greater value in spending money in some other way, no exchange will occur.

Objectives Should Guide Strategy Planning for Price

Pricing objectives should flow from, and fit within, company-level and marketing objectives. Pricing objectives should be *explicitly stated* because they have a direct effect on pricing policies as well as the methods used to set prices. Exhibit 9-4 shows the various types of pricing objectives we'll discuss.

Profit-Oriented Objectives

Target returns provide specific guidelines

Over the long term, and often over the short term, marketing managers should set objectives oriented toward making a profit. A **target return objective** sets a specific level of profit as an objective. Often this amount is stated as a percentage of sales or of capital investment. A large manufacturer such as Motorola might aim for a 15 percent return on investment. The target for Safeway and other supermarket chains might be a 1 percent return on sales.

A target return objective has administrative advantages in a large company. Performance can be compared against the target. Some companies eliminate divisions, or drop products, that aren't yielding the target rate of return. For example, General Electric sold its small appliance division to Black & Decker because it felt it could earn higher returns in other product-markets.

Some just want satisfactory profits

Some managers aim for only satisfactory returns. They just want returns that ensure the firm's survival and convince stockholders they're doing a good job. Similarly, some small family-run businesses aim for a profit that will provide a comfortable lifestyle.

Many private and public nonprofit organizations set a price level that will just recover costs. In other words, their target return figure is zero. For example, a government agency may charge motorists a toll for using a bridge but then drop the toll when the cost of the bridge is paid.

Exhibit 9-4 Possible Pricing Objectives

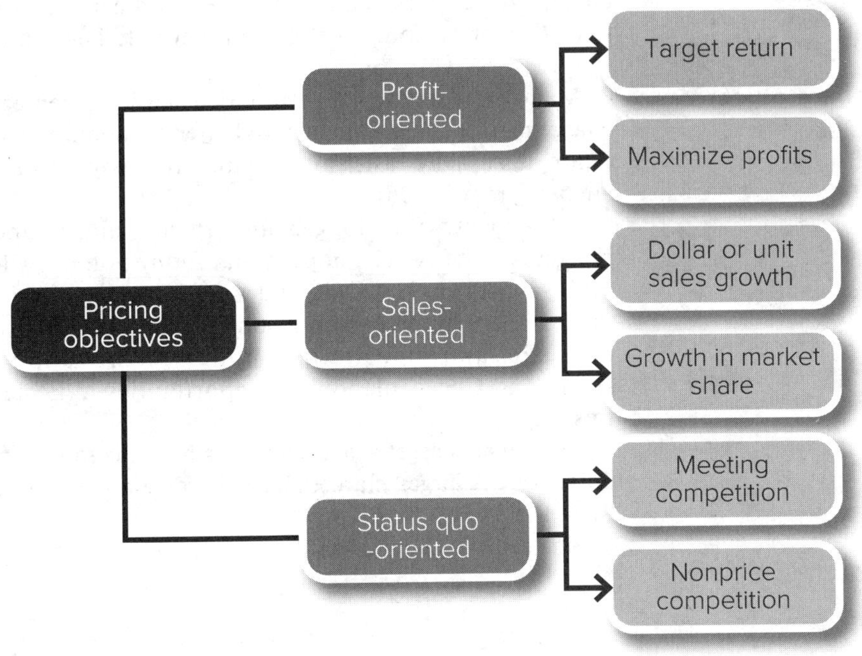

Similarly, firms that provide critical public services—including many utilities, insurance companies, and defense contractors—sometimes pursue only satisfactory long-run targets. They are well aware that the public expects them to set prices that are in the public interest. They may also have to face public or government agencies that review and approve prices.

Profit maximization can be socially responsible

A **profit maximization objective** seeks to get as much profit as possible. It might be stated as a desire to earn a rapid return on investment—or, more bluntly[3], to charge all the traffic will bear.

Pricing to achieve profit maximization doesn't always lead to high prices. Low prices may expand the size of the market and result in greater sales and profits. For example, when prices of cell phones were very high, only businesses and wealthy people bought them. When producers lowered prices, nearly everyone bought one.

If a firm is earning a very large profit, other firms will try to copy or improve on what the company offers. Frequently, this leads to lower prices.

Sales-Oriented Objectives

Sales growth doesn't necessarily mean big profits

A **sales-oriented objective** seeks some level of unit sales, dollar sales, or share of market—*without referring to profit.*

Some managers are more concerned about sales growth than profits. They think sales growth always leads to more profits. This sometimes makes sense over the short term. For example, many Procter & Gamble brands in product categories such as shampoo, soap, and diapers lost market share during the recent recession. When the economy began to recover, P&G kept prices low and sacrificed profits in order to grow with the recovering economy. It might also work well when products are in the introductory or early growth stages of the product life cycle. However, over the long term this kind of thinking causes problems when a firm's costs are growing faster than sales. Although some firms have periods of declining profits in spite of growth in sales, business managers should usually pay more attention to profits, not just sales.

Some nonprofit organizations set prices to increase market share—precisely because they are *not* trying to earn a profit. For example, many cities set low fares to fill up their buses, reduce traffic, and help the environment. Buses cost the same to run empty or full, and there's more benefit when they're full even if the total revenue is no greater.

Market share objectives are popular

Many firms seek to gain a specified share (percentage) of a market. If a company has a large market share, it may have better economies of scale than its competitors. In addition, it's usually easier to measure a firm's market share than to determine if profits are being maximized.

A company with a longer-run view may aim for increased market share when the market is growing. The hope is that future volume will justify sacrificing some profit in the short run. HP, Dell, and Acer have waged pricing battles in an effort to gain market share in the personal computer market. High market share offers economies of scale and negotiating power with suppliers. Companies as diverse as 3M and Coca-Cola look at opportunities in Eastern Europe and Southeast Asia this way.

Of course, market share objectives have the same limitations as straight sales growth objectives. A larger market share, if gained at too low a price, may lead to profitless "success."

Michelin wants its customers to know that its more efficient tires make them a good value. Lumension Security reminds customers of the high cost of lax computer security.
Left: Source: Michelin North America Inc.; Right: Source: Lumension Security, Inc.

Status Quo Pricing Objectives

Don't-rock-the-boat objectives

Managers satisfied with their current market share and profits sometimes adopt **status quo objectives**—don't-rock-the-*pricing*-boat objectives. Managers may say that they want to stabilize prices, or meet competition, or even avoid competition. This don't-rock-the-boat thinking is most common when the total market is not growing.

Sometimes firms in an industry make price changes very carefully—and only if others follow their lead. This tends to prevent price wars, which can drag down all firms' profits. For example, the airline industry typically raises prices collectively. One airline might add a fuel surcharge—if the others do not follow, that airline backs off and all maintain the status quo.

Or stress nonprice competition instead

A status quo pricing objective may be part of an aggressive overall marketing strategy focusing on **nonprice competition**—aggressive action on one or more of the Ps other than Price. Some companies that sell through the Internet originally thought that they'd compete with low prices and still earn high profits from volume. However, when they didn't get the sales volume they hoped for, they realized that there were also some nonprice ways to compete. For example, Zappos.com offers free shipping and guarantees that it will meet local shoe store prices. But it wins customers with its enormous selection of shoes, a website that makes it easy for customers to find what they want, and excellent customer service before and after the sale.

Most Firms Set Specific Pricing Policies—To Reach Objectives

Administered prices help achieve objectives

Price policies usually lead to **administered prices**—consciously set prices. In other words, instead of letting daily market forces (or auctions) decide their prices, most firms set their own prices. They may hold prices steady for long periods of time or change them more frequently if that's what's required to meet objectives.

If a firm doesn't sell directly to final customers, it usually wants to administer both the price it receives from intermediaries and the price final customers pay. After all, the price final customers pay will ultimately affect the quantity it sells.

Yet it is often difficult to administer prices throughout the channel. Other channel members may also wish to administer prices to achieve their own objectives. This is what happened to Alcoa, one of the largest aluminum producers. To reduce its excess inventory, Alcoa offered its wholesalers a 30 percent discount off its normal price. Alcoa expected the wholesalers to pass most of the discount along to their customers to stimulate sales throughout the channel. Instead, wholesalers bought *their* aluminum at the lower price but passed on only a small discount to customers. As a result, the quantity Alcoa sold didn't increase much, and it still had excess inventory, while the wholesalers made much more profit on the aluminum they did sell.

Some firms don't even try to administer prices. They just meet competition—or worse, mark up their costs with little thought to demand. They act as if they have no choice in selecting a price policy.

Remember that Price has many dimensions. Managers usually *do* have many choices. They *should* administer their prices. And they should do it carefully because, ultimately, customers must be willing to pay these prices before a whole marketing mix succeeds. In the rest of this chapter, we'll talk about policies a marketing manager must set to do an effective job of administering Price.

Price Flexibility Policies

One-price policy—the same price for everyone

One of the first decisions a marketing manager has to make is whether to use a one-price or a flexible-price policy. A **one-price policy** means offering the same price to all customers who purchase products under essentially the same conditions and in the same quantities. The majority of U.S. firms use a one-price policy—mainly for administrative convenience and to maintain goodwill among customers. But that is changing thanks to technology and the ability to identify different customer segments to which a firm wishes to charge higher or lower prices.

A one-price policy makes pricing easier. But a marketing manager must be careful to avoid a rigid one-price policy. This can amount to broadcasting a price that competitors can undercut, especially if the price is somewhat high. One reason for the growth of mass-merchandisers is that conventional retailers rigidly applied traditional margins and stuck to them. This left an opportunity for mass-merchandisers to undercut conventional retailers on price, allowing them to gain market share.

Flexible-price policy—different prices for different customers

A **flexible-price policy** means offering the same product and quantities to different customers at different prices. When computers are used to implement flexible pricing, the decisions focus more on what type of customer will get a price break. As firms learn how to analyze big data, more organizations are moving from a one-price policy to a flexible-price policy.

Pricing databases make flexible pricing easier

Various forms of flexible pricing are more common now that most prices are maintained in a central computer database. Frequent changes are easier. You see this when supermarket chains give loyalty club cardholders reduced prices on weekly specials. The checkout scanner reads the code on the package, and then the computer looks up the club price or the regular price depending on whether a club card has been scanned.

Dynamic pricing means prices change with demand

Dynamic pricing refers to pricing products at a particular customer's perceived ability to pay. This is the ultimate in price flexibility. The idea is to optimize revenue and profit by charging higher prices to customers willing to pay more and lower prices to those who do not see value at the high price but will buy at lower prices. Some companies use dynamic pricing as a means for changing prices over time. For example, airlines might raise or lower prices over time depending on how many seats are still available on a flight. Tickets purchased months in advance might have a lower price, but as the flight starts filling up, prices will rise as supply decreases. It can also work in the other direction; if United Airlines sees that early morning Tuesday flights from St. Louis to Miami are not selling well, the airline can lower the price to stimulate demand—perhaps encouraging some flyers to fly out on Tuesday morning instead of Monday night when there are fewer available seats. It is better to sell some seats at a discount than to have the flight leave with half the seats empty.

Sports teams are increasing ticket revenue by analyzing big data and implementing dynamic pricing. The idea is to charge higher prices for a better product. Initially, these teams simply charged higher prices for more popular weekend games as compared to midweek games. Now teams have adapted and change pricing even days before events—charging more when the weather is better or the matchup more intriguing. For example, the San Francisco Giants baseball team adjusts ticket prices to maximize attendance and revenue for each game. Ticket prices for each seat at each game are adjusted after crunching numbers that examine past ticket sales, the day of the week, time of the game, the opposing team's record, the pitching match-up, the going price at ticket resale sites like StubHub, and even the weather forecast. The Giants were expecting an additional $5 million in revenue the first year using the system. Other teams are following the Giants' lead.

Big data and predictive analytics vary prices by individual

Firms have long adjusted pricing for segments of customers. Now many firms use big data from loyalty cards or online shopping and predictive analytics to deliver customers individual prices. Many sources of big data can be read in real time, so pricing "experiments" can be run. For example, an online retailer can cut prices for a day or even a few hours to see whether it stimulates demand and raises profits. Another example of big data at work in real time is Office Depot.com's adjustment of prices depending on customers' browsing history and the physical location of the computer from which they are browsing.

Even brick-and-mortar retailers will use knowledge of individual customers to offer targeted price discounts to certain customers. It is not always a ploy to charge higher prices to customers more likely to pay them. For example, grocery store chain Safeway's Just for U loyalty program mines data to make unique offers to customers based on their previous shopping behavior. But they use the offers on products they were likely to buy anyway—with the expectation that customers will buy even more. Customers who buy lots of Cheerios are pleasantly surprised to receive a coupon for one dollar off their favorite breakfast cereal. Tracking data will show where that works and where it doesn't—and may reduce offers to customers that do not increase purchases.

"Surge" prices go up with demand

Car-sharing service Uber employs an analytical model for flexible pricing. Uber's "surge pricing" model adjusts prices to better match supply and demand for its service. When Uber sees demand for rides significantly exceeds supply—for example, on a rainy afternoon in a big city—prices are increased in an effort to raise the supply of drivers and reduce the demand for riders. Drivers, seeing the higher prices they will receive, are encouraged to work later than they might have otherwise wanted; riders, seeing the temporary price increase, may wait until later or seek another transportation option. Prices, which can rise to as much as 10 times the normal fare, fall back to normal when supply and demand stabilize.

Salespeople negotiate prices to the situation

Sometimes prices are negotiated and a price is determined by bargaining between the buyer and the seller. This type of flexible pricing is most common in the channels, in direct sales of business products, and at retail for expensive shopping products. Retail shopkeepers in less-developed economies typically use flexible pricing—shopkeepers start with high prices but bargain to try to make a sale at a price the customer will accept while still providing maximum profit to the seller. These situations usually involve personal selling, not mass selling. The advantage of flexible pricing is that the salesperson can adjust price—considering prices charged by competitors, the relationship with the customer, and the customer's bargaining ability. Flexible-price policies often specify a *range* in which the actual price charged must fall.

Too much price-cutting erodes profits

Some sales reps let price-cutting become a habit. This can lead to a lower price level and lower profit. A small price cut may not seem like much, but keep in mind that all of the revenue that is lost would go to profit. If salespeople for a producer that usually earns profits equal to 20 percent of its sales cut prices by an average of about 10 percent, profits would drop by half (see Exhibit 9-5)!

Disadvantages of flexible pricing

Flexible pricing does have disadvantages. A customer who finds that others paid lower prices for the same marketing mix will be unhappy. This can cause real conflict in channels. For example, the Winn-Dixie supermarket chain stopped carrying products of some suppliers who refused to give Winn-Dixie the same prices available to chains in other regions of the country. Similarly, companies that post different prices for different segments on a website that all can see often get complaints.

If buyers learn that negotiating is in their interest, the time needed for bargaining will increase. This can increase selling costs and reduce profits. It can also frustrate customers. For example, most auto dealers use flexible pricing and bargain for what they can get. Inexperienced consumers, reluctant to bargain, often pay hundreds of dollars more than the dealer is willing to accept. By contrast, CarMax has earned high customer-satisfaction ratings by offering haggle[4]-weary consumers a one-price policy.

Price-Level Policies–Over the Product Life Cycle

Marketing managers who administer prices must consciously set a price-level policy. As they enter the market, they have to set introductory prices that may have long-run effects. They must consider where the product life cycle is and how fast it's moving. And they must decide if their prices should be above, below, or somewhere in between relative to the market.

Let's look for a moment at a new product in the market introduction stage of its product life cycle. There are few (or no) direct substitute marketing mixes. So the price-level decision should focus first on the nature of market demand. A high price may lead to higher profit from each sale but also to fewer units sold. A lower price might appeal to more potential customers. With this in mind, should the firm set a high or low price?

Skimming pricing—feeling out demand at a high price

A **skimming price policy** tries to sell the top (skim the cream) of a market–the top of the demand curve–at a high price before aiming at more price-sensitive customers. Skimming may maximize profits in the market introduction stage for an innovation,

Exhibit 9-5 Impact of Price Cut on Profit

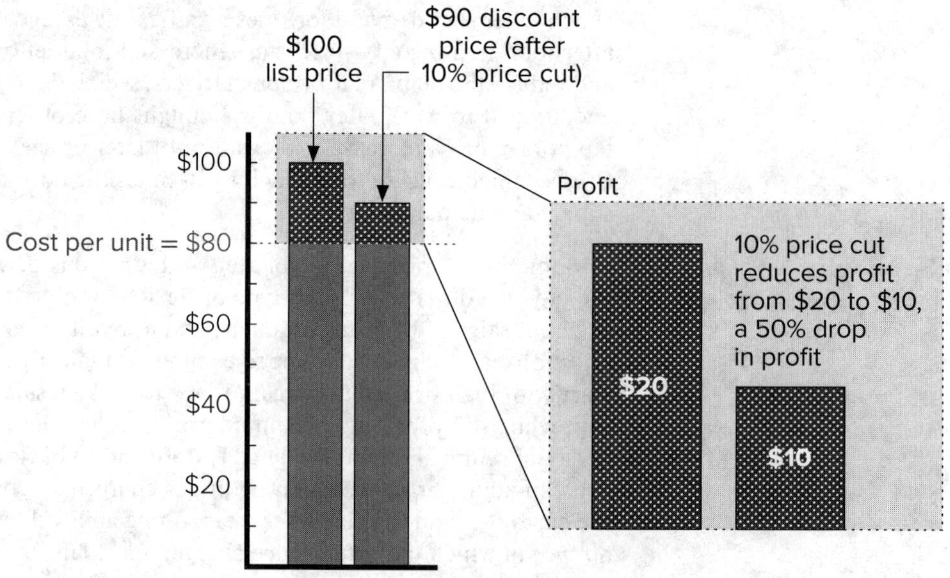

especially if there are few substitutes or if some customers are not price sensitive. Skimming is also useful when you don't know very much about the shape of the demand curve. It's sometimes safer to start with a high price that can be reduced if customers balk.

That is what happened to Apple when it introduced the first iPhones. The phone was originally sold for $600 but customers pushed back and it did not meet sales targets. A few months later Apple lowered the price by $200 and sales took off.

Price moves down the demand curve

A skimming policy often involves a slow reduction in price over time (see Exhibit 9-6). Note that as price is reduced, new target markets are probably being sought. So as the price level steps down the demand curve, new Place, Product, and Promotion policies may be needed too.

This is what happened when cellular phone service was first introduced. McCaw Cellular was the first to bring this product to market. Wireless phone calls cost $1 per minute and customers paid about $700 for a large clunky[5] phone. At these prices, business customers were about the only ones interested in buying. Over time, more competitors entered the market, prices fell, and more customers found value in the offering. Today, prices are much lower and cellular phones are widely adopted.

Penetration pricing—get volume at a low price

A **penetration pricing policy** tries to sell the whole market at one low price. This approach might be wise when the elite market—those willing to pay a high price—is small. This is the case when the whole demand curve is fairly elastic[6]. See Exhibit 9-6. A penetration policy is even more attractive if selling larger quantities results in lower costs because of economies of scale. Penetration pricing may be wise if the firm expects strong competition very soon after introduction. This was the strategy when Amazon first introduced its Echo voice-controlled smart speaker. Anticipating competition from Google, Microsoft, and Apple, Amazon offered the Echo at a low price and grabbed the early market share lead.

Of course, even a low penetration price doesn't keep competitors out of a market permanently. Product life cycles do march on. However, a firm that gets a head start in a new market can often maintain its advantage.

Introductory price dealing—temporary price cuts

Low prices tend to attract customers and trial. Therefore, marketers often use **introductory price dealing**—temporary price cuts—to speed new products into a market and get customers to try them. However, don't confuse these *temporary* price cuts with

Exhibit 9-6 Alternative Introductory Pricing Policies

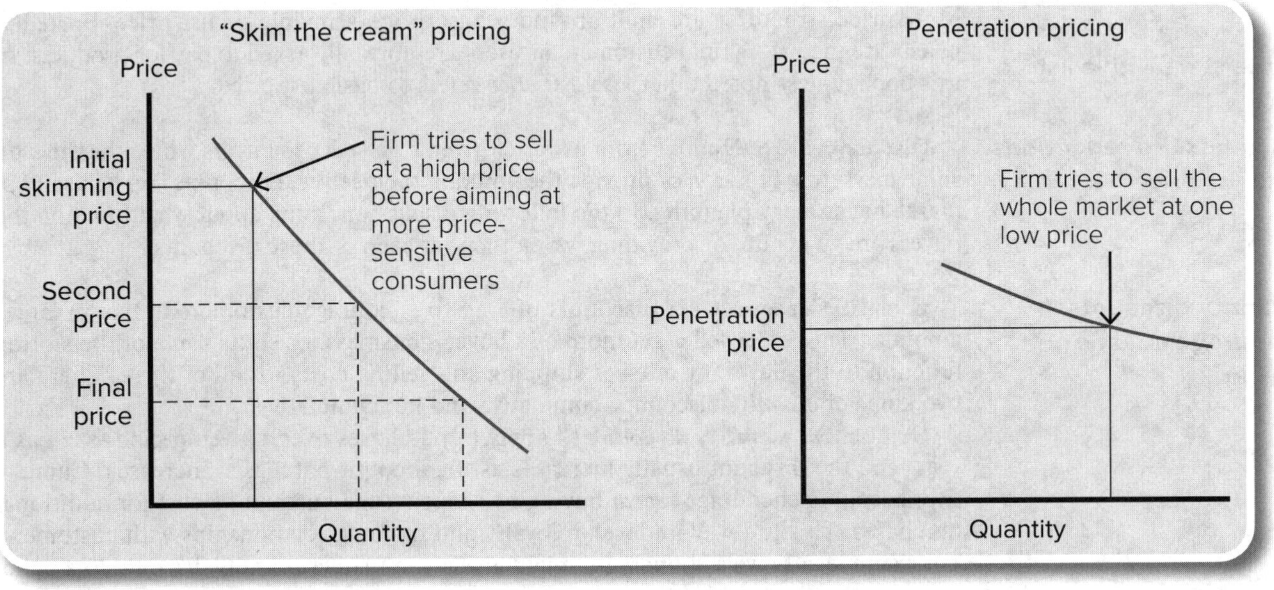

Marketers often use introductory price dealing—in the form of temporary price cuts, introductory coupons, or trade-in allowances—to speed new products into a market.
Left: Source: Spectrum Brands, Inc.; Right: Source: Google

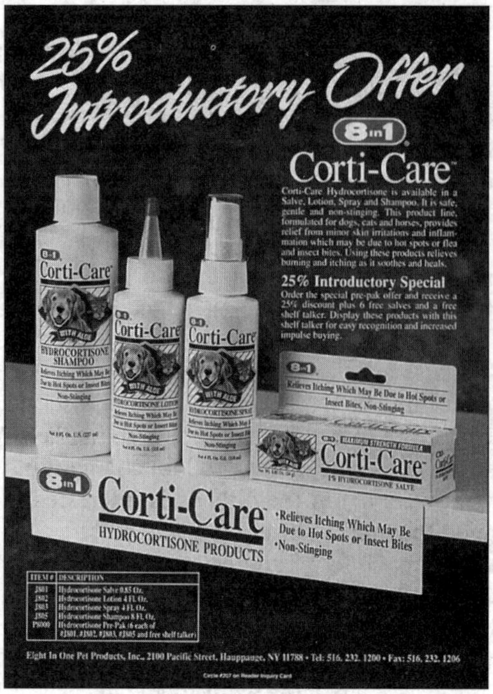

low penetration prices. The plan here is to raise prices as soon as the introductory offer is over. Hopefully by then target customers will have decided it is worth buying again at the regular price. Introductory price dealing should be part of a larger marketing strategy. For example, some developers of software applications (or "apps") for smartphones know that getting onto the store's list of "Top Apps" gets attention, which drives sales. So some app makers price the app low at launch to encourage sales, which moves it up the rankings. Then they raise prices to optimize profits.

Established competitors often choose not to meet introductory price dealing—as long as the introductory period is not too long or too successful. However, some competitors match introductory price deals with their own short-term sale prices to discourage customers from shopping around.

Discount Policies—Reductions from List Prices

Prices start with a list price

Most price structures are built around a base price schedule or list price. **Basic list prices** are the prices final customers or users are normally asked to pay for products. In this book, unless noted otherwise, *list price* refers to basic list price.

Discounts are reductions from list price

Discounts are reductions from list price given by a seller to buyers who either give up some marketing function or provide the function themselves. Discounts can be useful in marketing strategy planning. In the following discussion, think about what function the buyers are giving up, or providing, when they get each of these discounts.

Quantity discounts encourage volume buying

Quantity discounts are discounts offered to encourage customers to buy in larger amounts. This lets a seller get more of a buyer's business, or shifts some of the storing function to the buyer, or reduces shipping and selling costs—or all of these. There are two kinds of quantity discounts: cumulative and noncumulative.

Cumulative quantity discounts[7] apply to purchases over a given period—such as a year—and the discount usually increases as the amount purchased increases. Cumulative discounts encourage *repeat* buying by reducing the customer's cost for additional purchases. This is a way to develop loyalty and ongoing relationships with customers. For example, a Lowe's lumberyard might give a cumulative quantity discount to a building contractor who is not able to buy all of the needed materials at once. Lowe's wants to reward the contractor's patronage[8] and discourage shopping around. Along the same lines, Disney World wants to keep you on its properties and not at Universal's Islands of Adventure—so it offers discounts for multi-day passes.

A cumulative quantity discount is often attractive to business customers who don't want to run up their inventory costs. They are rewarded for buying large quantities, even though individual orders may be smaller.

Noncumulative quantity discounts apply only to individual orders. Such discounts encourage larger orders but do not tie a buyer to the seller after that one purchase. Lowe's lumberyard may resell insulation[9] products made by several competing producers. Owens-Corning might try to encourage Lowe's to stock larger quantities of its pink insulation by offering a noncumulative quantity discount.

Seasonal discounts—buy sooner

Seasonal discounts are discounts offered to encourage buyers to buy earlier than present demand requires. If used by a manufacturer, this discount tends to shift the storing function further along in the channel. It also tends to even out sales over the year. For example, Kyota offers wholesalers a lower price on its garden tillers if they buy in the fall, when sales are slow.

Service firms that face irregular demand or excess capacity often use seasonal discounts. For example, some tourist attractions, such as ski resorts, offer lower weekday rates when attendance would otherwise be down.

Payment terms and cash discounts set payment dates

Most sales to businesses are made on credit. The seller sends a bill (invoice) by mail or electronically, and the buyer's accounting department processes it for payment. Some firms depend on their suppliers for temporary working capital (credit). Therefore, it is very important for both sides to clearly state the terms of payment—including the availability of cash discounts—and to understand the commonly used payment terms.

Net means that payment for the face value of the invoice is due immediately. These terms are sometimes changed to net 10 or net 30, which means payment is due within 10 or 30 days of the date on the invoice.

Cash discounts are reductions in price to encourage buyers to pay their bills quickly. The terms for a cash discount usually modify the net terms.

2/10, net 30 means the buyer can take a 2 percent discount off the face value of the invoice if the invoice is paid within 10 days. Otherwise, the full face value is due within 30 days. And it usually is stated or understood that an interest charge will be added after the 30-day free-credit period.

Why cash discounts are given and should be evaluated

Smart buyers carefully evaluate cash discounts. A discount of 2/10, net 30 may not look like much at first. But the buyer earns a 2 percent discount for paying the invoice just 20 days sooner than it should be paid anyway. By not taking the discount, the company in effect is borrowing at an annual rate of 36 percent. That is, assuming a 360-day year and dividing by 20 days, there are 18 periods during which the company could earn 2 percent—and 18 times 2 equals 36 percent a year.

Some customers pay over time

Some firms help buyers who cannot afford to pay for their products all at once by offering some form of installment plan. Installment involves making small payments over time—usually with interest payments built in. This approach has been used to open rural markets in the developing countries of Africa and Latin America to portable solar energy. Many of these rural villages are located off the electric grid and rely on kerosene lamps for light. Kerosene isn't a healthy or economic alternative to electricity—but until recently, many of these customers had little choice. When low-cost solar power first became available, these customers couldn't afford the $50 to $100 cost to install a small rooftop system. Then many solar suppliers developed installment plans. Customers might pay $10 for installation and then $1.50 a week (half the price of kerosene) for perhaps a year or two.

Leases lower the perceived price

Another example is cars. Many are leased—where consumers pay a monthly fee over a specified time period (usually three years). A monthly payment of $199 a month sounds more affordable to most consumers than buying the car for $21,495. Of course at the end of three years, the person leasing a car has to purchase it or return it, while the purchaser still owns the car.

Consumers say "charge it"

Credit sales are also important to retailers. Credit cards are the most common method for customers to pay over time. Retailers usually accept credit cards from services such as Visa or MasterCard and pay a percentage of the revenue from each credit sale for the service. Some retailers also have aggressive promotions to sign up customers for their own credit cards because customers who carry a store's credit card may spend more money at the store. Generous credit terms such as "no interest or payments for one full year" do stimulate sales. However, credit that is too easy exposes retailers to the risk of losses when the economy turns down.

Credit cards raise ethical and legal concerns

There are also ethical concerns about credit card companies and retailers that make it too easy for consumers to buy things they really can't afford. The problem becomes worse when an unpaid balance on a credit card carries a very high interest rate. This can significantly increase the price a consumer pays. Even worse, it leaves many low-income consumers trapped in debt.

College students have traditionally been a target market for credit cards—in part because credit card issuers covet customers who don't have any previous card loyalties. Of course many students also arrive at college with no job, no income, few assets, and a sparse credit report. Wooed with free food or gifts, many sign up for cards and return home with significant debt. The U.S. Congress passed the Credit CARD Act of 2009, which offers protections for college-aged students. Anyone younger than 21 must now have a cosigner or prove he or she can repay any debt.

Trade discounts are often set by tradition

A **trade (functional) discount** is a list price reduction given to channel members for the job they are going to do. A manufacturer, for example, might allow a retailer a 30 percent trade discount from the suggested retail list price to cover the cost of carrying inventory and providing knowledgeable salespeople to demonstrate the manufacturer's products. Similarly, the manufacturer might allow wholesalers a *chain* discount of 30 percent and 10 percent off the suggested retail price. In this case, the wholesalers would be expected to pass the 30 percent discount on to retailers.

Special sales reduce list prices—temporarily

A **sale price** is a temporary discount from the list price. Sale price discounts encourage immediate buying. In other words, to get the sale price, customers give up the convenience of buying when they want to buy and instead buy when the seller wants to sell.

Special sales provide a marketing manager with a quick way to respond to changing market conditions without changing the basic marketing strategy. For example, a retailer might use a sale to help clear extra inventory or to meet a competing store's price.

In recent years, sale prices and deals have become much more common. Some retailers have sales so often that consumers just wait to purchase when there's a sale. Others check out a website such as www.fatwallet.com to figure out where the product they want is already on sale. At first it may seem that consumers benefit from all this. But prices that change constantly erode brand loyalty.

To avoid these problems, some firms that sell consumer convenience products offer **everyday low pricing**—setting a low list price rather than relying on frequent sales, discounts, or allowances. Some supermarkets use this approach.

Sale prices should be used carefully, consistent with well-thought-out pricing objectives and policies. A marketing manager who constantly uses temporary sales to adjust the price level probably has not done a good job setting the normal price or creating a marketing mix that offers sustainable competitive advantage.

Allowance Policies—Off List Prices

Allowances, like discounts, are given to final consumers, business customers, or channel members for doing something or accepting less of something.

Advertising allowances—something for something

Advertising allowances are price reductions given to firms in the channel to encourage them to advertise or otherwise promote the supplier's products locally. For example, Sony might give an allowance (3 percent of sales) to its retailers. They, in turn, are expected to spend the allowance on local advertising.

Stocking allowances—get attention and shelf space

Stocking allowances—sometimes called *slotting allowances*[10]—are given to an intermediary to get shelf space for a product. For example, a producer might offer a retailer cash or free merchandise to stock a new item. Stocking allowances are commonly used to get supermarket chains to handle new products. Supermarkets are more willing to give space to a new product if the supplier will offset their handling costs and risks. With a big stocking allowance, the intermediary makes extra profit—even if a new product fails and the producer loses money.

PMs—push for cash

Push money[11] **(or prize money) allowances**—sometimes called *PMs* or *spiffs*—are given to retailers by manufacturers or wholesalers to pass on to the retailers' salesclerks for aggressively selling certain items. PM allowances are used for new items, slower-moving items, or higher-margin items. They are often used for pushing furniture, clothing, consumer electronics, and cosmetics. A salesclerk, for example, might earn an additional $5 for each new model Panasonic DVD player sold.

Bring in the old, ring up the new—with trade-ins

A **trade-in allowance**[12] is a price reduction given for used products when similar new products are bought. Trade-ins give the marketing manager an easy way to lower the effective price without reducing list price. Sometimes producers want to get older products off the market or move them to a new market. Apple offered trade-in incentives for its iPhones and shipped the older models to developing countries that could not afford the higher price of a new phone.

Some Customers Get Something Extra

Coupons—more for less

Many producers and retailers offer discounts (or free items) through coupons distributed in packages, mailings, print ads, at the store, or online. By presenting a coupon to a retailer, the consumer is given a discount off list price. The fastest-growing distribution approach is online—where consumers can search for coupons and print them out, send them to their cell phone, or directly add them to their store loyalty card. This is especially common in the consumer packaged goods business—but the use of price-off coupons is also growing in other lines of business.

Retailers are willing to redeem[13] producers' coupons because it increases their sales and they usually are paid for the trouble of handling the coupons. For example, a retailer that redeems a 50 cents off coupon might be repaid 75 cents.

Rebates—cash back

Some firms offer **rebates**—refunds paid to consumers after a purchase. Sometimes the rebate is very large. Some automakers offer rebates of $500 to $6,000 to promote sales of slow-moving models. Rebates are also used on lower-priced items, ranging from Duracell batteries to Logitech webcams and Paul Masson wines. Rebates give a producer a way to be certain that final consumers actually get the price reduction. If the rebate amount were just taken off the price charged to intermediaries, they might not pass the savings along to consumers.

But rebates have their critics. Although rebates prompt many consumers to make a purchase, many rebates—even high-value rebates—are never redeemed. A few years ago

TiVo offered a $100 holiday season rebate, but half of the consumers eligible failed to even request their rebate. For many customers the paperwork and hassle deter them; others simply forget after they leave the store. The growing consumer backlash[14] against rebates and the threat of government regulation have prompted many firms to drop rebates from their marketing strategies.

Coupons, deals, and rebates can segment the market

Coupons, deals, and rebates can help marketing managers attract new customers or move customers who are interested in a product to take action and buy. However, many marketing managers want to sell not only to customers looking for a bargain but also to customers willing to pay full price. But it's hard for a firm to appeal to both groups with the same price. For instance, if a firm persists in offering only higher prices, then sales are lost to the price-sensitive customer who wants only the lowest price. On the other hand, if a firm lowers its prices to appeal to the bargain hunters, then profits will be low from all customers—even those willing to pay a higher price.

To appeal to both groups and maximize profits, many firms now offer a variety of coupons, deals, and rebates. These discounts are an effective way to segment the market. For example, bargain hunters are willing to spend the time and energy necessary to find discounts—before purchasing the firm's products—and probably would not purchase without them. This makes the discounts a useful part of the price equation for these shoppers. But other customers will still pay full price because they value the whole marketing mix. They don't need the added incentive of a deal and won't look for the discounts. As a result, a marketing manager can increase total profits by segmenting the market and targeting each group separately.

Ethical Dilemma

What would you do? A pricing consultant has suggested that your firm set a premium price for the paper-shredding machines it sells through office equipment stores—but that there be a $20 mail-in rebate with each unit. The consultant says his research shows that, when an office shredder[15] wears out, it's usually the administrative assistant who is sent to buy a replacement. The consultant says that many of these buyers will pick your firm's shredder, in spite of the higher price, so that they can pocket the rebate. At the end of his report he says, "This is an accepted way to motivate the decision maker. Think about all those executives who rack up frequent-flier miles on business trips and then use the free tickets they get for family vacations." Your boss has left the decision up to you.

Would you follow the consultant's advice? Why or why not?

List Price May Depend on Geographic Pricing Policies

Retail list prices sometimes include free delivery. Or free delivery may be offered to some customers as an aid to closing the sale. But deciding who pays the freight charge is more important on sales to business customers than to final consumers because more money is involved. Purchase orders usually specify place, time, method of delivery, freight costs, insurance, handling, and other charges. There are many possible variations for an imaginative marketing manager, and some specialized terms have developed.

F.O.B. pricing is easy

A commonly used transportation term is **F.O.B.**—which means "free on board" some vehicle at some place. Typically a location is associated with F.O.B. and often the terms *F.O.B. shipping point* or *F.O.B. destination* are used. Whatever place is listed refers to the point where title (ownership) passes from the seller to the buyer.

F.O.B. shipping point means that the buyer owns the product as soon as it is loaded onto a vehicle at the seller's point of shipment (perhaps its warehouse). The buyer then pays the cost of shipping, insurance, and other costs from the point of shipping. When something is shipped *F.O.B. destination,* the buyer owns the product when it is delivered.

The seller has responsibility for shipping costs and any damage that might occur in shipping.

F.O.B. shipping point pricing simplifies the seller's pricing, but it may narrow the market. Because the delivered cost varies depending on the buyer's location, a customer located farther from the seller must pay more and might buy from suppliers with lower shipping costs.

Zone pricing smooths delivered prices

Zone pricing means making an average freight charge to all buyers within specific geographic areas. The seller pays the actual freight charges and bills each customer for an average charge. For example, a company in Canada might divide the United States into seven zones, then bill all customers in the same zone the same amount for freight even though actual shipping costs might vary.

Zone pricing reduces the wide variation in delivered prices that results from an F.O.B. shipping point pricing policy. It also simplifies transportation charges.

Uniform delivered pricing—one price to all

Uniform delivered pricing means making an average freight charge to all buyers. It is a kind of zone pricing—an entire country may be considered as one zone—that includes the average cost of delivery in the price. Uniform delivered pricing is most often used when (1) transportation costs are relatively low and (2) the seller wishes to sell in all geographic areas at one price, perhaps a nationally advertised price.

Freight-absorption pricing—competing on equal ground in another territory

When all firms in an industry use F.O.B. shipping point pricing, a firm usually competes well near its shipping point but not farther away. As sales reps look for business farther away, delivered prices rise and the firm finds itself priced out of the market.

This problem can be reduced with **freight-absorption pricing**—which means absorbing freight cost so that a firm's delivered price meets that of the nearest competitor. This amounts to cutting list price to appeal to new market segments. Some firms look at international markets this way; they just figure that any profit from export sales is a bonus.

Pricing Policies Combine to Impact Customer Value

Look at Price from the customer's viewpoint

We've discussed pricing policies separately so far, but from the customer's view they all combine to impact customer value. So when we talk about Price we are really talking about the whole set of price policies that define the real price level. On the other hand, superior value isn't just based on having a lower price than some competitor but rather on the whole marketing mix.

Value pricing leads to superior customer value

Smart marketers look for the combination of Price decisions that results in value pricing. **Value pricing** means setting a fair price level for a marketing mix that really gives the target market superior customer value.

Value pricing doesn't necessarily mean cheap if cheap means bare-bones or low-grade. It doesn't mean high prestige either if the prestige is not accompanied by the right quality goods and services. Rather, the focus is on the customer's requirements and how the whole marketing mix meets those needs.

Honda is a firm that has been effective with value pricing. It has different marketing mixes for different target markets. From the $15,000 Fit to the $36,000 S2000 Roadster and $40,000 four-wheel-drive Pilot, Honda offers high quality at reasonable prices. Among fast-food restaurants, Wendy's was one of the first to create a Dollar Menu. This has helped give it a reputation for value pricing.

Companies that use value pricing deliver on their promises. They try to give the consumer pleasant surprises—like an unexpected service—because it increases value and builds customer loyalty. They return the price if the customer isn't completely satisfied. They avoid unrealistic price levels—prices that are high only because consumers already know the brand name. They build relationships so customers will come back time and again.

There are Price choices in most markets

Some marketing managers miss the advantages of value pricing. They've heard economists say that in perfect competition it's foolish to offer products above or below the market price. But most firms *don't* operate in perfect competition where what firms offer is exactly the same.

Most operate in monopolistic competition, where products and whole marketing mixes are *not* exactly the same. This means that there are pricing options. At one extreme, some firms are clearly above the market—they may even brag about it. Tiffany's is well known as one of the most expensive jewelry stores in the world. Other firms emphasize below-the-market prices in their marketing mixes. Prices offered by discounters and mass-merchandisers, such as Walmart and Tesco, illustrate this approach. They may even promote their pricing policy with catchy slogans such as "guaranteed lowest prices."

Value pricers define the target market and the competition

In making price decisions and using value pricing, it is important to clearly define the *relevant target market* and *competitors* when making price comparisons.

Consider Walmart prices again from this view. Walmart may have lower prices on electronics products such as flat-panel televisions, but it offers less expertise from the store's sales staff, less selection, and no help installing or setting up a new television. Walmart may appeal to budget-oriented shoppers who compare prices *and* value among different mass-merchandisers. But a specialty electronics store appeals to different customers and may not even be a direct competitor!

A producer of flat-panel televisions with this point of view may offer the specialty electronics store models that are not available to Walmart—to ensure that customers don't view price as the only difference between the two stores. Further, the specialty store needs to clearly communicate to its target market *how* it offers superior value. Walmart is certainly going to communicate that it offers low prices. If that's all customers hear, they will see no differences between retailers except for price. The specialty retailer must emphasize its expertise, selection, or the superior performance of its product line—so that target customers who value these differences know where to find them.

Meeting competitors' prices may be necessary

In a mature market there is downward pressure on both prices and profit margins. Moreover, differentiating the value a firm offers may not be easy when competitors can quickly copy new ideas. Extending our flat-panel example, if our speciality store is in a city with a number of similar stores with the same products, there may not be a way to convince consumers that one beats all of the others. In such circumstances there may be no real pricing choice other than to "meet the competition." With profit margins already thin, they would quickly disappear or turn into losses at a lower price. And a higher price would simply prompt competitors to promote their price advantage.

Often little choice on price in oligopoly situations

There may be little choice about Price in oligopoly situations. Pricing at the market—that is, meeting competition—may be the only sensible policy. To raise prices might lead to a large loss in sales, unless competitors adopt the higher price too. And cutting prices would probably lead to similar reductions by competitors—downward along an inelastic industry demand curve. This can lead only to a decrease in total revenue for the industry and probably for each firm. The major airlines faced these problems recently.

Differentiation earns a price premium

Even though competition can be intense, too many marketers give up too easily. They simply price their product the same as a competitor. There often is a way to differentiate their product, even if it is something that competitors dismiss as less important. Creative brands differentiate and charge a higher price to reflect the additional value customers place on the differentiation. The value customers perceive can be measured as *price premium*; that is, the percentage by which a price exceeds (or falls short of) a benchmark price. The benchmark price may vary, but it usually represents some measure of the average price of all competitors in the market.

Price and customer perceptions of quality

Prices also influence how customers view quality. Without other information, most customers associate higher prices with a higher-quality product. Marketing managers should be aware that charging lower prices than competitors might have a detrimental effect on how customers view relative product quality.

Online glasses retailer Warby Parker considered this issue when starting up. The first business plan called for selling eyeglasses that typically cost $500 for less than $50. Warby Parker figured it could be profitable at that price. However, upon reflection, Warby Parker's founders worried that the dramatic price gap might adversely affect customer perceptions of its product quality and optical-related services. Sure enough, research showed Warby Parker that prices below about $100 raised customer suspicions about the quality. So it priced its glasses at $95. It used some of the extra margin to offer better service. For example, it created a "Home Try-On Program" that allows customers to request up to five frames, try them on for five days, and then return the frames, all at no cost to the customer. Even with online rivals such as Zenni Optical and GlassesUSA.com charging half of Warby Parker's prices, Warby Parker continues to capture customers' trust, and consequently, prosper.

Value pricing fits with market-oriented strategy planning

There are times when the marketing manager's hands are tied and there is little that can be done to differentiate the marketing mix. However, most marketing managers do have choices—many choices. They can vary strategy decisions with respect to all of the marketing mix variables, not just Price, to offer target customers superior value. And when a marketer's hands are really tied, it's time to look for new opportunities that offer more promise.

Value can have societal and ethical dimensions

Value is a subjective appraisal. It may differ for each person. This can be more complicated when society has to pay part of the "price." This can be the case for many projects where the government is involved. For example, is it a good investment to build a new interstate highway or build a new school? All taxpayers contribute, but only some benefit.

The issue is the same for health care—especially because Medicare and Medicaid are government programs that pay for the health care of many older U.S. citizens. With an aging population and rising health care costs, value is becoming a growing concern in the health care debate. The breakthrough innovations in health care have costs and benefits that create challenges for a society deciding how they should be valued. Read more about this complicated value issue in *What's Next?* Putting a price (and value) on life.

Legality of Pricing Policies

This chapter discusses the many pricing decisions that must be made. However, some pricing decisions are limited by government legislation. The first step to understanding pricing legislation is to know the thinking of legislators and the courts. Our focus will be on U.S. legislation but most countries have similar laws. Still, marketing managers may find that some countries have more restrictive laws. Intel was fined $1.45 billion by European regulators for price discounting practices that were used to keep competitors out of the market.

Minimum prices are sometimes controlled

Unfair trade practice acts put a lower limit on prices, especially at the wholesale and retail levels. They have been passed in more than half the states in the United States. Selling below cost in these states is illegal. Wholesalers and retailers are usually required to take a certain minimum percentage markup over their merchandise-plus-transportation costs. The practical effect of these laws is to protect certain limited-line food retailers—such as dairy stores—from the kind of "ruinous" competition supermarkets might offer if they sold milk as a leader, offering it below cost for a long time.

What's Next? Putting a price (and value) on life

What is the value of one more day of life? One more month? One more year? These are the difficult decisions that doctors, patients, and public policy makers must make. Life-extending medical treatments can be very expensive, and although the costs are borne partly by patients, most of the cost falls on insurance companies and governments. As the United States gets older, health care expenses are rising. Decisions about the value of a day, month, or year may be *What's Next?* for lawmakers and voters.

A few years ago, doctors at Memorial Sloan-Kettering Cancer Center made a big decision: it decided to boycott the colorectal cancer drug Zaltrap. The required three-month treatment with Zaltrap cost over $30,000—more than twice as much as an equally effective competitive treatment. Both drugs had similar side effects and offered patients an average of 42 more days of life. Deciding to remove a potentially life-extending medicine from doctors' options because of its cost was unheard of.

Perhaps this choice shouldn't have been a big deal. In most product-markets, an equally effective product costing twice as much has no value, so it would not even be brought to market. But this is the world of medicine. When faced with life-threatening conditions, patients and doctors prefer not to think about cost when deciding on treatment.

The question of "value" gets more complicated when no equivalent treatments exist. Consider Novartis' "miracle pill," Gleevec, that treats a rare cancer—chronic myeloid leukemia. With an 80 percent survival rate 10 years from diagnosis, Gleevec has no equally effective competitors. But an annual supply cost to patients (and their insurer) is $100,000—every year!

Gilead Science's Sovaldi is another breakthrough, boasting a 95 percent rate of *curing* hepatitis C. The cure costs $84,000; a daily dose for 12 weeks breaks down to $1,000 a pill. A less expensive competing treatment has severe side effects and doesn't cure as many patients. Gilead claims that its cure *saves* the health care system in the long run; patients cured of hepatitis C will never experience—and the health care system won't incur the cost of—the longer-term tolls of this disease, which include liver scarring, cirrhosis, cancer, and organ failure.

Drug companies invest hundreds of millions of dollars in research, development, and in bringing a new product to market. Many new-product efforts fail along the way. High prices cover those costs and ensure future breakthroughs. Critics wonder if these companies are taking advantage of their situation. They wonder if the price justifies the value to both the individual and to society—which ends up paying much of the cost.

This is a What's Next? *that no one wants to face. But in the end, someone has to pay for breakthrough drugs. What do you think? Are the prices of these drugs fair? Do they deliver proportional value? How should a company determine prices for breakthrough drugs? Should society—because it pays through insurance and taxes—have a say about whether such drugs are covered by insurance plans?*

The United States and most other countries control the minimum price of imported products with antidumping laws. **Dumping** is pricing a product sold in a foreign market below the cost of producing it or at a price lower than in its domestic market. These laws are usually designed to protect the country's domestic producers and jobs. U.S. steelmakers have accused China of dumping and encouraged the U.S. government to take action.

Regulators can set prices

In some industries, often where there is little competition, a state government may control prices. For example, many utilities—such as electric and gas—have little or no competition to keep prices in check, so states will usually have a board that governs the prices they charge. To ensure all citizens have access to affordable auto insurance, most states control auto insurance rates as well. Still, to maintain competition, there are several important regulations in the pricing area.

You can't lie about prices

Phony list prices[16] are prices customers are shown to suggest that the price has been discounted from list. Some customers seem more interested in the supposed discount than in the actual price. Most businesses, trade associations, and government agencies consider the use of phony list prices unethical. In the United States, the FTC tries to stop such pricing—using the **Wheeler Lea Amendment**, which bans "unfair or deceptive acts in commerce."

A few years ago, some electronics retailers were criticized on these grounds. They'd advertise a $300 discount on a computer when the customer signed up for an Internet service provider, but it might not be clear to the consumer that a three-year commitment—costing more than $700—was required.

Price fixing is illegal—you can go to jail

Difficulties with pricing—and violations of pricing legislation—usually occur when competing marketing mixes are quite similar. When the success of an entire marketing strategy depends on price, there is pressure (and temptation) to make agreements with competitors (conspire). And **price fixing**—competitors getting together to raise, lower, or stabilize prices—is common and relatively easy. *But it is also completely illegal in the United States.* It is considered "conspiracy" under the Sherman Act and the Federal Trade Commission Act. To discourage price fixing, both companies and individual managers are held responsible. In a recent case, an executive at Archer Daniels Midland (ADM) Company was sentenced to three years in jail and the company was fined $100 million.

Different countries have different rules concerning price fixing, and this has created problems in international trade. Japan, for example, allows price fixing, especially if it strengthens the position of Japanese producers in world markets.

Producers may set minimum retail prices

Manufacturers usually suggest a retail list price and then leave it up to retailers to decide what to charge in their local markets. In fact, until recently the courts prohibited manufacturers from imposing a minimum price at which their goods could be sold. This was viewed as a form of price fixing and a violation of the Sherman Antitrust Act. However, the ruling in a recent Supreme Court case changes that. The case involved Leegin Creative Leather Products and Kay's Kloset, a retailer that had been discounting Leegin's handbags. To prevent the discounting, Leegin stopped selling to Kay's Kloset. Kay's Kloset brought suit and said that retailers should be free to set their own prices—which, in turn, would keep prices lower for consumers. However, Leegin argued that its strategy focused on building the reputation of its brand with excellent service and advertising. Its retailers couldn't provide that level of service and promotion if they didn't charge a price that offered a sufficient profit margin. Leegin also argued that if one retailer ignored the strategy and cut its price on Leegin products, other retailers would follow suit—and soon the retailers wouldn't be able to provide the backing Leegin bags needed to compete. The court ruling, which supported Leegin, marks an important change because it gives manufacturers more power to control retail pricing.

U.S. antimonopoly laws ban price discrimination unless . . .

Price-level and price-flexibility policies can lead to price discrimination. The **Robinson-Patman Act** (of 1936) makes illegal any **price discrimination**—selling the same products to different buyers at different prices—*if it injures competition.* The law does permit some price differences—but they must be based on (1) cost differences or (2) the need to meet competition. Both buyers and sellers are considered guilty if they know they're entering into discriminatory agreements.

What does "like grade and quality" mean?

Firms in businesses as varied as transportation services, book publishing, and auto parts have been charged with violations of the Robinson-Patman Act in recent, nationally publicized cases. Competitors who have been injured by a violation of the law have incentive to go to court because they can receive a settlement that is three times larger than the damage suffered.

The Robinson-Patman Act allows a marketing manager to charge different prices for similar products if they are *not* of "like grade and quality." But the FTC says that if the physical characteristics of a product are similar, then they are of like grade and quality. A landmark U.S. Supreme Court ruling against the Borden Company upheld the FTC's view that a well-known label *alone* does not make a product different from one with an unknown label. The company agreed that the canned milk it sold at different prices under different labels was basically the same.

But the FTC's victory in the Borden case was not complete. The U.S. Court of Appeals found no evidence of injury to competition and further noted that there could be no injury unless Borden's price differential exceeded the "recognized consumer appeal of the Borden label." How to measure "consumer appeal" was not spelled out, so producers who want to sell several brands—or dealer brands at lower prices than their main brand—probably should offer physical differences, and differences that are really useful.

©William D. Perreault, Jr., Ph.D.

Can cost analysis justify price differences?

The Robinson-Patman Act allows price differences if there are cost differences—say, for larger quantity shipments or because intermediaries take over some of the physical distribution functions. But justifying cost differences is a difficult job. And the justification must be developed *before* different prices are set. The seller can't wait until a competitor, disgruntled[17] customer, or the FTC brings a charge. At that point, it's too late.

Can you legally meet price cuts?

Under the Robinson-Patman Act, meeting a competitor's price is permitted as a defense in price discrimination cases. A major objective of antimonopoly laws is to protect competition, not competitors. And "meeting competition in good faith" still seems to be legal.

Special promotion allowances might not be allowed

Some firms violate the Robinson-Patman Act by providing push money, advertising allowances, and other promotion aids to some customers and not others. The act prohibits such special allowances, *unless they are made available to all customers on "proportionately equal" terms.*

How to avoid discriminating

Because price discrimination laws are complicated and penalties for violations heavy, many business managers follow the safest course by offering few or no quantity discounts and the same cost-based prices to *all* customers. This is *too* conservative a reaction. But when firms consider price differences, they may need a lawyer involved in the discussion!

CONCLUSION

The Price variable offers an alert marketing manager many possibilities for varying marketing mixes. This chapter began by discussing how a firm's pricing objectives may be oriented toward profit, sales, or maintaining the status quo. Clear pricing objectives help in making decisions about the firm's important pricing policies.

This chapter discussed the pros and cons of flexible pricing and some of the approaches that firms use to implement it. It also considered the initial price-level decision—skim the cream or penetration—that the marketing manager must make with new products at the introductory stage of their life cycle. We also discussed a variety of ways that marketing managers adjust the basic list price under different circumstances—by using different types of discounts, allowances, and transportation costs. These policies need to be clearly defined by the marketing manager.

The chapter described how the different components of price are traded off against the other marketing mix variables to create something of value for the customer. We also discussed value pricing and how to create a competitive advantage by offering customers superior value—which isn't the same as just offering lower and lower prices.

Pricing comes under greater scrutiny from the law than some other marketing mix variables. So it is important to understand key legal constraints that influence pricing decisions.

This chapter provided a foundation for understanding the objectives and policies that guide pricing decisions. This information provides input into the price-setting process, which we describe in greater detail in the following chapter when we look at both cost- and demand-oriented approaches to pricing.

JOYFUL MOMENT

I Never Work After Supper

A penny-pinching farmer didn't want his hired man to stop working. One morning, he told the farmhand, "It's such a nuisance to come in from the field, wash up for lunch and take time to eat. Why don't we save time and eat lunch now?"

The hired man agreed. The farmer's wife brought in some cold meat and fried potatoes, and the two men ate again.

When they had finished, the cheap farmer said, "While we're still at the table, let's have supper too." They were now served steak, boiled potatoes and mixed vegetables, and they ate once more.

"Now that the meals are out of the way," the farmer announced, "we can go out and work all day without interruption."

"Oh, no," the man answered. "I never work after supper."

WORDS AND EXPRESSIONS

1. **premium**: *n. /adj.* sum of money paid (regularly) for an insurance policy; reward; prize; bonus; addition to ordinary charges, price, etc. (like commission); of high quality 保险费；奖金；额外费用；优质的
   —We would like to see more premium gasoline provided in the market.
   我们希望市场上能提供更多的优质汽油。
2. **rebate**: *n./ vt./ vi.* to give a reduction in the price during a sale 回扣，折扣；打折扣
   —It goes against our principle to give rebate to our clients.
   给客户回扣有悖于我方原则。
3. **bluntly**: *adv.* (to say exactly what you think) without trying to be polite 直率地，不客气地，直言不讳地
   —She told me bluntly it was my own fault.
   她坦率地说那是我个人的错。
4. **haggle**: *v.* to argue about something before reaching an agreement, especially about the cost of something that you are buying 讨价还价
   —In many countries you have to haggle before you buy anything.
   在许多国家里买东西之前都得讨价还价。
5. **clunky**: *adj.* solid, heavy, and rather awkward 笨重的，老式的
   —At present, investments in the road system are based on clunky cost-benefit calculations.
   目前，道路系统投资还是基于古老的成本收益算法。
6. **elastic**: *adj.* able to be changed if the situation changes; not fixed 可伸缩的，灵活的
   —The new policy was sufficiently elastic to accommodate both views.
   新政策充分灵活地适用两种观点。
7. **cumulative quantity discount**: 累计数量折扣
   —Then we offer quantity discounts for larger orders.
   大量定购的话我们还有折扣。
8. **patronage**: *n.* the support and money given by someone to a person or a group such as a charity 资助，赞助，恩惠
   —I look forward to your continued support and patronage.
   我期待您继续支持，经常光顾。
9. **insulation**: *n.* a thick layer of a substance that keeps something warm, especially a building 隔热层，绝缘体
   —This can be counteracted only by very effective insulation.
   这只能用非常有效的绝缘来防止。
10. **slotting allowance** 安置补贴，货位补贴，上架费
    —The anti-monopoly law and the regulation of slotting allowance.
    反垄断法与上架费的法律规制。
11. **push money**: 提成，佣金
12. **trade-in allowance**: 旧货补贴，旧货折让折扣
13. **redeem**: *v.* to do something that makes people have a good opinion of you again after you have behaved or performed badly 挽回（声誉），补偿，弥补（过错）
    —He had realized the mistake he had made and wanted to redeem himself.
    他已经认识到了自己的错误，想要进行弥补。
14. **backlash**: *n.* a sudden, strong reaction against it 激烈的，强烈的反击，反弹
    —China's investment largesse also risks sparking a backlash.
    中国慷慨的投资也有激起反弹的风险。
15. **shredder**: 碎纸机
16. **phony list price**: 假目录价格
17. **disgruntled**: *adj.* unsatisfied 不满意的
    —It's inevitable that there will be the occasional disgruntled customer.
    偶尔会出现对你的服务不满意的客户，这是不可避免的。

EXERCISES

1. **Multiple choices**

(1) Which of the following items is not included in pricing objectives?

A. Profit-oriented objective. B. Flexible price-oriented objective.

C. Sales-oriented objective. D. Status quo-oriented objective.

(2) A ___ tries to sell the whole market at one low price especially when the elite market is small.

A. one-price policy B. flexible-price policy

C. skimming price policy D. penetration price policy

(3) The following statements concerning skimming price policy are correct EXCEPT ___.

A. skimming policy tries to sell the top of a market at a high price

B. skimming policy may maximize profits in the market introduction stage for an innovation

C. skimming policy is useful when you know very much about the shape of the demand curve

D. skimming policy usually involves a slow reduction in price over time

(4) Service firms that face irregular demand or excess capacity often use ___.

A. seasonal discount B. cash discount

C. cumulative quantity discount D. noncumulative quantity discount

(5) ___ are given to an intermediary to get shelf space for a product.

A. Push money B. Stocking allowances

C. Trade-in allowances D. Slotting allowances

2. Terms translation

(1) target return objective (2) one-price policy (3) penetration pricing policy (4) basic list prices
(5) allowances (6) quantity discounts (7) trade-in allowances (8) push money/prize money
(9) coupons (10) advertising allowances

3. True or false

(1) Pricing to achieve profit maximization doesn't always lead to high prices. ______

(2) A larger market share, if gained at too high a price, may lead to profitless "success." ______

(3) High market share offers economies of scale and negotiating power with suppliers. ______

(4) A skimming pricing policy is even more attractive if selling larger quantities results in lower costs because of economies of scale. ______

(5) There are two kinds of quantity discounts: cumulative and noncumulative. ______

(6) College students have traditionally been a target market for credit cards. ______

(7) In a mature market there is downward pressure on both prices and profit margins. ______

(8) Price fixing is illegal and considered to be "conspiracy" in the United States as well as in Japan. ______

(9) A major objective of antimonopoly laws is to protect competitors, not competition. ______

(10) There is little competition in some industries, for example, many utilities where a state government may control prices. ______

4. Fill in the blanks

(1) Almost every business transaction in our modern economy involves an exchange of money—__________—for something.

(2) Price has many dimensions. How each of these dimensions is handled affects __________.

(3) HP, Dell, and Acer have waged pricing battles in an effort to gain __________ in the personal computer market.

(4) __________ is most common in the channels, in direct sales of business products, and at retail for expensive shopping products.

(5) __________ encourage repeat buying by reducing the customer's cost for additional purchases.

(6) Many producers and retailers offer discount through __________ distributed in packages, mailings, print ads, at the store, or online.

(7) __________ give a producer a way to be certain that final consumers actually get the price reduction.

(8) Most firms operate in __________ competition, where products and whole marketing mixes are not exactly the same.

(9) __________ is pricing a product sold in a foreign market below the cost of producing it or at a price lower than in its domestic market.

(10) Price level and price flexibility policies can lead to __________.

5. Answer the following questions

(1) Illustrate how profit-oriented objectives affect pricing policies.

(2) What should a marketing manager consider when setting the price level for a product in the early stages of the product life circle?

(3) Why are cash discounts given and why should them be evaluated? Try to illustrate it using your own experience.

(4) How much do you know about allowance policies? Summarize them in brief.

(5) There are some important regulations in the pricing area to maintain competition, could you list some of them?

SUGGESTED CASES

13. Paper Products, Inc. (PPI) 17. Wise Water, Inc.

MARKETING ANALYTICS: DATA TO KNOWLEDGE

CHAPTER 9: CASH DISCOUNTS

Joe Tulkin owns Tulkin Wholesale Co. He sells paper, tape, file folders, and other office supplies to about 120 retailers in nearby cities. His average retailer-customer spends about $900 a month. When Tulkin started business in 1991, competing wholesalers were giving retailers invoice terms of 3/10, net 30. Tulkin never gave the issue much thought—he just used the same invoice terms when he billed customers. At that time, about half of his customers took the discount. Recently, he noticed a change in the way his customers were paying their bills. Checking his records, he found that 90 percent of the retailers were taking the cash discount. With so many retailers taking the cash discount, it seems to have become a price reduction. In addition, Tulkin learned that other wholesalers were changing their invoice terms.

Tulkin decides he should rethink his invoice terms. He knows he could change the percentage rate on the cash discount, the number of days the discount is offered, or the number of days before the face amount is due. Changing any of these, or any combination, will change the interest rate at which a buyer is, in effect, borrowing money if he does not take the discount. Tulkin decides that it will be easier to evaluate the effect of different invoice terms if he sets up a spreadsheet to let him change the terms and quickly see the effective interest rate for each change.

See Connect for the spreadsheet and questions needed to analyze this scenario.

10 CHAPTER TEN

Ethical Marketing in a Consumer-Oriented World: Appraisal[1] and Challenges

Although consumers want marketplace choice, we're not there yet globally. Someone in a rural village in Mozambique may catch a glimpse of the quality of life that consumers in advanced economies enjoy, but for that person this way of life may not seem real. What is real is the struggle of everyday life—living without electricity or running water—and perhaps worrying about malnutrition, disease, and hunger. Cell phone carriers see growth opportunities, even though average monthly billings are often less than $5 in some of the world's poorest countries. The vast majority of consumer-citizens in these societies still wonder if they'll ever have choices among a wide variety of goods and services—and the income to buy them—that most consumers in the United States, Canada, and other advanced economies take for granted.

The challenges faced by consumers and marketing managers in advanced economies seem minor by contrast. In England, for example, some consumers who live in villages that are off the beaten path instead may worry that they are not included in the 96 percent of the British population served by Tesco delivery vans. Tesco, the largest supermarket chain in England, created its online shopping service for groceries and other products just a few years ago, but now its fleet of vans makes hundreds of thousands of deliveries each week.

If shopping online for groceries has had a slower start in the United States, it may just be because many Americans are more interested in instant gratification. We expect the corner convenience store to have a selection of frozen gourmet dinners that we can prepare in minutes in our microwave ovens. Or if that's too much hassle, Domino's will deliver a hot pizza in less than 30 minutes—just tweet a pizza emoji. And Starbucks has our Caffè Latte ready when we pull up at the drive-through at 7:00 in the morning. Few of the world's consumers can expect and get so much of what they expect.

But is it a good thing that firms give us what we want? Think about how automakers offered SUVs to appeal to consumers. Although SUVs satisfy many of the needs of suburban lifestyles, most are gas guzzlers and pollute the air. On the other hand, when gas prices rose and consumer interest in the environment grew, producers responded with hybrid technologies and electric vehicles. A fleet of self-driving electric vehicles may be in our future—or we may not even own a car; instead we may simply call one to take us where we need to go. Of course, such adjustments take time.

Much national attention is now directed toward problems of obesity, especially among children. In the United States, more than a third of children and adolescents are overweight. The surge of obesity among children is a global trend. Nutritionists say that in the United States and elsewhere, the key culprits are too much fat, starch, and sugar in diets. World Health Organization experts say that today's levels of childhood obesity will lead to an explosion of illnesses (such as heart disease, type 2 diabetes, and hypertension), drain economies, create enormous suffering, and cause premature deaths. Many nutritionists and public health officials blame "big food"—processed food and fast food. When a group of overweight teens sued McDonald's, claiming that it made them fat, the widely publicized case was fodder for jokes on late-night TV shows. Although that suit went nowhere, some experts predict more lawsuits against fast food, drawing a parallel with the lawsuits against tobacco companies 30 years ago.

In some places, regulation nudges consumer behavior; for example, France and San Francisco have recently initiated a "soda tax" on sugary drinks. Should consumers have the right to choose high-calorie or high-fat foods if that's what they want? Should they pay more for their choices? And what if their choices raise health care costs for others?

When you think about the contrast between problems of starvation and too much fast food, it's not hard to decide which consumers are better off. But is that just a straw man comparison? Is the situation in less-developed nations one extreme, with the system in the United States and similar societies just as extreme—only in a different way?

And what about companies that gather data on consumers? In Western countries, the modern digital world allows firms to collect a great deal of customer data; they analyze those data using artificial intelligence to offer highly targeted products and promotions. Does this bring better products? Lead to less wasted promotion? And ensure that consumers see only advertising that interests them? Or is this an invasion of privacy? Will it lead to some consumers paying more while other, perhaps more "desirable," customers get all the good deals? Marketing managers and public policy makers must wrestle with these issues—and consumers must make sure their voices are heard, too.

Would society be better off if it didn't put quite so much emphasis on marketing? Do we need so many brands of products? Does all the money we spend on advertising really help consumers? It does keep the cost of television, the Internet, and other media low. Should we expect access to fast food any hour of the day—or to order groceries over the Internet and have a van deliver them to our front door? Conversely, do all these choices just increase the prices consumers pay without adding anything of value? More generally, does marketing serve society well?

We'll discuss these questions in this chapter. Now that you have a better understanding of what marketing is all about, and how the marketing manager contributes to the macro-marketing process, you should be able to decide whether marketing costs too much.

LEARNING OBJECTIVES

Throughout the text, we've discussed ways that marketing can help customers while also meeting a firm's objectives. We've also considered many related ethical and societal questions. In this chapter, we evaluate the overall costs and benefits of marketing to society. This leads into an explanation of how to prepare a marketing plan—because the marketing plan integrates all of the decisions in the marketing strategy planning process and thus guides the firm toward more effective marketing.

When you finish this chapter, you should be able to

1. understand why marketing must be evaluated differently at the micro and macro levels.
2. understand why this text argues that micro-marketing costs too much.
3. understand why this text argues that macro-marketing does not cost too much.
4. understand all of the elements of the marketing strategy planning process and strategy decisions for the Four Ps.
5. know how to prepare a marketing plan and how it relates to the marketing strategy planning process.
6. know some of the challenges marketers face as they work to develop ethical marketing strategies that serve consumers' needs.

How Should Marketing Be Evaluated?

We must evaluate at two levels

We've stressed the need for marketing to satisfy customers at a cost that customers consider a good value. So in this final chapter we'll focus on both customer satisfaction and the costs of marketing as we evaluate marketing's impact on society (Exhibit 10-1). As we discussed in Chapter 1, it's useful to distinguish between two levels of marketing. Managerial (micro) marketing concerns the marketing activities of an individual firm, whereas macro-marketing concerns how the whole marketing system works. Some complaints against marketing are aimed at only one of these levels at a time. In other cases, the criticisms seem to be directed to one level but actually are aimed at the other. Some critics of specific ads, for example, probably would not be satisfied with any advertising. When evaluating marketing, we must treat each of these levels separately.

Nation's objectives affect evaluation

Different nations have different social and economic objectives. Dictatorships, for example, may be mainly concerned with satisfying the needs of society as seen by the political elite. In some societies, the objectives are defined by religious leaders. In others, it's whoever controls the military.

Exhibit 10-1 Ethical Marketing in a Consumer-Oriented World

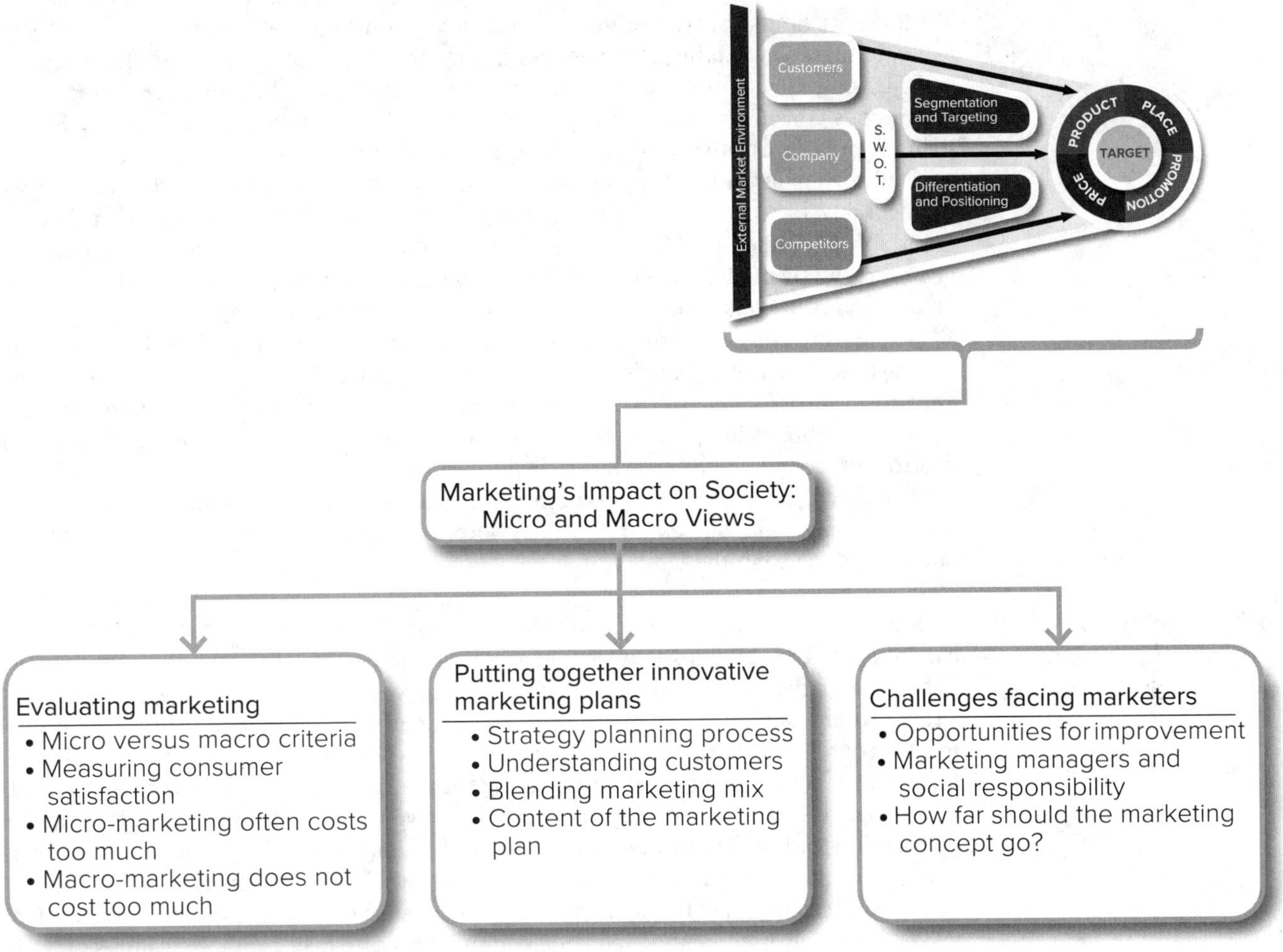

Consumer satisfaction is the objective in the United States

In the United States, *the basic objective of our market-directed economic system has been to satisfy consumer needs as they, the consumers, see them.* This objective implies that political freedom and economic freedom go hand in hand and that citizens in a free society have the right to live as they choose. The majority of American consumers would be unwilling to give up the freedom of choice they now enjoy. The same can be said for Canada, Great Britain, and most other countries in the European Union. To maintain focus, we will concentrate on marketing as it exists in American society.

Therefore, let's try to evaluate the operation of marketing in the American economy—where the present objective is to satisfy consumer needs *as consumers see them.* This is the essence of our system.

Can Consumer Satisfaction Be Measured?

Because consumer satisfaction is our objective, marketing's effectiveness must be measured by *how well* it satisfies consumers. There have been various efforts to measure overall consumer satisfaction—not only in the United States but also in other countries. For example, a team of researchers at the University of Michigan has created the American Customer Satisfaction Index based on regular interviews with tens of thousands of customers of about 230 companies in 43 industries. Similar studies are available for member countries of the European Union.

Satisfaction depends on individual aspirations

This sort of index makes it possible to track changes in consumer satisfaction measures over time and even allows comparison among countries. That's potentially useful. Yet there are limits to interpreting any measure of consumer satisfaction when we try to evaluate macro-marketing effectiveness in any absolute sense. One basic issue is that satisfaction depends on and is *relative to* your level of aspiration or expectation. Less prosperous consumers begin to expect more out of an economy as they see the higher living standards of others. Also, aspiration levels tend to rise with repeated successes and fall with failures. Products considered satisfactory one day may not be satisfactory the next day, or vice versa. Thirty years ago, most people were satisfied with a 21-inch color TV that pulled in three or four channels. But once you become accustomed to a large-screen HD model and enjoy all the options possible with a digital satellite receiver, on-demand programs, and a DVR, that old TV is never the same again.

In addition, consumer satisfaction is a highly personal concept. Thus, looking at the "average" satisfaction of a whole society does not provide a complete picture for evaluating macro-marketing effectiveness. At a minimum, some consumers are more satisfied than others. So, although efforts to measure satisfaction are useful, any evaluation of macro-marketing effectiveness has to be in part subjective.

Probably the supreme test is whether the macro-marketing system satisfies enough individual consumer-citizens so that they vote–in the ballot box–to keep it running. So far, we've done so in the United States.

There are many measures of micro-marketing effectiveness

Measuring the marketing effectiveness of an individual firm is also difficult, but it can be done. Expectations may change just as other aspects of the market environment change–so firms have to do a good job of coping with the change. Individual business firms can and should try to measure how well their marketing mixes satisfy their customers (or why they fail). In fact, most large firms now have some type of ongoing effort to determine whether they're satisfying their target markets. For example, the J.D. Power and Associates marketing research firm is well known for its studies of consumer satisfaction with different makes of automobiles and computers. And the American Customer Satisfaction Index is also used to rate individual companies.

Many large and small firms measure customer satisfaction with attitude research studies. Other widely used methods include comment cards, e-mail response features on websites, unsolicited[2] consumer responses (usually complaints), opinions of intermediaries and salespeople, market test results, and profits. Of course, customers may be very satisfied with some aspects of what a firm is doing but dissatisfied about other dimensions of performance.

In our market-directed system, it's up to each customer to decide how effectively individual firms satisfy his or her needs. Usually, customers will buy more of the products that satisfy them–and they'll do it again and again. That's why firms that develop really satisfying marketing mixes are able to develop profitable long-term relationships with the customers that they serve. Because efficient marketing plans can increase profits, profits can be used as a rough measure of a firm's efficiency in satisfying customers. Nonprofit organizations have a different bottom line, but they too will fail if they don't satisfy supporters and get the resources they need to continue to operate.

Evaluating marketing effectiveness is difficult, but not impossible

It's easy to see why opinions differ concerning the effectiveness of micro- and macro-marketing. If the objective of the economy is clearly defined, however–and the argument is stripped of emotion–the big questions about marketing effectiveness probably *can* be answered.

In this chapter, we argue that micro-marketing (how individual firms and channels operate) frequently *does* cost too much but that macro-marketing (how the whole marketing system operates) *does not* cost too much, *given the present objective of the American economy–consumer satisfaction.* Don't accept this position as *the* answer but rather as a point of view. In the end, you'll have to make your own judgment.

Micro-Marketing Often Does Cost Too Much

Throughout the text, we've explored what marketing managers could or should do to help their firms do a better job of satisfying customers–while achieving company objectives. Many firms implement highly successful marketing programs, but others are still too production-oriented and inefficient. For customers of these latter firms, micro-marketing often does cost too much.

Research shows that many consumers are not satisfied; but you know that already. All of us have had experiences when we weren't satisfied–when some firm didn't deliver on its promises. And the problem is much bigger than some marketers want to believe. Research suggests that the majority of consumer complaints are never reported. Worse, many complaints that are reported never get fully resolved.

The failure rate is high

Further evidence that too many firms are too production-oriented–and not nearly as efficient as they could be–is the fact that so many new products fail. New and old businesses–even ones that in the past were leaders in their markets–fail regularly too.

Generally speaking, marketing inefficiencies are due to one or both of these reasons:

1. Lack of interest in or understanding of the sometimes fickle[3] customer.
2. Improper blending of the Four Ps–lack of understanding of or adjustment to the market environment, especially what competitors do.

Either of these problems can easily be a fatal flaw–the sort of thing that leads to business failures. A firm can't create value if it doesn't have a clue what customers think or say. Even if a firm listens to the "voice of the customer," there's no incentive for the customer to buy if the benefits of the marketing mix don't exceed the costs. And if the firm succeeds in coming up with a marketing mix with benefits greater than costs, it still won't be a superior value unless it's better than what competitors offer.

The high cost of missed opportunities

Another sign of failure is the inability of firms to identify new target markets and new opportunities. A new marketing mix that isn't offered doesn't fail–but the lost opportunity can be significant for both a firm and society. Too many managers seize on whatever strategy seems easiest rather than seeking really new ways to satisfy customers. Too many companies stifle[4] really innovative thinking. Layers of bureaucracy and a "that's not the way we do things" mentality can snuff it out[5].

On the other hand, not every new idea is a good idea for every company. Many firms have lost millions of dollars with failed efforts to jump on the "what's new" bandwagon–without stopping to figure out how it is going to really satisfy the customer and result in profit for the firm. That is as much a ticket for failure as being too slow or bureaucratic.

Ethical Dilemma

What would you do? Your firm has a new strategy that will make its established product obsolete. However, it will take a year before you are ready to implement the new strategy. If you announce your plan in advance, profits will disappear because many customers and intermediaries will delay purchases until the new product is released. If you don't announce the new plan, customers and intermediaries will continue to buy the established product as their needs dictate, but some will be stuck owning the inferior product and won't do business with you again in the future.

How would you handle this situation? Explain the reasoning for your decisions.

Micro-marketing does cost too much, but things are changing

For reasons like these, marketing does cost too much in many firms. Despite much publicity, the marketing concept is not applied in many places.

But not all firms and marketers deserve criticism. More of them *are* becoming customer-oriented. And many are paying more attention to market-oriented planning to carry out the marketing concept more effectively. Throughout the text, we've highlighted firms and strategies that are making a difference. The successes of innovative firms—such as Nike, Cirque du Soleil, Amazon.com, LEGO, Apple, iRobot, Method, and GEICO—do not go unnoticed. Yes, they make some mistakes. That's human—and marketing is a human enterprise. But they have also shown the results that market-oriented strategy planning can produce.

Another encouraging sign is that more companies are recognizing that they need a diverse set of backgrounds and talents to meet the increasingly varied needs of their increasingly global customers. They're shedding "not-invented-here" biases and embracing new technologies, comparing what they do with the best practices of firms in totally different industries, and teaming up with outside specialists who can bring a fresh perspective.

Managers who adopt the marketing concept as a way of business life do a better job. They look for target market opportunities and carefully blend the elements of the marketing mix to meet their customers' needs. As more of these managers rise in business, we can look forward to much lower micro-marketing costs and strategies that do a better job of satisfying customer needs.

Macro-Marketing Does Not Cost Too Much

Some critics of marketing take aim at the macro-marketing system. They typically argue that the macro-marketing system causes a poor use of resources and leads to an unfair distribution of income. Most of these complaints imply that some marketing activities by individual firms should not be permitted—and because they are, our macro-marketing system does a less-than-satisfactory job. Let's look at some of these positions to help you form your own opinion.

Micro-efforts help the economy grow

Some critics feel that marketing helps create a monopoly or at least monopolistic competition. Further, they think this leads to higher prices, restricted output, and reduction in national income and employment.

It's true that firms in a market-directed economy try to carve out separate monopolistic markets for themselves with new products. But consumers do have a choice. They don't *have* to buy the new product unless they think it's a better value. The old products are still available. In fact, to meet the new competition, prices of the old products usually drop. And that makes them even more affordable.

Over several years, the innovator's profits may rise—but rising profits also encourage further innovation by competitors. This leads to new investments, which contribute to economic growth and higher levels of national income and employment. Around the world, many countries failed to achieve their potential for economic growth under command systems because this type of profit incentive didn't exist.

Increased profits also attract competition. Profits and prices then begin to drop as new competitors enter the market and begin producing somewhat similar products.

Is advertising a waste of resources?

Advertising is the most criticized of all micro-marketing activities. Indeed, many ads *are* annoying, insulting, misleading, and downright ineffective. This is one reason why micro-marketing often does cost too much. However, advertising can also make both the micro- and macro-marketing processes work better.

Advertising is an economical way to inform large numbers of potential customers about a firm's products. Provided that a product satisfies customer needs, advertising can increase demand for the product—resulting in economies of scale in manufacturing, distribution, and sales. Because these economies may more than offset advertising costs, advertising can actually *lower* prices to the consumer.

Consumers are not puppets

The idea that firms can manipulate consumers to buy anything the company chooses to produce simply isn't true. A consumer who buys a soft drink that tastes terrible won't buy another can of that brand, regardless of how much it's advertised. In fact, many new products fail the test of the market. Not even large corporations are assured of success every time they launch a new product. Consider, for example, the dismal fate of Pets.com and eToys.com, Ford's Edsel, Sony's beta format VCRs, Xerox's personal computers, and half of the TV programs put on the air in recent years. And if powerful corporations know some way to get people to buy products against their will, would companies such as Lucent, General Motors, and Eastern Airlines ever have gone through long periods losing hundreds of millions of dollars?

Needs and wants change

Consumer needs and wants change constantly. Few of us would care to live the way our grandparents lived when they were our age. Marketing's job is not just to satisfy consumer wants as they exist at any particular point in time. Rather, marketing must keep looking for new *and* better ways to create.

Does marketing make people materialistic?

There is no doubt that marketing caters to materialistic values. However, people disagree as to whether marketing creates these values or simply appeals to values already there.

Even in the most primitive societies, people want to accumulate possessions. The tendency for ancient pharaohs[6] to surround themselves with wealth and treasures can hardly be attributed to the persuasive powers of advertising agencies!

Products do improve the quality of life

Clearly, the quality of life can't be measured just in terms of quantities of material goods. But when we view products as the means to an end rather than the end itself, they *do* make it possible to satisfy higher-level needs. The Internet, for example, empowers people with information in ways that few of us could have even imagined a few decades ago.

Marketing reflects our own values

Critics say that advertising elevates the wrong values–for example, by relying on sex appeal to get attention–and generally sending the signal that what really matters most is self-gratification[7]. For example, GoDaddy.com sells Internet domain names and related services. Its stated objective for a Super Bowl ad was to create the most talked about ad ever, and it figured that a risqué[8] ad was the way to go. The ad that it ultimately aired (after trying another dozen or so ideas that were rejected as inappropriate for TV) was a spoof on Janet Jackson's "wardrobe malfunction" during the Super Bowl halftime show the previous year. The sexy woman dancing around in the commercial doesn't have anything to do with GoDaddy.com, but she did get a lot of attention and GoDaddy's awareness levels went up significantly. A survey showed that it was one of the four most liked commercials during the Super Bowl and the year, but also one of the four most disliked. There are thousands of other ads that rely on something related to sex to get attention. But is it advertising that creates interest in sex or something else? Experts who study values seem to agree that, in the short run, marketing reflects social values while in the long run it enhances and reinforces them. Further, many companies work hard to figure out their customers' beliefs and values. Then they refuse to use ads that would be offensive to their target customers.

Not all needs are met

Some critics argue that our macro-marketing system is flawed because it does not provide solutions to important problems, such as questions about how to help people who are homeless or uneducated, dependent children, members of minorities who have suffered discrimination, elderly poor people, and those who are sick. Many of these people do live in dire[9] circumstances. But is that the result of a market-directed system?

There is no doubt that many firms focus their effort on people who can pay for what they have to offer. But, as the forces of competition drive down prices, more people are able to afford more of what they need. And the matching of supply and demand stimulates economic growth, creates jobs, and spreads income among more people. In other words, a market-directed economy makes efficient use of resources. However, it can't guarantee that government aid programs are effective. It doesn't ensure that all voters and politicians agree on which problems should be solved first–or how taxes should be set and allocated. It can't eliminate the possibility of a child being ignored.

These are important societal issues. Consumer-citizens in a democratic society assign some responsibilities to business and some to government. Ultimately, consumer-citizens vote via the ballot box for how they want governments to deal with these concerns–just as they vote with their dollars for which firms to support. As more managers in the public sector understand and apply marketing concepts, we should be able to do a better job meeting the needs of all people.

Marketing Strategy Planning Process Requires Logic and Creativity

We've said that our macro-marketing system *does not* cost too much, given that customer satisfaction is the present objective of our economy. But we admit that the performance of many business firms leaves a lot to be desired. This presents a challenge to serious-minded students and marketers–and raises the question: What needs to be done?

We hope that this book has convinced you that a large part of the answer to that question is that the *effectiveness and value of marketing efforts in individual firms is improved significantly when managers take the marketing concept seriously–and when they apply the marketing strategy planning process we've presented.* So let's briefly review these ideas and show how they can be integrated into a marketing plan.

Marketing strategy planning process brings focus to efforts

Developing a good marketing strategy and turning the strategy into a marketing plan requires creative blending of the ideas we've discussed throughout this text. Exhibit 10-2 provides a broad overview of the major areas we've been talking about. Now we must integrate ideas about these different areas to narrow down to a specific target market and marketing mix that represents a real opportunity. This narrowing-down process requires a thorough understanding of the market. That understanding is enhanced by careful analysis of customers' needs, current or prospective competitors, and the firm's own objectives and resources. Similarly, trends in the external market environment may make a potential opportunity more or less attractive.

There are usually more different strategy possibilities than a firm can pursue. Each possible strategy usually has a number of different potential advantages and disadvantages. This can make it difficult to zero in on the best target market and marketing mix. However, as we discussed in Chapter 2, developing a set of specific qualitative and quantitative screening criteria–to define what business and market(s) the firm wants to compete in–can help eliminate potential strategies that are not well suited to the firm.

Careful analysis helps the manager focus on a strategy that takes advantage of the firm's strengths and opportunities while avoiding its weaknesses and threats to its suc-

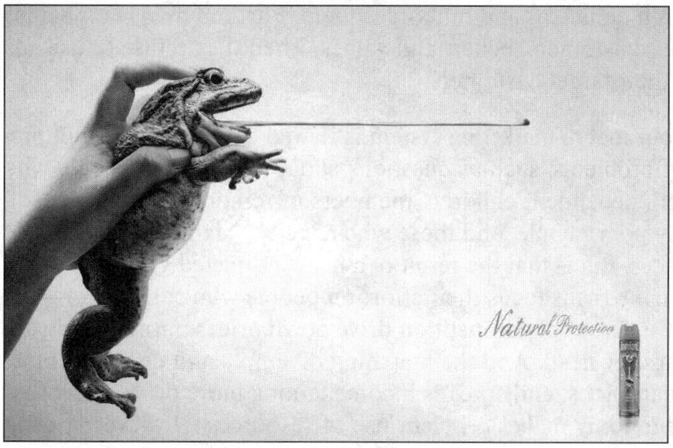

Micro-marketing does not cost too much when firms understand and address customer needs and wants with an effective marketing mix. Because some customers prefer not to use dangerous chemicals on their skin to keep bugs and mosquitoes away, Shieldtox Naturgard uses natural ingredients to offer continuous control of flying insects. Saridon's clever advertising reminds customers that its tablets are a good way to manage a headache.
Left: Source: Reckitt Benckiser Group plc.; Right: Source: Saridon

Exhibit 10-2 Overview of Marketing Strategy Planning Process

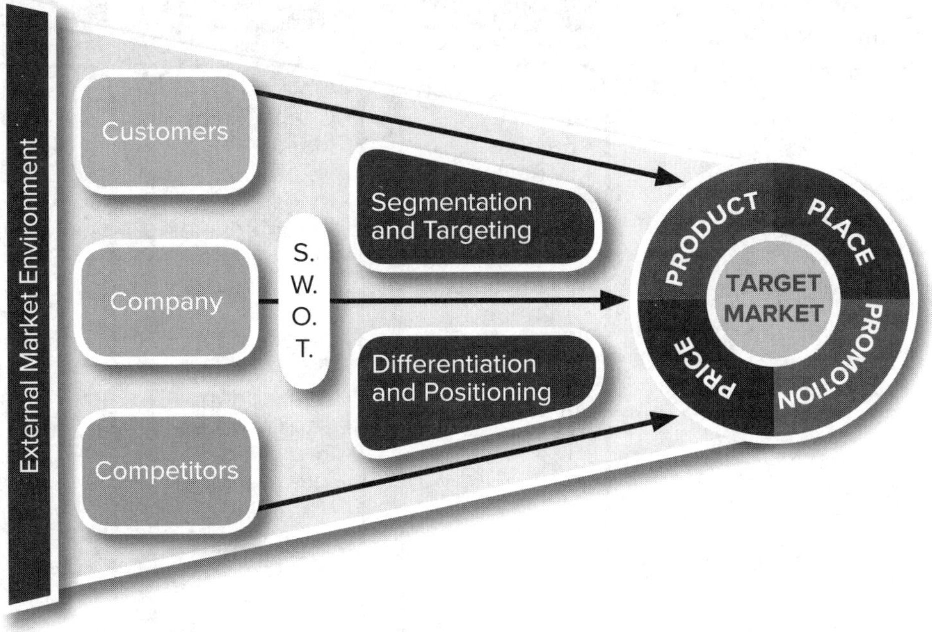

cess. These strengths and weaknesses can be compared with the pros and cons of strategies that are considered. For example, if a firm is considering a strategy that focuses on a target market that is already satisfied by a competitor's offering, finding a competitive advantage might require an innovative new product, improved distribution, more effective promotion, or a better price. Just offering a marketing mix similar to the competition's usually doesn't provide any real basis for the firm to position or differentiate its marketing mix as offering superior customer value.

Marketing manager must blend the Four Ps

Exhibit 10-3 reviews the major marketing strategy decision areas organized by the Four Ps. Each of these requires careful decision making. Yet marketing planning involves much more than just independent decisions and assembling the parts into a marketing mix. The Four Ps must be creatively *blended*—so the firm develops the best mix for its target market. In other words, each decision must work well with all of the others to make a logical whole.

In our discussion, we've given the job of integrating the Four Ps strategy decisions to the marketing manager. Now you should see the need for this integrating role. It is easy for specialists to focus on their own areas and expect the rest of the company to work for or around them. This is especially true in larger firms where the size of the whole marketing job is too big for one person. Yet the ideas of the product manager, the advertising manager, the sales manager, the logistics manager, and whoever makes pricing decisions may have to be adjusted to improve the whole mix. It's critical that each marketing mix decision work well with all of the others. A breakdown in any one decision area may doom the whole strategy to failure.

The Marketing Plan Brings All the Details Together

Marketing plan provides a blueprint for implementation

Once the manager has selected the target market, decided on the (integrated) marketing mix to meet that target market's needs, and developed estimates of the costs and revenues for that strategy, it's time to put it all together in the marketing plan. Thus, the plan basically serves as a blueprint for what the firm will do.

Exhibit 10-4 provides a summary outline of the different sections of a complete marketing plan. You can see that this outline is basically an abridged overview of the topics we've covered throughout the text. Thus, you can flesh out your thinking for any portion of a marketing plan by reviewing the section of the book where that topic is discussed in more detail.

Exhibit 10-3 Strategy Decision Areas Organized by the Four Ps

Product

- Physical good
- Service
- Features
- Benefits
- Quality level
- Accessories
- Installation
- Instructions
- Warranty
- Product lines
- Packaging
- Branding

Place

- Objectives
- Channel type
- Market exposure
- Kinds of intermediaries
- Kinds and locations of stores
- How to handle transporting and storing
- Service levels
- Recruiting intermediaries
- Managing channels

Promotion

- Objectives
- Promotion blend
- Salespeople
  - Kind
  - Number
  - Selection
  - Training
  - Motivation
- Advertising
  - Targets
  - Kinds of ads
  - Media type
  - Copy thrust
  - Prepared by whom
- Publicity
- Sales promotion

Price

- Objectives
- Flexibility
- Level over product life cycle
- Geographic terms
- Discounts
- Allowances

Marketing plan spells out the timing of the strategy

Some time schedule is implicit in any strategy. A marketing plan simply spells out this time period and the time-related details. Usually, we think in terms of some reasonable length of time—such as six months, a year, or a few years. But it might be only a month or two in some cases, especially when rapid changes in fashion or technology are important. Or a strategy might be implemented over several years, perhaps the length of the early stages of the product's life.

Although the outline in Exhibit 10-4 does not explicitly show a place for the time frame for the plan or the specific costs for each decision area, these should be included in the plan—along with expected estimates of sales and profit—so that the plan can be compared with *actual performance* in the future. In other words, the plan not only makes it clear to everyone what is to be accomplished and how—it also provides a basis for the control process after the plan is implemented.

A complete plan spells out the reasons for decisions

The plan outline shown in Exhibit 10-4 is quite complete. It doesn't just provide information about marketing mix decisions—it also includes information about customers (including segmenting dimensions), competitors' strategies, other aspects of the market environment, and the company's objectives and resources. This material provides important background information relevant to the "why" of the marketing mix and target market decisions.

Too often, managers do not include this information; their plans just lay out the details of the target market and the marketing mix strategy decisions. This shortcut approach is more common when the plan is really just an update of a strategy that has been in place for some time. However, that approach can be risky.

Managers too often make the mistake of casually updating plans in minor ways—perhaps just changing some costs or sales forecasts—but otherwise sticking with what was done in the past. A big problem with this approach is that it's easy to lose sight of why those strategy decisions were made in the first place. When the market situation changes, the original reasons may no longer apply. Yet if the logic for those strategy decisions is not retained, it's easy to miss changes taking place that should result in a plan being reconsidered. For example, a plan that was established in the growth stage of the product life cycle may have been very successful for a number of years. But a marketing manager can't be complacent and assume that success will continue forever. When market maturity hits, the firm may be in for big trouble—unless the basic strategy

Exhibit 10-4 Summary Outline of Different Sections of Marketing Plan

Situation Analysis

Company Analysis
- Company objectives and overall marketing objectives
- Company resources (marketing, production, financial, human, etc.)
- Other marketing plans (marketing program)
- Previous marketing strategy
- Major screening criteria relevant to product-market opportunity selected
  - Quantitative (ROI, profitability, risk level, etc.)
  - Qualitative (nature of business preferred, social responsibility, environment, etc.)
- Major constraints
- Marketing collaborators (current and potential)

Customer Analysis (organizational customers and/or final consumers)
- Product-market
- Possible segmenting dimensions (customer needs, other characteristics)
  - Qualifying dimensions and determining dimensions
- Identify target market(s) (one or more specific segments)
  - Operational characteristics (demographics, geographic locations, etc.)
- Potential size (number of people, dollar purchase potential, etc.) and likely growth
- Key economic, psychological, and social influences on buying
- Type of buying situation
- Nature of relationship with customers

Competitor Analysis
- Nature of current/likely competition
- Current and prospective competitors (or rivals)
  - Current strategies and likely responses to plan
- Competitive barriers to overcome and sources of potential competitive advantage

Analysis of the Market Context—External Market Environment
- Economic environment
- Technological environment
- Political and legal environment
- Cultural and social environment

Key Factors from Situation Analysis: S.W.O.T.
- S.W.O.T.: Strengths, weaknesses, opportunities, and threats from situation analysis

Marketing Plan Objectives
- Specific objectives to be achieved with the marketing strategy

Differentiation and Positioning
- How will marketing mix be differentiated from the competition?
- How will the market offering be positioned?
- Positioning statement

Marketing Strategy

Overview of the Marketing Strategy
- General direction for the marketing strategy
- Description of how the Four Ps fit together

Target Market(s)
- Summary of characteristics of the target market(s) to be approached

Product
- Product class (type of consumer or business product)
- Current product life-cycle stage
- New-product development requirements (people, dollars, time, etc.)
- Product liability, safety, and social responsibility considerations
- Specification of core physical good or service
  - Features, quality, etc.
- Supporting service(s) needed
- Warranty (what is covered, timing, who will support, etc.)
- Branding (manufacturer versus dealer, family versus individual, etc.)
- Packaging
  - Promotion and labeling needs
  - Protection needs
- Cultural sensitivity of product
- Fit with product line

Exhibit 10-4 Summary Outline of Different Sections of Marketing Plan—*continued*

Place
- Objectives
  - Degree of market exposure required
  - Distribution customer service level required
- Type of channel (direct, indirect)
  - Other channel members or collaborators required
  - Type/number of wholesalers (agent, merchant, etc.)
  - Type/number of retailers
  - How discrepancies and separations will be handled
  - How marketing functions will be shared
- Coordination needed in company, channel, and supply chain
  - Information requirements (EDI, the Internet, e-mail, etc.)
- Transportation requirements
- Inventory product-handling requirements
- Facilities required (warehousing, distribution centers, etc.)
- Reverse channels (for returns, recalls, etc.)

Promotion
- Objectives
- Major message theme(s) (for integrated marketing communications/positioning)
- Promotion blend
  - Advertising (type, media, copy thrust, etc.)
  - Personal selling (type and number of salespeople, compensation, effort allocation, etc.)
  - Publicity (earned, owned, social media)
  - Sales promotion (for customers, channel members, employees)
  - Interactive media
- Mix of push and pull required
- Who will do the work?

Price
- Nature of demand (price sensitivity, price of substitutes)
- Demand and cost analyses (marginal analysis)
- Markup chain in channel
- Price flexibility
- Price level(s) (under what conditions) and impact on customer value
- Adjustments to list price (geographic terms, discounts, allowances, etc.)

Marketing Information Requirements
- Marketing research needs (with respect to customers, Four Ps, external environment, etc.)
- Secondary and primary data needs
- Marketing information system needs, models to be used, and so on

Implementation and Control

Special Implementation Problems to Overcome
- People required
- Manufacturing, financial, and other resources needed

Control
- Marketing information systems and data needed
- Monitoring and analytics needed
- Criterion measures/comparison with objectives (customer satisfaction, sales, cost, performance analysis, etc.)

Budget, Sales Forecasts, and Estimates of Profit
- Costs (all elements in plan, over time)
- Sales (by market, over time, etc.)
- Estimated operating statement (pro forma)

Timing
- Specific sequence of activities and events, and so on
- Likely changes over the product life cycle

Risk Factors and Contingency Plans

and plan are modified. If a plan spells out the details of the market analysis and logic for the marketing mix and target market selected, then it is a simple matter to routinely check and update it. Remember: The idea is for all of the analysis and strategy decisions to fit together as an integrated whole. Thus, as some of the elements of the plan or market environment change, the whole plan may need a fresh approach.

Challenges Facing Marketers

Marketers face the challenge of preparing creative and innovative marketing plans, but that in itself will not improve the value of marketing to society. We need to face up to other basic challenges that require new ways of thinking.

Change is the only thing that's constant

We need better marketing performance at the firm level. Progressive firms pay attention to changes in the market—including trends in the market environment—and how marketing strategies need to be improved to consider these changes. Exhibit 10-5 lists some of the important trends and changes we've discussed throughout this text.

Most of the changes and trends summarized in Exhibit 10-5 are having a positive effect on how marketers serve society. And this ongoing improvement is self-directing. As consumers shift their support to firms that do meet their needs, laggard businesses are forced to either improve or get out of the way.

If it ain't broke, improve it

Marketing managers must constantly evaluate their strategies to be sure they're not being left in the dust by competitors who see new and better ways of doing things. It's crazy for a marketing manager to constantly change a strategy that's working well. But too many managers fail to see or plan for needed changes. They're afraid to do anything different and adhere to the idea that "if it ain't broke, don't fix it." But a firm can't always wait until a problem becomes completely obvious to do something about it. When customers move on and profits disappear, it may be too late to fix the problem. Marketing managers who take the lead in finding innovative new markets and approaches get a competitive advantage.

We need to welcome international competition

Marketers can't afford to bury their heads in the sand and hope that international competition will go away. Rather, they must realize that it is part of today's market environment. It creates even more pressure on marketing managers to figure out what it takes to gain a competitive advantage—both at home and in foreign markets. But with the challenge comes opportunities. The forces of competition in and among market-directed economies will help speed the diffusion of marketing advances to consumers everywhere. As macro-marketing systems improve worldwide, more consumers will have income to buy products—from wherever in the world those products come.

We need to use technology wisely

We live in a time of dramatic new technologies. Many marketers hate the idea that what they've learned from years of on-the-job experience may no longer apply when new technologies come along. Or they feel that it's the job of the technical specialist to figure out how a new technology can help the firm serve its customers. But marketers can't just pawn[10] that responsibility off on "somebody else." If that means learning about new technologies, then that is just part of the marketing job.

At a broader level, firms face the challenge of determining what technologies are acceptable and which are not. For example, gene research has opened the door to life-saving medicines, genetically altered crops that resist drought or disease, and even cloning of human beings. Yet in all of these arenas there is intense conflict among different groups about what is appropriate. How should these decisions be made? There is no simple answer to this question, but it's clear that old production-oriented views are *not* the answer. Perhaps we will move toward developing answers if some of the marketing ideas that have been applied to understanding individual needs can be extended to better understand the needs of society as a whole.

Exhibit 10-5 Some Important Changes and Trends Affecting Marketing Strategy Planning

Communication Technologies
The Internet and intranets
Satellite communications and Wi-Fi
Videoconferencing and Internet telephony
Growing use of smartphones
Consumer online "search" shopping
More interactive communications with customers

Role of Computerization
E-commerce, websites
Wireless networks
Scanners, bar codes, and RFID for tracking
Multimedia integration
"Cloud" computing
Mobile web access
Marketing analytics and predictive analytics
Artificial intelligence and intelligent agents
Augmented reality

Marketing Research
Search engines and web analytics
Online research—surveys, focus groups, online communities
Growth of marketing information systems
Decision support systems
Single source data (and scanner panels)
Data warehouses and data mining
Customer relationship management (CRM) systems
Big data

Demographic Patterns
Technology usage around the globe
Explosion in senior and ethnic submarkets
Aging of the Baby Boomers
Population growth slowdown in United States
Geographic shifts in population
Slower real income growth in United States

Business and Organizational Customers
Closer relationships and single sourcing
Just-in-time inventory systems/EDI
Web portals and Internet sourcing
Interactive bidding and proposal requests
Internet as source of information
E-commerce and supply chain management

Product
More attention to "really new" products
Growth of dealer brands and private label
Faster new-product development
R&D teams with market-driven focus
Role of customer experience
More attention to quality
More attention to service technologies
More attention to sustainable design
Category management
3-D printing
Patent trolls tie up patents
Internet of Things

Channels and Logistics
Internet selling (wholesale and retail)
More vertical marketing systems
Clicks and bricks (multichannel)
More multichannel shopping
Larger, more powerful retail chains
More attention to distribution service
Real-time inventory replenishment
Automated warehousing and handling
Cross-docking at distribution centers
Logistics outsourcing

Sales Promotion
Database-directed promotion
Point-of-purchase promotion
Trade promotion becoming more sensible
Event sponsorships
Customer loyalty programs
Customer acquisition cost analysis

Personal Selling
Post-sale customer service
Sales technology
Major accounts specialization
More telemarketing and team selling

Mass Selling
Interactive media (Internet ads, etc.)
Increasing role of publicity
More emphasis on earned and owned media
Role of customer reviews and ratings
Integrated marketing communications
Growth of more targeted media
Growth of interactive agencies
Consolidation of global agencies
Consolidation of media companies
Changing agency compensation
Shrinking media budgets
Social media
Inbound communications

Pricing
Value pricing
Overuse of sales and deals
Bigger differences in discounts
More attention to exchange rate effects
Lower markups on higher stockturn items
Use of "free" as a price
Comparison price shopping easier

International Marketing
More international market development
Global competitors—at home and abroad
Global communication over the Internet
New trade rules (WTO, EU, etc.)
More attention to exporting by small firms
International expansion by retailers
Impact of "pop" culture on traditional cultures
Tensions between "have" and "have-not" cultures
Growing income and population in emerging markets
Greater technology access in emerging markets

General
Economic decline
Privacy issues
More attention to profitability, not just sales
Greater attention to superior value
Addressing of environmental concerns
More pressure on marketing to demonstrate financial returns

Internet for consumers—sunny or partly cloudy

The Internet promised to create a more transparent business environment for customers. By shining "sunlight" on bad practices, the costs rise for firms producing a defective product or engaging in unethical behavior. In some ways this has proven to be the case. Early adopter customers review purchases on websites. Reports of a boring book, misleading product descriptions, poorly designed products, or bad customer service help prospective customers make more informed choices. On the other hand, there are growing reports of companies gaming the review system with fake reviews–leading consumers to question this source of information.

Along the same lines, companies must work hard to bury negative information about their brands. Sometimes this is justified, as the web allows anyone with a gripe (valid or not) to post complaints. But now marketing managers have become much more clever about controlling their brand image online. It wasn't too long ago that when typing "Nike" into Google, the first page of the search returned several links questioning the company's ethics and practices. Now the same search turns up only positive messages. In part this is because Nike has responded to critics and actively engages in more sustainable and socially responsible practices. It is also because Nike is more aware of how to manage search results to effectively bury its critics.

In general, the Internet has helped shine a light that helps consumers make more informed choices. The risk is that increasingly web-savvy brands find ways to clean up their image without cleaning up their practices.

We must consider *long-run* consumer welfare

Throughout this book we have emphasized the importance of the marketing concept–satisfying customers through a total company effort at a profit. Unfortunately, some firms take too short-run a view. They satisfy customers in the near term and take their profits, without worrying about longer-term problems. For example, some banks, mortgage brokers, and credit card companies made credit too easy to get. Some customers enjoyed this for a while, but many purchased homes or built up credit card debt that they couldn't afford. Although this helped companies earn high profits in the short term, many customers later defaulted[11] on loans. Eventually, such activities harmed customers–and wreaked havoc[12] on our global economy. Marketing managers must have a long-run view of customer satisfaction and recognize their social responsibility.

May need more social responsibility

Good business managers put themselves in the consumer's position. A useful rule to follow might be: Do unto others as you would have others do unto you. Sometimes called the "Golden Rule," this approach is found in many religions and philosophies. In practice, this means developing satisfying marketing mixes for specific target markets. It may mean building in more quality or more safety. The consumer's long-run satisfaction should be considered too. How will the product hold up in use? What about service guarantees? While trying to serve the needs of some target market, does the marketing strategy disregard the rights and needs of other consumers or create problems that will be left for future generations?

We need the truth

Promotion provides powerful ways to communicate with customers. Yet too many firms lapse into telling only half the truth. This is most obvious when there is a shift in consumer interest. For example, a firm's ad may accurately proclaim that its food product has no "trans fat"–but do consumers think that means it's healthy, low calorie, or even low in fat? Today we're also seeing a lot of incomplete or misleading "greenwashing" claims about firms' environmental practices and eco-friendly products. It's good for a firm to create a biodegradable package and promote it, but the cleaning product in the package shouldn't contain chemicals that will be harmful once they're in the sewer system.

Growing consumer cynicism about promotion is also a problem. As it gets worse, firms as well as consumers suffer. Regulations say that marketing communications shouldn't be false or misleading, but managers need to take seriously the responsibility to be truthful to their customers. Marketing communications should be helpful–not just legal. Managers who don't get this message are likely to learn a hard lesson from activists who spread criticisms of their firms across the web and other media. The potential harm to a brand's reputation from this sort of negative publicity has many firms cautious about overstating their claims, including ones related to sustainability efforts.

The environment is everyone's need

Marketers need to work harder and smarter at finding ways to satisfy consumer needs without sacrificing the environment. All consumers need the environment, whether they realize it yet or not. We are only beginning to understand the consequences of the environmental damage that's already been done. Acid rain, depletion of the ozone layer, global warming, and toxic waste in water supplies—to mention but a few current environmental problems—have catastrophic effects.

In the past, most firms didn't pass the cost of environmental damage on to consumers in the prices that they paid. Pollution was a hidden and unmeasured cost for most companies. That is changing rapidly. Firms are already paying billions of dollars to correct problems, including problems created years ago. The government isn't accepting the excuse that "nobody knew it was a big problem."

Consumer privacy needs to be protected

Marketers should be sensitive to consumers' rights and privacy. In this book, we describe how marketing managers collect and analyze data about customers. Many of these data are collected and analyzed without customers' knowledge. Organizations can abuse these rights. For example, credit card records—which reveal much about consumers' purchases and private lives—are routinely sold to anybody who pays for the file. Many people post a great deal of personal information on social networking websites such as Facebook, assuming they have some privacy. This is often not the case. Facebook sells this information to assist advertisers in finding their target market.

Most consumers don't realize how much data about their personal lives—some of them incorrect but treated as fact—are collected and available. A simple computer billing error may land consumers on a bad-credit list without their knowledge. Worse, poor security can result in identity theft. Marketing managers should use technology responsibly to improve the quality of life, not disrupt it. Yet where to draw that line differs depending on whom you talk to. Consider what is already happening and what might be coming in *What's Next?* Marketers use big data and analytics—cool or creepy?

May need to change laws and how they are enforced

One of the advantages of a market-directed economic system is that it operates automatically. But in our version of this system, consumer-citizens provide certain constraints (laws), which can be modified at any time. Managers who ignore consumer attitudes must realize that their actions may cause new restraints.

Before piling on too many new rules, however, some of the ones we have may need to be revised—and others may need to be enforced more carefully. Antitrust laws, for example, are often applied to protect competitors from one another—but they were originally intended to encourage competition.

Specifically, U.S. antitrust laws were developed so that all firms in a market would compete on a level playing field. But in many markets, that level playing field no longer exists. In our global economy, individual U.S. firms now compete with foreign firms whose governments urge them to cooperate with one another. Such foreign firms don't see one another as competitors; rather they see U.S. firms, as a group, as the competitors.

Laws should affect top managers

Strict enforcement of present laws could have far-reaching results if more price fixers, fraudulent or deceptive advertisers, and others who violate existing laws—thus affecting the performance of the macro-marketing system—were sent to jail or given heavy fines. A quick change in attitudes might occur if unethical top managers—those who plan strategy—were prosecuted, instead of the salespeople or advertisers expected to deliver on weak or undifferentiated strategies.

Laws merely define minimal ethical standards

Whether a marketer is operating in his or her own country or in a foreign nation, the legal environment sets the *minimal* standards of ethical behavior as defined by a society. In addition, the American Marketing Association's Statement of Ethics (Exhibit 1-7) provides basic guidelines that a marketing manager should observe. But marketing managers constantly face ethical issues where there are no clearly defined answers. Every

What's Next? Marketers use big data and analytics—cool or creepy?

Marketing managers use big data to build "social profiles" of individual consumers. Right now, a few companies create profiles using customers' clicks, conversations, Facebook "Likes," Twitter tweets, cell phone activity, and credit card and loyalty card purchases. With artificial intelligence and analytics software, they deliver unique promotional messages and offers. In exchange, customers give up some privacy.

This is an early indication of *What's Next?* in advertising and sales promotion. Is this new practice cool? Or is it creepy? To better understand how the big data revolution affects customers, let's take a closer look at how this might play out in real life by looking at how this impacts college students Nick and Shelby.

Nick often eats fast food and regularly receives texts with coupons for fast-food purchases. His family is not wealthy, and saving money is important. Nick's profile shows that he usually spends significantly more than the coupon amount, and computer analysis of Nick's photos and comments on Facebook suggest he is overweight. Soon Nick starts seeing ads for diets; he also receives a special introductory offer from a local health club. Cool or creepy? Nick's Facebook newsfeed and Twitter feed include "articles" from news sites on healthy eating with an emphasis on Kellogg's Special K diet products and weight-loss tips from South Beach Diet products. Cool or creepy? Some days, as Nick walks home from school, his Snapchat flashes a picture of an ice-cream cone (and a $0.50 off deal) just a block before he passes a Baskin-Robbins ice-cream store. Cool or creepy?

Shelby is from a wealthy family. Her friends know she works out regularly and maintains a healthy diet. Last week she was online reading articles about mountain bikes—now when she surfs the web, she sees ads for mountain bikes. Cool or creepy? As Shelby walks into her grocery store, her phone lights up with an offer for $1 off on Ben & Jerry's Greek Frozen Yogurt—she loves that stuff but rarely eats it unless she's feeling down. Did the grocery store know she and her boyfriend just broke up? Yes, it did; she posted a Facebook status update that morning. Cool or creepy? Shelby often receives direct-mail offers for low-interest credit cards; Nick doesn't get those. Does the financial institution figure that healthier behavior is a sign of self-discipline and, therefore, financial responsibility? Or is it just that her family is wealthier? Will insurance companies draw the same conclusions and adjust their rates accordingly? Cool or creepy?

Marketing managers see an opportunity to leverage big data and analytics to customize advertising, sales promotion, and pricing. Tracked by your cell phone's GPS, messages target your location. If a $0.50 coupon motivates Nick to buy ice cream, but it takes $1.00 off to move Shelby, each gets a different coupon. Shelby's wealthier background suggests a higher customer lifetime value than Nick, so department stores will offer her better deals, hoping to build brand loyalty. And those "articles" served to your news feed might be written by someone paid by a brand prominently featured in the article.

Cool or creepy? It probably depends on your values. As we move into a brave new world where customers surrender privacy (usually without their knowledge), you should have questions. *Do you want to trade your privacy for personalized marketing mixes? What do you have to gain or lose? Who owns your data? Should governments regulate this—or should it be up to you? There are no easy answers. Is this cool? Creepy? A little of both? A lot of both?*

marketing manager should make a personal commitment to carefully evaluate the ethical consequences of marketing strategy decisions.

On the other hand, innovative new marketing strategies *do* sometimes cause problems for those who have a vested interest[13] in the old ways. Some people try to portray anything that disrupts their own personal interest as unethical. But that is not an appropriate ethical standard. The basic ethical charge to marketers is to find new *and* better ways to serve society's needs.

Need socially responsible consumers

We've stressed that marketers should act responsibly—but consumers have responsibilities too. Some consumers abuse policies about returning goods, change price tags in self-service stores, and are downright abusive to salespeople. Others think nothing of ripping off businesses because "they're rich." Shoplifting is a major problem for most traditional retailers, averaging almost 2 percent of sales nationally. In supermarkets, losses to shoplifters are on average greater than profits. Online retailers, in turn, must fight the use of stolen or fraudulent credit cards. Honest consumers pay for the cost of this theft in higher prices.

Americans tend to perform their dual role of consumer-citizens with a split personality. We often behave differently at the cash register than we do on our soap box. For example, we say that we want to protect the environment, but when it comes to making our own purchase decisions, we're likely to pick the product that is more convenient or lower priced rather than the one that is the sustainable choice. We protest sex and violence in the media, but some of the most profitable websites on the Internet are purveyors of pornography. Parents complain about advertising aimed at children but use TV as a Saturday morning babysitter.

Unethical or illegal behavior is widespread. In a major survey of workers, managers, and executives from a wide range of industries, 48 percent admitted to taking unethical or illegal actions in the past year. Offenses included things such as cheating on expense accounts, paying or accepting kickbacks, trading sex for sales, lying to customers, leaking company secrets, and looking the other way when environmental laws are violated. Think about it—we're talking about half of the workforce.

As consumer-citizens, each of us shares the responsibility for preserving an effective macro-marketing system. And we should take this responsibility seriously. That even includes the responsibility to be smarter customers. Let's face it, a majority of consumers ignore most of the available information that could help them spend money (and guide the marketing process) more wisely. Consumerism has encouraged nutritional labeling, unit pricing, truth-in-lending, plain-language contracts and warranties, and so on. Many companies provide extensive information at their websites or in brochures. Government agencies publish many consumer buying guides on everything from tires to appliances, as do organizations such as Consumers Union. Most of this information is available from home over the Internet. It makes sense to use it.

How Far Should the Marketing Concept Go?

Should marketing managers limit consumers' freedom of choice?

Achieving a better macro-marketing system is certainly a desirable objective. But what part should a marketer play in deciding what products to offer?

This is extremely important because some marketing managers, especially those in large corporations, can have an impact far larger than they do in their roles as consumer-citizens. For example, should they refuse to produce hazardous products, such as skis or motorcycles, even though such products are in strong demand? Should they install safety devices that increase costs and raise prices that customers don't want to pay?

These are difficult questions to answer. Some things marketing managers do clearly benefit both the firm and consumers because they lower costs or improve consumers' options. But other decisions may actually reduce consumer choice and conflict with a desire to improve the effectiveness of our macro-marketing system.

Consumer-citizens should vote on the changes

It seems fair to suggest, therefore, that marketing managers should be expected to improve and expand the range of goods and services they make available—always trying to add value and better satisfy consumers' needs and preferences. This is the job we've assigned to business.

If pursuing this objective makes excessive demands on scarce resources or has an unacceptable ecological effect, then consumer-citizens have the responsibility to vote for laws restricting individual firms that are trying to satisfy consumers' needs. This is the role that we, as consumers, have assigned to the government—to ensure that the macro-marketing system works effectively.

It is important to recognize that some *seemingly minor* modifications in our present system *might* result in very big, unintended problems. Allowing some government agency to prohibit the sale of products for seemingly good reasons could lead to major changes we never expected and could seriously reduce consumers' present rights to freedom of choice, including "bad" choices.

CONCLUSION

Macro-marketing does *not* cost too much. Consumers have assigned business the role of satisfying their needs. Customers find it satisfactory and even desirable to permit businesses to cater to them and even to stimulate wants. As long as consumers are satisfied, macro-marketing will not cost too much—and business firms will be permitted to continue as profit-making entities.

But business exists at the consumer's discretion. It's mainly by satisfying the consumer that a particular firm—and *our* economic system—can justify its existence and hope to keep operating.

In carrying out this role—granted by consumers—business firms are not always as effective as they could be. Many business managers don't understand the marketing concept or the role that marketing plays in our way of life. They seem to feel that business has a basic right to operate as it chooses. And they proceed in their typical production-oriented ways. Further, many managers have had little or no training in business management and are not as competent as they should be. Others fail to adjust to the changes taking place around them. And a few dishonest or unethical managers can do a great deal of damage before consumer-citizens take steps to stop them. As a result, marketing by individual firms often *does* cost too much. But the situation is improving. More business training is now available, and more competent people are being attracted to marketing and business generally. Clearly, *you* have a role to play in improving marketing activities in the future.

The marketing strategy planning process presented in this book provides a framework that will guide you to more effective marketing decisions—and marketing that really does deliver superior value to customers. It also benefits the firm, through profits and growth. It's truly a "win-win" situation. And in our competitive, market-driven economy, managers and firms that lead the way in creating these successes will not go unnoticed. As effective marketing management spreads to more companies, the whole macro-marketing system will be more efficient and effective.

To keep our system working effectively, individual firms should implement the marketing concept in a more efficient, ethical, and socially responsible way. At the same time, we—as consumers—should consume goods and services in an intelligent and socially responsible way. Further, we have the responsibility to vote and ensure that we get the kind of macro-marketing system we want. What kind do you want? What should you do to ensure that fellow consumer-citizens will vote for your system? Is your system likely to satisfy you as well as another macro-marketing system? You don't have to answer these questions right now—but your answers will affect the future you'll live in and how satisfied you'll be.

JOYFUL MOMENT

Sam walks into his boss's office and says "Sir, I'll be straight with you, I know the economy isn't great, but I have over three companies after me, and I would like to respectfully ask for a raise."

After a few minutes of haggling the boss finally agrees to a 5% raise, and Sam happily gets up to leave. "By the way," asks the boss, "Which three companies are after you?" "The electric company, water company, and phone company!"

WORDS AND EXPRESSIONS

1. **appraisal**: *n.* the official or formal assessment of the strengths and weaknesses of someone or something 评估
—One of the most important tools for organizational improvement is the performance appraisal.
组织改进的最重要手段之一是业绩评估。
2. **unsolicited**: *adj.* not asked for 未经要求的；自发的
—She's always full of unsolicited advice.
她总是未被请求即提供一大堆建议。
3. **fickle**: *adj.* likely to change your opinion or your feelings suddenly and without a good reason（意见或感情）反复无常的，易变的
—She's so fickle—she's never been interested in the same man for more than a week!
她是如此变幻无常，喜欢同一个男人从未超过一星期。
4. **stifle**: *v.* to (cause to) be unable to breathe because you have no air 扼杀；使窒息
—Regulations on children stifled creativity.
对孩子们制定的各种规定压制了创造力。
5. **snuff sth. out**: phrasal *v.* to snuff out something such as a disagreement means to stop it, usually in a forceful or sudden way 消除；扼杀
—Retreating energy costs may yet snuff out even these faint, inflationary embers.
能源成本下降也可能会熄灭这微弱的通胀的余火。
6. **pharaoh**: *n.* a king of ancient Egypt 法老（古埃及国王）
—One of the most famous women in history, Cleopatra VII was the brilliant and beautiful last Pharaoh of Egypt.
克娄巴特拉七世是历史上最著名的女性之一，这个聪明、美丽的女人也是埃及最后一个法老。
7. **self-gratification**: *n.* great self-satisfaction 自我满足
—Some people seem to find it easy to resist temptation while others can be relied on to always yield to self-gratification.
一些人似乎很容易抵制诱惑，而其他人可能总是容易自我满足。
8. **risqué**: *n.* (of jokes or stories) slightly rude or shocking,

especially because of being about sex 粗俗下流的；有伤风化的

—We find ourselves laughing at risqué humor and embarrassing situations because they make us uncomfortable.

我们发现我们都会在尴尬时大笑，因为他们正在做一些我们感到不舒服的事。

9. **dire**: *adj.* very serious or terrible a situation or event is 严重的；可怕的

—The idea is that a new market can overcome the current one's dire problems.

这个想法是认为一个新市场能够克服并解决目前的可怕问题。

10. **pawn**: *n./v.* to leave a possession with a pawnbroker, who gives you money for it and can sell it if the money is not paid back within a certain time 典当；把…甩给…

—You can't pawn your old car off on me. I didn't go for it.

你别想把你的破车卖给我，我才不会有兴趣。

11. **default**: *v./n.* to fail to do something, such as pay a debt, that you legally have to do 拖欠，不履行债务；违约

—People who default on their mortgage repayments may have their home repossessed.

未能按期偿还抵押贷款者，其房屋可能会被收回。

12. **havoc**: *n.* confusion and lack of order, especially causing damage or trouble 破坏，毁坏；混乱

—The storm wreaked (= caused) havoc in the garden, uprooting trees and blowing a fence down.

风暴毁坏了花园，树被连根拔起，一排围栏也被刮倒了。

13. **vested interest**: a strong personal interest in something because you could get an advantage from it 既得利益

—As both a teacher and parent, she had a vested interest in seeing the school remain open.

身为教师兼家长，保证学校不被关闭符合她的既得利益。

EXERCISES

1. Multiple choices

(1) The objective of American market-directed economic system is to satisfy ___.

A. political elite's needs　B. religious leaders' needs

C. government planners' needs　D. customer needs

(2) For customers of ___ firms, micro-marketing often does cost too much.

A. highly successful　B. production-oriented and inefficient

C. customer-oriented　D. market-oriented

(3) Whether a marketer is operating in his or her own country or in a foreign nation, the legal environment sets the ___ standards of ethical behavior as defined by a society.

A. minimal　B. top　C. maximal　D. clear

(4) The major marketing strategy decision areas are organized by the Four Ps which are respectively Product, Place, Promotion, and ___.

A. Personal　B. Price　C. Publicity　D. Package

(5) Marketing strategy planning process requires logic and ___.

A. customer satisfaction　B. advertising　C. creativity　D. opportunities

2. True or false

(1) Nonprofit organizations have a different bottom line, so they will not fail if they don't satisfy supporters. ______

(2) If a firm listens to the "voice of the customer," there'll be an incentive for the customer to buy. ______

(3) If a firm succeeds in coming up with a marketing mix with benefits greater than costs, it still won't be a superior value unless it's better than what competitors offer. ______

(4) Advertising can also make both the micro- and macro-marketing processes work better. ______

(5) Firms can manipulate consumers to buy anything the company chooses to produce. ______

(6) Marketing's job is just to satisfy consumer wants as they exist at any particular point in time. ______

(7) In the short run, marketing reflects social values while in the long run it enhances and reinforces them. ______

(8) The marketing plan just provides information about marketing mix decisions. ______

(9) Marketing managers who take the lead in finding innovative new markets and approaches get a competitive advantage. ______

(10) Marketing managers must have a long-run view of customer satisfaction and recognize their social responsibility. ______

3. Fill in the blanks

(1) Many large and small firms measure customer satisfaction with ___________.

(2) ___________ frequently does cost too much but that ___________ does not cost too much, given the present objective of the American economy—consumer satisfaction.

(3) Good business managers put themselves in the ___________'s position.

(4) The basic ethical charge to marketers is to find new and better ways to serve ___________'s needs.

(5) Managers who adopt the __________ concept as a way of business life do a better job.

(6) Provided that a product satisfies customer needs, advertising can __________ demand for the product.

(7) Because these economies may more than offset advertising costs, advertising can actually __________ prices to the consumer.

(8) There is no doubt that marketing caters to __________ values. However, people disagree as to whether marketing creates these values or simply appeals to values already there.

(9) Experts who study values seem to agree that, in the short run, marketing reflects __________ while in the long run it enhances and reinforces them.

(10) A place for the time frame for the plan or the specific costs for each decision area should be included in the plan—along with expected estimates of sales and profit—so that the plan can be compared with __________ in the future.

4. **Answer the following questions**

(1) What criteria should be used to evaluate each level of marketing?

(2) List some reasons that lead to marketing inefficiencies.

(3) Why do some firms fail to identify new target markets and new opportunities?

(4) How far should the marketing concept go? How should we decide this issue?

(5) Should marketing managers, or business managers in general, refrain from producing profitable products that some target customers want, but that may not be in their long-run best interest? Should firms be expected to produce "good" but less profitable products? What if such products break even? What if they are unprofitable but the company makes other profitable products—so on balance it still makes some profit? What criteria are you using for each of your answers?

SUGGESTED CASES

17. **Wise Water, Inc.**
22. **Bright Light Innovations: The Starlight Stove**
25. **QXR Tools (QXR)**
26. **AAA Custom Castings, Inc.**
27. **Canadian Mills, Ltd.**
28. **Kingston Home Health Services (KHHS)**

Cases

Guide to the Use of These Cases

Cases can be used in many ways. And the same case can be analyzed several times for different purposes.

"Suggested cases" are listed at the end of each chapter, but these cases can also be used later in the text. The main criterion for the order of these cases is the amount of technical vocabulary—or text principles—that is needed to read the case meaningfully. The first cases are "easiest" in this regard. This is why an early case can easily be used two or three times—with different emphasis. Some early cases might require some consideration of Product and Price, for example, and might be used twice, perhaps regarding product planning and later pricing. In contrast, later cases, which focus more on Price, might be treated more effectively *after* the Price chapters are covered.

In some of the cases, we have disguised certain information—such as names or proprietary financial data—at the request of the people or firms involved in the case. However, such changes do not alter the basic substantive problems you will be analyzing in a case.

1. McDonald's "Seniors" Restaurant

Lisa Aham manages a McDonald's restaurant in a city with many "seniors." She has noticed that some senior citizens have become not just regular patrons, but patrons who come for breakfast and stay on until about 3 p.m. Many of these older customers were attracted initially by a monthly breakfast special for people aged 55 and older. The meal costs $1.99, and refills of coffee are free. Every fourth Monday, between 100 and 150 seniors jam Lisa's McDonald's for the special offer. But now almost as many of them are coming every day—turning the fast-food restaurant into a meeting place. They sit for hours with a cup of coffee, chatting with friends. On most days, as many as 100 will stay from one to four hours.

Lisa's employees have been very friendly to the seniors, calling them by their first names and visiting with them each day. In fact, Lisa's McDonald's is a happy place—with her employees developing close relationships with the seniors. Some employees have even visited customers who have been hospitalized. "You know," Lisa says, "I really get attached to the customers. They're like my family. I really care about these people." They are all "friends," and it is part of McDonald's corporate philosophy (as reflected in its website, www.mcdonalds.com) to be friendly with its customers and to give back to the communities it serves.

These older customers are an orderly group and very friendly to anyone who comes in. Further, they are neater than most customers and carefully clean up their tables before they leave. Nevertheless, Lisa is beginning to wonder if anything should be done about her growing "non-fast-food" clientele. There's currently not a crowding problem during the time when the seniors like to come. But if the size of the senior citizen group continues to grow, crowding could become a problem. Further, Lisa is concerned that her restaurant might come to be known as an "old people's" restaurant—which might discourage some younger customers. And if customers felt the restaurant was crowded, some might feel that they wouldn't get fast service. On the other hand, a place that seems busy might be seen as a "good place to go" and a "friendly place."

Lisa also worries about the image she is projecting. McDonald's is a fast-food restaurant (there are more than 35,000 of them serving more than 65 million people in more than 119 countries every day), and normally customers are expected to eat and run. Will allowing people to stay and visit change the whole concept? In the extreme, Lisa's McDonald's might become more like a European-style restaurant where the customers are never rushed and feel very comfortable about lingering over coffee for an hour or two! Lisa knows that the amount her senior customers spend is similar to the average customer's purchase—but the seniors do use the facilities for a much longer time. However, in actuality, most of the older customers leave McDonald's by 11:30, before the noon crowd comes in.

Lisa is concerned about another possibility. If catering to seniors is OK, then should she do even more with this age group? In particular, she is considering offering bingo games during the slow morning hours—9 a.m. to 11 a.m. Bingo is popular with some seniors, and this could be a new revenue source—beyond the extra food and drink purchases that probably would result. She figures she could charge $5 per person for the two-hour period and run it with two underutilized employees. The prizes would be coupons for purchases at her store (to keep it legal) and would amount to about two-thirds of the bingo receipts (at retail prices). The party room area of her McDonald's would be perfect for this use and could hold up to 150 persons.

Evaluate Lisa Aham's current strategy regarding senior citizens. Does this strategy improve this McDonald's image? What should she do about the senior citizen market—that is, should she encourage, ignore, or discourage her seniors? What should she do about the bingo idea? Explain.

2. Nature's Own Foods, Inc.

It is 2015, and Neal Middleton, newly elected president of Nature's Own Foods, Inc., faces a severe decline in profits. Nature's Own Foods, Inc. is a 127-year-old California-based food processor. Its multiproduct lines are widely accepted under the Nature's Own Foods brand. The company and its subsidiaries prepare, package, and sell canned and frozen foods, including fruits, vegetables, pickles, and condiments. Nature's Own Foods, which operates more than 30 processing plants in the United States, is one of the larger U.S. food processors—with annual sales of about $650 million.

Until 2015, Nature's Own Foods was a subsidiary of a major midwestern food processor, and many of the present managers came from the parent company. Nature's Own Foods' last president recently said:

> The influence of our old parent company is still with us. As long as new products look like they will increase the company's sales volume, they are introduced. Traditionally, there has been little, if any, attention paid to margins. We are well aware that profits will come through good products produced in large volume.

Alex May, a 25-year production manager, agrees with the multiproduct-line policy. As he puts it, "Volume comes from satisfying needs. We will can or freeze any vegetable or fruit we think consumers might want." May also admits that much of the expansion in product lines was encouraged by economics. The typical plants in the industry are not fully used. By adding new products to use this excess capacity, costs are spread over greater volume. So the production department is always looking for new ways to make more effective use of its present facilities.

Nature's Own Foods has a line-forcing policy, requiring any store that wants to carry its brand name to carry most of the 65 items in the Nature's Own Foods line. This policy, coupled with its wide expansion of product lines, has resulted in 88 percent of the firm's sales coming from major supermarket chain stores, such as Safeway, Kroger, and Winn Dixie.

Smaller stores are generally not willing to accept the Nature's Own Foods policy. May explains, "We know that only large stores can afford to stock all our products. But the large stores are the volume! We give consumers the choice of any Nature's Own Foods product they want, and the result is maximum sales." Many small retailers have complained about Nature's Own Foods' policy, but they have been ignored because they are considered too small in potential sales volume per store to be of any significance.

In late 2015, a stockholders' revolt over low profits (in 2015, profits were only $500,000) resulted in Nature's Own Foods' president and two of its five directors being removed. Neal Middleton (introduced earlier), an accountant from the company's outside auditing firm, was brought in as president. One of the first things he focused on was the variable and low levels of profits in the past several years. A comparison of Nature's Own Foods' results with similar operations of some large competitors supported his concern. In the past 13 years, Nature's Own Foods' closest competitors had an average profit return on shareholders' investment of 5 to 9 percent, whereas Nature's Own Foods averaged only 1.5 percent. Further, Nature's Own Foods' sales volume has not increased much from the 2001 level (after adjusting for inflation)—while operating costs have soared upward. Profits for the firm were about $8 million in 2001. The closest Nature's Own Foods has come since then is about $6 million—in 2004. The outgoing president blamed his failure on an inefficient sales department. He said, "Our sales department has deteriorated. I can't exactly put my finger on it, but the overall quality of salespeople has dropped, and morale is bad. The team just didn't perform." When Middleton e-mailed Shelley Walton, the vice president of sales, with this charge, her reply was:

> It's not our fault. I think the company made a key mistake in the late '80s. It expanded horizontally—by increasing its number of product offerings—while major competitors were expanding vertically, growing their own raw materials and making all of their packing materials. They can control quality and make profits in manufacturing that can be used in promotion. I lost some of my best people from frustration. We just aren't competitive enough to reach the market the way we should with a comparable product and price.

In a lengthy e-mail from Shelley Walton, Middleton learned more about the characteristics of Nature's Own Foods' market. Although all the firms in the food-processing industry advertise heavily, the size of the market for most processed foods hasn't grown much for many years. Further, most consumers are pressed for time and aren't very selective. If they can't find the brand of food they are looking for, they'll pick up another brand rather than go to another store. No company in the industry has much effect on the price at which its products are sold. Chain store buyers are very knowledgeable about prices and special promotions available from all the competing suppliers, and they are quick to play one supplier against another to keep the price low. Basically, they have a price they are willing to pay—and they won't exceed it. Then the chains will charge any price they wish on a given brand sold at retail. That is, a 48-can case of beans might be purchased from any supplier for $23.10, no matter whose product it is. Generally, the shelf price for each is no more than a few pennies different, but chain stores occasionally attract customers by placing a well-known brand on sale.

Besides insisting that processors meet price points, like for the canned beans, some chains require price allowances if special locations or displays are desired. They also carry non-advertised brands and/or their own brands at a lower price—to offer better value to their customers. And most willingly accept producers' cents-off coupons, which are offered by Nature's Own Foods as well as most of the other major producers of full lines.

At this point, Neal Middleton is trying to decide why Nature's Own Foods, Inc. isn't as profitable as it once was. And he is puzzled about why some competitors are putting products on the market with low potential sales volume. (For example, one major competitor recently introduced a line of exotic foreign vegetables with gourmet sauces.) And others have been offering frozen dinners or entrees with vegetables for several years. Apparently, Nature's Own Foods' managers considered trying such products several years ago but decided against it because of the small potential sales volumes and the likely high costs of new-product development and promotion.

Evaluate Nature's Own Foods' present situation. What would you advise Neal Middleton to do to improve Nature's Own Foods' profits? Explain why.

3. NOCO United Soccer Academy

Wesley Diekens came to the United States from the UK in 2005 on a soccer scholarship. Wesley grew up playing soccer on many competitive teams throughout high school and had a brief professional career in England. When St. Albans College recruited him to play soccer, he thought it would open his life to a grand adventure. That adventure changed his life.

While at St. Albans, Diekens met his future wife, Alyce Bilski, who also played soccer there. She graduated a year ahead of him and went to Fort Collins, Colorado, where she played on the semiprofessional Fort Collins Force women's soccer team. When Diekens finished college, he followed Bilski to northern Colorado. Bilski was captain of the Force and worked for the sports marketing company that owned the team.

Diekens got a job at a local meat packing plant, but soccer was his passion. He made the practice squad for the Colorado Rapids Major League Soccer team, but injuries cut his professional career short. Teaching soccer to kids became a new passion for Diekens. He has a natural talent for coaching. Diekens is charismatic, kids enjoy his easygoing demeanor and British accent, and he really knows soccer and how to teach the game to youngsters.

In 2009, Diekens founded the NOCO United Soccer Academy (NOCO standing for NOrthern COlorado). At first he trained small groups of young players aged 7 to 14. He grouped them by age and skill and conducted training sessions for small groups of five to seven at a local park. The first kids he attracted came by word-of-mouth as they quickly told friends and teammates about "this British guy who teaches soccer and makes it fun." His small after-school camps quickly grew to include more than 50 kids. Word continued to get around, and by the following summer Diekens conducted 10 different camps—and quit his job at the meat packing plant. He also trained 11 different NOCO United 3v3 soccer teams that competed in tournaments across the state and nation during the summer. All of his players had bright blue jerseys with the NOCO United name across the front, and the success of these teams made the jerseys a great promotion vehicle. In 2012, four of his teams competed in the national 3v3 soccer tournament, with one winning a national championship.

To keep up with the rapid growth, Diekens brought a few friends over from England to assist with training. Will Bowman moved to the United States to become Diekens' assistant director of coaching. Diekens and Bowman planned to work year-round as trainers and hire a couple of local coaches to help them conduct training sessions. During the summer he added a couple of local college soccer players and a few former teammates from England. The summer season works well for his British mates, because that is the off-season for those still playing professionally. Diekens is confident he can hire and train more coaches if he needs them to handle future growth.

Youth soccer is big in Colorado and across much of the United States. It is the largest participation sport for kids. Fort Collins is a soccer hotbed, and this has helped Diekens' business grow. He now trains about 600 kids per year. But he has even greater ambitions. For example, he would like to build a training facility; the space he currently rents is not always well suited to soccer. However, he figures he would need to double his business to justify the cost of the soccer complex he wants to build. So he is now wondering how to grow his business.

About 90 percent of his current customers live in Fort Collins, which has a population of about 150,000 people. Diekens believes awareness of his program is close to 100 percent among competitive soccer players ages 11 to 14—and is probably at about 40 percent among families with soccer-playing kids ages 6 to 10. Most of his customers are 10 to 13 years old and enroll in two to three NOCO United programs per year. He has also run a few camps in Boulder and Northglenn—both are about 50 miles from Fort Collins. These have been successful but are currently limited.

There are several small cities within 25 miles of Fort Collins. Loveland, a city of about 70,000, borders Fort Collins on the south. Greeley and Longmont, each with about 90,000 to 100,000 people, are about 25 miles away by interstate highway. These areas have very limited soccer training programs except for their competitive teams, and awareness of NOCO United is not very high. Those who have heard of his academy are often not familiar with its philosophy and programs. Diekens is not sure if parents in these communities would be willing to drive their kids to Fort Collins for training. If not, he would have to run his programs there.

Diekens knows that he wants to grow his business, but wonders how he can accomplish his goal. He currently sees a few options:

1. His current customer retention rate is pretty high: about 80 percent. However, when the kids reach 14 or 15 years old, other high school sports and activities make them less interested in extra soccer training. One option is to try to increase retention by developing programs targeted at kids older than 14.
2. Another option is to develop a marketing strategy that would encourage his current customers to buy more. He wonders if they have other needs that he might be able to serve.
3. Diekens could try to grow the business by entering new markets and acquiring new customers. His market penetration with kids 6 to 9 years old is still quite modest. He might develop new programs to better meet this group's needs.
4. Another new market option would be to serve more kids from Loveland, Longmont, and Greeley.

Evaluate Diekens' different options for growing NOCO United's customer equity. Develop a set of marketing strategy ideas for each of the options. What marketing research could Diekens perform to better assess his options?

4. Petoskey Tech Support

Claire Kelly is getting desperate about her new business. She's not sure she can make a go of it—and she really wants to stay in her hometown of Petoskey, Michigan, a beautiful summer resort area along the eastern shore of Lake Michigan. The area's permanent population of 10,000 more than triples in the summer months and doubles at times during the winter skiing and snowmobiling season.

Claire spent four years in the Navy after college graduation, returning home in June 2015. When she couldn't find a good job in the Petoskey area, she decided to go into business for herself and set up Petoskey Tech Support. Claire's plan was to work by herself and basically serve as a "for hire" computer consultant and troubleshooter for her customers. She knew that many of the upscale summer residents relied on home computers to keep in touch with business dealings and friends at home, and it seemed that someone was always asking her for computer advice. She was optimistic that she could keep busy with a variety of on-site services—setting up a customer's new computer, repairing hardware problems, installing software or upgrades, creating a wireless network, correcting problems created by viruses, and the like.

Claire thought that her savings would allow her to start the business without borrowing any money. Her estimates of required expenditures were \$7,000 for a used SUV; \$1,125 for tools, diagnostic equipment, and reference books; \$1,700 for a laptop computer, software, and accessories; \$350 for an initial supply of fittings and cables; and \$500 for insurance and other incidental expenses. This total of \$10,675 still left Claire with about \$6,500 in savings to cover living expenses while getting started.

Claire chose the technology services business because of her previous work experience. She worked at a computer "help desk" in college and spent her last year in the Navy troubleshooting computer network problems. In addition, from the time Claire was 16 years old until she finished college, she had also worked during the summer for Eric Steele. Eric operates the only successful computer services company in Petoskey. (There was one other local computer store that also did some on-location service work when the customer bought equipment at the store, but that store recently went out of business.)

Eric prides himself on quality work and has been able to build up a good business with repeat customers. Specializing in services to residential, small business, and professional offices, Eric has built a strong customer franchise. For 20 years, Eric's major source of new business has been satisfied customers who tell friends or coworkers about his quality service. He is highly regarded as a capable person who always treats clients fairly and honestly. For example, seasonal residents often give Eric the keys to their vacation homes so that he can do upgrades or maintenance while they are away for months at a time. Eric's customers are so loyal, in fact, that Fix-A-Bug–a national computer service franchise–found it impossible to compete with him. Even price-cutting was not an effective weapon against Eric.

From having worked with Eric, Claire thought that she knew the computer service business as well as he did; in fact, she had sometimes been able to solve technical problems that left him stumped. Claire was anxious to reach her $70,000-per-year sales objective because she thought this would provide her with a comfortable living in Petoskey. While aware of opportunities to do computer consulting for larger businesses, Claire felt that the sales opportunities for her services were limited because many firms had their own computer specialists or even IT departments. As Claire saw it, her only attractive opportunity was direct competition with Eric.

To get started, Claire spent $1,400 to advertise her business in the local newspaper and using Google AdWords. With this money she bought two announcement ads and 52 weeks of daily ads in the classified section, listed under "Miscellaneous Residential and Business Services." The Google AdWords ads appeared when locals searched for "computers," "tech support," or "computer repair." She also listed her business under "Computer Services" at Craigslist for Northern Michigan–updating this notice and information once a month. Further, she built a small website with just a basic home page, a page with her picture and experience, and a third page that lists the services she offers. She thought about creating a Facebook page and blog, but hasn't done that yet. She put magnetic sign boards on her SUV and has waited for business to take off.

At the end of three months, Claire had a few customers, but much of the time she wasn't busy and she was able to gross only about $300 a week. Of course, she had expected much more. Many of the people who did call were regular Eric customers who had some sort of crisis when he was already busy. While these people agreed that Claire's work was of the same quality as Eric's, they preferred Eric's "quality-care" image and they liked the fact that they had an ongoing relationship with him.

On occasion, Claire did get more work than she could handle. This happened during April and May, when seasonal businesses were preparing for summer openings and owners of summer homes and condos were ready to "open the cottage." The same rush occurred in September and October, as many of these places were being closed for the winter; those customers often wanted help backing up computer files or packing up computer equipment so they could take it with them. During these months, Claire was able to gross about $150 to $200 a day.

Toward the end of her discouraging first year in business, Claire Kelly is thinking about quitting. While she hates to think about leaving Petoskey, she can't see any way of making a living there with her independent technology services business. Eric seems to dominate the market, except in the rush seasons and for people who need emergency help. And the resort market is not growing very rapidly, so there is little hope of a big influx of new businesses and homeowners to spur demand.

Evaluate Claire Kelly's strategy planning for her new business. Why isn't she able to reach her objective of $70,000? What should Claire do now? Explain.

5. Resin Dynamics

Paige Chen, a chemist in Resin Dynamics' resins laboratory, is trying to decide how hard to fight for the new product she has developed. Chen's job is to find new, more profitable applications for the company's present resin products–and her current efforts are running into unexpected problems.

During the last four years, Chen has been under heavy pressure from her managers to come up with an idea that will open up new markets for the company's foamed polystyrene.

Two years ago, Chen developed the "foamed-dome concept"–a method of using foamed polystyrene to make dome-shaped roofs and other structures. She described the procedure for making domes as follows: The construction of a foamed dome involves the use of a specially designed machine that bends, places, and bonds pieces of plastic foam together into a predetermined dome shape. In forming a dome, the machine head is mounted on a boom, which swings around a pivot like the hands of a clock, laying and bonding layer upon layer of foam board in a rising spherical form.

According to Chen, polystyrene foamed boards have several advantages, such as:

1. Foam board is stiff–but can be formed or bonded to itself by heat alone.
2. Foam board is extremely lightweight and easy to handle. It has good structural rigidity.
3. Foam board has excellent and permanent insulating characteristics. (In fact, the major use for foam board is as an insulator.)
4. Foam board provides an excellent base on which to apply a variety of surface finishes, such as a readily available concrete-based stucco that is durable and inexpensive.

Using her good selling abilities, Chen easily convinced her managers that her idea had potential.

According to a preliminary study by the marketing research department, the following were areas of construction that could be served by the domes:

1. Bulk storage
2. Cold storage
3. Educational construction
4. Covers for industrial tanks
5. Light commercial construction
6. Planetariums
7. Recreational construction (such as a golf-course starter house)

The marketing research study focused on uses for existing dome structures. Most of the existing domes are made of cement-based materials. The study showed that large savings would result from using foam boards, due to the reduction of construction time.

Because of the new technology involved, the company decided to do its own contracting (at least for the first four to five years). Chen thought this was necessary to make sure that no mistakes were made by inexperienced contractor crews. (For example, if not applied properly, the plastic may burn.)

After building a few domes in the United States to demonstrate the concept, Chen contacted some leading U.S. architects. Reactions were as follows:

> "It's very interesting, but we're not sure the fire marshal of Chicago would ever give his OK."
>
> "Your tests show that foamed domes can be protected against fires, but there are no good tests for unconventional building materials as far as I am concerned."
>
> "I like the idea, but foam board does not have the impact resistance of cement."
>
> "We design a lot of recreational facilities, and kids will find a way to poke holes in the foam."
>
> "Building codes in our area are written for wood and cement structures. Maybe we'd be interested if the codes change."

After this unexpected reaction, management didn't know what to do. Chen still thinks they should go ahead with the project. She wants to build several more demonstration projects in the United States and at least three each in Europe and Japan to expose the concept in the global market. She thinks an interactive website and online video will also help spread the idea. She thinks architects outside the United States may be more receptive to really new ideas. Further, she says, it takes time for potential users to "see" and accept new ideas. She is sure that more exposure to more people will speed acceptance. And she is convinced that a few reports of well-constructed domes in leading trade papers and magazines will go a long way toward selling the idea. She is working on getting such reports right now. But her managers aren't sure they want to OK spending more money on "her" project. Her immediate boss is supportive, but the rest of the review board is less sure about more demonstration projects or going ahead at all—just in the United States or in global markets.

Evaluate how Resin Dynamics got into the present situation. What should Paige Chen do? What should Chen's managers do? Explain.

6. Dynamic Steel

Dynamic Steel is one of two major producers of wide-flange beams in the United States. The other producer is USX. A number of small firms also compete, but they tend to compete mainly on price in nearby markets where they can keep transport costs low. Typically, all interested competitors charge the same delivered price, which varies some depending on how far the customer is from either of the two major producers. In other words, local prices are higher in more remote geographic markets.

Wide-flange beams are one of the principal steel products used in construction. They are the modern version of what are commonly known as I-beams. USX rolls a full range of wide flanges from 6 to 36 inches. Dynamic Steel entered the field about 30 years ago, when it converted an existing mill to produce this product. Dynamic Steel's mill is limited to flanges up to 24 inches, however. At the time of the conversion, Dynamic Steel felt that customer usage of sizes over 24 inches was likely to be small. In recent years, however, there has been a definite trend toward the larger and heavier sections.

The beams produced by the various competitors are almost identical—because customers buy according to standard dimensional and physical-property specifications. In the smaller size range, there are a number of competitors. But above 14 inches, only USX and Dynamic Steel compete. Above 24 inches, USX has no competition.

All the steel companies sell these beams through their own sales forces. The customer for these beams is called a structural fabricator. This fabricator typically buys unshaped beams and other steel products from the mills and shapes them according to the specifications of each customer. The fabricator sells to the contractor or owner of the structure being built.

The structural fabricator usually must sell on a competitive-bid basis. The bidding is done on the plans and specifications prepared by an architectural or structural engineering firm and forwarded to the fabricator by the contractor who wants the bid. Although thousands of structural fabricators compete in the United States, relatively few account for the majority of wide-flange tonnage in the various geographical regions. Because the price is the same from all producers, they typically buy beams on the basis of availability (i.e., availability to meet production schedules) and performance (i.e., reliability in meeting the promised delivery schedule).

Several years ago, Dynamic Steel's production schedulers saw that they were going to have an excess of hot-rolled plate capacity in the near future. At the same time, development of a new production technology allowed Dynamic Steel to weld three plates together into a section with the same dimensional and physical properties and almost the same cross section as a rolled wide-flange beam. This development appeared to offer two key advantages to Dynamic Steel: (1) it would enable Dynamic Steel to use some of the excess plate capacity, and (2) larger sizes of wide-flange beams could be offered. Cost analysts showed that by using a fully depreciated plate mill and the new welding process, it would be possible to produce and sell larger wide-flange beams at competitive prices—that is, at the same price charged by USX.

Dynamic Steel's managers were excited about the possibilities because customers usually appreciate having a second source of supply. Also, the new approach would allow the production of up to a 60-inch flange. With a little imagination, these larger sizes might offer a significant breakthrough for the construction industry.

Dynamic Steel decided to go ahead with the new project. As the production capacity was converted, the salespeople were kept well informed of the progress. They, in turn, promoted this new capability to their customers, emphasizing that soon they would be able to offer a full range of beam products. Dynamic Steel sent several general information letters to a broad mailing list but did not advertise. The market development section of the sales department was very busy explaining the new possibilities of the process to fabricators at engineering trade associations and shows.

When the new production line was finally ready to go, the market reaction was disappointing. No orders came in and none were expected. In general, customers were wary of the new product. The structural fabricators felt they couldn't use it without the approval of their customers, because it would involve deviating from the specified rolled sections. And as long as they could still get the rolled section, why make the extra effort for something unfamiliar, especially with no price advantage. The salespeople were also bothered with a very common question: How can you take plate that you sell for about $460 per ton and make a product that you sell for $470 per ton? This question came up frequently and tended to divert the whole discussion to the cost of production rather than to the way the new product might be used or its value in the construction process.

Evaluate Dynamic Steel's situation. What should Dynamic Steel do?

7. Lake Pukati Lodge

Nestled in the high country of New Zealand's South Island is a getaway adventure playground unashamedly aimed at the world's very wealthy. Presidents, movie stars, and other such globe-trotters are the prime targets of this fledgling tourism business developed by Lake Pukati Lodge. The lodge offers this exclusive niche the opportunity of a secluded holiday in a little-known paradise. Guests, commonly under public scrutiny in their everyday lives, can escape such pressures at a hunting retreat designed specifically with their needs in mind.

A chance meeting between a New Zealand Department of Conservation investigator and the son of the former Indonesian president marked the beginning of this specialty tourist operation. Recognizing that "filthy rich" public figures are constantly surrounded by security and seldom have the luxury of going anywhere incognito, the New Zealander, Peter Slater, suggested that he and his new friend purchase a high-country station and hunting-guide company that was for sale. Slater believed that the facilities, and their secluded and peaceful environment, would make an ideal holiday haven for this elite group. His Indonesian partner concurred.

Slater, who was by now the company's managing director, developed a carefully tailored package of goods and services for the property. Architecturally designed accommodations, including a game trophy room and eight guest rooms, were constructed using high-quality South Island furniture and fittings to create the ambiance necessary to attract and satisfy the demands of their special clientele.

Although New Zealand has an international reputation for being sparsely populated and green, Slater knew that rich travelers frequently complained that local accommodations were below overseas standards. Because the price (NZ$700 a night) was not a significant variable for this target market, sumptuous guest facilities were built. These were designed to be twice the normal size of most hotel rooms, with double-glazed windows that revealed breathtaking views. Ten full-time staff and two seasonal guides were recruited to ensure that visitors received superior customized service, in fitting with the restrained opulence of the lodge.

The 28,000 hectares of original farmland that made up the retreat and backed onto the South Island's Mount Cook National Park were converted into a big-game reserve. All merino sheep on the land were sold, and deer, elk, chamois, and wapiti were brought in and released. This was a carefully considered plan. Slater, the former conservationist, believed that financially and environmentally this was the correct decision. Not only do tourists, each staying for one week and taking part in safari shooting, inject as much cash into the business as the station's annual wool clip used to fetch, but the game does less harm to the environment than sheep. Cattle, however, once part of the original station, were left to graze on lower river-flat areas.

For those high-flying customers seeking less bloodthirsty leisure activities, Lake Pukati Lodge developed photographic "safaris" and other product-line extensions. Horse-trekking, golfing on a nearby rural course (with no need for hordes of security forces), helicopter trips around nearby Lake Tekapo, nature walks, and other such activities formed part of the exclusive package.

While still in the early stages of operation, this retreat has already attracted a steady stream of visitors. To date, the manager has relied solely on positive word-of-mouth, publicity, and public relations to draw in new customers. Given the social and business circles in which his potential target market moves, Slater considers these to be the most appropriate forms of marketing communication. The only real concern for Lake Pukati Lodge has been the criticism of at least one New Zealand lobby group that the company is yet another example of local land passing into "foreign" hands, and that New Zealanders are prevented from using the retreat and excluded from its financial returns. However, this unwelcome attention has been fairly short-lived.

Identify the likely characteristics of the market segment being targeted by the company. Why are most target customers likely to be foreigners rather than New Zealanders? Suggest what expectations target customers are likely to have regarding the quality, reliability, and range of services. What are the implications for Lake Pukati Lodge? How difficult is it for Lake Pukati Lodge to undertake market research? Elaborate.

8. Carmine's Italian Restaurant

Rita Carmine, the owner and manager of Carmine's Italian Restaurant, is reviewing the slow growth of her restaurant. She's also thinking about the future and wondering if she should change her strategy. In particular, she is wondering if she should join a fast-food or family restaurant franchise chain. Several are located near her, but there are many franchisors without local restaurants. After doing some online research, she has learned that with help from the franchisors, some of these places gross $500,000 to $1 million a year. Of course, she would have to follow someone else's strategy and thereby lose her independence, which she doesn't like to think about. But those sales figures do sound good, and she has also heard that the return to the owner-manager (including salary) can be more than $150,000 per year. She has also considered creating a Facebook page for Carmine's Italian Restaurant but is not sure how that will help. She knows people go to Carmine's web page for directions and to see the menu—but why might she need Facebook or some other social media?

Carmine's Italian Restaurant is a fairly large restaurant—about 3,000 square feet—located in the center of a small shopping center completed early in 2013. Carmine's sells mainly full-course "home-cooked" Italian-style dinners (no bar) at moderate prices. In addition to Carmine's Italian Restaurant, other businesses in the shopping center include a supermarket, a hair salon, a liquor store, a computer repair business, and a vacant space that used to be a hardware store. The hardware store failed when a Home Depot located nearby. Rita has learned that a pizzeria is considering locating there soon. She wonders how that competition will affect her. Ample parking space is available at the shopping center, which is located in a residential section of a growing suburb to the east, along a heavily traveled major traffic route.

Rita graduated from a local high school and a nearby university and has lived in this town with her husband and two children for many years. She has been self-employed in the restaurant business since her graduation from college in 1998. Her most recent venture before opening Carmine's was a large restaurant that she operated successfully with her brother from 2004 to 2010. In 2010, Rita sold out her share because of illness. Following her recovery, she was anxious for something to do and opened the present restaurant in April 2013. Rita feels her plans for the business and her opening were well thought out. When she was ready to start her new restaurant, she looked at several possible locations before finally deciding on the present one. Rita explained, "I looked everywhere, but here I particularly noticed the heavy traffic. This is the crossroads for three major interstate highways. So obviously the potential is here."

Having decided on the location, Rita signed a 10-year lease with the option to renew for 10 more years, and then eagerly attacked the problem of outfitting the almost empty store space in the newly constructed building. She tiled the floor, put in walls of surfwood, installed plumbing and electrical fixtures, added an extra washroom, and purchased the necessary restaurant equipment. All this cost $240,000—which came from her own cash savings. She then spent an additional $3,000 for glassware, $4,000 for an initial food stock, and $4,250 to advertise the opening of Carmine's Italian Restaurant in the local newspaper. The paper serves the whole metro area, so the $4,250 bought only three quarter-page ads. These expenditures also came from her personal savings. Next she hired five waitresses at $550 a week and one chef at $1,100 a week. Then, with a $48,000 cash reserve for the business, she was ready to open. Reflecting her sound business sense, Rita knew she would need a substantial cash reserve to fall back on until the business got on its feet. She expected this to take about one year. She had no expectations of getting rich overnight. (Her husband, a high school teacher, was willing to support the family until the restaurant caught on.)

The restaurant opened in April and by August had a weekly gross revenue of only $4,800. Rita was a little discouraged with this, but she was still able to meet all her operating expenses without investing any new money in the business. She also got a few good customer reviews on Yelp. By September business was still slow, and Rita had to invest an additional $6,000 in the business just to survive.

Business had not improved by November, so Rita stepped up her advertising—hoping this would help. In December, she spent $2,400 of her cash reserve for radio advertising—10 late-evening spots on a news program at a station that aims at middle-income America. Rita also spent $1,600 more during the next several weeks for some Google Local advertising.

By April 2014, the situation had begun to improve, and by June her weekly gross was up to between $6,100 and $6,600. By March 2015, the weekly gross had risen to about $8,400. Rita increased the working hours of her staff from six to seven hours a week and added another cook to handle the increasing number of customers. Rita was more optimistic for the future because she was finally doing a little better than breaking even. Her full-time involvement seemed to be paying off. She had not put any new money into the business since summer 2014 and expected business to continue to rise. She had not yet taken any salary for herself, even though she had built up a small surplus of about $18,000. Instead, she planned to put in a bigger air-conditioning system at a cost of $10,000 and was also planning to use what salary she might have taken for herself to hire two new waitresses to handle the growing volume of business. And she saw that if business increased much more she would have to add another cook.

Evaluate Rita's past and present marketing strategy. What should she do now? Should she seriously consider joining some franchise chain?

9. Quiet Night Motel

Tristan Knaus is trying to decide whether he should make some minor changes in the way he operates his Quiet Night Motel or if he should join either the Days Inn or Holiday Inn motel chains. Some decision must be made soon because his present operation is losing money. But joining either of the chains will require fairly substantial changes, including new capital investment if he goes with Holiday Inn.

Tristan bought the recently completed 60-room motel two years ago after leaving a successful career as a production manager for a large producer of industrial machinery. He was looking for an interesting opportunity that would be less demanding than the production manager job. The Quiet Night Motel is located at the edge of a very small town near a rapidly expanding resort area and about one-half mile off an interstate highway. It is 10 miles from the tourist area, which has several nationally franchised full-service resort motels suitable for "destination" vacations. There is a Best Western, a Ramada Inn, and a Hilton Inn, as well as many mom-and-pop and limited-service, lower-priced motels–and some quaint bed-and-breakfast facilities–in the tourist area. The interstate highway near the Quiet Night Motel carries a great deal of traffic, because the resort area is between several major metropolitan areas. No development has taken place around the turnoff from the interstate highway. The only promotion for the tourist area along the interstate highway is two large signs near the turnoffs. They show the popular name for the area and that it is only 10 miles to the west. These signs are maintained by the tourist area's Tourist Bureau. In addition, the state transportation department maintains several small signs showing (by symbols) that near this turnoff one can find gas, food, and lodging. Tristan does not have any signs advertising Quiet Night Motel except the two on his property. He has been relying on people finding his motel as they go toward the resort area.

Initially, Tristan was very pleased with his purchase. He had traveled a lot himself and stayed in many different hotels and motels–so he had some definite ideas about what travelers wanted. He felt that a relatively plain but modern room with a comfortable bed, standard bath facilities, and free cable TV would appeal to most customers. Further, Tristan thought a swimming pool or any other nonrevenue-producing additions were not necessary. And he felt a restaurant would be a greater management problem than the benefits it would offer. However, after many customers commented about the lack of convenient breakfast facilities, Tristan served a free continental breakfast of coffee, juice, and rolls in a room next to the registration desk.

Day-to-day operations went fairly smoothly in the first two years, in part because Tristan and his wife handled registration and office duties as well as general management. During the first year of operation, occupancy began to stabilize around 55 percent of capacity. But according to industry figures, this was far below the average of 68 percent for his classification–motels without restaurants.

After two years of operation, Tristan was concerned because his occupancy rates continued to be below average. He decided to look for ways to increase both occupancy rate and profitability and still maintain his independence.

Tristan wanted to avoid direct competition with the full-service resort motels. He stressed a price appeal in his signs and brochures and was quite proud of the fact that he had been able to avoid all the "unnecessary expenses" of the full-service resort motels. As a result, Tristan was able to offer lodging at a very modest price–about 40 percent below the full-service hotels and comparable to the lowest-priced resort area motels. The customers who stayed at Quiet Night Motel said they found it quite acceptable. The hotel's online reviews at sites such as TripAdvisor.com and Hotels.com, although not numerous, were generally pretty positive. But he was troubled by what seemed to be a large number of people driving into his parking lot, looking around, and not coming in to register.

Tristan was particularly interested in the results of a recent study by the regional tourist bureau. This study revealed the following information about area vacationers:

1. 68 percent of the visitors to the area are young couples and older couples without children
2. 40 percent of the visitors plan their vacations and reserve rooms more than 60 days in advance
3. 66 percent of the visitors stay more than three days in the area and at the same location
4. 78 percent of the visitors indicated that recreational facilities were important in their choice of accommodations
5. 13 percent of the visitors had family incomes of less than $27,000 per year
6. 38 percent of the visitors indicated that it was their first visit to the area

After much thought, Tristan began to seriously consider affiliating with a national motel chain in hopes of attracting more customers and maybe protecting his motel from the increasing competition. There were constant rumors that more motels were being planned for the area. After some investigating, he focused on two national chain possibilities: Days Inn and Holiday Inn. Neither had affiliates in the area even though they each have about 2,000 units nationwide.

Days Inn of America, Inc. is an Atlanta-based chain of economy lodgings. It has been growing rapidly and is willing to take on new franchisees. A major advantage of Days Inn is that it would not require a major capital investment by Tristan. The firm is targeting people interested in lower-priced motels, in particular, senior citizens, the military, school sports teams, educators, and business travelers. In contrast, Holiday Inn would probably require Tristan to upgrade some of his facilities, including adding a swimming pool. The total new capital investment would be between $300,000 and $500,000, depending on how fancy he got. But then Tristan would be able to charge higher prices, perhaps $75 per day on the average rather than the $45 per day he's charging now.

The major advantages of going with either of these national chains would be their central reservation systems and their national names. Both companies offer nationwide, toll-free reservation lines, which produce about 40 percent of all bookings in affiliated motels. Both companies also offer websites (www.daysinn.com and www.holidayinn.com) that help find a specific hotel by destination, rate, amenities, quality rating, and availability.

A major difference between the two national chains is their method of promotion. Days Inn uses little TV advertising and less print advertising than Holiday Inn. Instead, Days Inn emphasizes sales promotions. In one campaign, for example, Blue Bonnet margarine users could exchange proof-of-purchase seals for a free night at a Days Inn. This tie-in led to the Days Inn system selling an additional 10,000 rooms. Further, Days Inn operates a September Days Club for travelers 50 and older who receive such benefits as discount rates and a quarterly travel magazine.

Days Inn also has other membership programs, including its InnCentives loyalty club for frequent business and leisure travelers. Other programs targeted to business travelers include two Corporate Rate programs and its new Days Business Place hotels. Not to be outdone, Holiday Inn has a membership program called Priority Club Worldwide. Both firms charge 8 percent of gross room revenues for belonging to their chain—to cover the costs of the reservation service and national promotion. This amount is payable monthly. In addition, franchise members must agree to maintain their facilities and make repairs and improvements as required. Failure to maintain facilities can result in losing the franchise. Periodic inspections are conducted as part of supervising the whole chain and helping the members operate more effectively.

Evaluate Tristan Knaus' present strategy. What should he do? Explain.

10. Cousin's Ice Center

Mark Cousin, the manager of Cousin's Ice Center, is trying to decide what strategies to use to increase profits.

Cousin's Ice Center is an ice-skating rink with a conventional hockey rink surface (85 feet × 200 feet). It is the only indoor ice rink in a northern U.S. city of about 450,000. The city's recreation department operates some outdoor rinks in the winter, but it doesn't offer regular ice-skating programs because of weather variability.

Mark runs a successful hockey program that is more than breaking even—but this is about all he can expect if he offers only hockey. To try to increase his profits, Mark is trying to expand and improve his public skating program. With such a program, he could have as many as 700 people in a public session at one time, instead of limiting the use of the ice to 12 to 24 hockey players per hour. While the receipts from hockey can be as high as $200 an hour (plus concession sales), the receipts from a two-hour public skating session—charging $5 per person—could yield up to $3,500 for a two-hour period (plus much higher concession sales). The potential revenue from such large public skating sessions could make Cousin's Ice Center a really profitable operation. But, unfortunately, just scheduling public sessions doesn't mean that a large number will come. In fact, only a few prime times seem likely: Friday and Saturday evenings and Saturday and Sunday afternoons.

Mark has included 14 public skating sessions in his ice schedule, but so far they haven't attracted as many people as he had hoped. In total, they generate only a little more revenue than if the times were sold for hockey use. Offsetting this extra revenue are extra costs. More staff people are needed to handle a public skating session—guards, a ticket seller, skate rental, and more concession help. So the net revenue from either use is about the same. He could cancel some of the less attractive public sessions—like the noontime daily sessions, which have very low attendance—and make the average attendance figures look a lot better. But he feels that if he is going to offer public skating he must have a reasonable selection of times. He has noticed the wide variation in the kinds of people attracted to the different skating sessions.

The Saturday and Sunday afternoon public skating sessions have been the most successful, with an average of 200 people attending during the winter season. Typically, this is a "kid-sitting" session. More than half of the patrons are young children who have been dropped off by their parents for several hours, but there are also some family groups.

In general, the kids and the families have a good time—and a fairly loyal group comes every Saturday and/or Sunday during the winter season. In the spring and fall, however, attendance drops by about half, depending on how nice the weather is. (Mark schedules no public sessions in the summer, focusing instead on hockey clinics and figure skating.)

The Friday and Saturday evening public sessions are a big disappointment. The sessions run from 8 until 10, a time when he had hoped to attract teenagers and young adult couples. At $5 per person, plus $1.50 for skate rental, this would be an economical date. In fact, Mark has seen quite a few young couples—and some keep coming back. But he also sees a surprising number of 8- to 14-year-olds who have been dropped off by their parents. The younger kids tend to race around the rink playing tag. This affects the whole atmosphere, making it less appealing for dating couples and older patrons.

Mark has been hoping to develop a teenage and young-adult market for a "social activity," adapting the format used by roller-skating rinks. Their public skating sessions feature a variety of couples-only and group games as well as individual skating to dance music. Turning ice-skating sessions into such social activities is not common, however, although industry newsletters suggest that a few ice-rink operators have had success with the roller-skating format. Seemingly, the ice-skating sessions are viewed as active recreation, offering exercise or a sports experience.

Mark installed some soft lights to try to change the evening atmosphere. The music was selected to encourage people to skate to the beat and couples to skate together. Some people complained about the "old" music, but it was "danceable," and some skaters really liked it. For a few sessions, Mark even tried to have some couples-only skates. The couples liked it, but this format was strongly resisted by the young boys who felt that they had paid their money and there was no reason why they should be kicked off the ice. Mark also tried to attract more young people and especially couples by bringing in a local rock radio station disc jockey to broadcast from Cousin's Ice Center—playing music and advertising the Friday and Saturday evening public sessions. Cousin's son even set up Facebook and Instagram pages for Cousin's, but only a dozen or so people "liked" the pages. All of this appeared to have no effect on attendance, which varies from 50 to 100 per two-hour session during the winter.

Mark seriously considered the possibility of limiting the Friday and Saturday evening sessions to people aged 14 and older—to try to change the environment. He knew it would take time to change people's attitudes. But when he counted the customers, he realized this would be risky. More than a quarter of his customers on an average weekend night appeared to be 13 or younger. This meant that he would have to make a serious commitment to building the teen and young-adult market. And, so far, his efforts haven't been successful. He had already invested more than $3,000 in lighting changes and more than $9,000 promoting the sessions over the rock music radio station, with very disappointing results. Although the station's sales rep said the station reached teenagers all over town, an on-air offer for a free skating session did not get a single response!

Some days, Mark feels it's hopeless. Maybe he should accept that most public ice-skating sessions are a mixed bag. Or maybe he should just sell the time to hockey groups. Still he keeps hoping that something can be done to improve weekend evening public skating attendance, because the upside potential is so good. And the Saturday and Sunday afternoon sessions are pretty good money-makers.

Evaluate Cousin's Ice Center's situation. What should Mark Cousin do? Why?

11. Running On

Carla Gomez is the owner of Running On—a retail store that sells shoes and accessories to runners. Carla is trying to decide what she should do with her retail business and how committed she should be to her current target market.

Carla started Running On retail store in 1994 when she was only 24 years old. At that time, she was a nationally ranked runner and felt that the growing interest in jogging offered real potential for a store that provided serious runners with the shoes and advice they needed. The jogging boom quickly turned Running On into a profitable business selling high-end running shoes—and Carla made a very good return on her investment for the first 10 years. From 1998 until 2008, Carla emphasized Nike shoes, which were well accepted and seen as top quality. Nike's aggressive promotion and quality shoes resulted in a positive image that made it possible to get a $5 to $7 per pair premium for Nike shoes. Good volume and good margins resulted in attractive profits for Carla.

Committing so heavily to Nike seemed like a good idea when its marketing and engineering were the best available. In addition to running shoes, Nike had other athletic shoes Carla could sell. So even though they were not her primary focus, Carla did stock other Nike shoes, including walking shoes, shoes for aerobic exercise, basketball shoes, tennis shoes, and cross-trainers. She also added more sportswear to her store and put more emphasis on fashion rather than just function.

Even with this broadened product line, Carla's sales flattened out—and she wasn't sure what to do to get her business back in growth mode. She realized that she was growing older and so were many of her longer-term customers. Many of them were finding that jogging isn't just hard work—it's hard on the body, especially the knees. Some were not running as often—and buying shoes less often. Other of her previously loyal runner-customers were switching to other, less demanding exercise programs. However, when she tried to orient her store and product line more toward these people, she wasn't as effective in serving the needs of serious runners—still an important source of sales for the store.

She was also facing more competition on all fronts. Many consumers who don't really do any serious exercise buy running shoes as their day-to-day casual shoes. As a result, many department stores, discount stores, and regular shoe stores have put more and more emphasis on athletic shoes in their product assortment. Many customers were growing more comfortable buying shoes online. When Carla added other brands and put more emphasis on fashion, she found that she was in direct competition with a number of other stores, which put more pressure on her to lower prices and cut her profit margins. For example, in Carla's area there are a number of local retail chains offering lower-cost and lower-quality versions of similar shoes as well as related fashion apparel. Walmart also expanded its assortment of athletic shoes—and it offers rock-bottom prices. Other chains, such as Foot Locker, have focused their promotion and product lines on specific target markets. Still, all of them (including Carla's Running On, the local chains, Walmart, and Foot Locker) are scrambling to catch up with rival category killers whose selections are immense.

In the spring of 2014 Carla tried an experiment. She took on a line of high-performance athletic shoes that were made to order. The distinctive feature of these shoes was that the sole was molded to precisely fit the customer's foot. A pair of these custom-made shoes cost about $170, so the market was not large. Further, Carla didn't put much promotional emphasis on this line. However, when a customer came in the store with a serious interest in high-performance shoes, Carla's sales clerks would tell them about the custom shoe alternative and show a sample. When a customer was interested, a mold of the customer's bare foot was made at the store, using an innovative material that hardened in just a few minutes without leaving a sticky mess. Carla sent the mold off to the manufacturer by UPS, and about two weeks later the finished shoes arrived. Customers who tried these shoes were delighted with the result. However, the company that offered them ran into financial trouble and went out of business.

Carla recently learned about another company that is offering a very similar custom shoe program. However, that company requires more promotion investment by retailers and in return provides exclusive sales territories. Another requirement is that the store establish a website promoting the shoes and providing more detail on how the order process works. Running On had a pretty basic website, so Carla knew she would have to spend some money to make this happen. In addition, all of a retailer's salesclerks are also required to go through a special two-day training program so that they know how to present the benefits of the shoe and do the best job creating the molds. The training program is free, but Carla would have to pay travel, hotel, and food expenses for her salespeople. So before even getting started, the new program would cost her several thousand dollars.

Carla is uncertain about what to do. Although sales have dropped, she is still making a reasonable profit and has a relatively good base of repeat customers, with the serious runners still more than half of her sales and profits. She thinks that the custom shoe alternative is a way to differentiate her store from the mass-merchandisers and to sharpen her focus on the target market of serious runners. On the other hand, that doesn't really solve the problem that the "runners" market seems to be shrinking. It also doesn't address the question of how best to keep a lot of the aging customers she already serves who seem to be shifting away from an emphasis on running. She also worries that she'll lose the loyalty of her repeat customers if she shifts the store further away from her running niche and more toward fashionable athletic shoes or fashionable casual wear. Yet athletic wear—women's, in particular—has come a long way in recent years. Designers such as Donna Karan, Calvin Klein, Georgio Armani, and Ralph Lauren are part of the fast-growing women's athletic wear business.

So Carla is trying to decide if there is anything else she can do to better promote her current store and product line, or if she should think about changing her strategy in a more dramatic way. Any change from her current focus would involve retraining her current salespeople and perhaps hiring new salespeople. Adding and maintaining a website isn't an insurmountable challenge, but it is not an area where she has either previous experience or skill.

Clearly, a real shift in emphasis would require that Carla make some hard decisions about her target market and her whole marketing mix. She's got some flexibility—it's not like she's a manufacturer of shoes with a big investment in a factory that can't be changed. On the other hand, she's not certain she's ready for a big change, especially a change that would mean starting over again from scratch. She started Running On because she was interested in running and felt she had something special to offer. Now she worries that she's just grasping at straws without a real focus or any obvious competitive advantage. She also knows that she is already much more successful than she ever dreamed when she started her business—and in her heart she wonders if she wasn't just spoiled by growth that came fast and easy at the start.

Evaluate Carla Gomez's present strategy. Evaluate the alternative strategies she is considering. Is her primary problem her emphasis on running shoes, her emphasis on trying to hang on to her current customers, or is it something else? What should she do? Why?

12. DrV.com—Custom Vitamins

Dr. Victoria van der Walt has to decide how to handle a complaint letter from a customer. When she received the letter, she passed it along to Paul Zimbalist, the firm's customer service manager, to get his recommendation. Now van der Walt has a reply from Zimbalist, and she must decide how to respond to the customer and determine if changes are needed in her company's customer service operations.

Dr. van der Walt has a reputation as a health and nutrition guru. Her fame grew after she published two books—both of which were very popular and received a lot of attention in the press. Five years ago, Internet entrepreneur Tania Cox approached her with the idea of creating a website to sell custom vitamins under Dr. Victoria's name.

van der Walt and Cox became partners, and the business enjoyed success in its first four years of operation. Cox handles the website technology, inventory, production, and shipping. Dr. van der Walt is the health expert, creates content provided on the website, and is in charge of marketing and customer service. The complaint letter and reply from Zimbalist follow:

Dear Dr. van der Walt,

I am a longtime fan of your books and like to visit your website for health tips. As a new grandmother, my health is even more important to me. I want to see my grandchildren graduate from high school, go to college, and have kids of their own.

You have made me a bit of a guru as well. I work out every day. People always ask me how I stay so fit and healthy. Having read both your books, I tell them they should exercise regularly and take vitamins and supplements for long-term health. I always recommend your DrV.com website and especially the section on your custom vitamins. That is my favorite part of your website. I really like that you take information about me and my medical history—and then recommend custom vitamins and supplements. I also like how you send me packages that each contain a daily dose.

But after my recent experiences, my loyalty to you and your company is now in jeopardy. Here is my story.

Six months ago, I went to the website to reorder my vitamins and supplements. The home page announced a new and improved health survey and custom health program. So I went through the survey and filled out all the details—it would have been nice if you had saved some of them from my previous survey. At the end of the survey the website offered me a 90-day supply of a custom set of vitamins and supplements selected for my specific needs. The $212 price was about $50 more than my previous 90-day supply, but I trusted your advice so I placed the order.

About two-and-a-half months later, I phoned your 800 number for DrV.com to place a refill order. The person on the phone was very nice and asked if I wanted to set up automatic refills. I said no because I hate those automatic programs. They remind me of those book clubs that automatically send you books you don't want if you do not reply fast enough. About a week later my order arrived—then two days later another identical order arrived. I did not understand this, but I figured I would eventually use them up and I kept everything (and I was billed for both orders—$424 on my credit card). I should mention there was no e-mail explaining this mystery delivery. I was a little annoyed and sent an e-mail to customer service seeking an explanation. I received an automated response, "Thank you for your inquiry; someone will get back to you within 24 hours." No one ever replied, but I forgot about it.

Then two weeks ago I received an e-mail from DrV.com telling me my refill order had been shipped and would arrive in a few days. But I did not place a refill order! I did not even need more vitamins because I was still working off the two 90-day supplies that I received three months ago. So I replied by e-mail that I did not want the order and to cancel it. A reply e-mail (from Sally) told me that I had signed up for automatic refill six months ago. I replied that I certainly had not and that I would not pay for the order that was being sent.

A few days later I received a call from Paul Zimbalist, your director of customer service. He told me that I had originally signed up for automatic refill and that was why I received vitamins. I told him that was impossible, and he told me that unless I checked some box on my original order that this was done automatically, "for my convenience." He said there were also several warnings and that I must have missed those. *Basically, I think he told me this was my fault. I did not like that one bit!!!*

Mr. Zimbalist told me the vitamins were on their way, but I could refuse delivery of them. He offered to let me have them for 20 percent off if I simply kept them. Unfortunately, the vitamins were on my doorstep when I arrived home that day. I had to take the vitamins to UPS to get them shipped back to you.

You guys are no longer very good at your business. You might have a great product, but I am now seeing other vitamin companies offering the same products. I have no doubt these other companies offer better customer service. If you want me back as a customer, I would expect a formal apology from Mr. Zimbalist and a free 90-day supply. Otherwise, I figure my business will be welcomed at one of your competitors. I will be sure all my friends know about my experience at DrV.com, and I intend to post a bad review at resellerratings.com, too.

Sincerely,
Maxine Slezak

Next is the reply that Paul Zimbalist sent to Dr. van der Walt concerning Maxine Slezak's letter.

Dear Victoria,

As per your request, I reviewed Mrs. Slezak's order history. Yes, she is a very good customer who spent almost $800 with us last year. And she is a member of our referral program—and we can count at least seven new customers she has directed to us in the last 18 months. But I want to clarify some of this particular situation.

- You might recall that our automatic refill program has been a big success. Since we instituted the program a year ago, our customer retention rate has jumped by 10 percent. There are occasional complaints, but given the large number of customers we serve, the complaints are really just a "drop in the bucket."
- When Mrs. Slezak placed her order six months ago, there were at least two different warnings about the automatic refill program—customers have to check a box at the bottom of the screen to "opt out" of the program. We all agreed that it was better to make them part of the program automatically, but to give them two chances to remove themselves from automatic delivery.
- I do not know if we replied to her e-mail asking for customer service help.
- I did not tell Mrs. Slezak that this was her fault, but I did tell her that when she signed up there were two chances for her to choose to not be part of the automatic refill program.
- Mrs. Slezak did not get an e-mail notifying her of the first refill order because that system was not yet in place. But this has now been fixed, and the e-mail notifying her when we ship shows that this works.
- I offered her 20 percent off, as is our standard policy when we make a mistake. Considering this was her mistake, I thought this was generous.
- If Mrs. Slezak had called and asked, I could have had UPS come out and pick up the package for return to us.

I do not recommend giving her a free 90-day supply. This may simply encourage her to complain again in the future. Besides, this was not our mistake. We may be better off without certain customers—and I think Mrs. Slezak falls into this category.

Feel free to call me if you have any more questions.
Paul

Assess the customer service operations at DrV.com. What should van der Walt do about Mrs. Slezak? What changes, if any, should van der Walt make to customer service and ordering operations?

13. Paper Products, Inc. (PPI)*

Stasia Acosta, marketing manager for Paper Products, Inc., must decide whether she should permit her largest customer to buy some of PPI's commonly used file folders under the customer's brand rather than PPI's own FILEX brand. She is afraid that if she refuses, this customer—Business Center, Inc.—will go to another file folder producer and PPI will lose this business.

Business Center, Inc. is a major distributor of office supplies and has already managed to put its own brand on more than 45 high-sales-volume office supply products. It distributes these products—as well as the branded products of many manufacturers—through its nationwide distribution network, which includes 150 retail stores. Now Lance Richardson, vice president of marketing for Business Center, is seeking a line of file folders similar in quality to PPI's FILEX brand, which now has more than 60 percent of the market.

This is not the first time that Business Center has asked PPI to produce a file folder line for Business Center. On both previous occasions, Stasia turned down the requests and Business Center continued to buy. In fact, Business Center not only continued to buy the file folders but also the rest of PPI's product lines. And total sales continued to grow as Business Center built new stores. Business Center accounts for about 30 percent

*Adapted from a case by Professor Hardy, University of Western Ontario.

of Stasia Acosta's business. And FILEX brand file folders account for about 35 percent of this volume.

In the past, PPI consistently refused such dealer-branding requests as a matter of corporate policy. This policy was set some years ago because of a desire (1) to avoid excessive dependence on any one customer and (2) to sell its own brands so that its success is dependent on the quality of its products rather than just a low price. The policy developed from a concern that if it started making products under other customers' brands, those customers could shop around for a low price and the business would be very fickle. At the time the policy was set, Stasia realized that it might cost PPI some business. But it felt wise, nevertheless, to be better able to control the firm's future.

PPI has been in business 28 years and now has a sales volume of $40 million. Its primary products are file folders, file markers and labels, and a variety of indexing systems. PPI offers such a wide range of size, color, and type that no competitor can match it in its part of the market. About 40 percent of PPI's file folder business is in specialized lines such as files for oversized blueprint and engineer drawings; see-through files for medical markets; and greaseproof and waterproof files for marine, oil field, and other hazardous environmental markets. PPI's competitors are mostly small paper converters. But excess capacity in the industry is substantial, and these converters are always hungry for orders and willing to cut prices. Further, the raw materials for the FILEX line of file folders are readily available.

PPI's distribution system consists of 10 regional stationery suppliers (40 percent of total sales), Business Center, Inc. (30 percent), and more than 40 local stationers who have wholesale and retail operations (30 percent). The 10 regional stationers each have about six branches, while the local stationers each have one wholesale and three or four retail locations. The regional suppliers sell directly to large corporations and to some retailers. In contrast, Business Center's main volume comes from sales to local businesses and walk-in customers at its 150 retail stores.

Stasia has a real concern about the future of the local stationers' business. Some are seriously discussing the formation of buying groups to obtain volume discounts from vendors and thus compete more effectively with Business Center's 150 retail stores, the large regionals, and the superstore chains, which are spreading rapidly. These chains—for example, Staples and Office Depot—operate stores of 16,000 to 20,000 square feet (i.e., large stores compared to the usual office supply stores) and let customers wheel through high-stacked shelves to supermarket-like checkout counters. These chains stress convenience, wide selection, and much lower prices than the typical office supply retailers. They buy directly from manufacturers, such as PPI, bypassing wholesalers like Business Center. It is likely that the growing pressure from these chains is causing Business Center to renew its proposal to buy a file line with its own name. For example, Staples offers its own dealer brand of files and many other types of products.

None of Stasia's other accounts is nearly as effective in retailing as Business Center, which has developed a good reputation in every major city in the country. Business Center's profits have been the highest in the industry. Further, its brands are almost as well-known as those of some key producers—and its expansion plans are aggressive. And now, these plans are being pressured by the fast-growing superstores, which are already knocking out many local stationers.

Stasia is sure that PPI's brands are well entrenched in the market, despite the fact that most available money has been devoted to new-product development rather than promotion of existing brands. But Stasia is concerned that if Business Center brands its own file folders, it will sell them at a discount and may even bring down the whole market price level. Across all the lines of file folders, Stasia is averaging a 35 percent gross margin, but the commonly used file folders sought by Business Center are averaging only a 20 percent gross margin. And cutting this margin further does not look very attractive to Stasia.

Stasia is not sure whether Business Center will continue to sell PPI's FILEX brand of folders along with Business Center's own file folders if Business Center is able to find a source of supply. Business Center's history has been to sell its own brand and a major brand side by side, especially if the major brand offers high quality and has strong brand recognition.

Stasia is having a really hard time deciding what to do about the existing branding policy. PPI has excess capacity and could easily handle the Business Center business. And she fears that if she turns down this business, Business Center will just go elsewhere and its own brand will cut into PPI's existing sales at Business Center stores. Further, what makes Business Center's offer especially attractive is that PPI's variable manufacturing costs would be quite low in relation to any price charged to Business Center—that is, there are substantial economies of scale, so the extra business could be very profitable—if Stasia doesn't consider the possible impact on the FILEX line. This Business Center business will be easy to get, but it will require a major change in policy, which Stasia will have to sell to Ramon Torres, PPI's president. This may not be easy. Ramon is primarily interested in developing new and better products so the company can avoid the "commodity end of the business."

Evaluate PPI's current strategy. What should Stasia Acosta do about Business Center's offer? Explain.

14. Schrock & Oh Design

Kevin Schrock and Katie Oh met while studying architecture in college. They became good friends and after graduating decided to start a modern architecture firm in Los Angeles. Schrock & Oh Design opened in 2011, specializing in contemporary residential and commercial projects.

Starting an architecture business in the midst of a recession was not easy. The business struggled in those first few years. But they loved what they did, scrimped and saved, and took whatever work they could get. The economy gradually improved. They soon built a modest business based mostly on word-of-mouth; Kevin noted that their only marketing investment was business cards and a small five-page website. They did not have the money to invest in much more. They survived and eventually built a bit of a reputation for their work.

Reputation and word-of-mouth were carrying Schrock & Oh Design only so far. They wanted to move their business to the next level. They started by advertising on Yahoo! and Google. Although this led to some initial inquiries, very few panned out into actual work. People seemed most interested in just asking questions, seeing photographs of their work, and learning more; they were just gathering ideas. These customers were early in the buying process. Kevin and Katie spent lots of time talking to customers but not much time designing and billing out. "It feels like we spend so much time educating these customers that in the end, we hardly make any money even if they do work with us on a design project," noted Kevin.

Their next foray was to start blogging. Katie was a pretty good writer and started a blog on the SchrockOhDesign.com website. She blogged about the industry—"Development Fact of the Day—China," which discussed a magazine article she read about architecture in *Metropolis Magazine* and "Is Prefab the Future," which described issues around the modern prefabricated home. Prefab homes were one of their competitors. Although low in cost, they are not easily customized to a customer's specific needs. Some of her posts generated traffic to the website, but few turned into leads for the design firm. When they looked at clickstream data, they found that most customers read the blog and then left the company's website.

They were stumped about where to go next. "We tried all the marketing we knew. We started with advertising, which did not seem to work. So we went to this new 'owned media' approach but that isn't getting us any business either," claimed Katie. "It doesn't seem like a Facebook page or Twitter feed is our best route either. Our goal is to attract qualified leads. We would like to attract customers who already know they want to build a contemporary home or commercial building—and then we can use our time with them to discuss what our design firm can do."

Evaluate Schrock & Oh Design's strategy so far. What would you recommend to help the architecture firm attract more qualified leads?

15. The Scioto Group

Theresa Campana owns The Scioto Group (named after a local river)—a manufacturers' rep agency. The Scioto Group sells similar products for noncompeting producers in the technology industry. She is deciding whether to add a new product line—serving another producer. She is very concerned because although she wants more lines, she feels that something is wrong with her latest candidate.

Theresa graduated from a large midwestern university in 2006 with a BS in business. She worked selling cell phones for a year. Then Theresa decided to go into business for herself and formed The Scioto Group. Looking for opportunities, Theresa placed several ads in her local newspaper in Columbus, Ohio, announcing that she was interested in becoming a sales representative in the area. She was quite pleased to receive a number of responses. Eventually, she became the sales representative in the Columbus area for three local computer software producers: Accto Company, which produces accounting-related software; Saleco, Inc., a producer of sales management software; and Invo, Inc., a producer of inventory control software. All of these companies were relatively small and were represented in other areas by other sales representatives like Theresa. The companies often sent her leads when customers from her area expressed interest at a trade show or through the company's website.

Theresa's main job was to call on possible customers. Once she made a sale, she would fax the signed license agreement to the respective producer, who would then UPS the programs directly to the customer or, more often, provide a key code for a website download. The producer would bill the customer, and Theresa would receive a commission varying from 5 to 10 percent of the dollar value of the sale. Theresa was expected to pay her own expenses. And the producers would handle any user questions, either by using 800 numbers for out-of-town calls or by e-mail queries to a technical support group.

Theresa called on anyone in the Columbus area who might use the products she sold. At first, her job was relatively easy, and sales came quickly because she had little competition. Many national companies offer similar products, but at that time they were not well represented in the Columbus area. Most small businesses needed someone to demonstrate what the software could do.

In 2008, Theresa sold $250,000 worth of Accto software, earning a 10 percent commission; $100,000 worth of Saleco software, also earning a 10 percent commission; and $200,000 worth of Invo software, earning a 7 percent commission. She was encouraged with her progress and looked forward to expanding sales in the future. She was especially optimistic because she had achieved these sales volumes without overtaxing herself. In fact, she felt she was operating at about 60 percent of her capacity and could easily take on new lines. So she began looking for other products she could sell in the Columbus area.

A local software company has recently approached Theresa about selling its newly developed software, which is basically a network security product. It is designed to secretly track all of the keystrokes and mouse clicks of each employee as he or she uses the computer—so that an employer can identify inappropriate uses of its computers or confidential data. Theresa isn't too enthusiastic about this offer because the commission is only 2 percent on potential annual sales of about $150,000—and she also doesn't like the idea of selling a product that might undermine the privacy of employees who are not doing anything wrong.

Now Theresa is faced with another decision. The owner of the MetalCoat Company, also in Columbus, has made what looks like an attractive offer. She called on MetalCoat to see if the firm might be interested in buying her accounting software. The owner didn't want the software, but he was very impressed with Theresa. After two long discussions, he asked if she would like to help MetalCoat solve its current problem. MetalCoat is having trouble with marketing, and the owner would like Theresa to take over the whole marketing effort.

MetalCoat produces solvents used to make coatings for metal products. It sells mainly to industrial customers in the mid-Ohio area and faces many competitors selling essentially the same products and charging the same low prices.

MetalCoat is a small manufacturer. Last year's sales were $500,000. It could handle at least four times this sales volume with ease and is willing to expand to increase sales—its main objective in the short run. MetalCoat's owner is offering Theresa a 12 percent commission on all sales if she will take charge of its pricing, advertising, and sales efforts. Theresa is flattered by the offer, but she is a little worried because it is a different type of product and she would have to learn a lot about it. The job also might require a great deal more traveling than she is doing now. For one thing, she would have to call on new potential customers in mid-Ohio, and she might have to travel up to 200 miles around Columbus to expand the solvent business. Further, she realizes that she is being asked to do more than just sell. But she did take marketing courses in college and thinks the new opportunity might be challenging.

Evaluate Theresa Campana's current strategy and how the proposed solvent line fits in with what she is doing now. What should she do? Why?

16. Hanratty Company

Joe Hanratty, owner of Hanratty Company, feels his business is threatened by a tough new competitor. And now Joe must decide quickly about an offer that may save his business.

Joe has been a sales rep for lumber mills for about 20 years. He started selling in a clothing store but gave it up after two years to work in a lumberyard because the future looked much better in the building materials industry. After drifting from one job to another, Joe finally settled down and worked his way up to manager of a large wholesale building materials distribution warehouse in Richmond, Virginia. In 2000, he formed Hanratty Company and went into business for himself, selling carload lots of lumber to lumberyards in southeastern Virginia.

Joe works with five large lumber mills on the West Coast. They notify him when a carload of lumber is available to be shipped, specifying the grade, condition, and number of each size board in the shipment. Joe isn't the only person selling for these mills—but he is the only one in his area. He isn't required to take any particular number of carloads per month—but once he tells a mill he wants a particular shipment, title passes to him and he has to sell it to someone. Joe's main function is to find a buyer, buy the lumber from the mill as it's being shipped, and have the railroad divert the car to the buyer.

Having been in this business for 20 years, Joe knows all of the lumberyard buyers in his area very well and is on good working terms with them. He does most of his business over the telephone or by e-mail from his small office, but he tries to see each of the buyers about once a month. He has been marking up the lumber between 4 and 6 percent—the standard markup, depending on the grades and mix in each carload—and has been able to make a good living for himself and his family. The going prices are widely publicized in trade publications and are listed on the Internet, so the buyers can easily check to be sure Joe's prices are competitive.

In the last few years, a number of Joe's lumberyard customers have gone out of business—and others have lost sales. The main problem is competition from several national home improvement chains that have moved into Joe's market area. These chains buy lumber in large quantities direct from a mill, and their low prices, available inventory, and one-stop shopping are taking some customers away from the traditional lumberyards. Some customers think the quality of the lumber is not quite as good at the big chains, and some contractors stick with the lumberyards out of loyalty or because they get better service, including rush deliveries when they're needed. Then came the mortgage crisis, and the residential housing market really slowed down, though not as bad in Richmond as in other parts of the country. Fortunately for Joe, the commercial market remained pretty strong and he had good relationships there—or Joe's profits would have taken an even bigger hit.

Six months ago, though, things got even worse. An aggressive young salesman set up in the same business, covering about the same area but representing different lumber mills. This new salesman charges about the same prices as Joe but undersells him once or twice a week in order to get the sale. On several occasions he even set up what was basically an online auction to quickly sell excess wood that was not moving fast enough. Many lumber buyers—feeling the price competition from the big chains and realizing that they are dealing with a homogeneous product—seem to be willing to buy from the lowest-cost source. This has hurt Joe financially and personally—because even some of his old friends are willing to buy from the new competitor if the price is lower. The near-term outlook seems dark, because Joe doubts that there is enough business to support two firms like his, especially if the markup gets shaved any closer. Now they seem to be splitting the shrinking business about equally, as the newcomer keeps shaving his markup.

A week ago, Joe was called on by Amy Balderas of Arbor Door and Window Co., a large manufacturer of windows, raised-panel doors, and accessories. Arbor doesn't sell to the big chains and instead distributes its quality line only through independent lumberyards. Amy knows that Joe is well acquainted with the local lumberyards and wants him to become Arbor's exclusive distributor (sales rep) of residential windows and accessories in his area. Amy gave Joe several brochures on Arbor's product lines. She also explained Arbor's new support program, which will help train and support Joe and interested lumberyards on how to sell the higher markup accessories. Later, in a lengthy e-mail, Amy explained how this program will help Joe and interested lumberyards differentiate themselves in this very competitive market.

Most residential windows of specified grades are basically "commodities" that are sold on the basis of price and availability, although some premium and very low-end windows are also sold. The national home-improvement chains usually stock and sell only the standard sizes. Most independent lumberyards do not stock windows because there are so many possible sizes. Instead, the lumberyards custom order from the stock sizes each factory offers. Stock sizes are not set by industry standards; they vary from factory to factory, and some offer more sizes. Most factories can deliver these custom orders in two to six weeks, which is usually adequate to satisfy contractors who buy and install them according to architectural plans. This part of the residential window business is well established, and most lumberyards buy from several different window manufacturers—

to ensure sources of supply in case of strikes, plant fires, and so on. How the business is split depends on price and the personality and persuasiveness of the sales reps. And given that prices are usually similar, the sales rep–customer relationship can be quite important.

Arbor gives more choice than just about any other supplier. It offers many variations in 1/8-inch increments—to cater to remodelers who must adjust to many situations. Arbor's online ordering system is state-of-the-art. The lumberyard can connect to the website, enter the specs for a window online, and within seconds get a price quote and estimated delivery time.

One reason Amy has approached Joe is because of Joe's many years in the business. But the other reason is that Arbor is aggressively trying to expand—relying on its made-to-order windows, a full line of accessories, and a newly developed factory support system to help differentiate it from the many other window manufacturers. To give Joe a quick big picture of the opportunity she is offering, Amy explained the window market as follows:

1. For commercial construction, the usual building code ventilation requirements are satisfied with mechanical ventilation. So the windows do not have to operate to permit natural ventilation. They are usually made with heavy-grade aluminum framing. Typically, a distributor furnishes and installs the windows. As part of its service, the distributor provides considerable technical support, including engineered drawings and diagrams to the owners, architects, and/or contractors.
2. For residential construction, on the other hand, windows must be operable to provide ventilation. Residential windows are usually made of wood, frequently with light-gauge aluminum or vinyl on the exterior. The national chains get some volume with standard-sized windows, but lumberyards are the most common source of supply for contractors in Joe's area. These lumberyards do not provide any technical support or engineered drawings. A few residential window manufacturers do have their own sales centers in selected geographic areas, which provide a full range of support and engineering services, but none are anywhere near Joe's area.

Arbor feels a big opportunity exists in the commercial building repair and rehabilitation market (sometimes called the retrofit market) for a crossover of residential windows to commercial applications—and it has designed some accessories and a factory support program to help lumberyards get this "commercial" business. For applications such as nursing homes and dormitories (which must meet commercial codes), the wood interior of a residential window is desired, but the owners and architects are accustomed to commercial grades and building systems. And in some older facilities, the windows may have to provide supplemental ventilation for a deficient mechanical system. So what is needed is a combination of the residential *operable* window with a heavy-gauge commercial exterior frame that is easy to specify and install. And this is what Arbor is offering with a combination of its basic windows and easily adjustable accessory frames. Two other residential window manufacturers offer a similar solution, but neither has pushed its products aggressively and neither offers technical support to lumberyards or trains sales reps like Joe to do the necessary job. Amy feels this could be a unique opportunity for Joe.

The sales commission on residential windows would be about 5 percent of sales. Arbor would do the billing and collecting. By getting just 20 to 30 percent of his lumberyards' residential window business, Joe could earn about a third of his current income. But the real upside would come in the long term by increasing his residential window share. Joe is confident that the housing market will turn around soon, and when it does he will be well-positioned for growth. To do this, he will have to help the lumberyards get a lot more (and more profitable) business by invading the commercial market with residential windows and the bigger markup accessories needed for this market. Joe will also earn a 20 percent commission on the accessories, adding to his profit potential.

Joe is somewhat excited about the opportunity because the retrofit market is growing. And owners and architects are seeking ways of reducing costs (which Arbor's approach does—over usual commercial approaches). He also likes the idea of developing a new line to offset the slow-growing market for new construction housing. But he is concerned that a lot of sales effort will be needed to introduce this new idea. He is not afraid of work, but he is concerned about his financial survival.

Joe thinks he has three choices:

1. Take Amy's offer and sell both window and lumber products.
2. Take the offer and drop lumber sales.
3. Stay strictly with lumber and forget the offer.

Amy is expecting an answer within one week, so Joe has to decide soon.

Evaluate Joe Hanratty's current strategy and how the present offer fits in. What should he do now? Why?

17. Wise Water, Inc.

Morton Rinke established his company, Wise Water, Inc., to market a product designed to purify drinking water. The product, branded as the PURITY II Naturalizer Water Unit, is produced by Environmental Control, Inc., a corporation that focuses primarily on water purification and filtering products for industrial markets.

Wise Water is a small but growing business. Morton started the business with an initial capital of only $20,000, which came from his savings and loans from several relatives. Morton manages the company himself. He has a secretary and six full-time salespeople. In addition, he employs two college students part-time; they make telephone calls to prospect for customers and set up appointments for a salesperson to demonstrate the unit in the consumer's home. He has built a small website that primarily provides detailed information and allows customers to request a call from a salesperson. By holding spending to a minimum, Morton has kept the firm's monthly operating budget at only $4,500—and most of that goes for rent, his secretary's salary, and other necessities such as computer supplies and telephone bills.

The PURITY II system uses a reverse osmosis purification process. Reverse osmosis is the most effective technology known for improving drinking water. The device is certified by the Environmental Protection Agency to reduce levels of most foreign substances, including fluoride, mercury, rust, sediment, arsenic, lead, phosphate, bacteria, and most insecticides.

Each PURITY II unit consists of a high-quality 1-micron sediment removal cartridge, a carbon filter, a sediment filter, a housing, a faucet, and mounting hardware. The compact system fits under a kitchen or wet bar sink. A Wise Water salesperson can typically install the PURITY II in about a half hour. Installation involves attaching the unit to the cold water supply line, drilling a hole in the sink, and fastening the special faucet. It works equally well with water from a municipal system or well water, and it can purify up to 15 gallons daily, so most people use it for drinking water. Wise Water sells the PURITY II to consumers for $395, which includes installation.

The system has no movable parts or electrical connections, and it has no internal metal parts that will corrode or rust. However, the system does use a set of filters that must be replaced after about two years. Wise Water sells the replacement filters for $80. Taking into consideration the cost of the filters, the system provides drinking water at a cost of approximately $0.05 per gallon for the average family.

There are two major benefits from using the PURITY II system. First, water treated by this system tastes better. Blind taste tests confirm that most consumers can tell the difference between water treated with the PURITY II and ordinary tap water. Consequently, the unit improves the taste of coffee, tea, frozen juices, ice cubes, mixed drinks, soup, and vegetables cooked in water. Perhaps more important, the PURITY II's ability to remove potentially harmful foreign matter makes the product of special interest to the growing number of people who are concerned about health and the safety of the water they consume. For example, there is growing controversy surrounding public fluoridation of drinking water—and many consumers are looking for filters that remove fluoride.

The number of people with health and safety concerns is growing. In spite of increased efforts to protect the environment and water supplies, there are still many problems. Hundreds of new chemical compounds—ranging from insecticides to industrial chemicals to commercial cleaning agents—are put into use each year. Some of the residue from chemicals and toxic waste eventually enters water supply sources. Further, floods and hurricanes have damaged or completely shut down water treatment facilities in some cities. Problems like these have led to rumors of possible epidemics of such dread diseases as cholera and typhoid—and more than one city has recently experienced near-panic buying of bottled water.

Given these problems and the need for pure water, Morton believes that the market potential for the PURITY II system is very large. Residences, both single-family homes and apartments, are one obvious target. The unit is also suitable for use in boats and recreational vehicles; in fact, the PURITY II is standard equipment on several upscale RVs. And it can be used in taverns and restaurants, in institutions such as schools and hospitals, and in commercial and industrial buildings.

There are several competing ways for customers to solve the problem of getting pure water. Some purchase bottled water. Companies such as Ozarka deliver water monthly for an average price of $0.60 per gallon. The best type of bottled water is distilled water; it is absolutely pure because it is produced by the process of evaporation. However, it may be *too pure.* The distilling process removes needed elements such as calcium and phosphate—and there is some evidence that removing these trace elements contributes to heart disease. In fact, some health-action groups recommend that consumers not drink distilled water.

A second way to obtain pure water is to use some system to treat tap water. PURITY II is one such system. Another system uses an ion exchange process that replaces ions of harmful substances such as iron and mercury with ions that are not harmful. Ion exchange is somewhat less expensive than the PURITY II process, but it is not well suited for residential use because bacteria can build up before the water is used. In addition, there are a number of other filtering and softening systems. In general, these are less expensive and less reliable than the PURITY II. For example, water softeners remove minerals but do not remove bacteria or germs.

Morton's first year with his young company has gone quite well. Customers who have purchased the system like it, and there appear to be several ways to expand the business and increase profits. For example, so far he has had little time to make sales calls on potential commercial and institutional users or residential builders. He also sees other possibilities such as expanding his promotion effort or targeting consumers in a broader geographic area.

At present, Wise Water distributes the PURITY II in the 13-county Gulf Coast region of Texas. Because of the Robinson-Patman Act, the manufacturer cannot grant an exclusive distributorship. However, Wise Water is currently the only PURITY II distributor in this region. In addition, Wise Water has the right of first refusal to set up distributorships in other areas of Texas. The manufacturer has indicated that it might even give Wise Water distribution rights in a large section of northern Mexico.

The agreement with the manufacturer allows Wise Water to distribute the product to retailers, including hardware stores and plumbing supply dealers. Morton has not yet pursued this channel, but a PURITY II distributor in Florida reported some limited success selling the system to retailers at a wholesale price of $275. Retailers for this type of product typically expect a markup of about 33 percent of their selling price.

Environmental Control, Inc. ships the PURITY II units directly from its warehouse to the Wise Water office via UPS. The manufacturer's $200 per unit selling price includes the cost of shipping. Wise Water needs to keep only a few units on hand because the manufacturer accepts faxed orders and then ships immediately—so delivery never takes more than a few days. Further, the units are small enough to inventory in the back room of the Wise Water sales office. Several of the easy-to-handle units will fit in the trunk of a salesperson's car.

Morton is thinking about recruiting additional salespeople. Finding capable people has not been a problem so far. However, there has already been some turnover, and one of the current salespeople is complaining that the compensation is not high enough. Morton pays salespeople on a straight commission basis. A salesperson who develops his or her own prospects gets $100 per sale; the commission is $80 per unit on sales leads generated by the company's telemarketing people. For most salespeople, the mix of sales is about half and half. Wise Water pays the students who make the telephone contacts $4 per appointment set up and $10 per unit sold from an appointment. A growing number of leads are coming from the company's website, largely due to search ads placed using Google AdWords and on Facebook.

An average Wise Water salesperson easily sells 30 units per month. However, Morton believes that a really effective and well-prepared salesperson can sell much more, perhaps 50 units per month.

Wise Water and its salespeople get good promotion support from Environmental Control, Inc. For example, Environmental Control supplies sales training manuals and sales presentation flip charts. The materials are also well done, in part because Environmental Control's promotion manager previously worked for Electrolux vacuum cleaners, which are sold in a similar way. The company also supplies print copy for magazine and newspaper advertising and tapes of commercials for radio and television. Thus, all Wise Water has to do is buy media space or time. In addition, Environmental Control furnishes each salesperson with a portable demonstration unit, and the company recently gave Wise Water three units to be placed in models of condominium apartments.

Morton has worked long hours to get his company going, but he realizes that he has to find time to think about how his strategy is working and to plan for the future.

Evaluate Morton Rinke's current marketing strategy for Wise Water. How do you think he's doing so far, and what should he do next? Why?

18. West Tarrytown Volunteer Fire Department (WTVFD)

Cheyne Morgan raced out the front door of the Target store where he worked as soon as his beeper sounded. In his pickup truck, he heard the call on his special radio scanner: "Highway 18 Fire Department, there is a grass fire at the old McCullough place. That's a mile down the old dirt road just past the Wilson house." The directions might appear cryptic to someone who had not grown up around West Tarrytown, but it was all Cheyne needed to know. Upon arriving at the fire, Cheyne quickly pulled on his fire-retardant bunker pants and boots. He left his Nomex hood, helmet, and fire pants in the back of his truck—he would not need them for this fire.

Less than 10 minutes from the time the call was placed, Cheyne and 20 other members of the West Tarrytown Volunteer Fire Department (WTVFD) had arrived at the old McCullough place. They were able to put out the fire in less than half an hour, but not before a football-field-size patch of grass was scorched. Their quick response saved the neighbor's barn and kept the fire from spreading to a nearby forest. A third straight year of drought has the crew on high alert.

Cheyne threw his gear in the back of his truck and headed back to finish his shift at Target. He had worked there as a department manager for two years, ever since he graduated from the local state college with a marketing degree. As he drove, Cheyne thought about what WTVFD chief Fran Holland recently asked him to do. Over the last few years, the fire department had more to do but fewer people to do it with. So Chief Holland asked Cheyne to draw up a marketing plan to recruit new volunteers.

Cheyne had already started to gather information for the marketing plan. From an online search he found that WTVFD was one of an estimated 30,000 volunteer fire departments in the United States and that these departments had almost a million volunteers. Cheyne was surprised that more than 75 percent of all U.S. firefighters were volunteers. West Tarrytown, a small city of just over 100,000 and hours from a big city, had only volunteer firefighters.

There are 48 firefighters currently in the WTVFD—down from 55 five years ago. Although there was a surge of interest in the year following the terrorist attacks in 2001, only a few of those volunteers remain. Over time, WTVFD has found that about half of new recruits quit before their three-year anniversary. Those who remain usually stay with the department until they can't keep up with the job's physical demands. Fran Holland has been chief for the last three years. She replaced long-time chief, Ken Reeb, who retired after being with WTVFD for more than 40 years—the last 10 as chief.

The current volunteers include 44 men and 4 women; more than half of the force is older than 40 years old, and Cheyne is 1 of only 5 volunteers younger than 30. Almost all of them started volunteering while still in their 20s or early 30s. The crew represents all walks of life, and their ranks include a lawyer, a real estate salesperson, a college professor, a carpenter, a stay-at-home mom, and a few guys from the local factory. Many entered firefighting for the thrill of it or because they hoped the experience might help them land a paid firefighting job in a bigger city. But most of the crew stay with it because they feel good about giving back to their community, view it as a hobby, and enjoy the camaraderie with the other firefighters.

Being a volunteer firefighter is much different than Cheyne thought it would be when he started. Last year he counted 238 hours volunteering for WTVFD, but less than a third of that was actually responding to emergencies. And fewer than half of the emergencies were actual fires. He spent about a quarter of this time in required training and drills. He had to be trained for the many different possible calls, including car accidents, hazardous chemical spills, and terrorist attacks. Another 20 percent of his time was spent in meetings and a similar amount helping with fund-raising. Depending on financial needs, WTVFD holds at least four fund-raising events a year—some years six or eight. These include annual activities such as a chili cook-off, pancake breakfast, and booth at the county fair—and as-needed events such as pie auctions, turkey shoots, and basketball tournaments.

The biggest requirement to be a volunteer firefighter is the willingness to make the time commitment. Cheyne's time commitment and allocation of hours is typical of all the firefighters at WTVFD. Volunteers have to be able to attend at least 80 percent of the twice-monthly drills—scheduled on the second and fourth Tuesdays of every month. Firefighters also have to live or work near the town of West Tarrytown so they can quickly respond to emergencies. They also have to be at least 18 years old and have a valid driver's license.

There is a physical ability test to make sure that firefighters can stand the rigors of the job. Although one doesn't have to be a weightlifter, the job requires volunteers to be in good physical shape.

WTVFD has never really had a marketing strategy or any formal promotion efforts. Most of Cheyne's fellow volunteers heard about WTVFD through word-of-mouth. People are always curious when a volunteer firefighter runs out the door from work or suddenly leaves a party. These occasions give volunteers a chance to tell others about what they do. Sometimes those questions bring someone out to see drills and to apply to become a volunteer. One of Cheyne's high school friends was a volunteer and he encouraged Cheyne to join up while Cheyne was in his junior year of college. But still, awareness of volunteer firefighting in the West Tarrytown area is very low. When Cheyne tells friends about his volunteer work, most are surprised and think the town has full-time paid staff fighting fires.

Cheyne thinks his marketing strategy should focus mostly on promotion. From his studies he remembers the AIDA model and integrated marketing communications. WTVFD does not really have an advertising budget and right now only a one-page informational website. He is pretty sure he could get some money to build a more robust website—especially because one of the recent recruits would do the work for free. Cheyne also wonders if his plan should focus only on gaining new recruits or if current volunteers might also be the target of new promotion. Cheyne also considers how and what he should communicate to his target market. He knows he will have limited funding for his efforts. Should he consider starting a Facebook page or blog? Maybe a website would be better—but what kind of information would be on the website? What about advertising or information sessions? Who should be his target market?

What are the promotion objectives Cheyne Morgan should include in his plan? What promotion methods should he use to achieve those objectives?

19. MyOwnWedding.com

Sterling Bassett is happy with her life but disappointed that the idea she had for starting her own business hasn't taken off as expected. Within a few weeks, she either has to renew the contract for her Internet website or decide not to put any more time and money into her idea. She knows that it doesn't make sense to renew the contract if she can't come up with a plan to make her website-based business profitable—and she doesn't like to plan. She's a "doer," not a planner.

Sterling's business, MyOwnWedding.com, started as an idea 18 months ago as she was planning her own wedding. She attended a bridal fair at the convention center in Raleigh, North Carolina, to get ideas for a wedding dress, check out catering companies and florists, and in general learn more about the various services available to newlyweds. While there, she and her fiancé went from one retailer's booth to another to sign up for their wedding gift registries. Almost every major retailer in the city—ranging from the Home Depot warehouse to the Belk department store to the specialty shops that handle imported crystal glassware—offered a gift registry. Some had computers set up to provide access to their online registries. Being listed in all of the registries improved the odds that her wedding gifts would be items she wanted and could use—and it saved time and hassle for gift-givers. On the way back from the fair, Sterling and her fiancé discussed the idea that it would be a lot easier to register gift preferences once on a central Internet site than to provide lots of different stores with bits and pieces of information. A list at a website would also make it easier for gift-givers, at least those who were computer users.

When Sterling got home, she did an Internet search and found several sites that focused on weddings. The biggest seemed to be www.theknot.com. It had features for couples who were getting married, including a national gift registry. The site featured products from a number of companies, especially large national retail chains; however, there was a search feature to locate people who provide wedding-related services in a local ZIP code area. Sterling thought that the sites she found looked quite good, but that they were not as helpful as a site could be with a more local focus.

The more Sterling and her fiancé discussed the idea of a website offering local wedding-related services, the more it looked like an interesting opportunity. Except for the annual bridal fair, there was no other obvious local place for consumers to get information about planning a wedding and buying wedding-related services. And for local retailers—florists, catering companies, insurance agents, home builders, and many other types of firms—there was no other central place to target promotion to newlyweds. Further, the amount of money spent on weddings and wedding gifts is substantial, and right before and after getting married many young couples make many important purchase decisions for everything from life insurance to pots and pans. Spending on the wedding alone can easily exceed the cost of a year of college.

Sterling was no stranger to the Internet. She worked as a website designer for a small firm whose only client was IBM. That IBM was the only client was intentional rather than accidental. A year earlier IBM had decided that it wanted to outsource certain aspects of its website development work and have it handled by an outside contractor. After negotiating a three-year contract to do IBM's work, several IBM employees quit their jobs and started the business. IBM was a good client, and all indications were that IBM could give the firm as much work as it could handle as it hired new people and prospected for additional accounts over the next few years. Sterling especially liked the creative aspects of designing the "look" of a website, and technical specialists handled a lot of the subtle details.

Before joining this new company, Sterling had several marketing-related jobs—but none had been the glamorous ad agency job she dreamed of in college as an advertising major. Her first job as a college graduate was with an ad agency, but she was in a backroom operation handling a lot of the arrangements for printing and mailing large-scale direct-mail promotions. In spite of promises that it was a path to other jobs at the agency, the pay was bad, the work was always pressured, and every aspect of what she had to do was boring. After six punishing months, she quit and went looking for something else.

When a number of job applications didn't turn up something quickly, she took a part-time job doing telemarketing calls for a mortgage refinance company. Sterling's boss told her that she was doing a great job reeling in prospects—but she hated disturbing people at night and just didn't like making sales pitches. Fortunately for her, that pain didn't last long. A neighbor in Sterling's apartment complex got Sterling an interview for a receptionist position at an ad agency. That, at least, got her foot in the door. Her job description wasn't very interesting, but in a small agency she had the opportunity to learn a lot about all aspects of the business—ranging from working on client proposals and media plans to creative sessions for new campaigns. In fact, it was from a technician at that agency that she learned to work with the graphics software used to create ad layouts and website pages. When the website design job came open at the new firm, her boss gave her a glowing recommendation, and in two days she was off on her new career.

Although Sterling's jobs had not been high-profile positions, they did give her some experience in sales promotion, personal selling, and advertising. Those skills were complemented by the technical computer skills of her fiancé (now husband), who made a living as a database programmer for a large software consulting firm. Taking everything as a whole, they thought that they could get a wedding-related website up and running and make it profitable.

There were several different facets to the original plan for MyOwnWedding.com. One focused on recruiting local advertisers and "sponsors" who would pay to be listed at the website and be allocated a web page (which Sterling would design) describing their services, giving contact information, and links to their own websites. Another focused on services for people who were planning to be married. In addition to an online wedding gift registry, sections of the website provided information about typical wedding costs, planning checklists, details about how to get a required marriage license, and other helpful information (including a discussion forum with comments about the strengths and weaknesses of various local suppliers). Sterling also started a blog that helped foster more feedback from customers. A man and woman could sign up for the service online and could pay the modest $20 "membership" fee for a year by credit card. Friends, family, and invited guests could visit the website at no charge and get information about wedding preferences, local hotels, discounts on local car rentals, and even printable maps to all of the churches and synagogues in the area.

When Sterling told friends about her plan, they all thought it sounded like a great idea. In fact, each time she discussed it, someone came up with another idea for a locally oriented feature to add to the website. Several friends said that they had tried national websites but that the information was often too general. But generating more new ideas was not the problem. The problem was generating revenue. Sterling had already contracted for space from an Internet service provider and created some of the initial content for the website, but she only had four paying sponsors, two of whom happened to be family friends.

Sterling started by creating a colorful flyer describing the website and sent it to most of the firms that had participated in the bridal fair. When no one sent back the reply coupon for more information, Sterling started to make calls (mainly during her lunch hour at her full-time job). Some stores seemed intrigued by the concept, but no one seemed ready to sign up. One reason was that they all seemed surprised at the cost to participate and get ad space at the website—$2,400 a year (about the same as a 1/16-page display ad in the Raleigh *Yellow Pages*). Another problem was that no one wanted to be the first to sign up. As one florist shop owner put it, "If you pull this off and other florists sign up, then come back and I will too."

Getting couples to sign up went slowly too. At first, Sterling paid for four display ads in local Sunday newspapers in the society section, sent information sheets about the website to clergy in the area, and sent carefully crafted press releases announcing the service to almost every publication in the area. She read a bit about search engine optimization and tried to design her site to be more easily found when potential customers were searching. One article that resulted from a press release got some attention, and for a few weeks there was a flurry of e-mail inquiries about her web page. But after that it slowed to a trickle again. More recently, she tried to use Google AdWords, which places ads next to Google search results when someone from the greater Raleigh area searches on the keyword *wedding*. She got a few more hits from this and wondered if she should increase the number of keywords—and wondered what the best keywords could be. She thought about creating a Facebook page but wondered how it would help. She knows that many brides are on Pinterest and wasn't sure if she should start her own page there.

Sterling's diagnosis of the problem was simple. Most people thought it was a great idea, but few couples knew where to look on the Internet for such a service. Similarly, potential advertisers—many of them small local businesses—were not accustomed to the idea of paying for Internet advertising. They didn't know if the cost was reasonable or if her site would be effective in generating business.

Sterling's life as a married person was going great and her job as a web page designer kept her very busy. Her free time outside of work was always in short supply because the young crowd at her office always had some scheme for how to keep entertained. So she wasn't about to quit her job to devote full time to her business idea. Further, she thought that once it got rolling she would only have to devote 10 hours a week to it to earn an extra $30,000 a year. She didn't have delusions of becoming a "dot-com millionaire." She just wanted a good locally oriented business.

However, it still wasn't clear how to get it rolling. After a year of trying on and off, she only had four paying ad sponsors, and one of them had already notified her that he didn't plan to sign up again because it wasn't clear that the website had generated any direct leads or sales. Further, it looked like anything she could do to attract more "members" would end up being expensive and inefficient.

Her parents offered her $10,000 to keep the idea alive. Sterling believes that proper promotion is the key. Now the question is how to budget this latest investment. She was thinking about doing some search advertising—that can be narrowly targeted to local people searching under "wedding," "wedding planning," and other keywords. She was also thinking about building up her owned media content on the site. While Sterling could create the pages at no cost, she felt she would need help creating content. She wondered about maybe going with some user-generated content. Social media was another possibility—Twitter? Facebook? So many choices, and time was Sterling's scarcest resources (oh yeah, money is scarce, too).

Sterling thinks the idea has real potential, and she's willing to do the work. But she's not certain if she can make it pay off. She doesn't want to lose her parents' money.

What is Sterling's strategy? What should she do? If she were to move forward, what strategy would you recommend? Does her financial goal seem realistic? Why?

20. Lake Russell Marine & Camp

Rusty Steuben, owner of Lake Russell Marine & Camp, is worried about his business' future. He has tried various strategies for two years, and he's barely breaking even.

Two years ago, Rusty bought the inventory, supplies, equipment, and business of Lake Russell Marine & Camp, located on the edge of Minneapolis, Minnesota. The business is in an older building along a major highway leading out of town, several miles from any body of water. The previous owner had sales of about $500,000 a year but was just breaking even. For this reason—plus the desire to retire to Arizona—the owner sold to Rusty for roughly the value of the inventory.

Lake Russell Marine & Camp had been selling two well-known brands of small pleasure boats, a leading outboard motor, two brands of snowmobiles and jet skis, and a line of trailer and pickup-truck campers. The total inventory was valued at $250,000—and Rusty used all of his own savings and borrowed some from two friends to buy the inventory and the business. At the same time, he took over the lease on the building—so he was able to begin operations immediately. Rusty had never operated a business of his own before, but he was sure that he would be able to do well. He had worked in a variety of jobs—as a used-car salesman, an auto repairman, and a jack-of-all-trades in the maintenance departments of several local businesses.

Soon after starting his business, Rusty hired his friend, Ginny Wooten. She had worked with Rusty selling cars and had experience as a receptionist and in customer service. Together, they handle all selling and setup work on new sales and do maintenance work as needed. Sometimes the two are extremely busy—at the peaks of each sport season. Then both sales and maintenance keep them going up to 16 hours a day. At these times it's difficult to have both new and repaired equipment available as soon as customers want it. At other times, however, Rusty and Ginny have almost nothing to do.

Rusty usually charges the prices suggested by the various manufacturers, except at the end of a weather season when he is willing to make deals to clear the inventory. He is annoyed that some of his competitors sell mainly on a price basis—offering 10 to 30 percent off a manufacturer's suggested list prices—even at the beginning of a season! Rusty doesn't want to get into that kind of business, however. He hopes to build a loyal following based on friendship and personal service. Further, he doesn't think he really has to cut prices because all of his lines are exclusive to his store. No stores within a five-mile radius carry any of his brands, although nearby retailers offer many brands of similar products. Right now, the Internet does not provide much competition, but he fears future price competition from online boat shows.

To try to build a favorable image for his company, Rusty occasionally places ads in local papers and buys some radio spots. He knows he should probably do some online advertising, but he has no idea how to do it. The basic theme of this advertising is that Lake Russell Marine & Camp is a friendly, service-oriented place to buy the equipment needed for the current season. Sometimes he mentions the brand names he carries, but generally Rusty tries to build an image for concerned, friendly service—both in new sales and repairs—stressing, "We do it right the first time." He chose this approach because, although he has exclusives on the brands he carries, there generally are 10 to 15 different manufacturers' products being sold in the area in each product category—and most of the products are quite similar. Rusty feels that this similarity among competing products almost forces him to try to differentiate himself on the basis of his own store's services.

The first year's operation wasn't profitable. In fact, after paying minimal salaries to Ginny and himself, the business just about broke even. Rusty made no return on his $250,000 investment.

In hopes of improving profitability, Rusty jumped at a chance to add a line of lawn mowers, tractors, and trimmers as he was starting into his second year of business. This line was offered by a well-known equipment manufacturer that wanted to expand into the Minneapolis area. The equipment is similar to that offered by other lawn equipment manufacturers. The manufacturer's willingness to do some local advertising and to provide some point-of-purchase displays appealed to Rusty. And he also liked the idea that customers probably would want this equipment sometime earlier than boats and other summer items. So he thought he could handle this business without interfering with his other peak selling seasons.

It's been two years since Rusty bought Lake Russell Marine & Camp—and he's still only breaking even. Sales have increased a little, but costs have gone up too because he had to hire some part-time help. The lawn equipment helped to expand sales—as he had expected—but unfortunately it did not increase profits as he had hoped. Rusty needed part-time helpers to handle this business—in part because the manufacturer's advertising had generated a lot of sales inquiries. Relatively few inquiries resulted in sales, however, because many people seemed to be shopping for deals. So Rusty may have even lost money handling the new line. But he hesitates to give it up because he doesn't want to lose that sales volume, and the manufacturer's sales rep has been most encouraging, assuring Rusty that things will get better and that his company will be glad to continue its promotion support during the coming year.

Rusty is now considering the offer of a mountain bike producer that has not been represented in the area. The bikes have become very popular with students and serious bikers in the last several years. The manufacturer's sales rep says industry sales are still growing (but not as fast as in the past) and probably will grow for many more years. The sales rep has praised Rusty's service orientation and says this could help him sell lots of bikes because many mountain bikers are serious about buying a quality bike and then keeping it serviced. He says Rusty's business approach would be a natural fit with bike customers' needs and attitudes. As a special inducement to get Rusty to take on the line, the sales rep says Rusty will not have to pay for the initial inventory of bikes, accessories, and repair parts for 90 days. And, of course, the company will supply the usual promotion aids and a special advertising allowance of $10,000 to help introduce the line to Minneapolis.

Rusty likes the idea of carrying mountain bikes because he has one himself and knows that they do require some service year-round. But he also knows that the proposed bikes are very similar in price and quality to the ones now being offered by the bike shops in town. These bike shops are service- rather than price-oriented, and Rusty feels that they are doing a good job on service; consequently, he is concerned with how he can be "different."

Evaluate Rusty Steuben's overall strategy(ies) and the mountain bike proposal. What should he do now?

21. GeoTron International (GTI)

GeoTron International (GTI) is a multinational producer of various chemicals and plastics with plants in the United States, England, France, and Germany. Its headquarters are in New Jersey.

Kenneth Shibata is marketing manager of GTI's plastics business. Kenneth is reconsidering his promotion approach. He is evaluating what kind of promotion–and how much–should be directed to car producers and to other major plastics customers worldwide. Currently, Kenneth has one salesperson dedicated to the automobile industry. This man is based in the Detroit area and focuses on GM, Ford, and Chrysler–as well as the various firms that mold plastics to produce parts to supply the car industry. This approach worked well when relatively little plastic was used in each car and the auto producers did all of the designing themselves and then sent out specifications for very price-oriented competitive bidding. But now the whole product planning and buying system is changing–and of course foreign producers with facilities in the United States are much more threatening as competitors.

How the present system works can be illustrated in terms of the team approach Ford used on its project to design the Flex, the full-sized crossover introduced as a 2009 model. For the Flex, representatives from all the various functions–planning, design, engineering, purchasing, marketing, and manufacturing–worked together. In fact, representatives from key suppliers were involved from the outset. The whole team takes final responsibility for a car. Because all of the departments are involved from the start, problems are resolved as the project moves on–before they cause a crisis. Manufacturing, for example, can suggest changes in design that will result in higher productivity or better quality, which is especially important at a time when Ford's initial quality ratings are beating those of Honda and Toyota.

The old approach was different. It involved a five-year process of creating a new vehicle in sequential steps. Under the old system, product planners would come up with a general concept and then expect the design team to give it artistic form. Next, engineering would develop the specifications and pass them on to manufacturing and suppliers. There was little communication between the groups and no overall project responsibility.

In the Flex project, Ford engineers followed the Japanese lead and did some reverse engineering of their own. They dismantled several competitors' cars, piece by piece, looking for ideas they could copy or improve. This helped them learn how the parts were assembled and how they were designed. Eventually, Ford incorporated or modified some of the best features into its design of the Flex. For example, the Flex uses a new design to seal the doors and eliminate wind noise.

In addition to reverse engineering, Ford researchers conducted a series of market studies. This led to positioning the Flex as an "anti-minivan." That positioning resulted in a decision to eliminate the sliding side doors and instead to use traditional hinged doors. That cut costs, but the savings were used for dress-up features, such as 19-inch aluminum wheels and a special new seat design that reduces movement in the seat and gives the car an even smoother drive. The Flex's optional refrigerator/freezer is another example of a feature that did well in concept tests.

Ford also asked assembly-line workers for suggestions before the car was redesigned and then incorporated their ideas into the new car. Most bolts have the same-sized head, for example, so workers don't have to switch from one wrench to another.

Finally, Ford included its best suppliers as part of the planning effort. Instead of turning to a supplier after the car's design was completed, Ford invited them to participate in product planning. For example, Microsoft's Sync system provides the Flex with voice control of the entertainment system.

Most other vehicles are now developed with an approach similar to this. GM, for example, used a very similar team approach to redesign its new Malibu. And major firms in many other industries are using similar approaches. A major outgrowth of this effort has been a trend by these producers to develop closer working relationships with a smaller number of suppliers. To some extent, this is a direct outgrowth of the decision to try to reduce unnecessary costs by using the same components for different vehicles. For example, the powertrain for the Flex is the same as the one used in Ford's Edge.

Many of the suppliers selected for the Flex project had not only the facilities, but also the technical and professional managerial staff who could understand–and become part of–the program management approach. Ford expected these major suppliers to join in its total quality management push and to be able to provide just-in-time delivery systems. Ford dropped suppliers whose primary sales technique was to entertain buyers and then submit bids on standard specifications.

Because many firms have moved to these team-oriented approaches and developed closer working relationships with a subset of their previous suppliers, Kenneth is trying to determine if GTI's present effort is still appropriate. Kenneth's strategy has focused primarily on responding to inquiries and bringing in GTI's technical people as the situation seems to require. Potential customers with technical questions are sometimes referred to other noncompeting customers already using the materials or to a GTI plant–to be sure that all questions are answered. But basically, all producer-customers are treated more or less alike. The sales reps make calls and try to find good business wherever they can.

Each GTI sales rep usually has a geographic area. If an area like Detroit needs more than one rep, each may specialize in one or several similar industries. But GTI uses the same basic approach–call on present users of plastic products and try to find opportunities for getting a share (or bigger share) of existing purchases or new applications. The sales reps are supposed to be primarily order getters rather than technical specialists. Technical help can be brought in when the customer wants it, or sometimes the sales rep simply sets up a conference call between GTI's technical experts, the buyer, and the users at the buyer's facility.

Kenneth sees that some of his major competitors are becoming more aggressive. They are seeking to affect specifications and product design from the start rather than after a product design is completed. This takes a lot more effort and resources, but Kenneth thinks it may get better results. A major problem he sees, however, is that he may have to drastically change the nature of GTI's promotion. Instead of focusing primarily on buyers and responding to questions, it may be necessary to try to contact *all* the multiple buying influences and not only answer their questions but help them understand what questions to raise—to find solutions. Such a process may even require more technically trained sales reps. In fact, it may require that people from GTI's other departments—engineering, design, manufacturing, R&D, and distribution—get actively involved in discussions with their counterparts in customer firms. Further, use of e-mail and a website might make ongoing contacts faster and easier.

While Kenneth doesn't want to miss the boat if changes are needed, he also doesn't want to go off the deep end. After all, many of the firm's customers don't seem to want GTI to do anything very different from what it's been doing. In fact, some say that they're very satisfied with their current supply arrangements and really have no interest in investing in a close relationship with a single supplier. Even with the Flex project, Ford wasn't 100 percent dedicated to the team approach. For example, when Ford's research showed that the target market viewed quiet and more comfortable seats as an especially important factor in purchases, Ford didn't turn to a supplier for help but rather assigned a team of its own design engineers to develop and test them in-house. Now some of what was learned on the Flex project is going to be used in redesigning other models.

Contrast Ford's previous approach of designing and producing cars to Flex's program management approach, especially as it might affect suppliers' promotion efforts. Given that many other major producers have moved in the program management direction, what promotion effort should Kenneth Shibata develop for GeoTron International? Should every producer in every geographic area be treated alike, regardless of size? Explain.

22. Bright Light Innovations: The Starlight Stove*

The top management team of Bright Light Innovations is preparing to meet and review its market situation. The team is a combination of students and faculty from Colorado State University's (CSU) Colleges of Business and Engineering: Dr. Bryan Wilson, Paul Hudnut, Ajay Jha, Sachin Joshi, Katie Lucchesi, Dan Mastbergen, Ryan Palmer, and Chaun Sims. They are excited about the Starlight Stove product they have developed—and passionate about the opportunity that it provides to improve the quality of life for some of the world's poorest people. They know they have a great technology, but they need a marketing plan to bring this product to market.

Every day, more than 2.4 billion people—more than one-third of the world's population—burn solid biomass fuel (wood, charcoal, dung, and coal) for cooking and heating. These fuel sources are usually burned indoors in open pits or traditional cook stoves. About two-thirds of the people using biomass fuel also have no electricity, so the open fires often burn into the night to provide light. These fires create indoor air pollution, which is a leading contributor to respiratory diseases. UN Secretary General Kofi Annan has called for greater energy efficiency and noted that "indoor air pollution has become one of the top 10 causes of mortality and premature death." It is estimated that this source of pollution contributes each year to the deaths of 1 million children younger than the age of 5, and it is a leading cause of miscarriage and women's health problems.

Hoping to address these consumers' needs for safe cooking and electricity, CSU's Engines and Energy Conversion Laboratory developed the Starlight Stove. The Starlight Stove's improved technology requires 50 to 70 percent less biomass fuel than traditional stoves. It also has a thermoelectric generator that converts heat from the stove into electricity that can power a small lightbulb or be stored in a rechargeable battery for later use. The technology has been refined, and the team believes it is ready to go to market.

There are other competing enclosed cookstoves, but none produce electricity. Solar panels can provide electricity, but they are expensive—costing $360 each. Micro-hydropower allows households to convert the power from streams and rivers into electricity, but homes must be close to a river, and water flow in many areas of the country is seasonal. These technologies—solar panels and hydropower—are understood by many consumers and are already in use in some areas. The Starlight Stove, on the other hand, offers a new technology, and that may slow its adoption.

The management team decided on Nepal as the initial target market for the Starlight Stove. Several factors made this market particularly attractive. The climate is relatively cold, and only 11 percent of the households have access to electricity, so the heat and electricity production of the stove are particularly beneficial. Eighty-eight percent of the population uses firewood as their main source of energy. In addition, deforestation creates environmental problems in Nepal because it contributes to erosion and flooding. So the social benefits of the Starlight Stove will be particularly appealing to the Nepalese government and aid organizations.

There are approximately 9.2 million households in Nepal, but the gross national income per capita is only about $400, with most adults making between $1 and $3 per day. Nepal is largely rural, with only 17 percent of the population living in urban areas. The country is divided into 75 districts. Each district is further divided into about 60 village development committees (a sort of local government) consisting of about 450 households. The similar characteristics of northern India—immediately south of Nepal—make it a logical follow-up market.

The Starlight Stove offers several benefits to this population. For example, the longer hours with light—thanks to the electricity—and less time required to collect wood or other fuel could allow families to earn money by weaving, farming, or producing other crafts. Family productivity could increase 20 percent or more per day. Or the added hours with light might allow children to gain an education. If the product were manufactured locally, it could provide jobs for the population and help them learn the benefits of technology.

With obvious benefits for such a large number of people, the Bright Light Innovations team could look to donations to subsidize the Starlight Stove for the Nepalese people. But the team has concerns about this traditional form of aid. Financing in the form of grants, government relief, or donations is

*This case is based on a business plan written by Ajay Jha, Sachin Joshi, Katie Lucchesi, Dan Mastbergen, Ryan Palmer, and Chaun Sims.

unreliable. If it is not renewed, projects wallow or die. Further, grants often fail to teach disadvantaged people skills and responsibility. So the team wants to create a sustainable venture that provides benefits for all—and has set up Bright Light Innovations as a for-profit business.

The management team has to make a number of marketing decisions. For example, it has to decide how to price the Starlight Stove. It estimates that the stove will cost about $60 to manufacture after setting up a plant in Nepal and expects that microfinancing organizations will provide loans for families. If units are sold for $80, the loan can be financed at 20 percent interest for three years with payments of $0.68 per week (microfinancing institutions typically collect on a weekly, or sometimes daily, basis). The team thinks that it will be easy to find a microfinancing institution to provide these loans. But the team is still unsure about whether this price will provide adequate margins for distributors.

The team also has to decide how to promote the stove to a population where less than half the adults can read. However, the team does have contacts with some business leaders, government officials, and nongovernmental organizations that may be able to provide advice and help.

What should be the marketing strategy of the Bright Light Innovations team for the Starlight Stove? Why?

23. Wire Solutions

Wendy Keating, marketing manager of consumer products for Wire Solutions, is trying to set a price for her most promising new product: a space-saving shoe rack suitable for small homes or apartments.

Wire Solutions—located in Ft. Worth, Texas—is a custom producer of industrial wire products. The company has a lot of experience bending wire into many shapes and also can chrome- or gold-plate finished products. The company was started 16 years ago and has slowly built its sales volume to $3.6 million a year. Just one year ago, Keating was appointed marketing manager of the consumer products division. It is her responsibility to develop this division as a producer and marketer of the company's own branded products—as distinguished from custom orders, which the industrial division produces for others.

Keating has been working on a number of different product ideas for almost a year now and has developed several designs for DVD holders, racks for soft-drink cans, plate holders, doll stands, collapsible book ends, laptop stands, and other such products. Her most promising product is a shoe rack for crowded homes and apartments. The wire rack attaches to the inside of a closet door and holds eight pairs of shoes.

The shoe rack is very similar to one the industrial division produced for a number of years for another company. That company sold the shoe rack and hundreds of other related items out of its "products for organizing and storing" mail-order catalog. Managers at Wire Solutions were surprised by the high sales volume the catalog company achieved with the rack. In fact, that is what interested Wire Solutions in the consumer market and led to the development of the separate consumer products division.

Keating has sold hundreds of the shoe racks to various local hardware, grocery and general merchandise stores, and wholesalers on a trial basis, but each time she has negotiated a price—and no firm policy has been set. Now she must determine what price to set on the shoe rack, which she plans to push aggressively wherever she can. Actually, she hasn't decided on exactly which channels of distribution to use. But trials in the local area have been encouraging, and as noted earlier, the experience in the industrial division suggests that there is a large market for this type of product. Further, she has noticed that a Walmart store in her local area is selling a similar rack made of plastic. When she talked casually about her product with the store manager, he suggested that she contact the chain's houseware buyers in the home office in Arkansas.

The manufacturing cost of her rack—when made in reasonable quantities—is approximately $2.80 if it is painted black and $3.60 if it is chromed. Similar products have been selling at retail in the $9.95 to $19.95 range. The sales and administrative overhead to be charged to the division will amount to $95,000 a year. This will include Keating's salary and some travel and office expenses. She expects that a number of other products will be developed in the near future. But for the coming year, she hopes the shoe rack will account for about half the consumer products division's sales volume.

Evaluate Wendy Keating's strategy planning so far. What should she do now? What price should she set for the shoe rack?

24. Fresh Harvest

Chelsea Skye-Rice, president of Fresh Harvest, is not sure what she should propose to the board of directors. Her recent strategy change isn't working. And Don Bartley, Fresh Harvest's only sales rep (and also a board member), is so frustrated that he refuses to continue his discouraging sales efforts. Don wants Chelsea to hire a sales force or do *something.*

Fresh Harvest is a long-time processor in the highly seasonal vegetable canning industry. Fresh Harvest packs and sells canned beans, peas, carrots, corn, peas and carrots mixed, and kidney beans. It sells mainly through food brokers to merchant wholesalers, supermarket chains (such as Kroger, Safeway, and Jewel), cooperatives, and other outlets, mostly in the Midwest. Of less importance, by volume, are sales to local institutions, grocery stores, and supermarkets—and sales of dented canned goods at low prices to walk-in customers.

Fresh Harvest is located in Wisconsin's beautiful Devil's Valley. The company has more than $28 million in sales annually (exact sales data are not published by the closely held corporation). Plants are located in strategic places along the valley, with the main offices in the valley as well. The Fresh Harvest brand is used only on canned goods sold in the local market. Most of the goods are sold and shipped under a retailer's label or a broker's/wholesaler's label.

Fresh Harvest is well known for the consistent quality of its product offerings. And it's always willing to offer competitive prices. Strong channel relations were built by Robert Skye, Fresh Harvest's former board chair and chief executive officer. Robert—who still owns controlling interest in the firm—worked the Chicago area as the company's sales rep in its earlier years, before his father stepped down as president and he took over in 1974. Robert was an ambitious and hardworking top manager—the firm prospered under his direction. He became well known within the canned food processing industry for technical/product innovations.

During the off-canning season, Robert traveled widely. In the course of his travels, he arranged several important business deals. His 1990 and 2001 trips resulted in the following two events: (1) inexpensive pineapple was imported from Taiwan and sold by Fresh Harvest, primarily to expand the product line; and (2) a technically advanced continuous process cooker (65 feet high) was imported from England and installed at one of Fresh Harvest's plants. It was the first of its kind in the United States and cut processing time sharply while improving quality.

Robert retired in 2010 and named his daughter, 35-year-old Chelsea Skye-Rice, as his successor. Chelsea is intelligent and hardworking. She has been primarily concerned with the company's financial matters and only recently focused on marketing problems. During her seven years as financial director, the firm received its highest credit rating and was able to borrow working capital ($5 million to meet seasonal can and wage requirements) at the lowest rate ever.

The fact that the firm isn't unionized allows some competitive advantage. However, changes in minimum wage laws have increased costs. These and other rising costs have squeezed profit margins. This led to the recent closing of two plants as they became less efficient to operate. Fresh Harvest expanded capacity of the remaining two plants (especially warehouse facilities) so they could more profitably operate with maximum use of existing processing equipment.

Shortly after Robert's retirement, Chelsea reviewed the company's situation with her managers. She pointed to narrowing profit margins, debts contracted for new plants and equipment, and an increasingly competitive environment. Even considering the temporary labor-saving competitive advantage of the new cooker system, there seemed to be no way to improve the status quo unless the firm could sell direct—as it does in the local market—thereby eliminating the food brokers' 5 percent commission on sales. This was the chosen plan, and Don Bartley was given the new sales job. An inside salesperson was retained to handle incoming orders and do some telemarketing to smaller accounts.

Don, the only full-time outside sales rep for the firm, lives in Devil's Valley. Other top managers do some selling but not much. Because he is Robert's nephew, Don is also a member of the board of directors. He is well qualified in technical matters and has a college degree in food chemistry. Although Don formerly did call on some important customers with the brokers' sales reps, he is not well known in the industry or even by Fresh Harvest's usual customers.

It is now five months later. Don is not doing very well. He has made several selling trips, placed hundreds of telephone calls, and maintained constant e-mail contacts with prospective customers—all with discouraging results. He is unwilling to continue sales efforts on his own. There seem to be too many potential customers for one person to reach. And much negotiating and wining-and-dining seems to be needed—certainly more than he can or wants to do.

Don insists that Fresh Harvest hire a sales force to continue its present way of operating. Sales are down, both in comparison to expectations and to the previous year's results. Some regular supermarket chain customers have stopped buying—though basic consumer demand has not changed. Further, buyers for some supermarket chains that might be potential new customers have demanded quantity guarantees much larger than Fresh Harvest can supply. Expanding supply would be difficult in the short run—because the firm typically must contract with growers to ensure supplies of the type and quality it normally offers.

Robert, still the controlling stockholder, has asked for a special meeting of the board in two weeks to discuss the present situation.

Evaluate Fresh Harvest's past and current strategy planning. What should Chelsea Skye-Rice tell Robert Skye? What should Fresh Harvest do now?

25. QXR Tools (QXR)

Pedro Gomez, president and marketing manager of QXR Tools, is deciding what strategy, or strategies, to pursue.

QXR Tools (QXR) is a manufacturer of industrial cutting tools. These tools include such items as lathe blades, drill press bits, and various other cutting edges used in the operation of large metal cutting, boring, or stamping machines. Pedro takes great pride in the fact that his company—whose $5.7 million sales in 2010 is small by industry standards—is recognized as a producer of a top-quality line of cutting tools.

Competition in the cutting-tool industry is intense. QXR competes not only with the original machine manufacturers, but also with many other larger domestic and foreign manufacturers offering cutting tools as one of their many different product lines. Over the years, this has had the effect of standardizing the price, specifications, and, in turn, the quality of the competing products from all manufacturers. It has also led to fairly low prices on standard items.

About a year ago, Pedro was tiring of the financial pressure of competing with larger companies enjoying economies of scale. At the same time, he noted that more and more potential cutting-tool customers were turning to small tool-and-die shops that used computer-controlled equipment to meet specialized needs that could not be met by the mass production firms. Pedro thought perhaps he should consider some basic strategy changes. Although he was unwilling to become strictly a custom producer, he thought that the recent trend toward buying customized cutting edges suggested new markets might be developing—markets too small for the large, multi-product-line companies to serve profitably but large enough to earn a good profit for a flexible company of QXR's size.

Pedro hired a marketing research company, MResearchPro, to study the feasibility of serving these markets. The initial results were encouraging. It was estimated that QXR might increase sales by 65 percent and profits by 90 percent by serving the emerging markets. The research showed that there are many large users of standard cutting tools who buy directly from large cutting-tool manufacturers (domestic or foreign) or wholesalers who represent these manufacturers. This is the bulk of the cutting-tool business (in terms of units sold and sales dollars). But there are also many smaller users all over the United States who buy in small but regular quantities. And some of these needs are becoming more specialized. That is, a special cutting tool may make a machine and/or worker much more productive, perhaps eliminating several steps with time-consuming setups. This is the area that the research company sees as potentially attractive.

The next strategy change made by Pedro was to have the sales manager hire two technically oriented marketing researchers (at a total cost of $85,000 each per year, including travel expenses) to maintain continuous contact with potential cutting-tool customers. The researchers were supposed to identify any present or future needs that might exist in enough cases to make it possible to profitably produce a specialized product. The researchers were not to take orders or sell QXR's products to the potential customers. Pedro felt that only through this policy could these researchers talk to the right people.

The initial feedback from the marketing researchers was most encouraging. Many firms (large and small) had special needs—although it often was necessary to talk to the shop foreman or individual machine operators to find these needs. Most operators were making do with the tools available. Either they didn't know customizing was possible or doubted that their supervisors would do anything about it if they suggested that a more specialized tool could increase productivity. But these operators were encouraging because they said that it would be easier to persuade supervisors to order specialized tools if the tools were already produced and in stock than if they had to be custom made. So Pedro decided to continually add high-quality products to meet the ever-changing, specialized needs of users of cutting tools and edges.

QXR's potential customers for specialized tools are located all over the United States. The average sale per customer is likely to be less than $500, but the sale will be repeated several times within a year. Because of the widespread market and the small order size, Pedro doesn't think that selling direct—as is done by small custom shops—is practical. At the present time, QXR sells 90 percent of its regular output through a large industrial wholesaler—Superior Mill Supply—which serves the area east of the Mississippi River and carries a very complete line of industrial supplies (to "meet every industrial need"). Superior carries more than 10,000 items. Some sales come from customers who know exactly what they want and just place orders directly by fax or at the firm's website. But most of the selling is by Superior's sales reps, who work from an electronic catalog on a laptop computer. Superior, although very large and well known, is having trouble moving cutting tools. It's losing sales of cutting tools in some cities to newer wholesalers specializing in the cutting tool industry. The new wholesalers are able to give more technical help to potential customers and therefore better service. Superior's president is convinced that the newer, less-experienced concerns will either realize that a substantial profit margin can't be maintained along with their aggressive strategies, or they will eventually go broke trying to overspecialize.

From Pedro's standpoint, the present wholesaler has a good reputation and has served QXR well in the past. Superior has been of great help in holding down Pedro's inventory costs—by increasing the inventory in Superior's 35 branch locations. Although Pedro has received several complaints about the lack of technical assistance given by Superior's sales reps—as well as their lack of knowledge about QXR's new special products—he feels that the present wholesaler is providing the best service it can. All of its sales reps have been told about the new products at a special training session, and new pages have been added to the electronic catalog on their laptops. So regarding the complaints, Pedro says, "It's just the usual things you hear when you're in business."

Pedro thinks there are more urgent problems than a few complaints. Profits are declining, and sales of the new cutting tools are not nearly as high as forecast—even though all research reports indicate that the company's new products meet the intended markets' needs perfectly. The high costs involved in producing small quantities of special products and in adding the marketing research team—together with lower than expected sales—have significantly reduced QXR's profits. Pedro is wondering whether it is wise to continue to try to cater to the needs of many specific target markets when the results are this discouraging. He also is considering increasing advertising expenditures, including some search engine advertising, in the hope that customers will pull the new products through the channel.

Evaluate QXR's situation and Pedro Gomez's present strategy. What should he do now?

26. AAA Custom Castings, Inc.

Mallory Rizocki, marketing manager for AAA Custom Castings, Inc., is trying to figure out how to explain to her boss why a proposed new product line doesn't make sense for them. Mallory is sure it's wrong for AAA Custom Castings, but isn't able to explain why.

AAA Custom Castings, Inc. is a producer of malleable iron castings for automobile and aircraft manufacturers and a variety of other users of castings. Last year's sales of castings amounted to more than $70 million.

AAA Custom Castings also produces about 30 percent of all the original equipment bumper jacks installed in new U.S.-made automobiles each year. This is a very price-competitive business, but AAA Custom Castings has been able to obtain a large market share with frequent personal contact between the company's executives and its customers—supported by very close cooperation between the company's engineering department and its customers' buyers. This has been extremely important because the wide variety of models and model changes frequently requires alterations in the specifications of the bumper jacks. All of AAA Custom Castings' bumper jacks are sold directly to automobile manufacturers. No attempt has been made to sell bumper jacks to final consumers through hardware and automotive channels—although they are available through the manufacturers' automobile dealers.

Tim Kingston, AAA Custom Castings' production manager, now wants to begin producing hydraulic garage jacks for sale through auto-parts wholesalers to auto-parts retailers. Tim saw a variety of hydraulic garage jacks at a recent automotive show and knew immediately that his plant could produce these products. This especially interested him because of the possibility of using excess capacity. Further, he says "jacks are jacks," and the company would merely be broadening its product line by introducing hydraulic garage jacks. (*Note:* Hydraulic garage jacks are larger than bumper jacks and are intended for use in or around a garage. They are too big to carry in a car's trunk.)

As Tim became more enthusiastic about the idea, he found that AAA Custom Castings' engineering department already had a patented design that appeared to be at least comparable to the products now offered on the market. Further, Tim says that the company would be able to produce a product that is better made than the competitive products (i.e., smoother castings)—although he agrees that most customers probably wouldn't notice the difference. The production department estimates that the cost of producing a hydraulic garage jack comparable to those currently offered by competitors would be about $48 per unit.

Mallory has just received an e-mail from Jesse Zachary, the company president, explaining the production department's enthusiasm for broadening AAA Custom Castings' present jack line into hydraulic jacks. Jesse seems enthusiastic about the idea too, noting that it would be a way to make fuller use of the company's resources and increase its sales. Jesse's e-mail asks for Mallory's reaction, but Jesse already seems sold on the idea.

Given Jesse's enthusiasm, Mallory isn't sure how to respond. She's trying to develop a good explanation of why she isn't excited about the proposal. The firm's six sales reps are already overworked with their current accounts. And Mallory couldn't possibly promote this new line herself—she's already helping other reps make calls and serving as sales manager. So it would be necessary to hire someone to promote the line. And this sales manager would probably have to recruit manufacturers' agents (who probably will want 10 to 15 percent commission on sales) to sell to automotive wholesalers who would stock the jack and sell to the auto-parts retailers. The wholesalers will probably expect trade discounts of about 20 percent, trade show exhibits, some national advertising, and sales promotion help (catalog sheets, mailers, and point-of-purchase displays). Further, Mallory sees that AAA Custom Castings' billing and collection system will have to be expanded because many more customers will be involved. It will also be necessary to keep track of agent commissions and accounts receivable.

Auto-parts retailers are currently selling similar hydraulic garage jacks for about $99. Mallory has learned that such retailers typically expect a trade discount of about 35 percent off the suggested list price for their auto parts.

All things considered, Mallory feels that the proposed hydraulic jack line is not very closely related to the company's present emphasis. She has already indicated her lack of enthusiasm to Tim, but this made little difference in Tim's thinking. Now it's clear that Mallory will have to convince the president or she will soon be responsible for selling hydraulic jacks.

Contrast AAA Custom Castings, Inc.'s current strategy and the proposed strategy. What should Mallory Rizocki say to Jesse Zachary to persuade him to change his mind? Or should she just plan to sell hydraulic jacks? Explain.

27. Canadian Mills, Ltd.*

Valerie Boudreau, marketing manager of Canadian Mills, Ltd.—a Canadian company—is being urged to approve the creation of a separate marketing plan for Quebec. This would be a major policy change because Canadian Mills' international parent is trying to move toward a global strategy for the whole firm, and Boudreau has been supporting Canada-wide planning.

Boudreau has been the marketing manager of Canadian Mills, Ltd. for the last four years—since she arrived from international headquarters in Minneapolis. Canadian Mills, Ltd., headquartered in Toronto, is a subsidiary of a large U.S.-based consumer packaged food company with worldwide sales of more than $2.8 billion in 2007. Its Canadian sales are more than $450 million, with the Quebec and Ontario markets accounting for 69 percent of the company's Canadian sales.

The company's product line includes such items as cake mixes, puddings, pie fillings, pancakes, prepared foods, and frozen dinners. The company has successfully introduced at least six new products every year for the last five years. Products from Canadian Mills are known for their high quality and enjoy much brand preference throughout Canada, including the Province of Quebec.

The company's sales have risen every year since Boudreau took over as marketing manager. In fact, the company's market share has increased steadily in each of the product categories in which it competes. The Quebec market has closely followed the national trend; however, in the past two years, total sales growth in that market began to lag.

According to Boudreau, a big advantage of Canadian Mills over its competitors is the ability to coordinate all phases of the food business from Toronto. For this reason, Boudreau meets at least once a month with her product managers—to discuss developments in local markets that might affect marketing plans. Although each manager is free to make suggestions and even to suggest major changes, Boudreau has the responsibility of giving final approval for all plans.

One of the product managers, Jackie Provence, expressed great concern at the last monthly meeting about the poor performance of some of the company's products in the Quebec market.

*This case was adapted from one written by Professor Roberta Tamilia, University of Windsor, Canada.

Table 1 Per Capita Consumption Index, Province of Quebec (Canada = 100)

Cake mixes	107	Soft drinks	126
Pancakes	87	Pie fillings	118
Puddings	114	Frozen dinners	79
Salad dressings	85	Prepared packaged foods	83
Molasses	132	Cookies	123

Note: An index shows the relative consumption as compared to a standard. In this table, the standard is all of Canada. The data show that per capita consumption of cake mixes is 7 percent higher in Quebec and pancake consumption 13 percent lower compared to all of Canada.

Although a broad range of possible reasons—ranging from inflation and the threat of job losses to politics—were reviewed to try to explain the situation, Provence insisted that it was due to a basic lack of understanding of that market. She felt not enough managerial time and money had been spent on the Quebec market—in part because of the current emphasis on developing all-Canada plans on the way to having one global strategy.

Provence felt the current marketing approach to the Quebec market should be reevaluated because an inappropriate marketing plan may be responsible for the sales slowdown. After all, she said, "80 percent of the market is French-speaking. It's in the best interest of the company to treat that market as being separate and distinct from the rest of Canada."

Provence supported her position by showing that Quebec's per capita consumption of many product categories in which the firm competes is above the national average (see Table 1). Research projects conducted by Canadian Mills also support the "separate and distinct" argument. Over the years, the firm has found many French-English differences in brand attitudes, lifestyles, usage rates, and so on.

Provence argued that the company should develop a unique Quebec marketing plan for some or all of its brands. She specifically suggested that the French-language advertising plan for a particular brand be developed independently of the plan for English Canada.

Currently, the Toronto agency assigned to the brand just translates its English-language ads for the French market. Boudreau pointed out that the present advertising approach assured Canadian Mills of a uniform brand image across Canada. Provence said she knew what the agency is doing, and that straight translation into Canadian-French may not communicate the same brand image. The discussion that followed suggested that a different brand image might be needed in the French market if the company wanted to stop the brand's decline in sales.

The managers also discussed the food distribution system in Quebec. The major supermarket chains have their lowest market share in that province. Independents are strongest there—the mom-and-pop food stores fast disappearing outside Quebec remain alive and well in the province. Traditionally, these stores have stocked a higher proportion (than supermarkets) of their shelf space with national brands, an advantage for Canadian Mills.

Finally, various issues related to discount policies, pricing structure, sales promotion, and cooperative advertising were discussed. All of these suggested that things were different in Quebec and that future marketing plans should reflect these differences to a greater extent than they do now. After the meeting, Boudreau stayed in her office to think about the situation. Although she agreed with the basic idea that the Quebec market was in many ways different, she wasn't sure how far the company should go in recognizing this fact. She knew that regional differences in food tastes and brand purchases existed not only in Quebec but in other parts of Canada as well. But people are people, after all, with far more similarities than differences, so a Canadian and, eventually, a global strategy makes some sense too.

Boudreau was afraid that giving special status to one region might conflict with top management's objective of achieving standardization whenever possible—one national strategy for Canada, on the way to one worldwide global strategy. She was also worried about the long-term effect of such a policy change on costs, organizational structure, and brand image. Still, enough product managers had expressed their concern over the years about the Quebec market to make her wonder if she shouldn't modify the current approach. Perhaps they could experiment with a few brands—and just in Quebec. She could cite the language difference as the reason for trying Quebec rather than any of the other provinces. But Boudreau realizes that any change of policy could be seen as the beginning of more change, and what would Minneapolis think? Could she explain it successfully there?

Evaluate Canadian Mills, Ltd.'s present strategy. What should Valerie Boudreau do now? Explain.

28. Kingston Home Health Services (KHHS)

Chelsea Kingston, executive director of Kingston Home Health Services, is trying to clarify her strategies. She's sure some changes are needed, but she's less sure about how *much* change is needed and/or whether it can be handled by her people.

Kingston Home Health Services (KHHS) is a nonprofit organization that has been operating—with varying degrees of success—for 25 years, offering nursing services in clients' homes. Some of its funding comes from the local United Way to provide emergency nursing services for those who can't afford to pay. The balance of the revenues—about 90 percent of the $2.2 million annual budget—comes from charges made directly to the client or to third-party payers, including insurance companies, health maintenance organizations (HMOs), and the federal government for Medicare or Medicaid services.

Chelsea has been executive director of KHHS for two years. She has developed a well-functioning organization able to meet most requests for service that come from local doctors and from the discharge officers at local hospitals. Some business also comes by self-referral—the client finds the KHHS name in the yellow pages of the local phone directory.

The last two years have been a rebuilding time—because the previous director had personnel problems. This led to a weakening of the agency's image with the local referring agencies. Now their image is more positive. But Chelsea is not completely satisfied with the situation. By definition, Kingston Home Health Services is a nonprofit organization. Yet it still must cover all its costs: payroll, rent payments, phone expenses, and so on, including Chelsea's own salary. She can see that although KHHS is growing slightly and is now breaking even, it doesn't have much of a cash cushion to fall back on if (1) the demand for KHHS nursing services declines; (2) the government changes its rules about paying for KHHS's kind of nursing services, either cutting back what it will pay for or reducing the amount it will pay for specific services; or (3) new competitors enter the market. In fact, the last possibility concerns Chelsea greatly. Some hospitals, squeezed for revenue, are expanding into home health care—especially nursing services—as patients are being released earlier from hospitals because of payment limits set by government guidelines. For-profit organizations (e.g., Kelly Home Care Services) are expanding around the country to provide a complete line of home health care services, including nursing services of the kind offered by KHHS. These for-profit organizations appear to be efficiently run, offering good service at competitive and sometimes even lower prices than some nonprofit organizations. And they seem to be doing this at a profit, which suggests that it would be possible for these for-profit companies to lower their prices if nonprofit organizations try to compete on price.

Chelsea is considering whether she should ask her board of directors to let her offer a complete line of home health care services—that is, move beyond just nursing services into what she calls "care and comfort" services.

Currently, KHHS is primarily concerned with providing professional nursing care in the home. But KHHS nurses are much too expensive for routine home health care activities—helping fix meals, bathing and dressing patients, and other care and comfort activities. The full cost of a nurse to KHHS, including benefits and overhead, is about \$65 per hour. But a registered nurse is not needed for care and comfort services. All that is required is someone who is honest, can get along with all kinds of people, and is willing to do this kind of work. Generally, any mature person can be trained fairly quickly to do the job—following the instructions and under the general supervision of a physician, a nurse, or family members. The full cost of aides is \$9 to \$16 per hour for short visits and as low as \$75 per 24 hours for a live-in aide who has room and board supplied by the client.

The demand for all kinds of home health care services seems to be growing. With more dual-career families and more single-parent households, there isn't anyone in the family to take over home health care when the need arises—due to emergencies or long-term disabilities. Further, hospitals send patients home earlier than in the past. And with people living longer, there are more single-survivor family situations where there is no one nearby to take care of the needs of these older people. But often some family members—or third-party payers such as the government or insurers—are willing to pay for some home health care services. Chelsea now occasionally recommends other agencies or suggests one or another of three women who have been doing care and comfort work on their own, part-time. But with growing demand, Chelsea wonders if KHHS should get into this business, hiring aides as needed.

Chelsea is concerned that a new, full-service home health care organization may come into her market and be a single source for both nursing services *and* less-skilled home care and comfort services. This has happened already in two nearby but somewhat larger cities. Chelsea fears that this might be more appealing than KHHS to the local hospitals and other referrers. In other words, she can see the possibility of losing nursing service business if KHHS does not begin to offer a complete home health care service. This would cause real problems for KHHS—because overhead costs are more or less fixed. A loss in revenue of as little as 10 percent would require some cutbacks—perhaps laying off some nurses or secretaries, giving up part of the office, and so on.

Another reason for expanding beyond nursing services—using paraprofessionals and relatively unskilled personnel—is to offer a better service to present customers *and* make more effective use of the computer systems and organization structure that she has developed over the last two years. Chelsea estimates that the administrative and office capabilities could handle twice as many clients without straining the system. It would be necessary to add some clerical help if the expansion were quite large. But this increase in overhead would be minor compared to the present proportion of total revenue that goes to covering overhead. In other words, additional clients or more work for some current clients could increase revenue and ensure the survival of KHHS, provide a cushion to cover the normal fluctuations in demand, and ensure more job security for the administrative personnel.

Further, Chelsea thinks that if KHHS were successful in expanding its services—and therefore could generate some surplus—it could extend services to those who aren't now able to pay. Chelsea says one of the worst parts of her job is refusing service to clients whose third-party benefits have run out or who can no longer afford to pay for other reasons. She is uncomfortable about having to cut off service, but she must schedule her nurses to provide revenue-producing services if she's going to meet the payroll every two weeks. By expanding to provide more services, she might be able to keep serving more of these nonpaying clients. This possibility excites Chelsea because her nurse's training has instilled a deep desire to serve people in need, whether they can pay or not. This continual pressure to cut off service because people can't pay has been at the root of many disagreements and even arguments between the nurses serving the clients and Chelsea, as executive director and representative of the board of directors.

Chelsea knows that expanding into care and comfort services won't be easy. Some decisions would be needed about relative pay levels for nurses, paraprofessionals, and aides. KHHS would also have to set prices for these different services and tell current customers and referral agencies about the expanded services.

These problems aren't bothering Chelsea too much, however—she thinks she can handle them. She is sure that care and comfort services are in demand and could be supplied at competitive prices.

Her primary concern is whether this is the right thing for Kingston Home Health Services—basically a nursing organization—to do. KHHS's whole history has been oriented to supplying *nurses' services.* Nurses are dedicated professionals who bring high standards to any job they undertake. The question is whether KHHS should offer less-professional services. Inevitably, some of the aides will not be as dedicated as the nurses might like them to be. And this could reflect unfavorably on the nurse image. At a minimum, she would need to set up some sort of training program for the aides. As Chelsea worries about the future of KHHS, and her own future, it seems that there are no easy answers.

Evaluate KHHS's present strategy. What should Chelsea Kingston do? Explain.

29. Kennedy & Gaffney (K&G)

The partners of Kennedy & Gaffney are having a serious discussion about what the firm should do in the near future.

Kennedy & Gaffney (K&G) is a medium-sized regional certified public accounting firm based in Grand Rapids, Michigan, with branch offices in Lansing and Detroit. Kennedy & Gaffney has nine partners and a professional staff of approximately 105 accountants. Gross service billings for the fiscal year ending June 30, 2010, were $6.9 million. See Table 1, which presents financial data for 2010, 2009, and 2008.

K&G's professional services include auditing, tax preparation, bookkeeping, and some general management consulting. Its client base includes municipal governments (cities, villages, and townships), manufacturing companies, professional organizations (attorneys, doctors, and dentists), and various other small businesses. A good share of revenue comes from the firm's municipal practice. Table 1 details K&G's gross revenue by service area and client industry for 2010, 2009, and 2008.

At the monthly partners' meeting held in July 2010, Robert Kennedy, the firm's managing partner (CEO), expressed concern about the future of the firm's municipal practice. Robert's presentation to his partners follows:

> Although our firm is considered to be a leader in municipal auditing in our geographic area, I am concerned that as municipals attempt to cut their operating costs, they will solicit competitive bids from other public accounting firms to perform their annual audits. Three of the four largest accounting firms in the world have local offices in our area. Because they concentrate their practice in the manufacturing industry–which typically has December 31 fiscal year-ends–they have "available" staff during the summer months.
>
> Therefore, they can afford to low-ball competitive bids to keep their staffs busy and benefit from on-the-job training provided by municipal clientele. I am concerned that we may begin to lose clients in our most established and profitable practice area.*

Sherry Gaffney, a senior partner in the firm and the partner in charge of the firm's municipal practice, was the first to respond to Robert's concern.

> Robert, we all recognize the potential threat of being underbid for our municipal work by our large accounting competitors. However, K&G is a leader in municipal auditing in Michigan, and we have much more local experience than our competitors. Furthermore, it is a fact that we offer a superior level of service to our clients–which goes beyond the services normally expected during an audit to include consulting on financial and other operating issues. Many of our less sophisticated clients depend on our nonaudit consulting assistance. Therefore, I believe, we have been successful in differentiating our services from our competitors. In many recent situations, K&G was selected over a field of as many as 10 competitors even though our proposed prices were much higher than those of our competitors.

The partners at the meeting agreed with Sherry's comments. Yet even though K&G had many success stories regarding their ability to retain their municipal clients–despite being underbid–they had lost three large municipal clients during the past year. Sherry was asked to comment on the loss of those clients. She explained that the lost clients are larger municipalities with a lot of in-house financial expertise and therefore less dependent on K&G's consulting assistance. As a result, K&G's service differentiation went largely unnoticed. Sherry explained

*Organizations with December fiscal year-ends require audit work to be performed during the fall and in January and February. Those with June 30 fiscal year-ends require auditing during the summer months.

Table 1 Fiscal Year Ending June 30

	2010	2009	2008
Gross billings	$6,900,000	$6,400,000	$5,800,000
Gross billings by service area:			
Auditing	3,100,000	3,200,000	2,750,000
Tax preparation	1,990,000	1,830,000	1,780,000
Bookkeeping	1,090,000	745,000	660,000
Other	720,000	625,000	610,000
Gross billings by client industry:			
Municipal	3,214,000	3,300,000	2,908,000
Manufacturing	2,089,000	1,880,000	1,706,000
Professional	1,355,000	1,140,000	1,108,000
Other	242,000	80,000	78,000

that the larger, more sophisticated municipals regard audits as a necessary evil and usually select the low-cost reputable bidder.

Robert then requested ideas and discussion from the other partners at the meeting. One partner, Rosa Basilio, suggested that K&G should protect itself by diversifying. Specifically, she felt a substantial practice development effort should be directed toward manufacturing. She reasoned that because manufacturing work would occur during K&G's off-season, K&G could afford to price very low to gain new manufacturing clients. This strategy would also help counter (and possibly discourage) low-ball pricing for municipals by the three large accounting firms mentioned earlier.

Another partner, Wade Huntoon, suggested that "if we have consulting skills, we ought to promote them more, instead of hoping that the clients will notice and come to appreciate us. Further, maybe we ought to be more aggressive in calling on smaller potential clients."

Another partner, Stan Walsh, agreed with Wade, but wanted to go further. He suggested that they recognize that there are at least two types of municipal customers and that two (at least) different strategies be implemented, including lower prices for auditing only for larger municipal customers and/or higher prices for smaller customers who are buying consulting too. This caused a big uproar from some who said this would lead to price cutting of professional services, and K&G didn't want to be price cutters: "One price for all is the professional way."

However, another partner, Isabel Ventura, agreed with Stan and suggested they go even further—pricing consulting services separately. In fact, she suggested that the partners consider setting up a separate department for consulting—like the large accounting firms have done: "This can be a very profitable business. But it is a different kind of business and eventually may require different kinds of people and a different organization. For now, however, it may be desirable to appoint a manager for consulting services—with a budget—to be sure it gets proper attention." This suggestion too caused serious disagreement. Partners pointed out that having a separate consulting arm had led to major conflicts, especially in some larger accounting firms. The initial problems were internal. The consultants often brought in more profit than the auditors, but the auditors controlled the partnership, and the successful consultants didn't always feel that they got their share of the rewards. There had also been serious external problems and charges of unethical behavior based on the concern that big accounting firms had a conflict of interest when they did audits on publicly traded companies that they in turn relied on for consulting income. Because of problems in this area, the Securities and Exchange Commission created new guidelines that have changed how the big four accounting firms handle consulting. On the other hand, several partners argued that this was really an opportunity for K&G because the firm handled very few companies listed with the SEC, and the conflict of interest issues didn't even apply with municipal clients.

Robert thanked everyone for their comments and encouraged them to debate these issues in smaller groups and to share ideas by e-mail before coming to a one-day retreat (in two weeks) to continue this discussion and come to some conclusions.

Evaluate K&G's situation. What strategy(ies) should the partners select? Why?

30. Paglozzi's Pizza Pies

Cassidy Newman, manager of the Paglozzi's Pizza Pies store in Flint, Michigan, is trying to develop a plan for the "sick" store she just took over.

Paglozzi's Pizza Pies is an owner-managed pizza take-out and delivery business with three stores located in Ann Arbor, Southfield, and Flint, Michigan. Paglozzi's business comes from telephone, fax, or walk-in orders. Each Paglozzi's store prepares its own pizzas. In addition to pizzas, Paglozzi's also sells and delivers a limited selection of soft drinks.

Paglozzi's Ann Arbor store has been very successful. Much of the store's success may be due to being close to the University of Michigan campus. Most of these students live within 5 miles of Paglozzi's Ann Arbor store.

The Southfield store has been moderately successful. It serves mostly residential customers in the Southfield area, a largely residential suburb of Detroit. Recently, the store advertised—using direct-mail flyers—to several office buildings within three miles of the store. The flyers described Paglozzi's willingness and ability to cater large orders for office parties, business luncheons, and so on. The promotion was quite successful. With this new program and Paglozzi's solid residential base of customers in Southfield, improved profitability at the Southfield location seems ensured.

Paglozzi's Flint location has had mixed results during the last three years. The Flint store has been obtaining only about half of its orders from residential delivery requests. Cassidy, the Flint store's new manager, believes the problem with residential pizza delivery in Flint is due to the location of residential neighborhoods in the area. Flint has several large industrial plants (mostly auto industry related) located throughout the city. Small, mostly factory-worker neighborhoods are distributed in between the various plant sites. As a result, Paglozzi's store location can serve only two or three of these neighborhoods on one delivery run. Competition is also relevant. Paglozzi's has several aggressive competitors who advertise heavily, distribute cents-off coupons, and offer 2-for-1 deals. This aggressive competition is probably why Paglozzi's residential sales leveled off in the last year or so. And this competitive pressure seems likely to continue as some of this competition comes from aggressive national chains that are fighting for market share and squeezing little firms like Paglozzi's. For now, anyway, Cassidy feels she knows how to meet this competition and hold on to the present residential sales level.

Most of the Flint store's upside potential seems to be in serving the large industrial plants. Many of these plants work two or three shifts, five days a week. During each work shift, workers

Table 1 Practical Capacities and Sales Potential of Current Equipment and Personnel

	11 A.M. Break	8 P.M. Break	2:30 A.M. Break	Daily Totals
Current capacity (pizzas)	48	48	48	144
Average selling price per unit	$ 12.50	$ 12.50	$ 12.50	$ 12.50
Sales potential	$ 600	$ 600	$ 600	$1,800
Variable cost (approximately 40 percent of selling price)*	240	240	240	720
Contribution margin of pizzas	360	360	360	1,080
Beverage sales (2 medium-sized beverages per pizza ordered at 75¢ a piece)†	72	72	72	216
Cost of beverages (30 percent per beverage)	22	22	22	66
Contribution margin of beverages	50	50	50	150
Total contribution of pizza and beverages	$ 410	$ 410	$ 410	$1,230

*The variable cost estimate of 40 percent of sales includes variable costs of delivery to plant locations.

†Amounts shown are not physical capacities (there is almost unlimited physical capacity), but potential sales volume is constrained by number of pizzas that can be sold.

are allowed one half-hour lunch break—which usually occurs at 11 a.m., 8 p.m., or 2:30 a.m., depending on the shift.

Customers can order by phone, fax, e-mail, or at the Paglozzi's website. About 30 minutes before a scheduled lunch break Paglozzi's can expect an order for several (5 to 10) pizzas for a work group. Paglozzi's may receive many orders of this size from the same plant (i.e., from different groups of workers). The plant business is very profitable for several reasons. First, a large number of pizzas can be delivered at the same time to the same location, saving transportation costs.

Second, plant orders usually involve many different toppings (double cheese, pepperoni, mushrooms, hamburger) on each pizza. This results in $11 to $14 revenue per pizza. The delivery drivers also like delivering plant orders because the tips are usually $1 to $2 per pizza.

Despite the profitability of the plant orders, several factors make it difficult to serve the plant market. Paglozzi's store is located 5 to 8 minutes from most of the plant sites, so Paglozzi's staff must prepare the orders within 20 to 25 minutes after it receives the telephone order. Often, inadequate staff and/or oven capacity means it is impossible to get all the orders heated at the same time.

Generally, plant workers will wait as long as 10 minutes past the start of their lunch break before ordering from various vending trucks that arrive at the plant sites during lunch breaks. (Currently, no other pizza delivery stores are in good positions to serve the plant locations and have chosen not to compete.) But there have been a few instances when workers refused to pay for pizzas that were only 5 minutes late! Worse yet, if the same work group gets a couple of late orders, they are lost as future customers. Cassidy believes that the inconsistent profitability of the Flint store is partly the result of such lost customers.

In an effort to rebuild the plant delivery business, Cassidy is considering various methods to ensure prompt customer delivery. She thinks that potential demand during lunch breaks is significantly above Paglozzi's present capacity. Cassidy also knows that if she tries to satisfy all phone or fax orders on some peak days, she won't be able to provide prompt service and may lose more plant customers.

Cassidy has outlined three alternatives that may win back some of the plant business for the Flint store. She has developed these alternatives to discuss with Paglozzi's owner. Each alternative is briefly described below:

Alternative 1: Determine practical capacities during peak volume periods using existing equipment and personnel. Accept orders only up to that capacity and politely decline orders beyond. This approach will ensure prompt customer service and high product quality. It will also minimize losses resulting from customers' rejection of late deliveries. Financial analysis of this alternative—shown in Table 1—indicates that a potential daily contribution to profit of $1,230 could result if this alternative is implemented successfully. This would be profit before promotion costs, overhead, and net profit (or loss). *Note:* Any alternative will require several thousand dollars to reinform potential plant customers that Paglozzi's has improved its service and "wants your business."

Alternative 2: Buy additional equipment (one oven and one delivery car) and hire additional staff to handle peak loads. This approach would ensure timely customer delivery and high product quality as well as provide additional capacity to handle unmet demand. Table 2 is a conservative estimate of potential daily demand for plant orders compared to current capacity

Table 2 Capacity and Demand for Plant Customer Market

	Estimated Daily Demand	Current Daily Capacity	Proposed Daily Capacity
Pizza units (1 pizza)	320	144	300

Table 3 Cost of Required Additional Assets

	Cost	Estimated Useful Life	Salvage Value	Annual Depreciation*	Daily Depreciation†
Delivery car (equipped with pizza warmer)	$11,000	5 years	$1,000	$2,000	$5.71
Pizza oven	$20,000	8 years	$2,000	$2,250	$6.43

*Annual depreciation is calculated on a straight-line basis.

†Daily depreciation assumes a 350-day (plant production) year. All variable expenses related to each piece of equipment (e.g., utilities, gas, oil) are included in the variable cost of a pizza.

and proposed increased capacity. Table 3 gives the cost of acquiring the additional equipment and relevant information related to depreciation and fixed costs.

Using this alternative, the following additional pizza delivery and preparation personnel costs would be required:

	Hours Required	Cost per Hour	Total Additional Daily Cost
Delivery personnel	6	6	$36.00
Preparation personnel	8	6	48.00
			$84.00

The addition of even more equipment and personnel to handle all unmet demand was not considered in this alternative because the current store is not large enough.

Alternative 3: Add additional equipment and personnel as described in alternative 2, but move to a new location that would reduce delivery lead times to 2 to 5 minutes. This move would probably allow Paglozzi's to handle all unmet demand—because the reduction in delivery time will provide for additional oven time. In fact, Paglozzi's might have excess capacity using this approach.

A suitable store is available near about the same number of residential customers (including many of the store's current residential customers). The available store is slightly larger than needed. And the rent is higher. Relevant cost information on the proposed store follows:

Additional rental expense of proposed store over current store	$1,600 per year
Cost of moving to new store (one-time cost)	$16,000

Cassidy presented the three alternatives to Paglozzi's owner, Skipper Kipnis. Skipper was pleased that Cassidy had done her homework. He decided that Cassidy should make the final decision on what to do (in part because she had a profit-sharing agreement with Skipper) and offered the following comments and concerns:

1. Skipper agreed that the plant market was extremely sensitive to delivery timing. Product quality and pricing, although important, were of less importance.
2. He agreed that plant demand estimates were conservative. "In fact, they may be 10 to 30 percent low."
3. Skipper expressed concern that under alternative 2, and especially under alternative 3, much of the store's capacity would go unused more than 80 percent of the time.
4. He was also concerned that Paglozzi's store had a bad reputation with plant customers because the prior store manager was not sensitive to timely plant delivery. So Skipper suggested that Cassidy develop a promotion plan to improve Paglozzi's reputation in the plants and be sure that everyone knows that Paglozzi's has improved its delivery service.

Evaluate Cassidy's possible strategies for the Flint store's plant market. What should Cassidy do? Why? Suggest possible promotion plans for your preferred strategy.

31. Silverglade Homes*

Brian Silverglade, who seven years ago founded Silverglade Homes in Asheville, North Carolina, is excited that he'll complete his first LEED-certified "green" home this month. The LEED (Leadership in Energy and Environmental Design) rating means that the home uses 30 percent less energy and 20 percent less water than a conventional house; it also means that construction waste going into landfills must also be reduced. The house will be the model home to showcase Brian's new development, which includes four more homes that he hopes to complete in the next six months.

Although Brian is excited, he is also nervous. Rising interest rates and an uncertain economy have reduced demand in the local housing market. People who do buy homes are more price-sensitive. That's a problem because building a green house

*Erik Hardy did the research for an earlier version of this case.

usually increases construction costs—but customers are not always aware of the benefits that come with the higher price tag. So Brian has to figure out how to find home buyers who are willing to pay a premium for his "green" homes.

Prior to building this home, Brian tried to make environmentally responsible building choices that didn't increase his costs. However, two years ago while at the National Association of Home Builders' convention in Orlando, Florida, Brian visited a booth that described LEED Certification, and it appealed to him. He also met a number of new suppliers who were offering sustainable building materials. When Brian returned from the convention in Orlando, Silverglade Homes salesperson Karen Toller told him that more home buyers were asking about environmental and energy-saving features. Brian thought the time was right to commit to building at least a few homes that met higher environmental standards.

Brian kept his eye out for a good piece of property for his project. Before long he found a three-acre parcel of land about 15 minutes from downtown Asheville. The land had a nice mix of hardwood trees and a small stream, but lacked the panoramic mountain views expected by high-end home buyers in the area. Nevertheless, Brian thought the property would be ideal for a small neighborhood of moderate-sized green homes. He purchased the land—and his first green project was under way.

Brian worked closely with a local architect, Katie Kelly, who had won several awards from the Green Building Council for her innovative designs. Katie proposed that each home follow a theme based on a classic Appalachian farmhouse design that would blend well with the rural surroundings and fit the concept of clustered development. Clustered development allows a builder to increase the number of home sites allowed if land is set aside for open space. For example, regulations usually required at least one acre for a rural home site. However, in a clustered development, the county would allow Brian to build five homes on 1.5 acres of his land if he dedicated the remaining 1.5 acres as open space controlled by a conservation easement.

Initially, Brian thought the additional two home sites and preservation of open space would be a huge benefit for his project. However, to get the development permit, he had to provide the county with a special land survey and biological inventory of the site. This extra survey work cost Brian $25,000 more than was normal.

Brian is behind schedule with construction because working with new types of materials has slowed him down. In some cases, his workers even had to be trained by factory representatives on the proper installation of materials. In addition, many of the materials in a LEED home—such as low-E windows, blown foam insulation, a high-efficiency furnace and water heater, and Energy Star appliances—have premium prices. As a result, Brian's LEED-certified homes cost about 10 percent more than conventionally built homes of the same size.

However, LEED homes do offer buyers a number of benefits. Toxin-free building materials help combat indoor air pollution—and green homes are less likely to have problems with mold or mildew. Energy and water savings for the homes Brian is building should be $2,000 to $3,000 per year. Plus, buyers can feel good that their homes produce fewer greenhouse gases, reduce dependence on fossil fuels, and send less construction waste to the local landfill.

Brian priced the five homes he is building at $250,000 to $300,000—about 10 percent more than similar non-LEED certified homes in the area. So far, the homes are getting a few looks, but none have sold and he hasn't had an offer. The feedback that Karen Toller hears is that people like the homes, but think that the price seems to be high; they like the general idea of owning a green home and saving money on energy, but they don't focus on the benefits. Perhaps that is because real estate agents in the area have little experience with green building and are used to talking about value in terms of "cost per square foot."

Karen Toller works full-time as a real estate agent—and Silverglade Homes is one of her clients. She receives a 1 percent sales commission for every Silverglade home that is sold. She typically writes the listing that all real estate agents can read on the Multiple Listing Service (MLS) website and also handles the contract to complete a sale. With no movement on Brian's new houses and with prime spring selling season coming up fast, Brian has asked Karen to meet with him to discuss ways to spark more interest in his development. Brian wants a plan that will bring people out to see his new homes and development—and a way to ensure that they are aware of the benefits he is offering.

Brian wonders what needs to be done to tell customers about the benefits of green building. Some other builders are advertising in local media and developing brochures to leave in a rack outside of their homes—but Brian has not needed to do that before. He wonders if he might be able to generate some inexpensive publicity by working with the local newspaper; it has run several feature stories about the environment but none about green building. He also thinks he needs to do more to convince real estate agents about the benefits of green housing. One idea is to ask someone at the Green Building Council or possibly his architect to put on a seminar, but Brian doesn't know if real estate agents will show up. He also wonders if putting signs in his model home to point out the environmental benefits might be helpful.

When Brian started his project, he thought his green homes would sell themselves, but now he wonders if he isn't ahead of his time.

What do you think of Brian Silverglade's marketing strategy so far? What promotion objectives should Brian set for his marketing strategy? What are the advantages and disadvantages of targeting communications at consumers as compared to real estate agents? What would you recommend as a promotion blend?

32. Mallory's Lemonade Stand (A)

Eleven-year-old Mallory is a budding entrepreneur. She is always coming up with new business ideas. In early summer 2015, her latest venture is a lemonade stand. Mallory is focused on making a high level of profits–she is saving for a new bike. Mallory is trying to to develop a marketing strategy to help her achieve this goal.

Last year, Mallory helped a friend with a lemonade stand. This year she wants to run her own business. Her parents expect her to pay for almost everything related to her business. Her dad built her a small lemonade stand–and although he donated his time, he did ask for the $12 in materials needed to build the stand. Mallory had to purchase other supplies as well. She bought a nice one-gallon pitcher for $5, and cups cost her $0.10. She figured out that sugar and lemons were costing her $0.30 for each 12-ounce cup she sold. Her parents let her use ice from the freezer–no cost there. Mallory initially planned to charge $0.75 per cup for her lemonade. Oh, and Mallory has a secret weapon. Her grandma had a little spice combination she put into lemonade that people just love–she knows from experience that once customers taste *her* lemonade they will be coming back for more.

Mallory is looking for help with some of her calculations, especially the final determination of an appropriate price. Answer the following questions:

1. *Which of Mallory's costs are* ***fixed costs?*** *These are the costs that will not change whether Mallory sells few or many cups of lemonade.*
2. *What are the* ***variable costs?*** *These are costs that change directly with Mallory's sales. They go up proportionately to Mallory's increased number of sales.*
3. *What is Mallory's* ***fixed-cost contribution per unit*** *(assumed selling price minus the variable cost per unit)?*
4. *How many cups of lemonade does Mallory need to sell to reach her* ***break-even point (BEP)?*** *Recall that the break-even point (in units) = (total fixed costs)/(fixed cost contribution per unit).*
5. *After conferring with her sister (a marketing major in college), Mallory considered four marketing strategies in addition to her original plan. Calculate the break-even point (in cups) for each (assume for the moment that each is an independent alternative):*
   a) *Mallory's family lives on a cul-de-sac and her parents said she has to sell from her driveway. This means her street gets limited traffic. She thinks creating two signs and placing them at the entrance of the cul-de-sac would make more people aware of her stand. The materials to make the signs cost $5. With this change what is her BEP?*
   b) *Mallory saw some fancier plastic cups that she thought might make her lemonade look nicer. The larger cups would go for $0.15 each, and because they were a little larger, costs for lemons and sugar would rise $0.05 per cup. With this change what is her BEP?*
   c) *Her sister said she was charging too much for a cup of lemonade. So Mallory considered charging $0.50 per cup instead of the planned $0.75. With this change what is her BEP?*
   d) *She also wanted to consider a higher price of $1 per cup instead of the planned $0.75. With this change what is her BEP?*
6. *What other information would be helpful to know before you make your final recommendation?*
7. *What else could Mallory do to deliver more value to her customers?*

More information on the terms in bold can be found in Chapter 18.

33. Mallory's Lemonade Stand (B)

It is March 2016 and Mallory has come a long way since last summer. Her lemonade was a hit–everyone raved about her secret formula (she added some special spices suggested by her grandmother). When Damien Cuban (billionaire investor) happened to drive through the neighborhood, he had a cup of Mallory's lemonade and offered to invest in the company. So Mallory's Lemonade Stand Lemonade will soon be found in a limited number of local Whole Foods Stores. Mallory had to figure out pricing once again. She started with the knowledge that retailers would want to sell her 20-oz. bottles for $2.00 at retail.

Mallory figured her costs as follows:

- $10,000 in fixed costs for various costs including some local advertising to support the Whole Foods launch.
- A co-packer (company that manufactures food products to specifications) will charge $0.50 for each 20-oz. bottle–including bottles, packages, and delivery.
- Mallory assumes she can sell 30,000 bottles.
- Mallory plans to charge Whole Foods $1.00 each for the bottles. Whole Foods will charge $2.00.
- Using average cost pricing, she is counting on a $5,000 profit.

1. *Assuming the numbers shown here, what is Whole Foods'* ***markup (percent)*** *on each bottle of Mallory's Lemonade Stand Lemonade?*
2. *Using Mallory's projected sales of 30,000 bottles, calculate Mallory's (a)* ***average fixed cost,*** *(b)* ***average variable cost,*** *(c)* ***margin*** *in dollars per bottle, and (d) total profit.*
3. *What is Mallory's profit if sales turn out to be only 15,000 bottles?*

When MLS Lemonade failed to meet sales targets, Whole Foods quietly dropped the line. But all was not lost. Damien Cuban was able to help her obtain a presence in a convenience store chain. Cuban suggested that Mallory use **marginal analysis** (which focuses on the changes in total revenue and total cost from selling one more unit to find the most profitable price and quantity). This approach recognized that price and quantity sold change together. Cuban called in a favor from a friend who is an expert in the beverage market. This woman was able to provide a well-informed estimate of how much Mallory could sell during her test at different prices. Fill out the table and suggest an appropriate price. Because the convenience store manager knew it would have a 50 percent markup, the first column is actually the store's purchase price and Mallory's selling price.

Mallory has partially filled out a spreadsheet with the numbers (see below). Finish this spreadsheet based on the following questions.

4. *Assuming the expert's estimates are accurate, what price maximizes revenue? What is that revenue?*
5. *Assuming the expert's estimates are accurate, what price maximizes profit? What is that profit?*
6. *What would help Mallory reduce the price sensitivity some customers may have for her lemonade?*

More information on the terms in bold can be found in Chapter 18.

Price (P)	Quantity	Revenue (P * Q)	Total VC	Total FC	Total Cost	Profit (Rev – Cost)
$3.00	0	$ 0	$ 0	$10,000	$10,000	–$10,000
$1.75	10,000	$17,500	$ 5,000		$15,000	$ 2,500
$1.40	15,000	$21,000			$17,500	$ 3,500
$1.20	20,000	$24,000	$10,000			
$1.00	30,000	$30,000	$15,000			
$0.85	45,000	$38,250				
$0.77	51,000	$39,270				
$0.70	55,000				$37,500	$ 1,000

图书在版编目（CIP）数据

国际市场营销：第十六版 = Essentials of Marketing: A Marketing Strategy Planning Approach, Sixteenth Edition：英文 /（美）小威廉·D. 佩罗，（美）约瑟夫·P. 坎农，（美）E. 杰尔姆·麦卡锡著；刘白玉，刘夏青，孙明玉改编. —北京：中国人民大学出版社，2020.4

ISBN 978-7-300-27984-8

Ⅰ. ①国… Ⅱ. ①小… ②约… ③E… ④刘… ⑤刘… ⑥孙… Ⅲ. ①国际营销—教材—英文 Ⅳ. ①F740.2

中国版本图书馆 CIP 数据核字（2020）第 046449 号

国际市场营销（第十六版）

小威廉·D. 佩罗（William D. Perreault Jr.）
[美] 约瑟夫·P. 坎农（Joseph P. Cannon） 著
E. 杰尔姆·麦卡锡（E. Jerome McCarthy）
刘白玉 刘夏青 孙明玉 改编

Guoji Shichang Yingxiao (Di-shiliu Ban)

出版发行	中国人民大学出版社		
社　　址	北京中关村大街 31 号	**邮政编码**	100080
电　　话	010-62511242（总编室）		010-62511770（质管部）
	010-82501766（邮购部）		010-62514148（门市部）
	010-62515195（发行公司）		010-62515275（盗版举报）
网　　址	http:// www. crup. com. cn		
经　　销	新华书店		
印　　刷	北京七色印务有限公司		
规　　格	215 mm × 275 mm 16 开本	**版　　次**	2020 年 4 月第 1 版
印　　张	20.5	**印　　次**	2022 年 7 月第 3 次印刷
字　　数	647 000	**定　　价**	58.00 元

中国人民大学出版社外语出版分社读者信息反馈表

尊敬的读者：

感谢您购买和使用中国人民大学出版社外语出版分社的 ______________ 一书，我们希望通过这张小小的反馈卡来获得您更多的建议和意见，以改进我们的工作，加强我们双方的沟通和联系。我们期待着能为更多的读者提供更多的好书。

请您填妥下表后，寄回或传真回复我们，对您的支持我们不胜感激！

1. 您是从何种途径得知本书的：

□书店　□网上　□报纸杂志　□朋友推荐

2. 您为什么决定购买本书：

□工作需要　□学习参考　□对本书主题感兴趣　□随便翻翻

3. 您对本书内容的评价是：

□很好　□好　□一般　□差　□很差

4. 您在阅读本书的过程中有没有发现明显的专业及编校错误，如果有，它们是：

____

____

____

5. 您对哪些专业的图书信息比较感兴趣：

____

____

____

6. 如果方便，请提供您的个人信息，以便于我们和您联系（您的个人资料我们将严格保密）：

您供职的单位：______________________________

您教授的课程（教师填写）：______________________

您的通信地址：______________________________

您的电子邮箱：______________________________

请联系我们：黄婷　程子殊　吴振良　王琼　鞠方安

电话：010-62512737，62513265，62515538，62515573，62515576

传真：010-62514961

E-mail：huangt@crup.com.cn　chengzsh@crup.com.cn　wuzl@crup.com.cn
crup_wy@163.com　jufa@crup.com.cn

通信地址：北京市海淀区中关村大街甲 59 号文化大厦 15 层　邮编：100872

中国人民大学出版社外语出版分社